Money, Power and Space

Money, Power and Space

Edited by

Stuart Corbridge, Nigel Thrift and Ron Martin

BLACKWELL
Oxford UK & Cambridge USA

Copyright © Basil Blackwell Ltd 1994

First published 1994

Blackwell Publishers
108 Cowley Road
Oxford OX4 1JF
UK

238 Main Street
Cambridge, Massachusetts 02142
USA

British Library Cataloguing in Publication Data
A CIP catalogue record for this book is available from the British Library.

Library of Congress Cataloging-in-Publication Data
Money, power, and space / edited by Stuart Corbridge, Nigel Thrift, and Ron Martin.
    p.   cm.
   Includes bibliographical references and index.
   ISBN 0-631-18199-7 (alk. paper). — ISBN 0-631-19201-8 (pbk.)
    1. International finance. 2. Capital movements. 3. Money market. 4. Money.
  I. Corbridge, Stuart. II. Thrift, N. J. III. Martin, Ron.
  HG3881.M594   1994   93-32882
  332—dc20   CIP

Typeset in 10.5 on 12.5pt Sabon
by Pure Tech Corporation, India
Printed in Great Britain by Hartnolls Ltd., Bodmin

This book is printed on acid-free paper

Contents

Figures

Tables

Contributors

Dr Patrick Bond, Planact, Yeoville, Johannesburg, South Africa.

Professor Gordon Clark, Department of Geography, Monash University, Clayton, Victoria, Australia.

Dr Stuart Corbridge, Department of Geography, University of Cambridge, England.

Professor Maurice Daly, Department of Geography, University of Sydney, New South Wales, Australia.

Dr Sheila Dow, Department of Economics, University of Stirling, Scotland.

Dr Chris Hamnett, Faculty of Social Sciences, Open University, Milton Keynes, England.

Dr Geoffrey Ingham, Faculty of Economics and Politics, University of Cambridge, England.

Professor Jane Jacobs, Department of Geography, University of Melbourne, Victoria, Australia.

Dr Andrew Leyshon, Department of Geography, University of Hull, England.

Professor Peter Marden, Department of Geography, Monash University, Clayton, Victoria, Australia.

Dr Ron Martin, Department of Geography, University of Cambridge, England.

Dr Michael Pryke, Department of Geography, Quenn Mary Westfield College, University of London, England.

Professor Susan Roberts, Department of Geography, University of Kentucky, Lexington, KY, USA.

Professor Susan Strange, Department of Economics, University of Warwick and London School of Economics, England.

Professor Nigel Thrift, Department of Geography, University of Bristol, England.

Professor Barney Warf, Department of Geography, Kent State University, Kent, OH, USA.

Professor Michael Watts, Department of Geography, University of California at Berkeley, USA.

Acknowledgements

The Editors are grateful to John Davey and Simon Prosser for their encouragement and advice in preparing the book for publication. We are also grateful to John Taylor for his excellent work in copy-editing the manuscript. The book is dedicated to our loved ones.

The authors, editors and publishers gratefully acknowledge the following for permission to reproduce copyright material: The Corporation of London for figure 15.4; Josy Ajiboye for figures 17.4 and 17.5.

The publishers apologize for any errors or omissions in the above list and would be grateful to be notified of any corrections that should be incorporated in the next edition or reprint of this book.

1

Money, Power and Space: Introduction and Overview

Stuart Corbridge and Nigel Thrift

Love and money may make the world go around . . . but love of money provides the raw energy at the center of the whirlwind. *(David Harvey, 1989a, p. 185)*

The essays in this collection place a concern for money, power and space at the centre of a continuing debate on the restructuring of the global political economy. Neither the editors nor the contributors subscribe to the view that money is all-important, or that a discussion of money should be undertaken independently of an analysis of the productive economy and its governing political institutions. But it is nevertheless our contention that money has been neglected by many social scientists, or marginalized in their accounts, even though many of the recent crises of global capitalism can be ascribed to the institutions and circuits of national and international money. If the 1950s and 1960s were the golden years of capitalism in the advanced industrial world (Marglin and Schor, 1990), then so were the 1970s and 1980s years of inflation, debts and deficits in the global economy more generally.

The comparative neglect of money in the social sciences (and especially human geography) is not easily explained. Social scientists are clearly familiar with the debt crises that have plagued so many countries since 1980, including the United States, and a good number of them are sensitive to the effects that unanticipated exchange rate movements can have on the profitability of trading enterprises. It is also widely acknowledged that the financial services industry is a major employer of labour in most parts of the world economy and that forms of monetary calculation are bound up with (and constitutive of) the wider cultural logics of modernity and modern societies (Simmel, 1990). Indeed, the making of money has often been adopted as a leitmotif for the 1980s, a decade in which, so the story goes, speculation and greed ran riot in many Western societies (Thrift and Leyshon, 1992).

Nevertheless, money is not usually to the fore in accounts of the crises of global capitalism (or, indeed, in accounts of the restructuring of the state socialist economies of Eastern Europe and the ex-Soviet Union). Most models of the transition from Fordism to post-Fordism in the 1980s have focused on changes in the labour process, whereby flexible production systems are said to have replaced mass production technologies in districts as disparate as Silicon Valley in California and the Third Italy in Southern Europe (Scott and Storper, 1986). Attention has also been focused on the internationalization of production as a means of restoring declining corporate rates of profitability (Frobel et al., 1980), on new social and gender divisions of labour (Sayer and Walker, 1992), and on the privatization of consumption as an organized capitalism gives way to a disorganized capitalism (or a capitalism organized more by markets than by states: Lash and Urry, 1987). Still another conceptual dualism holds that the modern world is in transition to a postmodern world. Central to this transition are those shifts already identified as part of the transition from Fordism to post-Fordism (Harvey, 1989b); but allied to this practical reordering of economy, society and space there is a reordering of social scientific theory and a more insistent account of the symbolic orders of (post) modern societies. Some prophets of postmodernism hold that the conventional metanarratives of the 1960s and 1970s – be they modernization theory, Marxism or neoclassical economics – are no longer appropriate to a postmodern world suffused in difference. Money, as the universal equivalent, somehow sits uneasily in this mental landscape.

There is much in these agendas that is of value and some parts of them will be reflected in *Money, Power and Space*. At the same time, it is apparent that rather more of the work conducted on the two 'posts' (post-Fordism and postmodernism) has been about visible fixed points and patterns of production than about the invisible spatial flows that link these nodes together. Most economic geographers continue to focus mainly upon individual factories or groups of enterprises, labour markets, new management practices, economies of scope, just-in-time systems and so on. Significantly, it is mainly in Australia, a country continually battered by flows of money capital, that a 'new economic geography' has emerged which is more sensitive to the intersections of financial and industrial capitals in the restructuring of space-economies. In the work of geographers like Robert Fagan (1990), Maurice Daly and Malcolm Logan (Daly and Logan, 1989), the centre stage is less often occupied by new production technologies than by a considered review of the role of leveraged buyouts, junk bonds and the Eurocurrency markets in the restructuring of industrial capitalism. (Manuel Castells has also focused upon a new 'space of flows', paying particular attention to the importance of information flows in the modern world economy: Castells, 1989.)

Money, in short, has been neglected in the social sciences in part because of a continuing focus in some quarters upon the static and the tangible (the fixed points of production). It has also been neglected because of the failure of many economically minded social scientists to engage with the related agendas of political scientists in a way that has now begun to happen in the case of the 'new international political economy' (Strange, 1988; Murphy and Tooze, 1991). Finally, it has been neglected by the Left because few there 'have perceived the main weakness of a modern global capitalist system to lie, not in the exploitation of labour nor in the oppression of the working class, but in the ability of its leading governments to run a monetary system stable and viable enough to sustain a global production system' (Strange, 1986, p. 85). Although 'Lenin is said to have declared that the best way to destroy the capitalist system was to debauch the currency' (Keynes, 1972, p. 57), many on the Left have still remained in thrall to a prevailing 'productionism'.[1]

This collection of essays seeks to redress this lack of balance. It also does so in recognition of the importance of money in the restructuring of contemporary capitalism. We have already referred to the global debt crisis and (by implication) to the trading imbalances that exist between the United States, on the one hand, and Germany and Japan on the other. But money has also been at the heart of a more vital and deep-seated restructuring of capitalism. The economic and political agendas of Reaganism and Thatcherism, not to mention those of Germany, Australia, New Zealand and a majority of developing countries after 1982/3, have been inspired by a desire to defeat inflation above all else. A concern for sound money policies – and thus, allegedly, for stable forms of capitalist regulation, calculation and exchange – has been associated with rising unemployment and falling aggregate demand in particular national economies and in the wider global economy. Many companies went to the wall when faced by high interest rates in the early 1980s. Many have again in the early 1990s. The lives of men and women in Belfast and Boston, Bombay and Brasilia have all been directly affected by so-called monetarist policies and/or by the related doctrines of structural adjustment. The restructuring of local economies cannot reasonably be understood except in relation to the disciplining of money, and the various disciplines imposed by money capital and the community of money.

Money has also been freely available to some groups and classes in some places at various times in the past twenty years; too freely, perhaps, in countries like Brazil and Mexico in the 1970s, and in the many nations hit by property booms in the 1980s. In the 1990s people are again having

---

1 An obvious exception to this rule has been the diverse school of regulation theorists (including Aglietta and Lipietz), who have tried to give money its due, in particular by including financial systems as a key moment in the regulation of capitalism (see Aglietta, 1982; Lipietz, 1987, 1989).

to come to terms with tight monetary policies in many countries as a previous disposition to issue new credit monies is reined in by a widespread 'return to the eternal verities of the monetary base' (Harvey, 1982, p. 254). The problem is that the victims of 'sound money' policies are rarely the same as the progenitors of the earlier round of easy money. When devaluation bites, it bites hardest and deepest in communities and households least able to resist the community of money. Crises, as Harvey points out: 'unravel as rival states, possessed of different money systems, compete with each other over who is to bear the brunt of devaluation. The struggle to export inflation, unemployment, idle productive capacity, excess commodities, etc., becomes the pivot of national policy. The costs of crises are spread differentially according to the financial, economic, political and military power of rival states' (Harvey, 1982, p. 329).

Money, Power and Space reflects upon the wisdom of Harvey's observation. The first part of the book is concerned mainly with the geopolitics of money and with debates about national and international systems of monetary transfer and regulation. It also considers different theoretical accounts of money and money capital, including those associated with monetarism, Keynesianism and Marxism (and hybrids thereof). The second part of the book is concerned with the intersections of financial and industrial capitals in particular national and regional economies. The third and final part of *Money, Power and Space* examines the community of money in its technological, cultural and aesthetic dimensions. It also attends to a series of struggles waged around competing interpretations of money. The remainder of this introduction offers a few words about each part of the book. Detailed summaries of each chapter are not provided here; we trust that a wide-ranging cast of authors have provided essays that speak for themselves.

The Geopolitics of Money

Money is indispensable to the organization and reproduction of any modern economy. It is money that 'permits the separation of sales and purchases in space and time' (Harvey, 1982, p. 245). But money comes in many different forms and the evolution of monetary systems has as much to do with power relations as it has with a search for solutions to certain technical problems relating to the issuance and regulation of money and credit.

The main technical problems that money systems and currencies must solve are those of liquidity, adjustment and confidence. As Gilpin points out,

> To assure liquidity, the system must provide an adequate (but not inflationary) supply of currency to finance trade, facilitate adjustment, and

provide financial reserves. To deal with the adjustment problem, the system must specify methods to resolve national payments disequilibria . . . The system must also prevent destabilizing shifts in the composition of national reserves. Such shifts can be caused by loss of confidence in the reserve currency or currencies. Each of these problems must be solved if an international monetary system is to operate efficiently and integrate the world economy. (Gilpin, 1987, pp. 118–19)

Geopolitics affects these problems because no one solution can satisfy all parties equally. Even when all countries have an interest in international monetary stability, some powerful countries will have an interest in so arranging international monetary affairs that a particular national interest is favoured. This seeming paradox, or contradiction, is mirrored by the $N-1$ problem in international finance: a situation where, in 'a monetary system composed of N countries, $N-1$ countries are free to change their exchange rate but one country cannot change its exchange rate, because its currency is the standard to which all other countries peg their currency values' (Gilpin, 1987, p. 138). (The 'obvious' solution to this consistency problem is to have a truly world money, not tied to any one issuing country; an 'obvious' solution only if one is prepared to overlook the fact that the modern world economy is made up of competing countries or nation states.) The paradox of absolute and relative gains highlights a persistent 'prisoner's dilemma' situation that is apparent in international monetary relations. It also confirms some commentators in the view that stable international relations can only be enforced when there is a strong and unrivalled hegemonic power in world affairs. The theory of hegemonic stability predicts that international economic and monetary relations will tend towards anarchy when there is no clear hegemon present to enforce a stable set of international rules and regulations (see Keohane, 1984; Corbridge, 1988; Eichengreen, 1992).

The international monetary system in the pre-modern era was stable for rather different reasons to those mentioned above. International currency units were then largely separated from national currency units and the national versus international question did not arise to the same extent. International trade prior to the sixteenth and seventeenth centuries was financed largely by gold and silver currencies, such as the dinar of the Arabs or the ducat of Venice. States had little incentive to debase their currency units precisely because competing currency units were available to international merchants. The debasement of currencies was left to local economies, where local monies 'were very much at the mercy of governments' (Gilpin, 1987, p. 120).

With the great influx of precious metals into Europe from the New World in the sixteenth and seventeenth centuries, the long-standing divide between national and international monetary systems was slowly eroded. National economies now became interdependent to a greater extent and economic theories were advanced to counter the mercantilist claim that states would remain strong only by accumulating specie money (gold and silver). Hume showed that a country accumulating specie money would encounter an increase in its domestic money supply, which would cause its domestic and export prices to rise. Imports would be sucked into such a country, with the result that a changed flow of trade would cause specie money to flow out of the country in due course.

Hume's price–specie flow mechanism provided intellectual support for the classical gold standard system, which governed international monetary relations from 1870 to 1914. Yet by this time money had already been 'transformed from a gift of nature to a creation of the state' (Gilpin, 1987, p. 121). The growth of world production and trade in the nineteenth century necessitated a growth in paper or 'political' monies, which would be backed by specie monies but not quite limited by them. The growth in fiduciary monies again raised the question of the balance to be struck between contending nation states and the wider international community. The classical gold standard worked well enough when Britain enforced the rules of the game: namely, that central banks of countries on the gold standard would buy and sell gold at a fixed price, and that private citizens could freely export and import gold (Cohen, 1977, p. 77; see also chapter 2 by Geoffrey Ingham). It also worked to the extent that governments were willing to maintain the stability of international monetary relations even at the cost of persistent bouts of deflation, devaluation and mass unemployment, and notwithstanding the scars imposed upon the dependent colonial countries by the tendency of the gold standard to erode their commodity terms of trade. The stability of the system also depended upon the willingness of France, Germany and the United States to accord to Britain the advantages conferred upon it in the form of leverage over international trade and capital movements.

The First World War brought the classical gold standard years to an end. After the War a gold-exchange standard system survived for a few years, but it depended too much on the continued strength of sterling at a time when Britain was in relative decline. In the interwar years, too, countries were keen to assert a degree of sovereignty over their 'own' economic affairs (however illusory), and some governments had learned that they could not ride roughshod over the living standards of their labouring classes (even if attitudes to the British General Strike of 1926 did confirm a willingness to suspend such sensitivities). In the 1930s the international monetary and economic systems fell into disrepair. Regional trading and monetary blocs emerged and competitive deflations were common (Eichengreen and Lindert, 1989). The Second World War was perhaps an obvious conclusion to the absence of international economic cooperation which was apparent in this decade.

The concluding years of the Second World War brought fresh attempts to provide an international monetary system that would respect national economic agendas while ensuring stability and growth for all. The Bretton Woods system, which was negotiated in 1944 (by Keynes and Dexter White above all), grounded this compromise in a system of fixed exchange rates, currency convertibility (mainly from 1958) and ostensibly national controls over employment, savings and interest rates (Wood, 1986). The International Monetary Fund (IMF) was set up to supervise this system and to assist countries in short-term balance of payments difficulties. As a last resort, a country in a state of 'fundamental disequilibrium' could change its exchange rates with international consent. In later years, the International Bank for Reconstruction and Development (the World Bank) would transfer some funds from the developed world to the developing world. The economies of Japan and Europe were themselves rebuilt after 1945 by massive infusions of US capital, most obviously in the form of military spending, but also by means of the Marshall Plan for Europe (1948–52).

The Bretton Woods years (from 1944 to the mid-1970s in formal terms; from 1958 to 1964 in its pure form) coincided with the golden age of capitalism in the developed world; years when even working class men and women 'had never had it so good' (to paraphrase Harold Macmillan). But it would be too easy to assume that the former guaranteed the latter. The Bretton Woods system doubtless did meet part of its brief (even if that brief was a pale shadow of Keynes's vision of an international world economy: Moggridge, 1992), but the system contained within itself three pressing contradictions.

The system depended, first of all, on the willingness of the United States – as the new hegemonic power – to maintain the value of the US dollar against gold. The Bretton Woods system proposed a gold–dollar exchange standard, wherein the US dollar would serve as the main international means of payment, but where the value of the dollar would remain fixed at a price of US $35 per ounce of gold. Central banks fearful that the United States was printing too many dollars could demand gold from the United States in return for accumulated dollar holdings (or IOUs). The problem was that an expanded international trade could only be financed by an increase in paper monies (US dollars) in excess of the rate of growth of US gold reserves. This is the so-called Triffin paradox (Triffin, 1960). At a certain point the system was bound to become a dollar standard (fiat money) system, and faith in it would then be proportional to the confidence that the rest of the world expressed in the capacity and the willingness of the United States not to print dollars to excess (see chapter 3 by Susan Strange).

Secondly, and relatedly, the stability of a dollar standard system could only be guaranteed to the extent that the United States was willing to subordinate its immediate national economic and political interests to wider system goals. In the 1950s and the early 1960s the United States did indeed act as a benevolent despot. Inflation was kept low in the

United States (even at the cost of a rate of unemployment higher than the OECD average), and political allies of the USA were allowed to pursue discriminatory trading practices against it. In the mid-to-late 1960s this system began to change. Faced with a costly war in Vietnam, with a run on US gold reserves initiated by De Gaulle's France, and with a rising US trade deficit, President Nixon moved finally, in August 1971, to close the gold–dollar window. Henceforth the US dollar would not be backed by gold. It would be backed only by the US Treasury and by international confidence in its value and trading worth. The USA now took steps to improve its export position by driving down the value of the dollar (Parboni, 1981). International liquidity was massively expanded by lax monetary policies in the USA and by a much expanded US balance of payments deficit. Other countries could react defensively to the USA by devaluing their own currencies, but this served only to suck inflation into their economies more quickly than was already the case. The OPEC oil price rises of 1973–4 did not make life any easier for oil-importing countries.

Finally, the planners of the Bretton Woods system assumed that there would be a relatively even rate of economic growth between countries in the postwar era (Brett, 1985). In the 1940s it was not envisaged that the very vitality of the postwar world economy would encourage massive flows of capital from the USA to Europe and Japan, and from these three regions to some newly industrializing countries. Yet it was the relative decline of the US economy that encouraged the USA to experiment with economic policies that were more exceptionalist than internationalist. The closing of the gold–dollar window in 1971 was one instance of such behaviour; another was the reaction of the USA to the OPEC oil price hikes of 1973–4. There is some evidence to suggest that the USA was not unduly worried by OPEC's actions. As an oil producer itself, the USA believed that the oil crisis would hurt its economic rivals much more than it would hurt the United States.

The breakdown of the Bretton Woods system in the 1970s was accompanied by a massive surge in inflation in both the developed and the developing worlds (see chapter 4 by Stuart Corbridge). Rates of inflation differed from country to country in part because of the strength of local labour movements and different government policies, but the main source of the global inflation in the 1970s was the large number of dollars put into circulation by the US authorities. The emergence of the Eurobanks, and the Eurobanking phenomenon, only expanded this pool of high-powered dollars and further increased openness in international economic affairs (and in the transmission and receipt of inflation). The Eurobanks also helped to define a new geography of international finance, as stateless monies moved offshore – or beyond national regulatory regimes – and increasingly came to rest in 'fictitious spaces', which played host to fictitious capitals. (For more on these distinctions, see chapter 5 by Susan Roberts.)

The Bretton Woods years finally came to an end in the late 1970s when the Carter, Schmidt and Callaghan governments took steps to rein in the global money supply. The early 1980s were years of high interest rates and tight money. They were also years of sharply fluctuating exchange rates, as governments sought once more to recover some of the economic powers they had previously surrendered to the international community (now they would surrender these powers to the markets). The early post-Bretton Woods era was an era of savage devaluations in the indebted developing world and in parts of Eastern Europe, as debts extended at floating interest rates in the late 1970s and early 1980s became liable for repayment at high real interest rates (and with the US dollar riding high in the foreign exchange markets: Corbridge, 1993). Meanwhile, in the United States, the first Reagan administration pursued an extraordinary mixture of lax fiscal policies and tight monetary policies. The upshot was that Americans were put back to work in the short term, but only at the cost of mounting export uncompetitiveness and massive external borrowing, mainly from Japan (Corbridge and Agnew, 1991; see also figure 1.1). In the late 1980s America's new exceptionalism became a matter of some concern within the United States, as well as outside its borders. As the US net external debt spiralled upwards towards US $1 trillion,[2] it became apparent that America's debt service obligations would remain high for many years to come, and that its creditors might want to have their debts serviced in the form of real US assets (real estate, equity), rather than in the form of a depreciating dollar (Congdon, 1988). In

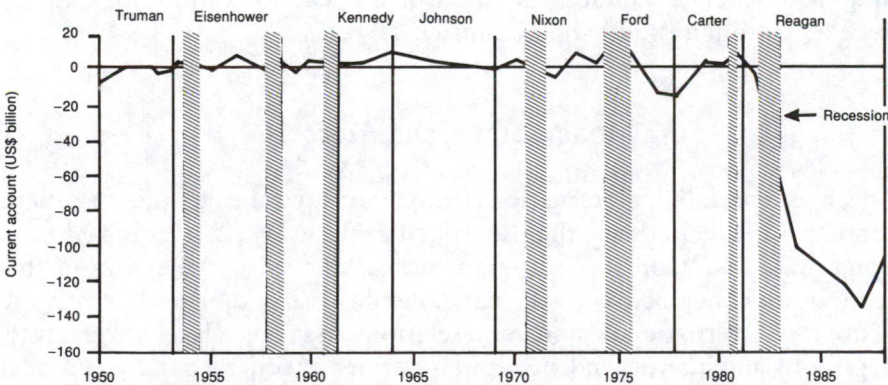

Figure 1.1 US international accounts, 1950–1988. Balance on current account in seasonally adjusted billions of dollars.
Source: IMF, *International Financial Statistics*, various issues.

---

2 The size of the net external debt of the United States is the subject of some debate. It is likely that the value of US assets abroad is higher than is conventionally suggested, not least because it is traditionally valued at historic cost (see also Eisner, 1986).

some quarters there was even talk of the United States becoming a dependent country (Tolchin and Tolchin, 1988).

Outside the United States, the main concern was that scarce international savings were flowing to the most powerful economy in the world and not to the rest of the international community (as history suggested they should do: Stallings, 1987). The developing countries' debt crisis and massive capital flight compounded this trend and ensured that future development would only be produced by means of a costly process of 'structural adjustment' in the present and near future. There was also concern that fluctuations in interest rates and exchange rates were causing unnecessary problems for businesses in open economies like the UK and the Netherlands.

In the late 1980s new attempts were made to balance the needs of individual countries and the wider international economy (Claassen, 1990). In Europe this took the form of a reinvigorated European Monetary System and a greater role for the European Currency Unit (the ecu, a quasi-stateless money). Germany would exercise leadership in an expanded European Community, with the Bundesbank coming in time to serve as Europe's central bank. Elsewhere, attempts at international cooperation were forged at the Plaza and Louvre accords of the mid-to-late 1980s, at various summit meetings of the G3 and G7 powers, and by means of the Baker and Brady proposals for debt crisis management. Japan, for its part, continued to build up a yen zone in the Pacific Rim and Tokyo continued to press its claims as a major financial centre (see chapter 6 by Andrew Leyshon). By 1990, significantly, Tokyo was beginning to challenge London as the world's leading centre for foreign exchange dealing (Budd and Whimster, 1992).

Money, States and Markets

The rise and fall of international monetary systems in the twentieth century is the main theme that ties together the essays in part I of *Money, Power and Space*. In their different ways, all five of the essays in this section are concerned with the fundamental issues that lie beneath the history of international monetary relations: issues such as sovereignty, hegemony and interdependence, and questions of order, anarchy and free-riding in international relations theory and practice. The essays in part II of *Money, Power and Space* are not unconcerned with these issues (see chapter 7 by Sheila Dow and chapter 11 by Ron Martin, in particular), but their particular focus is on the institutional geographies of international finance and national regimes of industrial and financial capitalism.

At first glance, the post-1978 international monetary system would seem to be a system without rules or reason, but this is not the case. Proponents of the post-Bretton Woods 'system' sometimes maintain that discipline is now imposed upon the community of money by financial markets that are about as perfectly informed and competitive as markets ever can be. The 'new international monetary system' is a system in which the evident volatility of interest and exchange rates, not to mention capital movements, is countermanded by new financial institutions and new instruments designed to share risks and to provide insurance for the market's major players. Securitization, or the raising of capital sums without the intermediation of banks (for loans) or the stock markets (for shares and rights issues), is one aspect of this new financial system. As Whimster and Budd (1992, p. 11) point out, securitization has the effect of reducing 'the integuments of physical assets to merely tradeable pieces of paper' (Whimster and Budd, 1992, p. 11).

Not surprisingly, securitization has gone hand in hand with globalization and deregulation as the financial services industry has tried to escape the constraints imposed by physical space and tangible resources (Hamilton, 1986). As a result, paper money has become an increasingly poor indicator of what money 'really is'. Moreover, innovations like swaps and rapidly growing futures markets (where time itself is discounted), and various instruments for hedging risks (such as floating rate notes), all make the point that the financial markets are now defined by a set of credit relationships with different time structures, etched in computer memories. The Eurobond market also took off in the 1980s, as lenders sought to protect themselves against the perils apparent in defaults on large-scale loans to syndicates of banks.

These various new instruments and institutions have in turn brought with them significant changes in the employment structures and geography of the financial services industry. In the 1980s, financial services became a proportionately larger employer of labour (and female labour especially) in most countries of the world (see figure 1.2), although in the recession of the early 1990s employment levels fell rapidly. A new geography of employment in financial services has also appeared since the late 1980s, with the emergence of regional financial centres in many countries (Gentle et al., 1991) and de-centred trading exchanges like NASDAQ. Face-to-face contacts remain important in the male dominated world of high-finance, but elsewhere new locational possibilities are being opened up by video screens and telephone trading.

The financial innovations of the 1980s should not lightly be discounted. There is evidence to suggest that venture capital is now more readily available in some developed and developing countries (the UK and India, for example) than was the case ten years ago and that both institutional and private investors have benefited from the reforms that have ended the quasi-monopoly positions enjoyed by the commercial banks (as compared to investment banks and building societies). The fact that financial capitalism has not yet collapsed is itself an important rejoinder to those who have bemoaned its 'inherent instability'! A prospective stability was also being restored by regional monetary systems like the

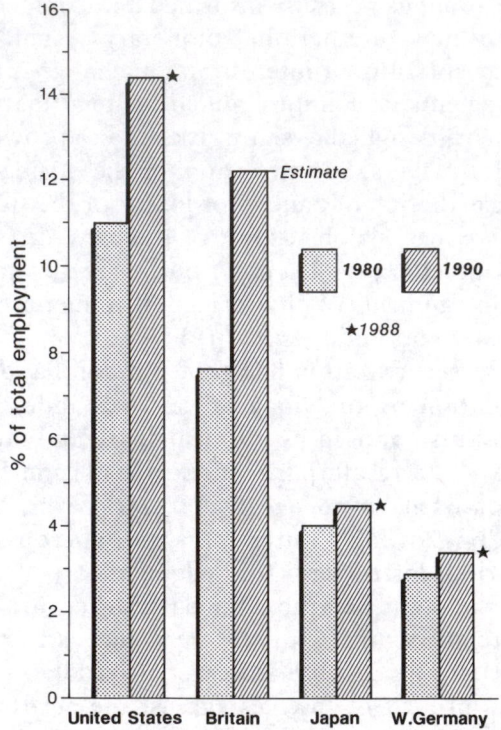

Figure 1.2   Employment in financial services: selected countries, 1980–1990.
Source: *The Economist*, 1992.

European Monetary System (see chapter 7 by Sheila Dow) – at least before the shocks of 1992–3 (see also Leyshon and Thrift, 1992).

Nevertheless, the liberalization of financial capitalism has not been without its costs. To begin with, there is widespread concern about the absence of effective reserve requirements in the global banking system. Notwithstanding the recent introduction of international capital adequacy guidelines by the Bank for International Settlements, the rate of expansion of international liquidity is still very much at the mercy of the banking industry and not at the behest of governments (Wachtel, 1986). This situation might cause problems, ironically, in those countries where governments are most committed to tight monetary targets. How can national money supplies be measured accurately and controlled in an era of global (and broad) money supplies? (As a 'global monetarist', McKinnon has long proposed that the world money supply should be controlled by a coordinated money supply policy on the part of the United States, Germany and Japan – the three countries that account for nearly two-thirds of the industrial world's output: McKinnon, 1984).

The absence of effective reserve requirements might also encourage further periods in which credit monies are lent in excess of the rate of expansion warranted by plausible estimates of medium-to-long term rates of economic growth in different regions. The continuing problems of some developing countries are an obvious testimony to a bout of uncontrolled lending in the 1970s and early 1980s. Further testimony comes from the troubled Savings and Loan Associations in the United States; associations that were encouraged through the 1980s to expand into financial markets and geographical regions in which many had little previous experience, with catastrophic results (Pizzo et al., 1991). As Keynes long ago pointed out, bankers are the most romantic and least realistic of men.

More worryingly, David Harvey has argued that capitalism can only live on tick, even if the credit mountains that then pile up must finally crash down upon the fragile built environments that take shape in their shadow. According to Harvey, 'The credit system is a product of capital's own endeavours to deal with the internal contradictions of capitalism. What Marx [shows] us is how capital's solution ends up heightening rather than diminishing the contradictions' (Harvey, 1982, p. 239). To put it one last way, when companies failed in the deflationary years of the gold standard era, they did so with disastrous consequences for the workers employed by those concerns (and their suppliers). When the crises of capitalism are such that the value of money itself is called into question, the deflationary consequences are likely to be even more long-lasting and much more generalized across space. On this reading, the prospects for the 1990s are none too pleasing.

A second point follows on from this. Although some barriers have been broken down in the 'new' world of international finance – both between countries and between institutions – many barriers still remain. Transaction costs and entry costs are by no means negligible and they still show considerable variation across space. Geography is not just a product or a victim of the locational preferences of financial institutions; it also shapes and constrains these preferences. National cultures of money-making and monetary regulation still matter, as the marked differentials that continue to exist in national interest rates (in supposedly interlocking and global money markets: Bayoumi, 1989) clearly attest.[3] To explain all such differentials by reference to 'risk premiums' is surely to risk a tautology. In the United Kingdom in 1991/2, real interest rates were up to six percentage points higher than corresponding rates in the United States, this despite the guarantees made to the markets by Britain's Conservative Government and by Britain's then membership of the European Exchange Rate Mechanism.

Apart from the obvious vagaries of national economic performance, the most important means by which such differences are perpetrated can

3 The work of Bayoumi found early apparent confirmation in the work of Feldstein and Horioka (1980). Rather different conclusions have been reached by Cooper (1991). For a more general review of global financial integration, see O'Brien (1992).

be found in the markedly different ways in which states manage the institutional relationships between finance and industry (Coakley and Harris, 1983; Murphy and Tooze, 1991). It is by now a commonplace observation that certain countries seem to have forged institutional relationships in which financial capital is closely linked in with industrial capital, thus approximating to Hilferding's (1981) concept of finance capital. German industrial companies continue to raise a majority of their capital by loans from banks that have a direct equity stake in the companies concerned. Similarly, in Japan, the *keiretsu* nearly always include banks and, in any case, certain banks have been moulded by the state into long-term savings institutions that offer favourable terms and low real rates of interest to industry (see chapter 6 by Andrew Leyshon). In other countries – and it is Australia, the USA and the UK that are usually singled out – the stock markets are more important sources of industrial finance with, so it is argued, a consequent tendency to short-termism in industries that are then geared to maximizing their annual or half-yearly or even quarterly statements. Industry in such countries is also more likely to be affected by the influence of the large pension funds that are among the chief owners of stocks and shares (see chapter 9 by Peter Marden and Gordon Clark and chapter 10 by Michael Pryke). It is a much argued point whether the latter, more open system is now becoming hegemonic in the world as a result of liberalization in countries like Japan in the 1980s and a complementary rise in the power of the financial markets (Thrift and Leyshon, 1992), or whether the former system of close ties between finance and industry, regulated by a strong central bank like the Bundesbank (Marsh, 1992), may make a comeback. (It is also worth noting that it is difficult to prove a direct link between different national systems of regulation and variations in national economic performance.)

The size and importance of the world's major financial institutions provides another reason for doubting the strong version of the 'efficient financial markets' thesis. Companies of the size and market capitalization of Citibank or Nomura or Salomon Brothers are not just financial actors like any other; they are major players and market *makers*. Such institutions can 'distort' otherwise efficient financial markets, although they need not necessarily do so. They can do this legally or illegally (as the recent scandals at Nomura and Salomon Brothers have indicated all too clearly). More significantly, perhaps, such institutions, together with market makers like Michael Milken, the ex-junk bond king, and Ivan Boesky, the disgraced insider dealer, can provide funds to companies whose aim is often to divide up and rule (such as the Hanson Group, albeit in the name of microeconomic efficiency), and to those small companies who want to take over some of the world's largest corporations by means of leveraged buy-outs. It is one of the great virtues of the 'new' Australian economic geography that the locational and employment effects of such restructuring *through the global financial markets* have been mapped out in some detail. Further work in this tradition is provided in this volume by Maurice Daly (chapter 8) and by Ron Martin (chapter 11). A common point of focus of their chapters is the institutional frameworks in and through which industrial and financial capitals are brought into local (and not so local) contact.

Money Politics and the Community of Money

The restructuring of 'real' communities by the community of money rarely goes uncontested, but the forms in which money is politicized vary from place to place, according to the effectiveness of different political coalitions and different local constructions of the powers of money. The essays in part III of *Money, Power and Space* address themselves directly to this issue: to the politics of money in the widest sense.

In most industrialized countries, struggles over the practices and meanings of money have usually been most visible when they have been connected to everyday life, and especially to the built environment. The built environment has been a symbol both of the power of money and of attempts to fend off Mammon over a long period of time. Whether it is John Wood the Elder's Bath, the result of an attempt to stand for ideals outside money (and a desperate scramble for the money to build it), Napoleon III's Paris, the result of an attempt to enshrine money (and brought about in part by the financial skills of the Rothschilds and the Pereire brothers), or the fierce struggle documented here by Jane Jacobs (chapter 15) to modernize the City of London's built environment as a functioning way-station for the space of money flows that Castells (1989) describes, the built environment nearly always declares a relation to money, whether enthusiastic or equivocal. Nowhere is this made clearer than in the case of ordinary domestic housing. (See chapter 12 by Chris Hamnett; see also chapter 13 by Barney Warf, which examines the relationship between financial deregulation and property speculation in the USA in the 1980s). The modern housing market sells islands of domesticity that can only now be built by means of sophisticated forms of financial engineering: from simple forms of credit, through linkage to insurance policies, to contemporary forms of securitization of mortgages. For many people it is the mortgage interest rate that remains the most potent sign of the power of money.

A related struggle has been over the closure of industrial plants. Throughout the 1980s the power of money was underlined by the seemingly magical ability of highly leveraged firms to buy out and restructure large corporations, often to the disadvantage of many local communities. In films like *Wall Street*, money is presented as a mobile, impersonal force wielded by greedy bad guys – the demonic new 'masters of the universe' (Wolfe, 1987) – to the detriment of working-class communities that embody all that is solid and worthwhile in the national character. It is an 'unreal world' in which numbers blast

> across screens; numbers which can be erased with the touch of a finger, or a loud voice. Numbers which point to imaginary properties or imaginary things. Companies with made-up names, whose productivity is measured by imaginary numbers concerning losses and gains. Money going in and out of hidden accounts. Money attached to nothing but imaginary numbers attached to made-up accounts, built on the transactions and imagined doings of imaginary companies. Careers built on who can best manipulate this imaginary political economy of signs. (Denzin, 1991, p. 91; see also Lewis, 1990)

No doubt there is considerable accuracy to this depiction. Yet, at the same time, as Zukin shows in her depictions of the fortunes of two steel communities in West Virginia and Michigan threatened by shutdowns, it was the intervention of ingenious investment bankers that allowed some steel plants to continue, notwithstanding the 'deep cultural antipathy to New York financial types' (Zukin, 1991, p. 125) registered by most local workers.

At the back of all this, for many people, is the problem of their own place in the financial system. Their place may be a strong one, shored up by trusts, insurance policies, shares and equity plans. This is the world of the rich and the powerful, or at least the comfortably off (Rubinstein, 1987; Marcus, 1992). It is certainly a very specific world. For example, in the United States the richest 10 per cent of the population own roughly 68 per cent of the nation's wealth. On one estimate, that 10 per cent includes at least 1,300,000 dollar millionaires, 700,000 people with assets worth upwards of US $10 million and 200,000 people with assets of more than US $20 million (Lapham, 1989). In the United States the rich and the powerful live in a relatively few areas, in the same kind of style that was described by Zorbaugh in his classic study of the 'Gold Coast' of Chicago (Zorbaugh, 1929). These communities of the monied can be compared with those of the poor, weighed down with debts. In the United States (as in some other OECD countries), the large retail banks are increasingly aiming to attract business from only the most wealthy two-fifths of the population (Christopherson, 1993), leaving the rest of the population to manage without easy access to formal sources of personal finance. The poor are being consigned to a twilight world of cheque-cashing services and unregulated loan-sharking (which is also rampant in the inner-city areas of the UK).

Los Angeles presents a good example of this new, bleak, financially divided landscape. Dymski and Veitch (1992) have shown how certain poorer areas of Los Angeles are systematically disadvantaged by a lack of access to a financial services infrastructure, with consequent detrimental

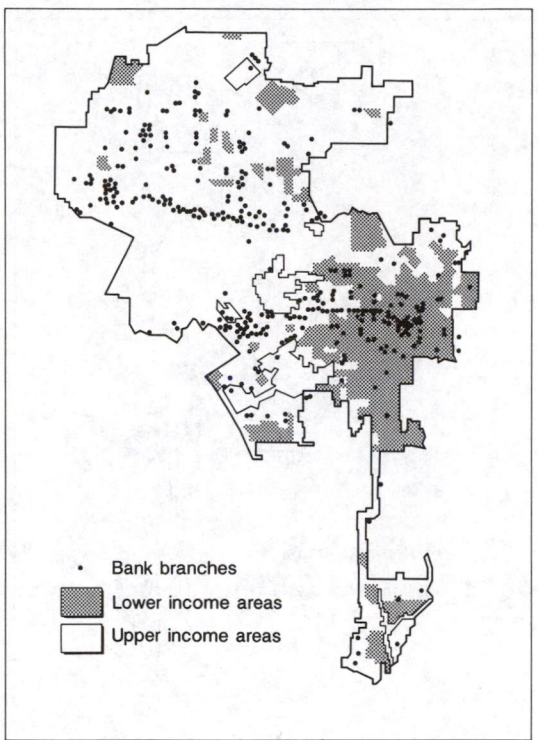

Figure 1.3 Access to bank branches across income areas in the city of Los Angeles. *Source*: Dymski et al., 1991.

results in terms of their ability to access funds for economic regeneration (figure 1.3). In particular, there is a clear under-representation of bank branches in lower-income and minority areas of Los Angeles (Dymski et al., 1991), and a large proportion of the black and Hispanic populations finds it difficult to obtain home loans. Not only are the number of loans made, and the amounts loaned, lower in 'minority' neighbourhoods than in comparable white neighbourhoods; there is also considerable evidence of 'redlining', with entire areas being deprived of mortgage finance (see figure 1.4). Finally, much of Los Angeles has effectively become an insurance no-go zone. In many poorer areas of the city, small businesses now find it impossible to get insurance because premiums are set at such a high level. Similarly, insurance on houses and cars is something that a large part of the population of Los Angeles is now denied (see figure 1.5). Needless to say, the problems of poorer Angelenos are mirrored in other poor communities throughout the developed and the developing world.

These and other struggles around the practices and meanings of money in turn have had important repercussions on what money is considered to stand for. These repercussions can be felt across the full range of geographical scales. Most obviously, battles continue to rage at the

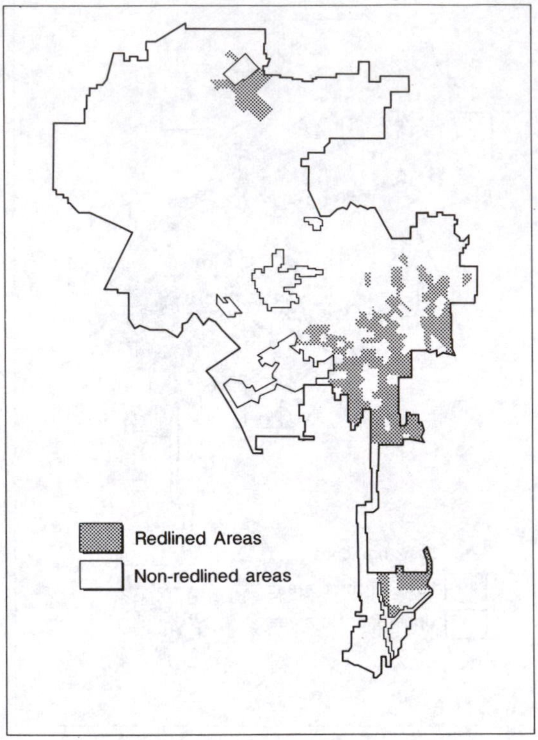

Figure 1.4 Redlined areas in the city of Los Angeles.
Source: Dymski et al., 1991.

international scale. There are activist alliances in the North demanding
an end to an international debt crisis which has put bank profits before
development and which throws workers out of jobs in some Northern
export industries (George, 1989). These alliances are mirrored by those
in the South that challenge the IMF for Imposing Misery and Famine and
that encourage women to take food from supermarkets under the banner
'Can't Pay, Won't Pay' (Walton, 1989). Still other activist groups have
encouraged women and men to set up their own financial institutions,
including the cooperative banks now common in parts of India and
Bangladesh. There are also battles at national scales over the course that
financial systems take: struggles, for example, over the imposition of
Sharia laws in certain Muslim countries, over the interest rates charged
to small businesses and over the ethical conduct of financial institutions
investing funds in environmentally unsound activities and/or countries
with poor human rights records. Finally, there are a whole series of local
battles. In the United States, a number of local coalitions have attempted
to manage the fall-out from the unbridled property speculation of the
1980s that was fuelled by financial deregulation. Other local coalitions
have tried more directly to intervene in local financial infrastructures,

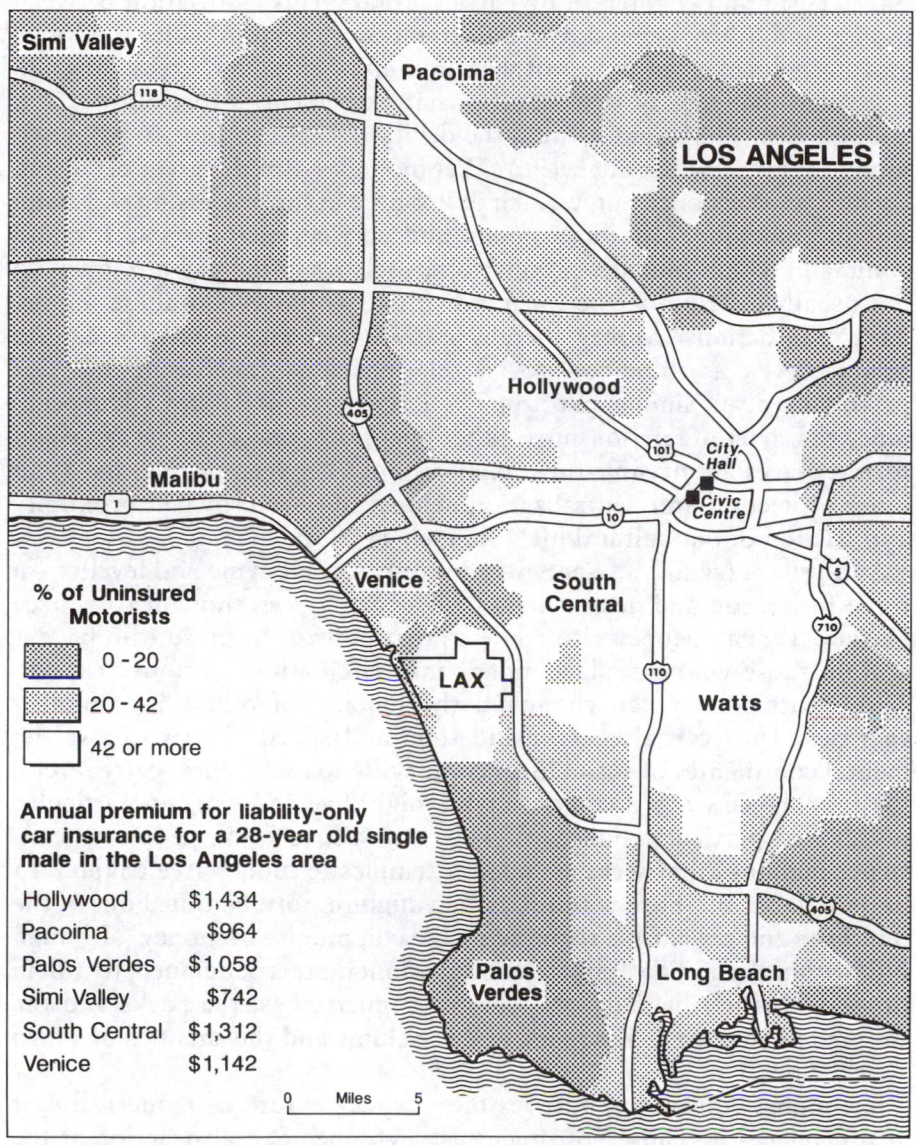

Figure 1.5 Insurance 'no-go' areas in the Los Angeles urban area.
Source: *Los Angeles Times*, 1993.

as in the case of the growing 'financial democracy' movement (Bond, 1990).

In most of these struggles, money and its makers are presented as corrupting agents, as tokens of that indifference (and affluence elsewhere) that is blind to the physical and emotional needs of people not able to avail themselves of money's undoubted powers (see chapter 14 by

Nigel Thrift and chapter 16 by Patrick Bond). This association between money and 'filthy lucre' draws our attention to certain wider questions and struggles over the power of the community of money. Freud long ago suggested that money is to adults what excrement is to children, and colloquialisms like tight-ass and the devil's ducats continue to pay testimony to this view (Greider, 1987). Yet money is also the great cynic and leveller, as Marx once put it. A ten dollar note in the possession of person A will command just those goods and services that person B could command with a similar ten dollar bill; societies in the pay of money do not usually discriminate between individuals at the level of these simple, daily transactions. Money thereby allows men and women a certain privacy, even as it renders social relations less transparent and less personalized. As Simmel put it in *The Philosophy of Money*: 'The pecuniary character of relationships, either openly or concealed in a thousand forms, places an invisible functional distance between people that is an inner protection and neutralization against the overcrowded proximity and friction of our cultural life' (Simmel, 1990, p. 477).

And yet . . . (again) . . . money is not only a great cynic and leveller – a force for reason and democracy as it has often been thought to be (see Harvey, 1989a). Money also confers great powers on those who have it and on those who can place money into circulation as money capital. Those with money can command the labours of others in capitalist societies. They can also command time and space, the two most elemental coordinates of social life. People with 'loadsamoney' can exercise the first choice when it comes to who might live and work in particular places and particular buildings. They can also employ people to construct buildings that serve as modern temples to money (see chapter 15 by Jane Jacobs). Those without money might in turn be tidied out of the buildings and pavements required by the community of money (although not without a fight). People without money are condemned to fill in those spaces left behind – the decaying inner cities, the parks and the shopfronts that serve as squats, and the slums and the shanties of Third World cities.

But money not only reinforces the abstract nature of modern life, it also produces it. Those postmodernists who bemoan abstraction at the level of epistemology sometimes forget that at the level of ontology the production of differences and distinctions is only made possible by concrete abstractions like money. Money forces us to act and think in abstract, depersonalized terms. This is especially true of modern forms of money, which have moved away from basic specie monies into the realm of electronic signifiers in which money refers only to itself.

Rotman (1989) makes just this point in his book *Signifying Nothing: the Semiotics of Zero*. Consider, says Rotman, how extraordinary modern money is and how difficult it is to define (and to escape). (Dickens makes a similar point when he confronts us with Dombey's son, Paul,

asking of his father, 'Papa! what's money?': Harvey, 1989a, p. 167.)
Consider, too, how fantastical are futures contracts and Eurobond markets, and how we, as supposedly sophisticated individuals, have placed
our faith first in gold and silver, then in paper monies, and now in
electronic representations of these paper tokens of 'real' value. Yet we
have no choice but to take (construct) money for granted in this way
(save in rapid inflations: Berti and Bombi, 1988). Fantastic as our faith
might be, it is a necessary faith. We must believe in the modern money
form because money greases the wheels of industry; money makes the
world go around. Money makes possible the complexity of modern life
and the extended divisions of labour that are at its core. Without global
money, there can be no global trade and industry; no modern forms of
globalization. While money is undoubtedly an abstraction, it is also
concrete. Money shapes the lives of men and women almost everywhere.
'Individuals', Marx wrote more than a century ago, 'are now ruled by
abstractions, whereas earlier they depended on one another' (Marx,
1973, p. 146). Money at once confers individual freedom and social
bondage; it is a contradictory social presence that embodies the contradictions of modern social life itself.

The problem is that complexity and contradiction are not always easy
to live with. The very ubiquity of money provokes not only local attempts to regulate its use, but also movements that challenge its very
right to be. At one level, perhaps, this challenge is apparent in the
well-observed trend for monied individuals to transfer their 'paper'
wealth into more tangible forms of cultural capital (Thrift and Leyshon,
1992). The idea that money should be laundered, or made clean, is still
a pervasive one in many Western societies (albeit less so in the United
States than in Europe and Japan).

More straightforwardly, the powers of money 'itself' continue to be
contested in those societies and regions on the boundaries between
'pre-capitalism' and capitalism. In his book *The Devil and Commodity
Fetishism in South America*, Michael Taussig (1980) recounts the events
surrounding the expanded use of paper monies in the peasant communities of the Cauca Valley in Colombia. One such tale concerns the
'baptism of the bills', a ceremony of baptism in which paper monies
usurp the name of a child to be baptized and thus claim certain powers
of reproduction. The baptized bills are said to call forth further bills, and
when such bills are passed into local cash registers they have been
'known' to make off with the entire contents of the till.

Taussig concludes that local people are here registering the apparent
power of money in the Cauca Valley to create wealth itself; a power
associated with urban traders and moneylenders especially. The Cauca
peasants are also registering the 'unnaturalness' of this act (the devil of
money in this case being opposed to the Christian ceremony of baptism).
If real wealth is produced only by land and labour, money can only be a

false god, which by its very nature must corrupt certain natural and pre-existing social and economic relationships. In short, the peasants of the Cauca valley are opposing a natural economy based on use-values (the world of gift exchange somewhat idealized by Taussig: see Parry and Bloch, 1989, p. 9) to a Satanic world of exchange value and easy money. Michael Watts tells a not dissimilar story in chapter 17 of this book. He focuses on the conflicting ways in which money mediates between relationships based upon oil wealth and Islam in modern Nigeria. In Hausaland, as in the Cauca Valley of Colombia, money is far from an unproblematical category.

The chapters in part III of *Money, Power and Space* confirm that money is more than just an economic phenomenon, even though it is often treated as the natural province of economists. Money is also a social and cultural relation bound up with asymmetries of power, which must vary from place to place. If the varied contributors to this volume – and the economists among them! – give a sense of these variegated worlds of money, then *Money, Power and Space* will have served its purpose.

References

Aglietta, M. (1982) World capitalism in the eighties. *New Left Review*, 137, 5–41.

Bayoumi, T. (1989) Saving-investment correlations. IMF Working Paper 89/66. Washington, DC: International Monetary Fund.

Berti, A. and Bombi, A. (1988) *The Child's Construction of Economics*. Cambridge: Cambridge University Press.

Bond, P. (1990) The new US class struggle: financial industry power versus grassroots populism. *Capital and Class*, 40, 150–81.

Brett, E. (1985) *The World Economy since the War: the Politics of Uneven Development*. London: Macmillan.

Budd, L. and Whimster, S. (eds) (1992) *Global Finance and Urban Living: a Study of Metropolitan Change*. London: Routledge.

Castells, M. (1989) *The Informational City*. Oxford: Blackwell.

Christopherson, S. (1993) How the state and the market are remaking the landscape of inequality. *Economic Geography* (forthcoming).

Claassen, E.-M. (ed.) (1990) *International and European Monetary Systems*. London: Heinemann.

Coakley, J. and Harris, L. (1983) *The City of Capital*. Oxford: Blackwell.

Cohen, B. (1977) *Organizing the World's Money: the Political Economy of International Monetary Relations*. New York: Basic Books.

Congdon, T. (1988) *The Debt Threat*. Oxford: Blackwell.

Cooper, S. (1991) Cross-border savings flows and capital mobility in the G7 economies. Bank of England Discussion Papers, Number 54.

Corbridge, S. (1988) The asymmetry of interdependence: the United States and the geopolitics of international financial relations. *Studies in Comparative International Development*, 23, 3–29.

Corbridge, S. (1993) *Debt and Development*. Oxford: Blackwell.

Corbridge, S. and Agnew, J. (1991) The US trade and budget deficits in global perspective: an essay in geopolitical-economy. *Society and Space*, 9, 71–90.

Daly, M. and Logan, M. (1989) *The Brittle Rim: Finance, Business and the Pacific Region*. Harmondsworth: Penguin.

Denzin, N. (1991) *Images of Postmodern Society*. London: Sage.

Dymski, G. and Veitch, J. (1992) Race and the financial dynamics of urban growth. University of California, Riverside: Department of Economics Paper, 92–21.

Dymski, G., Veitch, J. and White, M. (1991) *Taking It to the Bank: Poverty Race and Credit in Los Angeles*. Los Angeles: Western Center on Law and Poverty.

Eichengreen, B. (1992) Hegemonic stability theories and the international monetary system. In R. Cooper, B. Eichengreen, G. Holtham, R. Putnam and C. Henning (eds), *Can Nations Agree? Issues in International Economic Cooperation*. Washington, DC: Brookings Institution, 255–98.

Eichengreen, B. and Lindert, P. (eds) (1989) *The International Debt Crisis in Historical Perspective*. Cambridge, MA: MIT Press.

Eisner, R. (1986) *How Real Is the Federal Deficit?* London: Macmillan.

Fagan, R. (1990) Elders IXL Ltd: finance capital and the geography of corporate restructuring. *Environment and Planning A*, 22, 647–66.

Feldstein, M. and Horioka, C. (1980) Domestic savings and international capital flows. *Economic Journal*, 91, 17–31.

Frobel, F., Heinrichs, J. and Kreye, O. (1980) *The New International Division of Labour*. Cambridge: Cambridge University Press.

Gentle, C., Marshall, J. and Coombes, M. (1991) Business reorganization and regional development: the case of the British building societies movement. *Environment and Planning A*, 23, 1759–77.

George, S. (1989) *A Fate Worse than Debt*. Harmondsworth: Pelican.

Gilpin, R. (1987) *The Political Economy of International Relations*. Princeton, NJ: Princeton University Press.

Greider, W. (1987) *Secrets of the Temple: How the Federal Reserve Runs the Country*. New York: Simon and Schuster.

Hamilton, A. (1986) *The Financial Revolution: the Big Bang Worldwide*. Harmondsworth: Penguin.

Harvey, D. (1982) *The Limits to Capital*. Oxford: Blackwell.

Harvey, D. (1989a) *The Urban Experience*. Oxford: Blackwell.

Harvey, D. (1989b) *The Condition of Postmodernity*. Oxford: Blackwell.

Hilferding, R. (1981) *Finance Capital: a Study of the Latest Phase of Capitalist Development*. London: Routledge and Kegan Paul.

Keohane, R. (1984) *After Hegemony: Cooperation and Discord in the World Political Economy*. Princeton, NJ: Princeton University Press.

Keynes, J. M. (1972) *Essays in Persuasion*. London: Macmillan.

Lapham, L. (1989) *Money and Class in America: Notes and Observations on the Civil Religion*. London: Pan.

Lash, S. and Urry, J. (1987) *The End of Organized Capitalism*. Cambridge: Polity.

Lewis, M. (1990) *Liar's Poker*. Harmondsworth: Penguin.

Leyshon, A. and Thrift, N. (1992) Liberalization and consolidation: the single European market and the remaking of European financial capital. *Environment and Planning A*, 24(1), 49–81.

Lipietz, A. (1987) *Mirages and Miracles: the Crises of Global Fordism*. London: Verso.

Lipietz, A. (1989) The debt problem, European integration and the new phase of world crisis. *New Left Review*, 178, 37–56.

McKinnon, R. (1984) *An International Standard for Monetary Stabilization*. Washington, DC: Institute for International Economics.

Marcus, G. (1992) *Lives in Trust: the Fortunes of Dynastic Families in Late Twentieth Century America*. Boulder, CO: Westview Press.

Marglin, S. and Schor, S. (eds) (1990) *The Golden Age of Capitalism*. Oxford: Clarendon.

Marsh, D. (1992) *The Bundesbank: the Bank that Rules Europe*. London: Heinemann.

Marx, K. (1973) *Grundrisse*. Harmondsworth: Penguin.

Michaels, W. (1987) *The Gold Standard and the Logic of Naturalism*. Berkeley: University of California Press.

Moggridge, D. (1992) *Maynard Keynes: an Economist's Biography*. London: Routledge.

Murphy, C. and Tooze, R. (1991) *The New International Political Economy*. Boulder, CO: Lynne Reiner.

O'Brien, R. (1992) *Global Financial Integration: the End of Geography*. London: Pinter/RIIA.

Parboni, R. (1981) *The Dollar and Its Rivals: Recession, Inflation and International Finance*. London: Verso.

Parry, J. and Bloch, M. (1989) Introduction: money and the morality of exchange. In J. Parry and M. Bloch (eds), *Money and the Morality of Exchange*. Cambridge: Cambridge University Press, 1–32.

Pizzo, S., Fricker, M. and Muolo, P. (1991) *Inside Job: the Looting of America's Savings and Loans*. New York: Harper Perennial.

Rotman, B. (1989) *Signifying Nothing: the Semiotics of Zero*. London: Macmillan.

Rubinstein, W. (1987) *Elites and the Wealthy in Modern British History*. Brighton: Harvester.

Sayer, A. and Walker, R. (1992) *The New Social Economy: Reworking the Division of Labor*. Oxford: Blackwell.

Scott, A. and Storper, M. (eds) (1986) *Production, Work, Territory: the Geographical Anatomy of Industrial Capitalism*. Hemel Hempstead: Allen and Unwin.

Simmel, G. (1990) *The Philosophy of Money*. London: Routledge.

Stallings, B. (1987) *Banker to the Third World: US Portfolio Investment in Latin America, 1900–1986*. Berkeley: University of California Press.

Strange, S. (1986) *Casino Capitalism*. Oxford: Blackwell.

Strange, S. (1988) *States and Markets*. London: Pinter.

Taussig, M. (1980) *The Devil and Commodity Fetishism in South America*. Chapel Hill: University of North Carolina Press.

Thrift, N. and Leyshon, A. (1992) In the wake of money: the City of London and the accumulation of value. In L. Budd and S. Whimster (eds), *Global*

Finance and Urban Living: a Study of Metropolitan Change. London: Routledge, 282–311.

Tolchin, M. and Tolchin, S. (1988) *Buying into America*. New York: Times Books.

Triffin, R. (1960) *Gold and the Dollar Crisis*. New Haven, CT: Yale University Press.

Wachtel, H. (1986) *The Money Mandarins: the Making of a Supranational Economic Order*. New York: Pantheon Books.

Walton, J. (1989) Debt, protest and the state in Latin America. In S. Eckstein (ed.), *Power and Popular Protest: Latin American Social Movements*. Berkeley: University of California Press, 299–328.

Whimster, S. and Budd, L. (1992) Introduction. In L. Budd and S. Whimster (eds), *Global Finance and Urban Living: a Study of Metropolitan Change*. London: Routledge, 1–28.

Wolfe, T. (1987) *The Bonfire of the Vanities*. New York: Basic Books.

Wood, R. (1986) *From Marshall Plan to Debt Crisis: Foreign Aid and Development Choices in the World Economy*. Berkeley: University of California Press.

Zorbaugh, H. (1929) *The Gold Coast and the Slum*. Chicago: University of Chicago Press.

Zukin, S. (1991) *Landscapes of Power*. Berkeley: University of California Press.

Part I

The Geopolitics of Money

2

States and Markets in the Production of World Money: Sterling and the Dollar

Geoffrey Ingham

In the history of Western capitalism, only two national currencies have acted as formal world money. Both sterling and the US dollar had their values fixed in relation to gold and functioned as the global means of exchange and the numeraire against which the values of other currencies were measured. From around 1870 to 1914 and from 1945 to 1971, the gold–sterling standard and then the gold–dollar exchange system attempted to meet the fundamental requirement of market-based economic exchange – rational calculation of value through time and space. Without them it seems implausible that the world market economy could have expanded as rapidly as it did.

On first inspection, the explanation of these two national currencies' world roles seems obvious and straightforward. In Strange's (1971) terminology, they were the 'top currencies' – strong, freely available and therefore acceptable. But while market demand may determine the use of a currency for international transactions, it is by no means as obvious that the host state should actively manage the system; that is, stabilize the value of the currency, ensure the provision of adequate liquidity, provide the means for payments adjustments and act as lender of last resort. Nevertheless, the gold–sterling standard era and the gold–dollar exchange system have been generalized to form part of a theory of 'hegemonic stability' (for a general survey see Keohane, 1980). In its simplest version, the theory claims that the existence of an economic 'hegemon' leads to a liberal international economic order in which transactions are conducted by means of the hegemon's currency. When hegemonic predominance erodes the open international regime becomes disordered and ultimately devolves into a system of competing autarkist strategies – as in the interwar years. Kindleberger, whose analysis of the post-1929 depression is generally accepted as the precursor of the theory, did not explicitly relate economic strength directly to the assumption of a world monetary role. Rather, he argued prescriptively that the world economy could only be stabilized by a single lender of last resort (Kindleberger, 1973, chapter 14). Subsequent criticism and modifications have rendered the cruder interpretations less overtly materialistic and deterministic. Gilpin's position is perhaps representative of current thinking. In his view, the existence of a single dominant power is a necessary but not a sufficient condition for the development of an open world market economy based upon a stable international monetary system. Britain, for example, 'performed the task of international economic leadership because it had the power and the will to do so' (Gilpin, 1987, p. 127). This formulation mirrors Kindleberger's original ascription of the interwar international economic disorder to Britain's inability and the USA's unwillingness to assume the role of stabilizer.

In an effective critique of hegemonic stability theory, Ruggie has argued that the USA's unwillingness fully to assume international monetary responsibility and the subsequent breakdown of the Bretton Woods system was the result of a fundamental shift in the relations between state and market that developed from the 1930s onwards (Ruggie, 1982). Domestic stabilization by means of Keynesian demand management – which he refers to as 'embedded liberalism' – has necessarily clashed with any state's attempt to manage the value of its currency in line with the perceived needs of the international monetary system. In more general terms, he argues quite correctly that it is fundamentally mistaken to attempt to understand the mid twentieth-century international economic order in terms of a model drawn from a conception of the late nineteenth-century system. The equation 'pax Britannica is equal to pax Americana', Ruggie argues, is an extremely dubious proposition. Britain before 1914 and the USA after 1945 had different 'social purposes': the former was committed to *laissez-faire* liberalism, whereas the latter's market liberalism had become 'embedded' in the state managed New Deal and 'Great Society' programmes. He shows clearly that a state's 'purpose' in relation to international monetary arrangements cannot be deduced from the mere existence of superior economic power. However, he appears to accept the argument that the USA possessed the necessary power to manage the dollar as world money had its social purpose been different. In this respect, Ruggie holds to the same rather simplistic conception of power to be found in the hegemonic stability approach, which, I would argue, has two important limitations.

First, there does not appear to be a clear enough distinction between state and market power in the production and management of world money.[1] It is at least arguable, for example, that whatever its 'purpose',

1 In the production of forms of money, the modern state performs a crucial and necessary role. As Max Weber argued, 'a state today can insure the formal validity of a type of money as the standard in its own area of power'. Legal means of payment arise from the existence of debts – tax debts to the state and interest debts of the state. But as Weber continues in his critique of the 'state theory of money', money is also a

the American state had very few power resources with which to control or manage the global money markets that made their destabilizing appearance in the 1960s. The shift from market to state in the conduct of domestic economic affairs that Ruggie, following Polanyi, has emphasized did not, of course, lead to the elimination of the market in the production of money – domestically or internationally. Financial systems did, in fact, become more regulated in the efforts to stabilize national economies; but partly as a consequence of this domestic regulation international money markets became more detached from any particular host economy in a manner that was quite dissimilar to their pre-1914 linkages. After 1945, states and money markets became more spatially and economically dissociated and this internationalization of money and finance had historically particular origins. Although the Bretton Woods arrangements established the dollar as the major world currency, the international money and financial markets largely remained located in London. By the 1950s, the City's openness and lack of regulation attracted foreign bankers and dealers – expecially American – eager to escape the restrictions of their own financial systems. London's Eurocurrency markets conferred greater autonomy on international monetary transactions and played a part in the currency instability of the 1970s, which the major states were unable to control.

Second, in the analysis of power it is necessary to distinguish between power resources (e.g. wealth, manpower etc.) and the organizational means or infrastructural capacity to translate resources into action (see, for example, Mann, 1986, pp. 6–9). In this respect, the market capacity to transform a currency into a form of world money is not directly determined by the objective strength of the host economy. The production of international liquidity in its typical credit form requires an

means of exchange in market activity. Its effectiveness in this respect depends on 'the probability that it will be at some future time acceptable in exchange for goods in price relationships which are capable of approximate estimate' – that is, the market-determined substantive validity of money. An effective currency involves a close approximation between the formal and substantive validities of money. Purely market-produced money is restrictive and/or unstable; vagaries of supply and costs of production affect the substantive validity of metallic money and market competition renders bank-credit money even more volatile. Moreover, the market cannot set the standard – the fixed point – against which other values are measured, as bi-metallism has invariably demonstrated. Thus, Weber argued, valid and effective forms of money are the outcome of the interplay of market-based and state interests. This necessarily dual determination of valid money is especially problematic in the case of world money. Any attempt to secure the formal validity of money outside a given territory involves force or cooperation with markets that have a constant tendency to generate 'unofficial' or near-money, which stands in an uncertain relationship to the standard – for example, bills of exchange in the past and Eurocurrencies at present. See Weber (1978, pp. 166–93). On the relationship between state and market in the regulation of Eurocurrencies see Hawley (1984).

appropriate institutional structure: competent and trustworthy markets and banks. Once this dimension is taken into account, it becomes clear that the USA was not only unwilling but also incapable of managing world monetary affairs in the interwar and, to some extent, postwar years. After 1918, the USA possessed over 40 per cent of the world's gold reserves, yet the Federal Reserve was unable to prevent the failure of a third of all domestic American banks. Such was the Reserve's organizational incoherence that it was incapable of setting any clear goals (Palyi, 1972; Galbraith, 1975). In contrast, the Bank of England held less than 20 per cent of the world's gold reserves in 1900, but was the linchpin of the international monetary system (de Cecco, 1974).

The following brief account of the gold standard era and the Bretton Woods system focuses on the different combinations of state and market power resources in the production of the respective currencies as world money and stresses the importance of taking into account the institutional mediation between 'power' and 'purpose'.

The Gold–Sterling Standard

It is now widely accepted that the gold standard did not operate in the manner of the classical price–specie flow mechanism, nor even according to the modified model enunciated by the Cunliffe Committee, which recommended the return to gold in 1925 (Bloomfield, 1959; Williams, 1968; de Cecco, 1974). For much of the nineteenth century, including the gold standard era, most international transactions were denominated in sterling. It is, therefore, more accurate to refer to a gold–sterling standard: Britain's domestic currency, based on the pledge of convertibility, became universal money (Williams, 1968; de Cecco, 1974).

As world capitalism expanded during the nineteenth century, gold became relatively scarce in relation to economic transactions and the Bank of England's sterling liabilities to foreigners greatly exceeded the bullion stocks (Bloomfield, 1959; de Cecco, 1974). As Bloomfield has put it, the gold–sterling standard was able to operate with 'amazingly small reserves'. This quite remarkable system consisted of a complex structure of power resources and organizational capacities at the levels of both state and market, which were not a simple or direct result of the material strength of the British economy. Moreover, this intricate edifice was in a large part the unintended outcome of distinct patterns of development in which agents in the state and the market pursued their separate, but ultimately complementary, goals.

Gold, Sterling and Credit

Sterling's dominant role during the mid nineteenth century was in an obvious and direct way related to Britain's strength in production and trade; the latter ensured that sterling would become a key 'currency'. However, the British economy contained an enduring weakness – the balance of trade was in deficit throughout the nineteenth century and up to 1914. The 'workshop of the world' drew in vast quantities of raw materials and food to its industrial centres. In this respect, Britain was in an analogous position to the USA in the 1960s; it was a key currency country with a large trade deficit. But in contrast, Britain's economic power was never the simple result of her industrial strength. Unlike the USA a century later, Britain was also host to the world's 'clearing house' – the City. In this way Britain has played a unique role in world capitalism: no other industrial nation has ever contained a centre that has undertaken such a large share of the global economy's commercial, banking and financial intermediation. Furthermore, as I have argued at length elsewhere, the City's commercial capitalism was never a mere reflection of the productive domestic economy. Both its origins and its continued expansion through the long period of industrial decline must be seen as a partially independent development (Ingham, 1984, 1988).

On the one hand, geopolitical contingency played its part; during the eighteenth century, Amsterdam was the pre-eminent clearing house, but it never recovered from the French Wars. Huskisson's early free trade legislation of the 1820s and the return to convertibility in 1819 took advantage of the situation to make London 'the Emporium not only of Europe, but of America north and south' (Rothscild, 1832, quoted in Hitton, 1977). This was a quite intentional commercial (not industrial) strategy to create, in Huskissson's words, the Venice of the nineteenth century.

The City's activities were fundamental in the development of sterling as a key currency and in Britain's ability to sustain the gold standard with the onset of relative economic decline. First, commissions and brokerage fees from a wide range of commercial and financial intermediation, in themselves, transformed the trade deficit into a balance of payments surplus. Between 1861 and 1865, for example, the overall cumulative trade deficit was £60 million and income from re-exports (£46 million), shipping credits (£34 million) and financial services (£33 million) – that is, commercial earnings at £113 million – were almost exactly double the deficit on the trading account (Ingham, 1988).[2] From the last quarter of the nineteenth century to 1914, income from overseas investments grew to augment the 'invisibles' and to maintain the overall surplus and thus the gold standard. Second, the City made a more direct contribution to the operation of the international gold–sterling system. On the one hand, the City was a source of liquidity as London was not only the coordinating centre for international exchanges, but also the location at which the

2 The data are based on those compiled by Imlah (1958).

balances of trade were lodged. These flows of short-term capital were also an additional source of credit (Bloomfield, 1963). Furthermore, the entrepôt trade itself created sterling-based credit as merchant bankers made loans against commodities and securities. As a contemporary observed, 'What came to London became liquid and everything came to London. London therefore needed less gold than other centres' (Palyi, 1972, p. 115). Indeed, Tomlinson (1982, p. 64) has gone so far as to argue that, after 1860, the strength of sterling was not necessarily a result of the strength of the rest of the economy: 'Britain could only dominate the world economy . . . only so long as other nations chose to use the City of London as the contact point for their bilateral and multilateral transactions.' On the other hand, capital exports provided a means of adjustment for deficit countries and it must be borne in mind that the City performed a truly international role. Not only was British capital exported, the City was the central pool into which foreign capital flowed to be re-exported; that is, the means of international adjustment were distributed and not merely provided by Britain as 'hegemon' (Platt, 1980; Pollard, 1985).

Trust and Confidence

The central importance of trust and confidence in the operation of monetary systems is obvious, but is rarely considered as anything more than an *ad hoc* category in formal economic analysis. In the late nineteenth century, however, operators and successive Chancellors of the Exchequer were fully aware that economic phenomena did not act in a mechanical manner (Checkland, 1957). Within quite wide limits, trust and confidence were a substitute for gold. As Bagehot pointed out: 'The English people and foreigners too trust it [the Bank of England] implicitly. Every banker knows that if he has to prove that he is worthy of credit, however good may be his arguments, in fact his credit is gone; but what we have requires no proof. The whole rests upon an instinctive confidence generated by use and years' (quoted in Ingham, 1984, p. 259). Trust in Britain's monetary system was generated in part by the commitment to the legislation of 1819 and 1844, by which the state had enacted the formal validity of the gold standard. Within a few decades, monetary questions ceased to be a matter of dispute, and mistrust of the Bank of England's blatant self-seeking in the management of the currency gave way to unreflexive acceptance (Fetter, 1965). By the late nineteenth century, the relative size of the British economy was nowhere near large enough to dominate world monetary conditions (Cleveland, 1976). But the Bank of England was able to orchestrate the international system because the rest of the world held a large volume of liquid claims in sterling and 'such was the confidence in the parity of the pound that the sterling claims were regarded as free of exchange risk' (Cleveland, 1976, p. 19; see also Bloomfield, 1963).

The Pax Britannica and Empire

The temporal coexistence of the gold standard – first domestically and then globally – and the relative stability of the interstate system is almost exact. The year 1914 demonstrated the obvious fact and fulfilled the worst fears of the world's financial community that 'an international monetary system could not function in a general war' (Polyani, 1944). The truistic nature of the observation should not lead us to ignore its significance. The post-1815 balance of power system, which military and naval superiority had enabled Britain to impose on Europe, further occasional interventions and diplomacy backed by the threat of force all made their contributions to the geopolitical basis for the gold standard.

The Empire and, in particular, the physical control of Indian economic resources played a more direct role in Britain's ability to maintain the gold standard and manage the international monetary system. But the causal relations were neither simple nor one-way. The Empire did not serve Britain's economic dominance in the manner outlined by Hobson and Lenin, in what has become known as the theory of 'finance-capital imperialism' (Ingham, 1984, 1988).

However, India did play a pivotal role in the reproduction of the late nineteenth- and early twentieth-century trade and monetary system. During this period, Britain's largest trading deficits were with the USA and Europe; the largest surplus was with India (Saul, 1960). India maintained an overall trade surplus with the rest of the world through the exporting of primary products, and a large deficit with Britain through the importation of manufactured goods and the expenses of maintaining the Raj. (Indian industrial development was deliberately retarded – for political as much as economic motives – and her domestic market was virtually closed to non-British manufactures.)

This situation had two important consequences for the gold–sterling system. First, India's surplus with the rest of the world and deficit with Britain eased the latter's difficulties in dealing with international settlements on current account. Consequently, the City's invisible earnings – the liquidity that had been drained – could be returned to the international monetary system. Second, the Indian monetary reserves formed a *masse de manoeuvre* that supplemented those of the Bank of England and helped to cushion the effect of the threatening crises, which became more frequent as the world economic system expanded. Other possessions were used in a similar way; they were prohibited from realizing trade surpluses in gold and any sterling surpluses had to be deposited in London (de Cecco, 1974).

These market and state-based power resources were interdependent and mutually sustaining, and a threat to any one of them entailed a threat to the whole system. Thus, the gold standard's conditions of existence cannot be understood simply in terms of the relative success of the international monetary mechanisms; nor is it helpful to see it as a narrowly 'economic' phenomenon. Indeed, one is tempted to suggest that the optimism of the Bretton Woods planners was to some extent based on such a misconception, compounded by a belief that states could control such processes.

Organizational Capacity

Of course, the ability to produce and constantly to reproduce the gold–sterling standard was not the unmediated effect of possessing the adequate resources. The routine maintenance of the system was based upon and led to the further development of both market and state organizational capacities. At the highest level of generality these may be seen as networks of social interaction with two dimensions: the degrees of system and social integration (Lockwood, 1964; Giddens, 1979). On the one hand, those market and state institutions concerned directly with the routine management of the gold–sterling system – the Treasury, Bank of England and City – formed a highly interdependent and regularized network of exchanges (system integration). On the other hand, the face-to-face interaction between the individuals in the three groups formed a social network that cut across the institutional boundaries (social integration) (Ingham, 1984, chapter 6). Furthermore, in this instance, the social integration was based in part on class membership and the informal social relations of a common cultural milieu. The instrumental actions of the Treasury, Bank and City were embedded in social relations based on institutional and class membership (Granovetter, 1985).

By the late nineteenth century, the City–Bank–Treasury nexus comprised a highly integrated system in which the practices of any one institution were partly dependent on conditions provided by the others (Ingham, 1984). The City, in pursuit of profits based on the free trade–gold standard regime, saturated the world with sterling, provided a basis for the international monetary system and earned a surplus that, in turn, eased the management of the domestic financial and fiscal systems for the Bank and Treasury respectively. The City was left totally free of any outside control; *laissez-faire* was not merely ideologically sound, it also filled the state's coffers.

The Treasury's successful control of public expenditure maintained the state's solvency and (in both real and symbolic senses) supplied those conditions which the City was unable to produce for itself: the approximation of the formal and substantive validities of sterling. (Without customs duties and in the face of the political unacceptability of high rates of taxation, budgetary stringency was essential for the whole free trade–gold standard regime.) The task was made much easier when control of the entire state bureaucracy eventually passed to the Treasury – a situation without parallel in any other modern state.[3]

By the last quarter of the nineteenth century, the Bank of England's primary goal was the maintenance of adequate reserves for lending in last resort, first domestically and later for the international system. Thus the Treasury's parsimony and the Bank's prudence were complementary. Despite its belief in the self-equilibriating nature of the gold standard, the Bank was drawn inexorably into intervening in the money and exchange markets (Bloomfield, 1959; Cleveland, 1976). In this strategic management of the currency, the Bank operated quite independently of state control; it was the pivotal institution in the 'fiscal constitution', which comprised the 'Holy Trinity of Free Trade, the Gold Standard and Balanced Budgets' (Roseveare, 1969). The Bank's activities were made possible by efforts to centralize the domestic banking system under tight control. Just as the Treasury struggled with other branches of the state over expenditure, the Bank was engaged in quite intense conflict with the provinces over the burgeoning deposits of the joint-stock clearing banks. With the relative reduction of the Bank of England's reserve, there occurred a weakening of its market power at both domestic and international levels. Greater access to the clearing bankers' deposits was a means of resolving the problems and conflict between London and the provinces over this issue continued well into the twentieth century (de Cecco, 1974; Ingham, 1984). The joint-stock bankers were eventually subordinated and an unusually centralized domestic banking system emerged under very close central bank control.

However, these institutional relationships were not simply the outcome of efforts to maintain the gold standard; the Treasury's strict control of state expenditure and the Bank's domination of the financial system were independent sources of power for each agency in their respective institutional domain. Nevertheless, they comprised an unusually effective organizational capacity, and one that was sufficiently entrenched for successive governments to pursue a global role for the City and the currency long after the loss of economic power resources.

The dense interconnected network of social relations in the Treasury, Bank and City, which intertwined with a surviving aristocratic component of the ruling class, resulted in formidable managerial cohesion and expertise in the maintenance of the international economic regime by which they all profited, both in their respective institutions and as a class. They were of course fully aware of its value: the Bank of England 'has to keep a knowledge of men and force of character for use when

---

3 This position was the outcome of protracted intrastate conflict over the budget during the nineteenth century. Treasury control was originally based on *de facto* possession of the public purse and only gained *de jure* constitutional status in the 1920s in association with the return to gold.

required, as well as mere cash' (*Bankers' Magazine*, 1890, quoted in Checkland, 1957). The adept resolution of the Baring Crisis of 1890 demonstrated the force of this socially embedded organizational competence (Pressnell, 1968).

If credit is seen as an expression of socially generated trust, then it is difficult to exaggerate the importance of the social integration and codes of practice of the inner core of City merchant banks for sterling's liquidity. Indeed, Brown (1940) argued that the 'essence' of the gold standard was to be found 'in the whole institutional pattern that breathes life into these forms of law and practice'; that is, in his view, the pre-1914 London credit market.[4]

Origins

The classic international gold–sterling standard differed from the Bretton Woods system in a fundamentally important respect: it was unplanned. The creation of the resources and capacities to manage the international monetary system was the outcome of distinct (but partially related) strategies that were originally designed for the pursuit of separate interests. Furthermore, it would appear that the actual practice of global central banking began as an unreflexive activity:

> In the heyday of *laissez-faire* if the financial leaders of England had been told that they were the managers of the international gold standard and the international lender of last resort, they would have been as amazed as that character in Moliere's *Le Bourgeois Gentilhomme* who learned that, without knowing it, he had been speaking prose all his life. (Fetter, 1965, p. 256)

Bagehot had advocated the principle of the Bank's responsibility in the event of domestic crisis during his editorship of the *Economist* during the 1860s. By 1870, the Bank's internal conflict between profit-making and the retention of an unused hoard to halt crises had been resolved in the latter's favour.

It is obvious that the English monetary legislation of 1819 and 1844 to restore the domestic gold standard and reform the Bank of England was not intended to create a world bank and an international currency. But as I implied earlier, it is possible to detect the advocacy of a strategy at this time, which was designed to give Britain commercial hegemony – to make certain London's replacement of Amsterdam (Ingham, 1984). The gold standard and free trade were indivisibly part of Ricardian theory and Huskisson's policies in the 1820s. There was widespread opposition from manufacturers and artisans, who feared the deflationary

---

4 Brown (1940) stresses that the gold standard could not be understood outside British predominance as a commercial entrepôt.

consequences, and from those in the City who had taken advantage of inconvertibility and the instability of bimetallism. It was the desire to smash the corrupt system of state finance and to escape from the grasp of the 'money powers' that tipped the political balance in favour of the radical Tory 'economical reformers'. The Prime Minister, Lord Liverpool, believed that the monetary instability and the chaotic fiscal situation were a threat to the state's ability to discharge its primary responsibilities of preserving public order and guaranteeing defence against external threats.

From the outset, the construction of the monetary system, which later served the world, was shaped by the separate but complementary interests of both state and market. The gold standard and the London-based international clearing house system were to have a profound and long-term impact on the structure and performance of the British state and economy. Uniquely in the modern industrial capitalist world, the dominant section of the ruling class and the most powerful state agencies identified with and profited more from the international market economy than from the one in which they were at least nominally located (see Boyce, 1987). This class and the associated state institutions possessed the resources, the organizational capacity and a willingness borne of self-interest to struggle to prolong the life of the system even after the Second World War.

The Gold–Dollar Exchange Standard

In many crucial respects, the differences between the gold–sterling and the gold–dollar exchange standards appear to be more significant than their common identity as the base for world money. Instead of a relatively close integration of the constituent elements of state and market resources and organizational capacity, the Bretton Woods system contained a number of contradictions that became apparent in an ironic sequence of negative feedback effects as the intentionally planned system developed. I shall argue that the Bretton Woods system possessed an inbuilt lack of system integration; that is, a disengagement of state and market at the levels of both power resources and organizational capacity. This disengagement became overdetermined by the eventual territorial dislocation of the American state's means for maintaining the formal validity of the standard and the London-based market's setting of the substantive validities of the system's major currencies.

With hindsight, it would appear that the planners of the postwar international economic order set themselves an intractable problem: the reconciliation and integration of a liberal world trading system and the maintenance of stable high domestic employment. It was widely believed that capitalism could be managed and yet retain its liberal market basis.

Despite some ambivalence, it was a view that Keynes actively fostered: economic management had become a narrowly technical matter, like dentistry. Markets could be remote-controlled by means of the state's fiscal resources. With large increases in government expenditure, states had moved, with considerable variation, from supportive guardianship of their respective markets to become players with a more directive role. Thus, the Bretton Woods system was established by state power; the major negotiators were British and American officials and their advisors. Unlike in the post-1918 attempts at reconstruction, private bankers were almost entirely excluded and this indicated a remarkable loss of influence since the 1920s (Aronson, 1977). The gold–dollar exchange rate was fixed politically; but relatively little consideration was given to precisely how and to what extent markets would be involved in the provision of adequate liquidity and eventually in determining the exchange rates of the participating currencies.[5] Markets were to be subordinate in the new managed international monetary order. The outcome contained a profound irony: markets were to be the effective media through which the system was destabilized and then abandoned.

While this outcome may have occurred regardless of circumstances and events, the USA's dominant role transformed possibility into probability. The nature of America's articulation with the world economy and its chosen role in the international political system induced self-interested exploitation of its international monetary role, rather than its constructive management. In addition, the USA's domestic monetary and financial system was a singularly inappropriate one to take the transplanted world banking and monetary role. In short, America possessed neither the will nor the organizational capacity to perform the monetary roles that the possession of immense economic and military resources had thrust upon it after 1945.

Economic Resources and Integration into the World Economy

As early as the last quarter of the nineteenth century, the USA had overtaken Britain as the world's single largest industrial economy, and, with the defeat of Germany and the weakening of Britain after 1918, she possessed the single most powerful economy in the world. On this basis, it is frequently argued that the replacement of Britain's general world leadership or 'hegemony' developed throughout the interwar period and found its complete expression with the destruction of Europe and Britain's further impoverishment in the Second World War.[6] However, the model of Britain's nineteenth-century role is an inappropriate one for

5 For a detailed account of the negotiations see Gardner (1969) and van Dormael (1978).
6 For a discussion and critique of the 'heir to empire' thesis, see McKercher (1988).

Table 2.1 Exports and imports of goods
and services as a percentage of GNP

	1955	1979
USA	10.0	21.0
Japan	22.6	26.1
France	30.4	49.9
Germany	43.1	57.9
Great Britain	53.0	65.9

Source: Panic, 1988.

understanding the nature of American dominance and, in particular, is the source of some confusion in assessing the USA's role in the postwar international monetary system.

Although the USA accounted for over 40 per cent of the value of world output by the 1920s, she was an insular giant and as a national economy has continued to be relatively weakly integrated into the world economy (table 2.1). With such a relatively closed economy, the USA has never developed into the 'natural' centre for intermediation in international economic exchanges that London had been. In fact, by 1950, America showed a substantial deficit on financial and commercial services (Harris, 1961, p. 87). The spread of economic power outside the domestic economy did, in fact, increase rapidly during the 1920s until its abrupt halt in 1929; but the mode of expansion and influence was not in itself conducive to a world monetary role. American foreign investment was predominantly directed through domestically based financial–industrial combinations (Wilkins, 1974; Gilpin, 1975). These activities contributed relatively little to either world liquidity or the means for countries to make international payments adjustments.

Organizational Capacity

By the time the USA as a creditor nation with a balance of payments surplus was in a position to assume world monetary hegemony her banking and financial system had developed along quite different lines. The structure of American banking was largely conditioned by the decentralization and political fragmentation of the early state, the relative closure of the economy and the dominant positions of productive capital and agriculture.

Given the rapid domestic growth and Europe's financial strength, American banking was only marginally involved internationally in the early part of the century. However, domestic 'money trusts' (the near equivalent of continental Europe's 'finance-capital') expanded rapidly in the unregulated and decentralized conditions. Populist 'trust-busting' campaigns culminated in the Pujo Committee hearings, which recommended the foundation of the Federal Reserve – the idiosyncratic equivalent of a central bank – to regulate the finance-capitalists and stabilize the fragmented and crisis prone monetary system (1913).

The organization of the Federal Reserve had two important disabling effects on the imminent assumption of global economic power by the USA. First, little provision was made in structure and practice for dealing with international issues; by the 1920s, only two of the large staff of top officials were familiar with world financial conditions (Palyi, 1972). Second, its structure mirrored the decentralized character of the American polity and financial network; there were twelve regional reserve banks and of these only New York had any significant foreign dealings. Formally, the Federal Reserve System was controlled by the Federal Reserve Board in Washington under the chairmanship of the Secretary of the Treasury. However, the degree of decentralization and spatial dispersion between the constituent parts permitted conflicts and encouraged indecision and ineffectual compromise. To many observers, the Reserve appeared to be incompetent (Galbraith, 1975).

In fact, many disputes in the 1920s centred on the advocacy of economic internationalism by the Federal Reserve Bank of New York (which wished the city to take over London's world role) and the emerging transnational corporations (Block, 1977; Hogan, 1984). They found some support in the State Department, but were opposed by the Reserve Board and the Treasury, whose preferences more directly reflected the existing complection of the US economy. The latter's views prevailed after the 1929 stock market crash, the onset of depression and the domestic reconstruction of the New Deal (Block, 1977; Hogan, 1984). But for a while an internationalist lobby was active. Strong of the New York bank collaborated with Norman of the Bank of England to reconstruct and maintain the gold standard. Norman was acutely aware of the need for American support and this held out the promise of increased international business for New York. The period is often characterized as one of 'financial rivalry' in which the USA attempted to wrest international banking away from a weakened City (Costigliola, 1977). In fact, there existed a negotiated division of labour, which clearly indicated the different orientations of the two centres: high interest rates in London to direct short-term funds from New York and lower US interest rates, which would attract a share of long-term international borrowing.

Despite the rejection of the League of Nations, Washington was not completely economically isolationist. Hoover aimed to extend domestic state–market cooperation (associationalism) internationally; but this did not necessarily involve an interest in a liberal world order. It was an openingly self-seeking strategy; foreign cartels were denounced at the same time that the US government sponsored consortia in oil, radio and finance that 'amounted to multinational monopolies' (Hogan, 1984, p. 298). In other words, there was an internationalist 'will' in the 1920s, but it did not include a wish to take responsibility for the international monetary system.

Strong's death in 1928 and the crash of the following year ended New York's pretentions and the subsequent New Deal legislation (Glass–Steagall Act 1933, Banking Act 1935) strengthened state control over the financial markets. Monetary control including international aspects passed from the Federal Reserve to the Treasury, which was entirely preoccupied with domestic stabilization (Palyi, 1972; Galbraith, 1975; van Dormael, 1978).[7]

After 1931, the USA possessed the resources to stabilize the international monetary system, but even if the will had been there, the capability was absent. The American financial system could not have produced the necessary international liquidity (as opposed to a one-off stabilization) through a credit-providing network of banks and markets. On the contrary, before their regulation, they were independent sources of international instability.

This interwar legacy for the Bretton Woods system was to prove a crucial one. London had lost its gold, but its markets remained the most important single centre for global commercial and financial intermediation. On the other hand, the USA's capability for managing universal money was effectively diminished at the moment that its economic powers became paramount. Indeed, this judgement on the emerging 'hegemon' has been generalized: 'American strength in the new international order remained only potential strength. . . . Wealth means nothing in the hard world of global politics unless it is translated into tangible expressions of national potency' (McKercher, 1988, p. 441).

Bretton Woods and After: Markets against States

The Anglo-American negotiations were an attempt to resolve the conflict between national economic autonomy, the pursuit of full employment and the provision of a stable international means of exchange and payment. To this end, the original Keynes–White plan had favoured an 'adjustable peg' rather than fixed currency exchange rates in order to avoid drastic domestic deflationary adjustments. A world central bank was to be the source of liquidity and Keynes even favoured a stateless universal currency – the bancor. The US State Department and other domestic interests were wary of the possible costs of such internationalism and the eventual outcome was nearer to Williams's 'key currency plan' than Keynes's multilateralism (Block, 1977; van Dormael, 1978). Williams of the Federal Reserve Bank of New York simply wanted the

---

7 See also Frieden (1987, chapter 3). Frieden tends to overestimate the extent of American financial dominance and the bankers' political strength in the interwar years. For a more subtle analysis of the complexities see McKercher (1988).

dollar to take on the position of sterling under the old gold standard. The eventual scheme was based upon gold–dollar convertibility at US$35 per ounce, with a joint reserve role for sterling. The International Monetary Fund was to provide the borrowing facilities to enable capitalist states to make smooth economic adjustments and so maintain high levels of employment and steady growth. Until currency convertibilty in 1958, international financial and money markets were virtually inoperative and in all important respects the new international monetary system operated through state power and organizational media.

As Keynes had feared, it soon became clear that Europe's problems were too great for the Fund's resources and, moreover, Britain – the second largest contributor – was insolvent. In these circumstances, the American state had to take even more direct action to create the capitalist world system it favoured. Congress was eventually swayed by the State Department's argument that European prosperity was the best guarantee against the emergence of socialist governments. The Marshall Aid Plan provided US$12.5 billion – twice the amount that the IMF had at its disposal (Galbraith, 1975).

During the immediate postwar years of the 'dollar shortage', the USA maintained a large balance of payments surplus, but the American market-based financial system proved to be incapable of creating the necessary international liquidity. In the early 1950s, for example, New York's provision of trade-credit was only one-third of London's level in 1913 (Harrod, 1953; Clarke, 1965). In addition, gold tended to be hoarded in Fort Knox and Lower Manhatten, whereas in London before 1914 'gold was no sooner attracted than repelled'. The reserve function, which was shared in an *ad hoc* and uncertain manner by the IMF and the American state, was organizationally dissociated from the provision of the international means of exchange. Furthermore, it is arguable that the USA's acknowledged anxiety about exchange crises in the late 1950s was intensified by its social and spatial distance from the London markets, which became the centre for the transmission of any wavering confidence (Clarke, 1957). The contrast with the earlier integration of state and market in the Bank of England–City–Treasury linkage is an obvious one (see Ingham, 1984).

From the late 1950s onwards the liquidity problem was resolved, but in a quite contradictory manner. By this time, US military expenditure was fuelling a balance of payments deficit, but as Triffin explained to Congress, this provided the international means of exchange, but in a manner that undermined confidence in the USA's ability and willingness to maintain the gold–dollar exchange standard (Triffin, 1960). In fact, the very first year of convertibility had seen a speculative attack on the dollar. Liquidity and confidence were inversely related, whereas the converse had held during the gold standard era. As American arms spending increased, pressure mounted for the US government at least to appear seriously to be considering the problem. Various palliatives were produced: for example, greater central bank cooperation, the London gold pool, strengthening the IMF. Significantly, these were defensive measures against the markets; the USA took no effective steps to correct the cause of the dilemma. Speculative pressures were fuelled futher by expenditure on the Vietnam War and Johnson's Great Society programme. America's disinclination to reduce its spending brought charges of cynical manipulation, especially from the French. As guarantor of the standard, the USA was able simply to print the money to finance its geopolitical ambitions and domestic policies. Furthermore, excessive US demand created further destabilizing uncertainty by exporting inflation. In short, Bretton Woods was conferring special privileges, which many now considered the USA to be exploiting (Block, 1977; Gowa, 1983). Other states largely accepted the situation in return for the defensive shield provided by America's military strength. But developments were taking place in the international money markets over which the Western states had little control.

At this juncture, the basic dislocation of state and market in the Bretton Woods system produced a further telling contradictory effect. With convertibility, London began to enjoy a remarkable renaissance. Whereas New York was hampered by Federal Reserve regulation, London was a free 'self-regulating' centre with a considerable degree of expertise and a globally extensive network of banks and financial connections. The large non-US resident holdings of dollars that the deficit and the transnational corporations' activities had created were mobilized by the City into the Eurodollar market.[8] As the deficit mounted and the speculative fund grew, the market moved faster and a wave of instability spread over a range of currencies.

Predictably, efforts to resolve the contradiction simply led to its intensification. A range of Federal Reserve regulations and exchange controls to curb the outflow of long-term dollar investments were introduced during the 1960s (Aronson, 1977). The effect was simultaneously further to weaken New York's position as a centre for financial intermediation and the USA's position as reserve banker by stimulating foreign centres – especially the City. In short, the intended remedial action simply reduced the USA's capacity to withstand pressure on a system it was already incapable of managing. In a further ironic twist, many American banks evaded the controls by simply following the dollars and setting up branches in London; by the late 1970s they outnumbered British banks and had no doubt played their part in speculation against the dollar.

By 1971, the USA announced a trade deficit; a massive outflow of gold and calls for protection followed. The final crisis had been

8   For a general account of the offshore money markets see Mendelsohn (1980).

reached: Nixon suspended convertibility and soon after devalued the dollar. Henceforward, the markets determined both the status and the substantive validity of the 'paper dollar' as world money in the new regime of floating exchange rates. The system was formally negotiated by the major states, but in reality they were merely following the markets.

Conclusions

Generalizing from a small number of cases is obviously a hazardous procedure, but the failure to recognize singularity is a more serious matter. The theory of hegemonic stability implies a timeless structure in which dominance brings international stability and, thereby, more effective market competition. In turn, this weakens the hegemon and induces instability. This phase ends as the system is re-equilibrated under the new hegemon that emerges from the international competitive process. Thus, some adherents now suggest that Japan is, at least, objectively placed to take on financial leadership (Gilpin, 1987).

However, the differences in both the bases and extents of British and American dominance and monetary management seem too great to be accommodated comfortably by what is, in effect, a general equilibrium theory. It would appear to be more profitable to consider the development of the international monetary system as a single historical process marked by periods of relative stability/instability and punctuated by episodic crises that are related to changes in the distribution of power resources in indirect and extremely complex ways. Despite all its power, it is improbable that the USA would have developed into a willing and competent guardian of the dollar as world money had it not been for the Second World War. The devastation of Europe largely determined the formal role of the dollar and the advantages it bestowed on the USA. Bretton Woods simply delayed the advent of the *de facto* paper dollar 'standard' and the renewed power of the markets. As soon as the veil of the state-dominated 'transitional' Bretton Woods arrangements was lifted, the system's contradictory structure was revealed. In a real sense, this second instance of formal world money endured, with some difficulty, for a mere ten years – from convertibility to the Two Tier Agreement in 1968 (see Aronson, 1977; Gowa, 1983). Such observations give further emphasis to the contrast between Britain and the USA. Britain's world dominance straddled the periods of commercial and industrial capitalism and in several important respects her articulation with the world economy has had more in common with Venice and Holland than with the national economies of the twentieth century, for whom world monetary management would have been too costly under almost all circumstances.

References

Aronson, J. (1977) *Money and Power*. Beverly Hills, CA: Sage.

Block, F. L. (1977) *The Origins of International Economic Disorder*. Berkeley: University of California Press.

Bloomfield, A. I. (1959) *Monetary Policy under the Gold Standard, 1820–1914*. New York: Federal Reserve Bank.

Bloomfield, A. I. (1963) Short term capital movements under the pre-1914 gold standard. *Princeton Studies in International Finance*, 11, 1–48.

Boyce, R. (1987) *British Capitalism at the Crossroads, 1919–1932*. Cambridge: Cambridge University Press.

Brown, W. A. (1940) *The International Gold Standard Reinterpreted*. New York: Columbia University Press.

Checkland, S. G. (1957) The mind of the city, 1870–1914. *Oxford Economic Papers*, 9, 261–78.

Clarke, W. J. (1965) *The City in the World Economy*. Harmondsworth: Penguin.

Cleveland, H. van B. (1976) The international monetary system in the interwar period. In B. Rowland (ed.), *Balance of Power or Hegemony: the Inter-war Monetary System*. New York: New York University Press.

Costigliola, F. (1977) Anglo-American financial rivalry in the 1920s. *Journal of Economic History*, 37, 126–52.

de Cecco, M. (1974) *Money and Empire*. Oxford: Blackwell.

Fetter, F. W. (1965) *The Development of British Monetary Orthodoxy*. Cambridge, MA: Harvard University Press.

Frieden, J. (1987) *Banking on the World*. London: Hutchinson Radius.

Galbraith, J. K. (1975) *Money*. Harmondsworth: Penguin.

Gardner, R. N. (1969) *Sterling–Dollar Diplomacy*. New York: Columbia University Press.

Giddens, A. (1979) *Central Problems in Social Theory*. London: Macmillan.

Gilpin, R. (1975) *US Power and the Multi-national Corporation: the Political Economy of Foreign Direct Investment*. New York: Basic Books.

Gilpin, R. (1987) *The Political Economy of International Relations*. Princeton, NJ: Princeton University Press.

Gowa, J. (1983) *Closing the Gold Window: Domestic Politics and the End of Bretton Woods*. Ithaca, NY, and London: Cornell University Press.

Granovetter, M. (1985) Economic action and social structure: the problem of embeddedness. *American Journal of Sociology*, 91(3), 481–510.

Harris, S. (1961) *American Economic History*. New York: Columbia University Press.

Harrod, R. (1953) *The Dollar*. London: Allen Lane.

Hawley, J. P. (1984) Protecting capital from itself: US attempts to regulate the Eurocurrency system. *International Organisation*, 38(1), 17–49.

Hilton, B. (1977) *Cash, Corn and Commerce: the Economic Policies of the Tory Governments, 1815–1830*. Oxford: Clarendon Press.

Hogan, M. (1984) Revival and reform: America's search for a new economic order abroad. *Diplomatic History*, 8(4), 287–310.

Imlah, A. (1958) *Economic Elements in the Pax Britannica*. Cambridge, MA: Harvard University Press.

Ingham, G. (1984) *Capitalism Divided? The City and Industry in British Social Development*. London: Macmillan.

Ingham, G. (1988) Commercial capital and British development. *New Left Review*, 172.

Keohane, R. O. (1980) The theory of hegemonic stability and changes in international regimes, 1967–1977. In O. Holsti et al. (eds), *Changes in the International System*. Boulder, CO: Westview Press.

Kindleberger, C. P. (1973) *The World in Depression 1929–1939*. Harmondsworth: Penguin.

Lockwood, D. (1964) Social integration and system integration. In G. K. Zollschan and W. Hirsch (eds), *Explorations in Social Change*. Glencoe, IL: Free Press.

McKercher, B. (1988) Wealth, power and the new international order: Britain and the American challenge in the 1920s. *Diplomatic History*, 12(4), 411–41.

Mann, M. (1986) *The Sources of Social Power, vol. 1*. Cambridge: Cambridge University Press.

Mendelsohn, M. S. (1980) *Money on the Move*. New York: Praeger.

Palyi, M. (1972) *The Twilight of Gold*. Chicago: Henry Regnery Company.

Panic, M. (1988) *National Management and the International Economy*. London: Allen and Unwin.

Platt, D. C. M. (1980) British portfolio investment overseas before 1870; some doubts. *Economic History Review*, 2nd series, 32, 1–16.

Polanyi, K. (1944) *The Great Transformation*. New York: Rinehart.

Pollard, S. (1985) Capital exports, 1870–1914: harmful or beneficial? *Economic History Review*, 2nd series, 37, 489–513.

Pressnell, L. S. (1968) Banking reserves and the Baring crisis of 1890. In C. R. Whittlesey and J. S. G. Wilson (eds), *Essays in Money and Banking*. Oxford: Clarendon Press.

Roseveare, H. (1969) *The Treasury*. London: Allen Lane.

Ruggie, J. G. (1982) International regimes, transactions and change: embedded liberalism and the post war economic order. *International Organisation*, 36(2), 379–415.

Saul, S. P. (1960) *Studies in British Overseas Trade, 1820–1914*. Liverpool: Liverpool University Press.

Strange, S. (1971) *Sterling and British Policy*. London: Royal Institute of International Affairs.

Tomlinson, B. R. (1982) The contraction of England: national decline and the loss of empire. *Journal of Commonwealth and Imperial History*, 11(1), 58–72.

Triffin, R. (1960) *Gold and the Dollar Crisis*. New Haven, CT: Yale University Press.

van Dormael, A. (1978) *Bretton Woods: Birth of a Monetary System*. London: Macmillan.

Weber, M. (1978) *Economy and Society, vol. 1*. Los Angeles: University of California Press.

Wilkins, M. (1974) *The Maturing Multi-national Enterprise: American Business Abroad, 1914–1970*. Cambridge, MA: Harvard University Press.

Williams, D. (1968) The evolution of the sterling system. In C. R. Whittlesey and J. S. G. Wilson (eds), *Essays in Money and Banking*. Oxford: Clarendon Press.

3

From Bretton Woods to the Casino Economy

Susan Strange

The title of this book already suggests that there are important links between economics (money), politics (power) and geography (space). This chapter will try to explain why those links also have to include history. The reason is that history helps to explain why the links are what they are, and what social consequences follow from the way in which they interact.

They interact because we now have a worldwide market economy – but our political system is made up of 160 or so territorial states. The market economy is global. But the political system is inter-national; that is, it is divided among nation states. And the market economy and the state system exist side by side, each affecting the way the other functions. The common denominator of both is *power*. In the global market economy, the rich have power; and not only the rich who have money and can use it to make others do their bidding, but also those who control access to money, i.e. credit. This means not only governments but also banks and insurance companies, and other operators in financial markets. In the international political system, power is shared between governments. Some have more than others but they all acknowledge – at least most of the time – the right of other governments to the monopoly of the legitimate use of violence – political power – and, incidentally, their right to issue national forms of money, or currency.

One aspect of the global market economy is that it functions with the help of international banks and global capital markets – a whole system of creating, buying and selling credit money that in recent decades has developed somewhat independently of governments. We call this the global financial system. It coexists with what economists usually call the international monetary system. By that, they mean the relationship between national currencies – dollars, yen, Deutschmarks, francs, sterling and so forth. Obviously, the two interact so that the way the international financial system works affects the relative values of national

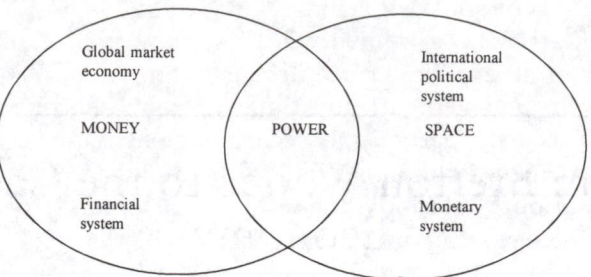

Figure 3.1 Money, power and space: system links.

currencies, just as the way in which governments manage their economies and currencies is reflected in the worldwide financial system. Yet the two are conceptually distinct. Figure 3.1 shows this diagrammatically.

Another way to think of it is, of course, historically. Start by imagining two trains running on parallel historical tracks. One train is called the international monetary system. The other is the worldwide financial system. The monetary system – like the political system of territorial states – has developed more slowly and changed less than the financial system. The latter has spread and grown immensely quickly in recent decades. But the progress of neither can be understood without the other. What we want to know is how the two systems function now, what the social consequences of their interaction are and what they may, or could, be in the future. In short, my concern as a political economist is with 'who gets what' as a result, in terms of costs and benefits, and risks and opportunities; and with the mix of values produced for human society as a whole by the functioning of the two systems. Only on that basis can we assess the alternative options for the future and the conditions under which this or that option would be feasible. But to understand that functioning, we need – as the green Michelin guidebooks like to say – *un peu d'histoire*.

In summarizing this historical background, I make no apology for seeming to overlap somewhat with chapter 2. Each of the contributors to this book has a slightly different interpretation to offer of the historical background. Each will draw different conclusions from history about the present and the future. Readers can have more confidence in their conclusions if they concur, knowing that on other things opinions may differ. My interpretation will emphasize the parallel but uneven development of the international monetary system and the global financial system in the period between the Second World War and the present. Yet my interpretation of this specific period will make more sense if – however briefly – I set it in the longer perspective of monetary and financial evolution from ancient times until the twentieth century.

As a political economist, I shall also try to show how the postwar progress of both trains was influenced by two important structures of the world system or international political economy. One is the security structure: the arrangements at any time whereby people are provided by others with security, particularly security against violence from states other than their own. Economists telling the monetary story often miss out the international relations dimension. The other structure I have called the knowledge structure (Strange, 1988). By that I mean the realm of ideas and the ways in which choices are made about the kind of knowledge to be valued and pursued and the means chosen for storing and communicating it. In my opinion, the choices made during and after the Second World War concerning both the international monetary system and the global financial system can only be explained in terms of this realm of ideas – the notions about the proper management of money and finance that people had at the time and the ideas they had derived from their own and their parents' past experience. That is why we have to go back to see where the two trains started from and to note some of the landmarks along their track to the present.

Of the early history of financial markets, and of currencies, we do not need for present purposes to know a lot of the detail. However, we should note that the origins of both are more ancient than most people realize. Bills of exchange to finance trade were used in Babylon and, long before the Roman emperors, rulers issued coins stamped with their own image and insisted that taxes were paid only in their currency. But from ancient times through until well into the nineteenth century, the coins – national currencies – were mostly made of either silver or gold, with copper for small change. Their relative value was therefore mainly determined by the relative supply of and demand for silver and gold. The value of silver was usually about one-fifteenth that of gold in terms of weight. Rulers had little control over this ratio, though they could – and did – use their power not only to exact taxes in coin or in services but also to cheat people by debasing coins, either by adding lead to silver or by issuing short-weight clipped coins. So it was only towards the end of the eighteenth and in the nineteenth centuries, when rulers began issuing bank-notes that were promises-to-pay in gold or silver, that the value of currencies came to be affected by the credibility, or otherwise, of their promises. The consequence was that some currencies – the dollars issued by the Continental Congress in the American War of Independence, for example – became completely worthless; 'not worth a continental' even became part of the language.

This new opportunity for rulers to issue paper money as well as or instead of coins reflected the fact that the transnational financial system had meanwhile evolved faster and changed more than the monetary systems. Although in Roman times there had been individual millionaires – like Croesus – who had money to lend, the institution of banking – the practice of profitable *intermediating* between savers and borrowers – only really took hold in Europe, and especially in Italy and Spain, in the fourteenth century. The bankers' wealth was soon translated – as with the Medicis in Florence – into political power. And sometimes this power was exercised transnationally when bankers lent to kings and princes. By the end of the nineteenth century, there was already a well-developed global financial system in existence, which effectively intermediated the savings of the richer countries into investment in agriculture, industry and the infrastructure of developing countries like the United States, Russia, Australia or Argentina. The bankers – sometimes egged on by governments playing the game of Diplomacy – took decisions affecting the lives and fortunes of people in faraway countries. Most of this transnational lending took the form of bonds, so that the banks passed on the risk of loss to the bondholders. When Tsarist Russia and the Ottoman Empire defaulted on their bonds, many bondholders suffered.

The progress of both trains came to an abrupt halt with the outbreak of war in 1914. In finance, the bankers took a back seat and transnational lending was left to governments, with the USA making large war loans to the Allies. In the international monetary system, the need to finance the war led in varying degrees to the inflation of currencies as governments issued more and more paper money and suspended their promises-to-pay in gold. By the end of the war in 1918, only the US dollar and some smaller neutral currencies had kept their market value and were still gold-convertible. Exchange rates between these and other currencies were highly volatile. In retrospect, people looked back to the prewar international monetary system – the so-called gold standard – as a golden age of currency stability. In their nostalgia, they often overlooked some important facts about the old gold standard. In the first place, it was really a gold–sterling standard; its stability owed more to the stable value of sterling in terms of gold, so that the global economy had a national currency that could be used for trade and investment which did not fluctuate in real terms. In the second place, governments did not stick to the textbook rules, so that its 'automatic' character was really a fiction. Finally, it was both short-lived – operating at most for forty years before the war (and if the USA is included only for less than two decades) – and far from universal, with all of China, most of Latin America and parts of Africa continuing to work on a silver standard.

Nevertheless, the nostalgia and the very real disorder in postwar currency values drove governments to seek ways to restore order to the international monetary system. But as with the League of Nations, their achievements fell far short of their desires. The 1922 Genoa conference was inconclusive. Britain's return to gold convertibility for sterling was mismanaged at too high a price. Thanks to French insistence on Germany paying reparations and the USA demanding repayment of British and French war loans, the system was restored on a precarious basis of short-term lending by the US banks, plus *ad hoc* cooperation between the US and British central bankers. Both were stopped dead by the 1929 Wall Street crash. First Britain, then the United States, was forced off gold, i.e. dollars and sterling could no longer be freely exchanged for gold and were merely paper currencies. And the main effect was felt in the global financial system where the flows of credit to indebted countries were suddenly and brutally cut off with exactly the same results for their development in the 1930s as were later experienced in the 1980s. Although liberal economists afterward blamed the long years of slump and depression on rising tariffs and trade protection, it is just as plausible that the hard times were as much if not more owing to the general dearth of credit and the failure of confidence in the capitalist system, of which Keynes complained and which he claimed only governments could remedy.

Bretton Woods

In any case, the 1930s Depression convinced the Americans and many Europeans that the world market economy could not be left to work by itself. Rules were needed. Exchange rates between currencies should be made more stable. Greater effort must be put into pulling down trade barriers. Poor countries should get some help with their postwar reconstruction and development. The United Nations must put more emphasis than the League of Nations had done on economic and social matters.

These convictions, in short, were in line with the Keynesian ideas about the role of states and markets that were shared at the time by the Roosevelt administration (1933–45) and by most European governments. Both thought history had shown that more conscious international management was needed to keep capitalist economies stable and growing. However much they disagreed on what the rules should be and what should be managed, they were agreed that something should, and could, be done to avoid any repetition of the waste and misery of the Great Depression.

Important as the prevailing climate of ideas certainly was, it was not the whole story. Power mattered too. While other developed economies were being disrupted and impoverished by the war, the US economy was booming as never before. Occupied or under attack, no allied government was in a position to argue with the Americans. Theirs was the wealth and the military power. Thus, when the British were told by the Americans that although supplies of arms, food and raw materials would be allocated wherever they would best serve the war effort, the same principle would not apply to finance, there was nothing Britain could do about it. With its gold and dollar reserves at rock-bottom, depleted before the USA came into the war in 1941, Britain had little real bargaining power. Nevertheless, because it was important to get allied agreement, Britain was consulted about the postwar monetary arrangements.

Both John Maynard Keynes for Britain and Harry Dexter White for the USA were asked to draw up blueprints for the future. But there was little doubt that it would be the American plan that would prevail over Keynes's more ambitious scheme for a really international currency. He called it 'bancor'. It was to take the place of gold as the pivot, or numeraire, around which other currencies moved and in which they were valued and their balance of payments was settled through a clearing union. With such a currency, the world's money supply could be expanded or contracted in line with global needs.

Harry White's plan was much more modest, in both size and concept. It proposed only that states would contribute according to their means to an international stabilization fund. Contributions would be made up of gold (25 per cent) and national currencies (75 per cent). In case of need, states could draw according to the size of their contribution, the conditions for drawing becoming harder as they reached the limit of their quota. In this way the fund would give temporary credit to countries with balance of payments deficits so that they need not devalue but could hold their exchange rates stable. The implicit assumptions – which proved false – were: that this would be enough to see the world economy through the transition from war to peace; that the world's major currencies would be more or less equally in demand; and that balance of payments deficits and surpluses would mostly be temporary, not structural, and would result from the trade account, not from financial flows.

White's stabilization fund became the model for the International Monetary Fund set up after agreement was reached at Bretton Woods in 1944 – basically between the Americans and British, with others like the French or Canadians being mere bystanders (Germany and Japan, of course, were not present, being enemy states). Alongside it, as a means of ensuring maximum membership, there was to be the International Bank for Reconstruction and Development. No one could draw on this World Bank who was not also a member of the IMF, bound by its rules to declare a fixed exchange rate in terms of gold.[1] Decisions in both the Bank and the Fund were to be taken by weighted vote – weighted, that is, according to the size of each member's quota. Since the US quota was far the largest, this meant that the USA alone had a veto. Nothing could be decided without American consent. And from the start it was the Americans who took all the key decisions in the development of the Fund.[2]

1 Effectively in dollars since, apart from the Swiss franc, the US dollar was the only currency freely convertible into gold at the fixed price of US $35 an ounce.
2 Typical of US dominance was that the size of the Fund was set by the amount of gold under control of the Executive, held in reserve at Fort Knox, Tennessee. This had been revalued in the 1930s by Roosevelt declaring unilaterally a higher price at which the US Treasury would buy gold. The difference between the old value and the new – about US $2 billion – could be contributed to the IMF; any more substantial transfer would require the consent of Congress. See Horsefield (1969, p. 43).

What was new in the international monetary system after Bretton Woods was that for the first time in history the governments of the leading economies had agreed on a set of rules, on a system of collective management. It was neither as impartial in its application nor as unalterable as textbooks sometimes suggest. But the underlying bargain was that states got access to a new source of credit to help them adjust to economic change. In return, they agreed, first, to declare a fixed exchange rate or par value for their currency, and, second, to intervene in markets so that the rate did not vary more than 1 per cent above or below parity, and to change the fixed rate or parity only in order to correct a 'fundamental disequilibrium' – whatever that might mean. So much for the first stage of membership. The second stage came with acceptance of Article VIII of the Bretton Woods Agreement, when members agreed to make their currencies freely convertible: that is, to do without official exchange controls over financial transfers – capital movements – as well as current payments for trade. In this way, the Fund's rules would contribute as much to the creation of an open, liberal world market economy as the parallel trade organization planned by the United States.

Cold War

Unfortunately, everyone had grossly underestimated the pains and problems of the postwar economic situation. The IMF was just not up to the job and its rulebook had to be largely set aside for most of the postwar decade. Even before the IMF was open for business, the United States thought it necessary to aid Britain unilaterally with a US $4.5 billion loan. And no sooner were the IMF and IBRD established than the political situation in Europe caused the USA to take a second and larger initiative – the Marshall Plan – which effectively put the whole IMF plan on ice from 1948 to 1952. The fact is that, although the IMF governors and executive directors continued to meet and take decisions, their place centre stage had been taken over by the US government. There was a worldwide shortage of dollars, but the USA was prepared to supply them on credit to Europe and Japan – and even some to poorer countries – in order to stop further expansion of the power and influence of the Soviet Union. The Cold War, in effect, changed the international monetary system. 'Containment', not 'stabilization', became the watchword.

Even with Marshall Aid and later NATO military aid, it was 1959 before the European economies were sufficiently recovered to risk giving up exchange controls and letting their currencies become freely convertible (i.e. into other currencies, like dollars). When at last they did so, and only then, was it legitimate to speak of a Bretton Woods regime.[3] But the regime was short-lived. Ten years later – or at the latest by 1971 – the system had changed out of all recognition. The dollar was inconvertible into gold and the world was on a paper dollar standard. Even though the IMF continued playing a role in the system – that of guardian-cum-governess to the indebted developing countries – its rule-book was in shreds, its role taken over by the Group of Seven industrialized countries, led, of course, by the United States.

What had happened to bring about this change? Basically, the Bretton Woods system was the victim of American success in avoiding a postwar slump and in priming the pump for the recovery of other countries' economies. That recovery put strains on what was, essentially, a gold-exchange standard or system. What that means is that because dollars were exchangeable for gold, and the USA had large gold reserves, other countries were content to hold dollars instead of gold as reserves. All was well as long as the USA had a payments surplus and the dollar shortage continued. But the economic recovery of the Europeans and later the Japanese turned the tables. A persistent US deficit appeared as trade became more balanced and as US military spending abroad and the foreign investments of US multinationals added further strains to the balance of payments. The probable outcome was foreseen even in the late 1950s. Robert Triffin, a Belgian professor of economics at Yale University, and Jacques Rueff, a French financial official, later advisor to De Gaulle, both foresaw a time when the system would no longer work. US deficits could be financed by other countries agreeing to hold gold-convertible dollars in their reserves. They were like IOUs in gold. But if the deficits continued, and the pile of IOUs went on growing, the time would soon come when they so dwarfed the size of US gold reserves that the credibility of the promises-to-pay in gold would be in doubt. If the system were not reformed in time, there would be a run on the US 'gold window' that would be like a run on a precarious bank. By way of reform, Triffin wanted a clearing union not unlike the original Keynes plan, in which the same rules applied to all, the USA as much as others. Rueff suggested buying time while reform was debated by doubling the price of gold in line with other postwar prices. In Washington, understandably, neither proposal found favour with President Kennedy or, after his death, President Johnson or President Nixon. Instead, Nixon eventually decided in August 1971 to slam closed the gold window and to use market pressures to get the dollar devalued. So ended Bretton

3   Even then, the regime hardly conformed to the rules in the original blueprint. That included a scarce currency clause, which laid on the surplus countries equal responsibility for restoring equilibrium; the USA, which should have done so, would have none of it. And the Fund, according to the rules, existed only to finance deficits on current account. But – against futile French protests – the USA disregarded this limitation on behalf of a valued ally when, after the Suez fiasco in 1956, Britain lost so much on capital account that it had to go for help to the IMF.

Woods, and with it, eventually, what has been aptly called the implicit bargain of the postwar alliance of affluent states. The bargain, never clearly stated but often hinted at, was that the USA would use its nuclear power to shield Europe and Japan from Soviet attack, and would pay the lion's share of the necessary defence costs. In return, the allies would not seriously question the right of the USA to run the monetary and financial systems as it thought best.

Freedom for Finance

This is a good moment to go back and look at what was happening to the second of our two trains: the global financial system. For it played a big part in the story of the 1960s just recounted, and an even bigger part in the 1970s and 1980s.

In the 1930s, it had been seriously slowed, if not put into reverse, as foreign lending dried up, creditors tried to collect on past debt as in the 1980s and the rich countries found various means to discourage foreign borrowers. In the war, naturally, it was at a standstill. Not really until the late 1950s did foreign financial business begin to pick up a little speed. How it did had important consequences for national currencies and for social groups in rich countries and poor ones.

(It is important to note that although we speak of the global financial system, this really referred only to the non-communist market economies. In the Soviet Union, its satellites and communist China finance was government-controlled. Credit was given by administrative order and there were no private financial institutions or markets. Inconvertible currencies and state-controlled trading at state-controlled prices frustrated efforts to create a multilateral payments system such as existed in the West.)

One big innovation was called the Eurodollar, and the market for loans of 'offshore' dollars (i.e. dollars held in banks outside the USA) that began in London. One reason for it was that New Deal precautionary rules kept interest rates artificially low on deposits in banks in the USA; but banks could borrow and lend at higher rates in London and make bigger profits. The other reason was that while the British (alone of the West Europeans) kept exchange controls on capital outflows of sterling, they raised no objection to banks, including British banks, taking in and lending out dollar deposits. The result was that the business, being profitable, unregulated and untaxed, flourished. By the late 1960s, movements of dollars in and out of the offshore markets were already adding to uncertainty and the instability of exchange rates. Allowing transnational Eurocurrency lending was the first big step in a long trend toward deregulating – liberalizing, if you prefer it – global finance and those who lived by it.

Credit creation – for that is what it was – in the Eurodollar market grew slowly in the early 1960s, then gathered speed while inconclusive negotiations were going on about monetary reform. By 1970 deposits totalled about US $10 billion, equal to the value of US gold reserves. The business really took off and began to have effects not only on the international monetary system but also on the real economy in the mid-1970s after the first OPEC oil price rise. This put billions of dollars in the hands of the oil-producing states. Rather than being banked in the USA, where they might be vulnerable to official interference or tax, these 'petrodollars' went to swell the volume of Eurocurrency business. There they were untaxed, anonymous and profitable. Flooded with petrodollars, the banks looked for borrowers. They found them in many developing countries hit by high oil prices and hungry for economic development. Compared with official 'aid' lent by Western governments or international organizations like the World Bank, these bankers' loans came with no awkward questions and imposed no hard performance requirements. And as inflation overtook interest rates in the middle 1970s, the real cost of borrowing like this was very low. It was all too easy. The snag was that the interest rate was variable. Loans were made at variable rates, at so much above the interbank rate in London, LIBOR. If LIBOR went up, so did the burden of servicing (i.e. paying interest) on the loans.

That was exactly what happened in the early 1980s, just when there was a big fall in commodity prices on which many LDCs still depended for their export earnings. It happened as a result of a change in US policy, which through most of the Carter administration had tolerated inflation and a weak dollar. Under Reagan, controls over the money supply were tightened, the price of borrowing naturally went up and indebted countries – not only Mexico and Poland, who were the first to suffer a debt crisis, but also France – felt the pinch. Big international banks that had lent imprudently but profitably to these countries found themselves lumbered with what were euphemistically called 'non-performing loans', i.e. loans that were paying no interest. Frightened of the effect on their own reputation, they more or less stopped lending. In 1974, confidence was shaken when Bank Herstatt in Germany and the Franklin National Bank in New York went bust, conjuring nightmares from the 1930s.

Meanwhile, the deregulating trend gathered speed in the financial system, led by the United States. In the mid-1970s, the USA abolished rules fixing the commissions charged by stockbrokers, and in other ways allowed banks and financial operators to compete much more vigorously with each other. This was supposed to make them more efficient, but it also made them take bigger risks and invent all sorts of new ways of creating and dealing in credit. As foreign exchange markets became more volatile with the end of Bretton Woods and the adoption of floating instead of fixed exchange rates, so financial markets became more speculative. Uncertainties bred hedging devices like futures and options. These in turn bred speculation. The speculation and the mobility of capital across frontiers meant that the value of any currency came to depend much more on financial flows moved by the moods of the market than on those moved by the balance of trade in the real economy. At the personal level of individual careers, this meant that the rewards of dealing in finance in Wall Street or the City of London far outdistanced the rewards of working for government or in industry. Within companies, the financial directors suddenly became key people, whose decisions about how to raise money and where to move it could greatly affect the firm's end-year profits. Popular novels like Paul Erdman's *Billion Dollar Killing*, plays like *Serious Money*, films like *Wall Street* and numberless magazine articles were quicker to note and reflect the trend to casino capitalism than were most professors of economics.[4]

Nor was it just Wall Street and the City that were affected. The very open, liberal economy that the postwar American governments had been at such pains to create meant that the casino phenomenon was world-wide; Tokyo, Hong Kong, Sydney and Toronto were all tied into one financial system. So when the USA continued its deregulation in the 1980s by allowing New York banks to conduct 'offshore' Eurodollar business without actually going offshore, every other government was under pressure to ease up on bank regulation – or risk the business moving elsewhere.

Change had the government authorities worried. Their central banks had been established precisely as watchdogs over private finance, to see that their keen pursuit of profit did not seriously harm the real economy. The authority of central banks rested on their ability to provide support – credit, in fact – in any panic or crisis threatening the commercial banks: in short to act as the lenders of last resort. But when the banks started more and more to function globally, and to operate secretly through tax havens in the Caribbean, new uncertainties arose over who was responsible for what and where. After 1974, the central banks came to a series of agreements among themselves, the Basle Concordats, to try and make up for the absence of a global lender of last resort. They tried to define more precisely the extent of their respective responsibilities. But though this reassured the markets, the BCCI affair in 1991 showed clearly how much the Bank of England, for instance, had relied on private account-ants, Price Waterhouse, for information about what was going on. Too little information, too late, finally led to the enforced closure of a large international bank with severe losses to the depositors, the employees and its main shareholder, the ruler of Abu Dhabi.

4 *Casino Capitalism* was the title I gave to a book about the monetary and financial history of the 1970s. See also Howard Wachtel's *The Money Mandarins* and Michael Moffitt's *The World's Money* for readable accounts of the build-up to the stockmarket crash of October 1987.

Conclusions

I began the story of two trains by posing the oldest question in politics: who gets what? States intervene in markets for credit and for currencies, but who loses and who benefits as a result of their intervention? What new risks are run and by whom? Who gets new opportunities to make money, to escape poverty, to avoid violence, to provide for a secure future for themselves and their families? This is always the bottom line of political economy. In short, what does the story of two trains tell us about the global system in which money, power and space interact? What values have been uppermost, have been given top priority by governments and by the markets?

First, we see that the evolution of global finance led to a debt crisis, which began in 1982 with the near-default of Mexico and continues to reverberate today. But really there were two crises, that of the creditors who had risked their business by lending too much; and that of the borrowers who had risked their economies by borrowing too much at variable rates of interest. The system coped – more or less well – with the first crisis so that there was no general international panic or crash. The 1987 stockmarket crash only lost share values that had previously been too much inflated; industry and confidence was quickly restored, thanks partly to the reassurance of governments through the central banks. But the system coped rather badly with the second crisis. The countries, like Brazil or Argentina, that had borrowed rashly and enjoyed a brief economic boom paid dearly for it in a lost decade or more of poor growth, low investment and flat or falling living standards for their people. Mexico, so close to the United States, was given special help; so was South Korea by the Japanese. The poor African countries, to whom the banks had lent little but who had mainly taken credit from rich governments, the World Bank or the IMF, became like wards of court, impoverished orphans that could no longer pretend to control their own economic destiny.

Second, we see that the system provided most credit to the rich countries, and especially to the United States. Not only did the debt crisis result in a very large net increase in financial flows from South to North instead of the other way round, but the surplus savings of the two newly rich industrial countries, Japan and Germany, were absorbed by the United States. Not only had the US deficit on its balance of payments persisted from the 1960s into the 1990s, its government's chronic fiscal deficit (i.e. shortfall of taxes to cover spending) had risen spectacularly in the 1980s to over US $200 billion a year. It was financed through the global financial system in which Japanese investors assured of high interest *and* political stability were free to buy US government securities. The payments deficit was similarly financed in large part by foreign firms, banks and individuals putting money into US shares, real estate and other investments.[5] Professor Triffin, the veteran critic of the international monetary system and especially of the post-1971 paper dollar standard, blames the allies of America for acquiescing in such an absurd situation. It was, he says, 'the political counterpart of their countries' dependence on the US nuclear umbrella as a crucial contribution to their own defence' (Triffin, 1991).

How long that acquiescence will survive the end of the Cold War, no one knows. But the interaction of the international monetary system and the global financial system is such that central banks are afraid of the effects on the latter if the Germans and/or Japanese imposed a 'hard landing' on the dollar. For that reason, there is a tacit common agreement not to rock the monetary boat.

Third, we see the financial system creating for business an asymmetry in costs and benefits, risks and opportunities parallel to that which the international monetary system creates for states. There is little doubt, even in the minds of ordinary people, that big, transnational business does better out of the new global game of finance than small, local business. True, there are risks from new competitors, risks of takeovers or mergers. But there are compensating opportunities. And vulnerability to the risks is much less than that of small producers and retailers. Epitomizing the pursuit of profit and the accumulation of wealth, the transnational enterprises whose names are known all over the world today give us a clue to the values that, compared with earlier times, are most prized in the structures of the political economy – that is, the wealth and the security of the established monetary and financial systems. By comparison, economic justice and the right of people to some autonomy in the running of their affairs and their businesses take second place.

Finally, we can discern a shift of power from state to market – a certain loss of national control over material life for the citizens of the state. The loss is much more apparent for small, weak, poor states than for large, rich and powerful ones. But liberalizing the world economy in monetary matters and in finance has brought political changes that have hit, first, the political systems of the former socialist, or centrally planned, economies. But it is by no means certain that in the longer run it will not also hit the political and social systems of the democracies, even the largest and richest. Uncertainty over the future of the economic system is matched by uncertainty in the political system.

References

Horsefield, J. K. (1969) *The International Monetary Fund 1945–1965. Vol. 1, Chronicle*. Washington, DC: International Monetary Fund.

5 According to the OECD, the total of US deficits for the six years 1984–9 was US $763 billion. Japan financed more than half of this deficit, Germany over a quarter.

Moffitt, M. (1983) *The World's Money: International Banking from Bretton Woods to the Brink of Insolvency*. London: Michael Joseph.

Strange, S. (1986) *Casino Capitalism*. Oxford: Blackwell.

Strange, S. (1988) *States and Markets*. London: Pinter.

Triffin, R. (1991) IMS – international monetary system – or scandal? Jean Monnet lecture series, European University Institute, Florence.

Wachtel, H. (1986) *The Money Mandarins*. Hemel Hempstead: Harvester Wheatsheaf.

4

Plausible Worlds: Friedman, Keynes and the Geography of Inflation
Stuart Corbridge

Introduction

> At the present moment people are unusually expectant of a more fundamental diagnosis; more particularly ready to receive it; eager to try it out, if it should be even plausible. But apart from this contemporary mood [mid-1930s], the ideas of economists and political philosophers, both when they are right and when they are wrong, are more powerful than is commonly understood. (*Keynes, 1973, p. 383*)

Since the late 1970s large parts of the world economy have been policed with an eye to the evil of inflation, and human geographers have joined with other social scientists in documenting the effects of this obsession with 'sound money'. The unemployment costs of economic restructuring have been counted for the UK, the USA and the OECD (Massey and Meegan, 1982; Scott and Storper, 1986), while the ravages of structural adjustment have been charted in the case of the indebted developing world (Watts, 1991; Riddell, 1992; Corbridge, 1993). Yet very few geographers have made a study of inflation itself,[1] or have pondered the counterfactual question quite reasonably advanced by the New Right: namely, 'how would (different parts of) the world economy have fared in the 1980s in the absence of monetarist and neo-monetarist policies designed to deal with the cancer of inflation?'

This chapter begins to address these issues, without directly confronting the counterfactual question. The second section maps out a historical geography of inflation since 1945 and briefly examines why inflation might be considered a danger for some economic agents. The third

---

1 Exceptions include Harvey (1982) and Sabin (1981). The case for a geography of inflation has also been argued by Gordon Clark (1985; see also Clark, 1984).

section outlines several of the monetarist accounts of inflation that emerged so forcefully in the 1970s. Although particular attention is paid to the work of Milton Friedman, I also consider a related body of work on the long-run Phillips curve, on rational expectations and on the nature of labour markets in unplanned economies. This section also pays attention to the political appropriation of some monetarist ideas by governments as diverse as the first and second Thatcher and Reagan administrations. At the same time, it does not seek to damn academic theories simply by association with such administrations (which themselves tend not to be popular with social scientists, and not least with human geographers). The fourth section presents a critique of the monetarist canon, both in technical terms and with regard to wider institutional, political, spatial and temporal parameters. It also develops another, more eclectic, theory of inflation and its consequences. This model might reasonably be described as Keynesian in tone and inspiration, and it has at its core an account of the changing position of the US political economy in the postwar global political economy. It also insists that inflation is bound up with a wider distributional struggle over the benefits and costs of economic activity.

The chapter does not discuss various Marxist theories of inflation. This is not because there are no such theories or because they are without value (Rowthorn, 1980; Parboni, 1981; Lipietz, 1985; Carchedi, 1991); it simply reflects my view that Marxist critiques are devalued by their failure to advance *plausible* alternative policies for dealing with inflation and other economic ills in a plainly complex world. The conclusion to the chapter takes up the question of plausible worlds at greater length.[2] Keynesian models are commended to human geographers because of their clear attachments to political economy, because of their evident concern for a practicable politics in an uncertain world economy, and because of the extraordinary relevance of Keynes's own work to the 1990s. Keynes never set much store by abstract economic principles – neither *laissez-faire* nor state socialism – and his studied eclecticism (not to mention his voice) is celebrated openly throughout this chapter.

Inflation in the Postwar World Economy

> Of the various purposes which money serves, some essentially depend upon the assumption that its real value is nearly constant over a period of time. The chief of those are connected, in a wide sense, with contracts for the *investment of money*. (*Keynes, 1972, p. 61; emphasis in the original*)

2   Notwithstanding the link to Keynes, the idea of 'plausible worlds' comes from the title of an important book by Geoff Hawthorn (1991).

Inflation is commonly defined as the rate at which the general level of prices is changing and, as such, it was not widely recognized as a social or economic problem in the OECD countries between 1950 and the end of the 1960s. This was the Golden Age of Capitalism (Marglin and Schor, 1990) when most citizens in the advanced industrial countries basked in conditions of fullish employment, annual rates of inflation of below 4 per cent and rates of real income growth as high as 4 and 5 per cent per annum. Real incomes doubled for most households in the OECD bloc between 1950 and 1970, during which time the British Prime Minister, Macmillan, told his fellow citizens that 'they had never had it so good'.

This was also the time of a hegemonic Keynesianism, both in academic circles and among policy-makers. In a telling commentary on the period, the Cambridge economist Wynne Godley has offered to 'come clean . . . and admit that, as a civil servant employed full time during the 1950s and 1960s on macroeconomic analysis, it was my belief that the simple system of ideas . . . outlined . . . above was nearly sufficient by way of economic theory for macroeconomic policy purposes' (Godley, 1984, p. 64). The ideas he refers to are: first, the belief that governments could sponsor real economic growth and full employment by expanding

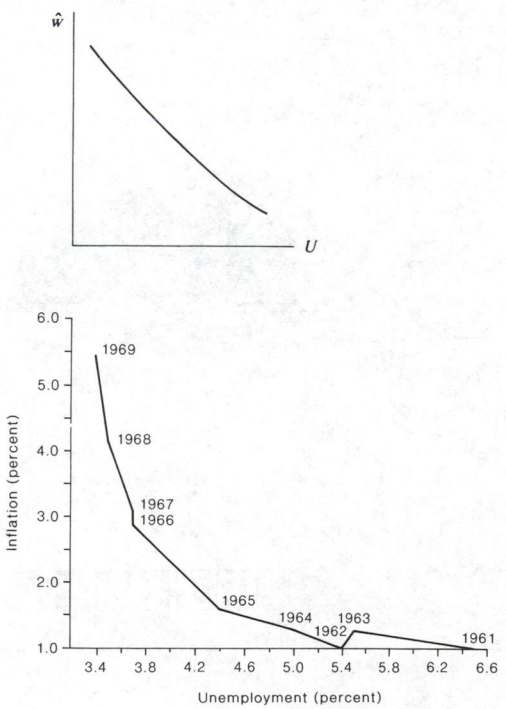

Figure 4.1 The original Phillips curve, and inflation and unemployment in the United States, 1961–1969.
Source: after Sachs and Larrain, 1993.

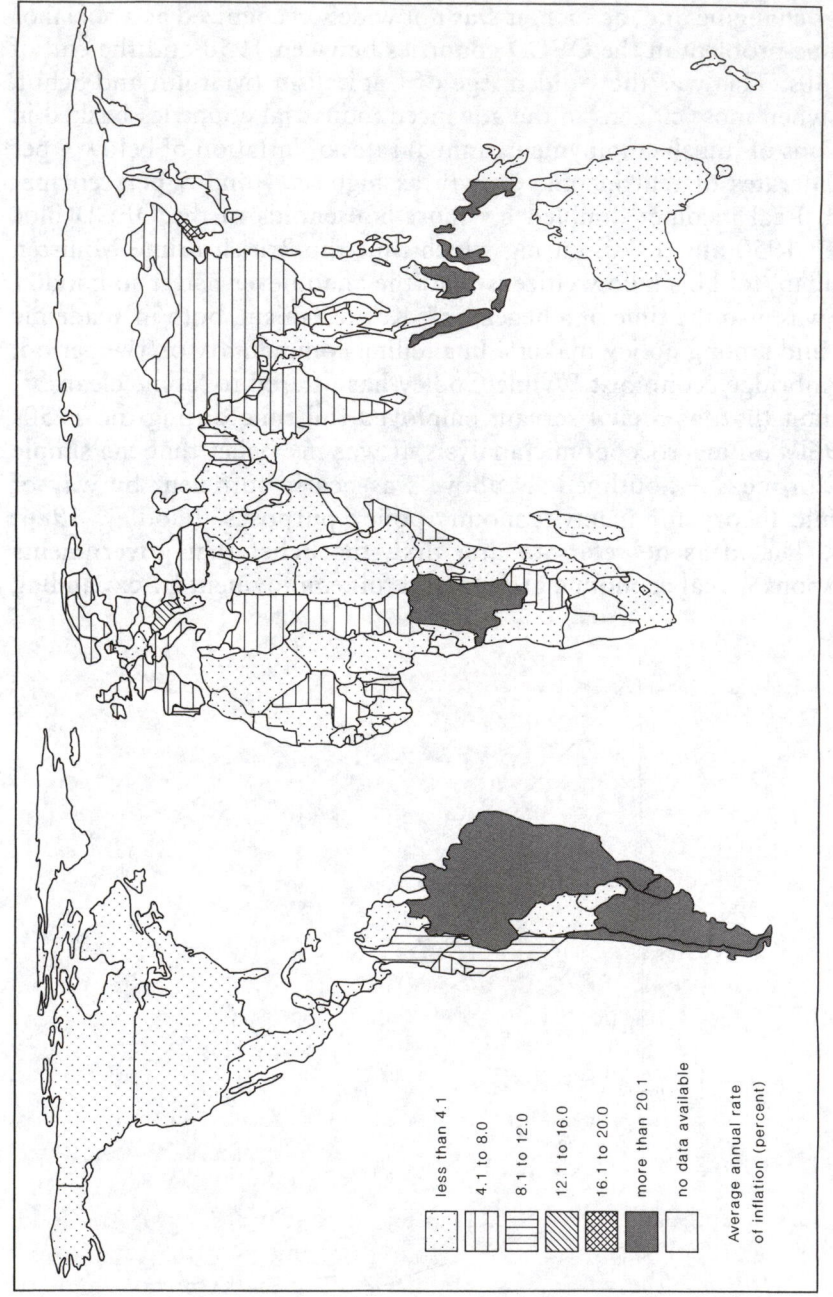

Figure 4.2 The global geography of inflation in the 1960s.
Source: World Bank data.

aggregate demand for goods and services; second, that subject to a balance of payments constraint, aggregate demand could be raised or lowered primarily by means of fiscal policy; and third, that 'Monetary policy under this system of ideas did not matter much, the quantity of money itself being a residual thrown up by everything else that happened which could be safely ignored' (ibid.).

This broad Keynesian perspective was consolidated by reference to the so-called Phillips curve. The early Phillips curve model (Phillips, 1958) suggested that governments could manage a trade-off between price stability and employment. More exactly, Phillips suggested an original equation written as $w = \text{constant} - bU$, where b is the coefficient determining the response of the nominal wage to the current unemployment rate. The Phillips curve further suggested that governments could commit themselves to full employment policies without great risk of inflation reaching more than 5 per cent per annum. Data from the United States in the 1960s seemed to bear Phillips out. Not only does the chart of inflation and unemployment in the USA between 1961 and 1969 follow quite closely the slope of the original Phillips curve (see figure 4.1), but inflation in the USA only once edged above 5 per cent in this period (in 1969, significantly). Other countries seemed to have achieved similar results. Figure 4.2 presents a map of average annual rates of inflation in the 1960s for most countries. If the eye is encouraged to linger on the OECD world-economy (as opposed to Latin America), the optimism of the Keynesian golden years seems to be vindicated. Inflation was a problem only to the extent that governments defined it as a problem in political terms. Where governments were especially keen to keep a lid on inflation – as in West Germany – a higher rate of unemployment could be 'chosen' by policy-makers.

In the 1970s the idea of a simple Phillips curve fell into disrepute. Figure 4.3 confirms that the supposed trade-off between inflation and unemployment broke down in the 1970s as a period of stagflation replaced the Golden Age (Bruno and Sachs, 1985). Rising unemployment and inflation went hand in hand throughout the OECD world-economy, and especially so in countries like Japan in the early 1970s and the UK and the USA in the later 1970s. Amid such conditions inflation forced itself back on to the agenda of economics, with a growing chorus of non-Keynesian economists rushing to denounce the short-run Phillips curve for its emphasis on nominal prices and for its failure to take account of workers' responses to anticipated changes in the price level.

We will return to the work of the monetarists shortly. In more general terms, the rise of 'creeping' inflation throughout most of the capitalist world economy brought into focus three apparent dangers in inflationism. A first danger concerns the conditions for economic stability. Ironically, it was Keynes in 1919 who popularized Lenin's dictum that 'the best way to destroy the capitalist system [is] to debauch the currency'.

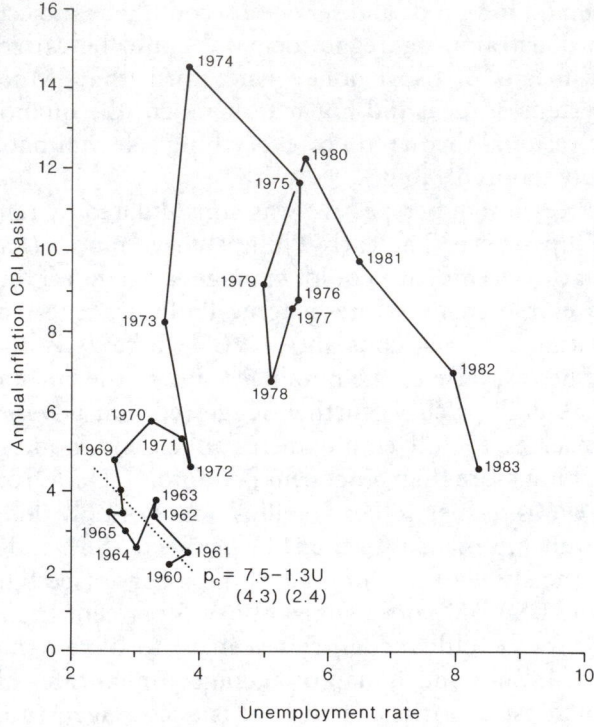

Figure 4.3   Unemployment and inflation in the large OECD economies, 1960–1983.

Keynes agreed: 'Lenin was certainly right. There is no subtler, no surer means of overturning the existing basis of society than to debauch the currency. The process engages all the hidden forces of economic law on the side of destruction, and does it in a manner which not one man in a million is able to diagnose' (Keynes, 1984, pp. 148–9). At the same time, Keynes believed that economic stability was threatened not so much by inflation itself, but by high and/or unstable rates of inflation. Others demur, pointing out that the threshold level of a dangerous inflationism can be quite low (Sargent, 1986). Inflation itself *is* then an economic evil, for it makes the process of economic calculation more difficult – more 'noisy', to use Friedman's term – than it needs to be. All inflations encourage economic agents to hold less money than they would otherwise choose to do, and thus to hold their wealth in less liquid forms than might be optimal from the point of view of the wider economy. Inflation might also encourage a certain conservatism in the face of uncertain future economic conditions and it has implications for the international competitiveness of countries with higher than average rates of price increases.

A second general objection to inflation is that it encourages governments to tax their citizens without their direct consent. Inflation taxes are perhaps most common in Latin America, but they are not unknown elsewhere. The tax works by courtesy of an inappropriate or belated indexation of wages. As long as marginal tax brackets are set in nominal terms, rises in nominal incomes will push people into higher tax brackets, thereby making them liable for higher marginal rates of taxation. As Sachs and Larrain (1993, p. 348) point out, 'A person whose real income is constant thereby suffers a gradual increase in her tax liabilities and a consequent loss of disposable income, simply because of inflation.' Perversely, inflation can also eat into the real value of the government's tax revenues because of significant lags in tax collection. This phenomenon was identified by Julio Olivera and Vito Tanzi in the late 1960s (Olivera, 1967) and it can quickly trigger a vicious circle of lower tax revenues, increased budget deficits, further inflation and renewed inflationary taxation. Again, it is not a phenomenon that economic managers would wish to encourage, although figure 4.2 suggests that it has been common enough in many Latin American countries.

A third objection to inflation is that it redistributes incomes in a broadly regressive manner. This is not always the case (particularly between countries), but inflation can be especially unwelcome for those workers unable to index their wages against prices, and for those who live mainly on fixed incomes (often welfare payments) and from their savings. Inflation tends to favour those in debt, who might benefit from low or even negative real rates of interest. More generally, 'Because the income elasticity of money demand is likely to be less than one, the inflation tax is likely to be regressive – that is, poorer people pay a higher proportion of their income as inflation tax than richer people do' (Sachs and Larrain, 1993, p. 351). Further criticisms of inflation – and its impact upon employment especially – are taken up in the next section.

Monetarist Accounts of Inflation

The view that *any* increase in the quantity of money is inflationary (unless we mean by *inflationary* merely that prices are rising) is bound up with the underlying assumption of the classical theory that we are *always* in a condition where a reduction in the real rewards of the factors of production will lead to a curtailment of their supply. (*Keynes, 1973, p. 304; emphasis in the original*)

The creeping inflation of the late 1960s and 1970s gave encouragement to a growing group of monetarist economists whose voices had been all but ignored in the 1950s and 1960s. These economists pointed out that Keynesian macroeconomics lacked a substantial microeconomic foundation, and that Keynesianism – unlike monetarism – was unable to predict the post-1960s phenomenon of stagflation.

The basis of the monetarist creed is the quantity theory of money and a particular reading of the equation of exchange: $MV = PY$ (where M is the quantity of money, V is the velocity of money turnover, P is the price level and Y is aggregate output). Now, the equation of exchange is nothing more than an identity. It simply states that the quantity of money multiplied by the number of times this money is spent in a given year is equal to nominal income (or the total amount spent on goods and services in that year). What is significant about the monetarist interpretation of the equation of exchange (from Irving Fisher to Milton Friedman and onwards) is that V is assumed to be fairly constant in the short run (governed as it is by certain institutional features of an economy), with the result that nominal income is determined almost wholly by changes in the quantity of money (M).

This is significantly different from the Keynesian or Cambridge approach to money demand. Keynes, following Marshall and Pigou, argued that people hold money for two main reasons: as a medium of exchange for carrying out transactions and as a store of wealth. More importantly, Keynes argued that because different individuals would choose to hold different amounts of money, so the apparently constant proportionality linking the demand for money to nominal income could be very inconstant indeed. More straightforwardly, Keynes did not believe that V was unimportant in the equation of exchange. He also did not assume that a rise in M could only prompt a later rise in P. Nominal incomes could also be affected by changes in M and, more importantly, the direction of causality was not unidirectional. The money supply could be credit-driven, with the demand for private bank credit being closely related to changes in business demand for working capital (after Michie and Wilkinson, 1992, p. 199). Milton Friedman has argued a very different line. According to Mishkin (1986, p. 420), 'Friedman's money demand function is essentially one in which permanent income is the primary determinant of money demand', so that, for Friedman, 'inflation is always and everywhere a monetary phenomenon'. Inflation emerges whenever governments put money into circulation in excess of a rate warranted by the growth of the real economy (Friedman, 1969).

However arcane these distinctions might seem, their policy-related dimensions are real enough. Friedman argued throughout the 1960s that the demand for money was largely insensitive to any single set of interest rates (an argument that was directly contrary to the Keynesian liquidity preference model of money demand). Friedman also argued that the money demand function is essentially stable. It then follows that there is a direct and predictable relationship between the rate of change of the money supply and the rate of inflation in subsequent years. Friedman also argued this case empirically. In an extraordinary survey of the monetary history of the USA conducted and published with Anne Schwartz (Friedman and Schwartz, 1963) – which was later extended to

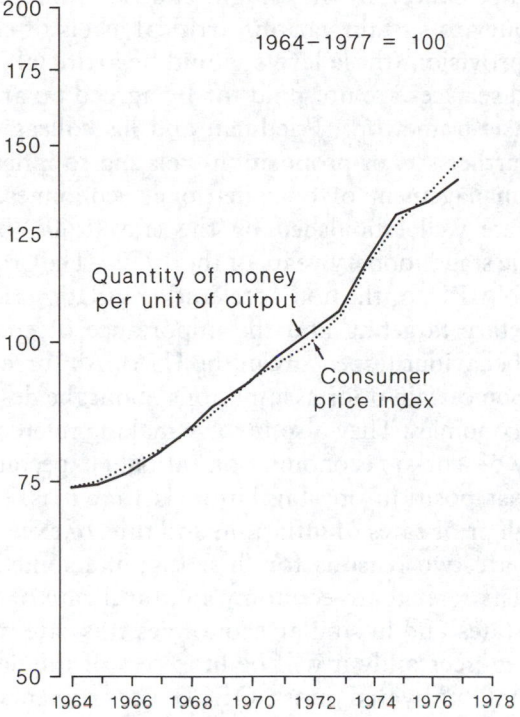

Figure 4.4 Money and prices in the United States, 1964–1977.
Source: after Friedman and Friedman, 1980.

include the UK (Friedman and Schwartz, 1982) – Friedman charted a close relationship between the rate of growth of the money supply and the rate of growth of inflation some one to two years later (see also figure 4.4).

Whether this relationship must hold in quite this form is a matter for debate and we will not go into it here. What matters is that the work of Friedman and Schwartz confirmed most monetarists in their view that inflations are sponsored by governments. This really is the nub of the matter. As Friedman has many times acknowledged, the analytical gap between him and most modern Keynesians is not too great (see Friedman, 1989, p. 23; see also Modigliani, 1977). Virtually all economists would agree that inflation is a monetary phenomenon. The disagreement is much more to do with the causes of inflation and the empirical dynamics of monetary expansion. For most Keynesians, as we shall see in the next section and as should be apparent already, there are many possible causes of inflation. For most monetarists, by contrast, inflation is a direct result of government attempts to stimulate the real economy by monetary infusions. Governments might do this for several reasons: they might believe, wrongly, that it is effective and has few costs (as per the simple Phillips curve), or they might choose to buy political support by printing money to sustain various artifical levels of employment and public service provision (these levels would be artificial in the sense that such goods and services are not paid for by agreed taxation).

Given this basic framework, Friedman and his colleagues were able to develop three further sets of propositions relating to inflation, unemployment and the management of open national economies. Some of these propositions were well established by the late 1960s, but most gained support amid the stagflationary years of the 1970s. The propositions I refer to concern: (a) NAIRU, or the non-accelerating inflation rate of unemployment; (b) monetary targeting and the importance of credibility; and (c) labour market behaviour (especially in the USA). All three sets of propositions depend upon certain prior assumptions about the desirability of open market-based economies. They also involve making reference to a new and associated body of work in economics on rational expectations.

The monetarist position on stagflation is that it is a necessary consequence of high prior rates of inflation, and thus of excess money supply growth. There are two reasons for this. Just like some modern Keynesians, monetarists refer to an economy's natural rate of unemployment. In the United States and in similar economies this rate might be as high as 5 or 6 per cent; certainly it will be in excess of the definitions of full employment that motivated most OECD governments in the golden years. It follows that attempts to maintain employment rates in excess of the warranted or natural rate can only lead to inflation (as per the equation of exchange). Governments print money to excess and overheat the economy. Empirical work by Friedman in the 1960s (Friedman, 1961, 1968), and by Phelps (1967; see also Phelps, 1970), suggested that the initial Phillips curve was inadequate (and too sanguine) because of its failure to model real wage rates and inflationary expectations. Friedman and Phelps suggested that the plot of the Phillips curve could itself shift upwards or to the right.

This observation led on to the concept of acceleration in relation to inflation. Friedman and Phelps argued that a trade-off between inflation and unemployment was only possible when the economy was already at its natural rate of unemployment. If unemployment is held above the natural rate inflation will fall. However, if unemployment is kept below its natural rate inflation will ensue, workers will anticipate a rise in inflation and will seek to defend real wages, inflation will rise further and unemployment will increase. This, of course, is the essence of stagflation. In more formal terms, Friedman and Phelps suggested that the long-run Phillips curve, far from sloping from top-left to bottom-right, is vertical; there is no trade-off between inflation and unemployment in the long run. The only rate of unemployment consistent with a stable inflation rate is the natural, or non-accelerating inflation rate of unemployment. Unemployment rates below NAIRU must trigger creeping and accelerating rates of inflation, such as were witnessed in the 1970s.

Many economists would accept some version of the NAIRU thesis. Not so many, however, would accept a second set of claims and policies that monetarists developed to deal with the stagflation of the 1970s. Monetarists, as we have seen, emphasize the responsibility of governments for funding inflation (by means of high budget deficits to maintain artificially high rates of inflation). Most monetarists deny or downplay other possible causes of inflation, such as labour militancy (acceded to by governments, they say), or cost-push factors like the 1973–4 oil price rises.

Given this emphasis upon government monetary policy, it follows that the monetarist cure for inflation is a credible money supply policy. This can take several forms. Although not a monetarist, Hayek has suggested that responsibility for money creation should be privatized and subjected to competitive pressures. Consumers of money would then choose to hold that form of money which best keeps its value (Hayek, 1976). Most monetarists do not go this far. Throughout the 1970s, Friedman and his followers argued that governments should both provide a consistent definition of their money supply (M0, M1, etc.), and publish targets of future rates of money supply growth over a one to five year period. Above all, these targets had to be credible and had to be stuck to, notwithstanding the short-term increases in unemployment which they might be expected to induce. In practice, this meant that responsibility for a country's money supply had to be taken out of the hands of government (a set of political actors willing to buy votes with public money) and entrusted to an independent central bank. Evidence has been produced which suggests that inflationary pressures are likely to be higher in countries with a non-independent central bank (such as the Bank of England) than in those countries with genuinely independent central banks (such as the German Bundesbank) (see Alesina, 1989).

Friedman was also among the first to argue that floating exchange rates are a necessary accompaniment to effective national monetary policies. A brief glance back to figure 4.2 reveals that the emergence of creeping inflation in the late 1960s (and the early 1970s for that matter) was not confined to a handful of OECD countries; it characterized the OECD region as a whole. Friedman was not surprised by this. Like McKinnon, and with several other monetarist and non-monetarist economists, he pointed out that under a system of fixed exchange rates the creation of high-powered money to excess in the USA was more or less bound to fuel inflation in the economies of the USA's main trading partners. In part, this would reflect the importance of arbitrage in the determination of international prices (a point argued strongly by Friedman). More straightforwardly, 'An expansion in domestic credit in one [powerful] country will tend to flow out through an increased payments deficit, on current or capital account or both, which will swell the reserves and – in the absence of complete sterilization – the money supplies of its trading partners' (Williamson and Milner, 1991, p. 411). Friends and rivals of the USA had but three choices in this situation: to continue to import inflation; to decrease their dependence on US dollar reserve holdings; or to press for a system of floating exchange rates (the option chosen by the Swiss and the West Germans in the early to mid-1970s). A system of floating exchange rates would in theory open up a window for national economic policy-making, specifically with regard to anti-inflationary measures through monetary policies. That such a system was all of a piece with the faith that most monetarists declare in liberalization and freely functioning (money) markets only heightened its appeal.

The third part of the broad monetarist perspective came from the field of labour economics. In the light of what we have said thus far it will be apparent that the adoption of monetarist policies to tackle creeping inflation is bound to increase unemployment in the short run (at least to the NAIRU). This was never likely to be popular with governments, especially in those countries that had long enjoyed a commitment to full employment. Happily, the blow could be softened in two ways. First, the monetarist camp had little difficulty in the 1970s in persuading some politicians that high inflation and high unemployment were likely to proceed in tandem. The evidence for this view was all around them and it was taken up by the UK Prime Minister, James Callaghan, at the Labour Party conference in 1976. Second, the emphasis that most monetarists placed on credibility and rational expectations was being reinforced by a related set of studies of the labour market in unplanned economies.

In the 1960s, most labour economists still worked with the traditional categories of full employment and structural, cyclical and frictional unemployment. Most economists also believed that 'unemployment is the worst scourge of a free enterprise system' (Woods and Ostry, 1962, p. 358; quoted in Osberg, 1984). Memories of the Great Depression of the 1930s had not yet been erased and few in the 1960s cared for the monetarist view that the Depression was caused by overly zealous monetary policies, as opposed to a lack of expansionary fiscal policies (Haberler, 1985). By the 1970s these seeming truths were being rendered problematic. We have already mentioned the work of Friedman and Phelps, but quite as important was the work of US-based labour economists, including Barro and Lucas. Lucas, in particular, promoted a micro-analysis of labour markets based on a study of search behaviour. Crudely summarized, he came to two main conclusions. To begin with, Lucas drew upon empirical studies of the US labour market in the early 1970s to suggest that the 'average' worker in the USA was employed for about 21 months, was then unemployed for one or two months, and then took up unemployment again. At any one time, therefore, perhaps 6 per cent of the US labour force would be unemployed, even in an economy supposedly at full employment. This work seemed to confirm the natural rate hypothesis. More importantly, Lucas went on to argue that such unemployment as there was in the USA was largely voluntary, and that America's pool of unemployed men and women was made up of people searching for a better or a different job, or simply trading off leisure time against unemployment for a brief period. In his judgement, 'the unemployed worker at any time can always find some job at once' (Lucas, 1978, p. 357).

The policy implications of this and other such work were not lost on some of the governments that came to power between 1979 and 1982. If unemployment was never structural but always voluntary it followed that unemployment was not an economic problem that needed to be tackled by government. Rather, it was a political problem (just as inflation was a political problem for Keynes). Insofar as long-term unemployment did exist, the long-term unemployed had to be convinced that work was available and that the option of not working was a poor option to take. This in turn might entail some cuts in benefits to make the labour market work more efficiently. Further, insofar as unemployment was a political problem for governments pursuing monetarist policies, the problem was unlikely to be long-lasting. This was the most important lesson that the work of Lucas seemingly held out to policy-makers. According to Lucas, unemployment was likely to be of short duration only and would affect workers more or less randomly and of their own volition. In such circumstances, government help for a specified and stable target population of the unemployed did not arise as a need or as a logical possibility. Moreover, the prospect was that while unemployment might rise to its natural rate in the wake of anti-inflation policies, the total rise in unemployment would not be large in most countries and in any case would be temporary and short-lived. Once workers learned to anticipate lower rates of inflation and the potential costs of unemployment, they would adjust their expectations of rewards in the labour market and act accordingly. The labour market would then return to its natural rate of unemployment, albeit, perhaps, at lower average real wage rates.

As recent work has reminded us, this was the message taken to heart by the first Thatcher and Reagan administrations. Monetary targeting had begun in earnest in Canada in 1975, but it became a stated and totemistic item of government policy mainly in the early 1980s and most obviously in the UK. The Thatcher Government drew explicitly on monetarism (or a version of it that suited its purposes) to declare war on inflation in the UK, and to build a new, freer economy based on sound money and real jobs. It was to this end that the UK's powerful trade unions were taken on by the UK Government, with the miners especially being faced down in the strike of 1984–5. It was to this end, too, that real interest rates were tightened by Paul Volcker in the USA (1979–83), notwithstanding the costs later to be imposed on the indebted developing world.

Quite why these policies were pursued with such a vengeance is a moot point. Many on the left in the UK saw Thatcherism as a means by which the power of the working class in Britain could be smashed, with the profits of capital being restored as a consequence. Many in the Third World see a not dissimilar motive in US interest-rate policies; policies intended to facilitate a transfer of wealth from the world's poor to the world's well-to-do. There is probably something in both these views.[3] What is also undeniable, however, is that both Thatcher and Volcker believed that their policies were in the national economic interest and that there was no viable alternative to these policies. They also believed – and were encouraged by some academics to believe – that the costs of their victories over inflation and sticky labour markets would be none too harsh (Lawson, 1992). Evidence to the contrary did little to dent this optimism. Writing some years later, Professor Patrick Minford, a supporter of the Conservative Government, concluded that 'The inflation battle, like many battles in history, did not go according to plan, and the plan itself could have been improved. But it was won' (quoted by Johnson, 1991, p. 38).[4]

Keynesian Accounts of Inflation

Thus inflation is unjust and deflation is inexpedient. Of the two perhaps deflation is, if we rule out exaggerated inflations such as that of Germany [in the 1920s], the worse; because it is worse, in

3 Keynes wrote famously of Mr Churchill's misuse of deflation for political ends and for a particular class interest. 'On grounds of social justice no case can be made out for reducing the wages of the miners. They are the victims of the economic juggernaut. They represent in the flesh the "fundamental adjustments" engineered by the Treasury and the Bank of England to satisfy the impatience of the City fathers to bridge the "moderate gap" between $4.40 and $4.86. . . . The plight of the coal miners is the first, but not – unless we are very lucky – the last, of the economic consequences of Mr Churchill' (Keynes, 1972, p. 223). In the UK, the idea that history repeats itself either as farce or as tragedy was itself made flesh in the economic policies of Messrs Major and Lamont in the early 1990s. The American economist James Tobin also put his finger on the politics of inflation (and thus monetarism) when he declared that 'it is gratuitously optimistic to think that fundamental distributional conflict can be resolved by shrinking the pie over which the parties are contesting' (Tobin, 1981, p. 39).
4 It matters to the wider argument of this chapter that the success or failure of monetarism in the UK in the early 1980s had surprisingly little to do with strict Friedmanite monetarism. UK Chancellor Geoffrey Howe tried to control the UK money supply by tight fiscal policies and high interest rates and not by direct control of the monetary base. Opposition politicians derided Howe's budgets as 'sado-monetaristic'.

an impoverished world, to provoke unemployment than to disap-
point the rentier. . . . For these grave causes we must free ourselves
from the deep distrust which exists against allowing the regulation
of the standard of value to be the subject of *deliberate decision*. We
can no longer afford to leave it in the category of which the
distinguishing characteristics are possessed in different degrees by
the weather, the birth-rate, and the Constitution – matters which
are settled by natural causes, or are the resultant of the separate action
of many individuals acting independently, or require a revolution to
change them. (*Keynes, 1972, p. 75; emphasis in the original*)

It would be idle to pretend that the adoption of sound money policies in
the 1980s was 'unsuccessful'. Inflation rates did fall in most OECD
countries between 1980 and 1985 and the importance of credible monetary targeting is now widely accepted. It is also unlikely that economic
managers in open advanced economies will allow future inflation rates
to exceed 10 per cent per annum. The questions that remain, of course,
concern the costs of the wars waged against inflation and the possibility
that inflation might have been tamed by less damaging economic policies.
It is in this context that a revitalized Keynesian economics remains a
vibrant intellectual force, and not least when it is allied to a geographical
imagination. A broad spectrum of Keynesian and post-Keynesian economists have called into question three main aspects of the monetarist
account of inflation and unemployment: its technical and empirical
specifications, its analysis of the proximate and structural causes of
inflation and labour market behaviour, and what Sachs and Larrain
(1993, p. 460) refer to as the 'sacrifice ratio' of sound money policies
in the 1980s. This general critique also throws into sharp relief an
alternative Keynesian model of the political economy of inflation and
unemployment.

Money Supplies in the Modern World Economy

Monetarist policies for dealing with creeping inflation depend upon a
model of the economy that makes some controversial assumptions about
the nature of the money supply and its real economic effects, and
about the nature of labour markets in the face of rational economic
expectations.

Consider, again, the equation of exchange whereby $MV = PY$. Critics
of monetarism deny that V can reasonably be assumed to be constant for
theoretical and policy purposes, and that an increase in M can provoke
a rise only in P and not in Y. In their judgement, such assumptions are
unwarranted and unpragmatic from the point of view of policy-making.
Although there is some empirical evidence to suggest that percentage
changes in velocity (V) decreased in the 1950s and 1960s in the USA, as

compared to the interwar years, there is also a substantial body of evidence that indicates that 'even in the short-run, velocity fluctuates too much to be viewed as a constant' (Mishkin, 1986, p. 406; on the basis of data from the Federal Reserve system), and that changes in velocity have increased again since the early 1970s. Moreover, as Mishkin points out, 'The percentage change in velocity (GNP/M1) from 1981 to 1982, for example, was −4.6%, while from 1980 to 1981 velocity grew at a rate of 5.5%. The difference of 10.1% means that nominal GNP was 10.1% lower than it otherwise would have been if velocity had kept growing at the same rate as in 1980–1981. The drop is enough to account for the severe recession that took place in 1981–1982' (Mishkin, 1986, p. 407). This last point is clearly very significant. If velocity is as unstable as published data suggest it is, it follows that an overriding emphasis upon the *M–P* relationship is unwarranted and is likely to be misleading. Rather, attention should be allowed to focus on each of the four elements of the equation of exchange and upon the reasons for the evident instability in *V*. Simply put, in most Keynesian models, *V* is likely to be unstable in the short run because of the different motives that economic agents have for holding money. These motives reflect conditions in the wider real economy, an observation that again suggests that a less causal role should be given to the supply of high-powered money (*M*).

A second technical problem facing monetarism concerns the definition and measurement of the money supply in an open economy. Friedman's reputation depends in large part upon his ability to demonstrate a causal relationship between a credible and consistent money supply indicator and a subsequent rate of inflation. Non-monetarists question whether such an association, even where it can be established, is necessarily causal or whether the direction of causality always runs from the money supply to the price level. They also question whether a consistent national indicator of high-powered money can be found for most countries in today's open and deregulated world economy. Friedman and Schwartz's most convincing empirical work examined the money supply–inflation relationship in the USA, largely before the 1970s. But the USA in this period was akin to a closed economy (certainly by comparison with the more open economies of Western Europe) and from 1945 the USA issued the main international unit of account. A close relationship between *M* and *P* might be expected in such circumstances, albeit not as close as the relationship that Friedman and Schwartz claimed to detect.

In the 1980s matters became a good deal more complicated. McKinnon (1984) now argued that the global money supply should be targeted and that the USA, Germany and Japan should coordinate their national money supply policies to this end. As a so-called 'global monetarist', McKinnon was perhaps more sensitive than Friedman to the possibility of imported inflation in a floating exchange rate system, and to the role played by the Eurobanks in multiplying the high-powered monies issued by governments. Economists less committed to monetarism were wary about going even this far. Most Keynesians consider the coordination of national money supply policies to be a matter of political economy and not of economics alone. Some have also pointed out that governments in the 1980s did not find it easy to target a consistent set of monetary aggregates (such as sterling M3), as demanded by many hard-line monetarists. The changing nature of money continued to erode the very condition of money supply stability upon which a practical monetarism might have been based. The publication of money supply targets continues in most OECD countries, but fewer economic agents are now willing to draw particular (as opposed to general) conclusions from the figures that governments put into circulation.

A third technical problem facing the wider monetarist imagination concerns the nature of rational economic expectations. The early work of Lucas and Thomas Sargent undoubtedly amounted to a breakthrough in postwar economic theory and we have already remarked upon the policy implications that it seemed to herald: namely, that in the wake of appropriate aggregate demand policies, 'the wage is set automatically at the appropriate nominal level to ensure full employment and zero inflation' (Sachs and Larrain, 1993, p. 466). In practice, though, labour markets have failed to clear in the way that some theorists of rational expectations were minded to predict. Perhaps unsurprisingly, most men and women do not act as if inflation will be zero in the next economic year just because a government has committed itself to a policy of zero inflation, however credible they think that government might be. Economic agents have memories and they tend to act with regard to past rates of inflation; the present and the future are not treated as blank pages informed only by an agent's own model of how the economy performs at this instant and at times hence. Most economic agents are also sceptical about promises made by governments, particularly when they know that governments have to buy the support of voters on a recurrent basis. In short, most economic agents do not behave as per the postulates of rational expectations theory. Their actions are shaped by a set of adaptive expectations and by the particular institutional frameworks in which they find themselves. As Keynes long ago pointed out, most people do not choose to be unemployed, but unemployment can persist for many years notwithstanding a collective disposition to seek work. In the real world, the unemployment costs of anti-inflation policies should not simply be assumed away.

The Causes of Inflation

A more general set of objections to monetarism concerns the possible causes of inflation, and in particular the inflations of the 1970s. Most Keynesians would accept that increases in the supply of high-powered money were largely contributory to the inflations experienced by many OECD countries in the 1970s (not to mention the steeper inflations so often apparent in Latin America). At the same time, they would doubt that such increases in the money supply were solely responsible for each and every inflationary episode. They would also contend that such increases in high-powered monies must themselves be explained with regard to a political economy of states and monies that moves far beyond the restrictive monetarist accounts of these issues.[5]

Consider, first, the range of possible causes of inflation to which a non-monetarist might make reference. An obvious starting point for the inflation of the 1970s is the exogenous price shocks brought about by the actions of OPEC in 1973–4. The oil price rises probably did encourage some governments to print money to excess (in monetarist terms), but only to ensure that the deflationary effects of current account adjustments would not have to be faced in a single financial year. The oil price rises also had a direct impact on inflation in many oil-importing countries, again through the balance of payments mechanism. Although some monetarists deny the existence of cost-push inflation in this form, Williamson and Milner, writing from what they call the 'eclectic mainstream' of economics, have no doubt that 'Higher oil prices gave a direct impulse to costs of production and thus to the rate of inflation' (Williamson and Milner, 1991, p. 415). This was especially the case in oil-importing developing countries, a point borne out by the changing global

---

5 It is here that Marxism comes into its own. Most Marxists would explain the rise of inflation in the 1970s in two main ways: first, as a means by which a building accumulation crisis in global capitalism could be bought off (literally) by an extension of credit monies and fictitious capitals in advance of production; and, second, as a means by which governments could disguise an underlying class struggle around the benefits of economic growth and the costs of economic crisis. Governments would regulate capitalism and legitimize their own power by printing money sufficiently in the short run to finance the continued production and consumption of collective goods. To an extent, these two explanations are at odds with each other. The first explanation, associated especially with David Harvey (1982, 1985), suggests that sooner or later the various local crises of capitalism will be generalized into a global crisis as anti-inflationary measures are provoked by an urgent need to 'return to the eternal verities of the monetary base' (Harvey, 1982, p. 254). Arguably, this is what happened in the 1980s, James Tobin's decade of deflation. The second explanation is then more problematic. Governments in some countries in the 1970s probably did legitimize their powers by an inflationary deficit financing which seemed to keep all economic classes happy (until it provoked an impending fiscal crisis of the state: see also Haggard and Kaufman, 1992). The savage deflations of the 1980s, however, showed that a toleration of inflationism was not a necessary condition of existence of government stability in the OECD world-economy. Many 'monetarist' governments survived without serious upset and in the UK were re-elected with increased majorities in the 1980s. As ever, there is a danger in most versions of Marxism of an unhelpful functionalism, which needs to be guarded against.

geography of creeping inflation in the 1970s. Plainly, inflation and geopolitics are not easily separated.

A not dissimilar set of arguments would hold with regard to wage-push inflation in the 1970s, and not least in a country like the UK where the power of organized labour was very great at the time. Monetarists like to argue that wage-push inflation is little more than a facade behind which cower governments too weak to set credible monetary targets and too frightened to persuade workers to accede to lower wage rises. If real wages are increasing faster than what might be called the warranted rate of increase, it is because governments are colluding with organized labour in promoting unemployment and in transferring wealth away from other groups of economic actors (including more entrepreneurial groups). It follows that a prices and incomes policy is both unlikely to work in practice (if trade unions remain strong) and poorly specified in theory (because it targets labour and not government). Many Keynesians would disagree. They might not fault all aspects of the monetarist case, but they would surely arrive at less dogmatic conclusions. Wages comprise an important component of the price of most goods and services and an increase in wages can be directly inflationary in certain circumstances. By the same token, efforts to control wages directly, by means of corporatist forms of economic management, have not always failed. A comparative (geographical) study of inflation and its management would

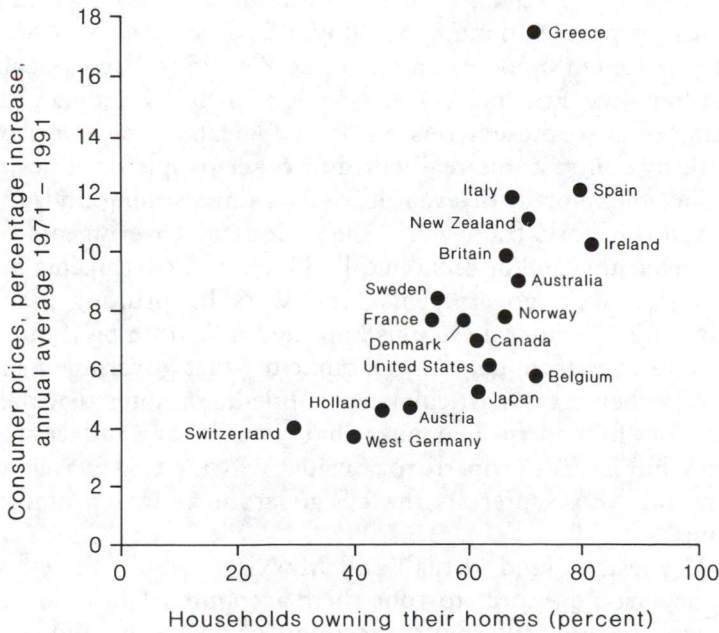

Figure 4.5 Home ownership and inflation, 1971–1991.

surely reveal 'successful' examples of prices and incomes policies, just as it would highlight several 'failures' in attempts to manage inflation by monetarist means. Clearly, a good deal of work remains to be done in this area. (Comparative geographical research is also beginning to establish a positive association between rates of inflation and home ownership in different countries: see figure 4.5. If this relationship is a significant one, it suggests that inflation *is* driven by the demand for credit through the private financial system, as many Keynesians have long maintained. This relationship probably strengthened in the 1980s, in the wake of more or less global financial deregulation: see O'Brien, 1992.)

A third broad cause of the inflations of the 1970s returns us to US monetary policy in the mid to late 1960s. Friedman is surely right to maintain that the emergence of a 'worldwide' creeping inflation in the late 1960s and 1970s (although not in the socialist world-economy) cannot reasonably be explained without reference to prior US money supply policies and the international transfer of inflation through the balance of payments. Friedman would also agree that the USA expanded its supplies of high-powered money in the 1960s to part-finance its war in Vietnam. In effect, the USA was now exercising its right to financial seignorage to press-gang international financial support for its geopolitical ambitions in South East Asia. The problem facing Friedman is not so much in recognizing the political conditions of existence of US money supply policies, but in his implicit suggestion that matters could have been otherwise. For Friedman and most monetarists, the world of 'politics' taints the purer and more logical world of 'economics'. Although he has often written in support of a broad set of political values – capitalism and freedom (see Friedman, 1962; Friedman and Friedman, 1980) – Friedman tends to present this work as logical to the point of being apolitical; by contrast, the real world of other people's politics remains murky and unexplored, or even decried as unreasoning and unreasonable. Given this basic framework, the actions of governments can only seem unpredictable and/or economically illiterate. Governments buy votes and they shouldn't; governments fund wars by printing money, but they shouldn't. The moral calculus appealed to is nothing if not precise, but it is surely far from helpful as a guide to what governments actually do and why they act in particular ways. Friedman notes that the war in Vietnam was funded in a manner that would have inflationary consequences, but he fails properly to consider why the USA was involved in Vietnam and whose interests the US government was promoting and protecting.

Most Keynesians (and virtually all Marxists) would be less circumspect. They would expect to root their accounts of inflation in these geopolitical concerns and to offer accounts of the nature and purpose of these concerns (see Hirsch and Goldthorpe, 1978). More to the point, because they are minded to focus on the political economy of inflation, most non-monetarists are unwilling to approach inflation as an economic malady alone (and to treat it by recourse to a narrow range of technical solutions). Inflation has many sources and many possible cures, each of which has distributional antecedents and consequences: it is worth repeating that inflation hurts (and benefits) different peoples and different regions in different ways. Inflation is also only one of many maladies facing most space-economies. To hitch one's stall to a totem like 'zero inflation' (as UK Prime Minister John Major did in the summer of 1992) is surely as misguided as declaring a belief in the simple Phillips curve. Inflation in itself is not always an overriding economic evil. Massive and unexpected rises in the rate of inflation are likely to be economically debilitating, but steady inflation rates of (say) 5 per cent and below probably should be lived with if the costs of lowering such rates are likely to be excessively high in output and employment terms (or morally unacceptable in terms of their distributional incidence). Again, this is in part an empirical matter: it largely depends on present and future behaviour in local labour markets (itself a major source of dispute between monetarists and non-monetarists). But it is also a political decision: it is a decision about the merits of what Keynes called 'deliberate decision'.

The Costs of Taming Inflation

If inflation has many possible causes, it follows that it can be treated and even tamed in different ways. Again, this is a topic that would repay comparative geo-economic research: how was inflation dealt with in different countries in the 1980s and with what measures of success and failure? In the present context, it will suffice to state that there are always alternatives to a given set of economic policies (notwithstanding Thatcherite incantations that 'there is no alternative': TINA), and to note that the events of the 1980s present us with a set of case studies with which we might begin to evaluate the costs of competing sets of economic policies.

In very broad terms, the questions that a geo-economist might work with are as follows: (a) how did rates of inflation fare in countries pursuing policies of tight monetary targeting as compared to those following a more eclectic mix of economic policies; (b) if inflation rates did drop sharply in nominally 'monetarist' countries (like the UK from 1979 to 1983), was this mainly because of these policies or because of the steep economic recession that monetarist policies induced; (c) assuming that a 'sacrifice ratio' (of lost economic activity per percentage point decline in annual inflation) can be calculated for most countries, what sort of correlation might exist between the sacrifice ratio and the promulgation of more or less restrictively monetarist policies; (d) insofar as the roots of the 1970s inflationism are to be found in the United States, and insofar as other countries still have to adapt to US monetary policies, how might one take account of the costs imposed on countries elsewhere in the world by the actions of the world's major economic power? (This last question has a particular relevance for countries in the indebted developing world. It also implies – even confirms – that the sort of economic accounting demanded by answers to questions (a) to (d) cannot only have recourse to national economic units. In the modern world economy the costs and benefits of any one set of anti-inflationary

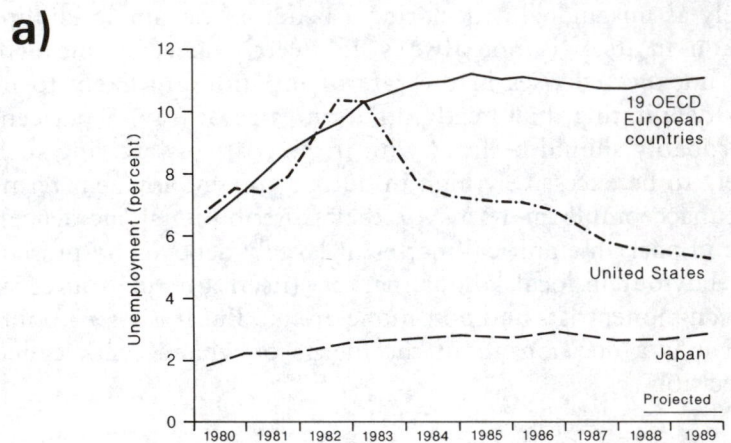

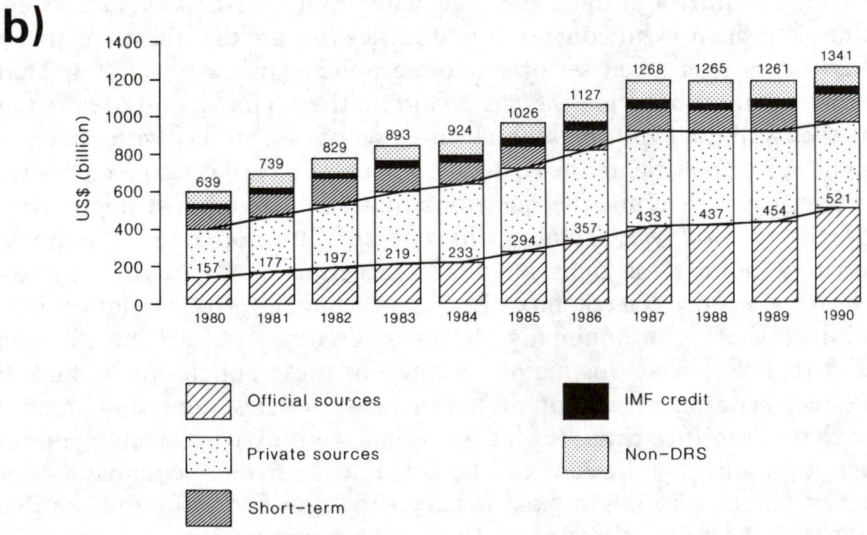

Figure 4.6 Unemployment (a), Third World indebtedness (b) and the war against inflation in the 1980s.

policies must also be considered for those countries (and regions and classes) not at the centre of global economic policy-making.)

This is not the place to offer even a preliminary answer to these questions. Let me say, instead, that my reading of some of the work that has been done in this area suggests: (a) that inflation rates in the 1980s did not always drop most precipitately in countries following broadly monetarist economic policies; (b) that economic recession did account for a good deal of the observed fall in national and international rates of inflation (Kaldor, 1986); and (c) that the so-called victory against inflation was a Pyrrhic victory – a victory surely not worth the price paid in the form of economic output forgone, persistent and much higher than anticipated rates of unemployment, and a lost decade of development in the indebted developing world. After two years of 'global monetarism', even the International Monetary Fund admitted in its 1982 *World Economic Outlook* that 'a disappointingly large proportion of the reduction in growth of aggregate nominal demand engendered by the tightening of monetary policy has taken the form of shrinkage in the growth of real economic activity, rather than lower inflation' (IMF, 1982, pp. 10–11; see also figure 4.6 and Osberg, 1984).

None of this means that a war (of sorts) against inflation was not worth waging, and monetarists can fairly ask 'what, precisely, were the alternative anti-inflationary policies that the opponents of monetarism had in mind?' (The beginnings of an answer to this last question come from those countries which saw their inflation rates fall by virtue of less costly and more eclectic anti-inflationary policies.) It does remind us, however, that the economic costs imposed by inflation have their counterpart in the economic costs that more often caught Keynes's imagination (idle hands and lost output), and that the maps of winners and losers from different sets of economic policies are rarely the same. The very best that one can say of the monetarist experiments of the 1980s is that they were associated with a decline in inflation, that they improved rates of profit in some countries and, more controversially, that they might have helped to lay the foundations of future economic growth and declining rates of unemployment. Whether these foundations were eroded in the late 1980s and early 1990s by a further dose of broadly monetarist policies, or by their premature abandonment, is another moot point. All one can say is that, at the end of 1992, a revitalized Keynesianism (or post-Keynesianism) is set to make a come-back. The signs are that pragmatism is coming back into fashion.

Conclusion: Geography, Economics and Plausible Worlds

All the same, I am afraid of 'principle'. Ever since 1918 we [the UK], alone amongst the nations of the world, have been the slaves

> of 'sound' general principles regardless of particular circumstances. We have behaved as though the intermediate 'short periods' of the economist between one position of equilibrium and another really were short, whereas they can be long enough – and have been before now – to encompass the decline and downfall of nations. Nearly all our difficulties have been traceable to an unfaltering service to the principle of 'sound finance' which all our neighbours neglected. . . . Wasn't it Lord Melbourne who said that 'No statesman ever does anything really foolish except on principle? (*Keynes, 1930; quoted in Moggridge, 1992, p. 499*)

The idea that Keynesianism might be coming back into fashion is more than just of biographical interest, or of relevance only to economic policy-makers. Just as Keynesianism signifies a certain pragmatism in economic policy-making, so also does it signify an intellectual position that is mistrustful of facile certainties and political finalism. Keynesianism, as I read it, is a philosophy that does not disavow principles so much as general principles. By the same token, a great virtue of Keynesian political economy is that it does not offer a set of self-evident truths that are meant to hold independent of time and place. Even the *General Theory* was written for a UK audience in the 1930s and Keynes, of course, was never much interested in the long run. In the long run we are all dead.

There are two conclusions in all this that I want to draw out here. A first conclusion concerns the subject matter of this chapter, namely inflation and the various policies advanced to deal with it. It is clear that the past twenty years have witnessed a revolution in economic and political thought, which has seen various forms of monetarism move from the periphery to the centre of public life. There are several reasons why this should be so, but not the least of them are intellectual. Monetarism has been expounded by several thinkers of the first rank and some of its propositions would seem to be supported by a good deal of empirical evidence. This remains the case notwithstanding the often poor economic record of nominally 'monetarist' governments in practice. The wider academic 'New Right' still needs to be closely engaged with.

At the same time, it seems clear to me that monetarism is deficient to the extent that it seeks explanations of economic outcomes in terms of proximate economic policies and with scant regard for the geopolitical context within which these policies are enacted. Like most forms of economics that grow out of the subjective preference paradigm (Edwards, 1985), monetarism is unable to advance an account of economic agency which escapes the reductive individualism of this tradition. Partly because of this reductionism, monetarism in practice has promoted a range of economic policies notable mainly for their narrowness and for their resistance to alternative accounts of economic maladies and alternative proposals for their cure. Its monomania has encouraged a political fundamentalism, which at times has seemed blind to the costs of the very policies it has so firmly propounded; not surprisingly, governments of a right-wing persuasion have been happy to take advantage of this.

Such fundamentalism is clearly at odds with the more pragmatic attitudes of Keynes and some of his followers (for none of whom, as Edwards (1985, p. 137) has it, 'the crisis is inflation'), and this brings me to my second set of concluding remarks. Insofar as this chapter is addressed to geography and geographers, its undertow takes the form of a critique of what often passes for critique in our subject. Geography has distinguished itself in recent years by its attention to some of the most pressing issues facing our 'world in crisis' (Johnston and Taylor, 1989). This is all the more remarkable at a time when large numbers of economists seem to have retreated entirely from real-world problems in favour of mathematics (a good servant, but a poor master, Keynes once observed),[6] and when the dialogue between economics and the other social sciences seems to be growing deafer year by year. But where some geographers can learn from economists is in the matter of critique. Most economists in the eclectic mainstream are happy to accept that our world is imperfect and that the benefits of any one set of economic and political actions will have an associated set of opportunity costs. Keynes understood this very well, even if his sensitivity to the long-term costs of short-run economic policies was not all that it might have been. Not all geographers take quite the same view. Although radical views are now falling from grace, geography for the past twenty years has been inspired by Marxism above all else. Again, there are good reasons for this, and many benefits have clearly flowed from it (not least Harvey's *The Limits to Capital*, 1982). One effect of this attachment to Marxism, however, has been a willingness to see critique mainly in destructive terms and with little regard for its constructive dimensions and responsibilities. Insofar as radical geography tends to associate most of the ills of the modern world with 'capitalism', it has sometimes seemed to suggest that the abolition of capitalism will provide a corresponding cure-all (see Peet, 1991).[7]

In the wake of the revolutions of 1989, I think few geographers now believe that the ills of capitalism can be made good by a transcendental form of socialism. In broader terms, though, the point surely is that all

6 Keynes was typically forthright on the matter in his *General Theory*. 'Too large a proportion of recent "mathematical" economics are merely concoctions, as imprecise as the initial assumptions they rest on, which allow the author to lose sight of the complexities and interdependencies of the real world in a maze of pretentious and unhelpful symbols' (Keynes, 1973, p. 298).

7 A similar antipathy to modernity – as opposed to some facets or consequences of modernity – has become apparent more recently in some quarters of human geography.

forms of critique are weakened to the extent that they do not also provide plausible accounts of how human affairs might better be arranged or managed. This in turn implies a willingness to argue counterfactually as well as consequentially; not just to ask whether actions A and B will have X and Y undesirable consequences, but also to ask whether another set of actions could have avoided these and other consequences, or in some way minimized their negative effects. Precisely because Keynesianism does not place its faith in some assumed future state of bliss, be it a free market paradise or a socialism unburdened by contradictions, it seems to me to be very well equipped to pose these questions. In this chapter on inflation I have tried to show that Keynesianism attends directly to the plausibility of the different worlds we are required to live in and that its proponents offer their advice on policy accordingly. Keynesians see inflation as one among many economic problems and one that has many causes and possible cures (which themselves vary from place to place). Sadly, a similar pragmatism isn't always apparent in the pronouncements of Keynesianism's intellectual and political rivals. Away from the eclectic mainstream of social science, it sometimes seems that a rigorous eclecticism is more often reviled than admired.

References

Alesina, A. (1989) Politics and business cycles in the industrial democracies. *Economic Policy*, April.

Bruno, M. and Sachs, J. (1985) *Economics of Worldwide Stagflation*. Oxford: Blackwell.

Carchedi, G. (1991) *Frontiers of Political Economy*. London: Verso.

Clark, G. (1984) Does inflation vary between cities? *Environment and Planning A*, 16, 513–27.

Clark, G. (1985) Guest editorial: a world of price inflation. *Environment and Planning A*, 17, 293–6.

Corbridge, S. (1993) *Debt and Development*. Oxford: Blackwell.

Edwards, C. (1985) *The Fragmented World: Competing Perspectives on Trade, Money and Crisis*. London: Methuen.

Friedman, M. (1961) The lag in effect of monetary policy. *Journal of Political Economy*, 69, 447–66.

Friedman, M. (1962) *Capitalism and Freedom*. Chicago: University of Chicago Press.

Friedman, M. (1968) The role of monetary policy. *American Economic Review*, 58, 1–17.

Friedman, M. (1969) *The Optimum Quantity of Money and Other Essays*. Chicago: Aldine.

Friedman, M. (1989) Quantity theory of money. In J. Eatwell, M. Milgate and P. Newman (eds), *The New Palgrave: Money*. Basingstoke: Macmillan, 1–40.

Friedman, M. and Friedman, R. (1980) *Free to Choose: a Personal Statement*. Harmondsworth: Pelican.

Friedman, M. and Schwartz, A. (1963) *A Monetary History of the United States, 1867–1960.* Princeton, NJ: Princeton University Press/NBER.

Friedman, M. and Schwartz, A. (1982) *Monetary Trends in the United States and the United Kingdom: Their Relation to Income, Prices, and Interest Rates, 1867–1975.* Chicago: Chicago University Press/NBER.

Godley, W. (1984) Confusion in economic theory and policy – is there a way out? In J. Cornwall (ed.), *After Stagflation: Alternatives to Economic Decline.* Oxford: Blackwell, 63–85.

Haberler, A. (1985) *The Problem of Stagflation: Reflections on the Microfoundation of Macroeconomic Theory and Policy.* Washington, DC: American Enterprise Institute.

Haggard, S. and Kaufman, R. (1992) The political economy of inflation and stabilization in middle-income countries. In S. Haggard and R. Kaufman (eds), *The Politics of Economic Adjustment.* Princeton, NJ: Princeton University Press, 270–315.

Harvey, D. (1982) *The Limits to Capital.* Oxford: Blackwell.

Harvey, D. (1985) The geopolitics of capitalism. In D. Gregory and J. Urry (eds), *Social Relations and Spatial Structures.* London: Macmillan.

Hawthorn, G. (1991) *Plausible Worlds.* Cambridge: Cambridge University Press.

Hayek, F. A. (1976) *Denationalization of Money.* London: Institute of Economic Affairs.

Hirsch, F. and Goldthorpe, J. (eds) (1978) *The Political Economy of Inflation.* London: Martin Robertson.

International Monetary Fund (1982) *World Economic Outlook, 1982.* Washington, DC: IMF.

Johnson, C. (1991) *The Economy under Mrs Thatcher, 1979–1990.* Harmondsworth: Penguin.

Johnston, R. and Taylor, P. (eds) (1989) *A World in Crisis? Geographical Perspectives,* 2nd edn. Oxford: Blackwell.

Kaldor, N. (1986) *The Scourge of Monetarism,* 2nd edn. Oxford: Oxford University Press.

Keynes, J. M. (1972) *Essays in Persuasion.* London: Macmillan.

Keynes, J. M. (1973) *The General Theory of Employment, Interest and Money.* London: Macmillan.

Keynes, J. M. (1984) *The Economic Consequences of the Peace.* London: Macmillan.

Lawson, N. (1992) *The View from No. 11: Memoirs of a Tory Radical.* London: Bantam

Lipietz, A. (1985) *The Enchanted World: Inflation, Credit and the World Crisis.* London: Verso.

Lucas, R. (1978) Unemployment policy. *American Economic Review,* 68, 353–7.

Marglin, S. and Schor, J. (eds) (1990) *The Golden Age of Capitalism: Reinterpreting the Post-war Experience.* Oxford: Clarendon/WIDER.

Massey, D. and Meegan, R. (1982) *The Anatomy of Job Loss.* London: Methuen.

McKinnon, R. (1984) *An International Standard for Monetary Stabilization.* Cambridge, MA: MIT Press.

Michie, J. and Wilkinson, F. (1992) Inflation policy and the restructuring of labour markets. In J. Michie (ed.), *The Economic Legacy, 1979–1992*. London: Academic Press, 195–217.

Mishkin, F. (1986) *The Economics of Money, Banking and Financial Markets*. Boston: Little, Brown and Company.

Modigliani, F. (1977) The monetarist controversy, or should we forsake stabilization policies? *American Economic Review*, 67, 1–19.

Moggridge, D. (1992) *Maynard Keynes: an Economist's Biography*. London: Routledge.

O'Brien, R. (1992) *Global Financial Integration: the End of Geography*. London: Routledge.

Olivera, J. (1967) Money, prices and fiscal lags: a note on the dynamics of inflation. *Banca Nazionale del Lavoro Quarterly Review*, September, 258–67.

Osberg, L. (1984) The Pyrrhic victory – unemployment, inflation and macroeconomic policy. In J. Cornwall (ed.), *After Stagflation: Alternatives to Economic Decline*. Oxford: Blackwell, 111–31.

Parboni, R. (1981) *The Dollar and Its Rivals: Recession, Inflation and International Finance*. London: Verso.

Peet, R. (1991) *Global Capitalism: Theories of Societal Development*. London: Routledge.

Phelps, E. (1967) Phillips curves, expectations of inflation, and optimal unemployment over time. *Economica*, 34, 254–81.

Phelps, E. (ed.) (1970) *Microeconomic Foundations of Employment and Inflation Theory*. New York: W. W. Norton.

Phillips, A. (1958) The relation between unemployment and the rate of change in money wages in the United Kingdom, 1861–1957. *Economica*, 25, November, 283–99.

Riddell, J. B. (1992) Things fall apart again: structural adjustment programmes in sub-Saharan Africa. *Journal of Modern African Studies*, 30, 53–68.

Rowthorn, R. (1980) *Capitalism, Conflict and Inflation*. London: Lawrence and Wishart.

Sabin, M. (1981) The spatial incidence of inflation in the United States 1967–1971: an economic-geographic perspective. Unpublished PhD thesis, Rutgers University, New Jersey.

Sachs, J. and Larrain, F. B. (1993) *Macroeconomics in the Global Economy*. Hemel Hempstead: Harvester Wheatsheaf.

Sargent, T. (1986) *Rational Expectations and Inflation*. New York: Harper and Row.

Scott, A. and Storper, M. (eds) (1986) *Production, Work, Territory: the Geographical Anatomy of Industrial Capitalism*. London: Allen and Unwin.

Tobin, J. (1981) The monetarist counter-revolution today: an appraisal. *Economic Journal*, 91, 29–42.

Watts, M. (1991) Visions of excess: African development in an age of market idolatry. *Transition*, 51, 124–41.

Williamson, J. and Milner, C. (1991) *The World Economy*. Hemel Hempstead: Harvester Wheatsheaf.

Woods, H. and Ostry, S. (1962) *Labour Policy and Labour Economics in Canada*. Toronto: Macmillan.

5

Fictitious Capital, Fictitious Spaces: the Geography of Offshore Financial Flows

Susan Roberts

Introduction

In a fundamental way money is the central enigma of capitalism. The peculiarly slippery nature of money has proven to be a problem for neo-classical economic analysis – prompting economists to make uncharacteristic confessions of perplexity (e.g. Hahn, 1981, p. 1; Howitt, 1989, p. 246). The realization that money only works because people believe in it underscores the fictitious quality of money. As Martin Amis puts it: 'If we all downed tools and joined hands for ten minutes and stopped believing in money, then money would no longer exist. We never will, of course. Money is the great conspiracy, the great fiction' (Amis, 1984, p. 384).

Simmel (1990, p. 148) acknowledged that money was significantly more than an economic fact, noting that it 'exercises its effects merely as an idea which is embodied in a representative symbol'. The insubstantial nature of money has been taken up recently in post-structuralist analyses (e.g. Spivak 1987). For Marx the evolution of the form of money was only part of its function in capitalism (Rosdolsky, 1977, part 2). Money, in the commodity–money–commodity circuit, turns relations 'upside-down' because money becomes the 'object *par excellence*' against which all else is measured – reducing 'everything to its own form of abstraction' (Marx 1976, chapter 3; Marx in Bottomore 1956, pp. 171–3; Marx in Hoare, 1975, p. 358). However, for Marx *credit* is 'money raised to a completely ideal form' where human beings (through their labour) are themselves 'transformed into money' (Marx in Hoare, 1975, p. 264–5). Marx thus specifically identified and defined credit money as fictitious capital (see Harvey, 1982, pp. 268–9; Foley, 1983, p. 99–100). Credit is fictitious because it is based on value which has yet to be created. Credit money when loaned as capital is reliant upon the future exploitation of labour and is 'some kind of money bet on production that doesn't yet exist' (Harvey, 1989a, p. 107). This leap into the future, courtesy of fictitious capital, allows the switching of 'over-accumulating circulating capital into fixed capital formation – a process that can disguise the appearance of crises entirely in the short run' (Harvey, 1982, p. 266). As Harvey argues, it is through credit, through today's fast-paced financial system, that capitalism displaces crisis, both temporally and spatially (Harvey, 1989a, pp. 160–72).

The explosion of fictitious capital formation in the Euromarkets in the 1960s and 1970s and the tremendously innovative variety of fictitious capital formation and deployment in the 1980s have visibly modified and altered cityscapes and social geographies in the rich countries of the world (e.g. Pryke, 1991). Meanwhile, scattered across the globe, a series of little places – islands and micro-states – have been transformed by exploiting niches in the circuits of fictitious capital. These places have set themselves up as offshore financial centres; as places where the circuits of fictitious capital meet the circuits of 'furtive money' in a murky concoction of risk and opportunity. Furtive money is 'hot' money that seeks to avoid regulatory attention and/or taxes. The Bahamas and the Cayman Islands, Luxembourg and Liechtenstein, Bahrain, Singapore and Hong Kong, Vanuatu and the Cook Islands are all part of a worldwide network of essentially marginal places which have come to assume a crucial position in the global circuits of fungible, fast-moving, furtive money and fictitious capital. These offshore financial centres are sites that dramatically evince the contrary and complex melding of offshore and onshore, of national and international, and of local and global.

The offshore financial centres are significant nodes in the geography of worldwide financial flows (see International Monetary Fund (IMF), 1990; Bank for International Settlements (BIS), 1991; Kochan, 1991, p. 73). According to IMF data the Cayman Islands is home to over 250 billion dollars in bank liabilities. The Caymans boast 546 banks from all around the world (Moore, 1992, p. 28). Yet there are only six 'high street' clearing banks in the Caymanian capital, George Town, where tourists can get traveller's cheques cashed and where local shopkeepers have accounts and so forth. In fact only 69 banks maintain a physical presence on the island (Crutchley, 1991, p. 136). The rest are to be found only as a brass or plastic name plate in the lobby of another bank, as a folder in a filing cabinet or an entry in a computer system. It is this lack of real entities, and the multitude of paper entities, that lends an air of illusion and make-believe to the offshore financial centres. Illusion turns to paradox when it is considered that fictitious capital is a way of pushing overaccumulated capital into fixed capital, whereas in the offshore centres the lack of fixity and physical presence is the salient characteristic. Yet for all this lack of substance the offshore financial centres are not insignificant. They are essential moments in the spectacularly fast and free-wheeling world financial system, allowing institutions to cope with volatility and 'manage' varieties of risk facing international capital. At the same time, the very existence of offshore financial centres is pointed to as a threat to international financial stability – most recently by those examining the activities of the Bank of Credit and Commerce International (BCCI).

This chapter focuses on the operations of offshore financial centres in the form of a growing collection of islands and mini-states. First, the nature of the offshore markets is outlined and the major changes therein are noted. Second, the distribution of offshore financial centres is considered – with particular attention being paid to the dynamics of the competition between them. Third, a closer look is taken at the Caribbean cluster of 'entreprenuerial islands' and at the Cayman Islands in particular. The promotion of an image of the Cayman Islands as an upstanding, solid and reputable financial centre is examined in the context of economic and geopolitical imperatives.

Offshore Financial Markets

What Does Offshore Mean?

The term 'offshore' is a relative one: it implies an 'onshore'. The designation 'offshore' is used in a number of different ways in various literatures. A company's offshore manufacturing is sometimes taken to mean all manufacturing not undertaken in the home country of the firm, and hence is synonymous with foreign. However, in financial circles the term has a less general meaning. Offshore markets are markets for currencies, loans, bonds and a host of other financial instruments which exist beyond the reach of regulation by the originating national economy. The offshore markets' *raison d'être* is simply that they are *less* regulated than the onshore markets with which they compete. The onshore and the offshore markets are not discrete entities; they are related because they compete with one another, and because the same financial intermediaries (such as banks) operate in both markets (Aliber, 1980). The closing of BCCI in July 1991 and the consequent unravelling of the bank's 'web' of involvements dramatically demonstrated the interlinking of onshore and offshore finance. Moreover, as onshore financial markets engaged in competive deregulation the distinction between onshore and offshore has become fuzzier (Hewson, 1982, pp. 406–7).

Fictitious Capital and the Euromarkets

The quintessential offshore market is the Eurocurrency market. The growth of the Euromarkets and the key changes in their composition and workings have been at the centre of the changing nature of the international financial system and are closely bound up with the shifting geography of international financial flows.

In the 1960s certain key elements of the Bretton Woods system of international financial regulation came to be regarded as disabling rigidities. In particular, the systems for regulating exchange rates and balance of payments imbalances came under pressure and were eventually abandoned. Several factors contributed to this change (see also chapter 3 by Susan Strange). First, as capital internationalized, especially as US firms became multinational corporations doing business in Europe and elsewhere, US banks recognized a need to provide services for these multinational clients. Second, the persistent balance of payments deficit of the USA *vis-à-vis* the rest of the world (reflecting the success of postwar economic recovery in Europe) meant there were large quantities of American dollars outside the USA. The dollar 'overhang' provided liquidity and confirmed the dollar as the *de facto* world currency. In an effort to encourage repatriation of dollars held abroad the US government enacted certain restrictive regulations, notably the Interest Equalization Tax (enacted 1963), and withholding tax requirements. With Regulation Q of the Federal Reserve Act, these regulations had the combined effect of fostering the growth of the Eurodollar market by reinforcing its attraction as a less regulated, and therefore a cheaper, place to do business (for details, see Versluysen, 1981, pp. 24–6; Johnston, 1982, pp. 12–14; Pippenger, 1984, pp. 282–4).

The uneven geography of economic growth since 1945 and the uneven geography of financial regulation thus combined to spur the growth of a huge market in dollars outside the USA. The Eurodollar market was (and remains) centred in London – a traditionally less-fettered financial centre than New York and a place where US banks in particular could make loans in dollars without having to comply with any reserve requirement.

The Euro*dollar* market became the Euro*currency* market as other currencies came to account for a significant share of the market, and although 'Euro' remains in the name of these offshore currency markets, Eurocurrency dealings are not carried out solely in Europe. The name is a vestige indicating the historical geography of the market but is somewhat misleading today (for discussions of the nomenclature see Machlup, 1972; Hogan and Pearce, 1982). A dynamic new geography of Euromarket centres and flows has been created, stretching from Panama to Switzerland and on to Singapore and beyond. The formation of offshore financial centres is tied to the growth and development of the Euromarkets themselves. The Eurocurrency markets grew tremendously in the late 1960s and 1970s. According to estimates by the BIS the net size of the Eurocurrency market enlarged from US $9 billion in 1964 to US $57 billion in 1970, and by 1981 it was US $661 billion (Pecchioli, 1983, p. 133). A big boost to the markets came in the shape of the increased oil revenues accruing to OPEC members after the 1973 price rises. These revenues were entrusted to (largely Western) banks and were 'recycled' via the Euromarkets. Just as the rise in oil prices had left some nations with extra dollars to deposit, so it had left many nations with a need to borrow dollars (hard currency) to pay for imports of oil to sustain their economies. These huge imbalances in international capital requirements were handled by the Euromarkets and the intermediation was accomplished by international banks. This is a powerful reminder of some key changes in the world financial system that the Euromarkets wrought or at least signalled. Under the Bretton Woods system, huge and persistent imbalances were presumed not to occur and such imbalances that did occur were to be attended to mainly by the IMF. However, the Euromarkets and the rise of the international commercial banks and their roles in recycling petrodollars marked a shift from a public supranational framework for dealing with asymmetry in the world economy to a quasi-private market process.

The Eurocurrency market is embedded in, and implicated in, all the major changes in the geography of international finance in the 1970s, including the internationalization of banking (particularly of US banking), the rise of OPEC as a force in the world economy and, stretching into the 1980s, the so-called Third World debt crisis. During the 1970s a long-standing pattern of capital transfer from the rich to the poor nations of the world was continued via the Eurocurrency markets. However, debts taken on by oil-importing countries became increasingly difficult to service as interest rates climbed throughout the 1970s.

The 1980s saw some significant alterations to the geography of offshore finance – at least Euromarket finance. First, the flow from rich to poor reversed. The Third World became a net exporter of capital by way of servicing its burgeoning debt, causing a 'role reversal' (Costello, 1986, p. 24). Robert Triffin, who was the first to note the paradoxes of the role of the USA and the US dollar in the post Second World War international financial system, has noted that:

> Economic logic as well as human concerns would require capital flows to move from the richer and more capitalized countries to the poorer and less capitalized countries, in order to accelerate their development and to enable them to finance levels of consumption indispensible to the very survival of their people. (Triffin, 1984, p. 137)

This 'role reversal' is further reinforced by the privileged position of the USA as the world's largest debtor, *sucking in surpluses* (*The Economist*, 1990; Corbridge and Agnew, 1991).

Second, while the Eurocurrency markets played a major role in international finance in the 1970s, it was the Eurobond or Euro-securites market that was the key factor in the 1980s. In addition to fixed-rate bonds, floating-rate notes and equity-related bonds, a whole host of derivative instruments, including swaps and options, as well as significant secondary markets, have appeared under the general trend of securitization.

> The remarkable expansion of markets for derivative products traded on organised exchanges or over the counter is perhaps the most striking development to have occurred in the financial markets during the 1980s. Although the characteristics of each individual instrument differ, all derivative financial products share the feature of not giving rise to an immediate flow of funds from one economic agent to another corresponding to the notional value of the contract. They have all been developed for the purpose of managing the risks associated with changes in asset prices, and the increase in volatility of interest rates, exchange rates and share indices in recent years is the factor which has contributed most to their success (BIS, 1990, p. 183).

This has compounded and heightened the fictitious nature of credit. The IMF itself has made this observation: 'Financial liberalization has made the financial system more competitive. At the same time, the process has involved changes in the nature, and possibly in the extent, of risk in the international financial system, with a pyramiding of financial transactions on a relatively small base of real transactions' (IMF, 1990, p. 1).

Third, securitization and the churning in the Euromarkets today are partly a result of attempts by international financial institutions to maintain profits and manage risk. Banks are less involved with straightforward deposit taking and loan making as a result of a marked shift to 'off balance sheet activity' (Khambata 1989). This shift was partly in response to capital requirements set up by the BIS for banks (Cates and Davis, 1987). Banks charge fees for off balance sheet activities and thus gain income without affecting their balance sheets and at the same time circumvent capital assets ratio guidelines. For their corporate clients banks now offer a multitude of services under the heading 'global custody'. Global custody services such as cash management, securities transfer, and corporate finance strategies such as mergers and acquisitions allow corporations to combine risk management and tax minimization strategies. Meanwhile the global custodians – the banks – profit from the fees paid for their services, despite having to make large investments in information and transactions processing technology (see Warf, 1989). Managing the risks inherent in today's world financial system means that corporations and banks (and institutional investors such as pension funds and insurance companies) must constantly be seeking flexibility. The ability to use the uneven global topography of taxation and regulation to gain advantage is now an imperative. As part of such 'strategies of flexibility', and especially through the banks' global custody services, offshore financial centres are important nodes in corporate networks of risk management and profit. For so-called 'high net worth individuals' banks also offer fee-based services under the heading of 'international private banking' (IPB). IPB services include tax avoidance or deferral schemes and trusts. IPB is a lucrative business for banks but one in which the risk of involvement with criminals seeking to hide ill-gotten gains is significant (Wacker, 1990). More generally, there is clearly a link between funds in IPB and flight capital (Gulati, 1988; Roberts, 1992).

Furtive Money

Money seeking to evade the attentions of regulatory authorities in one way or another may be called 'hot' money. Proceeds of securities fraud, trade in illegal drugs or other undeclared business income find their way into international circuits and together with flight capital are important components of the offshore financial markets. The 'fictitious and legitimate' is often hard to tell apart from the 'furtive and illegitimate'. Offshore financial centres have lately been particularly concerned to balance the need for secrecy (the preferred term is 'confidentiality') with effective supervision and regulation. Without secrecy, offshore financial centres would be unrecognizable. However, the 'secret money' business, as Walter (1989) puts it, means that offshore centres are vulnerable not only to the vagaries of the financial system, but also to the actions of powerful neighbours who might take exception to the activities hidden in an offshore financial centre. For example, the Caribbean centres are very aware of the presence and power of the USA. As part of the US 'War on Drugs', efforts have been made by US authorities to curtail financial activities of narcotics traffickers who do their money 'laundering' in the waters of the Caribbean Basin. US efforts to pressure offshore financial centres into compromising their strict secrecy laws have been very successful. This is not surprising in view of the asymmetry of power and the geopolitical preponderance of the USA in the Caribbean region. The Cayman Islands and other offshore financial centres have signed 'Mutual Legal Assistance Treaties', which enable US authorities to request and receive information about bank accounts and so on in cases of suspected criminal activity – including the laundering of drug profits and the stashing away of the gains from securities scams (such as penny stocks) (see Maingot, 1988; Pineau, 1988; Beaty and Hornik, 1989).

Offshore Financial Centres

Mapping the distribution of offshore financial centres involves making decisions about the definition of an offshore financial centre. Figure 5.1 includes all centres that are nodes in the Euromarkets – even though

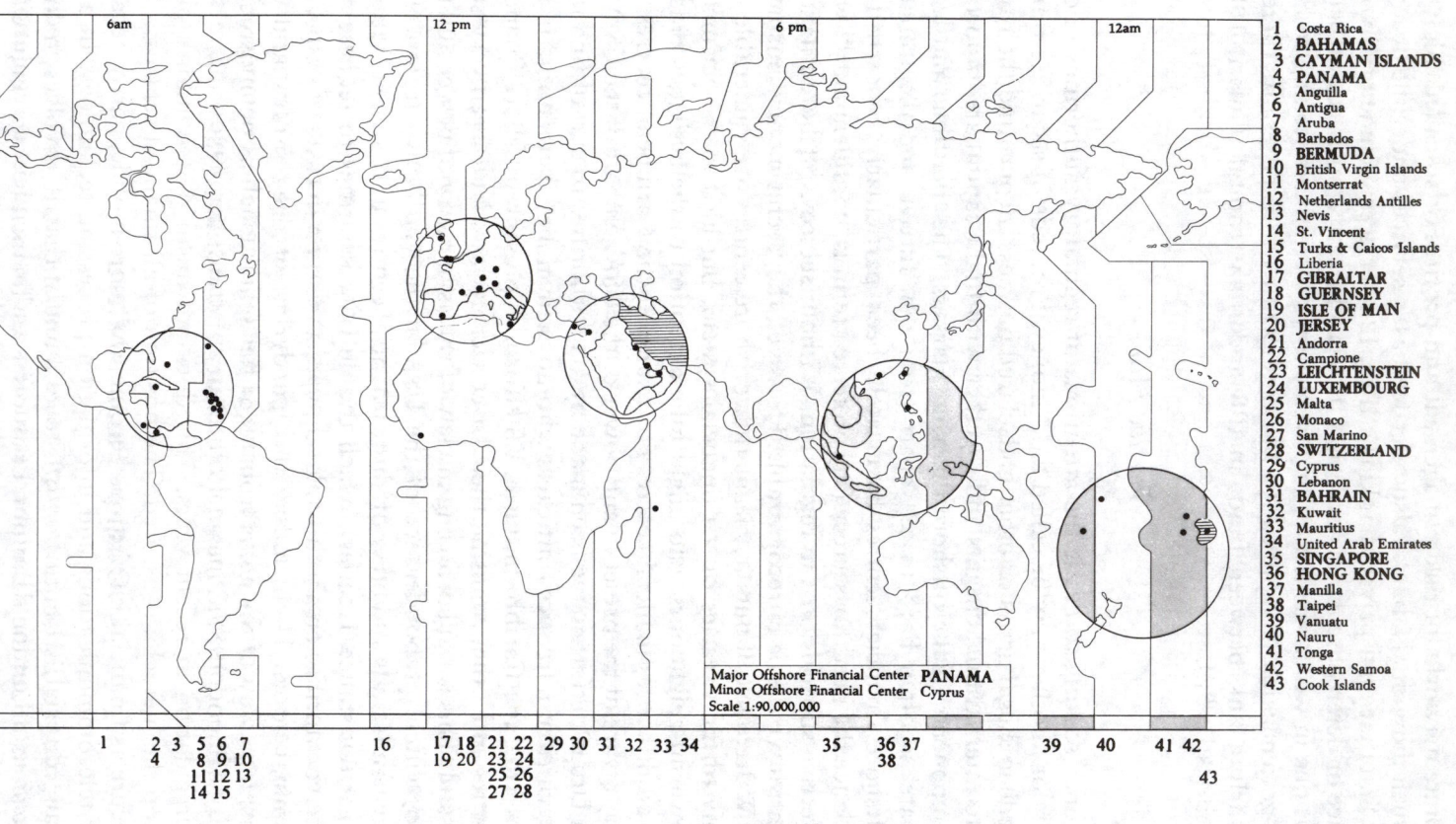

Major Offshore Financial Center **PANAMA**
Minor Offshore Financial Center Cyprus
Scale 1:90,000,000

Figure 5.1 World distribution of offshore financial centres.

some are formally onshore. In addition, several places which describe themselves as offshore financial centres but which may be little more than tax havens are shown. The latter are included because the distinction between a tax haven and a fully fledged offshore financial centre is not easy to draw, due to the fact that so many attributes of the older tax havens are now used in offshore financial dealings. Just as the offshore and onshore financial markets are inextricably linked – through financial institutions, currencies and so on – so the world of 'furtive money', of 'tax planning' and capital flight, is itself linked to the Euromarkets.

Competitive Deregulation and the Onshore Offshores

Each offshore financial centre competes with rival centres to attract financial institutions and individual investors, providing further evidence of the 'place-competition' noted in the geographic literature (e.g. Cox and Mair, 1988). Each centre's chief competitors are likely to be in the same spatial cluster. Additionally, the particular niche each centre has specialized in means that each centre competes with similarly specialized rivals worldwide. For example, the Cayman Islands' chief competitor in banking is the Bahamas, but in the case of captive insurance Cayman is pitted against Bermuda and Guernsey.

Offshore financial centres grew up in the 1970s in many places that were already tax havens. Fictitious capital (Eurodollars) and furtive capital (hot money) were intertwined from the beginning in the offshore centres. The Bahamas and the Cayman Islands in the Caribbean attracted banks which set up branches or subsidiaries to be used as 'booking centres' for their Eurocurrency dealings. By operating offshore booking centres international banks could act free of reserve requirements and other regulation. Offshore branches could also be used as profit centres (from which profits may be repatriated at the most suitable moment for tax minimization) and as bases from which to serve the needs of multinational corporate clients.

London emerged as the hub of the Euromarkets at their inception. It has managed to retain this central position despite deregulation in competing centres. This was achieved partly because of the comparatively loose regulatory style of the Bank of England and the booming of the City of London as a financial centre in an atmosphere favouring further deregulation in recent years. This does not mean that London's place atop the hierachy is assured. The position of all financial centres is less secure as financial institutions become ever more mobile, partly because of telecommunications and information processing technology. In a recent editorial, *The Economist* stated bluntly that it may be precisely *because* of London's Euromarket success and subsequent deregulation in rival places that it is now especially vulnerable:

London is right to worry. Of the three main financial centres, its position is the most fragile. In New York and Tokyo a small amount of international finance is perched on a vast domestic market. In London it is the other way around. The businesses it attracted in the past 30 years – international loans and deposits, offshore corporate bonds, worldwide fund management, cross-border trading of shares – could as easily be done in New York, Tokyo or elsewhere. Those national rules that money came to London to avoid – taxes, capital controls – loom far less large. (*The Economist*, 1991, p. 15)

In 1978 the New York Clearing House Association proposed that American states be allowed to enact legislation designed to capture some of the banking business that was going offshore. The Federal Reserve Board approved the proposal in 1980 and in December 1981 the first 'international banking facilities' (IBFs) were set up in New York. As Hultman (1990, p. 183) points out: 'Essentially, the authorization permits US banks to establish special adjunct facilities to accept deposits from foreigners free of reserve requirements and interest rate limitations.' In creating IBFs the US regulators relaxed two key regulations that had contributed to the involvement of US banks in, and hence the very growth of, the offshore Euromarkets a decade or more earlier. IBFs are no more than a segregated accounting unit of a bank, much like a shell or brass plate bank in the offshore centres (Cheng, 1981, p. 1). Bringing the offshore onshore as accounting units adds to the make-believe nature of 'offshore' banking: 'Accounts are booked at these institutions [IBFs] *as if* they were offshore' (Kane, 1987, p. 136; emphasis in original). The vast majority (over 80 per cent) of IBFs are located in New York, but California, Florida and Illinois each have over twenty (Hultman, 1990, p. 186). The geography of the IBFs illustrates the fierce competition to host even the paper offshore banking business. One commentator noted that 'Some have described the concept of the IBF as "hitching a line to an offshore banking branch and towing it to the United States" ' (Trivoli, 1981, p. 12). The efforts to attract, or repatriate, offshore banking have also to be seen in the light of a momentum favouring deregulation in the late 1970s and early 1980s. The ideological promotion of the virtues of unfettered markets meshed with New York's concern to retain its position as an international financial centre. It was thought that the IBFs would take a significant amount of business away from the Caribbean offshore centres. At first there did appear to be a slight movement onshore. However, political fears (for example, of asset seizure by US authorities) as well as the fact that offshore centres are not just used for Eurobanking have led to the retention of a major share of the Euromarket business by the offshore centres.

The Japanese Offshore Market (JOM) was established on 1 December 1986 (Sarver, 1988, p. 120). Tokyo was the last of the big three world financial centres to develop an offshore market at home. The JOM is a facility that allows the activities of the so-called Asian dollar market (the Eurocurrency market in Asia) to take place onshore in Tokyo. Thus Tokyo began competing with the extant Asian dollar centres of Singapore, Hong Kong and Bahrain. The JOM has been very successful and had grown to be twice as large as the US IBFs *by 1989* despite a heavier tax burden on offshore business (Sarver, 1988, p. 120; Jones, 1989, p. 4; BIS, 1990, p. 165). This does not mean that Japanese banks are not active in other offshore financial centres. They are a significant presence in the Bahamas, the Caymans, Panama and Luxembourg, as well as in the Asian centres (McDougall, 1989, p. 51).

Regional Blocs and the Dynamics of Competition

At the global, hemispheric and regional levels the various offshore financial centres compete to attract offshore businesses. Competition is partly confined to regional clusters (see figure 5.1) because in a globalized 24-hour financial system the time zone in which the centre is located assumes importance. The fact that both the Bahamas and the Caymans are in the same time zone as the eastern 'cores' of the USA and Canada (and particularly Miami and New York City) is crucial to their success. That Bahrain is the only centre in its time zone between the European and Asian markets has led several other places to see an opportunity to become rival offshore financial centres.

The time zone factor only partly explains the clustering of offshore financial centres shown on the map. The particular clusters that have developed may also be seen as groups of marginal places – often microstates and islands – which exist as adjuncts to one of the three financial blocs centred for the moment on London, Tokyo and New York City. The relationships between the dominant blocs and the adjunct offshore financial centres at their margins are contradictory, as the powerful countries treat the offshore centres at once as useful and as an irritating potential threat (see Brunet, 1986). Some offshore financial centres are more successful than others at surviving and prospering in such contradictory relationships. The more successful, diversified and established offshore centres may be contrasted with places that have not shaken off the tax haven label (Beecham and Benn, 1991; Kochan, 1991). The Gallagher Report, commissioned by the British government, highlights the difference between the Cayman Islands and an offshore financial centre such as Montserrat. Montserrat did not attempt to align itself with any bloc and by offering banking secrecy without even minimal regulation attracted criminal money and subsequently the attentions of the British and US governments (Gallagher, 1990). The Banking Supervisor of the Isle of Man has made this observation: 'offshore centres have to either attach themselves in terms of standards and licensing to one of the major blocs or remain outside and cater to business that either doesn't want to be related to a major bloc or needs to bypass them for some reason' (in Holstrom, 1988, p. 4).

Another example of a cluster of offshore centres aligning themselves with a dominant bloc is the South Pacific. Here the dominant economic bloc is comprised of Australia and New Zealand. Australian tax authorities are concerned about the amount of tax corporations are able to avoid by using the Pacific centres. According to one study, over half of Australia's top 200 companies use Vanuatu and the Cook Islands as part of their 'tax minimization' strategies (*Euromoney*, 1989b, p. 17). As in the case of the Caribbean centres, wider capital flows – in this case those of the Pacific Rim – are also relevant for the South Pacific offshore centres. For example, Vanuatu is linked into corporate financing and flight capital flows from Hong Kong (Johns, 1982, p. 224; Walter, 1985, p. 189; Naylor, 1987, p. 224). Attempts in the 1980s to use the US Trust Territories (especially the North Mariana Islands) as centres for suspect financial operations alerted the US authorities (Naylor, 1987, p. 307). Nauru, a speck in the Pacific Ocean north of Vanuatu, is listed in some tax haven directories (e.g. Spitz, 1983) and Tonga and Western Samoa are also considering becoming offshore financial centres (Walter, 1985, p. 189).

The Asian cluster of offshore financial centres is the locus of very active and growing financial markets. Singapore has been the hub of the Asian dollar market since its inception in 1968 at the urging of Bank of America (Versluysen, 1981, p. 94; Johns, 1982, p. 220; Daly and Logan, 1989, p. 100). Hong Kong remains a strong and diversified financial centre, despite recent capital movements out of Hong Kong by many of its wealthy (Hultman, 1991). The uncertainty over the transformation of Hong Kong from a British Colony to a Special Administrative Region of the People's Republic of China in 1997 has led to bids by Taipei (Taiwan) and Manila (the Philippines) to become offshore financial centres. Taipei issued its first offshore banking unit licences in 1984. However, this aspiring centre has only been somewhat successful owing to inconsistent policies, which have not always favoured offshore banking operations (Johns, 1982, p. 215; McDougall, 1989, p. 15). Manila has acheived modest success as an offshore financial centre attracting over twenty offshore banks, including several large American banks, on the basis of 1976 Offshore Banking Unit legislation (Sarver, 1988, p. 140). Nevertheless, Manila and Taipei do not look set seriously to challenge Singapore or Hong Kong as top Pacific Basin offshore financial centres.

Bahrain is the undisputed premier offshore financial centre in the Persian Gulf. It took the number one spot for the Middle East from Beirut in 1975, when the onset of the civil war in Lebanon caused many banks and financial organizations to look for an alternative base in the region. At various times Kuwait and Dubai (of the United Arab Emirates) have mounted challenges to Bahrain's pre-eminence – but so far neither has looked threatening. Even the Gulf War did not affect Bahrain's offshore sector as much as its rivals had hoped. Both Malta and Cyprus were 'anticipating growth on the back of turmoil in the Middle East' (Moore, 1992, p. 3). Indeed, in a distinct allusion to the Middle East, Cyprus casts itself as a 'financial oasis' and competes by emphasizing its traditional links with Lebanon and casting itself as a 'stepping stone to the European Community' (Central Bank of Cyprus, 1988, p. 4; *Euromoney*, 1992, p. 40).

In the Indian Ocean the island nation of the Seychelles is touted as a base for offshore company incorporation, and further south Mauritius is promoting itself as an offshore centre deliberately modelled on Singapore – according to statements by the Prime Minister (*Euromoney*, 1988a, p. 170). Mauritius claims that it hopes to serve the entire African continent but its traditional links are with South Africa. It seems to be lining itself up as a destination for flight capital as apartheid is destroyed (*Euromoney*, 1990, p. 18).

In the case of the European cluster there is a clear hierarchy among the many centres, with Switzerland at the top and places like Cyprus, Madeira and Malta presently struggling to establish themselves. Each centre has also specialized. Switzerland is an established centre for international private banking, whereas Luxembourg has built itself up as a major Eurocurrency and Eurobond centre (although lately it has been challenging Switzerland's hold on private banking, citing its lower costs as an advantage) (*The Banker*, 1989b, p. 67). Given greater European union after 1992, many micro-states in or near the European Community (EC) are jockeying for position as offshore centres to rival the more established centres attached to the EC. Malta, for example, has drawn up appropriate legislation 'after extensive study of related legislation in the Channel Islands, the Isle of Man and other offshore centres, with Chase Manhattan Bank acting as advisers' (*Euromoney*, 1988b, p. 26). Madeira, on the other hand, has ambitions to become an offshore base for Latin American corporations doing business with the EC, using the large Madeiran expatriate communities in countries such as Brazil and Venezuela (*Euromoney*, 1992, p. 58). Madeira has succeeded in attracting a few big name banks (*Euromoney*, 1988b, p. 17; *The Banker*, 1989a, p. 3; 1989b, p. 56). A whole host of other small marginal places are putting themselves forward as rivals to Switzerland, the Channel Islands and Luxembourg. Cyprus, Gibraltar, Monaco, Liechtenstein and even Andorra are all contenders for the title of offshore financial centre – although some are more serious about it than others. Several tax planners also cite the advantages that Austria, Hungary, the Netherlands and Belgium can each offer to certain types of operations, but these places are not properly offshore financial centres, and Dublin's 'International Financial Services Centre' is a significant financial centre based on tax concessions which operates as an adjunct to the EC.

The Caribbean Regional Cluster

In this section some themes which have been undercurrents thus far will be brought to the fore and explored with reference to the Caribbean offshore financial centres. Although Bermuda is an Atlantic island it will be included in the discussion, because functionally it is tied to the North American bloc in similar ways.

First, consideration will be given to the nature of competition between places for a share of the offshore financial markets. Why are so many places seeking to become fully fledged offshore centres? Second, what are the strategies employed in this inter-island competition to host offshore finance? In addressing these questions a closer look will be taken at the Cayman Islands.

Several recent changes in international finance make increased use of offshore entities likely. The securitization boom and changes in international banking are two of the main reasons. As banks face the 'fall-out' from their Third World loans and are subject to the BIS capital adequacy ratios, they are increasingly moving away from straightforward deposit-taking and loan-making and into off balance sheet activities (Cates and Davis, 1987; IMF, 1989, p. 7). Both global custody and international private banking often entail the use of offshore financial centres in 'global' networks designed to manage the risks inherent in the volatile world financial system and, at the same time, to profit from the churning markets and the uneven geography of regulation. As businesses, including institutional investors, have 'globalized' there has been an increase in the demand for international banking and other financial services which locate parts of their operations in the offshore financial centres (see Roberts, 1992). In addition, continued political instability, corruption and crime around the world mean that flight capital and 'hot money' are still looking for havens where they may stay or from which they may re-enter circuits of capital anonymously.

Given this 'demand' side to offshore financial centres, what about the 'supply' side? What makes so many Caribbean countries attracted to offshore finance? Small resource-poor island economies do not have many options for earning foreign exchange or more generally for development. Many aspiring offshore financial centres have seen neighbouring countries set themselves up as offshore financial centres. Offshore financial centres appear to offer a development model – one that ensures an inflow of hard currency in the shape of registration fees. That paper entities do not provide employment or demand much in the way of infrastructure may actually be attractive to many small countries. However, some are actively seeking to increase employment opportunities and therefore will favour offshore entities that maintain a physical presence in the centre. Often the less-developed offshore centres will specialize in offshore company formation rather than banking. The competition for offshore companies is fierce, with the Turks and Caicos and the British Virgin Islands in the Caribbean, for example, each attempting to be quicker and cheaper than the other (see *Euromoney*, Supplement May 1989). Whatever the strategy, the unspoken issue here is poverty. Many of the places indicated on the map in figure 5.1 are merely attempting to find ways in which they may bring some foreign exchange into their economies to supplement (and they may hope supplant) remittances from overseas, export earnings from primary products and income from tourism (see Gallagher, 1990). These offshore financial centres, actual and aspiring, are responding entrepreneurially to the changing world economy in which finance plays a major role. This is a twist on the theme of place entrepreneurialism noted elsewhere in the geographic literature (Harvey, 1989b). By existing at the margin, by offering flexibility, these places have located themselves at the juncture of circuits of fictitious and furtive capital, and by exploiting this position they may be said to benefit (McCarthy, 1979). However, when openness to the volatility of the financial system is combined with the geopolitical insecurity entailed in hosting flight capital and hot money, the inherent vulnerability (Commonwealth Secretariat, 1985) of small islands may be compounded in new ways.

The Cayman Islands and Its Reputation

The Cayman Islands is one example of a successful offshore financial centre. It is a British colony and claims to have the highest per capita GNP (about US $20,000 in 1992) in the Caribbean (*Euromoney*, 1992, p. 25). The Islands are a tourist destination for some 200,000 visitors a year. Another 400,000 disembark their giant cruise ships for a day ashore Grand Cayman (Cayman Islands Government, 1990b, p. 75). The Islands' government deliberately designed a development strategy based on tourism and offshore finance (Johnson, 1990). By combining an avowedly up-market tourism sector with a diversified financial sector the Caymans has undergone a rapid economic and social transformation from 'the Islands Time Forgot' (Maloney, 1950) to a sophisticated off-shore financial centre. The Caymanian capital George Town (on Grand Cayman) is host to over 540 banks from around the world which are licensed in the Caymans. In addition, there are some 24,000 companies registered here (more than one per person in the Caymans), about 60 per cent of which are purely offshore entities, together with over 350 captive (offshore) insurance companies registered in the Islands (Cayman Islands Government, 1990b; *Cayman Islands Yearbook*, 1991; *Euromoney*, 1992). There is also an aircraft register and a newly revamped ship register allowing the Caymans to compete with the likes of Liberia in the 'flag of convenience' business.

The vast majority of the banks registered on Grand Cayman do not maintain a physical presence in the Islands. Such banks are known variously as 'brass plate operations', 'shell branches' or 'paper entities'. These entities are used by the parent bank as 'booking centres' for their Euromarket activity. They are usually a link in a chain as part of a global strategy. Brass plate banks may be dormant – acting as a 'bolt hole' – a ready entity to which assets could be quickly transferred if another location seems threatened.

The Caymans Islands is one of the offshore financial centres (others include the Channel Islands) that are actively encouraging the creation of paper entities and discouraging the formation of staffed banking operations (Moore, 1992, p. 3). This is in contrast to their earlier position, which was to attract large well-known banks with staffed offices. The turn-around in policy has to be seen in the context of a small island (Grand Cayman) which has undergone tremendous economic growth and concomitant immigration over the past twenty years. Caymanians now make up only 67 per cent of the population (1989 census), and although the tourism industry is seen as the primary cause of the large influx of 'non-Caymanians', governmental controls over the issuance of work permits affect the financial sector (Roberts, 1992). In addition, it is deemed desirable to afford opportunities for educated Caymanians in the management echelons of the financial sector, positions that have been overwhelmingly held by expatriates – usually male and usually British or North American. The Caymans is looking to Jersey and Bermuda as examples of islands that have combined a successful offshore financial sector with a policy of controlled growth (Roberts, 1992). Such strategies are part of a wider and deeper questioning of the risks entailed in rapid economic growth for the social fabric of the Islands (see Jefferson, 1989, 1990; Roberts, 1992).

In contrast to the remarkably insubstantial nature of the financial sector itself, the Cayman Islands promotes itself as an offshore financial centre by emphasizing qualities of solidity, substance and good reputation. Offshore financial centres compete by keeping a close watch on rival centres and by seeking to pre-empt any deleterious effect that a change in another jurisdiction's laws might have. An offshore financial centre also watches its rivals for signs of a weakness that might be exploited (Kochan, 1991; Roberts, 1992). Any hint of political instablity, for example, can be used to steer potential business away from rival locations. The British Virgin Islands profited from Panama's troubles (e.g. surrounding the US invasion in December 1989) and the Cayman Islands' success has been in part the result of legislation enacted just in time to attract capital from the Bahamas during times of (perceived) instability there.

There are several participants engaged in the direct promotion of the Islands as an offshore financial centre. In the public sector the official

Government Information Service publishes brochures and leaflets, issues press releases and distributes material from the Government Statistics office. The Financial Secretary and occasionally the Governor go abroad as leaders of delegations seeking to publicize the Islands and perhaps negotiate special agreements. Such delegations have gone to Hong Kong, Japan, Sweden and Costa Rica in the past couple of years. Representatives are from professional associations such as the Cayman Islands Bankers' Association or the Cayman Insurance Managers' Association, and the Cayman Islands Chamber of Commerce is also involved in delegations. The Chamber of Commerce and the financial sector's industry associations publish materials outlining the attributes of the Caymans as an offshore financial centre and act as channels through which journalists and agencies can obtain information for articles in the trade presses. Public and private sector organizations are involved in the production of supplements for magazines (e.g. *Euromoney*, 1989a, 1992). Another way in which the Islands are promoted is through conferences. These include one-day seminars held in places 'onshore' that have been identified as sources of business. For instance, a one-day conference held at a New York City hotel in March 1990 was organized through a Washington DC law firm and featured several speakers, including the Cayman Islands Financial Secretary and lawyers and accountants from the USA and Cayman. Conferences are also held in the Caymans, such as the Cayman Islands Captive Insurance Conference in May 1989. This was organized by the Insurance Managers' Association and Tillinghast (a trade publisher) and it attracted over sixty overseas participants. The Superintendent of Insurance also leads a delegation to the North American Risk and Insurance Management Society's annual meetings. The Cayman Islands is one of a number of places (including Bermuda, the Bahamas, Hawaii and Ireland) that have exhibition booths at these meetings (*Business Insurance*, 1989; Hofmann, 1989).

In addition to these joint ventures between public and private sectors, individuals from the public and private sectors make presentations to colleagues and potential customers. These are often oral presentations, but may include slides, and several firms and banks employ professionally made videos (Roberts, 1992).

One important aspect of this public–private entrepreneurialism is the creation and promotion of a particular *image* of the Cayman Islands as part of a wider competitive strategy. Entrepreneurial islands do not compete as much by selling themselves as locations for offshore finance as by selling *images* of themselves. While an appropriate legislative framework, low costs and convenience are necessary attributes of a successful offshore financial centre, several less tangible factors are also important. The promotion of a certain image of the Islands is crucial in informing and affecting location decisions. The prospective client has to feel assured that his or her professional advisers are reputable and reliable, that there is no threat to the security or solvency of the institution and that the offshore centre itself is secure.

There are three related aspects of the Cayman Islands' image as an offshore centre that may be examined. These are: (a) the Islands as a safe and stable centre; (b) the Islands as a solid and substantial centre; (c) the Islands as a 'clean' and above-board centre.

Above all, potential clients must feel that their money is safe. Thus the sine qua non of a successful offshore financial centre is *stability*. Money is very cowardly and at even the hint of instability it will be moved elsewhere. Indeed, much of the Cayman Islands' early success can be traced to fears about the Bahamas at independence. Even in 1989, the Inspector of Banks and Trusts in the Cayman Islands noted in an interview that 'The Bahamas have Pindling [Prime Minister] and banks don't want to be in an unstable environment. It doesn't matter if you explain until you go blue in the face. If there is a hint of anything controversial the banks don't want to be involved. That's why we're so careful' (in *Euromoney*, 1989a, p. 68). The publicity materials of both the public and private sectors of the Caymans emphasize the Islands' political stability and racial harmony. Past disputes, such as that of 1962 over whether or not to opt for independence (albeit under Jamaica) or colonial status, and present-day discussions of constitutional change are not mentioned. Instead statements such as the following appear in almost every piece of promotional material: 'The Islands enjoy stable government having no racial or political problems. . . . The Islands have not sought independence despite pressure from her Caribbean neighbours and the UN. They have instead shown their firm determination to remain a British Crown Colony' (Cayman Insurance Managers' Association, n.d.; see also Gill, 1982). Corollaries of the Islands' colonial status, such as that Britain is responsible for the defence and external affairs of the Islands, that the law is based on English common law and that English is spoken, are also emphasized as being beneficial to the conduct of offshore financial business (e.g. Peat Marwick, 1989). More generally, the pomp and pageantry of the colonial government, with its venerable yet quaint British customs, are used to sell the Islands as changeless (and hence stable) to both tourists and financiers.

The infrastructure of the Islands – or more particularly of George Town, the capital in which the financial sector is clustered – is also stressed. Pictures of the modern office and bank buildings in George Town are employed frequently in promotional material and contribute to the image of the Islands as a modern, substantial and solid financial centre. The visual image of actual buildings is very important to inform and reassure prospective clients that the Cayman Islands is not a 'fly-by-night' financial centre. Several operations have videos or slide shows that introduce their services on the Cayman Islands and reinforce the solidity and substance of the built environment. During an interview with the author, an insurance manager described a slide presentation he had just given to New York and London based colleagues in his corporation as part of an effort to inform them of the activities of their Cayman office (and thus solicit appropriate referrals). He explained that 'We have to show them pictures of the modern office buildings in George Town so they see it is not all palm trees and mud huts here' (Roberts, 1992).

Why is stressing the solidity and stability of the islands so important in competing for offshore finance? At one level much of the business of offshore finance is about capital in flight. People or corporations engaged in moving money around out of fear of the sudden imposition of exchange or other controls are very concerned that their haven really *is* a haven. However, the changing fortunes of financial centres are clearly illustrated by the rapid change of Panama from a destination for flight capital to a source of it as the country was invaded by the USA in 1989. At another level the emphasis upon the solidity of the financial sector may be seen as an attempt to counter the intrinsic qualities of the shallow and fickle offshore market, which is a part of the contemporary international financial system marked by tremendous volatility and hypermobility enabled by deregulation and technology. Furthermore, a promotional strategy emphasizing the built environment of the Caymans may be interpreted as a direct response to the curiously fictitious nature of offshore finance itself.

The third major component of the image of the Cayman Islands as a financial centre is that of the Islands as a 'clean' financial centre. Cayman is especially anxious to be seen as having a reputation as a centre for respectable and legitimate international finance, and is keen to avoid a reputation as a money-laundering centre or as a haven for illegally gained funds. It is this concern that has motivated recent agreements with the geopolitically preponderant United States.

The Cayman Islands suffered in 1983 when the USA sought to apply its laws extraterritorially. The Bank of Nova Scotia in the USA was subpoenaed in connection with information relating to its Cayman branch. Eventually, despite protests from the Caymanian, British and Canadian governments, the USA succeeded in obtaining the information and in fining the Bank of Nova Scotia US $1.8 million (Pineau, 1988). In 1983 there were several articles in the US press linking the Caymans to money laundering. In addition, it was reported that Cayman businesspeople were harassed when entering the USA. These factors were effective in 'softening up' the Caymans and resulted in a Narcotics Agreement between the Caymans and the USA in 1984 (Roberts, 1992). This agreement allowed the US Attorney General to request the assistance of the Cayman Attorney General in obtaining information directly related to drugs cases. The Narcotics Agreement was a first stage agreement, and in 1986 the Mutual Legal Assistance Treaty (MLAT) was signed by the US, UK and Cayman governments. The MLAT extended the first agreement to cover crimes such as insider trading and securities frauds (such as penny stocks) as well as narcotics crimes. Although debate over the advisability of entering into agreements with the USA that compromise the legally protected confidentiality enjoyed by the financial sector was fierce, it is now generally agreed that the treaties have had a beneficial effect. However, the terms used to assess the impact of the MLAT are revealing. For example: 'The MLAT has helped the *image* of the Cayman Islands significantly' or 'The treaties have done a lot to enhance the Cayman Islands' *image* as a financial center' (from interviews with author; see Roberts, 1992). In describing the arrival of several large Japanese banks after the MLAT was signed, one banker noted that 'The last batch came over after the Cayman Islands sent a clear signal that we wanted to be a clean offshore center not a bucket shop place. . . . We never were a bucket shop but we didn't *control the image* and we didn't do active PR like we do now' (Roberts, 1992).

The explanation of the emphasis on the islands as a 'clean' financial centre lies in the real threat posed by a USA that is prosecuting a War on Drugs in the hemisphere. The Cayman Islands needs no reminders of its vulnerability to the USA and sees that without cordial relations its security, and hence its future, as an offshore financial centre is threatened.

The reputation of an offshore financial centre such as the Caymans is its most precious asset. It is also vulnerable to denigration. The particular image crafted and promoted by the public and private sectors in the Caymans has much to tell us about the nature and workings of an offshore financial centre and perhaps the international financial system as a whole, as simulacrum becomes everything as it feeds back into defining and legitimating existing relations (to employ Baudrillard's term after the fashion of Harvey, 1989a, p. 300). The promotion of the Islands contains dangers owing to the double role assigned to the regulatory authorities (as regulators and promoters), but has much deeper implications for the Cayman Islands. The necessity of social stability – or at least an image of social stability – means that on the one hand murmurings of discontent at the large number of expatriate professionals in the higher echelons of banking and the apparent relegation of Caymanians to clerical positions are taken seriously by the banks and the Bankers Association (for example, they provide scholarships). On the other hand, the government – notably the civil service – as well as the private sector, is in the business of denying social unrest or even political debate. The wish to reassure potential clients of the solidity of the built environment and, by implication, the 'realness' of the financial sector contradicts a stated policy of seeking to attract 'paper' business rather than financial business which requires offices and staff. The latter puts pressure on the already strained physical infrastructure of the islands as well as adding potentially to the controversial immigration of non-Caymanians. The promotion of the Islands as a 'clean' financial centre has meant that Cayman has complied with US wishes, and this is not universally regarded as admirable (Roberts, 1992).

It is not surprising that Caribbean islands which are, or aspire to be, offshore financial centres are acting as 'entrepreneurial islands'. Through joint public–private efforts the islands compete with one another to host mobile (or hypermobile) finance capital, which is itself seeking to counter, with flexibility, tremendous volatility and uncertainty in international finance.

Conclusion

Offshore finance is an essential and *characteristic* element of the contemporary world financial system. The interlinked but competing offshore financial centres help to define a new geography of finance. New patterns of offshore financial flows overlay and interact with older geographies of tax haven activity and present-day geographies of hot money flows. The offshore financial centres are nexuses where various intertwined circuits of global capital come into focus.

The role of fictitious capital is the defining characteristic of present-day global capitalism. As crises are temporarily resolved (or delayed) through fictions that rest on some future actualization (labour engaged in production), so new correspondingly contradictory spaces are created. The present uneven and paradoxical spatio-temporal configuration of capitalism is highlighted in the offshore markets for fictitious capital. Fictitious capital works through and in particular spaces which have come to evince the contradictory global-scale mix of risk and opportunity so typical of present-day capitalism. Offshore financial centres are at once on the margins and at the centre of global capitalism's displacement of crisis.

References

Aliber, R. Z. (1980) The integration of the offshore and domestic banking systems. *Journal of Monetary Economics*, 6, 509–26.

Amis, M. (1984) *Money: a Suicide Note*. Harmondsworth: Penguin.

Bank for International Settlements (1990) *60th Annual Report*. Basle: BIS.

Bank for International Settlements (1991) *61st Annual Report*. Basle: BIS.

The Banker (1989a) Paradise in Madeira. *The Banker*, January, 3.

The Banker (1989b) Madeira: place in the sun. *The Banker*, December, 56.

Beaty, J. and Hornik, R. (1988) A torrent of dirty dollars. *Time*, 18 December, 50–6.

Beecham, H. and Benn, D. (1991) Taking the heat offshore. *The International*, April, 19–26.

Bottomore, T. (ed.) (1956) *Karl Marx: Selected Writings in Sociology and Social Philosophy*. New York: McGraw Hill.

Brunet, R. (1986) *Atlas Mondial des Zones Franches et Paradis Fiscaux*. Paris: Reclus.

Business Insurance (1989) BI Atlanta guide. *Business Insurance*, 3 April.

Cates, D. and Davis, H. A. (1987) Revealing the invisible bank: disclosure of off-balance sheet activity. *Journal of Commercial Bank Lending*, 69(7), 9–18.

Cayman Islands Government (1990a) First estimates of Cayman Islands GNP. *Press Release*, 16 January, Cayman Islands Government Information Services.

Cayman Islands Government (1990b) *Statistical Abstract of the Cayman Islands 1989*. George Town: Cayman Islands Government Statistics Office.

Cayman Insurance Managers' Association (n.d.) *Cayman Insurance Managers' Association*. Brochure, George Town.

Cayman Islands Yearbook and Business Directory (1991) George Town: Cayman Free Press.

Central Bank of Cyprus (1988) *Annual Report 1987*. Nicosia: CBC.

Cheng, H.-S. (1981) From the Caymans. *Weekly Letter* (13 February). San Francisco: Federal Reserve Bank of San Francisco.

Commonwealth Secretariat (1985) *Vulnerability: Small States in the Global Society*. London: Commonwealth Secretariat Publications.

Corbridge, S. and Agnew, J. (1991) The US trade and budget deficits in global perspective: an essay in geopolitical-economy. *Society and Space*, 9, 71–90.

Costello, E. (1986) Offshore banking: securitisation leaves its mark. In A. Hendrie (ed.), *World Banking 1986*. London: FT Business Information, 24–6.

Cox, K. R. and Mair, A. (1988) Locality and community in the politics of local economic development. *Annals, Association of American Geographers*, 78(2), 307–25.

Crutchley, E. (1991) Stability and strength of the banking system. In *Cayman Islands Yearbook and Business Directory '91*. Goerge Town: Cayman Free Press, 135–51.

Daly, M. T. and Logan, M. I. (1989) *The Brittle Rim: Finance, Business and the Pacific Region*. New York: Penguin Books.

The Economist (1990) Without any help from my friends. *The Economist*, 14 April, 71.

The Economist (1991) Why London? Editorial. *The Economist*, 4 May, 14–15.

Euromoney (1988a) Towards a single market. *Euromoney*, Supplement, September.

Euromoney (1988b) Europe's new offshore banking centres. *Euromoney*, Supplement, December.

Euromoney (1989a) Treasure islands. *Euromoney*, Supplement, May.

Euromoney (1989b) South Pacific islands: into the mainstream. *Euromoney*, Supplement, September.

Euromoney (1990) Mauritius. *Euromoney*, Sponsored Supplement, September.

Euromoney (1992) The 1992 guide to offshore financial centres. Research guide. *Euromoney*, May.

Foley, D. (1983) Credit and fictitious capital. In T. Bottomore et al. (eds), *A Dictionary of Marxist Thought*. Cambridge, MA: Harvard University Press, 99–100.

Gallagher, R. (1990) *Report of Mr Rodney Gallagher of Coopers and Lybrand on the Survey of Offshore Finance Sectors in the Caribbean Dependent Territories.* London: HMSO.

Gill, C. S. (1982) *Incorporation and Investment in the Cayman Islands* (revised and updated). Grand Cayman: C. S. Gill (Attorney-at-Law).

Gulati, S. (1988) Capital flight: causes, consequences, and cures. *Journal of International Affairs,* 24(1), 165–85.

Hahn, F. (1981) *Money and Inflation.* Cambridge, MA: MIT Press.

Harvey, D. (1982) *The Limits to Capital.* Chicago: University of Chicago Press.

Harvey, D. (1989a) *The Condition of Postmodernity.* Oxford: Blackwell.

Harvey, D. (1989b) From managerialism to entrepreneurialism in urban govern-ance in late capitalism. *Geografisker Annaler B,* 71(1), 3–17.

Hewson, J. R. (1982) Offshore banking in Australia: consultant's report. In *Australian Financial System Inquiry: Commissioned Studies and Selected Studies. Part 2, Macroeconomic Policy: External Policy.* Canberra: Austra-lian Government Publishing Service, 403–738.

Hoare, Q. (ed.) (1975) *Karl Marx: Early Writings.* New York: Vintage.

Hofmann, M. (1989) Domiciles' exhibits vie for attention. *Business Insurance,* 24 April, 66–7.

Hogan, W. P. and Pearce, I. F. (1982) *The Incredible Eurodollar.* London: George Allen and Unwin.

Holstrom, L. (1988) The name of the game is tax efficiency. *Euromoney,* December supplement (Europe's New Offshore Banking Centres), 2–4.

Howitt, P. (1989) Money illusion. In J. Eatwell, M. Milgate and P. Newman (eds), *The New Palgrave: Money.* London: Macmillan, 244–7.

Hultman, C. W. (1990) *The Environment of International Banking.* Englewood Cliffs, NJ: Prentice-Hall.

Hultman, C. W. (1991) A note on the shifting comparative advantage in trade in financial services. *Banca Nazionale del Lavoro Quarterly Review,* 179, 481–7.

International Monetary Fund (1989) *International Capital Markets: Develop-ments and Prospects.* Washington, DC: IMF.

International Monetary Fund (1990) *International Capital Markets: Develop-ments and Prospects.* Washington, DC: IMF.

Jefferson, T. C. (1989) 1989–1990 Budget Address, delivered by the Financial Secretary to the Legislative Assembly, 17 November 1989. Grand Cayman: Cayman Islands Government.

Jefferson, T. C. (1990) Approaches to economic expansion. In *Cayman Islands Who's Who and Business Guide.* Grand Cayman: Star Communications, 368–76.

Johns, R. A. (1982) *Tax Havens and Offshore Finance: a Study of Transnational Economic Development.* New York: St Martin's Press.

Johnson, V. G. (1990) Understanding Cayman's rise as a financial centre. In *Cayman Islands Who's Who and Business Guide.* Grand Cayman: Star Com-munications, 141–55.

Johnston, R. B. (1982) *The Economics of the Euro-Market.* New York: St Martin's Press.

Jones, R. S. (1989) Japan's expanding role in world financial markets. *Columbia Journal of World Business,* 24(3), 3–9.

Kane, E. J. (1987) Competitive financial regulation: an international perspective. In R. Portes and A. K. Swoboda (eds), *Threats to International Financial Stability*. Cambridge: Cambridge University Press, 111–44.

Khambata, D. (1989) Off-balance sheet activities of US banks: an empirical evaluation. *Columbia Journal of World Business*, 24(2), 3–13.

Kochan, N. (1991) Cleaning up by cleaning up. *Euromoney*, April, 73–7.

McCarthy, I. (1979) Offshore banking centers: benefits and costs. *Finance and Development*, 16(4), 45–8.

McDougall, R. (1989) Empires of the yen: the East. *The Banker*, 139 (January), 50–60.

Machlup, F. (1972) Euro-dollars: once again. *Banca Nazionale del Lavoro Quarterly Review*, 101, 119–37.

Maingot, A. P. (1988) Laundering the gains of the drug trade: Miami and Caribbean tax havens. *Journal of Interamerican Studies and World Affairs*, 30(2/3), 167–87.

Maloney, J. (1950) The islands time forgot. *Saturday Evening Post* (New York), 8 April, 38–9, 83, 86, 89, 91.

Marx, K. (1976) *Capital. A Critique of Political Economy. Vol. 1.* Harmondsworth: Penguin.

Moore, P. (1992) Editorial, the 1992 guide to offshore financial centres. *Euromoney* Research Guide, May.

Naylor, R. T. (1987) *Hot Money and the Politics of Debt*. London: Unwin Hyman.

Peat Marwick (1989) *Starting a Captive Insurance Operation in the Cayman Islands*. Grand Cayman: KPMG Peat Marwick (accountants).

Pecchioli, R. M. (1983) *The Internationalisation of Banking: the Policy Issues*. Paris: OECD.

Pineau, W. (1988) Banking close-up. *Newstar* (Cayman Islands), August, 10–59.

Pippenger, J. E. (1984) *The Fundamentals of International Finance*. Englewood Cliffs, NJ: Prentice-Hall.

Pryke, M. (1991) An international city going 'global': spatial change in the City of London. *Society and Space*, 9, 197–222.

Roberts, S. (1992) The local and the global: the Cayman Islands and the international financial system. PhD dissertation, Geography, Syracuse University.

Rosdolsky, R. (1977) *The Making of Marx's Capital*. London: Pluto.

Sarver, E. (1988) *The Eurocurrency Market Handbook*. New York: New York Institute of Finance/Prentice-Hall.

Simmel, G. (1990) *The Philosophy of Money*, 2nd edn. London: Routledge (originally published 1907).

Spitz, B. (1983) *Tax Havens Encyclopedia*, issue 15. London: Butterworths.

Spivak, G. (1987) Speculations on reading Marx: after reading Derrida. in D. Attridge, G. Bennington and R. Young (eds), *Post-structuralism and the Question of History*. Cambridge: Cambridge University Press, 30–62.

Triffin, R. (1984) The European Monetary System: tombstone or cornerstone? In *The International Monetary System: Forty Years after Bretton Woods* (Conference Series 28). Boston: Federal Reserve Bank of Boston, 127–73.

Trivoli, G. W. (1981) The international banking facility – threat or opportunity? *The Bankers Magazine*, 164(5), 12–16.

Versluysen, E. (1981) *The Political Economy of International Finance*. New York: St Martin's Press.

Wacker, T. J. (1989) A macroview of private banking: marketing challenges and choices. In D. B. Zenoff (ed.), *Marketing Financial Services*. Cambridge, MA: Ballinger Publishing, 71–81.

Walter, I. (1989) *Secret Money*. London: Unwin Hyman.

Warf, B. (1989) Telecommunications and the globalization of financial services. *Professional Geographer*, 41(3), 257–71.

6

Under Pressure: Finance, Geo-economic Competition and the Rise and Fall of Japan's Postwar Growth Economy

Andrew Leyshon

Introduction

Fears about the possible impacts that the short-term imperatives of financial capital have had upon the industrial competitiveness of countries such as the United Kingdom and the United States have been voiced over a long period of time (for example, see Ingham, 1984; Anderson, 1987). More recently, concerns have arisen over the spectre of an increasingly speculative 'arbitrage economy' arising from successive rounds of financial innovation and re-regulation, and from the sharp increase in the number of financial institutions operating on a global scale, and the marked empowerment of financial capital that these changes have brought about (Clark, 1989; Gill and Law, 1989; Harvey, 1989; Minsky, 1989; Bond, 1990; Thrift, 1990; Hübner, 1991; Christopherson, 1992; Leyshon, 1992; Leyshon and Thrift, 1992).

Similar concerns over the speculative tendencies of financial capital are not unknown in Japan. Indeed, in common with one of the fundamental tenets of Marxist economic theory, the Confucian philosophy that underpins Japanese society identifies many of the activities concerned with the circulation of money as 'parasitic', which exist only by feeding off those economic agents who make a more concrete and material contribution

Many of the ideas developed in this chapter have emerged from investigations into the workings of the international financial system undertaken jointly with Nigel Thrift, whose consistent support and encouragement has been invaluable. I am extremely grateful for the helpful comments and observations made on an earlier, and considerably longer, version of this chapter by Stuart Corbridge, Andrew Cox, Stephen Gill, Phillip Jones, Kyo Ozeki and Adam Tickell. The usual disclaimers apply.

to society.[1] According to Ronald Dore (1987, p. 116), 'Confucian doctrine [places] "the merchant" at the bottom of the social hierarchy, inferior in usefulness to the peasant and the artisan.' Yet despite this underlying antipathy towards financial capital, trenchant criticisms of the kind that routinely appear within countries such as the UK and the USA are for the most part absent in Japan. In a key text, Dore (1986) has stressed the important role played by the financial system in facilitating industrial restructuring and the adoption of innovation-led competitive strategies. Japanese corporations have enjoyed both a plentiful supply of cheap credit and what Dore describes as an 'ability to wait': that is, being able 'to take low profits over a fairly extended period as long as one has one's banker's confidence in the long-run future' (Dore, 1986, pp. 71–2). This environment of patient money is said to have had important implications for the Japanese economy, for it has encouraged new firms to develop new industries and products, and existing firms to diversify into new sectors.

In many ways the Japanese financial system has been central to the process of postwar economic growth in Japan. Banks are located at the heart of many of the business groupings which dominate the institutional structure of the Japanese production base, while the provision of cheap and plentiful credit by the financial system to Japanese industry has played a critical role in Japan's economic success story. At the same time, the financial system in Japan has until recently been subject to a relatively high level of structural regulation, which was enforced by the state through the Ministry of Finance (MOF) and the Bank of Japan (BOJ). It was the structure of financial regulation in Japan which ensured that large volumes of cheap credit were available for industrial investment (Eccleston, 1986).

The Japanese financial system remains a distinctive and important component of the Japanese economic system, but since the early 1970s it has been undergoing a far-reaching process of restructuring, which has served to transform its postwar growth model. In short, the Japanese financial system has become less distinctive and has come more to resemble the financial systems of other core capitalist countries. This chapter will focus on the changing role of the financial system in Japan during the postwar period. The next section examines the organization of the financial system in the period between 1945 and 1970, during the years of rapid economic growth. During this period the financial system was subjected to a high level of structural regulation, which ensured that cheap credit was available to support rapid industrial expansion within a highly self-contained and self-generating economy. The third section looks at the period after 1970 when the financial system began to

---

1 For an excellent critique of the productivist and materialistic biases in Marxian economic theory see Boss (1990, pp. 89–118).

undergo important changes as Japan's role within the international economy increased. Internal pressures for change were later reinforced by external pressures in the form of geo-economic offensives conducted against Japan by the United States, which identified the Japanese financial system as a source of 'unfair' competitive advantage. These offensives have served greatly to transform the Japanese financial system, and led directly to a cycle of credit boom and bust in the late 1980s and early 1990s, which promises to have long-term implications for the future of Japanese capitalism. The conclusions to the chapter are presented in the last section.

Continuity and Change: Rebuilding the Postwar Economy

The shape of the Japanese financial system in the period up to 1970 bore the imprint of two very important processes of economic reform. The first was the Meiji Restoration of 1868, following which a concerted effort was made to modernize an economy that was more feudal than capitalist in its orientation. By the close of the nineteenth century, the Meiji rulers had succeeded in constructing a highly organized financial system, the structures of which were to prove very durable (Goldsmith, 1983). The purpose of this financial model, the various parts of which were modelled on institutional forms in operation in different countries in the West (Hayes and Hubbard, 1990, p. 139; Tamaki, 1990, p. 214), was clear: to harness domestic funds and to channel them into industrial production so as to achieve rapid industrial modernization. A second legacy of the Meiji Restoration was the underdeveloped nature of Japan's capital markets. To a large extent this feature could be explained by the nature of the financial system: the banking system and the government itself provided such a large proportion of investment funds, with much of the balance being sourced from internal financing, that capital markets were largely unnecessary. However, the underdevelopment of capital markets can also be explained by a distinctive form of industrial organization that evolved in Japan: the *zaibatsu*. These were alliances of firms held together under the umbrella of a holding company, which co-ordinated the activities of its constituent firms across a wide range of activities. The holding company function meant that a large proportion of equity was not traded, but held in trust on a long-term basis.

A second imprint upon the postwar financial system was left by the bureaucratic reformers working under the instructions of the Supreme Commander of the Allied Powers (SCAP) during the United States occupation of 1945–52. While the brief of the US reform programme was to create a new Japan from the ashes of the old, it was only partially successful. The reform programme was undermined by a critical contradiction in the US perception of the role of postwar Japan. On the one hand, the USA wished to combine demilitarization with democratization to prevent a resurgence of the military aggression observed in the 1930s and 1940s. At the same time, the USA wished to create a capitalist bulwark in Asia, sympathetic to US geopolitical objectives. This contradiction was to have important implications for the organization of the financial system and for Japanese capitalism as a whole.

The central plank of the reform programme was the dissolution of the *zaibatsu*, via the decentralization of their share capital, which began in 1945 (Adams and Hoshii, 1972; Cohen, 1987), and which was seen to be the single most important reform in the demilitarization process (Nestor, 1990). The abolition of the *zaibatsu* in this way also embodied the ethos of economic orthodoxy, which the United States wished to instil within the Japanese economy. This ethos was evoked still further in the Anti-Trust Act of 1947, which sought to prohibit monopolization and cartelization, and in particular to prevent the re-concentration and re-centralization of Japanese capital by outlawing holding companies, cross-company shareholdings and interlocking directorships between competitor firms. The Act also limited finance companies to a 5 per cent stake in any other company (Best, 1990, p. 174).

However, a wave of communist 'insurgencies' in Asia during the late 1940s, the most significant of which resulted in the formation of the People's Republic of China (PRC) in 1949, saw US policy-makers begin to question the merits of a complete overhaul of Japanese capitalism. In the light of the events unfolding in China, rather more concern began to be given to the possible implications of the economic chaos that would follow the comprehensive reconstruction of the Japanese economy to make it better resemble the American model. The birth of the PRC demanded a rapid re-evaluation of the SCAP reform programme, which according to Best was seen by elements of the US government as inimical to fending off the rise of communism in Asia:

> In the new context, the decentralization provisions within the Anti-Trust Act not only thwarted the re-emergence of Japanese Big Business, but limited the role of foreign investment in Japan by large American firms. The Pentagon procurement system, like all war planning agencies, is simplified by contracting with large rather than small businesses. Abruptly the SCAP industrial decentralization ideal was replaced by the imperatives of military procurement. A revised Antitrust Act came into effect in July 1949. Each of the anti-holding-company provisions of the 1947 Act was relaxed. (Best, 1990, p. 175)

The new imperatives of US geopolitics had a profound effect on the balance of power within the Japanese bureaucracy. The revival of economic orthodoxy in Japan, which was being reasserted within its natural constituency, the Ministry of Finance and the Bank of Japan, was nipped in the bud, and served to tilt the balance of bureaucratic power in favour of the Ministry of International Trade and Industry (MITI). SCAP began to support and encourage the productivist-orientated policies that had dominated Japanese economic policy-making in the prewar years.

This switch in the ideological foundations of Japanese economic development policy had several implications for the organization of the financial system. The most important was the continued underdevelopment of capital markets and the dominance of intermediated credit markets. The dissolution of the *zaibatsu* involved the de-concentration of corporate ownership, which was achieved by outlawing the holding companies and encouraging individual share ownership. The success of this policy in the short term meant that by 1949 an estimated 70 per cent of share capital was owned by individuals (Dore, 1987, p. 113). However, the repeal in that year of the 1947 anti-trust legislation opened the way for a re-concentration of share ownership and the formation of new industrial groupings to replace the *zaibatsu*. The centripetal forces unleashed in the equity market were for the most part driven by the old *zaibatsu* banks, which took it upon themselves to assume the coordinating role vacated by the holding companies:

> The banks became the foci for the re-establishment of many of the pre-war group affiliations during the 1950s . . . the term *kigyoshuden* came to be applied to the groups of enterprise which were linked through reciprocal shareholdings, trading links, and orientation to the same bank. Where the pre-war zaibatsu were structured vertically as pyramids through the family-controlled holding companies, the post-war *kigyoshuden* had a flatter, horizontal structure. (Scott, 1986, p. 162)

By 1950 the proportion of shares held by individuals had already fallen to around 60 per cent. Individual share ownership declined consistently thereafter (table 6.1). The reformation of the industrial groupings after 1949 saw companies purchase one another's shares not for their financial value but to express a business relation or alliance. Mutual share

Table 6.1 Percentage of shares held by selected shareholders in companies listed on the first section of the Tokyo Stock Exchange, 1955–1987

	1955	1965	1975	1979	1987
Government and local public bodies	0.4	0.2	0.2	0.2	0.8
Financial institutions	19.5	24.5	35.6	38.2	42.2
Investment trusts	4.1	6.2	1.7	2.0	2.4
Securities companies	7.9	6.1	1.5	2.1	2.5
Other corporations	13.2	17.3	25.5	25.3	24.9
Foreign corporations	1.5	1.6	2.5	2.4	3.6
Individuals and others	53.4	44.1	33.0	29.7	23.6

Source: Matsumoto, 1992, table 1.2.

ownership served to weld together the 'world of obligated long-term trading relationships which Japanese businessmen inhabit', being 'the expression of some other business relationship, not so much a relation in itself' (Dore, 1987, p. 113). Thus, the interlocking webs of corporate ownership can be interpreted as proactive, in that they were used to knit together the dense institutional matrix of Japanese capitalism. However, Dore also points to a defensive motive for the concentration of share ownership, arguing that the growing concentration of shareholdings in the 1960s was part of a collective movement organized to prevent Japanese companies falling prey to foreign corporations looking to pursue cross-border strategies of capital centralization: 'trade and capital liberalization threatened to bring foreign firms into Japan. The fear of takeovers by predatory American firms prompted what was called a "shareholding stabilization strategy". Firms sought to get a substantial share of their equity into the hands of other firms which could be relied on for support' (Dore, 1987, pp. 113–14).

The stabilization of share holdings in this way also brought about a stabilization of corporate governance in Japan, so that management teams enjoyed a rare freedom to disregard demands for short-term returns from the stockmarket. Individual share ownership was further discouraged in the late 1960s and in the early 1970s by the growing practice of issuing new share capital at market rather than at discounted prices (Dore, 1987, p. 114). The squeezing out of short-term financial pressures in this way also meant that the equity market became a very cheap source of capital. But it should be recognized that this was not a prime motive for the concentration of share ownership and the marginalization of external financial capital. This was just a welcome side effect of the pursuit of *kigyoism* and share stabilization. There was hardly any need to secure cheap credit within the capital markets, since the banking system already functioned as a source of almost unlimited, cheap credit.

The switch of emphasis towards continuity rather than change in SCAP policy in the late 1940s meant that the strong structural regulation applied to the Japanese financial system remained in place. The purpose of structural regulation in Japan was clear: to keep savers and investors separate from one another so that the intermediation of funds from one to the other could be acted upon by the bureaucracies of the state to ensure the supply of cheap credit to Japanese industry. The orchestration of funds intermediation in Japan was performed by the MOF through the BOJ. As with all systems of structural regulation, financial institutions submitted to restrictions on the range of activities in which they could engage for assurances over their economic security. In the Japanese case, banks were enjoined to lend large volumes of credit for industrial investment in the assurance that the BOJ and the MOF would prevent them ever going bankrupt should any of the loans turn sour (Zysman, 1983,

p. 244). In return for such assurances the banks willingly submitted to bureaucratic control over their lending activities.

Lending was encouraged by setting very low interest rates and by direct lending from the BOJ to the commercial banks. The provision of credit at artificially low prices meant that the market for credit never cleared. The commercial banks were drawn into 'overlending', while corporate borrowers were encouraged to 'overborrow'. This mutual dependence encouraged a fusion of interests between financial and productive capital, with banks in particular eager to 'acquire expert knowledge of the firm they deal[t] with' (Dore, 1986, p. 68).[2]

This was the system of finance that underwrote Japan's postwar industrialization, the scale of which was unprecedented. The dimensions of this exceptional economic growth performance have been outlined by Itoh (1990a, p. 140):

> In the 22 years from 1951 . . . Japanese GDP grew continuously and rapidly by 9.2 per cent per annum on average. . . . The annual growth rate was elevated from 8.9 per cent in 1951–61 to 9.4 per cent in 1961–73. These were remarkably high rates of growth in historical experience in the world. As a result, in the two decades until 1973, Japanese GNE (gross national expenditure) per capita multiplied 12.5 times in nominal yen and 4.9 times in real terms.

Bank-intermediated credit was pervasive during this time. Between 1965 and 1974 over 70 per cent of all funds raised in Japan were in the form of bank loans. It is difficult to question the importance of cheap, intermediated credit in facilitating the Japanese economic miracle. It was part of an internally coherent system of economic growth, that for the most part was characterized by *autocentricism*.[3] In the years of rapid economic growth Japan's export dependency, as expressed in the ratio of exports to GNP, was consistently lower than that of the United States or the United Kingdom over the same period (Itoh, 1990a, p. 155). Nevertheless, it should be noted that the internationalization of Japanese accumulation grew steadily during this period. Japan's low export dependency was a result of the rise in exports being matched by com-

2 It should be noted that the provision of cheap credit was a universal phenomenon, so that banks did not limit lending only to firms within their own business groupings (Goldsmith, 1983, p. 197; Zysman, 1983, p. 243; Dore, 1986, p. 68). The syndication of loans across the economy as a whole not only diversified risk but also deepened the dependency of the banks upon the production system as a whole, and encouraged the cooperative form of capitalism engendered by the *kigyoshuden*.

3 Samir Amin (1976, p. 76) describes autocentric accumulation as 'accumulation without external expansion of the system'. The growth of the Japanese economic system was for the most part self-funded, a product of the tight control exerted over the financial system, and self-generated, owing to the strong inter-corporate linkages within the industrial sector.

parable advances in the level of GNP, as the Japanese share of exported manufactured goods in the world economy more than doubled between 1957 and 1973, increasing from 5.5 to 11.5 per cent (Itoh, 1990a, p. 156).

However, while leading sectors of Japanese industry were becoming increasingly internationalized, the financial system remained strongly geared towards the intermediation of domestic savings and investments to facilitate domestic accumulation. Indeed, ports of entry and exit between the Japanese financial system and the international financial system were few and far between and were keenly guarded by the bureaucracies of the state. But by the mid-1970s the internal coherence of the Japanese financial system began to break down, as the Japanese economy entered a period of severe crisis. This was the catalyst for the restructuring of the Japanese financial system around the rubrics of re-regulation, internationalization and competition.

Under Pressure: the Japanese Financial System since 1970

Since the early 1970s the Japanese financial system has been profoundly restructured, a consequence of the faltering of the postwar growth model around this time. Whereas this model demonstrated an unusual fusion between financial and productive capital, more recently the financial system has taken on many of the characteristics of financial systems in other core capitalist countries. There has occurred a weakening of the level of bureaucratic control over the financial system and a diminution of the extent to which structural regulation governs the operations of financial institutions and markets. The weakening of these authority relations within the Japanese financial system has been paralleled by a reduction in the dependency relations flowing through the financial system. In particular, the degree to which productive capital is dependent upon the banking sector for finance has been diminished by the growing volumes of disintermediated credit circulating within the economy.

Japan's postwar financial system began to be restructured in the early 1970s as an inflationary surge destabilized the postwar growth economy. The major cause of the inflation lay in the dismantling of the system of international monetary management. The breakdown of the Bretton Woods agreement and the freeing of currencies from commodity money heralded an unprecedented increase in the volume of credit money circulating within the world economy, much of it emanating from the United States. Indeed, the United States used its liberation from the constraints of the gold window to expand its money supply both to stimulate domestic accumulation and to cause a depreciation of its currency, thereby improving the competitiveness of its producers in foreign markets.[4] In response, the financial authorities in Japan initiated an inflationary spiral of their own by lowering still further the cost of money in Japan, with the express intention that a rise in inflation would slow the rise of the yen against the dollar (Itoh, 1990a, p. 163). However, the inflationary spiral was given a further and unexpected spin in 1974 in the wake of the OPEC-inspired 'oil shock'. The quadrupling of oil prices had serious implications for an economy that relied on oil imports for over 90 per cent of its energy requirements. Japanese GDP fell by almost 4 per cent between 1973 and 1974, while wholesale prices increased by over 31 per cent, consumer prices by 24 per cent and wages by as much as 33 per cent in 1974 alone (Thorn, 1987, p. 9; Itoh, 1990a, p. 168). The rising cost of commodities and labour began to eat into profit levels, with the profit share of the manufacturing sector declining by over 60 per cent between 1970 and 1975 (Itoh, 1990a, p. 165).[5]

The autocentric growth model was clearly in trouble. The two main responses to the crisis were a switch in economic policy towards deficit financing and a greater emphasis on the internationalization of Japanese capital. These developments would irrevocably change the orientation of the Japanese financial system.

Deficit Financing and the Re-regulation of the Financial System

Despite the radical nature of Japan's productivist-orientated economic policy, the financial authorities had for the most part maintained an adherence to a strict fiscal orthodoxy by following the doctrines of the 'Dodge line' – Joseph Dodge being the banker despatched to Japan by President Truman in 1949 to tackle the accelerating inflation that accompanied the initial postwar reconstruction of the Japanese economy. The orthodox anti-inflation remedy prescribed by Dodge was that the Japanese government should run a balanced budget, and eschew any recourse to deficit financing (Hadley, 1989). The Japanese state did this for nearly twenty years, not least because the orthodoxy of the Dodge line supported the operation of the postwar economic growth model, ensuring that savings were used exclusively for the purposes of industrial development. Postwar recovery in Japan did *not* go hand in hand with the construction of a welfare state.

The scale of the crisis facing the Japanese economy in the early 1970s resulted in the wholesale rejection of the Dodge line. Between 1975 and 1979 the Japanese government borrowed heavily to engineer a deficit-led

4   For more on the United States' use of monetary policy as a competitive economic weapon see Parboni (1981, 1986), Evans (1988a) and Leyshon (1990, 1992). See also chapter 4, by Stuart Corbridge.
5   The *net profit share* is calculated by dividing net profits (including rent and interest) by net value added.

recovery out of recession. Government indebtedness, which stood at 13.2 trillion yen in 1973, increased to 22.8 trillion in 1975 and to 95.0 trillion in 1980, rising from 11.3 per cent to 39.7 per cent of GNP over the period (Itoh, 1990a, p. 171). The borrowed money, raised through the issue of government bonds, was used to increase domestic demand through an extensive state-led programme of infrastructure construction, which indeed helped to revive the domestic economy. Therefore, at the very moment that Keynesian economic demand management was being abandoned in favour of neoliberalism in North America and Western Europe, Japan's economic policy was moving in precisely the opposite direction.

That Japan was able to move in such a radically different direction bore testament to the continuing distinctiveness of its economy and its financial system. While more open capitalist countries found their freedom of manoeuvre within the field of monetary and fiscal policy increasingly constrained by the anti-inflationist sanctioning power of international financial capital (Leyshon and Thrift, 1992; Leyshon, 1992), Japan's relative immunity to the dynamics of the international financial system provided it with policy avenues that other states were being forced to relinquish. The strongly regulated nature of a 'closed' financial system meant that the Japanese authorities could bear the risk of incurring even higher inflation in the short term, if in the medium term this brought about an economic revival. However, the switch to deficit financing did not in the event bring about a rise in inflation. Indeed, inflation was actually reduced in the face of a demand-led revival, under the influence of two particularly important features of the Japanese economy. First, the pervasiveness of *kigyoism* plus rising levels of unemployment enabled firms to grow out of the crisis while at the same time resisting pressures for wage increases, thereby holding down demand in the personal sector. Second, despite the fact that an increasing volume of state expenditures was being directed towards welfare spending, it was not enough to undermine the high propensity to save within the Japanese population, and the diversion of funds into savings served further to offset inflation.

While the shift to deficit financing enabled the Japanese economy to grow out of recession in the short term, the reorientation of economic policy was to have long-term implications for Japanese capitalism as a whole. The growth of the government bond market destabilized Japan's financial markets. In an attempt to fund the deficits, in what was still an illiquid market for securitized debt, the MOF began to attach relatively high rates of interest to the bonds to make make them more attractive to investors. This introduced into Japan what was then the novel idea of competition for funds, which began to tip the balance of interests within Japan's financial markets away from borrowers and towards savers and investors (*Economist*, 1988). The attempt to dredge up new lenders to fund the budget deficits disturbed the long-run stability of the financial system, while the competition for funds saw money become more expensive. These changes generated a series of shock-waves throughout the financial system, which continued to reverberate through the 1980s. Growing competition saw the existing system of structural regulation come under increasing pressure. The unbalancing of the system, caused by the diversion of funds into a significantly enlarged government securities market, generated internal pressures for the liberalization of the financial system, as financial institutions looked for ways to attract back the funds that were being diverted into higher yielding investments.

Ironically, the issue of such large volumes of government debt served to wrest control of the process of credit allocation away from the state in the form of the BOJ and the MOF, as the price of credit increasingly became market rather than administratively determined (Suzuki, 1987, p. 26). Over the second half of the 1970s a growing proportion of funds circulating within the economy were doing so in disintermediated form, and therefore outside the existing system of structural regulation. Thereafter, the financial system began to move even further outside the control of the regulatory authorities as processes of financial innovation within the disintermediated section of the financial system spawned a series of derivative financial instruments and markets. The growth of disintermediated credit within the economy (table 6.2) forced the BOJ and the MOF to abandon their more interventionist mechanisms of monetary control, resorting to open market levers such as interest rate levels. The loosening of regulatory control over Japan's financial markets was accelerated by the process of internationalization that occurred in the wake of the crisis of the early 1970s.

The Internationalization of the Japanese Financial System

The second response to the crisis of Japanese capitalism in the early 1970s was to focus more strongly upon export-led growth. The leading

Table 6.2 Funds intermediation in Japan, 1965–1990 (fiscal year average, percentages)

	1965–74	1975–84	1985–90
Funds raised by domestic sectors	92.1	89.1	72.3
Loans from domestic banks	70.2	54.6	47.5
Securities	19.2	32.0	19.7
Government bonds	12.9	26.6	7.2
Foreign funds	2.7	2.5	5.1
Funds supplied to overseas market	7.9	10.9	27.1
Total funds supplied (trillion ¥)	20.4	58.6	122.9

Source: Kasman and Rodrigues, 1991.

manufacturing corporations, encouraged by MITI, began to move into new consumer-orientated industries, to engage in the radical reorganization of their labour processes and to implement export-led growth strategies. In consequence, Japanese corporations began to focus their attention on sectors such as automobiles and consumer electronics industries (Dicken, 1992, pp. 174–5), within which products were manufactured to new levels of quality and reliability through the use of quality circles and zero defect production routines, while the push into foreign markets saw Japan's export-dependency increase, although only marginally, over the course of the 1970s. The following list shows exports as a percentage of GNP, from 1947 to 1987 (Itoh, 1990a, p. 155):

1947	0.8
1956	10.0
1960	9.5
1965	10.0
1970	11.7
1975	11.2
1980	12.5
1985	13.5
1987	9.7

The internationalization of Japanese industry began to strain a financial system that was still first and foremost orientated towards the circulation of domestic capital. The high level of administrative control exercised by the MOF and the BOJ had encouraged a highly restrictive attitude towards foreign financial institutions in Japan. Only 18 foreign banks had branches in Japan in 1970 (Suzuki, 1987, p. 29) and the majority of those had been opened either before the war or during the occupation period of 1945–52 (Monroe, 1973, pp. 134–5). Thereafter, the barriers erected by the financial authorities were made virtually insurmountable. When Japanese banks sought to follow their manufacturing clients overseas in the early 1970s the restrictions on the entry of foreign banks to Japan were used by foreign financial authorities to prevent Japanese institutions gaining entry to their financial centres on the grounds of reciprocity. Given the growing demand for international financial services by Japan's rapidly internationalizing industrial sector, the financial authorities were forced to facilitate a greater degree of interaction between the domestic and international financial systems. During the course of the 1970s growing numbers of foreign financial institutions were allowed to enter Japanese financial markets,[6] while the internationalization of Japanese financial institutions accelerated. The

6 The number of foreign banks in Japan increased to fifty by 1975, while in 1972 the US firm Merrill Lynch was the first foreign securities house allowed to establish itself in Japan.

growing number of institutional pathways between the domestic and international financial markets encouraged the progressive internationalization of Japan's financial markets, and served further to integrate the Japanese financial system into the dynamics of the international financial system as a whole.

The internationalization of Japanese financial markets (see table 6.2) clearly contributed to a further diminution of regulatory control over the domestic financial system. Nevertheless, despite internationalization and the growth of a more disintermediated financial system by the end of the 1970s, the financial authorities in Japan still exercised a greater level of control over the circulation of financial capital in the economy than did their counterparts in other core capitalist countries. This state of affairs was to change in the 1980s as the United States launched a concerted geo-economic offensive against Japan, in a bid to eradicate the competitive advantages believed to be conferred upon Japanese producers by virtue of the structure of Japan's financial markets.

Taking on the Yen: United States Geo-economic Offensives against Japan in the 1980s

The United States has a tradition of attributing its trade deficits to the financial policies of its major trading partners. (*Haynes et al., 1986, p. 1*)

According to Michael Moran, the decision of the United States in the early 1980s to attempt to influence the course of financial restructuring within the Japanese financial markets was 'in an exact sense "critical": it marked a turning point in the history of the Japanese – and therefore the world – financial services revolution. This was not because American power was able to steamroller Japanese opposition, but because American intervention decisively altered the balance between the domestic coalitions formed in the Japanese arguments about reform' (Moran, 1991, p. 111). Moran argues that while the rigidities of the financial system had been steadily eroded by the wider restructuring of the Japanese economy since the early 1970s, 'the complexity of the interests lodged inside the key institutional actors like the multi-bureau MOF and the multi-member industrial trade associations – made the construction of a stable reforming coalition virtually impossible, and caused the process of regulatory change to grind forward in a slow and tortuous way' (Moran, 1991, p. 111).

The process of financial reform within Japan underwent a marked acceleration following the United States' geo-economic offensives, which formed part of a wider strategy to open foreign markets to United States service firms. The geo-economic offensives of the 1980s signalled a remarkable *volte face* in United States sentiment towards Japanese economic development. In the 1950s and for most of the 1960s the United States acted as sponsor and propagator of Japanese economic growth (Nestor, 1990), the most symbolic gesture of this support being the fact that the yen–dollar exchange rate remained unchanged between 1949 and 1971. The offensives of the 1980s were driven by two sets of grievances held by factions within the United States business and political community. First, there was a widespread feeling that Japanese industry was stealing an 'unfair' advantage in international markets through the prevailing yen–dollar exchange rate. The regulatory structure surrounding Japanese financial markets, it was argued, insulated low Japanese interest rates from the rest of the international financial system. The low rates of interest at home encouraged a large outflow of capital seeking higher returns abroad and the exchange of large volumes of yen into foreign currencies for the purpose of foreign investment, which had the further effect of depressing the yen in the foreign exchange markets (Thorn, 1987, p. 29). Out of these grievances emerged a distinctive *macroeconomic* arm of the geo-economic offensive, the objective being to restructure the conditions of credit creation and circulation in Japan, and in particular to bring about a greater integration with the dynamics of the international financial system as a whole. Macroeconomic conditions in Japan would then come into line with those prevailing in the other core capitalist countries.

The second set of grievances revolved around issues of reciprocity and equal access to national markets. Driven by the sentiments that saw the inclusion of services in the Uruguay Round of GATT (McCulloch, 1988), the United States sought to 'open [Japanese] financial markets to the largest American firms, in the conviction that the United States enjoys a comparative advantage over Japan in the financial services sector' (Moran, 1991, p. 109). Out of these grievances there emerged a *structural* arm of the geo-economic offensive, which sought to prise open Japan's domestic markets to foreign competition.

The first stage of this offensive was the opening of the yen–dollar negotiations between the United States Treasury Department and the MOF, culminating in the striking of the 'Yen–Dollar Agreement' in 1984.[7] The agreement considerably advanced the objectives of the structural arm of the geo-economic offensive (Moran, 1991, p. 110). By the end of the 1980s, discussions within the yen–dollar forum had succeeded in transforming a large part of the Japanese financial system:

> When negotiations began, the Japanese capital markets were heavily regulated. Interest rates were largely fixed; short-term money markets were in their infancy; there was little access for foreigners to the domestic bond market. Nor were there any foreign members of the Tokyo stock

7 The definitive account of the negotiations leading to the 'Yen–Dollar Agreement' is provided by Frankel (1984).

> exchange of foreign trust banks. The euroyen market was embryonic. Today [1989], about half of all bank deposits have been deregulated and largely reflect market interest rates. The Bank of Japan has taken an important step towards liberalising the money market. New short-term money market instruments have been introduced. A partial auction system in the government bond market has reduced the role of the traditional Japanese syndicate. Foreign firms have been admitted to the Tokyo stock exchange and entered the trust banking business. In the Euromarkets, the volume of yen offerings has grown 17-fold. (Mulford, 1989, p. 27)

The role of structural regulation was significantly reduced, as prices in the markets increasingly came to be determined by competition rather than by administrative allocation. This greatly improved the possibility of foreign financial institutions in Japan being able to carve out market shares for themselves, with the result that firms began to migrate to Tokyo in ever greater numbers during the 1980s. The macroeconomic objectives of the geo-economic offensive – the greater integration of Japanese financial markets with the international financial system – were to be served by the assertion of market forces and the penetration of the markets by foreign firms, which would increasingly act as conduits for funds entering and leaving the Japanese economy.

However, at the same time that the US authorities were negotiating the liberalization of Japanese financial markets, the chronic deterioration of the US budget and trade positions continued. In response, a new set of geo-economic pressures were placed on Japan, which took on a quite different complection from those that had gone before. In contrast to the bilateral yen–dollar negotiations, the multilateral agreements crafted by the Group of Five (G5) and the Group of Seven (G7) industrial nations, in a series of accords and agreements during the mid-1980s, pressed for Japan to *differentiate* its monetary conditions from the rest of the world economy. By 1985 the United States monetary authorities at last acknowledged the disastrous effects that the 'strong dollar' of the Reagan boom was having upon the international position of the United States economy (Corbridge and Agnew, 1991). In September 1985, under pressure from the United States, the finance minsters of the G5 nations agreed to facilitate a 'managed decline' of the dollar, which through careful intervention within the foreign exchange markets would prevent a decline of the dollar from turning into a collapse (Evans, 1988b). The 'Plaza Agreement', as it became known, had a transforming effect upon the role of Japanese finance within the international financial system. The value of the yen soared, and in a seven-month period increased from ¥240 to ¥170 to the dollar (Sampson, 1989, p. 79). By the beginning of 1988, the yen had appreciated a full 50 per cent to ¥120 to the dollar (Itoh, 1990a, p. 176). The rapid appreciation of the yen – described in Japan as *endaka* – led to a large outflow of Japanese financial capital from 1985 onwards as money flowed out into what had suddenly become much cheaper investments.

The volumes of capital migrating from Japan increased still further from the beginning of 1987 following the striking of the 'Louvre Accord' by the G7 countries. While the Plaza Agreement had succeeded in engineering a realignment of the yen–dollar rate in the foreign exchange markets, the attempt to manage the dollar's decline had seriously destabilized the foreign exchange markets. The signing of the Louvre Accord in February 1987 signalled the willingness of the leading industrial nations to reassert some semblance of order over an increasingly volatile macroeconomic environment. In particular, the Accord attempted to introduce a degree of stability into the foreign exchange markets (Evans, 1988b, pp. 13–14; Thompson, 1990, p. 61). But, if current exchange rate parities were to be maintained for the sake of international monetary order, some other way to redress Japanese–United States imbalances would have to be found. In a flat contradiction of the original macroeconomic goals of the United States' geo-economic offensive, Japan was enjoined by the other G7 nations to hold down interest rates within its financial system below those prevailing elsewhere in order to stimulate the domestic economy. The intention was that this would increase the volume of goods imported into Japan, lowering its trade surplus while at the same time encouraging accumulation within the other core capitalist countries.

These episodes of geo-economic intervention had profound economic implications in both the United States and Japan. While *endaka* secured a short-term improvement in the price competitiveness of United States producers over their Japanese rivals, the effects of which fed through into the trade balance (Hickok, 1989), the depreciation of the dollar against the yen also encouraged large inflows of Japanese money, particularly into property investments in large metropolitan centres in the United States (for example, see Davis, 1987; Warf, 1988; Rose, 1992). The earlier experiment with Keynesian deficit financing in Japan had been abruptly terminated in the wake of the 'second oil shock' of 1979–80, when the downturn at home and abroad meant that the size of the Japanese budget deficit offered the prospect of a severe fiscal crisis. In response the export-orientation of the Japanese economy continued to deepen throughout the early 1980s, especially in the wake of the economic boom in the United States after 1983. By 1984 Japan's exports were valued at a historically high figure of 13.5 per cent of GNP. The rapid rise in the international value of the yen precipitated a sharp fall in the volume of exports, upon which the Japanese economy was becoming increasingly reliant. Between 1985 and 1986 exports fell by 15.6 per cent, while the rate of GDP growth in Japan slowed by 4.7 per cent in 1985 to 2.7 per cent in 1986 (Itoh, 1990a, p. 177). *Endaka* was the stimulus for a marked increase in the volume of productive capacity decentralized from Japan as firms looked to establish new production facilities within markets in North America, Western Europe and South East Asia, thereby overcoming the problems of rapid currency appreciation (Dicken, 1992, p. 176).[8]

Endaka, the structural effects of the Yen–Dollar Agreement and the macroeconomic effects of the Louvre Accord combined to cause a major transformation in the trajectory of capitalist accumulation in Japan. The loosening of administrative control over many areas of the financial system occurred at the same time that the financial authorities were holding down interest rates below international levels to encourage accumulation, which made for a heady and potent brew. There was an explosion of credit creation in the Japanese financial system, which because of the now less restrictive regulatory regime found its way into increasingly speculative investments. As the official discount rate fell to 2.5 per cent in 1987 the money supply, as measured by a range of indicators, increased sharply. Whereas between 1975 and 1984 the total volume of funds intermediated in Japan averaged ¥58.6 trillion per annum, between 1985 and 1990 the comparable figure was ¥122.9 trillion per annum (Kasman and Rodrigues, 1991, p. 32). A further indicator was the scale at which the asset base of banks expanded. Between 1980 and 1990 the asset base of Japan's largest twenty banks increased by over 450 per cent (*The Banker*, 1990). A proportion of this cheap money was exported, but the majority of it found its way into domestic investments. Some of the money found its way into productive investment, but much of the remainder had a transforming effect upon Japan's securities markets.

The weight of newly created money chasing investment outlets drove up the value of Japan's financial markets, making them the largest in the world. At the same time, the re-regulation of the financial structure saw the development of new derivative financial markets in Tokyo, which were used first as hedging instruments against investments in securities, and then as purely speculative investments.[9] The wave of credit creation and financial innovation enabled Japanese productive capital to counter some of the problems created by *endaka*. By turning to the circuit of financial capital for an alternative source of profits many firms were able to overcome the loss of revenues caused by declining sales overseas. This was the era of *zaitech*, during which large Japanese manufacturing

8 Glasmeier and Sugiura (1991, p. 406) reveal that MITI introduced special programmes to help smaller firms deal with the problems of *endaka* and the internationalization of production complexes by giving assistance in moving their production offshore to retain their position in subcontracting networks.

9 A market for Japanese government bond futures was opened in 1985, a market in Nikkei Index futures was opened in 1987 (in Osaka) and a wider range of futures indices, which included Euroyen and Eurodollar interest rate futures, was introduced in 1989 (Hayes and Hubbard, 1990, pp. 175–6).

corporations began to derive large profits from financial activities. *Zai-tech* fund management arose out of the treasury functions of currency, option and futures dealing all transnational corporations undertake to manage financial risk in an increasingly volatile macroeconomic environment. But the plentiful supply of money in Japan enabled Japanese corporations to turn risk management strategies into money-making activities in their own right:

> [In 1987] Toyota . . . produced and exported 10 per cent less than in 1986 yet recorded profits of 180 billion yen of which no less than 160 billion came from trading in financial assets. Nissan converted a substantial operating loss into a small overall profit because of their *zaitech* profits. For the top ten exporters of electrical goods in 1987, the average contribution of money management profits to their total profits was . . . 49 per cent. (Eccleston, 1989, p. 234)

Zaitech profits not only enabled Japanese industrial capital to shrug off the effects of *endaka* but also served to break the dependency and authority relations that had long flowed through the financial system. The improved financial position of manufacturing companies enabled them to go a long way towards wiping out their historical financial deficits by paying off much of their bank-generated debt (Itoh, 1990a, p. 185). Indeed, in the new financial environment there was little need for Japanese corporations to turn to the banks for new cheap credit; this could be generated just as easily by tapping the international debt markets.

The production of such easy money encouraged speculative investments. The fortunes of the Japanese property market in the 1980s bore testament to the increasingly speculative use to which this new money was being put. The value of property in Japan increased by over 200 per cent between 1985 and 1991 (*Fuji Economic Review*, 1991), rapidly appreciating values in an already expensive property market. Between 1982 and 1988 the value of commercial property in Tokyo increased by almost 300 per cent, and by over 65 per cent in 1988 alone. A rash of large property developments saw an increasing volume of bank lending finding its way to the property development sector, so that by 1991 it was estimated that the property sector accounted for 10.6 per cent of total banking lending in Japan (Shreeve, 1992). As their more traditional manufacturing clients increasingly trawled the international financial markets in search of new credit, Japan's banks began to cast about at home in search of borrowers in order to maintain their spectacular rate of asset growth:

> Most of the lending was to the luxury end of the market, such as condominiums, hotels, sports facilities and (a Japanese favourite) golf courses. All normal standards of prudential banking and credit analysis disappeared. . . .

> Salomon Brothers reckon that 20–25% of total city bank loans were made to this speculative market; the Finance Ministry says the figure represents some ¥115 trillion (US$885 billion). Many of the companies were new, greedy, opportunistic, a familiar story of the 1980s. They lent money up to 90% – sometimes even 100% of the inflated value of a property. (Shreeve, 1992, p. 33)

Nevertheless, while the stockmarket and the property market were riding high no one seemed very much to mind. It was this growth in the value and size of financial assets in Japan that propelled more and more banks to the pinnacle of the international banking community, and encouraged the diaspora of banks and securities houses to international financial centres around the world (for example, see Rose, 1992). Once abroad, these institutions began aggressively to carve out market share by cutting margins to the bone, even at the cost of deferring profits, thereby replicating the competitive strategies of Japanese productive capital. The invincibility of Japanese financial power seemed confirmed in October 1987 when Tokyo remained relatively untouched by the global stockmarket crash, as concerted and coordinated action by the large securities houses, under the direction of the Ministry of Finance, served to prop up a market that all but collapsed in other financial centres (Alletzhauser, 1990). However, this gilded era for Japanese finance was shortly to come to an end and the era of cheap money was drawn to a close from 1989 onwards.

Ending the Money Boom

As the 1980s came to an end, asset price inflation began to take its toll on the Japanese economy. By 1990 inflation had risen to 3.9 per cent, its highest level for nine years. Inflation was not the only problem generated by the boom of the late 1980s. There was also a marked increase in social polarization (Sassen, 1991). Differential increases in levels of remuneration and rapid increases in the value of residential property – by the end of the 1980s, the average cost of residential property in Tokyo cost 10–12 times average salaries (Wagstyl and Thomson, 1990) – saw the flattened social structure of Japanese society, a product of the social restructuring undertaken during the occupation, begin to be extended as wealth became increasingly polarized. The emergence of a highly visible cohort of 'new rich' (Morioka, 1989; Itoh, 1990b)[10] was accompanied by the emergence within Japan of a growing underclass, made up almost

10 Occupational polarization was also coincident with a widening of gender differentials within the labour market. Most female employees remained located in clerical jobs and were expected to 'retire' on marriage. This stark level of labour market segregation ensured that even by the late 1980s average female earnings were only 52 per cent of average male earnings (Tasker, 1989, p. 120).

entirely of foreign immigrants, mostly of Korean and South East Asian extraction, who were allocated jobs at the lower end of the occupational hierarchy, mainly in menial service activities (Mammen, 1988; Sassen, 1991). By the late 1980s the growing polarization of Japanese society began to generate grave concerns within the Japanese bureaucracy. In 1990 a MITI report singled out the cleavage between property owners and non-owners as perhaps the most critical social problem facing Japan in the 1990s, with the force to generate divisive tensions strong enough to unravel the cooperative basis of society upon which Japan's postwar revival had in large part been founded (Thomson, 1990).

However, the critical bureaucratic intervention in the credit surge was made one year earlier. The Bank of Japan began to raise interest rates at the beginning of 1989, and they then moved upwards four more times in a fifteen-month period. By August 1991 the official discount rate had been raised to 6 per cent, compared to the rate of 2.5 per cent which had prevailed between 1987 and 1988.[11] This sudden appreciation in the cost of money served to burst the speculative bubble of the late 1980s, and marked an important moment in recent Japanese economic history, for three reasons in particular. First, it would appear that while raising the discount rate was justified by the rise in inflation, the tightening of monetary conditions was also driven by a wish to 'discipline' financial actors who were interpreted to be damaging the long-term economic competitiveness of the Japanese economy. Yasushi Mieno, governor of the Bank of Japan, argued that companies participating in financial markets had to recognize that values could 'move in two directions' (Thomson, 1991c), that is down as well as up. Money that had long been channelled into industrial investments was increasingly being channelled into investment vehicles of 'non-productive' and of 'fictitious' value. The growing integration of manufacturing companies with the circuit of financial capital was also seen to hold long-term dangers for the productive strength of the Japanese economy. The sentiment has been pointedly summarized by McCarthy (1992, p. 15): 'Japan . . . had its fling in the financial markets, but it [was] time to get back to what Japan is really good at – manufacturing.'

Second, the episode revealed how far the operation of the Japanese financial system had come to resemble that of other core capitalist countries. Formerly, the MOF and the BOJ would have attempted to control monetary aggregates through the use of structural regulation and moral suasion within the financial community. By the late 1980s the monetary authorities were now reliant upon the rather crude tool of interest rates as the principle mechanism of monetary policy (Kasman and Rodrigues, 1991, p. 20).

11   But note that in July 1991 the rate was subsequently lowered to 5.5 per cent and then to 5.0 per cent in November 1991 (*Fuji Economic Review*, 1992, p. 16).

Third, the raising of interest rates broke with the conditions of the Louvre Accord and as such represented an act of defiance by the Japanese authorities in the face of United States geo-economic pressure, and undermined the endeavours of the G7 to manage change within the international monetary and trade arenas. The new regime of expensive money slowed accumulation within the Japanese economy and stemmed the flow of imported goods into the country, while at the same time encouraging Japanese corporations to redouble their efforts within international markets. It was hardly surprising, therefore, that 1991 saw the Japanese trade surplus increase after four years of continuous decline (Thomson, 1992), precipitating a new round of United States and Japanese 'trade friction' (El-Agraa, 1988).

The ending of the era of cheap money was also to have severe consequences for Japanese financial capital. The regime of more expensive money generated what the Bank for International Settlements has described as a 'triple decline' in Japanese financial markets (Bank for International Settlements, 1991, p. 122). The decline in share prices was predictable, as the higher cost of money deterred further investment in securities with very high price–earnings ratios. However, the decline in the value of the Nikkei was such – a 40 per cent decline between January and September 1990 (Thomson, 1992) – that the stability of the whole financial system was severely shaken. The bond market also declined precipitously, as higher interest rates deterred new bond issuance, while the low rates of interest attached to extant bonds made them much less attractive as investment vehicles. The third element of the triple decline was the fall in the value of the yen in the foreign exchange markets, which reflected the wider financial turbulence in Japanese financial markets.

However, securities markets and the value of the yen were not the only phenomena to suffer a reversal of fortune. The new regime of more expensive money also took the sheen off property investments. Property in Japan traditionally generates a 3 per cent yield on investment; with interest rates at 6 per cent investments began to produce negative cash flows (Shreeve, 1992, p. 34). The volume of transactions in the market fell precipitously. In the six months to March 1991 an index of land prices in Japan's largest six cities fell by two points, the first decline recorded since 1975 (*Fuji Economic Review*, 1991). The problems caused by declining property values were exacerbated by the growing financial difficulties of Japanese financial institutions, many of which constituted an important part of the demand for commercial property. The declining values and falling turnover on the Tokyo Stock Exchange began to eat into the profitability of the securities houses, which had grown rich in the boom of the late 1980s. The commercial banks too began to suffer a precipitous decline in profitability. In consequence, much of the credit extended to the property sector began to turn bad, as did the other more speculative credits extended to other parts of the economy during the regime of cheap money. By 1991 it was estimated that between them the long-term credit banks, the commercial banks and the trust banks had accumulated ¥7,334 billion worth of bad debts (*Financial Times*, 1992). While problem debts were concentrated within the long-term credit and trust banks, the close links between financial institutions within different parts of the financial system ensured that the draining effects of the bad debts were disseminated through the financial system as a whole.[12] While this had the advantage of diffusing systemic risk, it also ensured that all financial institutions became implicated in a debt workout ranging across the entire financial system. Taking into consideration the wider changes in the organization of the Japanese financial system that occurred during the 1980s, the trajectory of Japanese financial capital in the 1990s is likely to be very different from what has gone before.

Conclusions

The rupturing of the structural organization of the Japanese financial system in the 1970s and 1980s served to erode its distinctiveness and has ensured its greater integration with the wider international financial system. This is likely to have a number of important implications for capitalist accumulation, not only within Japan but also within the wider world economy. Three developments are likely to be of particular significance.

First, the collapse of Japanese financial markets in the period after 1989 combined with the introduction of new multinational financial regulation to drain the financial system of the capacity readily to create new credit. New capital adequacy regulations imposed by the Bank for International Settlements (BIS) require that the total value of reserve capital should equal 8 per cent of bank assets (loans). These regulations, which were ostensibly introduced to reduce the level of systemic risk

12 It should be recognized, however, that the risk was also diversified among a large number of separate property developers and property brokers, of which there are up to 46,000 in Japan. Moreover, it has been estimated that only 10 per cent of urban land in Japan was turned over in property transactions between 1986 and 1990, and that the total volume of money estimated to have been lent to property companies comprises only 1.5 per cent of the total value of property in Japan (Wagstyl, 1991).

13 However, as Underhill (1991) reminds us, the process by which the BIS standards were arrived at was not insulated from the imperatives of the new geo-economic struggle. The capital–asset ratios finally agreed upon by the BIS were those originally proposed by Anglo-American regulators, which resulted in ratios being set at a level low enough not to favour German banks, which have long operated with relatively high capital–asset ratios, but high enough to force Japanese banks, which tended to operate with low capital–asset ratios, to submit to extensive asset reductions.

within the international financial system as a whole, would under normal circumstances have necessitated some adjustment within the Japanese banking system, where reserve requirements have traditionally been much lower than 8 per cent.[13] The financial crisis of the early 1990s necessitated an even more dramatic process of restructuring. The long-term shareholdings held by the banks constitute an important part of their capital base. Indeed, Japanese banks were allowed to use up to 45 per cent of the unrealized gains on their shareholdings as a contribution towards their reserve requirements. The sharp decline in the Nikkei revealed the fictitious nature of the value contained within these shareholdings.

The impact of the value of the stockmarket upon the ability of the banks to meet the BIS regulations is illustrated in table 6.3. On 16 March 1992, the Nikkei average fell below 20,000 for the first time since 1987, effectively eroding the capital base of many of the commercial banks. By the beginning of April 1992, the Nikkei had fallen to below 18,300. The decline of the Nikkei below levels at which the banks could cover their reserve requirements forced banks to begin 'shrinking' their assets; that is, selling off loans as securitized financial instruments within derivative financial markets (Corrigan and Waters, 1991). This development not only deepened the securitization of the Japanese financial markets but also sharply revealed the difficulties Japanese banks have in generating new credit.

The implications of this brake on new credit are likely to be rather more severe within the international arena than at home. Any new lending that the banks do make in this new environment is likely to be to

Table 6.3 Relationship between the Nikkei and Bank for International Settlements capital adequacy ratios

Nikkei average:	18,500	19,500	20,500	21,500	22,500	23,500	24,500
Bank			*Capital–asset ratios (%)*				
Dai-Ichi Kangyo	7.21	7.41	7.61	7.80	8.00	8.20	8.40
Mitsui Taiyo Kobe	7.06	7.30	7.35	7.35	7.35	7.35	7.35
Sumitomo	7.61	7.79	7.96	8.14	8.31	8.48	8.66
Fuji	7.51	7.70	7.90	8.09	8.28	8.48	8.67
Mitsubishi	7.39	7.59	7.80	8.01	8.21	8.42	8.63
Sanwa	6.99	7.19	7.39	7.59	7.79	7.99	8.18
Tokai	7.50	7.73	7.96	8.05	8.05	8.05	8.05
Daiwa	7.42	7.71	8.00	8.29	8.58	8.87	8.93
Hokkaido Takushoku	8.25	8.46	8.67	8.74	8.74	8.74	8.74
Bank of Tokyo	6.85	7.01	7.17	7.33	7.49	7.65	7.81
Kyowa Saitama	7.56	7.79	8.01	8.24	8.47	8.69	8.92
Average	7.40	7.61	7.80	8.97	8.12	8.26	8.39

Source: Alexander, 1992.

Japanese borrowers (Thomson, 1991a). The re-concentration of funds within Japan abruptly brought to an end the large outflows of capital that had characterized the 1980s. For the first time since 1980 Japan's long-term capital account in the first half of 1991 was in surplus, by as much as $7.78 billion (Butler, 1991). This repatriation of money served to deflate many international financial markets in the early 1990s.

The sudden withdrawal of international liquidity brings us to the second implication of the restructuring of the Japanese financial system: the generation of a savings shortage in Japan. The principal role of the strong system of structural regulation within Japan was to separate savers from borrowers, so that the bureaucracies of the state could intervene within the intermediation process in order to channel investments into productive uses. At the same time, structural regulation served to limit the amount of credit made available to individuals for fear that this would eat into savings and into the volume of money channelled into industrial investments. However, the loosening of controls on credit in the Japanese financial system saw a dramatic increase in the availability of personal credit, so that the level of household indebtedness rose significantly between 1975 and 1989, from 45 per cent to 92 per cent of disposable income (table 6.4). This inevitably has implications for the amount of savings that can be channelled into industrial investments in the future.

Third, and finally, the restructuring of the Japanese financial system has wrought great changes in the organization of Japanese capitalism itself. The legacy of the flirtation with *zaitech* is potentially damaging for Japanese productive capital. More than one company has collapsed under the weight of *zaitech*-generated debts, while many others have sown the seeds of crippling debt repayments in years ahead. For example, the warrant-bond market, which was eagerly tapped by Japanese corporations during the 1980s, generated cheap credit only when share prices were rising. The fall in share prices after 1989 meant that investors in the bonds were more likely to exercise their right to demand full repayment rather than, as previously, swap the repayments for equity

Table 6.4 Household indebtedness in selected countries, 1975–1989

Country	Debt as a percentage of disposable income			
	1975	1980	1985	1989
Japan	45	58	68	92
USA	67	77	83	96
Germany	62	76	88	87
UK	47	48	76	105
Canada	77	85	73	87

Source: Bank for International Settlements, 1991, p. 107.

in the borrowing company. It was estimated that the redemption of warrant bonds would cost Japanese companies US $154 billion in the three years to 1995 (Corrigan, 1991). Although the intervention of the MOF to push interest rates higher can be seen as a bid to restrain the excesses of the financial boom of the 1980s, by the 1990s financial capital in Japan was much less amenable to being subverted to productivist goals. The internationalization of Japanese financial capital was often accompanied by the adoption of a more independent, *rentier* orientation towards lending, as has been noted by Tickell (1992) in the case of Japanese banks based in the United Kingdom. There are early signs of a growing schism developing between productive and financial capitalism at home. In particular, the pressures of meeting the BIS capital adequacy ratios have forced a number of commercial banks to divest some of their long-term shareholdings in order to use the receipts of the sales to shore up their capital (McCauley and Zimmer, 1991). The growing number of 'free-floating' shares circulating within the Japanese equity market would perhaps support Thorn's contention that the unity of the business groups in Japan has undergone a marked decline (Thorn, 1987, p. 20).

However, it would be a mistake to underestimate the residual value and power of the business groupings within Japanese capitalism. The selling of long-term shareholdings has occurred as a result of exceptional external regulatory pressures upon Japanese financial capital, and does not represent a concerted bid to break down the system of long-term shareholdings. While the ability of the Japanese financial system to produce cheap intermediated credit has been undermined through processes of re-regulation and internationalization, as the Japanese financial system has been integrated into the international financial system as a whole, the prevailing structure of long-term shareholdings still confers upon Japanese firms significant savings in the raising of capital through the equity market (McCauley and Zimmer, 1991, p. 17). Moreover, it is these long-term shareholdings that continue to confer upon Japanese productive capital the ability to engage in strategies of competitive innovation on a long-term basis, and as such they serve as the linchpin to the long-term international competitiveness of Japanese firms.

It was perhaps not surprising, therefore, that the last of the United States geo-economic offensives of the 1980s, the Structural Impediments Initiative (SII), should explicitly target the business groupings as the phenomena that above all else conferred an 'unfair' competitive advantage upon Japanese capital. In a review of the progress of the SII talks, which began in 1989, US officials argued that the business groupings served to 'foster preferential group trade and anti-competitive activity, and impede foreign direct investment' (Thomson, 1991b, p. 5). Significantly, the US report remarked upon the 'problems' of cross-shareholdings. Clearly, the United States would like to sever the institutional link between financial and productive capital within the Japanese economy in the hope of undermining the competitive strength of Japanese capitalism as a whole. One cannot but notice the irony within this latest offensive. Not only did the hasty repeal of the anti-trust regulation by the occupation authorities of the United States on geopolitical grounds open the way for the formation of the business groupings but, given the recent economic histories of the two countries, the United States would surely do better not to try to make Japanese financial capital more like its own, but to make United States financial capitalism more like that of the Japanese. Whatever the outcome, the United States' continuing bid to remake Japanese financial capital is certain to have long-term implications not only for Japanese capitalism but also for the entire world economy.

Coda

After months in which they had appeared blind to the threat posed by falling share prices and an increasingly dismal stream of economic news, the [Japanese] government has acted to halt the deepening crisis in the domestic markets. At least for the time being. The government's overall Y10,700bn (£43bn) fiscal package . . . will increase public spending by an amount equivalent to building five Channel tunnels and extending London's Jubilee underground line with the spare change. Salomon Brothers, an investment bank, estimates that the programme will add Y7,600bn to aggregate demand, and boost gross national product by 1.66 per cent. (Butler, 1992)

References

Adams, T. F. M. and Hoshii, I. (1972) *A Financial History of the New Japan*. Tokyo: Kodansha International.

Alexander, J. (1992) Welcome to hard times. *The Banker*, January, 40–3.

Alletzhauser, A. (1990) *The House of Nomura*. London: Bloomsbury.

Amin, S. (1976) *Unequal Development: an Essay on the Social Formations of Peripheral Capitalism*. Hassock, Sussex: Harvester Press.

Anderson, P. (1987) The figures of descent. *New Left Review*, 161, 20–77.

Banker (1990) The top 100. *The Banker*, July.

Bank for International Settlements (1991) *61st Annual Report*. Basle: Bank for International Settlements.

Best, M. (1990) *The New Competition*. Cambridge: Polity Press.

Bond, P. (1990) The new US class struggle: financial industry power vs. grassroots populism. *Capital and Class*, 40, 150–81.

Boss, H. (1990) *Theories of Surplus and Transfer: Parasites and Producers in Economic Thought*. London: Unwin Hyman.

Butler, S. (1991) Reversing the flow of funds from Japan. *Financial Times*, 2 September.

Butler, S. (1992) Little cause for comfort. *Financial Times*, 1 September.

Christopherson, S. (1992) How the state and the market are remaking the landscape of inequality. Department of City and Regional Planning, Cornell University, Ithaca, NY (mimeo).

Clark, G. (1989) Remaking the map of corporate capitalism: the arbitrage economy of the 1990s. *Environment and Planning A*, 21, 997–1000.

Cohen, T. (1987) *Remaking Japan*. New York: Macmillan.

Corbridge, S. and Agnew, J. (1991) The US trade and budget deficits in global perspective: an essay in geopolitical-economy. *Environment and Planning D: Society and Space*, 9, 71–90.

Corrigan, T. (1991) Out of the money, into a problem. *Financial Times*, 20 February.

Corrigan, T. and Waters, R. (1991) Japan turns to securitization. *Financial Times*, 20 March.

Davis, M. (1987) Chinatown part two? The internationalization of downtown Los Angeles. *New Left Review*, 164, 65–86.

Dicken, P. (1992) *Global Shift: the Internationalization of Economic Activity*, 2nd edn. London: Paul Chapman.

Dore, R. (1986) *Flexible Rigidities: Industrial Policy and Structural Adjustment in the Japanese Economy, 1970–80*. London: Athlone.

Dore, R. (1987) *Taking Japan Seriously: a Confucian Perspective on Leading Economic Issues*. London: Athlone.

Eccleston, B. (1986) The state, finance and industry in Japan. In A. Cox (ed.), *State, Finance and Industry*. Hemel Hempstead: Harvester Wheatsheaf, 60–79.

Eccleston, B. (1989) *State and Society in Post-war Japan*. Cambridge: Polity Press.

Economist (1988) A survey of Japanese finance. *The Economist*, 10 December.

El-Agraa, A. (1988) *Japan's Trade Frictions: Realities or Misconceptions?* London: Macmillan.

Evans, T. (1988a) Money makes the world go around. In L. Harris, J. Coakley, M. Croasdale and T. Evans (eds), *New Perspectives on the Financial System*. London: Croom Helm, 41–68.

Evans, T. (1988b) Dollar is likely to rise, fall or stay steady experts agree. *Capital and Class*, 32, 10–15.

Financial Times (1992) Survey: Japanese financial markets. *Financial Times*, 27 March.

Frankel, J. A. (1984) *The Yen/Dollar Agreement: Liberalizing Japanese Capital Markets*, Policy Analyses in International Economics, No. 9. Washington, DC: Institute for International Economics.

Fuji Economic Review (1991) Land prices undergo a correction. *Fuji Economic Review*, September–October, 8–11.

Fuji Economic Review (1992) Statistical tables. *Fuji Economic Review*, January–February, 14–16.

Gill, S. and Law, D. (1989) Global hegemony and the structural power of capital. *International Studies Quarterly*, 33, 476–99.

Glasmeier, A. and Sugiura, N. (1991) Japan's manufacturing system: small business, subcontracting and regional complex formation. *International Journal of Urban and Regional Research*, 15, 395–414.

Goldsmith, R. W. (1983) *The Financial Development of Japan, 1868–1977*. New Haven and London: Yale University Press.

Hadley, E. (1989) The diffusion of Keynesian ideas in Japan. In P. Hall (ed.), *The Political Power of Economic Ideas: Keynesianism Across Nations.* Princeton, NJ: Princeton University Press, 291–309.

Harvey, D. (1989) *The Condition of Postmodernity: an Enquiry into the Origins of Cultural Change.* Oxford: Blackwell.

Hayes, S. L. and Hubbard, P. M. (1990) *Investment Banking: a Tale of Three Cities.* Boston, MA: Harvard Business School.

Haynes, S. E., Hutchison, M. M. and Mikesell, R. F. (1986) *Japanese Financial Policies and the Trade Deficit*, Essays in International Finance, No. 162. Princeton, NY: International Finance Section, Department of Economics, Princeton University.

Hickok, S. (1989) Japanese trade balance adjustment to yen appreciation. *Federal Reserve Bank of New York Quarterly Review*, 14(3), 33–47.

Hübner, K. (1991) Flexibilization and autonomization of world money markets: obstacles for a new long expansion? In B. Jessop et al. (eds), *The Politics of Flexibility.* Aldershot: Edward Elgar, 50–66.

Ingham, G. (1984) *Capitalism Divided? The City and Industry in British Social Development.* London: Macmillan.

Itoh, M. (1990a) *The World Economic Crisis and Japanese Capitalism.* London: Macmillan.

Ioth, M. (1990b) The Japanese model of post-Fordism. Paper presented at Pathways to Industrialization and Regional Development in the 1990s, Lake Arrowhead Conference Centre, University of California, Los Angeles (UCLA), 14–18 March.

Kasman, B. and Rodrigues, A. P. (1991) Financial liberalization and monetary control in Japan. *Federal Reserve Bank of New York Quarterly Review*, 16(3), 28–46.

Leyshon, A. (1990) Review essay: the United States in the world economy. *Environment and Planning A*, 22, 1267–74.

Leyshon, A. (1992) The transformation of regulatory order: regulating the global economy and environment. *Geoforum*, 23, 249–67.

Leyshon, A. and Thrift, N. (1992) Liberalisation and consolidation: the Single European Market and the remaking of European financial capital. *Environment and Planning A*, 24, 49–81.

McCarthy, T. (1992) How Japan works off its hangover. *The Independent on Sunday*, 23 February.

McCulloch, R. (1988) International competition in services. In M. Feldstein (ed.), *The United States in the World Economy.* Chicago: NBER, 367–406.

McCauley, R. N. and Zimmer, S. A. (1991) The cost of capital for securities firms in the United States and Japan. *Federal Reserve Board of New York Quarterly Review*, 16(3), 14–27.

Mammen, D. (1988) *Making Tokyo World City.* Report to the National Institute for Research Advancement, New York, Institute of Public Administration.

Matsumoto, K. (1992) *The Rise of the Japanese Corporate System: the Inside View of a MITI Official.* London: Kegan Paul International.

Minsky, H. P. (1989) Financial crises and the evolution of capitalism: the crash of '87 – what does it mean? In M. Gottdiener and N. Koninos (eds), *Capitalist Development and Crisis Theory: Accumulation, Regulation and Spatial Restructuring.* New York: St Martins Press, 391–403.

Monroe, W. F. (1973) *Japan; Financial Markets and the World Economy*. New York: Praeger, 134–5.

Moran, M. (1991) *The Politics of the Financial Services Revolution: the USA, UK and Japan*. London: Macmillan.

Morioka, K. (1989) Japan. In T. Bottomore and R. Brym (eds), *The Capitalist Class: an International Study*. London: Harvester Wheatsheaf, 140–76.

Mulford, D. (1989) Needed: bolder steps towards freer access. *Financial Times*, 29 November.

Nestor, W. (1990) *Japan's Growing Power over East Asia and the World Economy*. London: Macmillan.

Parboni, R. (1981) *The Dollar and Its Rivals: Recession, Inflation and International Finance*. London: Verso.

Parboni, R. (1986) The dollar weapon: from Nixon to Reagan. *New Left Review*, 15, 5–18.

Rose, P. S. (1992) *Japanese Banking and Investment in the United States: an Assessment of Their Impacts upon US Markets and Institutions*. New York: Quorom.

Sampson, A. (1989) *The Midas Touch: Money, People and Power from East to West*. London: Hodder and Stoughton.

Sassen, S. (1991) *The Global City: New York, London, Tokyo*. Princeton, NJ: Princeton University Press.

Scott, J. (1986) *Capitalist Property and Financial Power: a Comparative Study of Britain, the United States and Japan*. London: Wheatsheaf.

Shreeve, G. (1992) The price of success. *The Banker*, January, 33–8.

Suzuki, Y. (ed.) (1987) *The Japanese Financial System*. Oxford: Clarendon Press.

Tamaki, N. (1990) The Yokohama Specie Bank: a multinational in the Japanese interest, 1879–1931. In G. Jones (ed.), *Banks as Multinationals*. London: Routledge, 191–216.

Thompson, G. (1990) Monetary policy and international finance. In B. Hindess (ed.), *Reactions to the Right*. London: Routledge, 50–77.

Thomson, R. (1990) Japan's reservoir loses its depth. *Financial Times*, 21 September.

Thomson, R. (1991a) Regional banks return to basics. *Financial Times*, 21 February.

Thomson, R. (1991b) Talking gets tough in Japan trade debate. *Financial Times*, 24 April.

Thomson, R. (1991c) Japan may see changes to securities industry. *Financial Times*, 25 June.

Thomson, R. (1992) Japan's trade surplus up 50 per cent. *Financial Times*, 29 January.

Thorn, R. S. (1987) *The Rising Yen: the Impact of Japanese Financial Liberalization on World Capital Markets*. Singapore: Institute of South East Asian Studies.

Thrift, N. J. (1990) The perils of the international financial system. *Environment and Planning A*, 22, 1135–6.

Tickell, A. (1992) Banking on Britain? The role of Japanese banks in the British economy. Paper presented to the Annual Conference of the Institute of British Geographers, University College of Swansea, 7–10 January.

Underhill, G. R. D. (1991) Markets beyond politics? The state and the internationalisation of financial markets. *European Journal of Political Research*, 19, 197–225.

Wagstyl, S. (1991) Japan's banks offer property lifeline. *Financial Times*, 10 April.

Wagstyl, S. and Thomson, R. (1990) Sums of the rising land. *Financial Times*, 3 October.

Warf, B. (1988) Japanese investments in the New York metropolitan region. *The Geographical Review*, 78, 257–71.

Zysman, J. (1983) *Governments, Markets and Growth: Financial Systems and the Politics of Industrial Change*. Oxford: Martin Robertson.

Part II

Money, States and Markets

7

European Monetary Integration and the Distribution of Credit Availability

Sheila C. Dow

Introduction

The international monetary system in Europe is undergoing a process of change, induced partly by market forces and partly by the political programme of monetary integration. This programme, as set out in the Delors Report, is designed to remove national barriers from the financial system in Europe: barriers in the form of national exchange rate policies, national exchange controls on capital flows, national monetary policies and ultimately national central banks and national currencies. The aim is thus to create within Europe the equivalent monetary arrangements to those within any of the constituent states.

It is the purpose of this chapter to consider the implications of this process for the different members of the European Community, as nations and in terms of their constituent regions. Ultimately, economists are concerned with the implications of any development for output and employment, as indicators of welfare. So some consideration must be given, before addressing the issue at hand, to how money is relevant to output and employment. Private sector output and employment in an economy result from the decision-making of firms with respect to that economy: whether to set up a plant in that economy, or buy an existing one; how much to invest in expanding capacity; how much output, and of what sort, to produce; and how much labour to employ. (The structure of decision-making may also be affected by decisions with respect to merger, takeover and bankruptcy.) These decisions have an inherently monetary element, not least because a dominant goal of firms is to accumulate monetary profit. Not only do firms have the alternative of producing the output elsewhere, they can also choose not to produce (or

The author acknowledges the helpful comments and suggestions made on this chapter by Philip Arestis, Victoria Chick, Ronald Shone and the editors.

invest in increased production) at all. If the firm then has unused financial capacity, there is the alternative of buying financial assets. Otherwise the firm chooses not to incur debt. These decisions in turn are influenced by the financial choices made by households (how much to spend, how to allocate savings) and by financial institutions (how much to lend, under what terms and to whom).

The role of financial behaviour and the institutions governing it is thus complex, and interwoven with the 'real' side of the economy. Here we will put the spotlight on the 'bottom line' of this complex interaction, where money is seen at its most significant: the availability or otherwise of credit. The power of financial institutions is most evident in the decision on credit availability, which may constrain firms' output and employment plans. While this is conventionally discussed in the literature in terms of transactions costs and objective risk assessment by banks (see e.g. Stiglitz and Weiss, 1981), I will consider here the possibility that credit allocation has significant systematic elements. The ultimate concern here, therefore, is to consider whether and in what way particular types of borrowers in particular types of regional and national economy might find credit availability changed by financial integration of the sort being envisaged for Europe.

In the next section, some background is provided in an outline of the main features of the process of financial integration in Europe. This is followed by an outline of the conventional economic analysis of monetary integration, which focuses on the power of central banks to determine growth in the money supply, which in turn is seen as determining the domestic rate of inflation and thus international competitiveness. This account is representative of the bulk of the economics literature on monetary integration. The third section shifts the focus by questioning the ability of central banks to control the money supply, and questions the causal role of money with respect to inflation. An alternative framework for analysis is put forward, which focuses on the increasing power of the private-sector financial system to determine credit creation. This framework is elaborated with respect to monetary integration in Europe, and conclusions are drawn for the implications for the regional distributional aspects of credit creation.

The Path to Monetary Unification

In this section, a brief account is given of the process by which monetary unification in Europe is being approached. The first major concrete step towards monetary unification was taken in 1979, when the European Monetary System (EMS) was launched to maintain relative fixity between European exchange rates. A system of assigning responsibility for keeping currencies within set margins was agreed upon (the Exchange

Rate Mechanism, or ERM). A pool of foreign exchange reserves was established at the EC level to provide temporary support for currencies approaching the margins. The ecu was introduced as a new unit of account for defining these foreign exchange margins, and also for inter-governmental transactions within the EC. But, since its value is determined by the value of a weighted 'basket' of EC currencies, the ecu is not a monetary standard external to the EC. Other currencies, most notably the US dollar, provide the only external standard. While the ecu is not legal tender, its increasing use as a unit of account in private sector transactions has *de facto* transformed it into a means of payment (in the form of cheques drawn on ecu-denominated bank accounts, for example).

In the meantime, steps have been taken to promote economic (as opposed to monetary) union, notably harmonization of taxes and subsidies, and reduction of other barriers to intra-EC trade (see Commission of the European Communities, 1985). The aim is that goods and services, labour and capital will all flow freely on equal terms throughout the EC. A unified regulatory environment is envisaged, commonly referred to as a 'level playing field' on which the market players will compete. Increased competition in markets for goods and services will, it is hoped, generate efficiency gains.

As this economic integration has progressed, the need has become increasingly apparent for policy coordination to ensure balanced developments in the constituent economies. In particular, differing rates of inflation cannot be sustained with fixed exchange rates when the foreign sector in each member country is being exposed to increasing competition. Similarly, differing rates of growth of aggregate demand, which spill over into differing rates of growth of export demand, may also put pressure on some currencies. Exchange controls have provided some protection for the currencies of economies choosing more inflationary and/or more expansionary policies.

The phasing out of exchange controls is part of the remaining process of monetary unification (see Commission for the European Communities, 1988). Then the increasing cooperation over national monetary policy will become institutionalized in a European central banking arrangement. This has been a matter for recent negotiation. The possibilities ranged from a body to supervise the operation of the ERM, through a formal mechanism to coordinate national monetary policy, to a fully fledged European central bank independent of direct influence by national governments, and possibly even by government at the EC level. Much depended on whether or not national currencies continued to coexist with the ecu. The aim was to transform the ecu into a fully fledged currency that would be legal tender throughout the EC; some form of European central bank would be required to take responsibility for the ecu. The power and influence of this bank in relation to national central banks would be enhanced by the increasing integration of product and factor markets within the EC. But it would be limited if national currencies continued to circulate. Then there would always be at least one national currency that would be stronger than the ecu (since the ecu's value is roughly an average of national currencies); if at least one currency was persistently the strongest, then the attractiveness of the ecu as a store of value would be limited, and the power of the European central bank would wane relative to that of the country issuing the strongest currency. On the other hand the ecu would hold sway if the identity of the strongest currency changed frequently. The outcome of the Maastricht summit was a treaty that specified an independent central banking system consisting of a European System of Central Banks, made up from national central banks and a European central bank, i.e. the most radical of the possibilities noted above.

Maastricht also specified convergence conditions that must be satisfied before transition to full monetary union can be effected. The conditions refer to convergence of inflation, exchange rates and interest rates, and limitations on budgetary deficits; EMU *could* in principle still go ahead with divergent unemployment and economic growth, although such real divergence might in practice erode the political will to proceed. Thus, if the process of monetary integration increases regional and national disparities, the process itself will be impeded. Even if the divergence resulted from EMU after it was introduced, the resulting inter-EC balance of payments problems could make EMU unsustainable.

Whether or not monetary unification involves an exclusive common currency, it does involve a common monetary standard, and ultimately a unified banking system. The importance of distinguishing these features has been stressed by Chick (1991). She points out that not even all national financial systems have all of these features. The USA is an important counter-example, given the frequent references to monetary unification in Europe creating a 'United States of Europe'. The US dollar is based only on a very fragile monetary standard. The dollar is no longer tied to gold. The 'outside money' that underwrites the US banking system is the confidence held in the monetary authorities to ensure prudent financial behaviour and in the taxing power of government. Both of these are currently subject to scrutiny. A relatively high incidence of failure, particularly among state savings and loan companies, has raised concern about the adequacy of supervision, particularly as the financial system is undergoing structural adjustment as a result of de-regulation. Further, given the inadequacy of deposit insurance to cope with the scale of failures, general revenues have been devoted to meeting liabilities of failed institutions, raising concern about the fiscal health of the federal government.

In Europe too, in the absence of an outside monetary standard other than the dollar, confidence in the banking system will depend on the effectiveness of bank supervision and the capacity of the public sector to draw on fiscal resources. At a time of regulatory change as national financial markets are opened up to each other, and at a time of evolution in intergovernmental cooperation, confidence in the European banking system will be put to a severe test. Further, with respect to distributional considerations, it should be noted that even a long-standing national state like the USA does not have a unified banking system (although deregulation is breaking down state barriers to banking). Thus even if Europe becomes a common currency area, financial integration will depend on the degree to which national barriers to flows of finance and financial services are broken down; it is already clear that this had not been achieved by the target date of 1992.

In what follows I will focus on the implications of the aim of creating a perfect capital market in Europe (i.e. one with no barriers to capital flows), and consider whether there might be a case for challenging that aim. The aim is currently being pursued on the basis of conventional economic analysis of the beneficial implications of perfect capital markets. This analysis is outlined in the next section.

Mainstream Economic Analysis

Conventional economic analysis of monetary integration in Europe is conducted within a balance of payments framework with the presumption that balance of payments relations are always either in equilibrium or approaching equilibrium. The balance of payments can be represented by the following identity:

$$(X - IM) + (NKF) = \Delta R$$

where X is exports of goods and services and transfers in; IM is imports of goods and services and transfers out; NKF is net capital inflows; and ΔR is change in official foreign exchange reserves. $X - IM$ is then the current account and NKF the capital account. NKF is made up of short-term capital flows (resulting from portfolio adjustments, often resulting from foreign exchange speculation) and long-term capital flows (consisting of adjustment of long-term portfolios and of direct investment). In a unified currency area, where there is no need for foreign exchange reserves, the current and capital accounts must balance each other. They do not each need to balance to zero: net imports can be financed by net capital inflows. Such a situation would be characterized by a preference for spending over saving that was satisfied by inflows of net saving from elsewhere, i.e. it reflects preferences. These preferences, and thus these relationships, can be manipulated within a segmented national economy by the following measures:

1   Depreciating the domestic currency to make exports more competitive, to increase $(X - IM)$.
2   Reducing domestic monetary growth to reduce domestic inflation and thus increase competitiveness.
3   Imposing exchange controls and/or trade barriers to alter incentives with respect to capital and trade flows respectively.
4   Reducing the budgetary deficit to increase the volume of domestic saving available to finance domestic expenditure.

Monetary unification with a single currency would remove all but the fiscal measure (4) from the power of national governments and even then Maastricht seeks to limit the relative size of fiscal deficits. The balance of payments would then revert to the pattern determined by the free play of private sector preferences. Increased net imports, for example (possibly owing to a falling behind in international competitiveness), might not be financed by borrowing elsewhere, and would have to be curtailed in the same way as in subnational regions. The adjustment process would be automatic in the sense that curtailed capital inflows relative to current account spending would constitute a drain on the domestic money supply, which would in turn reduce domestic expenditure and thus prices. To the extent that the effect on prices operated with a lag, there might in the short-run be a fall in output and a rise in unemployment. But the costs involved are likely to be transitional, until unification is achieved with the harmonized inflation rates that that is expected to entail. Thereafter an economy with inflationary tendencies would benefit from the monetary discipline imposed by monetary unification. Each member state would have to accept the consensus EC rate of inflation that was the policy goal of the European System of Central Banks.

Monetary unification would, according to this approach, improve the efficiency with which credit is allocated, although the total availability of credit would be under the control of the European System of Central Banks. The complete removal of exchange controls, the emergence of a single European currency and the unification of financial regulation would remove constraints, reduce transactions costs and reduce uncertainty in international financial transactions. Local financial monopolies would be challenged by other European financial institutions, increasing the competitiveness with which credit and financial services in general are supplied. To the extent that national policy had previously inhibited the borrowing of foreign saving to finance domestic investment, monetary unification would make it easier for private-sector preferences to be met. The range of sources of funds would be increased, the cost of borrowing would be driven down by competition and the reduction in transactions costs and uncertainty would increase the volume of credit that would be supported by a given monetary base. The EC research report on monetary unification (Commission of the European Communities, 1990, chapter 10) allowed for the possibility of transitional problems for regions currently dependent on small local financial institutions which would not survive the onslaught of competition. But it was concluded that these costs would be transitional, until outside financial institutions became established in these local markets.

This approach can thus be characterized as envisaging trade within Europe as being driven by relative price competitiveness, which in turn would be enforced by monetary flows resulting from changes in competitiveness; the theory of inflation is a monetarist one, with the uniform rate of inflation in Europe being determined by the EC-level control of the aggregate European money supply. The creation of a perfect capital market would ensure that these stabilizing monetary flows were not impeded. The perfect capital market, too, would ensure an equalization of interest rates and an allocation of credit that was efficient, satisfying preferences of borrowers and lenders, subject to the constraint imposed on aggregate credit growth by the European central bank. Finally, and crucially, capital flows are seen as reallocating an existing stock of saving; the role of credit creation is not distinguished.

Monetary Integration and Endogenous Credit

There is a significant body of thought that challenges the notion that central banks can control the money supply in the first place. (This is called the *endogenous money* approach: see, for example, Kaldor, 1982; Dow and Saville, 1988; Moore, 1988; Wray, 1990.) As major participants in financial markets, central banks certainly influence the volume of credit. Indeed, by manipulating the cost of borrowed reserves and thereby also emitting interest rate signals that have conventional significance for financial markets, central banks can exert a disproportionate influence. But financial innovation has allowed banks to create an even larger inverted pyramid of credit on top of the reserve base, which in any case central banks are duty-bound to supply as lenders of last (or even in some cases first) resort. The more effective central banks are in supervising the banking system, and thus maintaining confidence in it, the greater the scope for enlarging the pyramid. This argument applies as much to a new European central bank as to any national central bank.

Germany might be thought to provide a counter-example that challenges the endogenous money approach. Germany is commonly regarded as holding the key to inflation control in Europe, given the apparent success of the Bundesbank in controlling the money supply in the past, and the low rate of inflation experienced in West Germany. The correlation between these two variables has been interpreted as implying causation, from low monetary growth to low inflation. But there are other institutional features of West Germany, notably the structure and context of wage-bargaining, that could well have accounted for the low rate of monetary growth. (Unification could provide a test of these two competing causal theories. Unification has disrupted both the structure of West German institutions and inflation expectations; if the virtuous circle is thus broken, the Bundesbank may be powerless to control inflation.)

The corollary of this argument is that European monetary unification may not produce a uniform inflation rate; continuing institutional and expectational differences between members could cause inflation rate differentials to persist. Members with relatively poor competitiveness would then have to undergo a more painful process of adjustment than is implied by the monetarist mechanism outlined above. The policy literature refers to the possibility of fast-track and slow-track members, the former being those that successfully harmonize inflation as a precondition for monetary union, and the latter being those for which reducing inflation is more difficult, preventing participation in monetary union. The debate over the speed with which monetary union should be completed has rested on different views as to the adjustment costs involved in slow-track members reducing their inflation with independent monetary policies, compared with the costs if it were to be achieved instead within monetary union. There is a general recognition, therefore, that there are some output and employment adjustments involved in the monetarist mechanism; but there is confidence that that mechanism is effective in determining the rate of inflation; and the greater the degree of monetary integration, the more effective it is.

If monetary unification cannot harmonize inflation some members will continue to have balance of trade problems until institutional and expectational changes with respect to wage bargaining and rates of investment are such that their competitive position improves. In the meantime, with only fiscal policy available as an adjustment tool, the extent of adjustment required in the short run will depend on the capital account. Much will therefore depend on the response of capital markets in general, and the banking system in particular. If credit is indeed created endogenously (i.e. substantially by the decisions of private-sector financial institutions), then it is within the power of these institutions to decide whether or not a trade deficit can be financed by borrowing. The alternative is generally downward adjustment of income and employment, which might even exacerbate an already weak competitive position; this effect could arise if, as is likely, competitiveness depends on economies of scale, and also if the adjustment process itself depresses long-term expectations.

Capital markets therefore have the power to determine whether or not economies must adjust to current account imbalance, or may indeed create a payments imbalance through the capital account itself. In the next section, I consider in more detail the evolution of banking systems using a framework that focuses on banks' evolving capacity to create credit under different institutional arrangements. This is developed in terms of the allocation of credit among economies with differing competitiveness. To differences in competitiveness must be added the further complication of differences in stage of evolution of indigenous banking systems prior to the removal of national barriers.

Evolution of Banking Systems and Credit Creation

The capacity of banks to create credit depends on the stage of evolution of the banking system. Chick (1991) has developed a stylized account of the stages of evolution of banking systems which suggests that this capacity in general increases with stage of evolution. Thus, the more developed the banking system, the more independent are private sector banks from reserves constraints, first in the form of specie, then as supplied by the central bank. The supply of credit can thus respond more to demand as the banking system becomes more established. Part of that process allows those banks expanding credit to borrow reserves from other banks. The greater the degree of integration between banks in the economy at issue (here, Europe), the more efficient is that interbank market, and the greater is an individual bank's independence from reserves constraints. An interbank market can be highly effective even without a unified banking system, as with the federal funds market in the USA. Then, with the evolution of the central bank's lender-of-last-resort facility and the emergence of liability management, the banking system as a whole can influence the volume of reserves, and thus the volume of credit in the system.

Chick also argues that, in later stages of banking development, credit creation also loses its dependence on 'real' economic activity. In their bid to maximize profits, possibly by the strategy of maintaining or increasing market share, banks actively seek to extend credit: the system becomes bank driven rather than bank borrower driven. Further, to fund expanding credit, banks innovate in new forms of borrowing instrument, but also offer ever higher returns on deposits. Depending on the underlying economic conditions, these higher deposit rates may then be reflected in ever higher interest charges on advances. These charges can only be supported by firms with sufficient market power to increase product prices accordingly, or by speculation in assets that promise a high enough return. The banks' drive for market share then encourages product market concentration (with inflation a by-product) and speculation in asset markets. But in market constrained circumstances, banks' profit margins suffer (see Howells, 1990), possibly resulting eventually in a process of concentration. Here we are concerned with how this process may affect and be affected by a breaking down of national barriers (different currencies, different regulatory frameworks, different market conventions and other barriers to entry). Are there categories of member states, or of regions within states, that will experience a change in credit availability as a result of financial integration? (There is a further dimension to the process which, although of great importance, will receive scant attention here. While all banking systems can be analysed in terms of Chick's sequential framework, there are different possible paths that these systems can take within the framework. Thus, for example, the regulatory and conventional nature of the German banking system differs from that of the British banking system. Financial integration in Europe thus involves creating a single market for banks at different stages of development, but also for banks that operate differently at similar stages of development.)

The first point to be made clear is that endogenous credit creation (the capacity of banks to create credit independently of central banks) does not mean limitless credit availability. (This point was made most forcefully in terms of given reserves by Tobin (1963); for a treatment using a broader perspective, see Dow and Dow (1989) and Wray (1990).) Banks allocate their resources to expanding market share among particular types of borrower, generally to the disadvantage of small firms. Small firms face greater difficulty in acquiring credit for a variety of reasons, most notably that the cost of acquiring pertinent information on the borrower and the purpose of the loan is typically high relative to the size of loan sought. It has been suggested further that regional economies have a two-tier banking system, whereby small, local firms are dependent on small, local banks while large firms have access to banks outside the region (i.e. there are systematic spatial constraints on capital mobility). Since local banks are more likely to be constrained in their capacity to create credit than large financial centre banks, small firms are more likely to be constrained in their access to credit for that reason too (see Moore and Hill, 1982; Dow, 1987).

Finally, credit availability and the charges attached to it depend on risk assessment. This assessment can rarely be fully quantified; default risk is ultimately in the realms of uncertainty (unquantifiable risk). Changes in banks' perception of this uncertainty will have consequences for the availability and cost of credit. Generally, the poorer the information on which the assessment is based, the greater the uncertainty attached to the assessment. More generally still, if confidence in the economy in general undergoes a change, there may be an overall change in credit availability, as banks seek to protect their interests by choosing instead to purchase existing financial assets (see Minsky, 1976, 1982).

Prior to financial integration, therefore, there may be general or particularized constraints on credit availability imposed by the banks themselves. To the extent that these constraints arise from geographically segmented markets, financial integration holds out the possibility of an easing of constraints as access to alternative sources of credit improves. McKillop and Hutchinson (1990) argue that the two-tier banking system argument applies more to the USA, which does not have a unified banking system, than to the UK, which does. The implication is that the constraints on credit availability to firms due to dependence on local banks will be reduced by the emergence of a unified banking system in Europe. Goodhart (1987), however, perceives a two-tier system as characterizing a financially integrated Europe, in that each tier will occupy market niches determined by information asymmetries; indeed, increased scale could allow new opportunities for market specialization. Branson (1990) concludes that the persistence of a tier of national banks would allow some scope for independent national monetary policy.

At the national level, greater access to banks elsewhere in Europe will open up new opportunities for borrowing. To the extent that this is the case, economies with balance of trade deficits may more readily finance these deficits by borrowing, thus avoiding painful income and employment adjustment. Similarly, economies experiencing weak economic growth owing to a lack of investment finance may attract funds from elsewhere in Europe. Costs in general should be reduced by a removal of exchange uncertainty, and the lower information costs and transactions costs associated with the removal of barriers to competition.

However, consideration must be given to how the original reasons for constraint will be affected by financial integration, and whether new sources of credit constraint might arise. If a two-tier banking system does emerge, then the greater access to credit will be enjoyed more by large firms operating in the EC-level banking tier; smaller firms will then bear the brunt of such adjustment as is not obviated by borrowing. This outcome could be modified if governments chose (and were allowed by EC rules) to use the element of monetary policy independence identified by Branson (1990) to encourage credit creation by the national tier of banks. If, however, the independence were used in a restrictive manner, it would be the small firms that would bear the brunt of higher interest rates and/or credit limits.

Financial integration will initially increase competition as national banks expand into each other's markets. But the eventual outcome is likely to be an increase in concentration in the banking sector. In particular, as the European Commission's (1990) research report points out, the small banks with local monopolies will be at a competitive disadvantage against large multinational banks. The historical evidence suggests that any second tier that emerges from this process of concentration will have quite limited scope; the process of concentration is well underway in the USA as a result of deregulation, for example. Molyneux (1989) argues that the concentration in Europe will result from takeovers of smaller rather than larger banks. But if the banking system becomes more concentrated, the incidence of remoteness from head office will increase, where that remoteness is not just a matter of physical distance, but also of culture, convention and social grouping. The uncertainty (and associated costs) attached to assessing the default risk of small borrowers is likely to be increased, and extended to larger borrowers. A concomitant of financial concentration will thus be industrial concentration, as large firms reap the advantages of integration and small firms bear the costs. This process has historical precedents, for example in Atlantic Canada (see Acheson, 1977; Brym and Sacouman, 1979).

There may be a further systematic spatial element to this process, to the extent that particular economies (national or regional) have and/or are perceived to have distinctive characteristics. The stages-of-banking framework has been developed in a spatial context by Chick and Dow (1988), who combine it with a centre–periphery characterization of regional economies. Peripheral economies are characterized by a relative dependence on primary and low-level secondary production, a high degree of outside ownership and relatively low levels of wealth. Centre economies, on the other hand, are characterized by high-level manufacturing and services, a concentration of head offices, in the financial as well as production sectors, and relatively high levels of wealth. To the extent that central and peripheral economies are financially integrated, centre capital will be made available to the periphery to finance investment. But a weakening in economic conditions in the periphery, which generally involves weakening exports, will be accompanied by a withdrawal of capital, creating problems on the capital account as well as the current account. Unless there is a mechanism for fiscal redistribution, or access to preferential public sector sources of finance, the only recourse is downward income adjustment in the periphery to reduce imports. The greater the degree of financial integration, the greater the dependence of the periphery on outside sources of capital, given the financial dominance of the centre.

The vulnerability of the periphery's capital account is exacerbated further by the attraction of centre's financial markets to periphery's savers. The financial centre enjoys a competitive advantage, in being able to offer higher returns than small, local institutions (see Kindleberger, 1987, pp. 75–7). But in addition, long experience of economic vulnerability in the periphery tends to generate endemic liquidity preference there, i.e. a preference for low-risk assets and a reluctance to borrow. The financial centre will tend to offer the most attractive low-risk assets, so that there will be a further inducement to capital outflow, which will be greatest when economic conditions in the periphery weaken. Falling export receipts, reduced inward investment and capital flight will thus tend to coincide, requiring income adjustment, sometimes at drastic speed. Each such experience reinforces the perceptions that led to the tendency for capital to flow out (credit not to be made available) at the first sign (however warranted) of weakening economic conditions.

It is being suggested here, therefore, that (*ceteris paribus*) financial integration in Europe will perpetuate some existing credit constraints and create new ones. New constraints are likely for small firms that previously had access to small local financial institutions, and for larger firms in peripheral regions that begin to encounter small-firm problems in a larger financial market. Generally, for regions, the existence of a unified national financial market is regarded as a satisfactory substitute for the capacity for exchange rate adjustment and independent monetary policy open to national governments facing balance of payments problems. It is the unified financial market that prevents the economic divergence that would otherwise threaten the functioning of a unified currency area. But if in Europe monetary integration were to promote divergence, this itself would threaten the success of the whole monetary integration programme; it would carry the seeds of its own destruction.

Finally, we must consider how this conclusion might be affected by integration among banking systems at different stages of development. This issue is most pertinent to the integration of Eastern Europe into Western financial markets. But it also has relevance to the existing EC membership, as nations but also as collections of regions that still have some institutional financial independence (see McKillop and Hutchinson, 1990). The evolution of banking systems has generally been in the direction of increasing scope to create credit along with falling costs (notably cost of reserves). While banks initially were constrained by reserves of precious metals, now they are constrained by their skill and efficiency in marketing loans and deposits within a (relatively) given interest rate structure. That skill and efficiency is most highly developed in the most advanced banking systems, which therefore will enter the free European financial market with a competitive advantage. The locus of control of the creation and allocation of credit will increasingly be concentrated in a few financial centres and this necessarily increases the geographical remoteness of some regions and the possible divergence between these regions and the financial centres. Here London may be the exception that proves the rule, in that it is likely to be one of these centres, although it is located in an economy that is in danger of being regarded as peripheral. Member nations with less developed banking systems should see an acceleration in stage-of-banking development as a result of financial integration. The common regulatory framework will reflect the practices of the most advanced banks and will thus accelerate development by indigenous banks. Tardiness in development, on the other hand, would encourage takeover by outside banks, constituting an alternative route to banking development. In either case, in aggregate, credit creation will be more unconstrained. But, at the same time, credit creation will become more bank-driven than deposit- or loan-demand-driven; further, the banks with most market power are likely to be those headquartered in the more advanced banking centres.

The caveat for EC members must be the same as for regions within a nation state with a unified banking system: fiscal policy provides an alternative means of buffering economies from adjustments that are judged to be irreversibly damaging. Kaldor (1970) pointed out that regional policy provides an alternative means of financing trade deficits; if effective, regional policy can prevent the economic divergence that the arguments outlined above might suggest as the likely outcome of market forces. Central government transfers can act as a substitute for capital inflows to finance balance of payments deficits. Similarly, within Europe, fiscal policy might be designed to make up for any inability to borrow to finance deficits. At the national level the government might use its market power to borrow to finance a budgetary deficit associated with a balance of trade deficit, or to finance a regional policy addressed at peripheral regions experiencing particular borrowing difficulties. But some national governments might find their liabilities adversely assessed by the integrated capital market. Then there would be a strong case for a regional policy at the Community level on a much larger scale than currently contemplated. If on balance it is judged that financial integration will lead to economic divergence, then fiscal policy provides the most promising antidote.

Conclusion

The most commonly perceived outcome of monetary integration in Europe is a unified inflation rate, maintained by money supply control on the part of the European System of Central Banks. The freeing up of capital flows is seen as the mechanism by which that unified inflation rate would be achieved; the by-product would be increased efficiency in the allocation of the given amount of credit allowed by the European central bank.

If, however, central banks cannot control the money supply, and if in any case the latter is the outcome rather than the cause of inflation, the problem of differing rates of competitiveness in Europe remains unaddressed by the plans for monetary integration. Indeed, it is possible that monetary integration could exacerbate differences in competitiveness, by reducing the availability of credit to peripheral regions. At the same time, the competitive process in the financial sector is likely to lead eventually to significant financial concentration, and a concomitant concentration in industry, increasing the dependency of peripheral regions. To counteract these trends, governments could look at measures to support the local banking system, with its important relationship with local industry; there might even be scope for an independent monetary policy with respect to these banks, by which the government could alleviate credit constraints. But, given the systemic nature of the processes of divergence between central and peripheral economies, an appropriate regional policy at the Community level is required. Further, if the provisions of

Maastricht are enacted, member governments will be severely constrained in their activities with respect to the financial sector.

Monetary integration is a mixed blessing. On the one hand, it provides borrowers and lenders with a wider market, with more instruments to choose from, at a lower cost. It may also ease the inflow of capital to finance investment in regions at a competitive disadvantage. Financial integration could promote economic convergence. But, on the other hand, financial integration can act even more powerfully to ease the flow of capital out of peripheral regions. At the same time the concentration in financial and goods markets can exacerbate the conditions that led these regions to fall behind in competitiveness in the first place. If, then, financial integration is the likely outcome of market and political forces, thought needs to be devoted to counteracting its negative effects on peripheral regions. In particular, more full consideration should be given to the role of regional policy (including fiscal transfers) on the one hand and policies to promote regional balance in the financial sector on the other. Not only might regional imbalance be an unfortunate side-effect of attempts to promote monetary integration, but also these side-effects might prevent the goal of full monetary integration being attained.

References

Acheson, T. N. (1977) The Maritimes and Empire Canada. In D. J. Bercuson (ed.), *Canada and the Burden of Unity*. Toronto: Macmillan.

Branson, W. H. (1990) Financial market integration, macroeconomic policy and the EMS. In J. Brago de Macedo and C. Bliss (eds), *Unity with Diversity within the European Economy: the Community's Southern Frontier*. Cambridge: Cambridge University Press.

Brym, R. J. and Sacouman, R. J. (1979) *Underdevelopment and Social Movements in Atlantic Canada*. Toronto: New Hogtown Press.

Chick, V. (1991) Some scenarios for money and banking in the EC, and their regional implications. University College London, mimeo.

Chick, V. and Dow, S. C. (1988) A post-Keynesian perspective on banking and regional development. In P. Arestis (ed.), *Post Keynesian Monetary Economics*. Aldershot: Elgar.

Commission of the European Communities (1985) *Completion of the Internal Market*. White Paper, Com (85) 310 (Final), Brussels.

Commission for the European Communities (1988) The creation of a European financial area: liberalisation of capital movements and financial integration in the Community. *European Economy*, 36.

Commission of the European Communities, Directorate-General for Economic and Financial Affairs (1990) One market, one money: an evaluation of the potential benefits and costs of forming an Economic and Monetary Union. *European Economy*, 44 (October).

Dow, A. C. and Dow, S. C. (1989) Endogenous money creation and idle balances. In J. Pheby (ed.), *New Directions in Post Keynesian Economics*. Aldershot: Elgar.

Dow, J. C. R. and Saville, I. D. (1988) *A Critique of Monetary Policy: Theory and British Experience*. Oxford: Clarendon.

Dow, S. C. (1987) The treatment of money in regional economics. *Journal of Regional Science*, 27, 13–24.

Goodhart, C. A. E. (1987), Structural changes in the British capital markets. In C. A. E. Goodhart (ed.), *The Operation and Regulation of Financial Markets*. London: Macmillan.

Howells, P. G. A. (1990) Bank liability management and monetary policy. *Cyprus Journal of Economics*, 3(1), 19–34.

Kaldor, N. (1970) The case for regional policies. *Scottish Journal of Political Economy*, 17 (November), 337–48.

Kaldor, N. (1982) *The Scourge of Monetarism*. Oxford: Oxford University Press.

Kindleberger, C. P. (1987) *International Capital Movements*. Cambridge: Cambridge University Press.

McKillop, D. G. and Hutchinson, R. W. (1990) *Regional Financial Sectors in the British Isles*. Aldershot: Gower.

Minsky, H. P. (1976) *John Maynard Keynes*. London: Macmillan.

Minsky, H. P. (1982) *Inflation, Recession and Economic Policy*. Brighton: Wheatsheaf.

Molyneux, P. (1989) '1992' and its impact on regional and local banking markets. *Regional Studies*, 23, 523–33.

Moore, B. J. (1988) *Horizontalists and Verticalists: the Macroeconomics of Credit Money*. Cambridge: Cambridge University Press.

Moore, C. L. and Hill, J. M. (1982) Interregional arbitrage and the supply of loanable funds. *Journal of Regional Science*, 22, 499–512.

Stiglitz, J. E. and Weiss, A. (1981) Credit rationing in markets with imperfect information. *American Economic Review*, 71, 393–410.

Tobin, J. (1963) Commercial banks as creators of 'money'. In D. Carson (ed.), *Banking and Monetary Studies*. Homewood, IL: Irwin.

Wray, L. R. (1990) *Money and Credit in Capitalist Economies: the Endogenous Money Approach*. Aldershot: Elgar.

8

The Road to the Twenty-first Century: the Myths and Miracles of Asian Manufacturing

M. T. Daly

The industrialization of Asia was, perhaps, the most spectacular economic happening of the second half of the twentieth century. Asian nations (more specifically those of the Pacific edge of Asia) compressed the process of industrialization; Japan achieved in 35 years an industrial transformation that had taken Britain and Germany over 50 years, and then Taiwan and the Republic of Korea (South Korea) reduced the span to 15 years. Moreover, this industrialization had an immediate effect on the rest of the world. By 1965, Japan had become the world's fourth biggest exporter of manufactured goods, and it ranked second by the mid-1980s. From the 1960s to the 1980s Taiwan rose from twenty-eighth to tenth, and South Korea (hereafter Korea) from thirty-third to thirteenth (Wade, 1990, p. 4). Between 1971 and 1980, China, Korea, Taiwan, Singapore and Indonesia had *annual* average growth rates of merchandise exports above 30 per cent and over the same years Korea, Taiwan, Thailand, Hong Kong, Singapore, Indonesia and Malaysia had annual growth rates of real GDP of 8 per cent or better, more than double the OECD average (*The Economist*, 16 November 1991, p. 4). This success focused attention on unravelling the secrets of Asia's success.

As alarming to their competitors as the trade inroads was the success of these nations in elaborately transforming their output, especially in the area of information technology: by the end of the 1980s Japan was an acknowledged leader, Taiwan's semiconductor houses were close to being world leaders in application-specific integrated circuits and the Korean semiconductor business was only around nine months behind Japan and USA in technology for large-capacity memory chips. Japan had become the world's richest nation (per capita) and a clutch of other Asian countries had displayed the world's fastest rates of income growth. The future of Asia was critical to the future shape of the world economy.

'By the early twenty-first century Japan, Taiwan, South Korea and China will probably have as much weight in the world economy as North America or Europe. Taiwan and South Korea will be as rich as Great Britain and Italy' (Wade, 1990, p. 4).

This chapter characterizes the emerging nature of Asian manufacturing as a system respondent to, and dependent on, the global geopolitical structure. It emphasizes the nature of corporate development in the major Asian nations (Japan, Korea and Taiwan) and relates that to the spread of manufacturing throughout the region. Essential to the argument is an understanding of the nature of corporate structures in Asian nations and how they have operated in conjunction with governments and financial structures to out-compete their Western rivals. Because of the changes in the broader geopolitical domain there is a fundamental challenge: Asian corporate structure will be forced to change if it is to be successful, and that change is of a significant nature.

The particular relationships created between finance and industry have been vital to Pacific Asia. The status of this relationship is critical to understanding the direction of change in the 1990s, especially in Japan. The other essential factor is the development of technology in the new industrial age, and Pacific Asia's place within this. Two major sections of the chapter address the issues of finance and technology. The final section assesses the positive and negative aspects of the challenges facing Asia.

The World Economic Order of the 1990s

The growth enjoyed by so many nations in the decades after the Second World War was a product of the liberal trading order established under the leadership of the USA. Principles and norms, such as the GATT and the Bretton Woods Agreement, and institutions, such as the IMF and the World Bank, were designed to produce a stable and open trading system. This regime gave Pacific Asian nations the broad opportunity to develop. Strategic political considerations (the perceived threat of China and the reality of wars in Korea, Malaysia and Indo-China) directed flows of funds and technology to Asia. The conversion of opportunity into growth, especially trade growth, was directed and buttressed by the governments of individual Asian nations, by the characteristics of Asian corporations and by the domestic control of both capital and imports.

The eventual collapse of outright US hegemony spelt the end of the old system that had so favoured Asia. Although there is debate over the extent of this collapse (Nau, 1990) and optimistic predictions that accommodations can be made to sustain the major working features of the old system (Keohane, 1984; Maswood, 1989), the reality is that the world faces a phase of reconstituting its organizational forms; and no one can know for certain just what structures will emerge. Investment and production will therefore, at least for the short term, face an unscripted, unknown and dramatically changing environment. It is uncertain whether Pacific Asia will be better placed than its competitors to succeed in the fluid atmosphere of the 1990s.

The reasons for this conclusion lie in two somewhat paradoxical features of the new environment: the emergence of what Ohmae (1989) and others have called Triad economics; and the compelling pace of technological change, which challenges the corporate organizational forms that were adequate for the previous period. The regionalization of markets, and perhaps production systems, favours Europe and North America, while Asian structures have adopted more quickly to the demands of the new technologies.

The term Triad derives from the proposition that the world will split into three major trading blocs, and that trade and economic cooperation within a specific regional cluster (Europe, North America or Asia) will eventually become greater than transactions between one cluster and another. Ohmae (1989, p. 6) also highlights the emergence of the 'interlinked economy', arguing that new products now rely on so many different technologies that it is impossible for most companies to maintain a lead in all of them. The fixed costs (over the short term) of technological development become immense if firms wish to compete in global markets. Corporate strategies, therefore, become much more difficult to devise. Technology, competition and the opportunities presented by the communications revolution of the late twentieth century demand a global structure. At the same time the structure has to accommodate the growing, and perhaps inevitable, protectionism of the Triad clusters.

Regionalism and globalization pose immense challenges to corporations seeking to succeed in the 1990s. The secret of Japan's successful assault on world markets lay in an emphasis on standard products and components rather than on a range of items tailored to different markets. Cost savings, through standardization and concentration, and quality control and reliability became the weapons. Integrated industrial policies designed to move companies in a timed sequence to improve consistently the value-added component became the setting. The giant trading companies (*sogo shosha*) provided the marketing edge.

The structures of the old global system allowed Japan to concentrate its production processes at home. When cost pressures or environmental concerns pushed manufacturing offshore it was generally to neighbouring Asian nations which acted as extensions of the export platform Japan had created at home. Of the top dozen Japanese firms producing motor vehicles, earth-moving equipment and electronic goods in 1986, half relied on exports for over 50 per cent of their sales and the remainder for over 25 per cent (James, 1989, p. 36).

Japanese, and other Asian, corporations now have to develop organizational forms that will work in the era of Triad economics. European and North American consortia have developed more flexible forms and more spatially distributed operating systems. US and European corporations have been investing in each other's regions over a long period. Within the USA in the 1980s EC countries invested over US $100 billion (to bring their cumulative investment to US $262 billion) and they employed two million workers, double the number of other foreign owners.

Japan has invested in the USA and Europe: US $53 billion from 1951 to 1987 in North America and US $21 billion in Europe. But it has been a case of too little, too late. Moreover, most of the investment has been in services, with finance, real estate and, more recently, communications being the focus. Relatively little has been invested in manufacturing. Even after the Plaza Agreement (and the subsequent outflow associated with the higher valued yen) services predominated (Steven, 1990, p. 87). US industrial investment in Europe was around 30 times the level of Japanese investment by the end of the 1980s.

Internationalization and Corporate Structures

Japanese Corporate Structures

As its firms captured ever larger shares of world markets it became accepted that Asia had produced the most effective corporate structures for successfully operating in the global arena; the *kigyo keiretsu* of Japan and the *chaebols* of Korea are outstanding examples. The *kigyo keiretsu* are large industrial groupings normally formed around a bank or a general trading company (*sogo shosha*). Surrounding the core are complex webs of subsidiaries and affiliates with large degrees of cross-shareholding; they operate in a wide variety of enterprises but do not possess an integrated corporate structure in the American or European sense. The global turnover of each of the major eight groups exceeds that of Exxon or General Motors. The leading 1000 Japanese companies belong to 17 *kigyo keiretsu* which account for 27 per cent of capital and 25 per cent of turnover in Japan (Eli, 1990, p. 5). Around the members of the *kigyo keiretsu* cluster a very large number of small firms engaged through sub-contracting arrangements in providing components of the production process. The total picture is of a dense interrelated manufacturing complex in Japan, replicated nowhere else in the world.

For more than 30 years after the Second World War relatively open markets were dominated by standardized products that were enormously responsive to cost reductions through scale economies. This system allowed fairly simple global strategies to be effective. It favoured the preferred option of Pacific Asian manufacturers: to rely on national (or regional) production bases which could exploit the special benefits of the *kigyo keiretsu* and *chaebol* systems. They then exploited weaknesses in the marketing and distribution systems of other countries.

The Japanese corporate form invoked the traditional concept of *ie*, or perpetual descent group. From this flowed the cornerstones of Japanese governance: implicit contracting founded on trust, extensive reciprocal shareholdings and implicit reciprocal trade agreements, managerial incentives aligned to overall corporate growth and early selective intervention in the case of problems by key stakeholders (Kester, 1991, p. 12). Culture provided the basic mix from which the distinctive Japanese corporate form was created, 'but it was the conflicting interests of diverse stakeholders that were the hammer and anvil used to forge the final corporate shape' (Kester, 1991, p. 52).

The system has received critical support from government. At least from 1952, when the Enterprises Rationalization Promotion Law was introduced, the government has provided subsidies, dialogue and direction to promote technological change. The choice always revolved around those technologies likely to transform the established existing pattern. The adoption of a systems approach to process and product design, the flexibility of the industrial structure, the capacity to identify crucial areas of future technological advance, the ability to mobilize large resources in technology and capital in pursuit of strategic priorities and the horizontal flow of information between firms has given Japan a crucial competitive edge (Freeman, 1988, p. 334).

The other significant factor in giving Japanese companies a competitive edge was the close association with banks, and the banks' association with government. Without a real securities market from the late nineteenth century through the early twentieth century the company–bank relationship became particularly intimate. The *zaibatsu* banks that emerged provided long-term credit and emergency funds as well as day-to-day banking needs.

The central role of the banks as credit providers continued in the postwar period. The banks are also at the centre of the information-sharing system that so marks the *kigyo keiretsu*. The banks help to stabilize corporate performance over time, and when problems appear they can make selective interventions. The special links between companies, banks and government are also cited as a reason why Japanese companies have been able to operate with a less stringent focus on profit maximizing.

The support systems inherent in the Japanese corporate structures have allowed them to operate with ambitions that were seemingly out of proportion to their resources and capabilities. They were driven by an obsession to win at all levels of the organization, and they sustained that obsession over a ten to twenty year quest for global leadership. Hamel and Prahalad (1989, p. 64) call this obsession strategic intent. This envisions a desired leadership position and establishes the criterion the organization will use to chart its progress and an associated active management programme. The Japanese exploited four approaches to competitive advantage in their global advances. They concentrated on building layers of advantage, they searched out weak spots ('loose bricks') in their competitors' armoury, they kept changing the terms of the engagement and they competed through collaboration (deskilling competitors through alliances and outsourcing deals). 'In the long run', Prahalad and Hamel (1990, p. 81) have observed, 'competitiveness derives from an ability to build, at lower cost and more speedily than competitors, the core competences that spawn unanticipated products.'

Japan as Exemplar

Japan charted its own industrial course and so became a model for others to follow. Korea, a land with even fewer resources than Japan, adopted much of the Japanese methodology and by the mid-1980s was widely acclaimed as having reproduced the Japanese miracle. By the mid-1980s within Asia the expectation, indeed the certainty, was that it was only a matter of time before nations such as Malaysia, Thailand and Indonesia repeated the lesson and achieved the desired status of a NIC (newly industrializing country).

Korea maintained a strong import-substitution regime for target industries and consumer goods organized through the *chaebols* which dominate the economy (in 1989–90 the four largest had sales equivalent to half Korea's GNP and 40 per cent of its exports). The *chaebols* were created by the actions of President Park Chung Hee and economic decision-making 'has been overwhelmingly a "top-down" process' (Song, 1990, p. 140). In the 1960s the economic ministries were run by retired army generals and colonels, and economic policy was run by command. Six five-year plans were introduced between 1962 and 1991, with the Economic Planning Board playing a central role in their preparation and implementation. Korean economic policy has been primarily political and security-oriented. As early as the 1970s, Korea was alarmed by the decline of US hegemony and made a deliberate thrust towards long-run future international competitiveness and industrial transformation (Woo, 1991, p. 11). The state shouldered the risk of investment in lumpy projects with a long gestation period. Crucial to the process was a credit-based financial structure controlled by the state. 'The Korean banking system exhibits the most extreme case of dependence on the state; unlike the privately owned Japanese banks . . . the Korean banks do not enjoy even limited autonomy with respect to criteria of lending and response to non-performing loans' (Woo, 1991, p. 12). The state influences investment patterns and sectoral mobility and permits highly leveraged firms to survive. On top of the basic financial structure Korea established a complex incentive scheme to facilitate structural mobility.

Policy loans (loans earmarked to specific sectors or industries at rates below the already subsidized bank loans) constitute a central pillar of this system; by the early 1980s there were 221 types of policy loans out of a total of 298 types of bank loans.

Taiwan, the other major success story of East Asia, contrasts with Korea in that the export base is dominated by small to medium firms (in 1985 accounting for 65 per cent of manufacturing exports and 40 per cent of total production). In this more differentiated environment the state has still played a key role. In many sectors public enterprise was used for the initial push (fuels, chemicals, mining, fertilizers, food processing) and in the 1950s and 1960s public enterprise played a large part in setting the synthetic fibres, metal and shipbuilding industries on their way. Established large-scale private firms were often exposed to administrative guidance, and the structure at large was supported by import controls, tariffs, entry requirements, domestic content requirements, investment incentives and concessional credit.

The financial system was rigidly controlled. The public enterprise sector was one of the largest outside sub-Saharan Africa and the communist bloc. The economic policies were dictated to a large degree by security considerations. 'Taiwan', Wade (1990, p. 113) concludes, 'manages its trade differently from many other developing countries, not less'.

Japan has had another significant, and recent, influence on the region, both as a producer of information technology and as a pioneer of new technology. The beginnings of the industry in the region came with the dispersal of various stages of semiconductor assembling from the USA (and to a lesser extent Europe): the first offshore plant was established by Fairchild Corporation in Hong Kong in 1962. The process of development of the industry since then has been well covered by Henderson (1989) and Scott and Angel (1988). The important result was that, by 1986, 91 out of 94 free-standing US assembly plants and 62 out of 65 independent sub-contractors were located offshore. When in March 1985 imports of semiconductors produced by US offshore plants were relieved of all duty, 85 per cent came from Asia.

By this time Japan had come to dominate the semiconductor industry and Korea and Taiwan were making great strides in developing their own industries. There has been a steady upgrading of the semiconductor branch plants of US companies in Singapore and Hong Kong, and a very substantial growth of Japanese plants throughout the region. As both wages and specializations increased in the NICs there were shifts to Malaysia and the Philippines (who collectively supplied 46 per cent of US imports by 1984: Scott and Angel, 1988, p. 1062). The various nations of Pacific Asia have tended to specialize in different kinds of devices related to the time of investment. Significant local complexes of producers supplying specialized services and inputs have developed around the cores of multinational firms.

In the 1980s Korea and Taiwan both moved to become major players in information technology. In the early 1980s two Korean firms, with government help, went from greenfields to operating plants for 64K DRAM chips in eight months (half the time it took in the USA and two-thirds that of Japan: Wade, 1990, p. 315). After surviving the mid-decade slump of the 1980s the government once again combined with the private sector to push into the frontiers of the industry. By 1988 Korea was the world's third biggest fabricator of large capacity memory chips. The Korean industry leader, Samsung, was shipping 1.5 million 1 megabit DRAMs a month by the end of 1988 (having produced zero a year before) and in 1989 produced more 1 megabit chips than all the US merchant producers together. Samsung introduced sample 4 megabit chips only six months after the world leader Toshiba, and in 1991 finished in a virtual dead-heat to produce the world's first 16 megabit DRAM semiconductor (*Far Eastern Economic Review*, 31 October 1991, p. 66). In 1990 Korea was the world's sixth largest producer of electronics; its US $24.1 billion was well behind the USA (US $199.1 billion) and Japan (US $188.9 billion) but was expected soon to overtake both France (US $26.1 billion) and Britain (US $26.1 billion). Only Germany (US $40.6 billion) seemed to be securely ahead among the European producers.

The history of the electronics industry in Taiwan has some distinct similarities to Korea's. From very early days the government fostered industrial technology through national science and technology development plans, and research and development institutes in strategic areas. The Industrial Technology Research Institute (founded in 1973) and the Hsinchu Science-based Industry Park (opened in 1980) are examples. Taiwan hoped to gain a competitive edge over Korea by concentrating on custom-tailored chips. In 1979 United Microelectronics was established to commercialize technology developed in public research laboratories. In 1986 a 256K DRAM chip was designed and in 1986 a 1 megabit chip. By the end of the 1980s Taiwan had the largest pool of chip design talent in Asia (outside Japan) – 58 design houses compared to 218 in Europe – and over 100 computer manufacturers compared to 60 in Korea (Wade, 1990, p. 106). In 1990 Taiwan ranked eighth in the world among electronic producers (US $14.1 billion). Singapore (US $13.2 billion) was ninth, Hong Kong eleventh (US $8.1 billion) and Malaysia fifteenth (US $6.1 billion) (*Far Eastern Economic Review*, 31 October 1991, p. 66).

The Sweep of Pacific Asian Growth

With good cause most attention has been paid to Japan and the larger Asian NICs in the considerable literature seeking to explain the growth of manufacturing and exports in the region. Less attention has been given to how the region as a whole is structured and to the growth of levels of intraregional trade in the 1980s.

At the centre of this regional change is the Japanese economy, and the dominating agent of change has frequently been Japanese investment. Japan in the 1980s replaced the USA, the pioneer investor in the region, as the major force. Foreign direct investment (FDI) throughout the world rose from a level of US $47.4 billion in 1980 to US $197.9 billion in 1989. The rate of growth was particularly rapid in the second half of the 1980s: 33.1 per cent (1985–9) compared to 12.5 per cent growth in merchandise trade and 14.0 per cent growth in services. In that period Japan became the world's largest source of FDI (US $44.1 billion in 1989). Taiwan's official levels of FDI (US $7 billion in 1989) placed it as a major investor, and in 1990 investment by Korean companies doubled to US $2.3 billion. The Asian NICs replaced Japan as the major investor in ASEAN and the ASEAN countries became the major focus of investment in Asia (supplanting the NICs).

Japanese overseas FDI has gone through three phases (see table 8.1). The first, from 1969 to 1973, paralleled Japan's maturing as a major force in world trading. Most of the US$8.3 billion of FDI was directed to labour-intensive manufacturing and trade-related services. Regional shares were fairly evenly distributed, with Asia attracting the largest share (24.2 per cent); the NICs were attractive for displaced Japanese manufacturing and countries like Indonesia and Australia were linked into the supply of Japanese raw materials.

The second phase began with Japan's recovery from the OPEC shock and lasted from 1978 to 1984. Japan dispatched US $49.2 billion, with North America overtaking Asia as the primary focus. In relative terms Asia's share did not change greatly (23.8 per cent of the total) but Europe's proportion fell by 9.4 per cent to 12.2 per cent. In this period the focus in Asia remained on manufacturing and resources: the NIC's manufacturing sector had grown more sophisticated, so that simpler and more labour-intensive manufacturing began to shift to Malaysia, the Philippines, Thailand and Indonesia.

The third phase (1986–9) followed the Plaza agreement and the resultant jump in the value of the yen. Japan rose to dominate world FDI

Table 8.1 Japanese FDI, 1969–1989 (US $ billion)

Region	1969–73	1978–84	1986–9
World	8.3	49.2	170.3
North America	1.9	16.1	82.1
Asia	2.0	12.0	21.0
Europe	1.8	6.0	34.0

Source: JETRO, 1991, p. 10.

with US $170.3 billion. North America took the major share of this (48.2 per cent) and Europe attracted US $34 billion while Asia slipped to fourth place with 12.3 per cent of the total.

Japanese investment in the USA and Europe has been dominated by investment in trade, services and finance. Financial deregulation and the problems of trade friction caused the initial shift to the developed countries (see table 8.2). Between 1975 and 1986, 67 per cent of Japanese FDI went into non-manufacturing investment, with 36.2 per cent going into finance and insurance, 23.0 per cent into real estate and 14.5 per cent into services. This distribution was not dissimilar to the FDI patterns of other major nations: non-manufacturing investment was the major part of US, German and UK FDI in the same period.

The Plaza agreement encouraged more FDI in manufacturing in the USA by Japan (although real estate and financial investments still dominated) and the single market legislation brought a similar shift in Europe. The higher priced yen pushed more manufacturing into Asia. Although Asia declined to become a relatively minor recipient of Japanese FDI, the greatly increased levels of these flows meant that very substantial sums were directed into countries such as Thailand, Malaysia, Singapore and Indonesia (US $11 billion from 1988 to 1990). In 1990, Japanese companies were opening up new factories in Thailand at the rate of one every two and a half days (*The Economist*, 16 November, 1991, p. 9). Japan continued investment in more sophisticated manufacturing in the NICs (US $3.4 billion in 1989). The total level of all FDI flowing into the ASEAN region climbed four-fold between 1987 and 1989 (to US $16.0

Table 8.2 Pacific Asia trade, 1989

Country	To USA		To Japan	
	US $ billion	% manufactures	US $ billion	% manufactures
World	493.6	72	209.6	41
Japan	97.1	95		
USA			48.3	53
NICs	66.4	94	28.0	63
Hong Kong	10.2	96	2.2	82
South Korea	20.5	95	12.9	67
Singapore	9.2	92	2.9	49
Taiwan	26.4	94	10.0	58
ASEAN	16.8	68	21.7	18
Indonesia	3.9	35	11.0	14
Malaysia	4.9	83	5.1	11
Philippines	3.3	78	2.1	18
Thailand	4.6	73	3.6	40

Source: *Far Eastern Economic Review*, 25 July 1991, p. 54.

Table 8.3 Japanese FDI in Asia, 1988–1990

Region	US $ billion		
	1988	1989	1990
Taiwan	0.37	0.49	0.45
Hong Kong	1.66	1.90	1.79
Singapore	0.75	1.90	0.84
Thailand	0.86	1.28	1.15
Malaysia	0.39	0.67	0.73
Indonesia	0.59	0.63	1.11

Source: Japan Ministry of Finance.

billion). Investment in the region by Asian NICs surpassed that of Japan in two of the four years between 1987 and 1990. The result was a great expansion of regional trade and a complex extension of integrated manufacturing. Trade among West Pacific nations grew at over 40 per cent per year in the three years to 1990, and in 1989 stood at US $256 billion or 40 per cent of world trade (see table 8.2).

There are two important aspects of Japanese investment in Asian manufacturing (see table 8.3). Within ASEAN, Japanese companies are producing a spatially specialized system of production; for example, there is an intaregional distribution of auto parts established by Japanese car-makers whereby production of different parts of certain models is shared among different countries. The high valued yen has weakened Japan's dominance as an exporter of consumer durables (electronic products and cars) and led to a domestic focus on capital goods (telecommunications and data processing equipment) and parts (semiconductors). The consumer goods industry has been effectively spread to form a regionally interrelated production system. Significantly, 70 per cent of Japan's trade has a Japanese company at either end of the transaction; the corresponding proportion for US companies is 20 per cent (*Far Eastern Economic Review*, 11 October 1990, p. 72).

Table 8.4 Japanese FDI in manufacturing: small and medium firms, 1980–1989 (percentages)

Region	1980	1985	1986	1987	1988	1989
World	100	100	100	100	100	100
Asia	57.6	63.5	64.9	72.7	65.6	64.7
NICs	36.4	30.7	47.0	46.3	26.8	20.4
China		21.1	10.8	6.4	8.1	7.9
Other Asia[a]	21.2	11.7	7.1	20.0	30.7	36.4

[a] Includes China 1980.

Source: JETRO, 1991, p. 32.

The second aspect has been the spread of small to medium Japanese firms throughout the region (see table 8.4). The number of such investments made throughout the world averaged 300 in the first half of the 1980s but then doubled each year to peak at 1625 in 1988. Manufacturing is the major part of this investment and most (67.4 per cent) of it occurs in Asia. There has been a pronounced shift to ASEAN countries: in 1986, 47 per cent of total investment was in Asian NICs, 10.8 per cent in China and only 7.1 per cent in the rest of Asia. By 1989, investment in the NICs had fallen to 20.4 per cent, China investment fell to 7.9 per cent and investment in the remainder of Asia (principally ASEAN) climbed to 36.4 per cent of the total. The ratio of joint ventures to wholly owned subsidiaries was two-to-one, with an emphasis on labour-intensive and low-tech mass-produced items. Japanese firms investing in the region procure equipment and machinery from Japan (72 per cent) but half of the raw materials locally (JETRO, p. 1991, p. 32).

The ASEAN nations used tax and other incentives to attract Japanese capital, which in turn reacted to the new order of a high-valued yen. The Malaysian ringgit dropped 63 per cent in value against the yen from 1985 to 1990. Thailand in 1984 introduced a basket of currencies against which to manage the baht and, with the US dollar having the heaviest weighting, rode down the trail of depreciation against the yen. This was a strong incentive for Japanese-owned electronics companies to establish in Thailand, Malaysia and the Philippines; 241 out of 340 were built between 1985 and 1990. As a result, US imports of consumer electronics from these countries jumped from US $7 million in 1988 to US $310 million in 1990. Malaysia is host to over 850 Japanese companies making a variety of goods from motorcycle batteries and marine cargo containers to electronic goods; 77 Japanese construction firms operate in Malaysia and Mitsubishi engineered the Malaysian-built Proton Saga car. Electrical products now dominate Malaysian industry, with a 1990 gross revenue of US $1.5 billion, ahead of food (US $1.21 billion) and petroleum refining (US$0.6 billion). The value of manufactured exports hovered between US $3 and 8 billion over the last years of the 1980s, three times the value of such traditional exports as petroleum, sawlogs, rubber and palm oil. Thailand's major industrial exports are textiles (1989: US $2.9 billion), footwear (US $0.5 billion) and integrated circuits (US $0.7 billion). Traditional exports such as rice (US $1.8 billion) and rubber (US$1.0 billion) are still very significant.

Within the Asian NICs there was a shift in inward FDI to higher value-added commodities: by 1990, 18.4 per cent of inward FDI was in chemicals and pharmaceuticals and 28.2 per cent in electric equipment and electronics. Korea's exports have been dominated by heavy and chemical industry products (US $33.6 billion in 1989), electronic and electrical products (US $16.3 billion) and light industry products (US $23.8 billion). Textiles had fallen relatively to US $14.1 billion. Taiwan's exports in 1990 were dominated by electronic products and information technology items (US $12.7 billion) but textiles and clothing were still quite important (US $10.3 billion).

The NICs entered periods of solid surplus in the second half of the 1980s. Taiwan's current account surplus was US $7.0 billion in 1984, peaked at US$18.0 billion in 1988 (when foreign reserves reached US $76.7 billion) and was US $11.3 billion in 1990. Korea's current account was US $0.9 billion in deficit in 1985, climbed into a surplus of US $4.7 billion in 1986, peaked at US $14.2 billion in 1988 then fell, recording a deficit of US $2.1 billion in 1990. Korea's external debt fell from US $46.7 billion in 1985 to US $29.4 in 1989, while reserves grew over the same period from US $7.7 billion to US $22.5 billion. The Asian NICs became exporters of capital (see table 8.5).

In 1989 Korean FDI rose by 93 per cent; there were 369 projects valued at US $0.927 billion, 49 per cent of which were in manufacturing (see table 8.6). Investments in South East Asia grew at three times the rate of general investments (*Business International*, 1990, p. 19). These investments are in textiles, footwear, household appliances and electronic and electrical equipment. From virtually nothing in 1986, official estimates of Taiwanese outward FDI rose to a cumulative total of around US $12 billion from 1987 to 1989. Official estimates are known to

Table 8.5 Pacific Asia investment flows, 1989 (US $ billion)

Country	Outflow	Inflow
USA	31.7	72.2
Japan	44.2	– 1.1
Australia	3.8	7.5
China	3.7	2.8
Singapore	0.1	4.0
Malaysia		1.8
Thailand	0.1	1.7
Korea	0.3	0.8
Indonesia		0.7
Philippines		0.5

Source: *Far Eastern Economic Review*, 25 July 1991, p. 55.

Table 8.6 South Korean FDI, 1980–1989 (US $ million)

Region	1980	1985	1986	1987	1988	1989
South East Asia	1.6	17.7	7.2	131.1	41.5	124.1
North America	11.1	10.8	76.1	71.4	41.6	31.7
Latin America	2.9	40.8	2.4	4.5	9.9	58.9
Europe	0.7	0.9	5.6	6.8	18.8	18.3
World	21.1	117.8	172.0	397.3	212.9	492.5

Source: Bank of Korea, 1990, p. 233.

underestimate seriously the true level of Taiwan's investments in South East Asia, Thailand and Malaysia (where Taiwan vies with Japan as the major investor). Singapore has shifted further into high-tech industries and established a range of tax incentives to attract international head-quarters, international procurement offices and international whole-saling. As Singapore moves towards international status as a service and high-tech centre it has invested strongly in labour-intensive activities in surrounding countries, particularly Malaysia and Indonesia. Hong Kong has become a major investor in China, with an emphasis on Guandong Province. Guandong Province, which has a population of 63 million people, traded HK \$400 billion (US \$50 billion) worth of goods in 1990: Hong Kong's GDP was only HK \$490 billion in that year. Hong Kong-financed factories in Guandong employed an industrial workforce three times that of the colony and 61 per cent of Hong Kong's imports from China came from these factories. Some 92 per cent of all foreign affiliates and 78 per cent of all FDI in China are concentrated in the coastal areas, and in the cities of Tianjin and Shanghai. By mid-1990 the coastal areas handled 78 per cent of China's total trade and 59 per cent of total industrial output. China sent a total of US \$240 billion of exports through Hong Kong in 1990. Manufactured exports increased from 53.4 per cent of exports in 1981 to 70 per cent in 1989 and these were comprised mainly of clothing and textiles. Close to 90 per cent of Hong Kong's electronic manufacturers have operations in China; a sure sign of the future (*Far Eastern Economic Review*, 16 May 1991, p. 66)

The fear of trade blocs engendered by the EC single market and the North American Free Trade Agreement has raised the question of defensive retaliation within Asia. Loosely, there has been talk of a yen bloc, given Japan's role as the centre of gravity of the region's economies. There is reluctance about this because of old fears concerning Japanese dominance, and the practical consideration that less than 12 per cent of the region's trade (excluding Japan's own trade) is denominated in yen and less than 15 per cent of the region's reserves are held in yen (*Far Eastern Economic Review*, 11 October 1990, p. 73).

Australia led the way in establishing the APEC (Asia-Pacific Economic Cooperation) framework. This was viewed suspiciously by ASEAN nations, largely because of the presence of the USA and Canada in the group. Its aims of providing an economic forum where issues such as trade can be discussed represents a vague response to the realities of the northern blocs.

In December 1990 Malaysia proposed the establishment of an East Asian Economic Grouping (EAEG), a trade bloc containing ASEAN with the East Asian economies and China that would exclude the USA, Europe, Australia and New Zealand. In October 1991 Thailand produced a modified proposal that would create within ASEAN an ASEAN Free Trade Area (AFTA); this would be phased in over 10 to 15 years, and would incorporate the Indonesian proposal of a Common Effective Preferential Tariff (CEPT) in the transition period. The problem with the idea is one that had always dogged ASEAN: the countries tend to produce similar items and have little trade with each other. The proportion of exports from countries in ASEAN to other ASEAN members has never exceeded 20 per cent, and in 1991 was only 10 per cent (*Far Eastern Economic Review*, 24 October 1991, p. 64).

Pacific Asia, which appears so threatening to Europe and North America, is not well equipped to retaliate against increased protectionism. The region covers an area of over 22 million square kilometres, contains almost 1.6 billion people with very little in terms of similar languages, cultures, religions or political systems, and has only one nation (out of 12) that has common borders with more than one other country; this is in a region spread across both the north and south hemispheres (Daly and Logan, 1989, p. 215). However much individual countries are reluctant to embrace the idea, and however reluctant the region's giant is to accept the leading geopolitical role, the essence of a regional response to world trends lies with Japan.

Into the Future: Nations, Regions and the Global Sphere

The Financial Mould

The struggles across the global geopolitical scene reflect the resurgence of nationalism (sprung from the collapse of the dual superpower administration of the world system) and the emergence of protectionist trade blocs. The contrasting fact is that production and marketing systems integrated over vast geographic areas are technologically more possible than ever before. Three factors in particular condition the ability of nations or regions to succeed in this situation:

- their place in the international financial markets and their ability to prosper from or control the effects of those markets;
- their ability to produce within the information-intensive production systems;
- their ability to produce and integrate a range of new technologies.

A Deregulated World

The global financial system was profoundly transformed after the final collapse of the Bretton Woods agreement in 1973. The primary change was a philosophical shift towards deregulation; while being accepted in principle, the fact of deregulation was not nearly as widespread as its advocates insisted. Asian nations in general resisted opening up their systems.

The image of a generally deregulated world system sprang from four sources:

1   The strength of the Euro- and Asia-dollar markets, whose volume of funds and freedom from government supervision allowed both corporations and governments to seek out better terms than regulated markets provided.
2   The quantity of money that the world had to absorb with the devaluations of the US dollar (the world's reserve currency) throughout the 1970s; the general growth of inflation; and the distributional shifts following the OPEC price rises. The brief period of monetarism in the early 1980s did little to arrest the problem: rather, it hastened the onset of the developing countries' debt crisis. It then shifted a mass of funds to the developed world, producing the superliquidity which fostered such results as the mergers and acquisition wave of the 1980s and the banking alarms of various nations.
3   The leaps in communication technology that made possible such things as 24-hour-a-day money markets, vast foreign exchange markets and effectively integrated world banking centres and tax havens.
4   The substantial rise in the power of the banks and other financial inter-mediaries (in a period of widespread industrial decay in the old industrial heartlands).

Instability in exchange and interest rates, mobility of funds, great liquidity, successive streams of new products to take advantage of the 'deregulated' markets and an emphasis on short-term profits were the trademarks of the new financial system.

From 1973 to 1988 the assets of the top 300 international banks increased seven-fold to US $15.43 trillion, a rate of increase that was double the growth of world GDP (De Carmoy, 1990, p. 111). By the end of the 1980s international trade was running at a level of around US $3000 billion per year while spot and forward exchange operations were between 50 and 75 per cent of that level *each day*. The financial world began to dominate the industrial world.

There were substantial shifts in the geographic division of financial power over two decades of change. Japan emerged as the clear winner. Japan became the world's major creditor nation and in the final years of the 1980s seven (and at one time eight) of the world's ten largest banks were Japanese. Japan became the major force in the principal money market centres, especially London. Japanese investors became dominant forces in the US securities market, and in the world's major property markets. The Japanese trade surplus did not fall after the Plaza Agreement, as expected, but rose to a peak of US $87 billion within two years.

Japan as a financial force

Japan had conquered the world's financial markets, just as before it had triumphed in so many of the world's manufacturing export markets. A long Japanese reign in the financial sphere seemed inevitable, and contributed substantially to the conclusion, drawn inevitably by so many, that the twenty-first century would belong to Pacific Asia. The proposition needs careful examination; the future shape of the Japanese financial system is critical not only for the future prospects of Asia but to the behaviour of the global financial system.

At their peak Japanese long-term capital exports were running at a level of US $42 billion above the current account surplus. Further, a number of investments had not been successful; between 1985 and 1987 Japanese life offices lost around US $40 billion on US Treasury bonds; and at the end of the decade Japanese investors lost heavily in both US and European property. Beyond 1988 the current account surplus slipped to be less than US $38 billion in late 1990 and forecasts for 1991 placed it between US $16 and 30 billion (*Fuji Economic Review*, January–February 1991, p. 7; *Mitsubishi Bank Review*, January 1991, p. 1250). Remarkably, the current account, after faltering early in 1991, rose to a level of US $60 billion by the end of the year. Japan's ability to sustain very high surpluses over the following decade, however, is debatable.

A number of domestic factors will influence Japan's financial status as well. Essentially, it will spend more at home and save less. A major outcome of the Structural Impediments Initiative was the agreement of the Japanese government to introduce a US $3010 billion programme of public works through to the year 2000. Private capital spending stayed at levels between 10 and 15 per cent higher in 1991 than in 1990 despite the introduction of tighter money policies. Consumer spending in 1990 reached a ten-year high (*Mitsubishi Bank Review*, October 1990, p. 1237), paralleling a decline in savings; in 1976, 23 per cent of disposable income was saved but in 1988 only 14.8 per cent (*Sumitomo Bank Economic Survey*, April 1991, p. 1). This is likely to continue: the population is ageing (by 2001, 21.2 per cent will be over 65 years of age compared to 13.8 per cent in 1985), tax and social security contributions have been climbing and home ownership (a key stimulus for saving) has become less possible because of high property prices.

Japanese finance, immensely strong to the world at large, has a degree of brittleness within. Property investment, both at home and abroad, became a Japanese obsession. The stock market soared to extraordinary levels. Manufacturing companies turned to *zaiteku*, financial engineering, as a major source of profit.

Urban property prices increased two and a half times over the 1980s. In 1990 Japan placed a theoretical value of US $14,000 billion on its property, land in Tokyo was selling at US $400,000 a square metre and Tokyo suburban houses were selling at 37 times average earnings. Land in Japan was valued as being four times as great as in the USA, a country 25 times larger.

Rising to its peak on 29 December 1990, the Nikkei stock market index stood at 38,915; the index had risen by 285 per cent between 1982 and mid-August 1987, and it then climbed a further 46 per cent to 1990 in defiance of the falls in other parts of the world. It fluctuated around a declining trendline throughout 1990 and 1991, reaching a low of 21,457 in 1991. In April 1992 it had fallen to 16,598, 57 per cent below the 1989 peak.

The problem in Japan is that all aspects of the financial system are intimately related. When Yasushi Mieno, head of the Bank of Japan, pushed up interest rates in 1990 and 1991 (eventually to a peak of 6 per cent) and restricted the money supply, alongside Ministry of Finance directives limiting lending for real estate, all segments of the Japanese system came under pressure.

The Tokyo Stock Exchange (TSE) has a very different market from those in other countries. Because of the immense web of cross-shareholdings associated with the *keiretsu*, 70 per cent of shares are normally never traded. The overheated markets pushed firms into issuing equity in the form of convertible bonds and warrant bonds; this, as well as the great earnings of the corporations, weakened their traditional dependence on the banks. Warrants are Eurobonds that give the buyer the option to purchase the bonds at fixed prices in four to five years time. By issuing dollar-denominated warrants in London and then using swaps to convert the money into yen the corporations were able to raise capital at what appeared to be very low (0.5 per cent) or negative rates of interest. This actually involved a numerical sleight-of-hand, as Kester (1991, p. 224) has demonstrated. The warrants were like time-bombs (and US $115 billion worth were issued between 1987 and 1989): harmless in a rising market but deadly in a collapsing market unless the options are mispriced in the company's favour. Even companies with abundant cash joined the rush. Toyota raised US $5.6 billion in the four years from 1986, and in 1990 more than 29 per cent of its operating profits came from *zaiteku*. As Kester (1991, p. 228) shows in a fairly typical year, 1987, were it not for *zaiteku* 47 of the largest 250 corporations would have shown no profit at all. In 1989 funds raised by companies on the TSE totalled US $175 billion, growing by 65 per cent in the year (*The Economist*, 24 March 1990, p. 81).

The giant life offices, always a significant force on the market, were induced into the speculative end of the system after 1984 by *tokkin* funds, which allowed them to separate speculative from stable funds and to gain tax advantages in the process.

Much of the capital raised on the stock market did not go into new production facilities but into the greater rewards offered in the stock and property markets. The fall in the stock market has occurred; and the property market has slipped significantly over recent years. In 1991 bankruptcies in Japan reached record levels, and most of these were property-related. By mid-year 1992, 70 per cent of property developers were reported as no longer paying the interest on their loans (*The Economist*, 11 April 1992, p. 72).

At the heart of both the shaky stock and property markets were the banks. In August 1990, Moodys downgraded the debt of Dai-Ichi Kagyo, the world's biggest bank, because in the year to 31 March 60 per cent of its profits had been generated by selling shares. From 1987 to 1989 Japanese banks raised US $42 billion in equity and equity-related finance. When the stock market fell it wiped out US $20 billion of bank capital, leading to a scramble to make it up. The cost of funds was then much greater (when the Ministry of Finance in June 1990 gave the banks the right to issue subordinated debt to raise funds some banks were looking at finance costing forty times that previously raised). In February 1991 the Industrial Bank of Japan lost its triple-A credit rating from Standard and Poor, and at the time it was the only Japanese bank with such a rating.

The property downturn affected the entire Japanese banking industry. In June 1990 the trust banks had 52 per cent of their total loans held against property collateral. The 30,000 lending institutions in the non-bank sector had a US $158 billion exposure to property (*The Economist*, 16 February 1991, p. 67). A major proportion of the funds of leasing companies and consumer-finance companies (which absorb 11 per cent of city bank funds) are on-lent for property. The biggest fears surround the 131 regional banks and the 452 *shinkin* (credit union) banks who married an over-exposure to property with a vigorous setting-up of *tokkin* accounts.

In 1991 banking frauds of the order of US $5 billion were exposed and security compensation deals worth US $1.3 billion came to light. Japan's major banks and security firms were involved. Ritual resignations were made by the heads of some organizations and eventually by the Minister of Finance. A deep malaise remained, however, at the heart of the Japanese financial system. As *The Economist* (17 August 1991, p. 13) observed:

> The scandals are sewn into the fabric of Japan's financial system, its corrupt politics and even of its business ways. They are systemic not only in nature but also in the risk they pose: the world's largest single source of capital and one of its top three financial centres is riddled with crookery, has been supervised by the blind or the complacent and could be facing collapse. Japan's dirt is dangerous stuff.

Japan cannot be isolated from the world financial system. Curiously, despite the number of Japanese institutions among the leading banks, they are relatively no more powerful than the American banks that preceded them. The proportional assets of the top ten, top twenty, top 100 and top 300 banks scarcely varied between 1973 and 1988 (De Carmoy, 1990, p. 115). What is more, the Japanese banks have not been very profitable. They adopted similar tactics to their industrial cousins: seeking 'loose bricks' in the fabric of world banking and then exercising their financial clout by pushing margins down to very slim levels. The average return on assets of Japanese banks from 1986 to 1989 was 0.34 per cent compared to British banks' 0.56 per cent and US banks' 0.47 per cent (*Euromoney*, September 1990, p. 113). The Japanese banks hid their true profit positions through transferring wrongly declared profits to offshore subsidiaries, leading Alicia Ogawa of SG Warburg Securities to comment: 'the tax fiddles revealed that they [Japanese banks] were in reality close to bankruptcy. They merely serve to demonstrate the delicate and fragile state of the Japanese banks' overseas operations' (*Euromoney*, September 1990, p. 115).

When in late 1987 the Bank for International Settlements (BIS) introduced new regulations that required banks to hold capital-to-assets ratios of 8 per cent by March 1993, the entire complection of Japanese banking was changed. To assist Japanese banks two tiers of capital were introduced, the second including subordinated debt and preferred shares. This allowed Japanese banks to count 45 per cent of the unrealized gains of their large shareholdings as capital. While the stock market boomed the banks had no problems; when the markets dived the capital requirements became a gigantic problem. A Nikkei index of 22,000 is seen as the bottom line in terms of Japanese banks' capability to meet the requirements. As the index slipped towards that level in 1990–1 the capital-raising efforts of the Japanese banks became more intense. This reverberated throughout the system, affecting especially the property elements.

Japanese banks were caught in a web of debt at home and abroad. They faced great challenges in meeting international capital requirements. Their traditional links to the industrial sector were punctured by the very success of *zaiteku*.

Japan will remain a significant force in the world financial scene, but the challenges both at home and abroad are such that it will be as much controlled by as controlling the system.

Asia in the 1990s

Asia's prospects for the next decade rest with Japan itself, and the way in which the regional economies can be integrated to withstand the threats of Europe and North America.

The key thing in Japan's favour is its commanding drive into high-tech industries. It has achieved this by various means.

(1) It has developed clear strategic intents, and built core competences that enable them to succeed. NEC, for example, is the only firm in the world to hold a top five position in mainframes, telecommunications and semiconductors. It clearly identified its interlinked goals in these areas and set about achieving the relevant competences in each. In the early 1980s NEC's sales were a third the level of the US GET corporation, but by 1988 NEC had increased its sales five-fold to US $21.9 billion, US $5.4

billion ahead of GET. Further, NEC had built across-the-board competences in each of its three main areas while GET had divested its television interests, had moved its switching, transmission and digital PABX operations into joint ventures and had closed down its semiconductor plants.

(2) Japanese companies have been brilliant exponents of competing through collaboration: they have used licensing, outsourcing and joint ventures to gain technology, to calibrate competitors' strengths and weaknesses, and to penetrate markets. Fujitsu's alliances with Siemens, STC and Amdahl or Matsushita's links with Thorn, Telefunken and Thomson illustrate the way these companies gained competitive edges against the giant Philips operation in Europe. Sales figures suggest that Japanese companies, in terms of brand share, are almost negligible in Europe; but through alliances Japanese companies account for a third of the value added in computer hardware manufacturing in Europe (Hamel and Prahalad, 1989, pp. 69–71).

(3) When necessary, Japanese companies have made strategic acquisitions; Sony's celebrated takeover of CBS is an example. Such acquisitions are generally not financially motivated (as were the majority of US and European takeovers during the mergers and acquisitions wave of the 1980s). They usually involved firms with whom the Japanese had prior production and marketing arrangements, and they then often proceeded through joint venture arrangements and finally led to equity positions.

Asia is at the competitive forefront of the next generation of information products. Japan's competitors have followed with some alarm Japan's progress in moving from being a follower in the technological race to becoming a leader. Between 1969 and 1981 Japan's compound growth rate of research and development (R&D) expenditure was 8.1 per cent compared to 1.8 per cent in the USA and 4.0 per cent in the EC. From 1981 to 1983 Japan sustained the same rate of growth as before while Europe slipped back to 2.5 per cent and the USA reached 3.8 per cent growth. As the second oil crisis abated Japan pushed its rate of R&D spending up to a compound 9.8 per cent, ahead of the USA's 7.3 and Europe's 6.0 per cent (James, 1989, p. 79). In terms of the Index of Comparative Advantage in High Technology Trade (OECD = 1.00) Japan moved from a low level of 0.72 in 1963 (USA 1.27, EC 1.01) to equal the USA in 1978 (1.27) and then to surpass the USA by 1985 (Japan 1.42, USA 1.25, EC 0.80).

In terms of total spending on R&D intensive industries (aerospace, electronics, computers, drugs, electrical machinery) Japan's spending had passed that of the EC by 1984 (28.8 per cent of world R&D spending compared to the EC's 26.1 per cent), and was close to the USA's level of 31.2 per cent. In 1970 Japan accounted for only 15 per cent of high-tech R&D spending whereas the USA had 35.4 per cent and the EC 33.0 per cent. Japan between 1970 and 1984 had doubled its spending on medium intensive R&D (cars, chemicals, non-electrical machinery, non-ferrous metals) to 21.5 per cent of the world total, and had maintained its spending on low intensity R&D (food, beverages, ferrous metals, fabricated metal products, paper, printing, textiles) while the USA had lowered its expenditure (James, 1989, pp. 89–90).

Japan and other Pacific Asian nations are likely to continue their high-performance record in R&D because the importance of research is accepted throughout the whole community: governments assist and reward research developments, and firms direct enormous resources to the process. As Kodama (1989, p. 201) has shown, in the latter part of the 1980s the R&D expenditure of major Japanese firms exceeded capital expenditure, often by large amounts. Japan's six largest electronic companies spend on R&D more than the total R&D spending of all but the five largest OECD countries (Walsh, 1988, p. 42).

Japanese corporations have hundreds of different projects under way at the same time, and this leads to introductions of new products at regular intervals. Resource allocation is not made on the basis of single products, however, but a whole series of products and extensions and variations. As Ohmae (1989, p. 83) has observed, many US companies are beguiled by the experience of the Manhattan Project; they rely wholly on elaborate and expensive R&D. The Japanese method is to run multiple projects with short lives (at NEC the average life of a project is under six months). Thus, cultivating core competences does not involve vastly outspending rivals on individual elements. Rather, it is the structure and environment of the R&D that counts. The traditional view of a linear sequence from basic research to product development to production and marketing gives way under the Japanese system to an interactive process requiring intensive traffic in facts, ideas and information within and beyond firms (Bureau of Industry Economics, 1991, p. 16). The corporation, in Kodama's terms (1989, p. 201) shifts from being a place for production to being a place for thinking.

While Japan and other Asian nations will maintain a high profile at the cutting edges of technology their success will be dependent on transforming the 'export-island' corporate structures into production systems that can overcome the barriers of a more protectionist world. The ability to do this is greatly complicated by the problems facing the finance industry. Japan in its profligate days of offshore investment gave manufacturing a low priority; the more limited capital availability of the 1990s will scarcely be sufficient to redress this.

Japan's attitudes to finance were in tune with its overall view of the world. As it became the world's biggest creditor nation and the world's largest earner of trading surpluses Japan sought to protect its own finance system from the rest of the world. This was impossible and the strains inevitably became too great. The stock market and banking crises of the early 1990s were the result.

The intimate relations between finance and industry in Japan have seen the financial problems rapidly translate into industrial difficulties. Despite the *zaiteku*, bank loans in 1992 were equivalent to 90 per cent of GNP in Japan compared to 37 per cent in the USA. The banks themselves were the major target in the selling which sent the Nikkei Index plumetting in the first half of 1992. Bad debts, the general tightness of money and the 1993 threat of the BIS requirements savaged the view of bank capital adequacy. In one week in early April 1992 bank shares fell by 28 per cent with those of the Industrial Bank of Japan diving by 41 per cent and those of Fuji Bank falling by 39 per cent (*The Economist*, 11 April 1992, p. 71).

The collapse of the stock market has challenged the delicate web of cross-shareholdings that hold together the *kigyo keiretsu*. Banks are less capable of performing the salvage operations that they performed in the past while the collapsing share market and falling profits place each element of the groupings under strain. The special features of the system that served the Japanese export island so well in the open trading decades from the 1950s begin to look precarious in the restricted era of the 1990s.

Japan might be the heart of the Pacific Asian economy but it is not the whole. Might the more highly integrated regional economy be capable of relating to external challenges and the problems of Japan itself? The answer is probably no.

There is no clear shape to the emerging regional structure. Japanese, Korean and Taiwanese investment and manufacturing growth have created an East Asian industrial core with strong linkages to the ASEAN periphery. This represents the most obvious form of regional cohesion but there are many other complicating regional forces. China is a conundrum. Its size and resources make it a potentially massive influence. Along its southern borders it is re-creating the Hong Kong miracle many times over, and China has strong links offshore through the wealthy and powerful network of overseas Chinese businessmen throughout Asia. Concepts such as the EAEG grouping suggest another arrangement: the creation eventually of a giant customs zone with some equality of positions within and a common bond against the outside world.

At another level other forces are at work. North and South Korea, China and Russia have explored a giant free trade area near their common borders. Singapore has taken a leading role in linking the economies of Malaysia and Indonesia with itself. Thailand has become a major investor from Burma in an arc across Indo-China. And to the north Central Asia, with its array of newly independent countries (Azerbaijan, Kazakhstan, Uzbekistan, Kirghizia and Tajikistan) introduces another complication to the maze that is regional Asia.

Without doubt Pacific Asia, with the world's largest population, the world's youngest population, the world's fastest growing population and the fastest growing incomes, will remain a vital and dominant segment of the world's economy. Its economic passage in the 1990s, however, will not be as comfortable or as predictable as the seers of the early 1980s believed.

References

Bureau of Industry Economics (1991) *Networks: a Third Form of Organization*. Discussion Paper 14. Canberra: AGPS.

Business International (1990) *Taiwan*. London: Economist Intelligence Unit.

Daly, M. T. and Logan, M. I. (1989) *The Brittle Rim: Finance, Business and the Pacific Region*. Ringwood, Victoria: Penguin.

De Carmoy, H. (1990) *Global Banking Strategy*. Oxford: Basil Blackwell.

Eli, M. (1990) *Japan Inc.: Global Strategies of Japanese Trading Corporations*. London: McGraw-Hill.

Freeman, C. (1988) Japan: a new national system of innovation. In G. Dosi et al. (eds), *Technical Change and Economic Theory*. London: Pinter, 330–48.

Hamel, G. and Prahalad, C. K. (1989) Strategic intent. *Harvard Business Review*, May–June, 63–76.

Henderson, J. (1989) *The Globalisation of High Technology Production*. London: Routledge.

James, B. G. (1989) *Trojan Horse: the Ultimate Japanese Challenge to Western Industry*. London: Mercury.

JETRO (1991) *White Paper on Foreign Direct Investment*. Tokyo: Japan External Trade Organization.

Keohane, R. O. (1984) *After Hegemony: Cooperation and Discord in the World Political Economy*. Princeton, NJ: Princeton University Press.

Kester, W. C. (1991) *Japanese Takeovers*. Boston: Harvard Business School Press.

Kodama, F. (1989) How research investment decisions are made in Japanese industry. In D. Evered and S. Harnett (eds), *The Evaluation of Scientific Research*. Chichester: John Wiley, 201–14.

Maswood, S. J. (1989) *Japan and Protection*. New York: Routledge.

Nau, H. (1990) *The Myth of America's Decline*. Oxford: Oxford University Press.

Ohmae, K. (1989) *The Borderless World*. London: Fontana.

Prahalad C. K. and Hamel, G. (1990) The core competence of the corporation. *Harvard Business Review*, May–June, 79–91.

Scott, A. J. and Angel, D. P. (1988) The global assembly operations of US semiconductor firms: a geographic analysis. *Environment and Planning A*, 22, 1047–67.

Song B. N. (1990) *The Rise of the Korean Economy*. Oxford: Oxford University Press.

Steven, R. (1990) *Japan's New Imperialism*. London: Macmillan.

Wade, R. (1990) *Governing the Market*. Princeton: Princeton University Press.

Walsh, V. (1988) Technology and the competitiveness of small countries. In E. Andersen and B. A. Lundvall (eds), *Small Countries Facing the Technological Revolution*. London: Pinter, 37–66.

Woo, J. E. (1991) *Race to the Swift*. New York: Columbia University Press.

9

The Pension Fund Economy: the Evolving Regulatory Framework in Australia

Peter Marden and Gordon L. Clark

Introduction

One of the most significant developments in modern economies in recent years has been the rapid expansion of private pensions. The growth in private pension funds has affected all liberal democratic societies since the end of the Second World War, and is now making a large impact on Australian life. Presently, there are 3.7 million Australians covered by some 150,000 superannuation (pension) schemes. These schemes cover approximately 47 per cent of the total workforce, 80 per cent of which are company-based schemes. It is estimated that the schemes are valued at about A $60 billion dollars and constitute 17 per cent of the value of the Australian stock market (Plowman and Weaven, 1988). Thus, the emergence of the private pension system has had profound consequences for savings and investment. This is reflected in the fact that the superannuation industry is now one of the fastest growing industries in Australia.

The shift from a reliance on public social security arrangements as the normal form of retirement income maintenance to an increasingly privatized system of deferred benefit is now an essential feature of federal government economic policy, regardless of political party. However, as with all changes in public policy objectives, there have been costs and benefits associated with this shift in emphasis and policy. Of particular importance are the long-term economic and social implications of this shift, and its impact throughout the community. Above all, the growth of private pensions brings with it an expansion in the professionalization of investment and financial intermediation. Hence, questions concerning social justice, law and morality become an imperative normative context for matters of investment management. Therefore, the regulation and control of the investment function, the role of fiduciaries and the whole question of discretionary powers have increasingly come under scrutiny. Thus, the significance of private pensions in Australia and other developed economies must be viewed not simply from the basis of their long-term economic implications; other social objectives and obligations to the community are a fundamental part of this growing industry. It remains to be seen whether our inherited institutions are up to the task of managing the pension fund phenomenon.

In this chapter we attempt to place the growth of pensions within a theoretical context whereby the capital–labour relation, the role of the state and crucial legal processes are principal concerns. We suggest that the development of private pensions in Australia has emerged largely from the federal government's attempt to adjust macroeconomic policy to control real wages through the principle of deferred benefit. The legislative and institutional framework established within this political context has facilitated the growth in pensions, and is therefore fundamental to the regulation of occupational superannuation. In particular, the interpretive and adjudicative procedures of the Industrial Relations Commission, through a case-by-case approach to matters relating to pensions, has been crucial to the direction and pace of this development. In particular, we address the possible future direction of private pensions in Australia. Our key argument here is that the incredible growth in the pension fund economy demands that adequate regulatory control is forthcoming. Hence, the current crisis in the administration of corporate regulation in Australia may pose significant problems for effective regulatory control in this area. Either way, the equitable management and control of workers' pensions must be the critical area of concern for public policy formulation.

The Pension Fund Economy

Since the end of the Second World War all liberal democratic societies have experienced rapid growth in private pension funds. The economic, political and social implications of pensions, and the institutions involved in their regulation and management, are critical areas of concern for issues of social justice. The expansion of pension fund arrangements has brought to the forefront questions concerning the structure and functioning of capitalism, particularly the capital–labour relation and the role of the state. The question is: how do we conceptualize this phenomenon? Do orthodox economic theories of private pensions provide us with appropriate insight? Can we rely upon a Marxist critique of capitalism to be the viable alternative? If indeed we are witnessing a new era of capitalism generated by the peculiarities of pensions, as some commentators have suggested, what then is the nature of this development? Moreover, is it valid to assert that the growth in pensions fundamentally changes the labour contract?

Although in many respects social security and private pension issues are interrelated, it is important to point out for analytical purposes that they occupy different areas of interest (see Williamson et al., 1985). Both may indeed perform functions necessary for the reproduction of social welfare and stability. However, the mechanisms for control attributable to each system are quite different. For example, pensions are essentially a privatized form of wage deferrals and deferred benefit, while social security arrangements are an immediate public form of income maintenance derived from general revenue. Social security programmes predominantly reflect relations of control whose immediate reference is the sphere of state relations and public policy implementation and application. The private pension system, however, has its immediate reference point in the social relations of control through production relations and the labour contract. The distinction is important in the sense that welfare policies and social security programmes have been established by the state in most liberal democratic societies for a considerable time. The emergence of private pension schemes, however, is a relatively new phenomenon by comparison. Furthermore, it should be understood that the issue of control through pension or social security systems derives from the conceptual framework of the welfare state posited by neo-Marxists (see Frankel, 1983). This body of thought will be evaluated below, particularly as it relates to pensions. For the moment, we will examine the theoretical and empirical validity of the pension fund economy as a concept describing contemporary liberal democratic societies.

The phrase 'pension fund economy' is attributable to no one in particular. None the less, there is little doubt among commentators that the growth in pensions is bringing about profound changes in the economies of advanced capitalist societies. In many respects, these issues are most apparent in the United States, the one country with a long history and experience in the regulation of private pensions. In the USA private pension plans have increased considerably since 1945. In the first five years after the war, the proportion of the private non-farm workforce covered by plans increased from 19 to 48 per cent. By the end of the 1970s about 40 per cent of retirees were receiving US $35 billion of private pension benefits annually to supplement social security. The contributions to such plans amounted to US $70 billion a year, or approximately 6 per cent of wages and salaries, and aggregate assets exceeded US $400 billion. Between 1940 and 1980 private pension funds expanded from US $2.4 billion to a staggering US $400 billion (Munnell, 1982, p. 7). Today there are nearly one million plans in operation in the United States. Further, an overwhelming majority of workers in firms with at least 100 employees are covered by plans (Schieber, 1991). This growth has been accompanied by the expansion of other institutional investors, which now own almost one-third of the value of stocks on the New York Stock Exchange. Moreover, private pension trusts are the largest investors in the stock market. Further, the three major institutions (insurance companies, mutual funds and the pension industry) account for half the traded volume of the New York Stock Exchange (Munnell, 1982, p. 114). It is clear that in the United States pension funds are playing an increasingly important role in financial markets. This is largely because of the size of their holdings and their allocation across financial assets. In 1950 pension reserves accounted for 1.9 per cent of total household wealth; in 1980 pension reserves exceeded 6.0 per cent of household wealth. Moreover, pension investments are highly concentrated in financial securities. In 1983, pension funds owned close to 15 per cent of all corporate stock, 26 per cent of corporate bonds and 5 per cent of federal, state and local government securities (Kotlikoff and Smith, 1983, p. 2). Hence, with pension funds currently owning a substantial portion of the stock in US corporations it is not difficult to see how their voting powers can profoundly affect corporate policy (see Bodie and Papke, 1991).

In their exhaustive study of pensions in America, Kotlikoff and Smith (1983, pp. 2–3) concluded that pensions may be affecting the nation's rate of saving in two ways. First, employer-sponsored pensions represent a substitute for households' retirement saving, but the rate of substitution may be greater or less than dollar for dollar. A major feature of pension benefit saving is the illiquidity of the investment. Young households unable to gain direct access to these funds, or to borrow against the assets from financial institutions, may be reducing their consumption and raising their total saving above its alternative value. The tax-free accumulation of capital income within pension funds may provide incentives for increased total household saving to the degree that these tax advantages are impacting upon marginal household consumption decisions and not simply altering the allocation of a given amount of household saving between pension and non-pension saving vehicles. Second, pensions could be altering national saving if workers over- or underestimate the extent of retirement income forthcoming from their pension arrangement. Moreover, stockholders of companies with unfunded pension benefit liabilities may similarly over- or undervalue these liabilities. Such practices would make the stock market more vulnerable in the sense that valuations would impact upon shareholders' perceptions of their net true worth, and obviously result in a change in stockholders' consumption patterns. Thus, institutional investors carrying out speculative trading based on these perceptions could lead to stock market volatility.

The effect of pensions on saving is, undoubtedly, an important consideration. However, further research is required before any firm conclusions can be drawn on this issue. Munnell and Yohn (1991) argue that there are many complicating factors making it almost impossible to determine *a priori* the effect of pensions on saving. For example, the illiquidity of pension promises and uncertainty about the value of future benefits raises the question as to whether individuals reduce their other saving dollar for dollar in response to promised future benefits. Moreover, the taxation regime further complicates the analysis, particularly favourable tax provisions for compensation in the form of deferred pension benefits (see Munnell and Yohn, 1991). For example, does the higher net rate of return for pension saving cause employees to increase their total saving?

Notwithstanding the complexities of such questions the spread of private pensions continues. The coverage of private pension plans in the United States is extensive to say the least. In 1979 an estimated 30.2 million of 67.3 million private sector workers were covered under these schemes. Approximately 70 per cent of these 30.2 million were male, 89.3 per cent were white, 56.3 per cent were over the age of 40, 40.1 per cent had post-high school education, 34.1 per cent earned more than US $15,000 per year, 49.8 per cent were white-collar workers and 44.1 per cent worked in manufacturing (Kotlikoff and Smith, 1983, p. 4). Moreover, private pension plan participants are highly concentrated in large plans: 78.06 per cent belong to plans with one thousand or more covered workers. Another striking statistic is that almost half of all private pension participants are enrolled in union plans, even though only 25 per cent (in 1983) of the total private workforce belonged to unions (Kotlikoff and Smith, 1983, p. 5).

The development of pension funds in Australia will be discussed at length throughout the rest of this chapter. For the moment, it is worth noting that in 1988 pension funds accounted for some A $60 billion and 17 per cent of traded volume in the Melbourne stock market (Plowman and Weaven, 1988, p. 4). Moreover, as of June 1990, 49 per cent of all full-time employees were covered by employer-sponsored superannuation (see figure 9.1). Space does not permit elaboration of the extent of

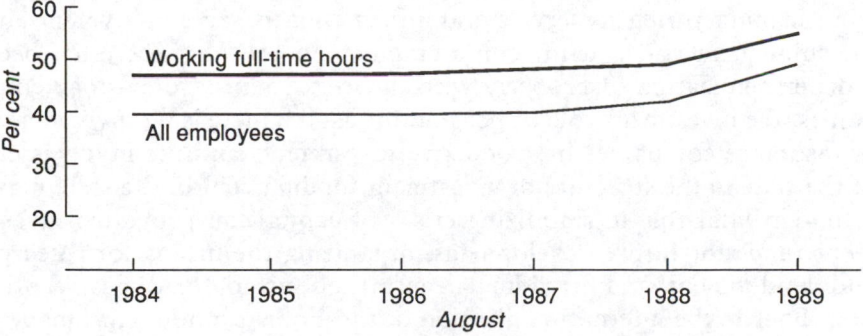

Figure 9.1 Employees in main job: proportion of employees receiving a superannuation benefit, August 1984 to August 1989.
Source: ABS, 1989.

pension coverage in other modern economies; suffice to say that coverage in Britain, Sweden and France is similarly extensive, albeit quite different in structure and organization (see Lucas, 1977; Pontusson, 1984; Lynes, 1985). On the basis of these studies, it is clear that since the end of 1945 there has been a considerable expansion in pension coverage for workers in advanced capitalist societies. But does this trend mean that we can confidently claim that we have entered into a pension fund economy with specific, and unique, configurations on the channelling of investments? Despite the semantics of such a debate we can assert that there has been a growth of financial intermediation in the capitalist world, whereby the role of financial intermediaries in the major financial markets has increased substantially. To this extent, the proportion of financial claims (stocks, bonds and other debt instruments) held by individual investors or households has decreased significantly since the end of the Second World War, and the proportion held by financial intermediaries (banks, thrift institutions, insurance companies, pension plans and investment companies) has increased. We now examine this phenomenon more closely within a theoretical context.

Theoretical Perspectives on the Pension Fund Economy

Essentially, the common problem with all economic theories of pensions is that they have been unable to advance a satisfactory explanation for the existence of public pension plans (Nektarios, 1982). Similarly, the Marxist accounts have found difficulty in coming to terms with recent changes in the social structure of contemporary capitalism. Of course, the extent and nature of these changes are subject to continuing debate, but some dominant features can be advanced (see Turner, 1989).

First, there has been a relative decline in the proportion of traditional, blue-collar working classes in the total employment structure of modern capitalist societies. This has resulted from the widely recognized shift from manufacturing to service and information based employment and the subsequent rise in white-collar employment. Second, there has been a depersonalization of property with the expansion of joint-stock companies, the investment role of pension funds, the increasing involvement of insurance companies in productive investments and the involvement of the state in the structure of investment funding. Third, the state plays a fundamental role in stabilizing crises of capitalism, providing investment funds for future development, organizing the means for research and development, and providing a centralized system for wages negotiation. Fourth, the internationalization of the global economy has made it continually difficult for nation states to manoeuvre effectively in the organization of their own internal economies in relation to powerful world economic trends. Fifth, although there has been a relative decline in real wages for most workers, there has paradoxically been a trend towards increased consumption through the expansion of financial and distributional systems.

Despite the significance of all the above trends, we would argue that it has been the rapid expansion of private pension funds in the capitalist world that has presented Marxist critiques of market-based economies with their greatest challenge. Through the extension of private pensions to average employees, workers have become joint investors with individual companies and management, resulting in an apparent shared responsibility for continued productivity and profit. Hence, although the labour contract has not fundamentally altered in the sense that salaries and wages in exchange for work time are still the dominant arrangement between capital and labour, there is none the less a subtle imperative for capital–labour cooperation, recognizing the mutual benefits to both parties in maintaining the value of promised pensions.

It is important to note that these changes in the capital–labour relations of capitalism, in particular the increasing significance of the financial sphere, are not solely derived from either the political or economic sphere of social life. Rather, they have emerged through significant developments in legal policy and practice, and are given expression in the regulatory processes continually at work in capitalist society. This does not deny the importance of economic and political imperatives, but suggests that pension fund capital formation and professional investment management as a central development in market-based economies have brought to the forefront critical questions concerning legal principle and liability. Hence, the nature of the pension fund economy is derived not simply from a combination of private sector forces and state intervention, but also from the regulatory outcomes of administrative law. As we have argued elsewhere, an adequate theory of regulation in capitalist society must move beyond economic imperatives by giving attention to the regulatory practices of agencies and the rules of adjudication (see Clark, 1992; Marden, 1992). In the case of pensions and matters of control in investment management, the social obligations of fund managers and the behaviour of corporations may at times come into conflict with community norms and existing laws – it is here that due attention to legal policy will not go unrewarded, particularly within the context of social justice.

According to Robert C. Clark (1981, pp. 562–74), the history of capitalist enterprise in the United States can be meaningfully organized into four distinct stages. These stages are like generations that overlap with one another; there are no clear lines of demarcation, although each has its own time of rapid growth. The first stage is the *age of the entrepreneur*, who may also be labelled the 'bourgeois capitalist' or 'robber baron'. This was the age of the promoter-investor-manager and large-scale business corporations, and was primarily a nineteenth-century phenomenon. The key distinctive feature was the emergence of the corporation as a form of business organization. The correlating legal policy instrument was the increased enactment of general incorporation statutes and enabling laws.

The second stage is the *age of the professional business manager*, which reached maturity in the early decades of the twentieth century. This individual emerged when the entrepreneurial function was split into ownership and control. The corresponding institution of the age was the modern public-held corporation. This second stage required the legal system to provide stable relationships between professional managers and public investors, seemingly designed to keep the former accountable to the latter. However, it also aimed to place full control of business decisions in the managers' hands. The key legal policy instrument was the enactment of the federal securities laws during the Depression. This second stage created the modern conception of corporation law, and focused on the relationships of corporations and their fiduciaries to public security holders.

The third stage categorized by Clark is the *age of the portfolio manager* which grew since the beginning of this century, reaching its peak in the 1960s. The characteristic institution is the institutional investor, or financial intermediary. This stage is noted for the incredible expansion of professional investment managers. For Clark (1981, p. 564), the increasing separation of the decision concerning how to invest from the decision to supply capital for investment 'is one of the most striking institutional developments in our century'. Since the beginning of the century in the United States, the proportion of savings channelled through various financial intermediaries has grown steadily, to where approximately eighty cents of every dollar saved can now be located with some intermediary. As is to be expected, the role of financial intermediaries in the major financial markets has also increased dramatically.

The fourth stage outlined by Clark is the *age of the savings planner* and is currently in its infancy. In the preceding stage, the capital ownership function was split into the decision to supply capital funds and active investment management, which became increasingly professionalized. However, this fourth stage splits capital supplying into the possession of beneficial claims and the decision to save, a function that has also become increasingly professionalized. For example, decisions concerning the method and extent of saving are being made by group representatives on behalf of individual members. Hence, present collective consumption is being deferred in favour of future consumption. Moreover, the role of new professional savings planners is a major characteristic of this fourth stage, inasmuch as the sponsors and administrators of large corporate pension plans are rarely actively involved in the investment function. This important development sees the investment function being contracted out to bank trust departments, insurance companies, investment advisory firms and investment management services. Individuals who bargain over employee pension plans, such as the corporate officers and union representatives, occupy key roles. In addition, the financial intermediaries' officers responsible for marketing benefit packages and the government decision-makers formulating and implementing social security policy also play central roles.

In sum, Clark's evolutionary model reveals that the shift from one stage to another is characterized by two features: increased division of labour and increased participation in the profits of capitalist enterprise. As each stage progresses, distinct aspects of the capital-mobilizing process are split off and professionalized. This process creates a set of institutional arrangements that facilitate a greater portion of the population obtaining a share in capital income. Thus, the first stage is marked by a small elite group with direct claims on capital income. The second and third stages, however, are characterized by a wider dispersal of those with claims on capital income. In stage four, the term 'capitalists' can be applied to all participants in employee benefit plans, and includes a significant portion of the population with substantial investment claims. A greater sharing of the benefits of capitalist enterprise by a greater number, however, has also led to the concentration of discretionary powers in the hands of professional managers and group representatives. Hence, with the increase of the share in benefits there has been a decrease in the actual power of the individual saving function.

The above trends, as outlined by Clark, were also discussed a few years earlier by Drucker (1976) in his use of the phrase 'pension fund socialism'. In this insightful work, Drucker argued that if socialism is defined as ownership of the means of production by the workers, then the United States 'is the first truly Socialist country' (p. 1). Through the establishment of pension funds, American employees have considerable claims through their shares of equity capital, and this is growing as time passes. For Drucker, the American pension fund represents a more substantial shift in ownership than at any time since the end of feudalism. This development has major implications for theory:

> The shift to an economy in which the 'worker' and the 'capitalist' are one and the same person, and in which 'wage fund' and 'capital fund' are both expressed in and through 'labor income', is radical innovation and at odds with all received theory. That the 'capital fund' is created out of labor income – and payments into a pension fund, whether made by employer, employee, or both, are 'deferred wages' and 'labor costs' – is perfectly sound Marxism. But it is totally incompatible with both classic economic theory and Keynesian neoclassicism. That this 'capital fund' is in turn channelled back through 'labor income' – which is what pension payments are – is again perfectly sound classical theory. But it is totally incompatible with Marxism, even at its most revisionist. (Drucker, 1976, p. 34)

Despite Drucker's optimistic claims regarding the rapid development of private pensions in the United States, we argue that he overstates the implications for the capital–labour relation. To suggest that this trend fundamentally alters this relationship to the extent that workers are now capitalists is ambitious to say the least. For example, recent work by Gordon L. Clark (1993) concerning pensions and corporate restructuring in the United States suggests that the dominance of capital over labour is still very much a part of contemporary capitalism. Clark has been particularly concerned to highlight a disturbing trend whereby some corporations are restructuring with the objective of illegally avoiding early retirement pension obligations (see Clark, 1990a, b). It is also important to make a distinction between workers gaining a greater share in capital income and the issue of ownership and control, for although pension funds have grown to an enormous size in the United States, there is little worker control over these huge funds (Mathews, 1989). We will return to this concern later in the chapter. For now, however, we need to examine how the development of private occupational superannuation (pensions) has occurred in Australia.

Australian Corporatism and Pensions

The rapid increase in pension schemes has been part of a systematic policy orientation, on behalf of the federal government, to control wage increases through the principle of deferred benefit. Thus, to a large extent, this development has been primarily a response to economic conditions and is seen predominantly as the solution to some of the problems facing the Australian economy. It has also been achieved through an active strategy by the trade union movement in their push for a 'social wage'. Hence, the increasing importance of pensions in Australian society can be viewed as the result of these two concurrent developments. More importantly though, the emergence of private pensions has occurred through a corporatist consensus-based political agenda known as the Accord. With this model of macro-policy planning, both unions and government have achieved their respective, yet incomplete, objectives regarding macro/micro economic reform and wages.

The adoption of the corporatist model has, therefore, been the preferred response to economic problems and pensions – a critical component in this approach. What are some of these economic problems? There is little doubt that Australia is currently facing a savings crisis. On average, Australian households are saving approximately 9 per cent of their post-tax income, compared with 12 per cent at the end of the 1970s. And although there has been an increase in the business sector over the same period, it has not been sufficient to offset the dramatic fall in household saving. One of the consequences of this fall has been an increasing dependence on overseas savings and a spiralling foreign debt. Australia's net foreign debt rose to A$103 billion (US $78 billion) at the end of March 1989 – a rise of A$7.2 billion during the quarter. Gross debt rose by A$5.3 billion to A$128.6 billion (US$97 billion). Net debt was 31.7 per cent of GDP at the end of March, the same ratio reached in 1985–6. Debt had dropped to 30.6 per cent of GDP by 1987–8 but rose again in financial year 1988–9 as Australia's poor trade performance brought the current account deficit to a record high of more than A$17 billion. The rise in debt will put further pressure on the current account of the balance of payments because of the interest payments required to service it. Interest payments accounted for about A$6.6 billion of the current account deficit in the first three quarters of the year (see Clark, 1989).

It is quite clear that unless Australia can increase national savings, there is little chance for improving either the current account or the foreign debt situation. Moreover, it is important to note that households constitute the largest group of savers in the Australian community. Thus, household savings are a major influence on savings level. One of the policy measures used by the federal government to increase savings and investment and reduce consumption has, of course, been the attempt to facilitate and encourage superannuation schemes. The simple economic logic behind this policy is that increasing contributions to schemes will increase the savings level and provide a pool of local investment funds, while simultaneously decreasing levels of consumption. The success of this strategy remains to be seen. This is largely owing to the fact that some savers may simply substitute one form of saving for another when offered superannuation tax concessions. Indeed, it has been argued that the security of superannuation may actually lower voluntary saving (see Clark, 1989).

Although the superannuation coverage for workers has fallen short of early predictions made by the federal government there has been a substantial increase in the number of workers receiving a superannuation benefit. For example, the proportion of employees receiving a superannuation benefit (i.e. belonging to a superannuation scheme or fund arranged by their employer) was steady from 1984 to 1988 at about 40 per cent (Australian Bureau of Statistics, 1989). By August 1989, however, the proportion had increased to 47 per cent (refer to figure 9.1). This increase would include the impact of the spread of occupational superannuation following the 1990 National Wage Case Decisions. There was a similar increase in the proportion of private sector (full-time in main job) employees receiving a superannuation benefit, which was estimated at 48 per cent in 1989 compared with 41 per cent in 1988. In figure 9.2 there is a breakdown of full-time recipients of superannuation by industry and sex. The proportion of full-time public sector employees also rose from 71 per cent in 1988 to 73 per cent in

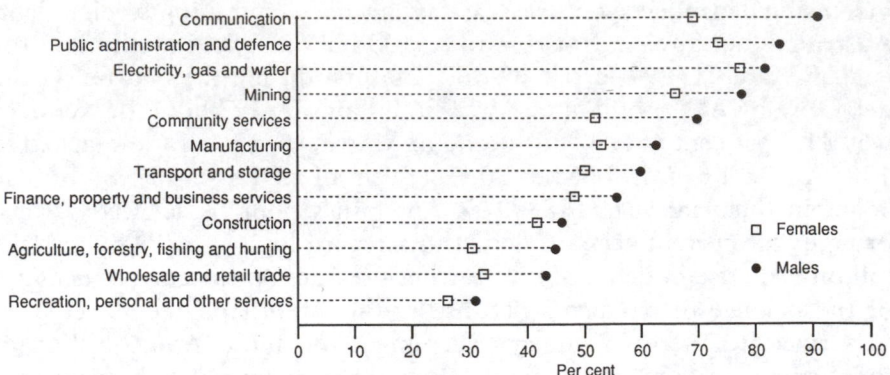

Figure 9.2 Full-time employees in main job: proportion of employees receiving a superannuation benefit by industry, August 1989.
Source: ABS, 1989.

1989. Relatively large increases were recorded for part-time employees. In 1988 the proportion of such employees receiving a superannuation benefit was 13 per cent for public sector employees and 7 per cent for those in the private sector. In 1989, these ratios had risen to 21 per cent and 14 per cent respectively (Australian Bureau of Statistics, 1989).

Whether federal government predictions concerning superannuation coverage will be realized in the near future is debatable. None the less, the extent of the coverage so far is a clear example of the government's intentions regarding the use of employer-financed pensions to facilitate macroeconomic adjustment in the light of severe problems facing the Australian economy. It also forms a central component in their labour relations agenda and wages policy. The challenge has been to initiate these adjustments without encountering the wrath of the trade unions who, through national Wage Case Decisions, have had to put aside their claims for wage increases by accepting pension fund investments as an alternative. This has largely been achieved through a consensus-based corporatist arrangement between the Australian Labor Party (ALP) and the Australian Council of Trade Unions (ACTU). But how durable is this arrangement? And what, if any, lessons can be learned from overseas experiences regarding this arrangement, particularly as it relates to pensions? To answer these questions we first briefly examine some of the central propositions of corporatism.

Corporatism – or more correctly neo-corporatism (see Schmitter, 1979; Crouch, 1982) – involves the centralization of decision-making by key groups in society, such as business, unions and government, on the basis of cooperation and consensus. It can be considered a form of pluralism in that it discards the authority of the state (see Rawson, 1986). In this regard, corporatism is consistent with the radical extension of pluralism – namely elite theory – which sees society as a pyramid with groups of social elites at the pinnacle. Hence, access to political power is restricted to the elites, and the majority are limited to symbolic political processes. Corporatism regards the state, in its relations with other institutions, as being autonomous and independent. There is some debate about just how corporatism should be viewed. For example, should it be viewed as a political structure, an economic system, a system of interest representation or an institutional pattern of policy formation, or perhaps more broadly as simply a system of politico-economic organization (see Crouch, 1979)?

Space does not permit a more thorough elaboration of some of the theories of corporatism presented here (for a useful summary see Dabscheck, 1989). Needless to say, there does appear to be a revised interest in the concept, particularly linking theories of the state and democracy with notions of justice (see Sainsbury, 1988). Moreover, continued interest in theories of capitalist regulation concerned with analysing the relationship between regulatory agencies, interest groups and the state is also bringing about a systematic re-evaluation of some of the central propositions of corporatist theorists, albeit from within a particular socio-theoretical perspective. It is important to note that these approaches differ from the more conventional perspectives on regulation, such as *capture theory*, which views the state and regulatory bodies as instruments used and manipulated by private interest groups from within an orthodox supply and demand framework. They also differ from another traditional model of regulation known as *bargaining theory*, which views regulators (individuals residing over regulatory bodies) as being independent from competing interest groups (see Posner, 1974; Wilson, 1980). Thus, the important aspect of recent theoretical developments in regulation theory has been the realignment with corporatist theory, and how this convergence provides a useful framework from which to examine the phenomenon of pensions in Australian society.

As previously mentioned, there are two significant factors concerning the rise of private pensions in the Australian setting, namely a state-led response to macroeconomic conditions and the corporatist arrangement between the ACTU and the ALP. These conditions have led to some landmark decisions regarding the bargaining power of trade unions over superannuation issues in National Wage Case rulings. A key factor has been the ACTU's agreement with the federal government to refrain from raising real wages and reducing working hours below 38 per week, in return for increased bargaining power over pension benefits. This has occurred as a direct result of the Prices and Incomes Accord, and of what Niland (1986, p. 12) refers to as the 'corporatism of social contracts'. Such a corporatist arrangement may be considered to be 'new' in the Australian experience. However, a brief look at pensions, unions and collective bargaining in the United States reveals that similar conditions prevailed there in the late 1940s and early 1950s. We argue that the evolution of pensions in the United States contains fundamental insights into possible future developments in Australia (see Clark, 1990a, 1993). Hence, it is necessary to highlight some of the landmark decisions that provided unions with the same rights over pension bargaining that we in Australia are now experiencing.

Since the Second World War, American industrial unions, such as the United Steelworkers of America (USWA) and the United Auto Workers (UAW), have played central roles in the growth and expansion of private pension coverage. This has largely been achieved because these unions were so successful in establishing pensions as legitimate and imperative subjects for collective bargaining. The unions were also fundamental in the developing political and legal constituencies for the federal regulatory framework, such as the Employee Retirement Income Security Act of 1974 (ERISA), established to protect workers' pension rights. The ERISA was the first comprehensive pension law passed by congress and served a two-fold purpose: to protect workers' pension rights by federal government guarantee and to broaden the coverage of pension benefits to include many non-union employees.

The significance of major industrial unions, particularly the USWA, in generating the growth and expansion of private pension plans was made possible by landmark decisions of the National Labor Relations Board (NLRB) and the federal courts in the late 1940s, the most significant being the suit brought by the USWA against the Inland Steel Corporation. In sum, the NLRB's decision in this case, and the US Supreme Court's decision to review and overturn a lower court's ruling in *Inland Steel* v. *NLRB*, made pension benefits a legitimate and mandatory subject for collective bargaining. The company argued that it was not mandated to bargain over the conditions of its pension plan. The union, however, argued that the rules, conditions and benefit levels of pension plans were subjects that should be deemed fundamental to the wages and conditions of employees. The company maintained that wages should be interpreted narrowly as constituting compensation for the completion of assigned work tasks. Thus, pension benefits were not earned wages and therefore not subject to negotiation. In a very important decision, the NLRB maintained that 'we are not convinced and find that the term "wages" as used in Section 9(a) must be construed to include emoluments of value, like pension and insurance benefits, which may accrue to employees out of their employment relationship. There is indeed an inseparable nexus between an employee's current compensation and his future pension benefits' (Clark, 1990a, p. 152).

The decision of the NLRB was a major contributing factor which facilitated the growth and expansion of pension benefits in the postwar US economy. The bargaining over pension benefits by trade unions became a legal right at a time when their ability to gain further wage increases was limited by political and economic concerns. At the time (*circa* 1950) there was growing concern from within both government and the corporate sector concerning the push for increased wages from powerful trade unions. Moreover, pension plans were viewed by unions and the US federal government as a means by which wage concessions could be gained without risking the obvious possibility of macro-economic instability in wages and prices: inflation. This is just the kind of circumstance faced by unions and the government in Australia now. It would not be an exaggeration to claim that superannuation as a form of deferred wages is a policy available to many governments in all kinds of settings.

It would be erroneous, however, to suggest that the role of unions in the spread of private pensions in the United States was the result of a corporatist arrangement. Rather, it was largely owing to the then entrepreneurial nature of American unions and the shared willingness of unions and the Truman Administration to provide new channels of income security for union members. Thus, we cannot really speak of an American corporatist political model, and its emergence in the near future seems unlikely. None the less, unions have played a vital role in gaining federal government support for their legitimate claims for pension rights protection, as the passage of ERISA in 1974 indicates. Of course, much the same has occurred in Australia, but unlike in the United States this has largely derived from corporatist developments, where there has been a more resolute collaboration between business, unions and government in the economic sphere. Of particular importance has been the regulatory regime established through legislative and statutory provisions. Hence, the role of the state has been fundamental to the development of occupational superannuation in Australia. It is to this area that we now turn.

The Evolving Regulatory Framework

The federal government has used income tax concessions as the key policy instrument in controlling and regulating the development of superannuation. It must be remembered that the Commonwealth does not have power to legislate on superannuation directly, but it does have complete taxation powers, and it has used these to gain effective control. There is little doubt that the decade of the 1980s was the most significant in the history of superannuation development in Australia. It was the decade where major taxation reform was initiated, based on the numerous findings of various task forces and committees constituted to report on superannuation. In particular, the government was concerned to reverse the trend that was occurring in the early 1980s, whereby superannuation funds were actively promoted by some as a means of minimizing income tax. In 1982, this trend was considerably reduced by the determination of the Australian Taxation Office that the level of deductible contributions was to be partly determined by the extent that a superannuation fund lent money back to the sponsoring employer (the higher the loan-back, the lower the contributions). In 1985 the government declared that loan-backs would be restricted to a maximum of 10 per cent of the assets of superannuation funds, with the objective of eliminating the use of superannuation as a means of tax avoidance.

In 1984, the Hawke government announced the most significant changes to legislation affecting the taxation of superannuation in 25 years (see Mercer Campbell Cook and Knight, 1987, for detail). Of particular importance was the abolition of the long-standing 30/20 rule, which had required that 30 per cent of a fund's assets (at cost) be invested in government securities, including 20 per cent in Commonwealth government securities. In 1985, the government also introduced the controversial income/assets test for eligibility for social security pensions. In November of the same year, the dollar limits on the maximum lump sum benefits were removed, so that the maximum benefit has become seven times final average salary, for all levels of salary. One of the most significant events, however, was the September hearing of the National Wage Case, with the ACTU arguing for a 3 per cent 'productivity' national wage increase being granted in the form of superannuation benefits. On this issue, the employers sought a High Court ruling that the Arbitration Commission could not hear this matter on the grounds that superannuation was not an industrial issue. The High Court ruled that the Arbitration Commission could have jurisdiction over superannuation. Subsequent to that ruling, the Commission determined that there was no justification for an across-the-board 3 per cent productivity rise, but that individual unions could negotiate such productivity increases with individual companies or industry bodies. Subject to certain conditions, the Arbitration Commission would ratify such agreements.

Two very significant legislative provisions were enacted by the Hawke government in 1987 and have had major implications for the direction of occupational superannuation in Australia. The first of these was the Occupational Superannuation Standards Act 1987 (OSSA); the second was the establishment of the Insurance and Superannuation Commission (ISC), which was created under the Insurance and Superannuation Commissioner Act 1987. The OSSA (Act No. 97 of 1987) was assented to on 5 November 1987 and proclaimed to commence on 21 December 1987. The Act has been consolidated to incorporate amendments made from its commencement by the Taxation Laws Amendment Act (No. 4) 1987 (Act No. 138 of 1987). It should be recognized that the OSSA and other related legislative provisions were outcomes of a long-incubated system of legal control of occupational superannuation at the end of 1987. This legal/institutional regulatory framework is still evolving, as demonstrated by recent changes, including the Taxation Laws Amendment Act

(No. 2) 1989, the Income Tax Rates Amendment Act (No. 2) 1989, the Taxation Laws Amendment (Superannuation) Act 1989 and the Income Tax (Fund Contributions) Act (No. 2) 1989.

The regulations contained within the OSSA, and carried out by the ISC, are the principle regulatory measures by which the government regularly assesses and evaluates the development of occupational superannuation. When taken in consideration with the various changes to the tax regime relating to superannuation, it becomes considerably difficult for trustees and superannuation practitioners to engage in schemes outside the general interest of members. By signing the prescribed certificate on the annual return under the requirements set out by the OSSA, trustees accept the primary responsibility for ensuring that funds comply with the necessary conditions. The ISC monitors a fund's compliance with the requirements, largely on the basis of the annual return and the audit certificate. Moreover, the Commission has the power to investigate those funds where non-compliance is suspected, and random routine examinations are frequently conducted. The incentive for fund managers to comply is strongly influenced by the tax concessions available.

The level of assets of the insurance and superannuation bodies for which the Commission has supervisory responsibility is currently approaching \$160 billion (ISC, 1989). These regulatory obligations have enabled the Commission to monitor the investment performance of particular funds and fully to scrutinize any anomalies that may arise from insurance companies' solvency. Ownership of assets is fundamental in the effective monitoring process and insurers are relied upon to claim assets correctly for solvency purposes. It is important to note that many insurance companies are increasingly making use of investment managers in the control and management of investment portfolios. The ISC does not object to this situation, with the understanding that expert advice and service is a viable strategy. However, under the OSSA it is not permissable for a situation to arise where control of the insurer's funds is placed under the complete discretion of the manager such that he or she becomes in law the owner of the assets. Thus, the insurance company at all times must take full responsibility for all investment decisions and have complete control over those assets.

Other important considerations are issues concerning related company assets, which are dealt with under Section 30 of the Insurance Act 1973. Section 30 provides that related company assets (greater than 25 per cent ownership or control), unless approved by the Commissioner, are not eligible assets for the purposes of a company's authority to engage in insurance activities. Approvals in relation to this section are not given as a matter of course, inasmuch as companies seeking approval of such assets need to establish a case having regard to the criteria set out in the Act. The Commission argues that there is always a degree of uncertainty about whether the insurer is, in reality, in fiduciary control of assets placed in the hands of a related company or whether other interests in those assets might take precedence over the interests of policy-holders. Recent significant financial failures of a number of company groups have prompted the need to restrict the movement of funds between insurer

Table 9.1 Outcomes of superannuation disputes before the Industrial Relations Commission, 1987 to March 1990

Appellant	Respondent	Dispute	Outcome	Justice(s)	Date	Case listing (AILR)
Whitehand[a]	Jenkins (liquidator)	Refusing to pay surrender value	Dismissed	Ormiston	6/2/87	29(8), 146
Magda Woods	Email Ltd	Conflict over pay-out	Upheld	Fisher	22/5/87	29(14), 253
Anthony Squires (Aust) p/l[b]	Spielman	Error of principle	Dismissed	Full bench	7/10/87	30(1), 4
FCUA[c]	Royal Automobile Association (SA) Inc.	Choice of fund	Upheld	Eglington	28/3/88	30(14), 278
Every and Ors	Clyde Industries Ltd	Unfairness of benefits	Dismissed	Bauer	29/3/88	30(10), 186
AJA[d]	Bell Publishing	Choice of fund	Dismissed	Laing	10/6/88	30(16), 307
Royal Automobile Association (SA) Ltd	FCUA	Choice of fund	Dismissed	Full bench	30/6/88	30(18), 354
ATWU[e] and Anor	R. E. Spence and Co. p/l	Range of funds	Upheld	Merriman	5/7/88	30(16), 307
Electrolyte Zinc Co. (Aus.)	TWU (Tas.)[f]	Claim for ill-health benefit	Dismissed	Gozzi	18/7/88	31(7), 127
Dillon	Burns Philip Finance Ltd and Ors	Fairness of collateral arrangement	Upheld	Bryson	20/7/88	30(21), 413
Wilson	NEI Pacific Ltd	Definition of ordinary time earnings	Upheld	Sweeney	10/8/88	30(24), 469
AMIEU (WA)[g]	Action Food Barns and Ors	Choice of fund	Dismissed	Full bench	8/2/89	31(8), 143
Child Care Industry	FMWU[h]		Dismissed	Full bench	8/6/89	32(8), 387

Appellant	Respondent	Dispute	Outcome	Justice(s)	Date	Case listing (AILR)
Robe River Iron Association	AMWSU and Ors[i]		Dismissed	Full bench	7/8/89	32(8), 142
FMWU (NT)[j]	Australian Development Ltd		Dismissed	McKenzie	15/9/89	32(8), 84
Bellmist p/l	AMWUEQ[k]		Dismissed	Moynihan	30/2/90	Case 30, 1989[l]

Notes: [a]Supreme Court; [b]Supreme Court, Court of Appeal; [c]Federal Clerks' Union of Australia; [d]Australian Journalist Association; [e]Australian Timber Workers' Union; [f]Transport Workers' Union; [g]Australian Meat Industry Employees' Union; [h]Federated Miscellaneous Workers' Union; [i]Amalgamated Metal Workers' and Shipwrights' Union; [j]Federated Mining Workers' Union; [k]Amalgamated Metal Workers' Union of Employees Queensland; [l]Case number listed in *Decision Summary IRC*, 20 April 1990.

and related company. In order to meet the minimum solvency requirements under the Act, some insurers are seeking approval of certain related body corporate assets, and these are being dealt with on a case-by-case basis. It is quite clear, however, that the Commission is becoming increasingly concerned with a general industry trend towards greater reliance on related body corporate assets for solvency purposes.

Another vital regulatory institution involved in the administration and management of superannuation is the Industrial Relations Commission (IRC). The IRC became a critical factor in the development of occupational superannuation when the federal government decided that employer contributions to superannuation funds should be adopted as a wage-fixing principle in 1986. This decision effectively provided a process of distributing national productivity in a form other than wage increases. It was of immediate appeal to the government, as it was a way of negating a 'wages blow-out' while finding favour with the ACTU's policy objective of employer-financed superannuation for all workers. The government announced that all employees should receive a 3 per cent productivity-based superannuation benefit through award restructuring, ratified by the Arbitration Commission. The awards provide the actual agreement with the necessary provisional amendments, and since 1986 superannuation has been incorporated under federal/state awards. The role of the Commission is to ensure that agreements are implemented in an orderly and rational basis and properly phased in, consistent with the state of the economy.

The role of the IRC is fundamental to an understanding of how occupational superannuation in Australia is regulated. However, owing to the numerous complex differences that can arise in collective bargaining procedures, and the variations across industries, the Commission has adopted a case-by-case approach (an example of this process can be found in table 9.1, which lists the outcomes of various disputes before the Commission between 1987 and 1990). In its adjudication it has avoided blanket prescriptions in matters relating to superannuation, and the above principle has provided the guidelines by which the Commission operates in its decision-making process. The important point here is that the IRC will interpret the legislation in accordance with the statutory provisions contained within the relevant Acts. However, with the exception of tax amendments, regulation relating to superannuation through the arbitration process is left to the discretion of the appropriate court. Hence, it is through the workings of case law and legal practice that the Commission is establishing its own regulations. In this regard the workings of case law as practised by the Commission take on considerable significance for how superannuation as a social objective develops in Australia. Indeed, the Commission's role is critical to the evolution of the regulatory framework in both pace and direction.

Questions of Regulation

The power of finance capital and corporate restructuring strategies raise some fundamental concerns about the ability of our current institutions to deal adequately with problems regarding superannuation as they arise. What are some of regulatory dilemmas posed by this shift? Moreover, could competing interests precipitate a crisis of regulation? Disregarding for the moment the broader political questions regarding labour relations, there are clearly some unresolved legal and moral questions about superannuation that need urgent consideration. First and foremost are questions over who owns the excess assets derived from overfunded pension funds and the problems arising out of asset reversion upon plan termination. We argue that not nearly enough attention has been paid to these fundamental concerns in Australia and, considering the push for enterprise bargaining and a more deregulatory approach to the whole question of labour–capital relations, such matters are of prime concern. As pointed out earlier, there is much that we can learn from the pension experience of the United States. Of particular concern is how the courts and legislators have dealt with these problems as they have arisen. Moreover, since these problems have emerged within a decentralized industrial relations system, the lessons for the Australian labour movement become all the more essential. However, before addressing the institutional and policy issues we need first to understand the nature of these unresolved legal questions concerning pensions.

In recent years, pension funds in both the United Kingdom and the United States have become overfunded by growing well beyond the value needed to satisfy current liabilities. In short, high interest rates and higher than expected investment yields have been responsible for this growth. The result has been burgeoning pension funds which have become attractive sources of cash and venture capital to their sponsors (see Butler, 1985; Nobles, 1987). From this situation a simple question emerges: if occupational pension schemes are 'overfunded', who is entitled to benefit from surplus assets? A clear trend that has emerged revolves around the ability of employers to extract surplus assets by breaching or changing their scheme's rules. Moreover, some employers have abused fiscal privileges by deliberately overfunding their pension schemes for the purpose of corporate gain. In this regard, excess funds have been used for a variety of corporate activities, such as payment of merger and acquisition debts, purchasing company stock to prevent unfriendly takeover attempts and improving financial balance sheets to assist in the attraction of new capital. These activities have been especially pronounced with the advent of asset reversion upon plan termination.[1] The problem for many corporations was that they had no effective access to excess funds, and so as a result some companies amended their pension scheme provisions to allow for recapture of excess assets in the event of plan termination. In the case of the USA, this action has been sanctioned by the courts, which have upheld the right of employers to amend plans for asset reversion (Butler, 1985). The point is, when plans (usually defined benefit type) become overfunded and subsequently terminated the sponsor satisfies accrued liabilities and recaptures the excess that could otherwise have accrued as future benefits to plan participants. In this context, the retirement income security of plan participants is diminished when overfunded plans are terminated before benefits have fully accrued. As such, termination of overfunded plans and the recapture of excess assets raise serious questions about the rights of the participants to share in the accrued benefit. The major concern is the ease with which companies have been able to terminate overfunded plans. For example, between 1979 and 1985, more than five hundred overfunded pension plans were terminated by plan sponsors, with the total asset reversions going to employers (Butler, 1985, p. 257). Moreover, between 1980 and 1987, employers in the USA have terminated and recovered assets not obligated for pension benefits from more than 1635 plans. The aggregate employer recovery from these terminations has approximated to $18 billion, or greater than 45 per cent of the plans' aggregate assets (Stein, 1986, pp. 130–1).

One of the main reasons why such a situation has occurred in the USA derives from the inability on the part of legislators to provide adequate provisions to deter such corporate activity. The ERISA of 1974 set minimum vesting and funding standards, required considerable reporting of

---

1 Reversion means returning to the sponsoring employer excess assets which remain after termination and satisfaction of all the liabilities of a defined benefit pension plan.

pension finances and mandated the purchase of insurance to guarantee benefits in the event of plan termination. The enactment of the ERISA was an attempt by the federal government to regulate the pension system. However, this attempt has not been without its problems, as evidenced by the numerous regulatory revisions designed to extend the scope of government oversight (see R. Clark, 1991). For example, at the time when the ERISA was enacted, Congress did not foresee the dramatic growth of overfunded pension plans, nor apparently the ability of companies to circumvent the ERISA's prohibition against removing assets from ongoing plans under the guise of terminations. Hence, terminations have threatened the retirement income security of many workers. There have been attempts to reduce these practices, such as the Plan Termination and Reversion Control Act of 1985. However, according to some commentators this Act lacks sufficient incentives to prevent employers from terminating defined benefit plans that are in the best interest of employees (see Butler, 1985).

Despite the obvious unethical activities of some companies regarding pension fund asset reversion, there is still a fundamental question remaining as to who really owns the excess assets. Essentially, the debate in the USA centres on three possible legal options. First, retain the status quo by allowing employers to recapture excess assets. Second, change the system by allocating excess assets to plan participants. Third, establish a 'hybrid' method whereby plan participants and the employers could share the excess funds (Abbott, 1989). It would appear that the first of these options has been the most widely adopted since the courts have generally ruled in favour of the employer in such cases. Hence, although employee groups have actively opposed this situation, they have not been successful in obtaining judicial relief or motivating governmental agencies into taking effective preventative action. Courts have rejected arguments that employers owe plan participants a fiduciary duty to use excess assets in their favour, or a duty to refrain from amending a plan just prior to termination so as to benefit from asset reversion (Stein, 1986).

In the United States, reversion is allowed under the rationale that the excess funds are in trust owing to 'erroneous actuarial computations' (see Abbott, 1989). An example can be seen in the experience of the UK regarding pensions schemes which are currently overfunded (Nobles, 1987). Essentially, following the poor performance of the stock market in the early 1970s, scheme actuaries were pessimistic about the likely performance of the schemes' assets when calculating the contribution rates required to fund pension liabilities. Similarly, they took a pessimistic view of their schemes' liabilities in the sense that they assumed a high rate of earnings inflation and a reasonably stable workforce. In sum, the value of the assets held by pension schemes is much greater, and their liabilities are much less, than predicted when contribution rates were fixed years earlier. Conversely, if actuaries are overly optimistic regarding the performance of schemes' assets, then underfunding occurs. Whether funding assumptions create a surplus depends, of course, on changes in the economy, but it also depends, in part, on the method of funding adopted.[2] However, the real dilemma lies with entitlement, and this has been problematic for adjudicators.

The dilemma for policy-makers stems from the divergent expectations of the various parties involved in occupational pension schemes. The point is that, if plans are to operate solely in the interest of members, there is a case for restricting the employer from extracting surplus assets. However, a problem arises in that if you reduce the level of benefit for employers, you also remove any incentive on their part to fund plans. Another consideration is that if excessive modification of plan sponsors' options occurs without due care, underfunding could very well result. As some commentators have pointed out, since the employer bears the risk of investment losses, participants get the best of both worlds: a guaranteed benefit based on the plan formula in addition to a bonus if the employer funds the plan successfully (see Abbott, 1985). Hence, there is considerable pressure on the employer to ensure that the chosen plan performs well and accrues the necessary benefits for the participants. Part of the solution may involve legislation that facilitates the ability of employers, under specific circumstances, to withdraw a portion of excess assets while the plan continues to operate. Such an amendment would allow the employer to receive a reversion while still enabling the participants to continue to accrue future benefits. The point about conditional employer withdrawals is that although the excess assets remain for the benefit of the participants, an employer may use the funds under strict regulation. In this regard, the issue of equity concerning employees is

2 The most widely used method in the UK over recent years has been the 'aggregate funding method'. This method aims at equating a scheme's liabilities with its assets. It treats the expected benefits as liabilities, and the expected contributions, investments and derived income as assets, and sets a contribution rate whereby the present value of the assets equals that of the liabilities. The objective of this method is to achieve solvency on the basis that the fund is ongoing, and it does not guarantee that the fund will be able to meet its liabilities if it is terminated. Another funding method, known as the 'projected unit method', requires the actuary to calculate the schemes accrued liabilities with reference to projected future salaries, and then compare this figure with the market value of the scheme's assets. However, rather than absorbing any discrepancy by altering the contribution rate (as with the aggregate funding method), this method allows the discrepancy to be eliminated as soon as possible. Hence, for a surplus, lower contributions, increased benefits or even a refund of contributions may apply. Conversely, for a deficit, increased contributions, special injection of capital or decreased benefits would ensue. The projected unit method aims to equalize liabilities and assets throughout the life of the scheme, but the method also makes the scheme funding very sensitive to short-term changes in the value of the scheme's assets (see Nobles, 1987, for more detail).

indirectly resolved because assets are returned to the plan, while the incentive for employers to engage in plan termination is also reduced. The balance, it seems, lies in accommodating the legitimate needs of business in financial distress while preventing any detrimental effect on the retirement income security of plan participants (Butler, 1985).

Accommodation of the interests of both employers and employees regarding excess plan assets cannot be achieved unless the legal concept of 'ownership' is clearly resolved. Hence, we need to look more closely at the arguments presented by both parties. The employers' claim to surplus assets is firmly premised on notions of fairness, on the basis that they should realize the excess value under defined benefit plans because they bear the risk of a decline in the value of plan assets. If the plan's assets are insufficient to meet the benefit obligations then the employer must make additional contributions. To this end, it is considered only fair that they should benefit from a rise in value in the event of plan termination. The argument, therefore, is one of simple symmetry in that the party who bears the risk of poor investment performance is entitled to the fruits of superior investment performance. On the other hand, employees have argued that the excess assets in an overfunded pension plan represent cost-of-living protection for retiree benefits, and that had the ERISA required employers to grant these increases, these excess assets would not exist. This argument is strengthened by the fact that employers' contributions should be viewed as a substitute for current wages, as reflected in the opinion of the National Labor Relations Board in *Inland Steel Co.* v. *NLRB* (see Clark, 1990a, for details of this case). Thus, there is some basis for arguing that excess assets should be distributed to plan participants upon termination.

It is important at this stage to be aware of the fundamental differences between defined benefit and defined contribution funds, particularly with regard to how pension plan overpayment occurs and in terms of funding liability (see Marden and Clark, 1993). In a defined contribution plan, the trustees are responsible for applying and investing the funds to maximize the coverage of benefits for the beneficiaries. The obligation on the part of the employer is to make a predetermined contribution to the plan for each employee. In defined benefit plans, however, the employer must provide the plan with sufficient funds in order to guarantee each beneficiary the amount and type of benefits established in the collective bargaining agreement. Because of the uncertainty surrounding investment, the employer's funding obligations will vary over time. Hence, the contribution rate is actuarially calculated by the trustees so as to ensure that the employer meets the funding requirements. Because of the structural and operational differences between the two types of plans, overpayments are generated from different sources. The primary cause of overpayments to defined contribution plans derives from employer error, whereas for defined benefit plans overpayments are largely the result of trustee error. With defined benefit plans, the trustees have greater knowledge regarding the funding requirements of employers, and on the basis of this knowledge levels of contributions are determined. Hence, trustee error is a frequent cause of overfunding with such plans.

It is clear, therefore, that the role of trustees should be carefully examined, in terms not only of their responsibilities for providing accurate actuarial advice but, even more importantly, of their legal liability in cases of pension fund surplus entitlement. This will of course depend on whether the trustee has the discretionary power to postpone winding up to augment benefits. If these powers exist, then trustees have to consider their legal duty before allowing asset reversion to the employer. However, the exact nature of their legal duty is not always clear, particularly in the case of pensions (see Nobles, 1987). It is clear that the trustees have a legal obligation to the employer for the aforementioned reasons, yet they also have an obligation to ensure that the long-term interests of the beneficiaries in terms of employee benefits are not undermined. In this situation, both employer and employee are beneficiaries and the duty on the part of the trustee is to act fairly between different beneficiaries. The actions of trustees therefore rest on a very difficult interpretation of what constitutes 'fairness' in terms of balancing the rights of both beneficiaries.

The question of pension fund surplus entitlement and asset reversion and the problems arising out of overfunded schemes present enormous implications for the regulatory framework developing around the spread of occupational superannuation. The important question is: do we in Australia have the appropriate institutional capacity to deal with problems as they emerge? Can we envisage a wider role for the courts concerning the unresolved legal and moral questions that have arisen in both the UK and the USA about reversions and entitlement? The point is that, with the current emphasis from both government and the trade union executive regarding enterprise bargaining and the expressed willingness to move away from the previous centralized system of wage bargaining, these questions take on a sense of urgency. It is to these institutional and regulatory issues that we now turn.

Conclusions

Let us begin with the axiomatic claim that pension rights for workers demand an appropriate regulatory regime consisting of adequate statutory and institutional protection. The principle presents no dilemma and is largely unproblematic for well-intentioned policy-makers determined to engage protective mechanisms on the fundamental ideal of equity and justice. However, as we have seen, the practice of adjudication is fraught with unresolved legal and moral questions which have tended to work in favour of the employer regarding entitlement and asset reversion in cases of overfunded pension plans. In the case of the United States, the adjudication process has highlighted serious anomalies in the provisions of the ERISA, which have led in many cases to erroneous assumptions and improper interpretation by the courts. This situation has largely emerged because Congress did not give serious attention to the problem of pension plan assets reverting to employers when the ERISA was first drafted in 1974.

The underlying principle of the ERISA was to stabilize the funding of defined benefit plans and to increase employee security in promised retirement incomes. To achieve this, the ERISA effected three significant changes in the law. First, it introduced minimum vesting standards to which all funded plans would have to adhere. Second, it increased the employer's minimum annual plan contributions to ensure that plans were adequately funded and provided rigorous new standards for plan fiduciaries and their investment of plan assets. Finally, it also created the Pension Benefit Guaranty Corporation (PBGC) to insure defined benefits.[3] The establishment of the ERISA was based on a widespread sentiment that existing regulations were inadequate in the face of the growing magnitude and complexity of the nation's private pension system. However, the evolving regulatory crisis since its promulgation points to the tensions inherent in keeping pace with such an increasingly complex phenomenon as the private pension system. The lessons for Australia are obvious, yet none the less complex.

In this chapter we have we outlined how the regulatory framework evolved to facilitate the growth of occupational superannuation in Australia. The Occupational Superannuation Standards Act (OSSA) of 1987, along with the creation of the Insurance and Superannuation Commission (ISC) and the increased jurisdiction over superannuation of the Industrial Relations Commission (IRC), represent the structure of our regulatory framework. The main objective of this regulatory regime was to extend coverage of superannuation for the Australian workforce, and to ensure that this coverage is properly undertaken in accordance with the provisions set out in legislation. Up to this time, the legislative response to the spread of superannuation has been adequate in terms of coverage (although there is still some way to go) and the elimination of past inequities. However, whether the existent legislative and institutional capacity to deal with some of the problems raised in this chapter is also adequate remains to be seen. At the moment, we are undergoing

3 The PBGC insures certain benefits in covered defined benefit plans that become insolvent (see ERISA 4021–22B). It should also be noted that not all benefits under a plan are guaranteed by the PBGC (see ERISA 4022–22B). The PBGC also has considerable regulatory powers to investigate whether plans are solvent, ERISA 4003 (a); involuntarily to terminate insolvent plans, ERISA 4042 (a); and to supervise the voluntary termination of covered defined benefit plans, ERISA 4041.

some of the most dramatic changes to the industrial relations system since the Accord was established in 1983. This begs the important question: what effect will these changes have on the regulation of superannuation? It is no small point to keep in mind that the conditions surrounding the private pension system in the United States have emerged out of a decentralized system where enterprise bargaining is dominant. In stating this, we do not necessarily imply that similar problems will automatically arise in Australia. Nevertheless, when one considers the recent action brought against Westpac concerning the misuse of pension fund assets, and the dilemma facing the Victorian government regarding its acutely underfunded pension scheme for its public servants, then it may not be an over-statement to suggest that a crisis is looming.[4]

At the moment it is not difficult to find information on how to plan for your retirement income. Indeed, a brief perusal in any large bookshop will reveal a plethora of publications concerning retirement planning and superannuation. This is not surprising considering the complexity of the issue for many people in the workforce, and they are no doubt welcomed as useful guides. However, as we have demonstrated in this chapter, there are some very important unresolved questions and issues to be dealt with concerning the fastest growing industry in Australia if a crisis in regulation is to be avoided. To this end, strategic unionism, with its current emphasis on the benefits of enterprise bargaining, will have to ensure that the protection of workers' pension rights occupies a central position on its reform agenda. Similarly, it behoves the federal government to ensure that proper legislative protection is forthcoming, and that the institutional framework is in no way weakened throughout this time of restructuring.

References

Abbott, J. H. (1989) Legislating reversions: a mistaken path leading to drastic results. *San Diego Law Review*, 26(5), 1100–44.

Australian Bureau of Statistics (1989) *Employment Benefits Australia August 1989*. Canberra: Australian Government Publishing Service.

Bodie, Z. and Papke, L. (1991) Pension fund finance. Working Paper series 90–4. Pension Research Council, Wharton School of the University of Pennsylvania, Philadelphia.

Butler, C. A. (1985) Pension plan terminations and asset reversions: accommodating the interests of employers and employees. *University of Michigan Journal of Law Reform*, 19, 257–74.

Clark, D. (1989) *Student Economic Briefs 1989/90*. Sydney: The Financial Review Library.

4 At the time of writing the case of Westpac was yet to be heard in the Supreme Court and information about the case was virtually non-existent because of the rules of *sub judice*.

Clark, G. L. (1990a) Restructuring workers' pension rights and the law. *Environment and Planning A*, 22, 149–68.

Clark, G. L. (1990b) Location management strategy and workers' pensions. *Environment and Planning A*, 22, 17–37.

Clark, G. L. (1992) 'Real' regulation: the administrative state. *Environment and Planning A*, 24, 615–28.

Clark, G. L. (1993) *Pensions and Corporate Restructuring in American Industry: the Crisis of Regulation*. Baltimore: Johns Hopkins University Press.

Clark, R. (1981) The four stages of capitalism: reflections on investment management treatises. *Harvard Law Review*, 94, 561–82.

Clark, R. (1991) Population aging and retirement policy: an international perspective. Working Paper Series 91–7, Pension Research Council, the Wharton School of the University of Pennsylvania.

Crouch, C. (1979) *The Politics of Industrial Relations*. Glasgow: Fontana/Collins.

Crouch, C. (1982) *Trade Unions: the Logic of Collective Action*. London: Fontana.

Dabscheck, B. (1989) *Australian Industrial Relations in the 1980s*. Oxford: Oxford University Press.

Drucker, P. (1976) *The Unseen Revolution: How Pension Fund Socialism Came to America*. New York: Harper & Row.

Frankel, B. (1983) *Beyond the State? Dominant Theories and Socialist Strategies*. London: Macmillan.

Insurance and Superannuation Commission (ISC) (1989) *Annual Report 1988–89*. Canberra: Australian Government Publishing Service.

Kotlikoff, L. and Smith, D. (1983) *Pensions in the American Economy*. Chicago: University of Chicago Press.

Lucas, H. (1977) *Pensions and Industrial Relations: a Practical Guide for All Involved in Pensions*. Oxford: Pergamon Press.

Lynes, T. (1985) *Paying for Pensions: the French Experience*. London: STICERD.

Marden, P. (1992) 'Real' regulation reconsidered. *Environment and Planning A*, 24, 751–67.

Marden, P. and Clark, G. L. (1993) *Private Pensions (Superannuation) in Australia*. Clayton, Victoria: National Key Centre in Industrial Relations, Monash University.

Mathews, J. (1989) *Age of Democracy: the Politics of Post-Fordism*. South Melbourne: Oxford University Press.

Mercer Campbell Cook and Knight (1987) *Superannuation Planning in Australia*, 4th edn. Sydney: CCH Australia Ltd.

Munnell, A. (1982) *The Economics of Private Pensions*. Washington, DC: The Brookings Institution.

Munnell, A. and Yohn, F. (1991) What is the impact of pensions on saving? Working Paper Series 90–3, Pension Research Council, the Wharton School of the University of Pennsylvania.

Nektarios, M. (1982) *Public Pensions, Capital Formation, and Economic Growth*. Boulder, CO: Westview Press.

Niland, J. (1986) Gaining against the tide: Australian unionism in the 1980s. Working Paper No. 62, Department of Industrial Relations, University of New South Wales.

Nobles, R. (1987) Who is entitled to the pension fund surplus? *The Industrial Law Journal*, 16, 164–84.

Plowman, D. and Weaven, G. (1988) Superannuation: a union perspective. Industrial Relations Working Papers, School of Industrial Relations and Organizational Behaviour, University of New South Wales.

Pontusson, J. (1984) *Public Pension Funds and the Politics of Capital Formation in Sweden*. Stockholm: Arbetsliuscentrum.

Posner, A. (1974) Theories of economic regulation. *Bell Journal of Economics and Management Science*, 5, 335–58.

Rawson, D. (1986) Industrial relations and the art of the possible. In R. Blandy and J. Niland (eds), *Alternatives to Arbitration*. Sydney: Allen and Unwin, 273–97.

Sainsbury, D. (ed.) (1988) *Critical Perspectives and New Interpretations*. Stockholm: Almquist and Witzsell.

Schieber, S. (1991) Can our social insurance systems survive the demographic shifts of the 21st century? Working Paper Series 91–3, Pension Research Council, the Wharton School of the University of Pennsylvania.

Schmitter, P. (1979) Still the century of corporatism? In P. Schmitter and G. Lehmbruch (eds), *Trends towards Corporate Intermediation*. Beverly Hills, CA: Sage, 7–52.

Stein, N. P. (1986) Raiders of the corporate pension plan: the reversion of excess plan assets to the employer. *American Journal of Tax Policy*, 5(1), 117–90.

Turner, B. (1989) *Citizenship and Capitalism: the Debate Over Reformism*. London: Allen and Unwin.

Williamson, J., Shindal, J. and Evans, L. (1985) *Ageing and Public Policy: Social Control or Social Justice?* Springfield, IL: Charles C. Thomas Publishing.

Wilson, J. Q. (1980) *The Politics of Regulation*. New York: Basic Books.

10

Urbanizing Capitals: towards an Integration of Time, Space and Economic Calculation
Michael Pryke

Introduction

> The urban process exists within the community of money, is framed by the concrete abstractions of space and time, and internalizes all the vigor and turbulence of the circulation of capital under the ambiguous and often shaky surveillance of the state. (*Harvey, 1985a, p. 38*)

This chapter is essentially exploratory and stems from an interest in the interaction of economic and social forces that merge in the production and reproduction of the built form within a market economy. The chapter focuses on the economic processes that underlie decisions to invest through spatial matrices. The influence of social space in the urban process is thus very much part of the chapter's main arguments.[1]

Against the specific economic environment of the UK during the 1980s, outlined in the first section, the overall aim is to give movement to the broader context in which property investment is realized. The next section approaches this aim from within a structure of building provision and social relations of rent framework. In turn this is linked to the

This chapter is essentially an edited version of chapters 4 and 5 of my PhD thesis. Thanks are due to my supervisors Doreen Massey and John Allen, in the Faculty of Social Sciences, the Open University. I am also very grateful to Grahame Thompson and Allan Cochrane for comments on an earlier draft, and give many thanks to those people who kindly cooperated in the research. Needless to say, the usual disclaimers apply. A first draft of this chapter was presented in 1991 to the Eighth Urban Change and Conflict Conference, University of Lancaster, sponsored by the ISA (Research Committee 21).

1 See Harvey (1985a, 1990, p. 496) on the need for space to play a more 'active' moment in accounts of urban processes.

respective 'institutional settings' and 'calculations' (Thompson, 1978) of the developers of and investors through the built form, thus allowing the regearing of the pace and form of building provision during the 1980s, and its implications, to be better understood.

The key economic processes within such regearing are informed, moreover, through an interpretation of economic power: the ability of financial capital to 'constrain and regulate' (Harris, 1988, p. 10) the economic actions of other agents.[2] The power contained within financial markets, it is suggested (in line with Harvey, 1989, p. 194), should be viewed generally as determining the pace, the times, that is, in which spaces must be turned over (to put it colloquially) if capitals are to remain profitable through time. The (re)production of the built environment is no exception to this rule (see Harvey, 1982).

In this chapter this power is attributed to the main investors through the built form, the long-term financial institutions. The 'long-term' funds (LTFs) of composites or insurance companies, together with the pension funds, have been the traditional main direct and indirect investors through commercial (industrial, retail and office) property in the UK (Clayton and Osborne, 1965; Briston and Dobbing, 1978; DOE/PAG, 1980). Their changing requirements as investors have influenced the forms that commercial building provision have taken.

The investors' links, directly and/or indirectly, with the property company sector contain differentially influential economic strengths. While property companies (noted in later sections as 'young' trader developers and more 'mature' investment companies[3]) have made innovative use of direct and indirect institutional funding and short-term bank capital, their financing ability has been restrained historically by the overall investment requirements, the overall economic power, of the investing institutions.

Additionally, it is contended, there is a need to recognize both the direct *shaping* of economic power by intermediaries engaging with the institutions in the formulation of investment flows and its more indirect *mediation* by those agents active in the new issue and secondary markets of the City's capital market, a market with which the (listed) property sector must negotiate. The chapter is thus grounded in the specific economic and social milieu of 'the City', the financial markets of the City of London.

Over the period covered by this chapter, which extends from the early to the mid 1980s,[4] there was an increased need for investments to

2 For early reminders of the absence of power in explanations of economic processes see the essays in Rothschild (1971).
3 It should be stressed that there is little new about these traders. They are simply young merchant capitalists of the type seen in previous booms.
4 The quotes that appear in this chapter are taken from semi-structured interviews with representatives from a selection of case study financial institutions, property companies and City securities houses (see Appendix 1; see Pryke, 1988, for further details).

Table 10.1 The emergence of yield gaps between average and prime property and UK equities and long gilts, 1978–1986

Year	FT All Share	Gilt yield	Offices average	Offices prime	Retail average	Retail prime	Industrial average	Industrial prime
1978	5.54	12.47	6.69	4.5	7.44	4	8.22	6.25
1979	5.75	12.99	6.12	4.35	6.74	3.85	7.91	6
1980	6.32	13.79	6.14	4.25	6.35	3.75	7.89	6.25
1981	5.89	14.75	6.18	4.5	6.15	3.5	8.29	6.25
1982	5.7	12.88	6.19	4.5	6.01	3.5	8.37	6.25
1983	4.81	10.8	6.4	4.8	6.04	3.75	8.81	6.8
1984	4.62	10.69	6.53	4.75	5.64	3.5	9.14	6.75
1985	4.47	10.62	7.12	4.75	5.61	3.65	10.19	7.5
1986	4.01	9.87	7.86	5.75	5.72	4	11.43	8.25

Notes: Financial statistics: FTA All Share Dividend Yield and Calculated Gross Redemption Yield on Long Gilts; average yearly figures used for both. The yield gap is calculated by simply subtracting average or prime property sector yield from the FTA dividend yield or gilt yield.

Source: Ellis, 1986

'perform' over a shorter period;[5] capitals, in a way, had to describe a briefer circuit. Both production and the time of circulation had to be speeded up[6] and new vehicles to circulate a changed mix of capitals through the production of the built form were required. One such vehicle is outlined in the penultimate section.

Overall, the chapter points to the implicit 'financial-property-engineering'[7] that stemmed from altering investment requirements during the 1980s, the force and design of which demonstrate the effects of economic power in motion, flowing from financial circuits into a 'productive' sector of the economy.

Economic Context: the 'Institutions' and the 'Property Companies'

The UK's economic environment changed dramatically at the beginning of the 1980s, the details of which have been covered elsewhere (e.g. Aaronovitch and Smith, 1981; Bleaney, 1983; Coakley and Harris, 1983; Brett, 1985; Fine and Harris, 1985; BZW 1987; Coutts et al., 1990). This section thus concentrates simply on what are felt to be the main features that affected the attractiveness of investing through the commercial built form.

Long-term Institutions

Nationwide, the performance of the property market varied greatly as average yields on virtually all sectors of the market rose (table 10.1). Unequal sectoral and geographical economic performance, together with rapidly changing building specifications, quickly influenced the rental and capital growth potential of commercial property and exerted a major influence on property investment returns, and consequently formed a critical element in the allocation of new investment monies. In a sense, the particularity of place was sharpening the particularity of investment decisions.

As table 10.2 indicates, from 1982 to around 1984 institutional property investment policy became one of active portfolio managment.

---

5 This is often referred to popularly as short-termism (see e.g. Utiger, 1988; Marsh, 1990; Ball, 1991; Williams, 1991). Although the notion of short-termism omits any notion of power, it does at least place a useful emphasis on the City's financing position and begins, albeit roughly, to recognize some of the outcomes of this role.
6 For the importance of time in the process of circulation see Marx (1967, pp. 128–9, 158). The need for speed in production was 'helped' by new building techniques and management/contractual systems.
7 I am grateful to Grahame Thompson for this term, written communication 22 November 1991.

Table 10.2 Long-term funds', private and other public sector pension funds' quarterly net acquisition of new and existing property, 1979(1)–1986(3), £ million

Year	\multicolumn{6}{c}{Long-term funds}						\multicolumn{6}{c}{Other public sector pension funds}						\multicolumn{6}{c}{Private pension funds}					
	AAE	ARE	AAN	ARN	NIE	NIN	AAE	ARE	AAN	ARN	NIE	NIN	AAE	ARE	AAN	ARN	NIE	NIN
1979	84.4	53.1	30.4	3.1	31.1	27.3	–	–	–	–	71.1	5	48.8	8.7	13.5	0	40	13.5
	131.1	49.1	78.2	7.1	82	71.1	–	–	–	–	65.5	5.6	42.8	9.5	7	0	33.4	7
	195.5	52.1	–	–	131.1	0	–	–	–	–	35.4	7.4	41.4	12.7	21.5	0	28.8	21.5
	274.8	43.6	–	–	231.3	0	–	–	–	–	58	7	50	10.3	19.5	0.1	39.7	19.5
1980	194.5	30.2	–	–	91	75.7	89.2	3.7	6.1	0	127.5	6.2	86.5	21.8	17.2	0	64.7	17.2
	237.9	62.4	–	–	75.9	96.7	137.6	34	6	0	105.6	6	48.5	4.8	15.4	0.4	43.8	15
	209.2	30	–	–	85	96	64.6	1.8	5.3	0	76.2	5.3	61.3	4.3	27.7	2	57	25.7
	294.8	25.8	–	–	144.4	138.5	120.5	3.7	14.6	0	116.8	14.6	53.3	9.5	20.2	0	43.9	20.2
1981	297.3	32.6	–	–	107.4	130.6	60.7	8.3	9.5	0	64.4	9.3	89.4	25.2	13.5	0.2	70.1	15.1
	275.1	40.9	–	–	121.1	129.2	81.4	11.3	17.2	0	61	12.8	81.4	11.3	17.2	0	70.2	17.2
	296	49.4	–	–	129.2	125.5	107.9	12.5	9.8	0.1	72.2	7.2	107.9	12.5	9.8	0.1	95.4	9.7
	176.6	66.8	127.7	1.2	109.8	126.5	101.1	14.4	2.1	0	86.7	2.1	106	28.1	8	0.2	77.9	7.9
1982	163.1	77.5	132.9	2.6	69	118	61.5	– 12.5	46.7	0	90.5	52.4	73.8	23.4	12.4	0.1	59.8	12.2
	194	86.3	116.8	0	217.3	0	44.9	19.1	24.2	0.1	40.5	42.7	97.5	7.8	7	0	97.6	9.1
	195.4	79.7	156.7	0.3	105.5	156.4	57	38.9	30.1	0	18.1	30.1	112.6	10.3	18.3	0	112.1	20.7
	235.6	60.4	144.1	9.8	175.2	134.2	60.7	37.5	14.7	0	23.2	14.7	0	23.2	14.7	64.9	34.2	11.6
1983	163	80	144	1	95	143	46	51	18	0	14	21	105	27	7	0	96	7
	173	86	109	1	101	108	87	24	29	0	40	32	55	42	8	10	15	– 2
	94	118	165	1	– 14	164	56	28	12	0	49	12	81	42	14	0	43	14
	213	189	213	14	9	182	65	32	15	0	31	15	119	66	15	0	53	15

	AAE	ARE		NIE	AAN	ARN			NIN								
1984	177	221	94	17	−29	81	86	17	30	0		49	24	128	32	14	0	115	19
	196	153	162	4	51	159	70	25	21	0		49	7	104	50	25	0	75	20
	184	96	143	1	93	142	74	32	20	6		27	10	36	32	40	0	24	19
	257	179	134	2	78	132	94	29	5	0		65	5	92	31	19	0	61	19
1985	189	110	109	1	79	108	51	27	20	0		17	22	131	92	16	0	29	14
	399	184	140	0	215	140	58	62	8	1		3	8	72	111	17	0	−37	17
	179	198	154	0	−19	154	63	37	9	0		25	7	137	63	107	0	79	58
	309	288	164	7	21	157	66	37	3	0		29	3	150	64	19	0	86	19
1986	217	135	115	2	82	149	67	101	4	0		−34	4	97	89	23	0	10	23
	484	335	147	1	113	146	93	192	15	0		−100	1	93	192	15	0	−78	16
	402	177	196	7	225	189	65	101	4	0		−36	4	97	98	33	0	−1	33

Figures are at cash values.

Notes: In 1979 and in the second quarter of 1982 new buildings are included in 'land and existing buildings etc.' to avoid disclosing investment activity by individual insurers. Prior to 1979 new buildings were included in 'Land, existing buildings, property and ground rents'. 'Cash values': net investment is the difference between payments made for assets acquired and payments received for assets realized.

AAE, assets acquired existing; ARE, assets realized existing; AAN, assets acquired new; ARN, assets realized new; NIE, net investment existing; NIN, net investment new. New buildings include purchase of newly constructed buildings and expenditure on the construction of new buildings commissioned by a company or fund, or expenditure on existing buildings.

Source: *Business Monitor* MQ, MQ5.

This involved directing (limited) investment monies into refurbishing existing property and rationalizing existing portfolios (interviews).[8] In 1982, for instance, authorizations were reduced by as much as a half of the previous year's figure, as direct developments were cut back sharply (interviews). To get within narrowing portfolio target figures for weighting in various sectors, and in an effort to generate 'internally' new investment monies and to improve overall property investment performance, an accelerated sales programme was implemented during the year by the property investment departments of many institutions[9] (interviews). And as inflation declined the exact role that property was to play in their investment portfolios had to be rethought.

In the first half of the 1980s (and indeed beyond) the distribution of holdings of both LTFs and pension funds remained biased towards UK and foreign equities, and (after abolition of exchange controls in 1979) overseas investment rose generally, as overseas investment limits slackened. By the end of 1986, for example, UK shares and overseas assets made up 68 per cent of pension fund and 47.1 per cent of LTF investment portfolios; in contrast, property, in aggregate, was to make up only 8.4 and 13.9 per cent respectively of total holdings at market value, the lowest level for pension funds since 1968 and for LTFs since 1972. In the year to December 1986 pension funds allocated only 1.2 per cent of annual cash flow to UK property investment; LTFs allocated only 8.1 per cent. These sums compared with 37.5 and just under 50 per cent of investment cash flow allocated to UK equities respectively (see tables 10.3 and 10.4).

The Property Company Sector

The re-emergence of positive real interest rates, reaching historically high levels between 1984 and 1986 (Chick, 1988, p. 31), constrained the activity of property companies in the early 1980s. The fall in interest rates after 1986, however, signalled more activity by both the traders and the investment companies. Yet with the ongoing financial regearing provoked by changing institutional investment demand, this activity was fed in the main by substantial increases in the amounts of interest-bearing capital employed, especially by the emerging property *trading* companies, as well as the property *investment* companies (e.g. Carr, 1986; Warburg Securities, 1987a). The amount of bank lending outstanding to property companies rose from £4062 million in 1983 to £37,092 million in 1990.[10]

8 See IPD (1986, 1987) for useful background data.
9 This 'turning' of portfolios is less open to pension funds because of their more restrictive legal setting.
10 Figures are at August for each year and are taken from 'Analysis of bank lending to UK residents', published by the Bank of England.

Table 10.3 Long-term funds' and private pension funds' annual percentage shares in gilts, equities and property, 1962–1986

Year	Long-term funds				Pension funds			
	BGS[a]	Property	Ordinary shares	Overseas assets	BGS[a]	Property	Ordinary shares	Overseas assets
1962	18.9	9.1	29.3	5.4	24.6	2.4	44	3.5
1963	18	8.9	29.7	5.9	21.4	2.2	46.1	3.3
1964	16	9.5	28.1	6.5	19.3	2.9	45.9	3.2
1965	16.3	9.6	28	5.9	18.4	3.1	46.6	3.2
1966	16.5	10.6	25.3	5.7	18.3	4.2	44.9	2.7
1967	16.6	10	28.9	5.7	17.5	5	47.8	2.9
1968	13.7	9.4	36.9	5.2	13.1	6.3	54.5	3
1969	13.7	11	34.7	4.8	13	8.9	50.3	3
1970	14.2	12.1	31.8	6	12.4	11.8	46.2	3.1
1971	15.9	11	38.8	4.7	13.7	10	52.2	3
1972	13.7	10.9	42	5.5	10.4	10.3	53.3	5
1973	13.4	16.1	33.7	5.6	11.9	15.4	41.8	5.7
1974	13.8	22.2	18.4	5.1	13.6	17.4	32.9	5.7
1975	16.1	20.7	28.9	4.5	15.7	14	46.9	6
1976	20.1	21.4	26.2	5.1	22.2	11	44.8	7
1977	25.8	19.4	29.5	3.2	24.9	9.8	47.1	4.8
1978	25.1	22	28.9	3.6	24.3	10.8	46.9	5.8
1979	26.4	24.1	27.8	3.2	24.3	13.3	45.4	5.8
1980	27.1	22.9	29.6	4.2	22.5	17.9	43.8	9.4
1981	24.8	23.7	30.2	5.7	20.3	18.7	43.4	12.2
1982	28.3	19.9	30.5	7.4	21.9	14.2	43	13.2
1983	26.6	17.8	32.8	9.3	20.5	11.8	43.5	15.9
1984	25	17.3	32.5	12.1	18.4	11	47.7	14.1
1985	23.4	15.5	33.1	11	17.4	9.8	49.6	15
1986	19.8	13.9	35.2	11.9	15.3	8.4	50.7	17.3

Note: Structure of portfolio is at year end; figures expressed in percentages. BGS, British government securities.

Source: Data 1962–84 from *BEQB* December 1986, table B. Figures for 1985 and 1986 calculated from *Financial Statistics*, May 1988, tables 7.13 and 7.14.

Implications

The restructuring of investment prioities among the institutions meant that different forms and proportions of financial capital (of which the rise in bank lending is a clear example) had to be combined to fund development programmes, which in turn introduced different times into the whole development process. It is the resulting interchange, as it were, between this mix of capitals and space-time that is felt to be integral to understanding the physical transformation of places in the 1980s. The next section therefore attempts to establish a framework for conceptualizing this process.

Table 10.4 Long-term fund and private sector pension fund annual investment to cash flow into selected assets, 1963–1986

Year	Long-term funds					Pension funds				
	LTF FIS	LTF BGS	LTF O/S	LTF property	LTF O/S assets	PPF FIS	PPF BGS	PPF O/S	PPF property	PPF O/S assets
1963	30.7	19.1	17.8	10.3	3.1	32.4	− 8	60.4	8	1.3
1964	30.5	14.6	19.6	9	3.5	19.2	− 0.4	56.8	6.8	− 0.9
1965	34.9	9.3	10.7	15.1	1.1	37.5	19.1	36	8.1	1.8
1966	35.8	4.8	13	19.3	0.7	36.3	19.8	35.2	6.5	1.1
1967	21	31.5	20.9	15	− 10.9	21.2	13.8	46	13.6	2.3
1968	21.9	15.4	5.7	15.3	17.7	12.6	0.2	56.7	22.2	3.3
1969	13.5	16.7	15.2	25.5	2.4	29.9	7.9	27.1	25	5.1
1970	6.8	17.9	10.9	22.6	17.3	16.1	− 1.4	45.1	21.5	5.8
1971	10	41.1	40.1	19.5	− 9.6	8.5	31.4	47.3	10.7	4.1
1972	10.8	20.9	34.4	10.3	13.5	3.2	− 3.3	44.3	14.7	11.8
1973	3.3	22.5	14.4	21.7	9.5	1.9	27.9	− 7.1	32.2	13.1
1974	2.3	7.9	8	29.9	− 0.3	− 1.2	36.9	− 12.6	30	− 0.7
1975	2.9	67.6	16.7	21.8	0.9	3.7	34	58.9	13.2	7.2
1976	− 2.8	74.6	12.5	19.1	1.1	0.1	49.9	31.1	17.4	3.1
1977	− 0.5	61.5	16.6	12.4	1.2	− 0.4	32.4	37	13	2.7
1978	− 1.4	58	17.2	11.7	2.9	− 2.9	38.4	35.2	10.6	11.8
1979	− 0.4	59	19.1	13.7	2.6	− 1.1	45.8	26.7	9.9	10.3
1980	− 1.4	44.7	17.9	16.7	11.7	− 0.9	36.2	33.7	9.8	23.5
1981	− 0.1	36.5	19.9	16.6	14.2	0.2	25.5	25.2	12.5	29.6

Year	LTF					PPF				
1982	3.9	28.7	25.2	15.7	19.5	0.6	9.1	30.5	11.8	39.2
1983	5.2	30.3	21.8	12.2	19.2	1.2	35.9	18.2	7.6	19.4
1984	4.5	28.7	24.1	9	9.1	2.3	31.8	32	8.7	7.5
1985	n/c	24.5	45.4	10.4	16.1	n/c	28.5	41	4.8	26.2
1986	n/c	10	49.9	8.1	11.2	n/c	13.7	37.5	1.2	26.5

Figures in percentages.

Notes: annual investment of cash flow at year end. LTF, long-term funds; PPF, private pension funds; FIS, fixed interest securities; n/c, not calculated for 1985 and 1986; BGS, British government securities (from 1981 includes index linked gilts); O/S, listed UK ordinary shares and unit trust units; O/S Assets, overseas assets. For 1985–6 includes all overseas securities and short term assets (and loans and mortgages for pension funds only). Property, for 1985 and 1986 includes UK property (and property unit trusts for pension funds only). Cash flow represents percentage of total annual net acquisition on various investment media; figures for totals in cash values..

Source: 1963 to 1986 *BEQB*, December 1986, table B. Figures for 1985 and 1986 calculated from *Financial Statistics*, May 1988, tables 7.13 and 7.14.

Building a Conceptual Framework: 'Structures of Building Provision'

In orthodox analyses of property development (see e.g. Cadman and Austin-Crowe, 1978; Barras, 1983; Cadman, 1984; Barras and Ferguson, 1987; Des Rosiers, 1987), terms such as 'insurance companies', 'pension funds' and 'property companies' are taken as given categories (Allen, 1983); economic agents are grouped together chiefly because they exihibit certain observable attributes. Trends, in other words, are identified among aggregate variables and patterns; their related data are then disaggregated into 'separate components' (insurance companies and pension funds are property related examples) and given explanatory status.

Although perhaps a helpful first stage, all that has been achieved is 'essentially classification by outcome rather than cause' (Massey and Meegan, 1985, p. 7; see also Wyn Williams, 1981, p. 33; Sayer, 1984). This is of little use, it is suggested, if spatially specific outcomes of economic processes are what need to be explained, as allowance is made neither for the spatial and temporal content of these processes nor for the nature of the influences motivating 'components'. The force behind observed trends can be better understood, it is contended, by examining the processes that propel and guide the economic agents that constitute these components.

The position of the long-term financial institutions in the development process and the relevance of this position to the style of property-financial-engineering in the 1980s can be analysed by employing Michael Ball's concept of a 'structure of building provision' (SBP) (e.g. Ball, 1977, 1979, 1985a, b, 1986). A SBP encompasses the historically and socially determined processes of land development and is used to inform later sections that focus on the long-term financial institutions and their links with the property sector. The pivotal financial role of the institutions, as promoters and consumers of the built environment, in a sense as a collective financial engineer, is felt to be essential to understanding the transient form of, say, the structure of office provision.[11] It is additional concepts that give expression to this transience that must now be looked for.

Urbanizing Capitals: Space, Time and Momentum

Of the attempts that have been made to understand the interrelationship of the agents involved in the production of the built environment (e.g. Lamarche, 1976; Massey and Catalano, 1978; Boddy, 1981), few have tried to incorporate a circuits of capital type argument into a spatial

11   This, and very many other insights into the analysis of building provision, have been gained from the work of Michael Ball.

context. Harvey's (1982) pioneering work has been the most influential in dealing with the 'production of spatial configurations' and the 'built environment'.

Harvey's starting point gives primary importance to capital's (un-problematic) drive for accumulation through the built form.[12] Spatial relations – the determinants of the profitability of development – are demoted to secondary importance (Mingione, 1981, p. 69; Harvey, 1982, p. 396). The see-saw between the spatial and the accumulation process is quite often omitted (Saunders, 1986, p. 255), while the complexities of the different time-costs of space for the capitals involved are unproblematized through a largely undifferentiated view of clearly defined (and easily definable) fractions of capital.

The perception of risks, and the required flow of returns, will be subject to change through time, and differ between capitals within 'fractions'. There is no surety that the returns from property investment will be positive. An important risk is demand, both 'long-term' and short-term, so that there is a close relationship between specific spatial relations and accumulation. By bringing in the particularity of place, the apparently unproblematical and functional correspondence of capitals becomes complex. Figuratively, the straight lines that connect capitals become squiggles. And as the abstract focuses in on the concrete, the formation of explanation must then take on board the spatial. Another problem then arises: the particular is not stationary; a place has a spatial history that evolves through the same time, but at a different momentum to the capitals involved in its (re)production. Thus there is a need to (re)introduce and (re)emphasize the influences of space and time into the whole equation, if an answer to the question of how capitals are urbanized is to be approached.

Pace and Form

A central issue thus revolves around the nature of returns required by capitals. For the long-term institutions and property companies alike, a – if not *the* – final determinant of the return received from monies advanced will be the rent achievable from the completed scheme. Property rent, as an equity type investment, is then put squarely in the context of financing and investment criteria (see Massey and Catalano, 1978, pp. 121–2). Thus, the 'rôle that rent plays' (Allen, 1983, p. 196) for each type of agent, whether a long-term institution or a property company, needs to be specified in relation to the respective settings and calculations. It then becomes possible to go some way in explaining two important elements in the urbanization of capitals.

12 For criticisms of the lack of 'space' in Harvey's arguments see Mingione (1981), Ball (1983) and Saunders (1986).

First, how do certain influences that impinge upon a structure, such as changing investment criteria, break through and dictate, if only for a short time, the pace and form of building provision? Second, why, at certain moments, are previously dominant agents, such as property investment companies, surpassed by others, such as property traders? These issues are considered in the next section, which draws upon a critical realist[13] approach in understanding the calculation of returns. The following section then takes up calculation in more detail.

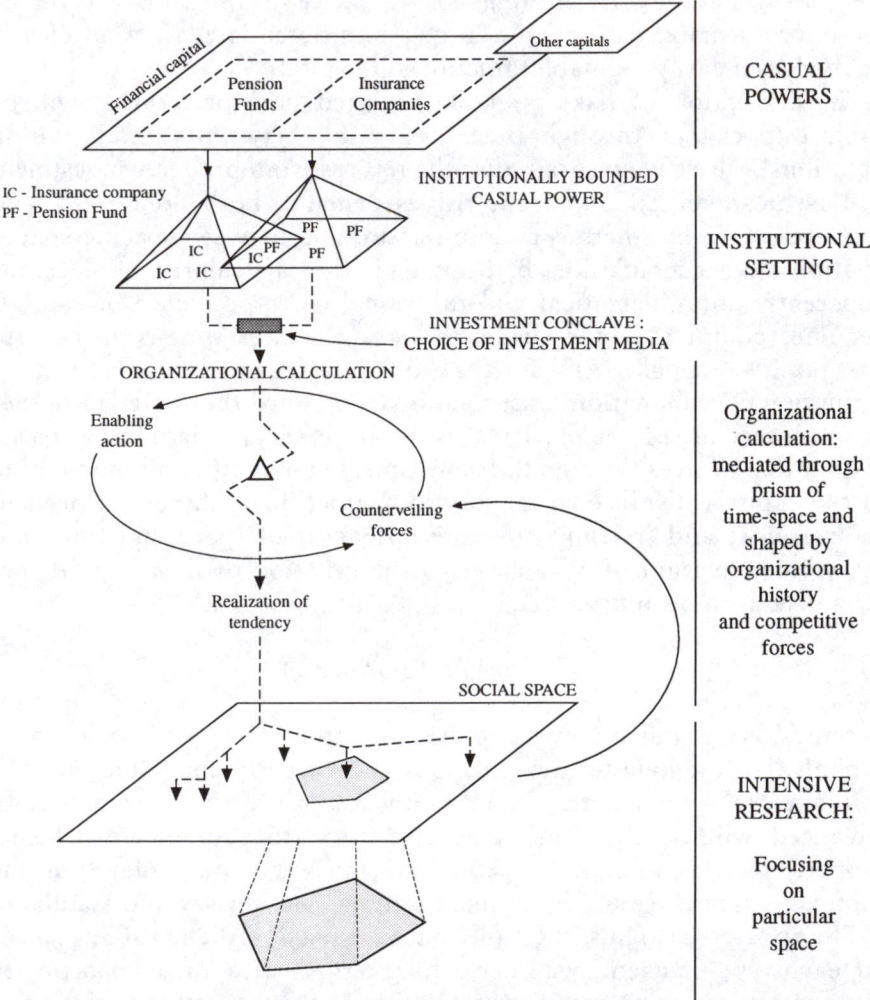

Figure 10.1 The setting of insurance company and pension fund property investment.

13   See Sayer (1984) for a detailed exposition of the critical realist approach.

Internal Structures and Organizational Strategies

In laying stress upon that which capacitates and limits specific capitals, the idea of different organizational strategems is introduced and a move away from simply juggling with either official labels or 'fractions of capital' is encouraged. Thompson (1977), for example, has argued that although the identification of fractions at the theoretical level is a satisfactory distinction, in practice capital is capable of acting as an amalgam of capitals. Distinctive characteristics of one fraction are 'visible' in the transactions of others. The problem becomes one of re-tackling the less visible internal structures of these 'collectives'.

The aim is not solely to look at the causal powers or the logic of financial capital (figure 10.1) but to understand such powers as tendencies, internalized and 'set in motion' (Bhaskar, 1978, p. 50) at the level of the organization. In this way the 'necessary characteristics' of financial capital can be understood in terms of the mediating influences of the prism of time-space, in which spatial relations, the yield contours noted above, enter into organizational calculations. Similarly, the circumstances under which innate powers are 'realized' may be better explained.

Thompson's (1978, 1986) question – 'How are profits calculated under capitalism?' – begins to uncover these circumstances as it shifts the angle of approach towards the manner, techniques and purposes of an organization's system of calculation. While the end result may not be a dramatically different (re)grouping of economic agents, such points as varying rates of return, different exposures to direct market competition and market analysis (especially in respect of the insurance companies and the life funds of composites, as well as the property companies) are given primary emphasis – which allows access to 'the force behind observed trends'.

Calculation: Institutional and Organizational

Calculation may take two forms: first, it may be akin to a firm's self-analysis of its competitive position, in accordance with arithmetical or accounting principles; in a second sense, calculation 'refers to the context in which such calculations take place and is concerned with elucidating the conditions of existence of calculative mechanisms and their effects'. Both interpretations involve the notion of agency and constraints upon action. Agency is placed in a wider context in the second sense, where exogenous factors acting upon non-homogeneous firms or organizations are introduced into the arithmetic, so that the particular assessment of an *organization's* competitive position, for example, is viewed as a profitability or competitive strategy expressed in terms of its wider '*institutional setting*' (Thompson, 1986, pp. 8–9; see also Thompson, 1978, p. 403).

A firm's *potentiality* to 'act' is thus understood as being relative both to its nature – as a type of capital, or amalgam of capitals – and to the social, legal and competitive constraints, each of which may change through *time*, imposed upon it by the institutional framework in which it is located. It is worth remembering here that all of these calculations must be played out (at some stage) through social space.

To grasp these calculative processes calls for a prior understanding of the nature of the capitals involved, in particular the characteristics of the pension funds and LTF, of, that is, money dealing capital.

The Institutions as Capital(s)

Always inherent in money and finance under capitalism is a tendency toward maximum flexibility; financial capital always seeks to be independent of constraints and the banks and financiers that control it seek to obtain maximum profit with maximum liquidity. (*Fine and Harris, 1985, p. 41*)

Accounts of the involvement of long-term institutions in the property development process, as initiators and facilitators, present their logic

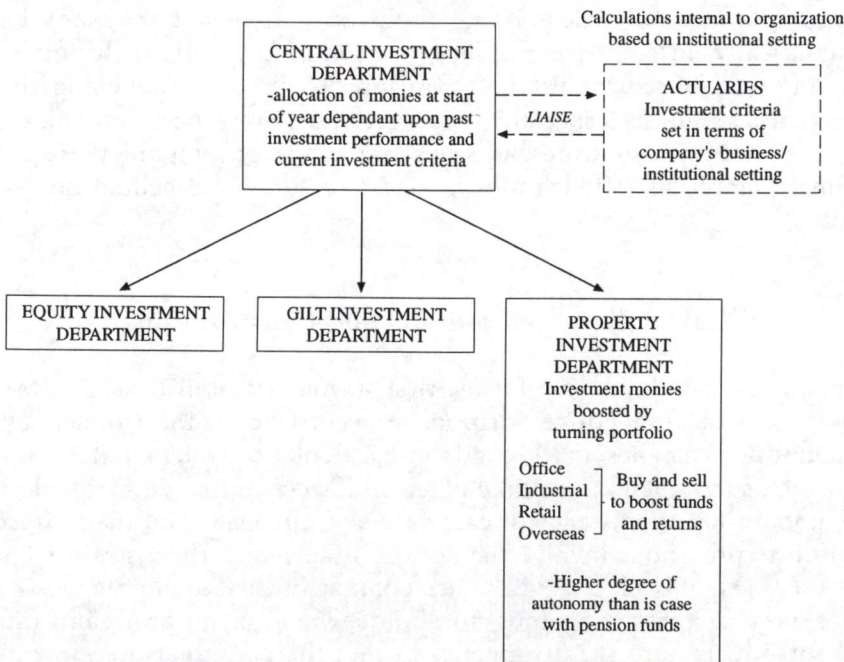

Figure 10.2 Organization of an insurance company's investment departments.

almost exclusively in terms of interest-bearing capital (e.g. Boddy, 1981). Yet from a glance at the reports and accounts of insurance companies, for example, it is plain that they operate simultaneously across a range of different economic relations. Thus, as figures 10.2 and 10.3 attempt to illustrate, it is important to recognize the ways in which the different tentacles of institutional investment – acting, all at once, as interest-bearing capital, money-dealing capital and so on – are coordinated by a central investment department, which establishes overall returns that correspond to relative institutional settings.

The institutions' role is thus broadened to show them as 'mobilizers' or 'managers' of money capital (Massey and Catalano, 1978; Harvey, 1982)[14] and in so doing introduces questions about the 'form' of the advance and 'reflux' (Marx, 1984, pp. 428–32) – the getting back to the

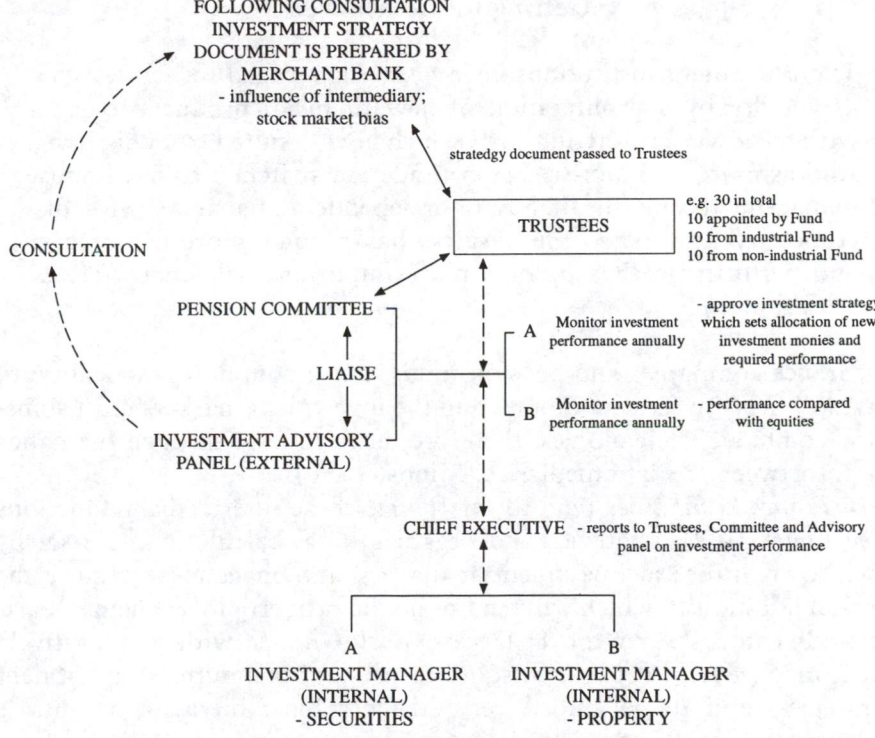

Figure 10.3 Organization of a pension fund's investment department.

14 Here I follow the work of Coakley and Harris (1982, 1983) and Ingham (1984), which stresses the need for flexibility among financial institutions and in which the City is conceptualized overwhelmingly in terms of money capital. Some slight differences between these authors is acknowledged (see Coakley and Harris, 1982, p. 18; 1983, p. 5), as are critiques of Ingham's approach (see Anderson, 1987; Barratt Brown, 1988; Calincos, 1988; Ingham, 1988).

starting point – of investment monies. The question of why a required 'form and reflux' should change then arises and the analysis moves on, from a focus on what separate 'fractions' of capital do separately, to a focus on what institutions do as an amalgam of capitals, and how, with the help of intermediaries, their *tendencies are realized*.

Turning from the abstract to the City, a place which itself is a culturally specific concretion of the 'social relations of money capital' (Harris, 1978, p. 313, 1976),[15] the accent returns to the manner in which City agents acquire their share of profits gained from money dealing. The next section questions how, and for what reasons, the City guides money capital, (in)directly into various spheres of production and directly into speculation.

Getting to the Market

> The investment institutions have been encouraged to higher levels of activity by a proliferation of new financial products together with the lower transaction costs which have resulted from Big Bang. And as more and more pension funds are switched from in-house management into the hands of independent managers with discretionary powers, so the business has become more competitive and performance has become more important. (*Financial Times, 1987a, p. 6*)

Insurance companies and pension funds face a common practicality: to invest, 'their' investment monies and the investment markets must somehow combine. Their monies, therefore, have to pass through the hands of go-betweens or intermediaries (Minns, 1980).

Insurance companies tend to internalize these intermediary functions (see figure 10.2); strategies and organizational calculations are set by their own in-house investment managers and investment teams, the newest addition to which will tend to be the property investment department. In contrast, even for the largest *pension funds* (with comparatively large management departments and investment committees) investment strategies tend to be guided very strongly by a hierachy of outside financial advisors (interviews), groups for whom money dealing is their sole purpose (figure 10.3). Moreover, within the constraints of any fund's trust deed, the influence of the 'nature and practices' of these advisors is of obvious importance (see Lee, 1986, para. 20.58, p. 471), giving a stock market bias to pension funds' calculations (see Minns, 1980; see also Wilson Committee, 1978a, p. 134; Philipp, 1981; Plender,

15 See also Harris (1976), Coakley and Harris (1983, p. 91) and Minns (1983, pp. 106, 109, 111) for further emphasis on social relations of money.

1982; Lee, 1986; *Financial Times* 1985, 1987b),[16] as the data in tables 10.3 and 10.4 and the above quote suggest.

The appeal of varying economic relations, the attraction and changing 'manner' of the advance and required 'form' of reflux of money capital through time, can be better understood, it is argued, by holding in mind the existence and influence of these investment conclaves and inter-mediaries.

The next section offers an example of the changing form of reflux required by LTFs resulting from changes to their institutional setting.

New Institutional Settings: the Example of Life Funds

The mid-1980s saw significant changes in the institutional setting of life companies (ABI, 1984–7, 1987; Diacon, 1985; Warburg Securities, 1986, 1987b; Savory Milln, 1987). Prior to the restrucuring of the savings industry in the mid-1980s, each type of life company was located in a relatively clearly demarcated (Diacon, 1985; BEQB, 1986, p. 547; Savory Milln, 1987) institutional setting, within which intrasectoral competitive calculations were worked out. However, the Financial Ser-vices Act 1986 altered dramatically the borders of dominance of these companies (*Insurance Age*, 1983, p. 26; *Financial Times*, 1986a, 1987a), changing marketing practices and investment strategies (interviews), in many cases prior to the implementation of the new legislative frame-work.

As remarked above, changes to institutional settings alter organiza-tional profitability. Yet how does this alteration feed through into the investment strategy? The interconnection between the two types of cal-culation can be seen, for instance, when the wider influence of the savings environment dictates a particular type of long-term savings product, which, if it is to compete in a new market, demands a different set of profitability horizons or strategems (Goford, 1985, pp. 99, 107). The post-1986 product range, typified by the sharp growth of linked and single premium business and the rise of portable pensions following the Social Securities Act 1986, led to a major restructuring within the life industry (e.g. Finance Act, 1986; Savory Milln, 1987).[17]

Single premium business, unlike whole life and endowment contracts, provide the life offices with a much greater uncertainty in terms of the

16   See also the annual reports and accounts of various pension schemes.
17   It should be noted that all types of long-term fund (whether composites, mutuals or pure life funds) may manage pensions either as corporate schemes or company funds, or through unit linked pensions business. Inflows from these areas of business may be invested through property. These funds or schemes will be subject to the same degree of competiveness and legislative change, and so on, as are pure pension schemes; hence the overlap of settings in figure 10.1 (see Pryke, 1988).

flow of new business and requisite investment assets (Dodds, 1979, p. 37; Diacon, 1985, Section C3.10, p. 76). The different performance criteria that the new institutional setting requires affect the attractiveness of different investment media in various ways (see Wilson Committee, 1978b, p. 80; Moody, 1981, p. 81). Insurance companies will have to consider the structure of bonus payments, the maintenance of a capital reserve and a shareholders' fund. Each of these will have to be 'fed' (in part) by investment income (actual or capitalized) in order for liabilities, in the form of new policies, to be attracted in the first place.

A key part of the new product–investment equation is the quality of investment returns and the timing of their flow. As interview material strongly suggests, some media, like equities, may be able to provide the required short-term performance, while a medium such as property will be less suited.

Liabilities, Investment Income and Competition: Bonuses, Investment Cushions and Write-ups

The need to provide *bonuses*, which relate to with-profits type business (see Wilson, 1983, p. 38; Greenwell Montagu, 1986), is a reminder that insurance companies are subject to competition. Although bonuses may seem removed from institutional property investment, the links between the returns achieved from investment media in general and the returns to individual funds are important chiefly because returns on investments must be sufficient to cover quoted bonuses (Wilson Committee, 1978a, appendix D, p. 96; *Financial Times*, 1986a).

Different media, such as gilts, equities and property, offer qualitatively and quantitatively different returns. To make up the cost of bonuses life companies may utilize the unrealized gains on property and equities in the form of an *investment cushion* or revaluation reserve, which simply refers to the difference between current market value and written book value of assets; the higher the market over the book value, the greater the investment cushion will be. (There will also tend to be some relationship between investment returns and the size of a company's revaluation reserve.) To take another example, some of the major life companies make use of *write-ups* to cover bonus payments, which allow yields on funds to be boosted by taking into account (unrealistic) investment growth (Greenwell Montagu, 1986, p. 25, table 6).

The links between investment policy and organizational calculations now need to be illustrated.

Investment Performance

A major attraction in holding the shares of any company is the potential for continued and, especially in sector terms, high *dividend* growth. For insurance companies dividend growth, reserves and the payment of bonuses are interlinked and (obviously) related to a comparative profitability (see e.g. Dodds, 1979; *Planned Savings*, 1982; Wilson, 1983; *Investors Chronicle*, 1986; Savory Milln, 1987).

While profitability of general insurance business, overseas and, increasingly, unit-linked business of the life fund, and possibly investment earnings on the shareholders' funds, are relevant, perhaps the major influence on dividend growth is the performance of LTFs' *main life funds* (Warburg Securities, 1987a, b, c; Greenwell Montagu, 1987). This is because it is possible to transfer surpluses to the with-profit policyholders, who then benefit in the form of reversionary and terminal bonuses. The distribution of *bonuses*, therefore, is very important to the competitive ability of life companies (including mutuals) to attract policyholders, and maintaining market share is essential to protecting share price (*Planned Savings*, 1982, p. 56).

Bonus rates are speculated on in the sense that they are related to 'actual and expected values', critical to which is the expected rate of investment earnings. (Other factors to be borne in mind are expenses, mortality, and surrenders and lapses.) Because of the bonus loading of life companies, which arises from the ratio of with- and without-profits business, life funds historically have had only to be able to show a modest return on investments to meet either the sum assured or the declared bonuses. (Any shortfalls could also be boosted by profits from non-participatory business.)

New forms of competition filtered through to the investment strategies of the insurance companies (Greenwell Montagu, 1986) changing the game to one of *projecting* high maturity values based on present bonus rates; namely, the higher the projected maturity value, the higher the sales of new policies. Recent competition, moreover, meant that both reversionary and terminal bonuses – which relate respectively to income and capital gains[18] – were combined in order to boost estimates, which in turn made the investment strategy more exacting. Although projections are by no means guarantees, both types of bonuses, and therefore investment returns, have to be high if the company is going to retain or increase market share[19] (Savory Milln, 1987, p. 12).

The resultant drive for performance was a (if not *the*) major source of pressure put on the investment departments of, particularly, the life

18 In unit-linked business, projections take a different form: they correspond (more or less) to current returns from investment units.

19 Reversionary bonuses, which tend to be reliant on investment reserves, are guaranteed, unlike terminal bonuses. Although a cut in reversionary bonuses would be apt in a recessionary climate and with low interest rates, no cut is expected because of 'strong commercial pressure': such a move would be seen as 'weakness' by the market and damage new business prospects for insurance intermediaries (Warburg Securities, 1991).

funds (the major fund, recall, to invest through property). Because of the critical importance of investment earnings to bonus declarations and dividend growth and thus market share (Greenwell and Montagu, 1986, p. 21), and despite the potential to boost bonuses from other sources, as used to be the case, the *main life funds* had to show high and competitive *short-term* performance (interviews).

As this section has illustrated, market forces were redefining calculation. The marked change in investment patterns of life funds should be interpreted in terms of changes in their institutional setting that 'set in motion' readjustments in the arithmetic of the profitability criteria of individual insurance companies. These criteria, together with the bullish environment of which they were necessarily a part, were to have major effects on the financial and spatial strategies of the property company sector; directly, as a result of the downturn in investment demand, and indirectly, via the growing general demand for 'performance'.

An Overview of the Spatial Sensitivity of Property Company Share Capital

> It's not just about levels of profit on cost. It's more about the profit you earn, the capital return, on the time employed. Someone who makes 20 per cent on cost in four years is only half as bright as someone who makes 20 per cent on cost in two years. (*Interview with property developer*)

This section is concerned with coercive, *indirect* economic power: the influence of 'market pressure' on the activities of property companies. This force is understood here to include the long-term institutions as dealers in the equity of property companies, and introduces, somewhat tangentially, but purposefully, the role of analysts and brokers in mediating the requirements of economic agents, here property companies, and the capital market.

This mediation is achieved in an accounting cum social discourse (Hopwood, 1984, 1986, p. 14), which, it is contended, spreads the power of money dealing capital.[20] One immediate effect is that organizational strategies have to fit with accounting principles – earnings per share and net asset value are property examples used here (see below) – in addition to economic categories (Cooper and Hopper, 1988, p. 3), such as cost and profit, in order for a firm to be able to articulate with

---

20 This comes through quite strongly from the confidential reports on property company activity prepared by City analysts and supplied to institutional investors. The increased use of information technology in compiling an accounting record of property company activities further extends the power of this discourse.

outside agents (see e.g. Allen, 1986). This section also outlines the valuation of a property company's shares in terms of the (often ignored) influence of the market and 'City opinion' on the actions of property companies, a theme taken up in more detail in the next section.

Some general points about share capital should be mentioned before we go any further. Money lent to a company can be either in return for interest, in the case of a loan, for example, or, as in the case of shares, in return for dividends and earnings. Share capital in the UK is raised through the Stock Exchange, which is characterized by a rapid turnover in paper rights to the equity of companies. Once a company issues shares or 'goes public' it may return to the market for a 'cash call' in order to raise further equity. Put simply, the capital value of property company shares will be determined heavily by its ability to sell developments at or above the costs of production and/or to retain high-yielding schemes in its investment portfolio.

Institutions holding property company shares (as with shareholdings generally) will require satisfactory income returns and capital growth. Market performance ultimately must be met. For example, in the late 1960s one investment company case study, acting as an 'investment vehicle' for its investors, was given a 'rude awakening' in the form of institutional pressure to show results. The company had to choose a development programme that would produce immediate returns following 'orders' to perform.

The growth of property companies, moreover, from trader developer to development investment company, will tend to create a particular locational or spatial policy of its own, even where the company bypasses the institutions for direct property funding. Such a policy will be related to strategies calculated in terms of particular market perceptions and to the consequent aptness of qualitatively and temporally different profit opportunities requisite to meeting those expectations.

How Does the Market Assess Property Company Shares?

Mountleigh meets City expectations with £35m. (*Financial Times*, 22 January 1988)

MEPC lifts asset value 21% to 533p. (*Financial Times*, 26 November 1987)

The first of the headlines above is taken from a brief article in the *Financial Times* reporting the interim figures of what was, at the time, a newly listed property trading and development company. The latter announced the end-of-year figures of the UK's second largest property investment and development company, which showed annual profits of £80.2 million. In aiming to meet the 'top end of City estimates', how do the different forms of 'listed' merchant capital set about achieving the type of profits expected of them by the market, by the City?

A Few Notes on the Listed Property Sector in the 1980s

> There is this problem that profits are non-repeatable. It is a finite thing: there are only so many schemes and there's only so much profitability. (*Interview with a property sector analyst*)

There are different ways of 'pleasing the investment markets'. *Developer traders* will be selling their ability to maintain and produce development profits. Indeed, they emphasized this by going to the market on an earnings per share (EPS) basis.[21] *Property investment companies* tend to hold development profit as an unrealized capital surplus by retaining the development in an investment portfolio, where any capital uplift at financial year end is shown as a valuation surplus.[22] (For trader developers profit is taken through to the profit and loss account on sale.)

Investors will be buying shares in trading companies in anticipation of receiving a stream of earnings and dividends that can only be delivered if sufficient development profit can be achieved to service short-term loans. Trader developers will thus be tempted by 'off pitch' schemes, in new areas, where there is a chance of making greater development profit. At the same time this must be balanced against maintaining market credibility, which is sensitive to letting risks and rental growth.

Markheath, a listed developer trader that emerged in the 1980s, to take an example, failed to recognize the spatial particularities of money dealing capital. The company was unsuccessful in selling sufficient development schemes by the financial year-end to meet market expectations and 'turned in' a £2.39 million loss, rather than an expected profit of £1.5 million. As one sector analyst commented, 'the company's credibility in the City suffered dramatically' (interview), leading to a very low price–earnings ratio, thus making it very difficult to issue paper. As the same analyst added, 'they blew it completely and it takes a while to forget' (interview).

The problem the developer traders faced was that if they were to meet estimated profit growth, then a certain number of successful schemes had to be undertaken each year and, as development profits are non-repeatable, more and more schemes were required to keep profits flowing through to feed dividend growth. Yet, importantly, the market will be

21   According to one analyst, of approximately twenty property companies that went to the market between 1981 and 1986, only an estimated four or five labelled themselves as investment companies.

22   Although trading activities can be used to 'fortify the cycle of profits', the main influence on an even and maintainable profits profile for investment companies will come from having a substantial investment portfolio.

looking at growth and assets *per share* rather than simply 'gross assets' or 'gross profit'. It was this last factor which, in part, lay behind the early success of the *trading companies* from the early 1980s and contrasted starkly with the plight of *property investment companies*, whose portfolios were showing slow growth in the face of rising yields over the same period.

The shift was quite dramatic. One analyst estimated the amount raised through shares by the property company sector, in the twelve months to April 1987, to be in the region of £1.5 billion, almost all raised by developer traders rather than property investment companies. (It is estimated that the institutions allocated only £1.3 billion to direct property investment over that same period.) The attraction of the traders was that they provided performance, thus enabling them to outstep the investment companies.

The property traders, however, soon found that they had to stabilize their profit rate and become like investment companies. A steady, upward moving stream of profits became the market requirement and not rapidly fluctuating profits, which are associated with income tied solely to development profits. The traders thus started to turn themselves into investment companies in order to build up an asset base to protect share price, and to be in the position where they would have to rely less on development profits – or at least that was the plan. Just as this metamorphosis tended to influence development strategy in the medium term, it also involved approaching the City more immediately to raise equity capital.

Equity Issues and Spatial Sensitivity

In general, raising money through equity issues will increase asset value. For the trading company, although there will be a slowdown in growth of earnings per share, it is relatively easier to raise money through a rights issue than it is for investment companies that tend to trade at a discount to asset value (in which case an equity issue will dilute asset strength). The qualification in both cases is that there should be a good reason for the issue in the eyes of institutional shareholders.[23]

As the Markheath example suggests, anticipating the reaction of the City's investors to issues is very much part of raising money for both types of merchant capital.[24] What is more, as noted above, brokers are pivotal in playing property market strategy against the indirect power of the institutions and the market's general 'sensitivity'. (Share price is also used by bankers to judge market sentiment; thus share performance and

23 See Pryke (1993) for further examples of this.
24 For investment companies, although NAV would remain unaffected, the side-effect of adverse market opinion would be compounded through a downrating of market capitalization.

the institutional support for a company may be highly influential in the availability and cost of *debt* finance.) As one analyst explained, pow wow with the institutions is a delicate business: 'it has to be manipulated quite well by the broker to judge the institutions' reactions: "how much stock will they take?", "how many times can you call on the market for money?", "how well do you have to perform to justify tapping the market so often?" That's the real trick, keeping a balance' (interview). As this quote and this section suggest, the 'invisible hand' of credibility acted continually as a coercive force on the main components of the property sector, the investment companies and the trader developers alike, stimulating them to maintain market share price, but from different starting points.

The *trader developers* began their listed life with a small equity base and thereby were able to show exceptional share price movement in the mid-1980s, and meet the performance required by the bull market. The *investment companies*, in contrast, generally found it very difficult to produce a growth of over 10 per cent per annum on their investment portfolios (mainly owing to low capital growth, income gearing and larger equity bases), a growth less than half that produced by the 'more exciting' traders. They had to reconsider, therefore, the quality of profits that they were offering to the equity market, which was showing an aggregate return three times the rate they offered.

One well-known investment company can be used to illustrate the problem confronting the mature end of the sector. Despite having an investment portfolio 30 per cent based in the City of London, Land Securities managed an asset growth of only 6 per cent in the financial year to 1986. The sheer size of the company's investment portfolio (and here capital growth at revaluation of the investment portfolio is ignored), however, meant that Land Securities had to carry out *more* developments than a trader simply to *match* the latter's level of performance. Thus 'dynamized' by the market, Land Securities, like other investment companies, had to 'step up their activity to make themselves attractive to the institutions' (interview, property sector analyst).

This renewed development activity had to pay heed to how credible development programmes appeared to the market. The market expected from such companies a smooth flow of returns over the longer term. To achieve these returns the investment companies' calculations had to be mapped on to particular spatial matrices (see Pryke, 1994). Social space, in other words, became an exacting ingredient – more so, perhaps, than was the case for traders – in the 'realization of tendencies'.

'Figuring Out' Calculation and Property Investment

Figure 10.4 attempts to pull together the main emphases of previous sections. The figure highlights the main economic links between a

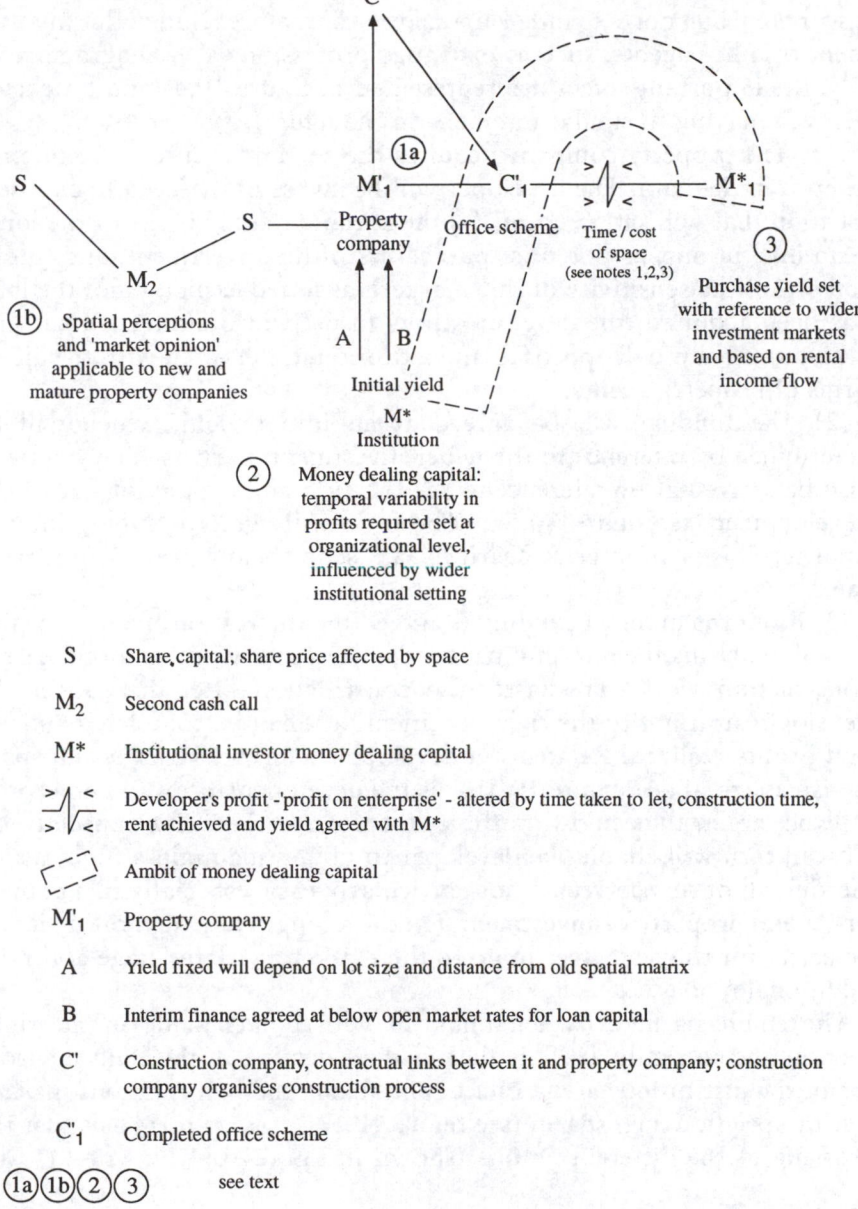

S	Share capital; share price affected by space
M_2	Second cash call
M*	Institutional investor money dealing capital
>/< >/<	Developer's profit -'profit on enterprise' - altered by time taken to let, construction time, rent achieved and yield agreed with M*
⬚	Ambit of money dealing capital
M'_1	Property company
A	Yield fixed will depend on lot size and distance from old spatial matrix
B	Interim finance agreed at below open market rates for loan capital
C'	Construction company, contractual links between it and property company; construction company organises construction process
C'_1	Completed office scheme
(1a)(1b)(2)(3)	see text

Figure 10.4 Example of a forward funding arrangement in the City of London in the mid-1980s.

property trader developer and a long-term institution involved in a so-called forward funded scheme, one of the 'new' vehicles engineered for circulating capitals through the built form in the 1980s, in a new spatial matrix on the fringes of the City of London.[25] Following Boddy (1981) the ties between the developer and the construction company are also noted but not expanded upon (the diagram excludes the involvement of other agents, such as exchange professionals[26]). Diagrammatically, the important stages are represented in figure 10.4 (and bracketed below, referring to similar numbers on the figure).

(1a) The property company acquires the site and secures an economic interest in the land. The developer will be aware of the need to choose a location that will satisfy (directly) the specific requirements of the long-term institutions, as potential purchasers of the investment, and (indirectly) (1b) the sensitivity of the 'market', as noted earlier. Once the land has been acquired, the developer, now in need of building finance and take-out money, will approach an institution, quite often with the aid of firms of property agents.

(2) The funding will be agreed at an initial yield, which will be determined by reference to the wider investment markets. The yield will also be arrived at by reference to the location and capital lot size of the development (see figure 10.5a). The fund will agree to supply interim finance. This is an interest-bearing loan, set at below prevailing market rates.

(3) From the moment funding is agreed the interest on the loan begins to add up. Using the interim finance, the developer will then organize the construction work. The faster the construction rate, the sooner the development (built to the right specifications) can be completed and let, and profits realized. Relatedly, a development in the 'right' social space is also essential (see figure 10.5b), as the developer's profit on enterprise will be larger, thus boosting the chance of meeting City expectations. This in turn will enable the developer to obtain/maintain a high rating. Getting all of this correct is not particularly easy, especially in a climate of general property disinvestment. On the strength of a high rating it will be easier for the developer to go to the market at a later stage and raise additional money.

The emphasis here (which links up with points made in the third section and in figure 10.1) is that in their dealing in the built environment, the institutions are in effect capitalizing the rent relations marked out by specific social spaces (see figure 10.5c). It is on this basis that the crossing of the different ambits (shown in figure 10.4 by $M^*-M^*_1$) of

25 The issue of different types of landownership is left out of this example, but see Pryke (1988, chapter 6).
26 The important role of office agents in the fluidity of this purely economic structure should nevertheless be acknowledged (see Pryke, 1994).

money dealing and merchant capitals is meant to signify the quite particular financial specifications of each. The latter, the trader developer, is looking for a profit on enterprise from a swift sale of the finished and let scheme. The institution, the former, is looking to hold an income producing investment.

In circulating through the built environment, picking out space with increasing care during the 1980s, the long-term institutions act as two types of capital. To arrive at the initial or purchase yield, the calculation is carried out while they are wearing their money dealing hat. When they agree to fund the development costs (also known as interim finance) the institutions act, straightforwardly, as interest-bearing capitalists. In this

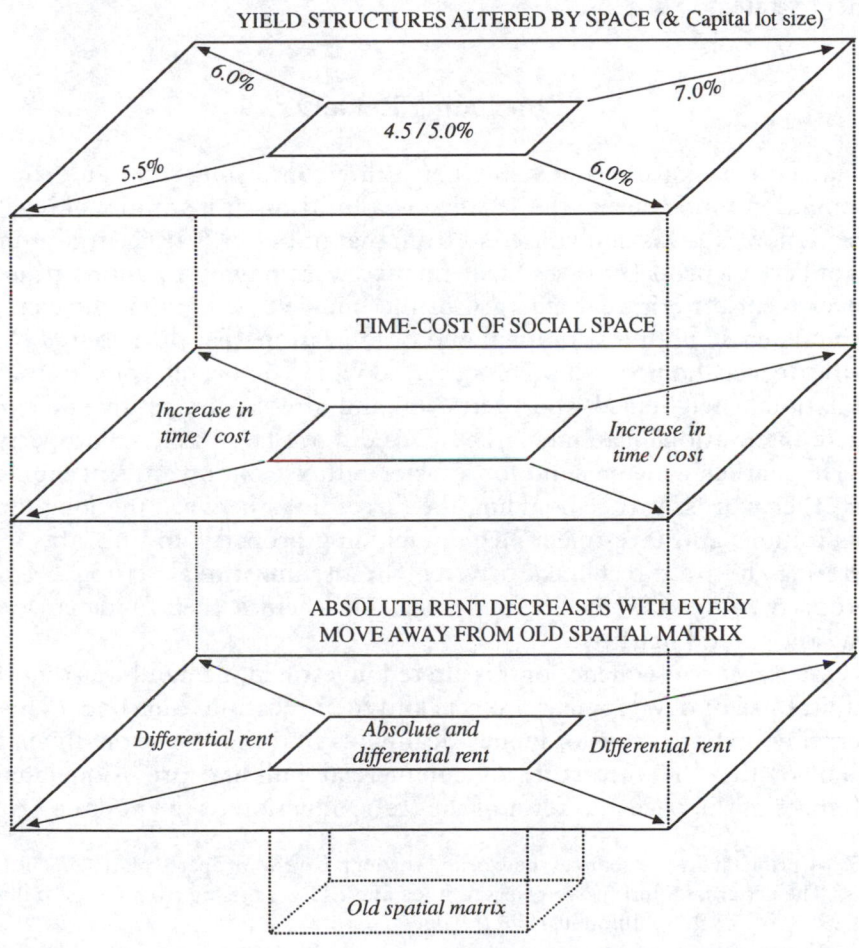

Figure 10.5 Yield structures and space.

last relationship they are (supposedly) also removed from the risks involved in establishing an income producing investment (in this case, in a new spatial matrix).

The form and reflux of this interim finance is not the same as the form and reflux expected from the purchase of the development and holding it as an investment. When a building is held as an investment, a qualitatively specific and quantitatively workable (and rising) income yield and capital gain are required.[27] These investment qualities are broadly similar to the form and reflux of returns available from dealing in equities and gilts. In part because of the frequently cited 'long-term nature' of property investment, it is the money dealing characteristics of the long-term institutions, established in their respective institutional and organizational settings, that ('in the last resort') determine their overall property investment strategy.

Concluding Remarks

Against a background of rising net inflows into long-term and superannuation funds during the 1980s, the allocation of institutional investment monies[28] was quite different from that of the 1970s. The traditional suppliers of property investment finance were having to adjust to new investment criteria that emerged in the mid-1980s. In sum, the change stimulated at both institutional and organizational levels favoured high performance, liquid media. This occurred within an overall context of low inflation,[29] heightened 'short-termism' and a more competitive deregulated, international capital market. This did not bode well for property.

The market-wide demand for a faster reflux from investment monies, in other words, was remoulding the direct links between the long-term institutions and investment media, including property. In turn, this was altering the (in)direct links between the organizational settings of the property companies, the life funds, pension schemes, their fund managers and the capital market.

One *direct* consequence of this altered investment demand was that the capital size of development projects and their location came under closer scrutiny by both types of money dealing capital that sit at the financial apex of the UK's structure of commercial building provision. Sharp changes in the pace and form of the (re)production of the built environ-

27   A property investment can be worked through careful property management.
28   The net annual inflows to pension funds and LTF was rising from £4762 million in 1978 to £17,958 million in 1986 (*Financial Statistics*).
29   Even if inflation were to return, which would affect the calculations of both the institutions and property companies, the freedom now to invest overseas would mean that for the institutions UK property would be unlikely to play the same function as it did prior to 1979 (interviews).

ment were provoked. Driven by another aspect of the economic power of money dealing capital, this time working *indirectly* through the stock market, the property sector increased its reliance on bank lending in order to carry out sufficient developments to meet market expectations. Social space was 'turned over' in accordance with reworked or re-engineered time–cost frameworks. Different sets of calculation and their associated times had to be urbanized through what was, by the mid-1980s, a sharply fragmented space economy, much of which was unacceptable to money dealing capital.

Despite the resultant optimistic switch to supplying owner-occupiers, the use of interest-bearing capital presented what should have been a familiar problem, as one property trader commented: 'someone has to work out how to sell these buildings at the end of the day' (interview). With the specific reflux, the specific time schedule, demanded by this form of financial capital, under which interest grows 'no matter whether it is awake or asleep, at home or abroad' (Marx, 1984, p. 393), the days ahead for many property developers and their bankers were set to be long and costly. For the rest of us, the effects of yet another 'turbulent' spell of 'creative destruction', spurred on by an economic power mediated through the City, are only too apparent.

Appendix: Interviews

Semi-structured interactive interviews were held during 1986/7 with representatives from the organizations listed below. An outline of these interviews is available from the author. The semi-structured nature of the interviews enabled a discussion about property development and investment generally and the City in particular (based on general market trends and conditions) to be combined with a particular company's organizational history. This interview method also allowed scope for comparisons to be made between different 'groups' of companies, and between companies within 'groups'. The quotes used in the text are therefore indicative of general and particular spatial patterns and economic processes, for instance; where quotes are exceptional they are introduced as such.

Long-term Financial Institutions

- Senior Regional Surveyor, PosTel
- Property Investment Assistant, British Petroleum Pension Scheme
- Property Investment Manager, Imperial Group (T)
- Property Investment Assistant, Electricity Supply
- Chief Surveyor and Property Director, Prudential
- Estates Manager, Norwich Union
- Investment Manager, Pearl (T)
- Property Investment Manager, Guardian Royal Exchange Properties
- Property Investment Manager, Sun Life Properties

- Surveyor, Scottish Amicable (T)
- Deputy Property Investment Manager, Commercial Union Properties
- Executive Director, Eagle Star
- Property Investment Manager, CIS

Note: (T) = telephone interview.

Property Investment and Trading Companies

- Deputy Chairman and Deputy Managing Director, CLRP/Land Securities
- Director (Property Development), MEPC
- Chief Surveyor, British Land
- Managing Director (Finance), Town and City Properties
  Chief Surveyor and Director, Town and City Properties
- Surveyor, Haselmere Estates (Rodamco)
  Finance Director, Haselmere Estates (Rodamco)
- Surveyor, Hammerson Group
- Surveyor, Trafalgar House
- Director, Wates City Properties
- Director, Rosehaugh
- Surveyor, London and Edinburgh Trust
- Managing Director, Mount Row/Speyhawk
- Director, Oldham Estates (MEPC)

Property Sector Analysts

- Senior Property Analyst, Hoare Govett
- Senior Property Analyst, CL Alexanders Laing and Cruickshank
- Property Analyst, Rowe and Pitman, S. G. Warburg

References

Aaronovitch, S. and Smith, R. (1981) *The Political Economy of British Capitalism: a Marxist Analysis*. London: McGraw Hill.

ABI (1984–7) *Quarterly Figures for New Life Assurance*. London: Association of British Insurers (yearly).

ABI (1987) *Insurance Statistics 1982–1986*. London: Association of British Insurers.

Allen, D. (1986) Strategic financial management. In M. Bromwich and A. Hopwood (eds), *Research and Current Issues in Management Accounting*. London: Pitman, 47–51.

Allen, J. (1983) Property relations and landlordism – a realist approach. *Environment and Planning D: Society and Space*, 1, 191–203.

Anderson, P. (1987) The figures of descent. *New Left Review*, 161, 20–77.

Ball, Sir J. (1991) Short-termism – myth or reality? *National Westminster Bank Quarterly Review*, August, 20–30.

Ball, M. (1977) Differential rent and the role of landed property. *IJURR*, 1(1), 380–403.

Ball, M. (1979) A critique of urban economics. *IJURR*, 3(3), 309–32.

Ball, M. (1985a) Land rent and the construction industry. In M. Ball et al. (eds), *Land Rent Housing and Urban Planning: a European Perspective*. London: Croom Helm, 71–86.

Ball, M. (1985b) The urban rent question. *Environment and Planning A*, 17, 503–25.

Ball, M. (1986) The built environment and the urban question. *Environment and Planning D: Society and Space*, 4, 447–64.

Barras, R. (1983) A simple theoretical model of the office-development cycle. *Environment and Planning A*, 15, 1381–94.

Barras, R. and Ferguson, D. (1987) Dynamic modelling of the building cycle: 1. Theoretical framework. *Environment and Planning A*, 19, 353–67.

Barratt Brown, M. (1988) Away with all the great arches: Anderson's history of British capitalism. *New Left Review*, 167, 22–51.

BEQB (1986) Life assurance company and private pension fund investment, 1962–84. *Bank of England Quarterly Bulletin*, 76(4), 546–57.

Bhaskar, R. (1978) *A Realist Theory of Science*. Brighton: Harvester Press.

Bleaney, M. (1983) Conservative economic strategy. In S. Hall and M. Jacques (eds), *The Politics of Thatcherism*. London: Lawrence and Wishart.

Boddy, M. (1981) The property sector in late capitalism: the case of Britain. In M. Dear and A. J. Scott (eds), *Urbanization and Urban Planning in Capitalist Society*. London: Methuen.

Brett, E. A. (1985) *The World Economy since the War: the Politics of Uneven Development*. London: Macmillan.

Briston, R. and Dobbing, R. (1978) The growth and impact of 'institutional' investors: a report to the Research Committee of the Institute of Chartered Accountants of England and Wales. In *Institutional Investors*. London: ICA.

BZW (1987) *Barclays de Zoete Wedd Equity-gilt Study*. London: Barclays de Zoete Wedd.

Cadman, D. (1984) Property finance in the UK in the post-war period. *Land Development Studies*, 1, 61–82.

Cadman, D. and Austin-Crowe, L. (1978) *Property Development*. London: F. and F. N. Spod.

Calincos, A. (1988) Exception or symptom? The British crisis and the world system. *New Left Review*, 169, 97–106.

Carr, W. I. (1986) *Property Investment Report*. London: W. I. Carr.

Chick, V. (1988) Sources of finance, recent changes in bank behaviour and the theory of investment and interest. In P. Arestis (ed.), *Contemporary Issues in Money and Banking*. London: Macmillan.

Clayton, G. and Osborn, W. T. (1965) *Insurance Company Investment: Principles and Policy*. London: George Allen and Unwin.

Coakley, J. and Harris, L. (1982) Industry, the city, and the foreign exchanges: theory and evidence. *British Review of Economic Issues*, 4(10), 15–36.

Coakley, J. and Harris, L. (1983) *The City of Capital*. Oxford: Basil Blackwell.

Cooper, D. J. and Hopper, T. M. (1988) Introduction: financial calculation in industrial and political debate. In D. J. Cooper and T. M. Hopper (eds), *Debating Coal Closures*. Cambridge: Cambridge University Press.

Coutts, K., Godley, W., Rowthorn, B. and Zezza, G. (1990) *Britain's Economic Problems and Policies*. London: Institute for Public Policy Research.

Des Rosiers, F. (1987) Finance and property: the role of institutional property investment in British and Canadian real estate. *Progress in Planning*, 28(2), 77–193.

Diacon, S. R. (1985) The UK insurance industry: structure, developments and market prospects to 1990. London: Staniland Hall.

Dodds, J. C. (1979) *The Investment Behaviour of British Life Insurance Companies*. Guildford: Croom Helm.

DoE/PAG (1980) *Structure and Activity of the Development Industry*. London: HMSO.

Financial Times (1985) Fund managers: not so myopic. *Financial Times*, 29 November, 6.

Financial Times (1986a) UK Provident had 'weak investment strategy'. *Financial Times*, 14 April, 14.

Financial Times (1986b) Seeking out life companies' potential in a changing market. *Financial Times*, 23 June, 22.

Financial Times (1987a) Life industry's future takes shape. *Financial Times*, 14 February, 5.

Financial Times (1987b) Pension fund investment. *Financial Times*, 21 May, insert.

Fine, B. and Harris, L. (1985) *The Peculiarities of the British Economy*. London: Lawrence and Wishart.

Goford, J. (1985) The control cycle: financial control of a life assurance company. *Journal of the Institute of Actuaries Students' Society*, 28, 99–114.

Greenwell Montagu (1986) *Insurance Commentary*, June. London: Greenwell Montagu Research.

Harris, L. (1976) On interest, credit and capital. *Economy and Society*, 5(2), 145–77.

Harris, L. (1978) The science of the economy. *Economy and Society*, 7(3), 285–320.

Harris, L. (1988) Alternative perspectives on the financial system. In L. Harris et al. (eds), *New Perspectives on the Financial System*. London: Croom Helm.

Harvey, D. (1982) *The Limits to Capital*. Oxford: Basil Blackwell.

Harvey, D. (1985a) *Money, Time, Space, and the City*. Cambridge: University of Cambridge Department of Land Economy/Granta Editions.

Harvey, D. (1985b) *The Urbanization of Capital*. Oxford: Basil Blackwell.

Harvey, D. (1989) *The Condition of Postmodernity*. Oxford: Blackwell.

Harvey, D. (1990) Review of Logan, Molotch, 'Urban Fortunes: the Political Economy of Place'. *Environment and Planning D: Society and Space*, 8, 495–6.

Hopwood, A. (1984) Accounting and the pursuit of efficiency. In A. Hopwood and C. Tomkins (eds), *Issues in Public Sector Accounting*. Oxford: Phillip Allan.

Hopwood, A. (1986) Management accounting and organizational action: an introduction. In M. Bromwich and A. Hopwood (eds), *Research and Current Issues in Management Accounting*. London: Pitman.

Ingham, G. (1984) *Capitalism Divided? The City and Industry in British Social Development*. London: Macmillan.

Ingham, G. (1988) Commercial capital and British development: a reply to Michael Barratt Brown. *New Left Review*, 169, 45–65.

Insurance Age (1983) What would life be like without LAPR? *Insurance Age*, July, 26–7, 55.

Investors Chronicle (1986) How life companies work. *Investors Chronicle*, 10 January, 10–12.

IPD (1986) *The IPD Annual Review 1986*. London: Investment Property Databank.

IPD (1987) *The IPD Annual Review 1987*. London: Investment Property Databank.

Lamarche, F. (1976) Property development and the economic foundations of the urban question. In C. G. Pickvance (ed.), *Urban Sociology: Critical Essays*. London: Methuen.

Lee, E. M. (1986) *An Introduction to Pension Schemes*. London: Institute of Actuaries.

Marsh, P. (1990) *Short-termism on Trial*. London: Institutional Fund Managers' Association.

Marx, K. (1967) *Capital, Volume II*. London: Edward Arnold.

Marx, K. (1984) *Capital, Volume III*. London: Lawrence and Wishart.

Massey, D. and Catalano, A. (1978) *Capital and Land*. London: Edward Arnold.

Massey, D. and Meegan, R. (1985) Introduction: the debate. In D. Massey and R. Meegan (eds), *Politics and Method: Contrasting Studies in Industrial Geography*. London: Methuen.

Mingione, E. (1981) *Social Conflict and the City*. Oxford: Basil Blackwell.

Minns, R. (1980) *Pension Funds and British Capitalism*. Guildford: Heinemann.

Minns, R. (1983) Pension funds – an alternative view. *Capital and Class*, 10, 104–16.

Moody, R. (1981) The life office as institutional investor. *CII Journal*, 5 February, 80–4.

Phillip, A. (ed.) (1981) *Pension Funds and Their Advisers*. London: AP Financial Registers.

Planned Savings (1982) Life office profits – a fair share for policyholders. *Planned Savings*, October, 56–70.

Plender, J. (1982) *That's the Way the Money Goes: Financial Institutions and the Nation's Savings*. London: Deutsch.

Pryke, M.D. (1988) Urban land 'values' and the changing role of financial institutions: a case study of the city of London. Unpublished PhD thesis, Faculty of Social Sciences, The Open University.

Pryke, M. D. (1994) Looking back on the space of a boom. *Environment and Planning A* (in the press.)

Rothschild, K. (ed.) (1971) *Power in Economics*. Harmondsworth: Penguin.

Saunders, P. (1986) *Social Theory and the Urban Question*, 2nd edn. London: Hutchinson.

Savory Milln (1987) *The Finance War Part I: the Life Industry*. London: Savory Milln.

Sayer, A. (1984) *Method in Social Science: a Realist Approach*. London: Hutchinson.

Thompson, G. (1977) The relationship between the financial and industrial sectors in the United Kingdom economy. *Economy and Society*, 6, 235–81.

Thompson, G. (1978) Capitalist profit calculation and inflation accounting. *Economy and Society*, 7, 395–429.

Thompson, G. (1986) Introduction. In G. Thompson (ed.), *Economic Calculation and Policy Formation*. London: Routledge and Kegan Paul.

Utiger, R. (1988) The stock market and industry. *Interchange*, Spring, 7–13.

Warburg Securities (1986) *Life Assurance: Annual Review*. London: S.G. Warburg Securities.

Warburg Securities (1987a) *Property: Review of 1986 and Prospects for 1987*. London: S. G. Warburg Securities.

Warburg Securities (1987b) *Life Assurance: Annual Review*. London: S. G. Warburg Securities.

Warburg Securities (1987c) *Composite Insurance: Annual Review*. London: S. G. Warburg Securities.

Warburg Securities (1991) *Life Assurance: Annual Review*. London: S. G. Warburg Securities.

Williams, P. (1991) Time and the city: short-termism in the UK, myth or reality? *National Westminster Bank Quarterly Review*, August, 31–8.

Wilson Committee (1978a) (I) Written evidence by the National Association of Pension Funds. (II) Transcript of the oral evidence given by the National Association of Pension Funds 8 November 1977. *Evidence on the Financing of Industry and Trade*, 3, 129–85.

Wilson Committee (1978b) (I) Written evidence by the insurance companies associations. (II) Transcript of the oral evidence given by the insurance companies associations 8 November 1977. *Evidence on the Financing of Industry and Trade*, 3, 55–128.

Wilson, K. (1983) *British Financial Institutions*. London: Pitman.

Wyn Williams, S. (1981) Realism, Marxism and human geography. *Antipode*, 13(2), 31–8.

11

Stateless Monies, Global Financial Integration and National Economic Autonomy: the End of Geography?

Ron Martin

The end of geography, as a concept applied to international financial relationships, refers to a state of economic development where geographical location no longer matters in finance, or matters much less than hitherto. In this state, financial market regulators no longer hold full sway over their regulatory frameworks, such as the nation-state or other typical regulatory jurisdictional territories . . . . The end of geography is a challenge to all participants in the world economy, to developing as well as developed economies, to public and private policy makers, to producers and consumers of financial services. It involves the debate over the role of the nation-state, the integration of nations and the disintegration of existing federations. (*O'Brien, 1992*)

Introduction: the Globalization Issue

Over the past few years the concept of 'globalization' has attracted increasing attention within the social science literature. In international economics and politics, for example, the term has already become part of the standard lexicon (Holland, 1987; Gill and Law, 1988; Wallerstein, 1991; McGrew and Lewis, 1992), though not without voices of dissent (such as Gordon, 1988; Hirst and Thompson, 1992). Likewise, economic geographers have also begun to give prominence to the 'globalization' process and the 'global economy' (for example, Thrift, 1986; Wallace, 1990; Peet, 1991; Dicken, 1992). There is in fact a widespread acceptance that an accelerating and deepening globalization of capitalism is under way which raises several fundamental problems of analysis, theory and policy. For one thing, exactly what is meant by the concepts of 'globalization' and the 'global economy'? Different authors use these terms in different ways and with varying degrees of precision. Yet another issue concerns the relationship between the global and the local, as expressed by such notions as the 'global–local interplay' and 'glocalization' (Dunford and Kafkalis, 1992; Swyngedouw, 1992). A third and fundamental problem has to do with the impact of globalization on the nature and role of the nation state. Must we now adopt a more 'globalized' framework of analysis, or does the nation state still provide a satisfactory and meaningful entity with which to understand the workings and regulation of capitalism? In many ways, the question of the powers and autonomy of the state is central to the globalization issue.

There are already three divergent schools of thought on this matter. Probably the most prominent is the view that transnationalization and globalization are seriously undermining the national basis of the nation state considered as a geographically bounded set of political, economic and social relations. The argument is that capital is overcoming the constraints of national economic organization and regulation, subordinating nation states to global markets and forces that cross national boundaries. Global capitalism is without its own state, and this is seen as potentially destabilizing (Radice, 1984; Gordon, 1988; MacEwan and Tabb, 1989; Picciotto, 1991; Reich, 1991; Crook et al., 1992). At the other extreme there are those who argue that the claim that the nation state is being undermined by globalization is greatly exaggerated, and that individual states still exercise substantial independence and authority in the regulation and management of their domestic political economies (Porter, 1990; Pooley, 1991; Hirst and Thompson, 1992). Still others see the dichotomy between nation states and global capital as a false one; for them the current transnationalization of capital is a process of reorganization of the state into the 'transnational state' and, simultaneously, of the system of national regulation into one of global regulation (McMichael and Myhre, 1991).

Nowhere are these processes and debates more pertinent than in the realm of money. Much of the expanding corpus of economic and geographical literature on the globalization of capitalism has focused on the processes and implications of industrial internationalization and transnationalization. Important though this aspect of globalization undoubtedly is, it is within the financial sphere that globalization is arguably most developed, reflecting the much greater fungibility and convertibility of the money capital form. This globalization and mobility of finance capital represents one of the most significant elements in the emergence of what Castells (1989) terms the new 'space of flows' that now dominates and transcends the historically constructed 'space of places'. Indeed, according to some observers the process of financial globalization is already sufficiently well advanced to signal the 'end of geography' with respect to monetary structures and relationships (O'Brien, 1992; see also Wachtel, 1986; Ohmae, 1990).

My aim in this chapter is to examine this contention. First, to set the scene, the trend towards financial globalization is charted in terms of some of the main financial developments that have taken place over the past two decades. The subsequent section looks at the geography of this globalization process and argues, contrary to the 'end of geography' thesis, that place remains fundamentally important to the structure and operation of the global financial system. The discussion then turns to the implications of global financial integration for the nation state and national policy autonomy.

Globalization and the Growth of a Supranational Financial System

The international movement of money and finance capital has long been a characteristic feature of modern industrial capitalism (Kindleberger, 1987). But as with industrial development itself, it is possible to distinguish certain (overlapping) phases in the historical evolution of the financial system of advanced capitalist countries (table 11.1 gives a stylized representation; see also Rybczynski, 1988). Generalizing across the specific experience of individual countries, the earliest stage, associated with industrialization, was essentially a 'regional' and 'bank-orientated' system, based on a network of regional banks using local sources of capital and savings to channel into private industry. A relatively high degree of regional autonomy in banking and investment capital was typical of this phase. To the extent that international movements of money took place, they were mainly associated with financing overseas trade. As the advanced capitalist countries moved into the mature stage of industrial development, so their financial systems became much more spatially and organizationally centralized. In this second, 'national' or 'market-orientated', phase, national capital markets largely replaced regional banks as sources of funds. And as regional financial autonomy was being lost to central institutions, these in turn became increasingly international in their operations, not only financing trade but also helping to channel capital into investment overseas. The latest, contemporary, phase, associated with the passage to a late- or post-industrial era, marks the onset of a further shift in the nature of the financial system towards a 'transnational' and 'securitized' form. Capital and money markets are separating from industry, money has been commodified, and as national financial centres become increasingly globalized and globally integrated, it is now national monetary autonomy that is being challenged.

By globalization in this context is meant a movement beyond a system based on inter-national financial transactions between nations. Nor is it simply synonymous with multinational banks and finance houses, or the process of internationalization associated with the increasing presence of

Table 11.1 The evolution of the financial system

Regional and bank-orientated	→	National and market-orientated	→	Transnational and securitized form
Associated with industrialization phase of economic development		Characteristic of industrial maturity phase of economic development		Associated with post-industrial and transnational phase of economic development
Banks main source of external funds needed by private sector firms		Capital markets main source of funds, using savings of private investors		Bulk of funds obtained through capital and credit markets, using mainly resources of institutional investors
Industrial growth financed by loans, risk capital and profits		Capital markets channel personal and other savings into industry; risk spread across shareholders		Separation of capital and money markets from industry and commodification of money; proliferation of monetary products
Regional and national banking system; local sources of capital important		Concentration and centralization towards national banking and capital markets; loss of regional financial autonomy; emergence of internationalization		Development of globally integrated system of world financial centres; loss of national financial autonomy to supranational economy of stateless monies

such multinational companies in domestic finance markets. Globalization combines these elements with a strong degree of *integration* between the different national and multinational parts. It refers to the emergence of truly transnational banks and financial companies that integrate their activities and transactions across different national markets. And above all it refers to the increasing freedom of movement, transfer and tradability of monies and finance capital across the globe, in effect integrating national markets into a new supranational system. This process of globalization stems from a number of interrelated changes that have been remoulding financial markets in the advanced industrial economies since the early 1970s: the progressive deregulation of money and financial markets, both internally and externally; the introduction of an expanding array of new financial instruments and monetary products, allowing riskier, bigger and more easily tradable financial investments; the emergence and role of new market actors, especially institutional investors such as large pension funds; and the spread of new communications and information technologies that have extended and accelerated financial transactions. Of these developments, deregulation of markets and technological innovation have been particularly influential.

The postwar period up until the early 1970s was one of generally closely regulated national financial markets. The rates of exchange between national currencies were fixed and stabilized by multilateral agreements under the Bretton Woods–IMF system, while most national governments also operated controls on the scale of currency outflows and capital leakages abroad. Although during the 1960s some European countries began to relax some of those controls, the United States actually extended its regulatory framework (in particular, the Kennedy–Johnson Interest Equalization Tax). Already in this period, with Europe having reached trading parity with the United States and the dollar progressively weakening, Bretton Woods was under increasing strain. Its final demise between 1971 and 1973, and the subsequent introduction of floating exchange rates, ushered in a substantially deregulated world monetary order and stimulated the internationalization and transnationalization of financial markets.

One of the most significant of these has been the Eurodollar market (Pilbeam, 1992). According to Susan Strange (1971, p. 207), the Eurodollar market was the 'great technological breakthrough of international finance in the mid-twentieth century'. It had its origins in dollar deposits transferred to Europe in the immediate postwar years by Communist Bloc countries seeking to avoid their possible sequestration by the United States.[1] In the 1950s, activity in the Eurodollar system was minimal, and it was not until the 1960s that deposits of 'offshore' dollars began to grow, promoted by the continuing US balance of payments deficit and the movement of dollars abroad by US banks and large independent wealth-holders, so as to avoid the restrictive financial regulations introduced by the US government (especially the Interest Equalization Tax and Regulation Q). As a result, from modest beginnings of about US $11 billion in 1964, the size of the Eurodollar system had grown to an estimated US $40 billion by the end of the decade.[2] From the start, large

1 After the Chinese Revolution in 1949, the United States took steps to freeze Chinese accounts in American banks. To evade this move, the Chinese managed to transfer most (though not all) of their accounts into the Russian-owned Bank Commerciale pour l'Europe du Nord in Paris. As the Cold War escalated, Russia moved its own overseas dollar holdings into a branch of its Moscow Narodny Bank situated in the City of London (Wachtel, 1986).

2 There are several different estimates of Eurodollars. Two basic sources are: the figures published by the Bank for International Settlements, which are net of interbank transactions, but which in early years exclude offshore deposits outside of Europe; and the estimates produced by Morgan Guaranty Trust Company, a New York supranational bank, which include all Eurodollar centres but give less detail on intrabank and interbank activities. The estimates used in this chapter are net of all interbank transactions but include all centres and exclude Eurocurrencies other than dollars.

international borrowers tapped this supply of funds, particularly American multinationals, which were increasing their overseas investment in Europe and elsewhere during this period.

The real take-off came, however, after the 1973–4 quadrupling of oil prices by the OPEC countries. These placed a substantial part of their hugely inflated earnings of 'petrodollars' in Eurodollar accounts in the offshore branches of American banks, mainly in Europe. As the 1970s continued so the OPEC surpluses grew, and almost all of these found their way into the Eurodollar system, only to be lent out through the so-called 'petrodollar recycling' process. Given that the traditional loan recipients, the multinational corporations, were unable to absorb this rapidly expanding supply of Eurodollars, the banks sought out new lending opportunities in the form of huge loans to less developed countries in the Third World, particularly Latin America. By the late 1970s the Eurodollar pool had grown to more than US $400 billion. Spurred on by the revolution in information processing and communications, the rapid growth of the Eurodollar system continued apace during the 1980s, reaching US $1 trillion by 1984 and an estimated US $2.8 trillion by the end of the decade (figure 11.1).

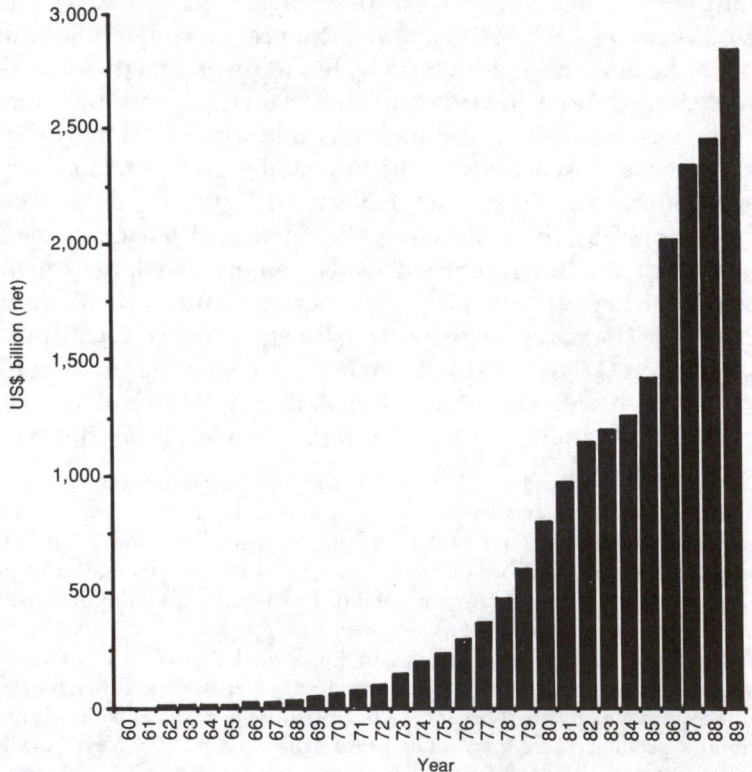

Figure 11.1 The growth of stateless money: size of the Eurocurrency market, 1960–1989.

Even by the end of the 1970s, the Eurodollar market could be characterized as a 'vast, integrated global money and capital system, almost
totally outside all government regulation, that can send billions of "stateless" currencies hurtling around the world 24 hours a day' (*Business
Week*, 1978, p. 76). Not only were Eurodollars the first truly supranational form of money, they fostered various other related innovations
in international finance. For one thing, the Eurodollar market helped to
breed a stateless banking system, a world of offshore trading dominated
by a few dozen giant banks that operate in every corner of the globe.
Throughout the 1960s, London was the prime location for Eurodollar
activity, but during the 1970s, as the British government increasingly
regulated foreign banks, trading operations were progressively switched
to other less-regulated havens, such as Hong Kong, Singapore and especially the Bahamas and Cayman Islands. With modern computer technology coming on-line in the mid-1970s, it did not take long for these
new offshore banking sanctuaries to become important players in the
game. Similarly, in the same way that new offshore banking locations
proliferated so did the range of offshore currencies: by the 1980s,
Eurocurrency markets had also developed in Deutschmarks, French
francs, sterling, yen and other currencies, although the US dollar still
dominates the system. A further related product of the growth of the
Eurocurrency system has been the development of an associated market in Eurobonds, essentially securitized loans denominated in Eurocurrencies.[3] By the end of the 1980s the annual value of new Eurobond
issues had exceeded £200 billion, helped by considerable product innovation in trading techniques, such as floating rate notes and convertible
bonds.

These developments in the stateless monies of the Euromarkets have
been paralleled by the dramatic growth and increasing globalization of
all the other major types of traded financial services.[4] The switch to
floating exchange rates, the growth in the need for foreign currency
associated with the growth in international trade, the abolition of exchange controls and the mushrooming of the international investment
flows of portfolio investors, life insurance companies and pension funds
have all combined to generate a rapid expansion in the market for
foreign exchange. The United States foreign exchange market alone

---

3 According to Smith (1992), the first Eurobond issue was for the Italian Autostrada
Group in 1963.
4 In addition to deposit-taking, that is demand and time deposits in foreign onshore
accounts and Eurodeposits in offshore accounts, these services include: international
trading and dealing in foreign currencies, forward exchange contracts, financial
futures, options etc.; international trade services; international lending; international
securities business; and other investment banking activities, including merger and
acquisition services (see Walter, 1988).

expanded twelve-fold between 1977 and 1987 (Cross, 1988). The total volume and institutional shares of foreign exchange trading are difficult to measure, because of the geographical dispersion of the activity and sheer number and often short-term nature of the deals. However, in 1979 the *daily* turnover on the world's major foreign exchange markets was reckoned to be about US $100 billion; by 1989 this was estimated to have increased to more than US $400 billion (*Euromoney*, January 1990); that is, an annual trading total probably in excess of US $100 trillion. It is, furthermore, a market that is highly concentrated. Foreign currencies are mostly traded in six world financial centres: London, New York, Frankfurt, Bahrain, Singapore and Tokyo (*The Economist*, 1992). And within these centres the market is dominated by just a handful of global players: some 60 per cent of the world's foreign exchange trade is accounted for by the top twenty transnational banks.

The volume of international banking, and the markets for syndicated loans, for the financing of cross-border merger and acquisition activity, and for international securities, all experienced unprecedented growth during the 1980s. From less than US $200 billion in the early 1970s, the total external liabilities of international banks (as recorded by the Bank for International Settlements) had reached US $1.3 trillion by 1980, and then rose sharply over the ensuing decade to more than US $6 billion by 1990. Syndication effectively became internationalized in the late 1960s and early 1970s, when loans based on Eurodollars appeared. As with essentially domestic syndications, such loans enable sovereign or multi-national borrowers to obtain funds from a group of banks, which in turn sell parcels of loans to smaller banks. The level of syndicated loans increased sharply in the 1970s, as large sums were lent by US and UK banks to Latin American countries. But following the subsequent defaults of many of the latter, sovereign lending fell sharply during the 1980s, and instead the leading banks switched their lending to corporations seeking finance for overseas investment and acquisition projects. Over the course of the decade, the annual flow of syndicated loans increased more than five-fold, from US $89 billion in 1980 to US $471 billion in 1989.

Merger and acquisition activity has long been part of the structural dynamic of the capitalist economies: equally long-standing is the provision of financial services in connection with this process. The 1980s saw an explosion in merger-acquisition activity, both within and between the main capitalist nations (Green, 1990; Cosh et al., 1992), and a dramatic increase in foreign direct investment (Julius, 1990). For example, between 1985 and 1989 the asset value of world merger and acquisition deals, both domestic and cross-border, increased from about US $300 billion to US $1 trillion. Within this total, the value of cross-border deals rose particularly rapidly, from about US $50 billion to almost US $300 billion. This recent rapid growth of the merger and acquisition market, especially of cross-border activity, reflects the operation of several factors. The internationalization of economic activity, and the moves to a Single European Market and a North American Free Trade Agreement, have encouraged many industrial and service sector firms to merge globally in search of economies of scale and scope and to acquire overseas firms in order to raise market shares and by-pass protective national trade barriers. In addition, the marked structural changes of the 1980s, producing sharp falls in the profitability of previously strong sectors, have left large numbers of big, cash-rich American, German, Japanese and British corporations seeking to diversify into new markets via overseas acquisition. At the same time, the global deregulation of banking activities and the opening up of world stockmarkets to foreign buyers have promoted a range of new instruments for financing merger and acquisition activity. The two processes have thus been mutually reinforcing.

While an international market in equities and bonds can be traced back to the early nineteenth century (primarily through London), the real move towards a global equities market came during the 1980s. Aided by the outright abolition of exchange controls in several countries on the one hand, and the opening up of national stock exchanges to foreign financial institutions on the other, this growth was stimulated by two factors: the desire of many multinationals to become truly global by having shareholders from several countries match their business interests, and the trend for fund managers to diversify their portfolios across different markets. Although the global equity market remains in its early stages, by 1986 cross-border trading had reached US $750 billion. This fell back after the worldwide stockmarket crash of October 1987, but has recovered since. Furthermore, the number of Third World stockmarkets has been growing, encouraged by the World Bank and the International Finance Corporation: there are now some thirty-five equity markets in developing countries, and some of these (Brazil, India, Malaysia, Korea and Taiwan) are bigger than many medium-sized European stockmarkets.

The growth of 'stateless' monies and the emergence of internationally integrated markets in an expanding array of financial services and products represent two aspects of the globalization of finance. A further dimension has been the growth of global or stateless banks and finance institutions that have offices around the world and dominate trading. Most financial product markets are characterized by a high degree of institutional concentration: typically, the top twenty institutions in a market account for between 40 and 60 per cent of worldwide transactions (Smith, 1992). Moreover, some of these institutions are leading players across several different product markets, with names such as Citicorp, Chase Manhattan, Merrill Lynch, Barclays, National Westminster, Warburg, UBS (Switzerland), Bank of Tokyo and Nomura consistently recurring. With their large asset bases, these leading institutions are in a better position than smaller ones to develop more extensive global networks and to offer more products and services; in short more able to achieve economies of scale and scope. By their multi-locational strategy of establishing branches in most if not all of the world's major financial centres, these major global actors themselves constitute a further dimension to the globalization process.

The process of global financial integration is thus firmly established, and may be expected to continue, although its pace and shape will depend upon future developments in the deregulation and competition policies of individual countries and upon further innovations in financial information technologies. Recent and anticipated regulatory changes in Europe (the integration of capital markets provided by the Single Market), in the United States (with the new SEC Rule 144A, which deregulates the US debt securities market, and expected changes to the Glass–Steagall laws to remove the separation between commercial and investment banking) and in Japan (the possible repeal of Article 65, the equivalent of the US Glass–Steagall provision) will drive the trend towards 'seamless' markets for many securities and related derivatives, in much the same way that a 'seamless' global market in foreign exchange exists today. Added to this, continued technological innovations in screen-based trading, automatic clearing and paperless settlement systems will also contribute to the further standardization and global integration of finance markets by the end of the 1990s (Smith and Walter, 1991).

The Geographies of Global Financial Integration

One of the claims of the 'end of geography' thesis is that this integration of world financial markets has undermined the significance of location, in the sense that the new communications technologies considerably widen the choice of geographical location of financial firms and allow them to serve widely dispersed markets regardless of where they happen to be. In assessing the validity of this claim it is necessary to conceptualize the impact of globalization in terms of two counterforces. In principle, modern telecommunications technologies render the need for financial centres increasingly obsolete: new banking and trading technologies, such as local area networks (LANs), on-line transaction processing (OLTP) and electronic data interchange (EDI), not only increase the range of financial services, but also confer considerable locational freedom on institutions. Market participants no longer have to be in the same centre, the same country or even the same continent for trading to take place: in terms of contact between financial firms and institutions, new information technologies allow propinquity without proximity.

Under this scenario, then, the spatial expression of global integration would be an increasing locational dispersal and specialization of markets: a relative shift of financial activity away from the established global metropolitan centres towards smaller, provincial locations, nearer to final customers.

Certainly there has been some decentralization of financial services employment towards provincial centres over the past years, as, for example, in the United Kingdom. Much of this, however, has been of back offices, leaving the head offices and primary business within the national capitals. Indeed, an equally plausible geographical trajectory of global integration is that the new technologies will actually reinforce the concentration of expertise and business within existing major centres, in that firms located in the latter can now easily access customers and funds wherever these are located. In other words, the new technologies allow firms even greater possibilities to develop economies of scale and scope through concentrating activities in a relatively small number of leading financial centres, selling and servicing global products from a few strategic locations. Thus, while the speed of information communication has annihilated *space* (Castells, 1989; Harvey, 1989) it has by no means undermined the significance of location, of *place*. The agglomeration economies generated by the established nexus of institutionalized financial skills, expertise and supporting specialist cognate services in leading financial centres, such as London, New York, Tokyo, Osaka, Chicago, Paris, Frankfurt, Hong Kong and Singapore, gives them a strong competitive advantage over other, smaller, national or provincial centres. In theory, then, both these divergent forces, of decentralization and dispersal, and of centralization and concentration, are consistent with global financial integration, and it is the dynamic tension between them that will shape the evolving geography of the global financial system.

Technological innovation is only one of the forces at work, and its impact is dependent upon a second, that of deregulation. The wave of financial deregulation that has swept through the OECD nations over the past decade and a half has unleashed a new process of global competition. There are two interrelated aspects to this competition: between the major global financial centres themselves, as the prime financial market locations, and between financial institutions. From the late 1950s to the early 1970s financial globalization was stimulated by the uneven geography of market regulation, and competition between the world's major financial centres was largely shaped by the regulatory contours between them. Now, with widespread deregulation and the move towards an increasingly 'even playing field', competition has become far more intense, and more global. The 'offshore' financial centres now face a much more open and competitive global market, and deregulation within the OECD countries, itself a competitive process,

has virtually removed the particular geographical and market monopoly advantages their centres were able to enjoy by virtue of restricting
the entry of outsiders. The world's major financial centres are now
in direct competition, albeit over an expanding volume of trade
and range of products (Bingham, 1991). And in confronting this new
environment, the competitive differences of place – differences in costs,
specialist skills, market opportunities, broad regional affinities, customs,
any remaining restrictions, etc. – assume hightened importance as each
centre seeks to maintain and improve its position within, and its share
of, the global market in finance (Smith, 1992). Considerable employment and wealth accrue to financial centres, with wider benefits (such as
invisible earnings) for the national economy in which they are located.[5]
It is not surprising, therefore, that national governments have become
increasingly sensitive to the competitive standing of their financial centres, and to the need to ensure that this standing is not eroded or
compromised.[6]

In short, global integration does not spell the 'end of geography' as far
as the continuing overwhelming locational and trading influence of the
world's financial centres is concerned; however, it does mean that market
activity has become extremely sensitive to even small differences in the
competitive advantage and trading performance of different financial
centres. The top world centres, London, New York and Tokyo in particular, show no signs of losing their overall dominance, but as capital and
trading become ever more mobile so markets shift more readily from one
centre to another in response to differences and changes in transaction
costs, liquidity, profits and other dimensions of relative attractiveness.
During the 1980s there were some significant shifts among the leading
centres in their shares of particular financial markets. For example,
London increased its historical monopoly of the global foreign equity
market still further over the decade (it accounts for about 80 per cent of
total world turnover), whereas Tokyo and New York, both far less
prominent in this market, saw their shares fall (Bank of England, 1991).

5 There may also be distinct disadvantages to the national economy of hosting a
world financial centre. Land and labour costs may be forced up, and internal regional
imbalance may be exacerbated. The economy may face risks owing to over-dependence
on a single sector, and the operation of domestic monetary policy may be compromised by the need to nurture or defend an internationally dominant financial
centre (a point taken up later in the chapter). Finally, the financial sector may actually
be 'parasitic', diverting valuable capital and human resources from other branches of
the domestic economy (see Tobin, 1984).
6 For example, in the case of London the implication of the Bank of England in the
collapse of BCCI, the huge losses recorded by the Lloyds insurance market and more
recently the abandonment of the Stock Exchange's computerized paperless settlement
system TAURUS have certainly dented the established reputation (but perhaps also
the complacency) of the financial City.

Table 11.2 International banking by country

Country	1980	1985	1989
UK	27.0	25.4	20.5
Japan	5.0	10.8	20.6
USA	13.4	13.3	10.0
'Offshore centres'	10.7	18.5	18.4
France	10.8	7.1	6.7
Germany	5.5	3.2	3.7
Switzerland	4.5	6.4	5.7
Belgium	4.2	3.8	3.5
Luxembourg	6.7	4.1	4.2
Italy	2.3	2.2	1.8
Netherlands	4.7	2.6	2.8
Canada	2.7	2.3	1.3

Outstanding lending as percentage share of total market
(BIS reporting area)

Source: Bank of England Quarterly Bulletin, 1989.

In the case of international banking, however, both London and New York, the traditional leaders, experienced a decline in their shares of global lending (in part because of retrenchment following the Third World debt crisis), while Japan and the 'offshore' centres increased their shares substantially (table 11.2).

These movements in the relative trading position of the major centres have been inextricably bound up with changes both in the shares of global financial markets accounted for by institutions of different nationalities and in the nationality mix of institutions within each centre. In London, for instance, between the mid-1970s and the end of the 1980s the number of foreign banks almost doubled, the greatest influxes being of Japanese and West European institutions. Whereas in 1975 Japanese banks accounted for 13 per cent of all international bank lending out of London, by 1989 their share had increased to 35 per cent. Over the same period the share of US banks in international lending out of London fell from 38 to 13 per cent, and that of UK banks from 22 to 17 per cent. On a global scale, a similar restructuring of market segments according to the nationality of institutions has been under way (table 11.3). Thus, in the foreign exchange markets, US institutions have lost ground to UK, Japanese and Canadian firms, whereas the market for syndicated loans has become increasingly controlled by US and UK institutions, and Japanese firms have assumed the leading position in the Eurobond markets. The different roles and relative performance of the major financial centres thus reflect the complex interplay of three intersecting geographies: the relative competitive advantage of the different centres as trading locations, the global geography of different financial

Table 11.3   Country shares, by nationality of institution, of selected
international financial markets

Nationality of institution	Foreign exchange transactions (%)			Syndicated bank loans (%)			Eurobonds (%)		
	1980	1985	1989	1980	1985	1989	1980	1985	1989
United States	63.1	57.0	50.2	49.7	75.4	74.9	36.5	59.7	28.3
United Kingdom	2.2	16.8	23.3	13.3	9.3	16.4	10.8	7.3	3.4
Japan	0.7	3.8	6.1	2.9	3.2	0.0	7.0	10.3	52.9
Canada	1.9	4.3	7.2	15.4	9.3	3.7	3.0	2.9	0.0
France	12.8	8.3	0.0	8.3	0.0	1.6	13.1	3.4	5.4
Switzerland	18.0	5.0	0.0	0.0	2.8	1.5	4.8	6.3	2.1
Germany	0.0	0.0	0.0	7.5	0.0	0.0	24.7	10.1	7.9
Others	1.3	4.8	13.2	2.9	0.0	1.9	0.1	0.0	0.0

Note: Country refers to the aggregate share of the global market accounted
for by the institutions of a given nationality, regardless of where they operate,
and not to the share of a given national location.

Sources: Euromoney; Smith, 1992.

product markets and the global geography of different national groups
of financial institutions.

Within this context, there is the key question of whether increasing
global integration is likely to promote greater convergence or divergence
between the major centres in terms of their mix of different financial
products and services. An 'end of geography' perspective would imply
convergence, with the leading financial centres functioning as linked,
largely undifferentiated 'trading nodes' within essentially uniform
worldwide markets. Against this, Ricardian comparative advantage theory suggests that market deregulation and free trade should serve to
accentuate existing patterns of specialization and dominance, as centres
focus on the particular markets in which they already have a competitive
edge, whether for historical, economic or geographical reasons. Under
this scenario, different financial centres would be the primary markets
for different global financial products and services. Evidence can be
invoked to support both these views. For example, although London still
leads the foreign exchange market, both New York and Tokyo have been
catching up. Likewise, since the early 1980s Tokyo has emerged as a
serious challenger to London's position in international banking. On the
other hand, London's grip on the foreign equity and international bond
markets has increased. In reality, of course, comparative advantages are
not static, but constantly in flux as both local circumstances and global
conditions change. In this respect, London can not assume that its
traditional strengths of a long financial history and institutionalized

expertise will be sufficient to guarantee its continuing competitive edge, even though it also enjoys the special trading advantage of being uniquely situated astride the international time zones. One major consideration of relevance here is the possibility that, geographically, global finance will evolve in the same direction that the systems of trade and foreign direct investment seem to be moving, into a 'triad' of three major regional blocs, America, Europe and the Pacific Rim (Schott, 1991; United Nations, 1991), based upon three corresponding world financial centres, New York, London and Tokyo, each having obvious competitive advantages with respect to its own regional bloc.

Financial Globalization and the Nation State

Whatever trajectory the geographical structure of global financial integration takes, however, the question of national economic sovereignty remains a central issue. According to the 'end of geography' argument, financial market regulators are no longer able to exert control over their regulatory territories, since rules no longer apply solely to or can be easily enforced within specific geographical borders, such as nation states. As a result, it is contended, financial globalization is undermining that most symbolic of geographical entities, national economic sovereignty. As national financial markets have become increasingly integrated on a global scale, and the boundaries between domestic and foreign financial business have become increasingly blurred, so the 'openness' and vulnerability of the national economy to external financial shocks has increased and the ability of governments to exercise national policy autonomy has declined (Ohmae, 1990; O'Brien, 1992). In going transnational, money has outflanked the nation state by nullifying national economic policy (Drucker, 1993).

There can be no doubting the political significance of the national economic sovereignty issue. The difficulties surrounding the movement towards monetary union within the European Union in large part revolve around the reluctance of member states to relinquish their autonomy in the realm of monetary policy and to abandon their national currencies for a common, supranational, European unit of account. Control of the money supply, of interest rates and to some extent of the exchange rate and capital flows has traditionally been seen as quintessential to national economic sovereignty, and the development of national economic policy has always been predicated on the assumption that the state has effective jurisdiction over these monetary and financial variables. This emphasis on national economic sovereignty in turn derives from the view of the nation state within economic theory. In all of the main schools of economics, the nation state is viewed as an essential unit of economy, and its role as an 'economic actor' is taken for granted. It is a conception that can be traced to the model of nineteenth-century 'national capitalism', in which nation states represented the geographically bounded areas of economic organization, accumulation and regulation. This notion of the 'national economy' is anchored in the institutions of central banking, the national currency, national income and national industry, and it underpinned the classical economics of *laissez-faire* and free trade, and even more so its twentieth-century successor, Keynesian macroeconomic demand management.

As Radice (1984, p. 116) points out: 'The national economy is privileged in Keynesian theory for the purely practical reason that the nation-state system defines geopolitical space with the necessary features convenient for the theory: a common currency, common laws, and shared institutions.' The central elements in that theory are all *national* aggregates or averages: output, employment, investment, consumption, rate of interest, real wage, price level, money supply; the 'national economy' is both the key theoretical object and the effective political space for state intervention. The Keynesian model of the national economy not only assumes but also requires a high degree of financial autonomy, or what Keynes himself called 'self-sufficiency'. Unconstrained financial speculation, unrestricted outflows of capital, savings and currency, and external fixity of the exchange rate: these and other threats to the state's control of the monetary system not only serve to disrupt the key relationships of the domestic economy (for example, between income, savings and investment), but also limit the scope for and impact of state monetary and fiscal policies as counter-cyclical stabilizers. Writing in the interwar years of international economic depression and disorder, Keynes himself was under no illusion about the importance of these effects: 'economic internationalization embracing the free movement of capital and of loanable funds as well as of traded goods may condemn [a] country to a much lower degree of material prosperity than could be attained under a different system' (Keynes, 1933, pp. 762–3). Of all aspects of economic and social life, he argued, 'let finance be primarily national' (ibid., p. 758).[7] Although subsequent Keynesians, and perhaps Keynes himself by the end of the Second World War, took a more sanguine view of cross-border finance, postwar Keynesianism remained wedded to a 'national model' in which governments carried out macroeconomic policy at the national level supported by the Bretton Woods system of financial management at the international level. Indeed, Bretton Woods itself was nothing other than a system of national regulation, made viable by a stable set of international linkages.

7 Keynes's 'nationalism' with respect to money derived from his basically monetary view of national economic disorder, and the need for the state authorities to keep the national money supply consistent with low or zero inflation. But it also reflected his strong 'anti-Americanism' during the interwar years, especially his fear of the power of American money (see Skidelsky, 1992).

The unrestricted movement of finance capital was seen as incompatible with this model.

Essentially the same emphasis on the nation state characterizes the French school of regulationist economics that has proved so influential in economic geography in recent years. Here too the national economy is prioritized as the key unit of analysis, and both local and global economic and regulatory processes are subordinated to those of individual nation states. In particular, the system of national monetary management is a crucial component of the 'mode of regulation', the ensemble of institutional forms, networks and norms that ensure compatibility of market behaviour, social relations and economic accumulation.[8] The form and function of the national mode of regulation distinguishes the specific pattern of economic accumulation in a given nation state from that in another. Even though regulationists recognize the global extension of capital circuits, in the form of global Fordism and possibly now an emerging global post-Fordism, they insist on the primacy of the national dimension and on conceptualizing the world economy as a system of interacting national regimes (Aglietta, 1982; Lipietz, 1987, 1992).

Most forms of economics, in fact, assume that capital fractures primarily along the boundaries of nation states and that the latter are sovereign actors over their domestic spaces. The rise of 'stateless monies' and the global integration of financial markets clearly challenge these assumptions. The very process of competitive financial deregulation by nation states has 'disarmed' them against the hypermobility of finance capital that deregulation has helped to unleash (Bienefeld, 1992). In contrast to the 1960s, the contemporary international monetary order is considerably more anarchic and volatile, and appears to have seriously undermined the possibilities for national autonomy. Individual countries seem caught in a classic prisoners' dilemma: they have moved to open up their financial systems to international competition and market forces in an attempt to attract growth, yet simultaneously have exposed themselves to financial speculation and global instability, against which national action is largely inhibited by the deregulated and globalized nature of the present system (cf. Preston and Windsor, 1992). Financial and money market fluctuations now move around the globe almost instantaneously (as was demonstrated only too vividly by the worldwide stockmarket

8 The use of the term 'regulation' in this context is thus much wider than the more specialized sense in which it has been used thus far in this chapter. The latter refers to the specific legal and jurisdictional framework governing financial markets and transactions. In regulation theory the term refers to the whole nexus of political, legal and institutional rules and procedures, social practices, market norms, and customs and conventions that regulate and stabilize economic accumulation. For useful general surveys of regulationist economics see Boyer (1990) and Jessop (1990). Critical assessments of the use of regulationist perspectives within economic geography are contained in Dunford (1990) and Tickell and Peck (1992).

crash on Black Wednesday in October 1987), and without much regard
to underlying national conditions. Similarly, the vast majority of daily
foreign exchange transactions on the leading global markets are purely
speculative and this, combined with the sheer scale and rapidity of
trading, makes them potentially destabilizing, causing unwarranted and
unwanted changes in national domestic monetary policies.

In some quarters this increasing national 'openness' to global financial
flows and fluctuations is seen as both desirable and inevitable, as an
integral part of a movement towards a new liberal economic world order,
towards 'global neoclassicism' (Schor, 1990). In contrast to Keynesians
and regulation-theorists, adherents of global neoclassicism by-pass the
nation state and take the world as their basic unit of analysis. For them,
provided there are no national regulatory barriers, and given modern
telecommunications technologies, cross-border flows of finance capital
should occur as easily as interregional flows in the national Keynesian
model. This means that marked differences in financial conditions and
returns between nations can only be temporary, as offsetting capital
flows will be rapid and powerful. Some go further and see global
financial integration as leading to a single world money market and
a single world capital market, with perhaps even a single world money, a
single world monetary policy, and equalization of interest rates and rates
of return. National regulations will be ineffective because economic
agents will evade them. Rather, the role of nation states is reduced to one
of trimming policy only if the national direction veers too far from the
world direction (see Kindleberger, 1987, chapter 4). The pattern to be
achieved would thus be similar to the integration of money and capital
markets and the pursuit of a common monetary policy within a single
country, such as the United States.

Under global neoclassicism the loss of national policy autonomy is
unavoidable in the face of the power of market economic forces. Any
attempt by a government to follow a discretionary economic policy or to
regulate its financial markets will be futile and self-defeating. In the same
way that neoclassicals previously stressed the need for and benefits of
open commodity trade, global neoclassicism stresses the need for capital markets to be liberalized. The loss of national sovereignty through
financial globalization is assumed to be compensated for by the increased
allocative efficiency of capital markets in terms of the demand for and
supply of loanable funds and investment finance. This, at least, has been
the message of governments, policy-makers and the financial elite in the
leading capitalist countries over the past decade and a half. Since the late
1970s there has been a marked trend towards governmental passivity
and accommodation in the face of financial markets, initially in the
United States and the United Kingdom, and then in other OECD countries that followed suit in order not to be out of step with the leaders. All
this has been rationalized on the grounds that global financial integra-

tion is an ineluctable process with its own economic logic, that free markets in money and capital are more efficient than regulated ones, and that rolling back state regulation in order to facilitate and encourage global financial competition is thus the only effective policy option.

However, none of these claims is self-evident. While global neoclassicism has captured the imagination of numerous economic theorists and policy-makers alike, its validity as a model for explaining or prescribing the changing nature of financial markets and national sovereignty can be questioned (Banuri and Schor, 1992). The increasing global integration of financial markets and loss of national economic autonomy has not necessarily been because of some inexorable logic of late capitalism, or because of the driving imperatives of global competition. For it has undoubtedly been politically engineered, promoted by those same capitalist nations which, already containing the leading world financial centres, stood to gain most from encouraging a 'free market' in global finance. In this context, the deregulation of financial and stock markets in the USA and UK was part of the overall economic policy reorientation of Reagan–Thatcher conservative ideology, with its blind faith in the free market. But in both cases, it also represented a reassertion by the state of an underlying disposition towards financial interests after several decades of welfare and national industrial–economic concerns. If the post-war Keynesian period had been one of 'managerial welfare capitalism', the past two decades have seen the advent of 'money manager capitalism' (Minsky, 1989). The crux of this change is that financial institutions have demanded and been granted less regulation and more protection at the same time that nation states themselves have prioritized the financial sphere and substituted monetary goals and policies for the employment and welfare priorities of the past. A new 'bankers' bargain' (Pringle, 1992) has replaced the former 'social bargain' with industry and labour, and in the process the state has ceded a considerable degree of its economic and political power to financiers, most of whom are trans-national rather national in orientation. This combination of the state's inclination towards financial interests and its deregulation of financial institutions has reduced the room within which policy-makers can manoeuvre. It is a bargain that has encouraged more risky activity, raised the likelihood of panics and bankruptcies, and rendered government ever more captive to the sentiments of the market. The loss of national autonomy to global finance is thus not some benign outcome or necessity of world market forces, but has a political origin.

Nor are the assumed mechanisms and benefits of global neoclassicism as prominent as protagonists of the model suppose. Certainly controls on capital and currency movements are at their lowest for more than fifty years; and while the lack of regulations and restrictions does not of itself validate the global neoclassical model, it does remove a significant barrier to its functioning. Likewise, the volume of cross-border capital flows and the increasing international integration of money and finance markets appear consistent with global neoclassicism. Further, existing evidence suggests that for those OECD countries where legal restrictions on capital flows are absent, interest rates on identical short-term assets do tend to equalize. Even so, these observations do not necessarily prove that world financial markets are moving inexorably towards a perfectly functioning global unity. For one thing, national geography still remains significant in certain financial relationships. National savings and investment rates, for example, continue to be highly correlated (Epstein and Gintis, 1992), whereas the global neoclassical model predicts they should be virtually uncorrelated. Similarly, the model suggests that with integrated markets, rapid transmission of information and hypermobile capital, the nationality mix of assets in investors' portfolios should be in rough proportion to the size of each nation in the world economy; but in practice nationals disproportionately hold assets of their own countries. Third, the equalization of short-term interest rates is not matched by the equalization of profit rates, which continue to show marked differences among the leading capitalist countries. Perhaps even more importantly, financial markets do not necessarily clear or function in the competitive demand–supply way that global neoclassicism assumes. Capital does not always gravitate to where it is most needed or where the highest returns can be offered, but instead is typically rationed in various ways so that credit is given only to the safer borrowers or to those 'less creditworthy' customers willing or forced to accept additional special charges and penalties. In short, financial markets do not operate in a Walrasian manner, but are as much political as economic in character, founded on and shaped by unequal relations of power between lenders and borrowers.[9]

The global neoclassical argument that nation states should adopt a passive, accommodative stance towards financial markets is thus suspect; the more so because it is assumed that such markets are composed of myriads of small, autonomous price-taking actors, that cartels are difficult to organize and that there is no centralized rationing of funds. The global financial system is simply not like that. The institutional players in this game are very large and powerful.[10] On the one side, the world's financial markets are organized by very large global banks and securities houses, by the G7 capitalist nations and the International Monetary Fund. On the other side, most investors and borrowers are also large institutions, such as pension funds, transnational corporations and nation states themselves. The ·importance of these large actors

9 Illustrated only too clearly by the part played by Northern states, banks and agencies in exacerbating and policing the Third World debt crisis.
10 The past decade has seen an increasing number of international bank mergers and takeovers, thus consolidating the degree of concentration and centralization of global banking capital.

throws the global neoclassical view of how world financial markets work into serious doubt. Alliances, negotiation, coercion, enforcement, rationing and secrecy abound (Walter, 1985). As Schor (1990, p. 17) argues, it 'seems that we have not only price-takers but price-makers, collusion as well as competition, and capital rigidity alongside capital mobility'. The sheer size and power of big institutions and large players means that they exert considerable influence over 'market' outcomes.

The shift towards a deregulated, globally integrated financial system, where markets are freed from and take precedence over intervention and control by nation states, does not therefore hold out the unequivocal promise of increased efficiency and wealth stressed by those who subscribe to a global neoclassical view of contemporary trends. Indeed, the evidence thus far suggests that the disadvantages may seriously outweigh the benefits. Compared to the postwar Keynesian era of fixed exchange rates and capital controls, the past decade and a half has seen considerable global and local financial instability (for example, the Third World debt problem and its impact on domestic banking in the USA and UK, the October 1987 crash of the US stockmarket, the October 1989 stockmarket scare, numerous financial and securities trading scandals – including junk bonds, bank failures and insider-dealing – and boom and bust in financial rentals and property markets in leading financial centres such as London and Tokyo). It is questionable whether this 'casino capitalism' (Strange, 1986) and the much riskier financial environment that now prevails (*The Economist*, 1993) are to be preferred to a regulated system. In order to assess exactly how far the retreat of the nation state has been imposed by the technological and competitive forces of globalization, and what the implications for policy autonomy are in an era of global financial integration, we require an approach that does not attribute everything to the imperatives of the market. To understand the changing contours of national sovereignty we also need to take into account the assertion of financial interests against state power, the actions of large financial institutions, the power of the banks, states and international agencies of the North over the debtor nations of the South, and the desire of Northern states themselves to conform to the dictates of the world financial markets that their centres dominate.

Conclusions: Money, Power and Space

There can be no doubt that global financial integration has substantially altered and circumscribed the effective economic boundaries of the nation state. But to depict this dilution of national autonomy as the 'end of geography' is to take too narrow a view of the relationships between money, power and space. Even in the global neoclassical vision of unregulated and perfectly functioning world capital markets and complete capital mobility, financial flows and accumulation would be inherently uneven: savings and funds would continue to concentrate in the high growth countries, in much the same way that regional imbalances in the movement of capital occur between regions within the monetary union of a nation state. But unlike a single country, where various fiscal and automatic governmental transfers tend to offset regional balance of payments deficits and disparities in capital accumulation, in a world of financially integrated nation states there is no equivalent international mechanism of balance of payment adjustment among nations. Contributions to and disbursements from such agencies as the IMF, the IBRD, the World Bank and other similar bodies are not sufficient to perform this compensating equalization role. In this respect, global financial integration is a highly asymmetric process, and is likely to accentuate uneven development, especially between the capital-rich North and the indebted South (Frieden, 1989).

Financial globalization is not 'obliterating geography'; rather it is reconfiguring the geographies of money, power and dependency. As nation states have decoupled themselves from banking capital and relinquished control over international monetary transactions, so there has been a substantial shift of power to a globally integrated hierarchy of financial centres, led by London, New York and Tokyo, and the major financial institutions located in them. These sites now shape and control the international spaces of financial flows. They constitute a system of geographical 'refuge centres' within nation states, located within and dependent upon national economic, social and political infrastructures, yet substantially shielded from national regulation. At the same time, different centres and different national institutions specialize in different circuits of the global capital market, and in this sense global finance still retains a national component. Previous conceptions of the 'place' for the state as geographically bounded limit our ability to comprehend the relationships between finance capital and the nation state in this complex terrain of global money.

This would not matter, perhaps, but for the increased disarray and instability that now characterizes the world financial system. The orderly and sensible movement of funds is far from guaranteed, and it is *within the nation state* that the instabilities of global money appear. If financial markets fail to fulfil their required functions, pressure for government intervention and regulation could mount. Opinions are divided over the case for and form of such re-regulation (see Adelman, 1988; Friedmann, 1991). One route would be to reimpose national systems of control and regulation, along the lines of those now being dismantled. However, the very fact of global financial integration renders the feasibility and effectiveness of this response highly doubtful. An alternative response would be to introduce new forms of regulation based on international cooperation: if markets have gone global in their geography, so too should the institutions of regulation (Soroos, 1987). This might be in the form of supranational regulation involving governing bodies outside the bounds of nations, or transnational regulation, involving the coordination of nation state policies through multilateral agreements. Such plans have their problems, of course, not least the difficulty of securing the international cooperation necessary for their implementation.[11] But whatever the form, the case for re-regulation is strong: the power of global money over national economic space has already been allowed to extend too far.

References

Adelman, C. C. (ed.) (1988) *International Regulation: New Rules in a Changing World Order*. San Francisco: Institute for Contemporary Studies.

Aglietta, M. (1982) World capitalism in the eighties. *New Left Review*, 136, 5–42.

Bank of England (1989) London as an international financial centre. *Bank of England Quarterly Bulletin*, November, 516–28.

Bank of England (1991) Global equity turnover: international comparisons. *Bank of England Quarterly Bulletin*, May, 246–9.

Banuri, T. and Schor, J. (eds) (1992) *Financial Openness and National Autonomy*. Oxford: Clarenden Press.

Bienefeld, M. (1992) Financial de-regulation: disarming the nation state. *Studies in Political Economy*, 37, 31–58.

Bingham, G. T. R. (1991) The changing face of the global financial market. *Journal of International Securities Markets*, 5, 191–3.

Boyer, R. (1990) *The Regulation School: a Critical Introduction*. New York: Columbia University Press.

Business Week (1978) Stateless monies: a new force on world economies. *Business Week*, 21 August, 76–85.

Castells, M. (1989) *The Informational City*. Oxford: Basil Blackwell.

Cosh, A. D., Hughes, A. and Singh, A. (1992) Openness, innovation and share ownership: the changing structure of financial markets. In T. Banuri and J. B. Schor (eds), *Financial Openness and National Autonomy*. Oxford: Clarenden Press, 19–42.

Crook, S., Pakulski, J. and Waters, M. (1992) *Postmodernization: Change in Advanced Society*. London: Sage.

Cross, S. Y. (1988) The growth and changing character of the foreign exchange market. In S. K. Kaushik (ed.) *International Capital Markets: New Directions*. New York: Institute of Finance.

Dicken, P. (1992) *Global Shift: the Internationalization of Economic Activity*, 2nd edn. New York: Guildford Press.

Drucker, P. (1993) *Post-capitalist Society*. Oxford: Butterworth-Heinemann.

Dunford, M. (1990) Theories of regulation. *Society and Space*, 8, 297–322.

11 This issue is closely bound up with the question of hegemonic leadership. The weakening of US hegemony has been a key factor behind both the deregulation of global finance and the loss of the stable postwar regime of international cooperation and agreement this hegemony helped to underpin (see Walter, 1991).

Dunford, M. and Kafkalis, G. (eds) (1992) *Cities and Regions in the New Europe: the Global–Local Interplay and Spatial Development Strategies*. London: Bellhaven.

Economist (1992) A survey of financial centres. *The Economist*, 27 June.

Economist (1993) A survey of international banking. *The Economist*, 10 April.

Epstein, G. and Gintis, H. (1992) International capital markets and the limits of national economic policy. In T. Banuri and J. B. Schor (eds), *Financial Openness and National Autonomy*. Oxford: Clarenden Press, 166–97.

Frieden, J. (1989) *Banking on the World: the Politics of International Finance*. Oxford: Basil Blackwell.

Friedmann, H. (1991) New wines, new bottles: the regulation of capital on a world scale. *Studies in Political Economy*, 36, 9–42.

Gill, S. and Law, D. (1988) *Global Political Economy: Perspectives, Problems and Policies*. Hemel Hemstead: Harvester Wheatsheaf.

Gordon, D. M. (1988) The global economy: new edifice or crumbling foundations? *New Left Review*, 168, 24–64.

Green, M. B. (1990) *Mergers and Acquisitions: Geographical and Spatial Perspectives*. London: Routledge.

Harvey, D. (1989) *The Condition of Postmodernity*. Oxford: Basil Blackwell.

Hirst, P. and Thompson, G. (1992) The problem of globalization: international economic relations, national economic management, and the formation of trading blocs. *Economy and Society*, 21(4), 357–96.

Holland, S. (1987) *The Global Economy*. London: Weidenfeld and Nicolson.

Jessop, B. (1990) Regulation theories in retrospect and prospect. *Economy and Society*, 19, 153–216.

Julius, D. (1990) *Global Companies and Public Policy: the Growing Challenge of Foreign Direct Investment*. London: Pinter.

Keynes, J. M. (1933) National self-sufficiency. *Yale Review*, 22, 4.

Kindleberger, C. (1987) *International Capital Movements*. Cambridge: Cambridge University Press.

Lipietz, A. (1987) *Mirages and Miracles: the Crises of Global Fordism*. London: Verso.

Lipietz, A. (1992) *Towards a New Economic Order: Postfordism, Ecology and Democracy*. Cambridge: Polity Press.

MacEwan, A. and Tabb, W. K. (eds) (1989) *Instability and Change in the World Economy*. New York: Monthly Review Press.

McGrew, A. G. and Lewis, P. (1992) *Global Politics*. Cambridge: Polity Press.

McMichael, P. and Myhre, D. (1991) Global regulation versus the nation-state. *Capital and Class*, 43, 83–106.

Minsky, H. P. (1989) Financial crises and the evolution of capitalism: the crash of 1987 – what does it mean? In M. Gottdiener and N. Komninos (eds), *Capitalist Development and Crisis Theory: Accumulation, Regulation and Spatial Restructuring*. London: Macmillan, 391–403.

O'Brien, R. (1992) *Global Financial Integration: the End of Geography*. London: Pinter.

Ohmae, K. (1990) *The Borderless World: Power and Strategy in an Interdependent Economy*. New York: Harper Business.

Peet, R. (1991) *Global Capitalism*. London: Routledge.

Piccioto, S. (1991) The internationalization of the state. *Capital and Class*, 43, 43–64.

Pilbeam, K. (1992) *International Finance*. London: Macmillan.

Pooley, S. (1991) The state rules, OK? The continuing political economy of nation-states. *Capital and Class*, 43, 65–82.

Porter, M. E. (1990) *The Competitive Advantage of Nations*. London: Macmillan.

Preston, L. E. and Windsor, D. (1992) *The Rules of the Game in the Global Economy*. Boston: Kluwer Academic.

Pringle, R. (1992) Financial markets versus governments. In T. Banuri and J. Schor (eds), *Financial Openness and National Autonomy*. Oxford: Clarendon Press, 89–109.

Radice, H. (1984) The national economy: a Keynesian myth. *Capital and Class*, 22, 111–40.

Reich, R. B. (1991) *The Work of Nations; Preparing Ourselves for 21st-Century Capitalism*. London: Simon and Schuster.

Rybczynski, T. M. (1988) Financial systems and industrial restructuring. *National Westminster Bank Quarterly Review*, November, 3–13.

Schor, J. (1990) Financial openness and national autonomy, Discussion Paper 1523, Harvard University Institute of Economic Research, Cambridge, MA.

Schott, J. J. (1991) Trading blocs and the world trading system. *The World Economy*, 14(1), 1–18.

Skidelsky, R. (1992) *John Maynard Keynes: the Economist as Saviour, 1920–37*. London: Macmillan.

Smith, A. D. (1992) *International Financial Markets: the Performance of Britain and Its Rivals*. Cambridge: Cambridge University Press.

Smith, R. C. and Walter, I. (1991) Reconfiguration of global financial markets in the 1990s. In R. O'Brien and S. Hewin (eds), *Finance and the International Economy, Vol. 4*. Oxford: Oxford University Press, 143–68.

Soroos, M. S. (1987) *Beyond Sovereignty: the Challenge of Global Policy*. Columbia: University of South Carolina Press.

Strange, S. (1971) *Sterling and British Policy*. London: Oxford University Press.

Strange, S. (1986) *Casino Capitalism*. Oxford: Basil Blackwell.

Swyngedouw, E. (1992) The mammon quest. 'Glocalisation', interspatial competition and the monetary order: the construction of new scales. In M. Dunford and G. Kafkalis (eds), *Cities and Regions in the New Europe*. London: Belhaven, 39–67.

Thrift, N. J. (1986) The geography of world economic disorder. In R. J. Johnston and P. J. Taylor (eds), *A World in Crisis? Geographical Perspectives*. Oxford: Basil Blackwell, 12–76.

Tickell, A. and Peck, J. A. (1992) Accumulation, regulation and the geographies of post-Fordism: missing links in regulationist research. *Progress in Human Geography*, 16, 190–218.

Tobin, J. (1984) On the efficiency of the financial system. *Lloyds Bank Review*, June.

United Nations (1991) *The Triad in Foreign Direct Investment*. New York: United Nations Centre on Transnational Corporations.

Wachtel, H. M. (1986) *The Money Mandarins: the Making of a Supranational Economic Order*. New York: Pantheon Books.

Wallace, I. (1990) *The Global Economic System*. London: Unwin-Hyman.

Wallerstein, I. (1991) *Geopolitics and Geoculture*. Cambridge: Cambridge University Press.

Walter, A. (1991) *World Power and World Money: the Role of Hegemony and International Monetary Order*. Hemel Hemstead: Harvester Wheatsheaf.

Walter, I. (1985) *Secret Money: the World of International Financial Secrecy*. London: Allen and Unwin.

Walter, I. (1988) *Global Competition in Financial Services: Market Structure, Protection and Trade Liberalization*. London: Harper and Row.

Part III

Money Politics and the Community of Money

12

Restructuring Housing Finance and the Housing Market

Chris Hamnett

Introduction

Private housing in capitalist economies is a commodity that is predominantly produced, financed, exchanged and often owned for profit. Because houses are very expensive both to build and to buy mortgage finance is crucial, and the availability and cost of this finance plays a key role in the structure and operation of the housing market. The 1980s have been a decade of major change in many countries in the structure of financial services and housing finance. These changes have had important consequences for housing markets, and the objective of this chapter is to examine some of these changes and their implications.

The relationships between financial services and housing markets are complex, but several key links and issues can be identified. First, there is the key role of finance in funding house purchase. This has become progressively more important as home ownership has grown in importance and house price inflation has increased the volume of finance necessary to support the home ownership market. Given the problems associated with bank lending to the Third World (Thrift and Leyshon, 1988; Dicks, 1991), and the perceived security of domestic mortgages, lending for home ownership became increasingly attractive in the 1980s.

The structure of housing finance varies between countries (Lomax, 1991; Haffner, 1991), and in some Mediterranean countries, such as Italy and Greece (Emmanuel, 1990), there has traditionally been strong reliance on private savings and family loans for house purchase. But in most Western countries some form of institutional mortgage finance has been established since the interwar period or before. There has frequently been a specialist circuit of housing finance at a privileged rate of interest. But during the 1980s there has been a move towards the deregulation and liberalization of financial services, which has had a considerable effect on the structure of housing finance. In particular, there has been a trend away from specialist circuits of housing finance towards a system in which the commercial banks and other financial institutions compete to lend. This has not been without its problems, however, and Britain and the USA have both experienced crises in housing finance and housing markets in the 1980s.

Second, the rapid house price inflation of the 1970s and 1980s has seen a trend in some countries, notably Australia, Canada, the United States and Britain, for home ownership to shift from its traditional role of providing a roof over people's heads and a set of residential use values to providing an investment and a source of capital gains. The extent to which this has taken place is very variable and a strong investment orientation to home ownership may be restricted to certain very specific groups. None the less, the exchange value of housing is now a major consideration in house purchase decisions, and Sternlieb and Hughes (1972) have suggested that the USA is now a post-shelter society where investment considerations are paramount. Whether or not this is true, there is no doubt that deregulation and competition have greatly increased the availability of mortgage finance, and enabled households to increase their mortgage debt and to extract equity for consumption. This has had important implications both for house prices and for the economy as a whole.

Thrift and Leyshon (1992) also argue that luxury housing has become an important 'positional good', which is keenly sought and conveys social status in certain groups. This is particularly important in certain major global cities, where the rise of financial services has meant that there is a considerable demand for housing from the high-income workers in this sector. This has served to inflate house prices and to raise demand for housing from international banks and other financial institutions for their staff.

Third, the restructuring of housing finance and housing's growing role as an investment good have had major spatial consequences. The importance of financial institutions in structuring the geography of the housing market was first identified by Harvey (1974) in his pioneering analysis of Baltimore, where he showed how federal mortgage insurance, institutional lending practices and landlord investment and disinvestment behaviour created a series of spatially differentiated housing markets. Subsequent research by Boddy (1976), Duncan (1976), Hamnett and Randolph (1988) and Sarre et al. (1988) has confirmed the importance of mortgage lending practices in the structuring of housing markets.

Harvey (1978) subsequently outlined a theory of urbanization under capitalism, which argued that periodic crises of over-accumulation within what he termed the primary circuit of capital resulted in shifts of capital into the secondary circuit in the built environment. This was followed up by substantive empirical analysis by King (1989) and Badcock (1992), which critically examined the importance of capital switching and value transfer in the urban areas of Melbourne and Adelaide. Badcock showed that Adelaide had experienced a major value transfer from its suburbs to the inner city during the 1970s and 1980s, though he is critical of the economic determinism of Harvey's thesis, and points to the importance of political factors in capital switching.

Work by Thorns (1981, 1989), Hamnett (1983), Saunders (1990), Dupuis (1992) and Harris (1987) has also identified the geographically and temporally variable nature of house price inflation and capital gains from the housing market. There is considerable debate, however, over the extent to which the differentials between the top and bottom end of the housing market are widening or narrowing. Thorns (1982) has argued that a process of cumulative inequality operates whereby high-priced areas show larger gains than low-priced areas, though work on Britain refutes this (Hamnett, 1992, 1993).

The final link is that between housing markets, mortgage debt, housing wealth and the macroeconomy. This is not a new concern. In the 1930s the Depression caused problems for millions of American homeowners who could not keep up payments on their houses and it threatened to bring down the mortgage finance institutions with it. This potential crisis was resolved by strong federal intervention in the mortgage industry to insure savings and loans against bad debts. Subsequently, it has been argued by Harvey (1974) that the US government used new housing construction as a counter-cyclical Keynesian economic regulator, and Walker (1981) and Florida and Feldman (1988) have argued that suburbanization has functioned as a key regulator in the development of US Fordism.

The debate over the relations between the housing market and the wider economy has recently manifested itself in Britain, where it has been argued that rising house prices in the 1980s led to rising personal wealth, greater home equity extraction, greater consumer spending and a fall in the savings ratio. Conversely, the fall in house prices and sales and the growth of housing debt from 1989 onwards has been linked to the fall in consumer spending, a rise in the savings ratio and the onset of recession. The private housing market is now thought to play a key role in economic growth in Britain.

There is not space to consider all these issues here, and the chapter therefore focuses on the changing structure of housing finance and its implications, particularly in Britain and the USA, and the relations between the housing market and the macroeconomy in Britain.

The Changing Structure of Housing Finance

The international financial system has witnessed major changes during the 1980s. In particular, the dominance of intermediated bank credit and specialist institutions has been replaced by what Leyshon and Thrift (1992) term 'a new regime of credit creation' brought about by the Third World debt crisis. This new regime has been characterized by the growth of dis-intermediated credit, securitization and deregulation (Budd and Whimpster, 1992). Leyshon and Thrift suggest that 'The transformation of the process of credit creation was paralleled by a reorientation of the spatial movement of credit flows' (p. 56) as the Third World was cut off from new funds and the international financial system became more spatially concentrated within a core of industrial nations (Thrift and Leyshon, 1988; Dicks, 1991).

The structure of housing finance has not been immune from these changes. On the contrary, the 1980s saw marked changes in the housing finance system in many countries. As Robin Leigh Pemberton, Governor of the Bank of England, pointed out in a speech to the World Congress of Building Societies and Savings Associations in 1986:

> Housing finance has not been immune from the pressures of new technology, greater interest rate volatility, and deregulation. In a number of countries new intermediaries have entered the market for housing finance, which in many cases has been dominated by specialists. A range of factors has encouraged newcomers to enter the field. The difficulties encountered with international lending, in particular, lending to less developed countries and for oil-related projects, have encouraged major international banks to concentrate more heavily on personal banking – a key element of which is seen to be the provision of loans secured on a first mortgage. Mortgage lending for owner-occupation is seen as highly attractive in view of the security offered by the underlying asset: and the favourable tax treatment and social security safety net offered in many countries. (Leigh Pemberton, 1986, p. 529)

Ball (1990) has commented that:

> From being relatively isolated from the mainstream of the financial world, house mortgages have become one of the keystones of the much talked about financial supermarkets of the future. Even the flow of funds into housing finance is being internationalised, with mortgage backed securites and bonds increasingly traded on and between the major financial centres and large scale loans raised on the Euromarkets. The world of mortgage finance has been irrevocably changed. (Ball, 1990, p. 1)

Lomax (1991) suggests that one of the consequences of the liberalization and deregulation of the financial system, and the reduction in the barriers to entry to the housing finance industry, has been convergence of national housing finance systems. This has been characterized by a greater degree of competition, the rise of multipurpose financial institutions and the blurring of the distinction between commercial banks and specialist mortgage institutions. In addition, there has been a decline of credit rationing and greater reliance on prices as a means of market clearing, greater financial innovation and expansion of the range of mortgage, saving and wholesale instruments.

Lomax (1991, p. 60) argues that 'although the moves towards increased wholesale funding, securitisation and de-regulation apply widely, the pace of change has varied markedly between countries' and that a distinction can be drawn between developments in the USA and the UK and those in countries which have higher entry barriers. The rest of this chapter concentrates on changes in the USA and the UK. For a discussion of the housing finance system in Germany see Ball et al. (1986) and Muellbauer (1991).

The Changing Structure of Mortgage Finance in Britain

Traditionally building societies operated on a separate financial circuit from that of the rest of the economy. (*Building Societies Association*, 1988)

The 1980s saw a dramatic change in the structure of mortgage finance in Britain. Until the early 1980s the building societies enjoyed 'a near monopoly over mortgage provision' (Callen and Lomax, 1990) and, because the savings market was highly segmented, they were largely insulated from competition over retail deposits. Competition between societies was restricted through cartel arrangements, and the Building Societies Association recommended interest rates that all the larger societies followed. These were often below prevailing market rates and were changed only infrequently. The objective was to keep the mortgage rate down to protect existing borrowers. The banks were largely excluded from mortgage lending as a result of government credit controls. As a result, building societies failed to meet demand and mortgage rationing was commonplace. Because of the controlled mortgage rate, there was little incentive for building societies to use wholesale funding even if this had been permitted, and no wholesale funding institution could enter the market because its interest rates would be totally uncompetitive (BSA, 1988).

In the 1980s the market environment altered radically in *three* main ways. First, changes in lending restrictions allowed the banks to enter the mortgage market in a major way. Second, marked changes in the legislation governing the building societies permitted them to behave more like the banks. Third, greater competition for savings and rising interest rates meant that wholesale funding could compete with retail funding and allowed the entry of new lenders selling securitized loans to institutions. As a result of the desire to sell mortgages and other products a number of large banks, insurance companies and building societies also diversified into estate agency, frequently with disastrous results. Each of these developments is dealt with in turn below.

Until 1980 the Bank of England operated a supplementary special deposits scheme (the corset) designed to restrict banks' ability to lend and control credit growth. But the abolition of foreign exchange controls in 1979 meant that it was easy to channel lending via overseas subsidiaries and circumvent the corset. Thus, the corset was abolished in mid-1980 and, as a result, 'The banks responded by expanding their business in the mortgage market, which was seen as profitable and low risk. This occurred at a time when the recession meant that corporate lending was risky and, chastened by the LDC debt problems, the banks were looking for safer ways to boost margins and strengthen or diversify their balance sheets' (Callen and Lomax, 1990, p. 503). In addition, the banks attempted to make more use of their extensive branch network to attract new customers and to boost sales of insurance, pension and mortgage products. Increased competition had several key effects. The banks introduced interest-paying current accounts in 1985 to compete with the building societies, and between 1981 and 1986 the BSA abolished its system of recommended rates. But, as Callen and Lomax (1990) comment, 'In the context of these developments, the Building Societies faced a key disadvantage in that the banks were better able to compete in the traditional business of the building societies than were the building societies in the business of the banks.'

The reason was that under the 1962 Building Societies Act societies could only lend on mortgages secured on freehold or leasehold properties, and their other assets had to be either fixed assets or a very limited range of government securities and bank deposits. Their funding was restricted to retail savings. The banks, by contrast, were much less restricted in their funding, and could offer a variety of money transmission facilities as well as savings accounts. As a result, the banks made significant inroads into the mortgage market in the early 1980s, after the abolition of the corset. The banks' share of new mortgage lending rose from under 10 per cent in the 1970s to 40 per cent in 1982 and 1983. Conversely, the building society share fell dramatically from 80–100 per cent in the late 1970s to 50 per cent in 1982–3.

After considerable pressure from the building societies to reduce their growing competitive disadvantage *vis-à-vis* the banks the government introduced the Building Societies Act 1986. This act provided a new legislative framework for the societies and permitted a gradual deregulation of the activities they could undertake and the products they could offer to both investors and borrowers. One of the most important changes was that building societies were permitted to obtain up to 20 per cent of their total funding from wholesale money market sources. This was raised to 40 per cent in 1988 and the societies have made increased use of this facility, particularly as the cost of retail funding rose owing to increased competition from the banks and the end of the interest rate cartel (Boddy, 1989).

The building societies also made considerable innovations in new saving products. In the early 1970s ordinary share accounts made up nearly 90 per cent of all building society retail deposits, but they accounted for under 10 per cent by 1989. There has been a corresponding increase in the importance of short notice and instant access accounts, whose share rose from zero in 1974 to 17 per cent in 1982 and 83 per cent in 1989 (Callen and Lomax, 1990). As a result of these changes the building societies increased their share of new mortgage lending to over 70 per cent in the mid–late 1980s. But this was achieved in part by offering generous mortgage to income and mortgage to property price ratios to win back market share, and the building societies suffered more than the banks from bad debts and repossessions in the early 1990s.

The third major change in the British mortgage finance market in the 1980s arose via the entry of a new type of mortgage lender and the creation of a secondary mortgage market. The Building Societies Association (1988, p. 13) noted:

> The normal pattern in the United Kingdom has been for the institutions which have made mortgage loans to continue to service them and to hold them on their balance sheets. There are, however, in effect three separate components of the mortgage lending process – origination, servicing, and holding the loan. . . . The establishment of a secondary mortgage market necessarily entails the splitting of the origination from the holding functions [and] involves the sale of housing finance loans from one institution to another, or the issuing of securities backed by housing finance loans.

The Building Societies Association report added that

> An institutional investor will purchase mortgage loans or mortgage backed securities only if the yield on them is higher than that on competing investments of similar riskiness, for example government securities. It follows that a secondary mortgage market could not exist if the mortgage rate was held significantly below other rates of interest. . . . The deregulation of the financial system over the past few years has, not surprisingly, led to a mortgage market being established at a . . . significant margin over money market rates. This has opened up the mortgage market to institutions funded entirely on wholesale markets, and has . . . resulted in a shift of power away from the providers of mortgage loans and towards the providers of mortgage applicants, that is largely estate agents, but also insurance intermediaries.

Four commercial banks, the Bank of Ireland, TSB, Chemical Bank and the Canadian Imperial Bank of Commerce, have been originating loans for the secondary market, but the major addition has been three new mortgage lenders, the National Home Loans Corporation (HLC), the

Mortgage Corporation and the Household Mortgage Corporation (HMC).

The Mortgage Corporation was set up in April 1986 by the American investment bank Salomon for the prime purpose of originating investment quality mortgages. The HMC was set up in July 1985 with sixteen financial institutions as major shareholders and gets its business from ten life companies. NHLC was set up in September 1985 with a stock market listing. It obtains business through a panel of life insurance companies and their intermediaries (BSA, 1988).

Business boomed for the new lenders during the late 1980s as the number of transactions soared and lenders competed to offer attractive terms to potential borrowers. Between May 1987 and September 1988 there were twenty-three issues by eight different mortgage originators, totalling just over £3 billion. But they achieved market share by offering high mortgage to income and high mortgage to purchase price ratios. This was successful while house prices were rising rapidly but with the housing market slump from 1989 onwards, the new wholesale lenders have suffered badly from bad debts and repossessions. The NHLC recorded losses of £89 million in 1991 and has ceased taking new business.

The Consequences of the Liberalization and Deregulation of Housing Finance

In the 1960s and 1970s . . . forces for instability were kept in check by a system of rationing of mortgages and other consumer credit. That system was abandoned as financial liberalisation was more and more deeply absorbed in the British economy in the 1980s. (*Muellbauer, 1991*)

What have been the consequences of the liberalization and deregulation of mortgage finance in Britain? The problems created by the boom in mortgage lending and house prices in the late 1980s and the subsequent housing market slump from 1989 to 1992 were clearly identified by the Governor of the Bank of England as early as 1986. Robin Leigh Pemberton (1986, p. 530) warned that:

In the United Kingdom, house prices appear to have followed an inexorable upward path over the last three decades. . . . But there is no economic law that dictates that house prices will necessarily travel in an everupward direction. Indeed, mortgage lenders in a number of continental European countries are only too well aware of the difficulties encountered as a consequence of the weakness of house prices during the early 1980s. Lending policies should not be based on the premise that house price rises will continue apace.

He pointed specifically to four potential problems:

1   Interest rates for borrowers would increase and tight margins would compel lenders to take a more hard-nosed attitude towards arrears and repossessions.
2   Lenders would face compressed risk/reward ratios, which could lead to some lenders being forced out of business.
3   Lenders should avoid the temptation to relax loan to income ratios to increase business. It would be unwise in a period of low inflation and high real interest rates for borrowers and mortgage lenders to rely on inflation to reduce the real cost of servicing the mortgage.
4   Lenders should avoid raising loan to value ratios as this could pose problems regarding security if arrears and defaults increase and property values fail to rise.

Unfortunately, almost all of Leigh Pemberton's fears have come to pass. In the competition to win and retain market share some mortgage lenders offered very high mortgage to income and mortgage to valuation ratios on the assumption that rising incomes and house price inflation would raise property values and reduce mortgage repayments as a share of income. But to control the inflationary boom caused by the Conservatives' lax monetary policy and tax cuts in the late 1980s, interest rates were doubled between mid-1988 and late 1989 from 8 to 15 per cent (Smith, 1992). As a result, the mid-1980s boom in house prices and sales volume collapsed in southern Britain. Sales fell by almost 40 per cent between 1988 and 1989, and by mid-1992 house prices in southern Britain (where the mid-1980s inflation was greatest) had fallen by 25–30 per cent from their 1988 peak. At the same time, Britain moved into a deep recession and unemployment rose sharply to almost three million. As a result, large numbers of owners have been unable to maintain their mortgage repayments and have had their homes repossessed. As Breedon and Joyce (1992, p. 175) comment,

> What has made the current downturn in the housing market unusual is the combination of falling *nominal* house price and high loan to value ratios for most recent buyers. This has led to a greatly increased number of home owners whose outstanding mortgage debt is greater than the value of their property (i.e. they have negative equity). This means that, whereas in the past the usual causes of arrears and possesions would have led homeowners either to sell their properties or to negotiate further loans to avoid possession, this course of action has increasingly not been available. Those experiencing repayment difficulties have therefore sometimes had little choice but to enter arrears and eventually be possessed. Those most likely to get into difficulty are those first-time buyers who purchased at the height of the 1988–89 boom and those who borrowed at high loan to value ratios.

It has been estimated (Bank of England, 1992) that about a million home owners who bought since 1988 now have negative equity. In

London, the South East and East Anglia, where the house price boom and bust has been most marked, the Bank estimates that two-thirds of first-time buyers who have bought homes since 1988 have negative equity. They estimate that the average negative is £6,000 but 20 per cent of those affected have negative equity over £10,000. Total negative equity totals about £6 billion. For many recent first-time buyers the results have been disastrous. Not only does this trap many people in their homes, but high mortgage interest rates and unemployment have meant that many home owners have been unable to meet their mortgage repayments. Unable to sell their houses to pay off the mortgage, they have had their homes repossessed (Wriglesworth, 1992).

The scale of mortgage arrears and repossession problems in Britain as a result of the recession and the housing market slump is considerable. At the end of 1991 a total of 589,000 mortgages (6 per cent) were 3 months or more behind with their payments, 184,000 were 6–12 months in arrears and 91,740 were over 12 months in arrears, compared to 10,500 in 1988. The number of mortgage repossessions in 1991 reached 75,540, almost a five-fold increase on the 15,800 in 1989 (Council of Mortgage Lenders, 1992).

The government pays mortgage interest via income support to those buyers unable to meet their mortgage repayments. In 1979 there were 98,000 claimants and annual payments totalled £31 million (£64 million at current prices). But the number of claimants rose sharply during the 1980s and by 1990 they totalled 310,000 at an annual cost of £554 million. This is a three-fold increase in the number of claimants and almost a nine-fold increase in cost from 1979 to 1990.

Where the size of their debts exceeds the value of the house, the lenders have simply been able to recoup the difference from the insurers, who provided cover for any mortgage over a given proportion, usually 80 or 90 per cent, of the valuation. The scale of the insurance losses on mortgage insurance in Britain has been considerable. It is estimated that they have amounted to £1.5 billion in 1991 and several companies have lost £300–400 million each. The Town and Country Building Society, which made high loan to income ratios and reinsured borrowers itself, was taken over in 1992 by the Woolwich at the behest of the Building Societies Commission to prevent any problems.

The Estate Agency Debacle

It is appropriate here to discuss another consequence of the financial deregulation and liberalization in Britain, namely the major losses incurred by a number of financial institutions as a result of their decision to expand into estate agency (real estate sales) during the late 1980s. The rationale for this decision was the view that estate agents offered great potential for originating loans and selling a wide variety of other financial services at the point of house purchase through their existing network of offices. In addition, estate agency was perceived to be a profitable business in its own right, and control of what was a fragmented small business sector offered a prospect of higher margins. This view had considerable logic. The principal problem lay in the timing and financing of the expansion. The first institution to expand was Lloyds Bank, which set up Black Horse Agencies in 1982 following its acquisition of a medium-sized estate agency chain. Lloyds was soon joined by other banks, including Hambros and the Trustee Savings Bank. Subsequently, the Building Societies Act 1986 and the Financial Services Act 1986 allowed building societies and insurance companies to diversify into estate agency which they did with great gusto. The Halifax, Nationwide Anglia and Abbey National building societies all set up their own estate agencies as did insurance companies such as General Accident, Royal Life, and Legal and General (Beaverstock et al., 1992).

> In each of these cases, the motives given for corporate expansion were essentially similar; to increase mortgage lending and to set up 'one-stop property shops' which could offer a full range of property-related financial services (home contents insurance, life policies, pensions etc.). Banks, building societies and insurance companies justified their entry into estate agency business as the product of rational business strategies. (Beaverstock et al., 1992, p. 171)

Unfortunately for most of these institutions, the timing and the methods of their expansion were badly misjudged. They chose to expand by purchasing existing estate agent chains, generally at a considerable premium, rather than establishing their own chains from scratch. As a result,

> an acquisition war broke out in the estate agency sector and gathered pace after 1986. The large institutions were bent on buying as many estate agency firms as possible [and] . . . takeover fever was heightened by the boom in the UK housing market . . . which meant that estate agency fee income rose to unprecedented levels. . . . The buying spree undertaken by the large financial conglomerates became particularly frenetic in 1987 and 1988. (Beaverstock et al., 1992, p. 173)

Beaverstock et al. (1992) provide figures that suggest that the institutions collectively spent between £1 and £2 billion in acquiring estate agency firms. They paid £300,000–400,000 per branch, and a high multiple of annual fee earnings. Prudential Property Services, for example, paid £125 million for 337 branches, an average of £371,000 per branch. Yet is has been estimated that the cost of setting up a new branch from scratch was only £75,000–100,000.

Unfortunately for the institutions, the peak of the buying spree coincided with the peak of the housing market boom, which suddenly collapsed in 1989 in southern Britain. Fee income and profits both slumped while overheads remained constant. As a result, most of the estate agency chains began to lose large sums of money and began to retrench. In 1989 the fifteen largest estate agency firms had losses of £170 million. Between December 1988 and December 1989 Nationwide closed 116 branches and Black Horse Agencies closed 41. The most dramatic losses, however, were suffered by the Prudential, which lost £23 million in the first half of 1990. It closed over 100 branches between December 1988 and May 1990, and a further 175 in July 1990. In May 1991 it sold its property services division for £13.5 million, a 90 per cent loss on the original capital invested. In some cases, individual estate agents have been able to buy back their chains of offices for a fraction of what they were paid initially.

The estate agency debacle is a direct result of the financial liberalization of the 1980s. It represents an example of collective institutional misjudgement, and the perils of expansion at the peak of a boom. More generally, the financial deregulation in the early and mid-1980s has clearly played a role in the subsequent boom and slump in the private housing market in Britain. First, the greater availability of mortgage finance and the breakdown of the building societies cartel meant the individuals found it much easier to borrow than before. Second, the competition between financial institutions meant that much higher mortgage to income and mortgage to purchase price ratios could be obtained. Traditional lending caution disappeared in the struggle to maintain or increase market share. As a result more marginal buyers were tempted into the market and the rapid rise in demand and finance helped to push up house prices to unsustainable levels. When mortgage interest rates rose and house prices fell, many recent buyers had no safety margin. Overgeared and overcommitted, they fell victim to the inevitable correction in prices and demand. But it would be a mistake to assume that deregulation was the sole, or even the major, cause of the boom and slump. As will be argued later in the chapter, government fiscal and economic policy also played a major role in creating a boom and slump in Britain in the 1980s and early 1990s.

American Housing Finance and the Crisis of the Thrifts

Until 1980 the Savings and Loans Associations (S and Ls) occupied a very similar position in the American housing finance system to the building societies in Britain. They comprised a separate circuit of housing finance which was regulated and protected by government. Like the building societies, their major role was the provision of mortgage finance, generally at a subsidized rate (Ball, 1990).

The origins of government regulation of the S and Ls date back to the depression of the 1930s, when the inability of many borrowers to meet their mortgage repayments caused a number of S and Ls to collapse. In order to prevent the collapse of the entire housing finance system, the federal government established the Federal Home Loan Bank System for S and Ls, and an extensive programme of mortgage and institutional insurance, including the Federal Deposit Insurance Corporation and the Federal Savings and Loan Insurance Corporation. These measures shored up the S and Ls' greatly expanded housing credit and mass home ownership, and shifted a substantial amount of the risk involved in mortgage lending to the government. They also facilitated 'a new fixed rate, long term, self-amortising mortgage instrument; a national secondary mortgage market; and tax incentives for thrifts to specialise in mortgage lending' (Meyerson, 1986, p. 466).

The latent problem with the system was between the fixed rate mortgages offered to borrowers and the need for the S and Ls (thrifts) to raise money from lenders at variable rates of interest. This began to surface in the mid-1960s, as Meyerson (1986, pp. 466–7) points out:

> The thrifts did very well for much of the postwar period. Armed with Regulation Q which set a ceiling on the amount of interest financial institutions could pay to depositors (with thrifts allowed to pay one quarter per cent more than commercial banks), they could charge borrowers two to three points more than the deposit ceiling and still offer a reasonable mortgage rate. But all this changed dramatically with the steep and unprecedented rise in interest rates beginning in the mid 1960s. As rate conscious depositors withdrew their savings in favour of alternative, less regulated investments, and as deposit rates rose faster on returns on mortgage portfolios, thrifts were forced to dip dangerously into surplus funds, sell non-liquid assets at a loss, and/or merge with other institutions to accommodate these deposit losses and low earnings. The mortgage market was deeply affected.

The basic problem of the S and Ls prior to the 1980s was the well-known one of borrowing short and lending long. But unlike other financial institutions, the S and Ls held long-term fixed interest mortgages and funded them with highly liquid passbook deposits. As Ball (1990, pp. 85–6) notes,

> In an era of volatile and rising nominal interest rates after 1966, the S & Ls would have had severe problems even if they could charge any interest rate on . . . deposits. At times of rising interest rates, if S & Ls had matched the interest rates offered elsewhere, their outstanding loan committments fixed at earlier lower rates would have made their operations unprofitable. If conversely, they did not match general interest rates then their net inflow of funds would dry up, leaving them with a liquidity crisis as outstanding mortgage debt could not be called in to bridge the funding gap.

According to Ball, the solution adopted by the S and Ls to this dilemma was the flawed one of trying to expand out of trouble by issuing more mortgages at higher interest rates in an attempt to change the composition of their mortgage portfolios. As he puts it,

> When faced with declining profitability at times of crisis . . . S & Ls consequently had a strong incentive to issue as many new mortgages as possible as long as the interest rate on them was greater than the average return on their outstanding holdings, because in this way the short-term profitability of their mortgage business was enhanced. Prudency or longer-term expectations of interest rate movements would suggest that such a growth strategy was unwise. When interest rates rose even further than the levels fixed on the additional mortgages, S & Ls ended up with even larger, unprofitable mortgage portfolios. So since the 1960s, thrifts have faced an environment which has encouraged them to adopt a 'growth or bust' strategy in which new business would hopefully take away the problems inherited from the past. (Ball, 1990, p. 94)

Not surprisingly, this strategy could not survive and the difficulties of the S and Ls came to a head in the early 1980s, particularly in 1981–2, when three-quarters of them made losses, and 1500 S and Ls disappeared through failure or merger between 1980 and 1986 (Ball, 1990). The result of this crisis was the abolition of interest rate controls and deregulation, with the introduction of the Depository Institutions Deregulation and Monetary Control Act 1980 and the Garn–St Germain Depository Institutions Act 1982. Ball states that the aim of the former was:

> to free regulated deposit taking institutions, commercial banks as well as thrifts from the constraints of interest rate controls which were losing them substantial deposits to money market funds. . . . It also enabled S & Ls to invest in consumer loans and commercial paper up to 20 per cent of their assets, and it abolished some lending restrictions. The aim of the second act was to speed up interest rate deregulation and particularly to reduce S & Ls' dependence on the mortgage market. They could now invest in tangible personal property for lease or sale up to 10 per cent of their assets, in a wide range of consumer, commercial and agricultural loans, and had restrictions lifted on loan to valuation ratios and on lending first mortgages only. (Ball, 1990, p. 101)

In addition, the 1982 Act permitted thrifts to increase consumer loans from 20 to 30 per cent of assets and to increase non-residential mortgage loans from 20 to 40 per cent of assets. The Act also directed federal regulators to devise a new, federally insured, high interest rate account offered by commercial banks and thrifts, which would be equivalent to and competitive with the high-yielding money market funds. The Act abolished the 0.25 per cent deposit rate advantage that the thrifts had previously enjoyed over commercial banks.

The Act's capital assistance plan also authorized federal regulators temporarily to increase the net worth (assets minus liabilities) of thrifts that had at least 20 per cent of their loans in mortgages, through government backed promissory notes. The government would pay off the notes to a thrift institution's creditors only if the thrifts failed. 'This enabled numerous thrifts to stay afloat without merging during 1983' (Meyerson, 1986, pp. 467–8). As Meyerson (1986) comments, the result of this federal legislation, together with the regulatory changes on a state and local level, brought dramatic changes in the financial structure of the United States, which have 'succeeded in substantially deregulating and homogenizing the financial system, producing a restructuring that has not been equalled for half a century. These developments, like the financial restructuring of the 1930s, are having a tremendous impact on housing in the United States' (p. 465). The S and Ls managed to overcome the early 1980s crisis by 1984 with a programme of new mortgages, sales of mortgages, relaxation of accounting rules and federal rescue plans. But the fundamental problems remained unaddressed and, as Ball (1990, p. 86) has perceptively commented, 'The problem of the 1980s was that the deregulators gave the S & Ls even more rope with which to hang themselves.'

As the S and Ls were permitted to extend their lending out of housing and into riskier commercial property, with losses underwritten by government, they were encouraged to expand into the booming real estate markets in the South, which subsequently turned sour. These problems were intensified by new managements who lent mortgages on speculative real estate developments whose value often proved doubtful. In addition, deposit rates offered were often unrealistically high and failed to maintain a good spread between deposit rates and investments in relatively secure activities. Meyerson (1986, p. 481) suggested that 'there is evidence that these investments, particularly in real estate development, may become the final push in the ultimate decline of the thrift industry. In the 1930s widespread thrift collapse was due to massive home loan default; in the early 1980s, to high interest rates, and now, additionally, to losses on high-risk loans.' When she wrote in 1986 there had already been runs on thrifts in Ohio and Maryland:

> as depositors responded to the reckless investment strategies of some privately-insured institutions. These savings and loans had been aggresively seeking rapid deposit growth, paying very high interest rates, and thus needed high-return investments. Many of these went sour leaving them with a large portfolios of non-earning assets. The deregulatory and volatile interest rate environment brought a new wave of management to the formerly conservatively managed thrifts: aggressive risk-taking businessmen who often purchased thrifts to finance their own real estate development activities. (Meyerson, 1986, p. 483)

Meyerson's fears proved prophetic. The Garn–St Germain Act allowed the thrifts to engage in a much greater level of non-housing lending, which was more profitable but much riskier, and, by ensuring that such lending was federally insured, it inadvertently created a moral hazard problem of major proportions in that there was no direct penalty for bad loans and financial failure. The government would pick up the tab if things went wrong. And pick up the tab it has. By the early 1990s, the total sum necessary to bail out bankrupt, and sometimes criminally run, thrifts had risen to an estimated US $500 billion – an average of US $2000 for each American citizen. According to Hall (1992, p. 5), the grave weaknesses of the federal deposit insurance scheme intensified the problems of the industry: 'The major defects in this scheme lie in the levying of flat rate premiums and the provision of blanket coverage up to the US $100,000 level. By eschewing a link between the premium and the riskiness of an institution, potentially serious "moral hazards" are created for the managers of the institutions thereby establishing a perverse system of incentives.' Hall adds that 'the flawed deposit insurance arrangements combined with the opportunities posed by deregulation served to deepen the crisis as many S & Ls choose to gamble their way cut of their predicament' (p. 7).

In conclusion, it is appropriate to quote Ball (1990): 'the 1980s deregulation process failed to understand the nature of the competitive processes it unleashed and the incentives it gave to particular players in the market'.

Housing Finance, Consumer Spending and the Wider Economy

The idea that the housing market may play a key role in the wider economy is not new. House building accounts for a significant proportion of GDP and it has long functioned as a key indicator of economic conditions. When the house building industry is booming, the economy is also booming. But there has also been a long standing neo-Marxist view that the construction industry functions as a Keynesian regulator, used by government for counter-cyclical demand management. Thus Harvey (1974) argues that housing policy is part of the wider government objective of the orderly accumulation of capital, economic growth and social and political stability. It functions, among other things, 'To ensure short-run stability and iron out cyclical swings in the economy at large by using the construction industry and the housing sector as a partial Keynesian regulator' (Harvey, 1984, p. 244).

This argument was developed further by Checkoway (1980), Walker (1981) and Florida and Feldman (1988) regarding the crucial role of suburbanization in American capitalist development. The regulationist thesis deployed by Florida and Feldman argues that the suburban owner-occupied single family house 'opened up new markets for automobiles, home appliances and consumer products, as well as a wide range of public and private services' (p. 197). They argue that 'US Fordism was inextricably tied to suburbanisation which enhanced consumer demand and set the preconditions for a temporary cycle of self-reinforcing growth' (p. 188). They do not suggest, however, that the 'suburban solution' (Walker, 1981) was the only possible solution. Rather,

> housing's crucial place in US Fordism was the product of unique historical conditions. While the productivity increases of Fordist production opened up a space for rising wages and mass consumption, the emergence of consumption patterns organised around suburbanisation was the result of a period of class formation, class conflict and attendant patterns of state intervention. (Florida and Feldman, 1988, p. 188)

Although the case for housing construction as an important economic regulator is well established, this does not of course mean that it will necessarily be used as such. On the contrary, there is a strong case to be made that the Thatcher Governments allowed new private house building to fall sharply in each of the last two recessions. And public housing construction was sharply cut back in 1979 and continued to fall during the early 1980s recession and subsequently. Housing construction has not been used as an economic regulator under Thatcherism. It has been sacrificed to the ideology of free-market competition and if anything it has functioned to reinforce major booms and slumps in the wider economy (Hamnett, 1989, 1993b).

Home Ownership, Housing Wealth and the British Economy

The late 1980s and early 1990s have seen an extensive debate in Britain over the role of house price inflation and housing wealth in stimulating consumer spending and the economy as a whole. The debate revolves around the relationship between rising house prices and home equity during the late 1980s, the increase in consumer spending between 1986 and 1988 and the associated fall in the saving ratio (the proportion of personal income that is saved). The concern has been reversed in the early 1990s and debate now centres on the links between falling house prices and sales, higher levels of mortgage debt, stagnant consumer spending, the rise in the saving ratio and the continuing recession.

The theoretical basis of the debate is very simple. Basic consumption theory postulates that as wealth increases so does consumer spending. Thus, because housing is a major component of personal wealth in Britain it is argued that rising house prices lead to increases in personal wealth. As a result, many home owners felt able to spend more and reduce their savings, to extract equity from their homes, or to borrow against the increase in the value of assets. As consumer spending accounts for a large proportion of national expenditure, house price inflation is a major determinant of demand and, hence, of the overall growth of the economy. The housing market is thus seen to play a key role in economic growth in Britain (Foley, 1991).

As Pannell (1992, pp. 6–7) puts it,

> with consumers accounting for two-thirds of all spending in the UK, the spending, saving and borrowing decisions of households have direct and pronounced effects on the well-being of the economy as a whole. . . . The sharply rising value of dwellings owned by the personal sector was a major factor inflating the paper wealth of households, especially during the height of the property market in 1986–88. . . . The consequent increase in individuals' sense of well-being may have helped to increase the readiness of the personal sector to spend and to borrow, thereby reinforcing the whole process and stimulating overall economic activity.

This argument has been reiterated by numerous informed commentators. Robin Leigh Pemberton (1986), the Governor of the Bank of England, suggested that 'The leaking of lending secured on a first mortgage, but used for other purposes, may well play a significant role in fuelling the expansion of consumer spending, and the entry of the building societies into the consumer lending market next year is likely to intensify competition in this area yet further.' This proved very perceptive and in 1991, giving evidence to the House of Commons Treasury and Civil Service Select Committee, Leigh Pemberton suggested that the sharp rise in house prices in the late 1980s has had major effects:

> Feeling richer, individuals saved less, and spent more. There was, of course, always an element of illusion in this feeling of greater wealth: house owners benefited in a tangible, durable sense only if they were prepared to move down-market or leave less to their heirs. But the impression, however false – of rising wealth – must have been a potent force encouraging higher levels of borrowing.

In the early 1990s the argument was reversed to explain the recession. Falling house prices in southern Britain, high levels of mortgage debt, negative housing equity and building of household savings were, it was argued, leading to a reduction of consumer spending and economic slowdown. Thus Will Hutton (1991), Economics Editor of the *Guardian*, stated that:

> Over the next 6–9 months, the shape of the recovery will depend almost entirely on the behaviour of the British consumer – and in turn on the

housing market. The housing market is important because with 70% of households owner occupied and 44% holding mortgages, the trend in prices and turnover has a vital import on both the feel-good factor and incomes that effect consumption.

Hamish MacRae (1992), the *Independent*'s Economics Editor, also commented that 'The scale of the 1988–89 consumer boom was underestimated because the forecasters did not fully appreciate the link between the housing market and people's willingness to spend. People were prepared to run down their savings partly because they felt that had made such a large profit on their houses.' Pannell (1992, p. 8) suggested that 'The weakness of house prices and low level of housing market activity may well have caused the personal sector to reassess the realisability of its equity tied up in home ownership and concluded that for the time being it needs to have a larger stock of liquid financial assets than in the past.' Finally, John Major, then Chancellor of the Exchequer, said in the Government's 1990 Autumn Financial Statement that 'The weak housing market has probably contributed to the moderation of consumer spending, just as the buoyancy of the housing market in the previous two years . . . contributed to its earlier strength' (quoted in *Housing Finance*, February 1991).

In a nutshell, the owner-occupied housing market is now widely seen to be a crucial component of economic health in Britain. How valid is this interpretation?

The aggregate empirical evidence is persuasive. Home ownership levels rose from 55 per cent in 1980 to 68 per cent in 1990 and national average house prices doubled between 1983 and 1989. During the same period the value of physical assets (predominantly dwellings) owned by the personal sector doubled from £553 billion to £1137 billion, the proportion of net personal wealth accounted for by dwellings rose from 44 to 52 per cent and total net personal wealth almost doubled from £1043 billion to £1939 billion.

Financial liabilities also doubled from £178 billion in 1984 to £343 billion in 1988, and house purchase loans as a proportion of financial liabilities rose from 61 per cent in 1984 (£109 billion) to 70.5 per cent (£242 billion). Although the rise in liabilities has been more than matched by the rising value of assets, the ratio of debt to disposable personal income rose sharply during the 1980s, rising from 57 per cent in 1980 to 115 per cent in 1990. Simultaneously, the personal sector saving ratio (which measures personal sector savings as a percentage of personal disposable income) fell from a peak of 13 per cent in 1981 to a low of 4 per cent in 1988.

Pannell (1992) suggests that 'The sharp tightening of monetary policy in 1988–89 prompted a significant correction by the personal sector. With around half of net wealth accounted for by home ownership and lending for house purchase making up about two thirds of personal sector borrowing . . . the housing and mortgage markets have borne the brunt of this adjustment.' There is convincing evidence for this. The personal saving ratio has risen sharply from a low of 4.1 per cent in the first quarter of 1988 to 10.9 per cent in the third quarter of 1991. Consumer spending has fallen in real terms in 1991, and despite the sharp fall in interest rates, personal sector borrowing has fallen sharply. Net new lending for house purchase has fallen since 1988 and the amount outstanding on consumer credit agreements has also fallen. A number of analysts have constructed econometric models to show the relationships between the owner-occupied housing market, borrowing, mortgage debt, equity extraction and consumer spending. Lee and Robinson (1990) argue that:

> the fall in the savings ratio is linked to a rise in borrowing, much of it mortgage borrowing. This borrowing provides important opportunities for the extraction of cash from the housing market (not necessarily by those who do the borrowing). The number of these opportunities for cash withdrawal is linked to turnover in the housing market. The value of such cash withdrawals depends on the price of housing.

Carruth and Henley (1990) argue that the level of housing market activity, particularly equity extraction, was very important in explaining consumer spending in the late 1980s:

> the housing market operates in such a way as to allow households additional freedom in their choice of income level. During periods of housing market boom, households may adjust their income upwards by moving house and withdrawing equity . . . for spending purposes. . . . There has also been widespread publicity about individuals taking second mortgages on existing property because of favourable borrowing rates, and then using the money for spending.

Carruth and Henley (1990) attempted to estimate the effect of activity in the housing market on aggregate consumer spending and indirectly on personal saving behaviour. They argue that the main macroeconomic forecasters failed to predict the boom in spending in the late 1980s because they did not incorporate house prices, housing wealth and equity extraction in their equations. When this is done, their results suggest 'the potential for a huge growth in HEW fuelling the spending boom' over the period 1986–9. They show that between 1982 and 1989 the proportion of houses sold relative to the total owner-occupied housing stock rose from 12 to 15 per cent. In 1988, the total value of traded housing equity was £100 billion, and they estimate that households had the ability to withdraw up to 12 per cent of this traded equity, a total of £12 billion per annum. This may have added up to 4 per cent of consumer spending in 1988, when it experienced a remarkable growth of 7 per cent. They also speculated that 'the dramatic termination of the housing boom, in response to a sharp tightening of monetary policy combined with rising inflation should have a considerable dampening effect on consumer spending'. This proved very perceptive.

The evidence on equity extraction from the owner-occupied housing market appears to support this thesis. Holmans's (1991) painstaking study of home owners' equity extraction from 1970 to 1990 shows that equity extraction increased rapidly during the mid-1980s. It does not, however, seem to support the recessionary thesis. Housing equity extraction fell only slightly in 1989 and 1990 and in real terms was back to the pre-boom levels of 1986–7. It seems, however, that the form of equity extraction in the late 1980s had changed. It was now less associated with moving and much more strongly linked to remortgaging. This may reflect the desire of home owners to reduce the interest costs on credit cards and other loans by remortgaging on property at much lower rates of interest. It is a residual category, however, and is therefore prone to considerable error.

Housing Wealth and Consumer Spending: the Contrary View

Not surprisingly, the argument outlined above is challenged by the Council of Mortgage Lenders, who, like the Building Societies Association before them, consistently reject any view which links mortgage finance or house price inflation to economic problems. Thus, Costello and Coles (1991) argue that

> It has frequently been alleged that equity withdrawal by individuals borrowing on mortgage for purposes other than house purchase was a major impetus behind the recent consumer boom. But a number of developments enhanced the personal sector's capacity to borrow for consumption reasons during the last decade . . . it is largely irrelevant that some borrowing was secured against privately-owned homes as the level of borrowing would probably have grown regardless of the form in which the assets were held. . . . The housing market cannot be held to account for the recent consumer boom and present recession . . . house price inflation and consumer spending are largely a function of the same set of factors.

And Pannell (1992, p. 7) argues that 'While the release of pent-up demand for mortgage finance and rising house prices were, in retrospect, a natural corollary of financial market deregulation, the effects were undoubtedly amplified by the . . . lax management of the macro economy in the mid to late 1980s.'

This argument has some merit. It has simply been assumed that because (a) house prices and wealth have risen, (b) consumption spending is positively linked to wealth, and (c) consumer spending rose sharply in the late 1980s, then (d) the increase in consumer spending was a function of rising house prices. As Costello and Coles (1991, p. 14) point out, 'The fact that these two variables move in tandem is not sufficient reason to conclude that the increase in housing wealth was the main factor explaining the rise in consumer spending during the late 1980s.'

There is no causal evidence for this, and Costello and Coles claim that rising consumer spending and rising house prices are both the result of the same set of factors. These are:

1   Lax monetary policy and low interest rates during the late 1980s.
2   Rapid growth in real incomes. Costello and Coles suggest that as in the house price booms of the 1970s, rising house prices were accompanied by rising incomes and consumer spending.
3   Reductions in income tax during the late 1980s when the government cut the basic rate of tax by 2 per cent and greatly reduced higher rates of tax.
4   Financial deregulation, which increased the number and competitiveness of lenders and made borrowing easier.

Folely (1991) has argued that the wealth effect of a house price boom can be overstated, and suggests that 'Other factors may lie behind the sharp upturn in equity withdrawal in the 1980s. It seems more likely that it is de-regulation of the financial markets allied to the collapse of the building society cartel at the beginning of the decade, which is the main cause' (p. 2).

This is not to argue that the state of the home ownership market does not have an impact on the wider economy. There is no doubt that a strong housing market with a high level of sales generates considerable housing-related spending on home furnishings, consumer durables and DIY as well as a boom for the house building industry and its materials suppliers. This spending will have considerable multiplier effects throughout the economy as a whole. There can also be little doubt that a high level of sales combined with rapidly rising house prices allows home owners to extract much more equity from their homes and divert some of this to consumption spending. Rising prices and housing wealth may also allow home owners to spend a higher proportion of their income on consumption.

Conversely, there can be little doubt that a slump in the volume of transactions and falling house prices will have a generally depressive effect on the economy, particularly when many households have a high level of mortgage debt. Falling real wealth and greater debt will, other things being equal, tend to encourage households to rebuild their savings, cut debts and reduce consumption.

What is disputed is the view that the home ownership market now holds the key to economic recovery, and that all that is required to jump start the economy is a new surge in housing demand and sales. As

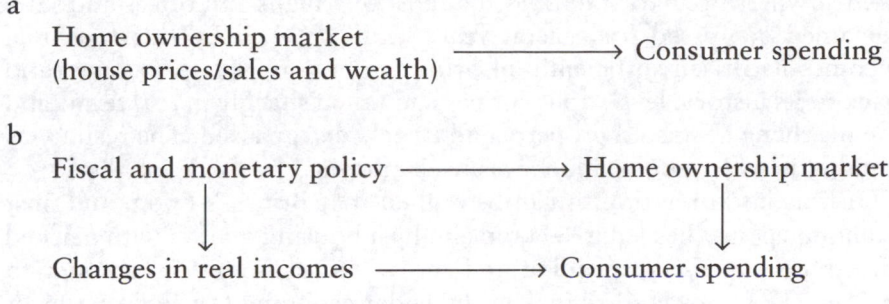

Figure 12.1 Two models of home ownership and consumer spending.

Costello and Coles point out, the fallacy of the argument is that causation is seen to lead directly from the housing market to consumer spending and economic growth. While there is undoubtedly a causal link between the housing market and consumer spending, it is not the only one, nor necessarily the most important. The problem with the view that the housing market is the key to consumer spending is that it ignores the other, and arguably more important, causal links. In a nutshell it misinterprets an indirect secondary causal link as being the primary direct causal link. The home ownership market reinforces booms and slumps in the wider economy, but it does not directly cause them.

For a more comprehensive analysis of the determinants of consumer spending and economic growth it is necessary to look at changes in real income, and government fiscal and monetary policy. Figure 12.1 gives a simplistic (housing determined) and a more sophisticated model of the links between the home ownership market and consumer spending.

The boom in the home ownership market in Britain in the mid-1980s was fuelled by *three* factors: first, financial deregulation in the early 1980s; *second*, a massive cut in higher rates of tax in the 1987 budget (abolition of marginal tax rates of over 40 per cent), which resulted in a large increase in disposable income for higher income groups; and third, the reduction in interest rates to a ten-year low in mid-1988. These policies generated a housing boom of major proportions but they also generated a consumer boom of equal proportions. Not surprisingly, the increase in interest (and mortgage) rates from late 1988 to 1991 (from 10 to 15 per cent), which was designed to cut back consumer spending and reduce inflationary pressures, also had the effect of triggering a sharp contraction in the grossly over-inflated home ownership market.

A similar pattern can be discerned in previous booms. In the early 1970s a cut in interest rates led to the Barber boom and to the first house price boom (from 1971 to 1973), when national average house prices doubled. In response to inflationary pressures and high consumer spending the government raised interest rates by 5 per cent in November 1973. The effect was precisely the same as in the late 1980s. The over-heated home ownership market collapsed almost overnight and prices and sales remained depressed for several years until 1976–7. By this time real incomes had risen sufficiently to bring the house price to income ratio back to its historic level, house prices had fallen sharply in real terms and the overhang of unsold property had largely disappeared. The result was another housing boom, which was itself curtailed by rising interest rates.

On this interpretation, it can be argued that Britain's boom and bust economic policy has led to a boom and bust housing market with marked effects on consumer spending and the wider economy. To attempt to explain the booms and slumps in the wider economy largely in terms of booms and slumps in the home ownership market is to misinterpret cause and effect.

There is no doubt that financial deregulation in the early 1980s led to a major expansion of mortgage lending, which permitted (but did not directly cause) house price inflation by virtue of the ease with which it was possible to get 95 per cent mortgages and high mortgage to income ratios. There is also no doubt that the inflated home ownership market permitted owners to reduce their savings, extract equity and increase consumer spending. But to attribute these consequences solely to the housing market, and to ignore the effects of tax cuts, low interest rates and rising real incomes on consumer spending, is to overlook the key determinants.

Conclusions

The 1980s saw the introduction of government moves, particularly in Britain and the USA, to deregulate and liberalize financial institutions and markets in order to encourage greater competition and efficiency. One result of these changes has been that the previously separate circuits of mortgage finance have become increasingly integrated into the wider circuits of finance capital.

However, although deregulation has allowed new and existing financial institutions to enter the mortgage market (with beneficial consequences for mortgagees), the increase in competition and the desire to retain or increase market share meant that lenders in Britain were not as careful as previously about the security of their loans and the ability of borrowers to repay. As a consequence of these lending policies, the number and the volume of loans rose dramatically. While house prices continued to rise so did lenders' security. But when the inflationary house price bubble burst, as it did in the South at the end of 1988, and sales volume and prices began to fall, the level of repossessions and the number of mortgagees with negative equity rose sharply. As a result, confidence in ownership and rising house prices has been broken and the market in Britain has become much less stable. Many financial institutions, particularly insurance companies, have lost money, perhaps two hundred thousand households have lost their homes as a result of repossession and more than a million home owners now own a home worth less than the outstanding mortgage debt. In the USA the deregulation of the Saving and Loans Associations has also had dramatic consequences. As a result of the defects in regulation (thankfully not present in Britain) and in the federal insurance scheme, the S and Ls were encouraged to gamble their way out of trouble in the 1980s with disastrous results. It is now estimated that the eventual cost of bailing out the S and Ls could amount to US $500 billion: an average of US $2000 for every man, woman and child in the USA.

In addition to these problems within the housing market and the mortgage finance industry, the slump in the home ownership market in Britain has compounded the early 1990s slump in consumer spending and economic growth. While it did not cause the current recession, the housing market slump has not helped. Rather than the housing market being used as a counter-cyclical economic regulator, as Harvey has suggested, it seems that, in Britain at least, the home ownership market has acted to reinforce and magnify booms and slumps in the wider economy. If this interpretation is correct, the deregulation of housing finance may have let a genie out of a bottle which will be hard to control. The phrase 'as safe as houses' may become an anachronism, depicting a safe and well-regulated golden age now past.

References

Badcock, B. A. (1992) Adelaide's heart transplant, 1970–88: 1. Creation, transfer and capture of 'value' within the built environment. *Environment and Planning A*, 24, 215–41.

Ball, M. (1990) *Under One Roof: the International Financial Revolution and Mortgage Finance*. Hemel Hempstead: Harvester Wheatsheaf.

Ball, M., Martens, M. and Harloe, M. (1986) Mortgage finance and owner occupation in Britain and West Germany. *Progress in Planning*, 26, 185–260.

Bank of England (1991) Recent sectoral financial behaviour. *Bank of England Quarterly Bulletin*, February, 83–9.

Bank of England (1992) Negative equity in the housing market. *Bank of England Quarterly Bulletin*, Month, 266–8.

Beaverstock, J., Leyshon, A., Rutherford, T., Thrift, N. and Williams, P. (1992) Moving houses: the geographical re-organisation of the estate agency industry in England and Wales in the 1980s. *Transactions of the Institute of British Geographers*, NS, 17(2), 166–82.

Boddy, M. (1976) The structure of mortgage finance: building societies and the British social formation. *Transactions of the Institute of British Geographers*, NS 1(1), 58–71.

Boddy, M. (1989) Financial deregulation and UK housing finance: government–building society relations and the Building Societies Act 1986. *Housing Studies*, 4(2), 92–104.

Breedon, F. J. and Joyce, M. A. (1992) House prices, arrears and possessions. *Bank of England Quarterly Bulletin*, May, 173–9.

Budd, L. and Whimster, S. (eds) (1992) *Global Finance and Urban Living*. London: Routledge.

Building Societies Association (1988) Changes in building society fundraising. *BSA Bulletin*, 56, October.

Callen, T. S. and Lomax, J. W. (1990) The development of the building societies sector in the 1980s. *Bank of England Quarterly Bulletin*, November, 503–10.

Carruth, A. and Henley, A. (1990) The housing market and consumer spending. *Fiscal Studies*, 27–38.

Checkoway, B. (1980) Large builders, federal housing programmes and post-war suburbanisation. *International Journal of Urban and Regional Studies*, 4, 21–45.

Costello, J. and Coles, A. (1991) The housing market and the wider economy. *Housing Finance*, February, 14–19.

Davis, E. P. and Saville, I. D. (1982) Mortgage lending and the housing market. *Bank of England Quarterly Bulletin*, September, 390–8.

Dicks, M. J. (1987) The financial behaviour of the UK personal sector. *Bank of England Quarterly Bulletin*, May, 223–33.

Dicks, M. J. (1991) The LDC debt crisis. *Bank of England Quarterly Bulletin*, November, 498–507.

Doling, J. and Ford, J. (1991) The changing face of home ownership: building societies and household investment strategies. *Policy and Politics*, 19(2), 109–18.

Drayson, S. J. (1985) The housing finance market: recent growth in perspective. *Bank of England Quarterly Bulletin*, March, 80–91.

Duncan, S. S. (1976) Self-help: the allocation of mortgages and the formation of housing sub-markets. *Area*, 8(4), 307–16.

Dupuis, A. (1992) Financial gains from owner occupation: the New Zealand case, 1970–88. *Housing Studies*, 7(1), 27–44.

Emmanuel, D. (1990) Trends in housing markets and finance and subsidies in the 1980s: the case of Greece. *Urban Studies*, 27, 931–50.

Florida, R. L. and Feldman, M. A. (1988) Housing in US Fordism. *International Journal of Urban and Regional Research*, 12(2), 187–209.

Foley, P. (1991) As safe as houses. *Lloyds Bank Economic Bulletin*.

Haffner, M. (1991) Fiscal treatment of owner-occupiers in the EC: a description. Paper presented at the conference on Housing and housing Policy, Oslo, June.

Hamnett, C. (1983) Regional variations in house prices and house price inflation, 1969–81. *Area*, 15(2), 97–109.

Hamnett, C. (1989) The political geography of housing in contemporary Britain. In J. Mahan (ed.), *The Political Geography of Contemporary Britain*. Basingstoke: Macmillan, 208–23.

Hamnett, C. (1992) The geography of housing wealth and inheritance in Britain. *The Geographical Journal*, 158, 307–21.

Hamnett, C. (1993a) The spatial impact of the British home ownership market slump, 1989–91. *Area*, 25, 217–27.

Hamnett, C. (1993b) Running housing policy and the British housing system. In R. Maidment and G. Thompson (eds,) *Managing the United Kingdom*. London: Sage.

Hamnett, C. and Randolph, W. (1988) *Cities, Housing and Profits*. London: Hutchinson.

Harris, R. (1987) Boom and bust: the effects of house price inflation on home ownership patterns in Montreal, Toronto and Vancouver. *Canadian Geographer*, 304, 302–15.

Harvey, D. (1974) Class monopoly rent, finance capital and the urban revolution. *Regional Studies*, 8, 239–55.

Harvey, D. (1978) Urbanization under capitalism: a framework for analysis. *International Journal of Urban and Regional Research*, 2, 101–31.

Holmans, A. (1991) Estimates of housing equity withdrawal by owner occupiers in the United Kingdom 1970 to 1990. Government Economic Service Working Paper no. 116, November.

Hutton, W. (1991) Housing is where the recovery is. *Guardian*, 23 September.

Kessler, D. and Wolff, E. N. (1991) A comparative analysis of household wealth patterns in France and the United States. *Review of Income and Wealth*, series 37, 3, 249–65.

King, R. J. (1989) Capital switching and the role of ground rent: 1. Theoretical problems. *Environment and Planning A*, 21, 445–62.

Leigh Pemberton, R. (1986) Structural change in housing finance. *Bank of England Quarterly Bulletin*, December, 528–31.

Leyshon, A. and Thrift, N. J. (1992) Liberalisation and consolidation: the Single European Market and remaking of European financial capital. *Environment and Planning A*, 24, 49–81.

Lomax, D. (1982) The banks and the housing market. *National Westminster Quarterly Bank Review*, 2–12.

Lomax, J. (1991) Housing finance – an international perspective. *Bank of England Quarterly Bulletin*, February, 55–66.

MacRae, H. (1992) More savings – but not yet. *Independent*, 12 May.

Meyerson, A. (1986) The changing structure of housing finance in the United States. *International Journal of Urban and Regional Studies*, 10(4), 465–97.

Muellbauer, J. (1991) Anglo-German differences in housing market dynamics: the role of institutions and macro economic policy. Unpublished paper, Nuffield College, Oxford.

Pannell, B. (1990) Trends in the personal sector balance sheet. *Housing Finance*, 8, 17–19.

Pannell, B. (1992) The outlook for personal sector borrowing. *Housing Finance*, 13, 6–9.

Sarre, P., Skellington, D. and Phillips, D. (1988) *Ethnic Minority Housing: Explanations and Policies*. Aldershot: Avebury.

Saunders, P. (1990) *A Nation of Home Owners*. London: Unwin Hyman.

Smith, D. (1992) *From Boom to Bust: Trial and Error in British Economic Policy*. Harmondsworth: Penguin.

Sternlieb, G. and Hughes, J. W. (1972) The post-shelter society. *Public Interest*, 39–47.

Thorns, D. C. (1981) The implications of differential rates of capital gains from owner occupation for the formation and development of housing classes. *International Journal of Urban and Regional Research*, 5, 205–17.

Thorns, D. C. (1982) Industrial restructuring and change in the labour and property markets in Britain. *Environment and Planning A*, 14, 745–65.

Thorns, D. C. (1989) The impact of homeownership and capital gains upon class and consumption sectors. *Society and Space*, 7, 293–312.

Thrift, N. and Leyshon, A. (1988) The gambling propensity: banks, developing country debt exposures and the new international financial system. *Geoforum*, 19(1), 55–69.

Thrift, N. and Leyshon, A. (1992) In the wake of money: the City of London and the accumulation of value. In L. Budd and S. Whimster (eds), *Global Finance and Urban Living*. London: Routledge.

Walker, R. (1981) A theory of suburbanisation: capitalism and the construction of urban space in the United States. In M. Dear and A. Scott (eds), *Urbanisation and Urban Planning in Capitalist Society*. London: Methuen.

Wood, G. A. and Bushe-Jones, S. (1990) Financial deregulation and access to home ownership in Australia. *Urban Studies*, 27(4), 583–90.

Wriglesworth, J. (1992) Housing market: the debt trap. *UBS Phillips and Drew Economic Briefing*, no. 262, 9 June.

13

Vicious Circle: Financial Markets and Commercial Real Estate in the United States

Barney Warf

The formation of economic landscapes in industrialized nations is intimately intertwined with capital markets and the institutions that control the supply of investment funding (commercial and savings banks, insurance firms, pension funds etc.). However, the linkages between the built environment and capital markets have been infrequently spelled out, especially from perspectives other than neoclassical economics. The availability and price of finance capital – in the forms of mortgages, commercial loans, and direct investments – heavily condition where, when and how much commercial and residential property will be constructed at any given time and place. Given that most financial institutions have the vast bulk of their net assets tied up in commercial, not residential, property, this omission is truly startling.

The financial mediation of property relations became a pressing object of analysis precisely as urban political economy underwent a sustained retheorization of rent and land use in the 1970s. In the classical view, rent was regarded as a parasitic remnant of precapitalist social relations (Haila, 1988). Harvey (1974) and Harvey and Chatterjee (1974) were instrumental in reformulating the Marxist theory of rent, particularly in the context of the availability of residential mortgage capital. More recently, Harvey (1985) theorized the production of the built environment as part of the 'secondary circuit' of capital, the materialization of liquid capital in the urban landscape, and thus as fundamental to the process of capital accumulation (see also Scott, 1980).

The importance of finance–commercial property relations is further underscored by the renewed recognition given to space by social theory. It is increasingly apparent to many observers that the built environment is not some passive actor in the interrelations between capital and real estate (Checkoway, 1980; Sbragia, 1988). Rather, geography – in the form of materialized capital assets – also reverberates actively to shape subsequent conditions of capital investment and disinvestment. This double-sidedness of finance and spatial relations became particularly obvious in the United States in the 1980s.

This chapter investigates the relations between finance capital and commercial real estate in the USA in the past decade. Under the impetus of deregulation, much of this period was dominated by the dizzying upward spiral of the stock market, the steady globalization of national capital markets and an enormous surge of commercial real estate construction. The chapter opens with a brief review of the structural changes that profoundly altered US capital markets over the past two decades. Next, it examines how commercial banks seized the opportunities this sea-change created. Third, it turns to the banks' cousins, the savings and loans, their disastrous foray into commercial real estate and the spatial repercussions of the enormous federal bail-out that attempted to save them at public expense. Towards the end of the decade, the inevitable effects of overproduction made themselves painfully evident. The fourth part of the chapter accordingly documents the effects of overinvestment in commercial real estate as the new built environment of the 1980s turned, like Frankenstein's monster, upon its creators. Finally, some reflections upon the implications of this process for urban political economy are offered in the conclusion.

Letting the Genie Out of the Bottle: Deregulation

The dramatic changes in US finance and real estate markets that unfolded in the 1980s must be understood within the context of the profound transformation in global capitalism that began in the 1970s, including: the collapse of the Bretton Woods agreement in 1971 and the subsequent shift to floating exchange rates; the oil crises of 1974 and 1979 and the subsequent recession in the West; the explosive growth of Third World debt; the steady deterioration in the competitive position of the USA and the concomitant rise of Japan, Germany and the newly industrializing nations; the emergence of 'flexible' specialization and computerized production technologies; the steady growth of multinational corporations and their ability to shift vast resources across national boundaries; the global wave of deregulation, privatization and the lifting of state controls in many industries; and the integration of world financial markets through telecommunications systems.

Beginning in the 1970s, the US government undertook a series of actions that had far-reaching consequences in many industries, particularly real estate. In 1974, money market mutual funds were introduced, which sharply increased competition for core banking deposits. In 1979, the Federal Reserve changed from a policy of stabilizing interest rates to a policy of slowing money growth in order to combat inflation; real (post-inflation) interest rates rose accordingly. Meanwhile, a wave of deregulation removed government controls in several industries, including the Securities Acts Amendments of 1975, the Airline Deregulation Act of 1978, the Motor Carriers Act of 1980 and the dissolution of American Telegraph and Telephone Corporation's monopoly of telecommunications in 1984. In finance, deregulation was even more dramatic: in 1980, Congress passed the Depository Institutions Deregulation and Monetary Control Act, and in 1982, the Garn–St Germain Act, which permitted thrifts (savings and loans) to compete more directly with commercial banks and eliminated geographic limitations on savings and loans lending. Financial markets also saw the relaxation of interstate banking regulations (Holly, 1987), the removal of restrictions governing pension and mutual fund portfolios, the abolition of fixed commissions on stock market transactions, the approval of foreign memberships on stock markets and the continuing debate over the repeal of the Glass–Steagall Act, which has separated commercial from investment banking since its implementation in 1933.

The effects of deregulation were amplified through the macroeconomic policies of the Reagan Administration. Chief among these was the Economic Recovery Program, which instigated a series of federal tax cuts legislated through the Economic Recovery and Tax Act of 1981, the Tax Equity and Fiscal Responsibility Act of 1982 and the Omnibus Reconciliation Act of 1981. As the US financial history of the 1980s clearly indicates, the tax cuts produced a series of rising federal budget deficits, often on the order of US $130 billion or more annually, which markedly altered the macroeconomic position of the USA, turning it into the largest debtor nation in the world. As federal government spending soaked up over one-half of the total investment funding in the USA, real interest rates soared, attracting a huge influx of foreign capital, particularly Japanese, German and Canadian, much of which found its way into commercial real estate. In Los Angeles, for example, one-half of the commercial real estate downtown is owned by Japanese firms; in Minneapolis, one-half is owned by Canadian corporations; in New York City, 20 per cent of the commercial office space is owned by foreign firms, particularly Canadian and Japanese corporations (Port Authority of New York and New Jersey, 1991; see also Thrift (1987) and Budd and Whimster (1992) in the case of London). Finally, the Congressional Tax Reform Act of 1986 made it unprofitable for developers to build or hold unoccupied space (Mahar, 1991), increasing their desperation in the search for tenants, many of whom became unwilling to buy in the increasingly overbuilt commercial real estate market.

The effects of these policy changes were dramatic. The abundance of investment capital, deregulation of the financial industry and inflation, which created negative real interest rates, conspired to allow developers to turn substantial profits by erecting skyscrapers, offices, hotels and shopping malls whenever possible. Eager for investment capital, many builders turned to traditional sources, the commercial banks. As other financial institutions (e.g. insurance companies, savings and loans) penetrated this lucrative market, in which profits greatly exceeded those in residential real estate, the urge to lend, speculate and invest in commercial real estate began to acquire symptoms of a feeding frenzy. Downs (1985) argued that these changes eliminated the institutional and legal barriers between the traditionally distinct residential and commercial real estate markets, intensifying competition within a single market that integrated the other two.

At this juncture, it should be noted that the surge in the supply of investment capital for commercial real estate construction occurred parallel to a pronounced restructuring in the role of the local state (Harvey, 1989; Leitner, 1990). Faced with slow economic growth, widespread political resistance to higher taxes and growing demands for public services, many state and municipal governments eagerly courted new property developments with an eye on job and tax revenue generation. Thus, the construction of new offices, hotels, convention centres and sports stadiums was often effectively subsidized through tax holidays, rebates, subsidies, zoning changes, training programmes, low-interest loans and a host of other 'development instruments', generally legitimized under the ideology that 'growth' is good for everyone (Logan and Molotch, 1987). In the process, traditional public sector redistributive functions were often abandoned or scaled back. That growth might be a mirage in the long term, or that its costs could be severe and unevenly distributed, rarely mattered to local politicians intent on securing investment in the short run.

In short, the changes of the 1980s liquidated the relatively stable division of markets and lending sources that had existed since the 1930s (commercial banks in commercial property lending, thrifts in residential lending), increased the liquidity and level of competitiveness of finance capital as new institutional players entered the commercial market and markedly altered the role of the local state in attracting development. The two institutions most heavily affected by these developments were commercial banks and the savings and loans institutions.

Commercial Banks, Commercial Property

Traditionally, the largest players in US commercial property markets have been commercial banks. Barred since the implementation of the Glass–Steagall Act in 1933 from speculating in securities, and shut out from residential real estate by the savings and loans institutions, commercial banks have made loans for the construction of office towers, hotels and convention centres their bread and butter. In 1990, US banks

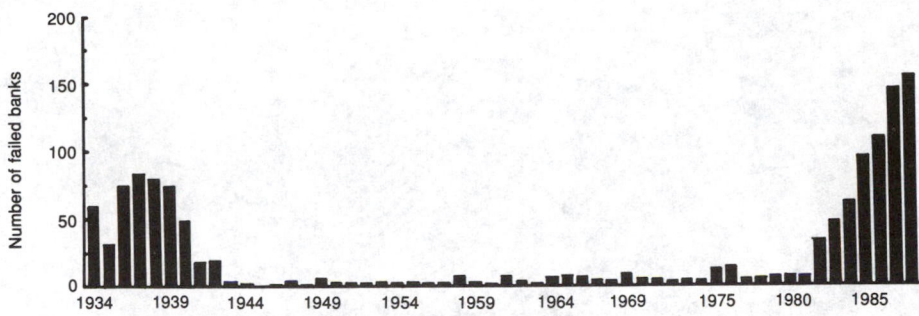

Figure 13.1 US commercial bank failures, 1934–1988.
Source: unpublished Resolution Trust Corporation data.

carried more than US $400 billion in commercial real estate loans (Mahar, 1991, p. 21).

Much of the attention paid to the growing crisis of US commercial banks has focused on the critical role of Third World debt, which affects primarily the large 'money centre' banks headquartered overwhelmingly in New York. As banks throughout the USA became increasingly involved in commercial real estate, however, the growing crisis in US banking extended progressively throughout the banking hierarchy (Quint and Freed, 1991). Buffeted by mismanagement, deregulation, depressed local economies and an overbuilt commercial real estate market – all of which conspired to raise markedly the proportion of non-performing loans – many banks in the 1980s collapsed altogether or tottered precariously on the brink of bankruptcy. Between 1985 and 1988, more than 640 US banks failed, equivalent to 45 per cent of the national total of bank failures since the Great Depression (figure 13.1). These failures have significant consequences for banking as an industry (for example, causing a plummet in their stock prices) and for local communities, where they represent disruptions in flows of payments and reduction in sources of investment capital. Bank failures are also important as a matter of public policy: between 1985 and 1988, the Federal Deposit Insurance Corporation (FDIC) dispersed roughly US $15.5 billion through payoffs or assumptions of deposits in 1046 banks, or 12.1 per cent of the nation's total banks (Mayer, 1990; Sherrill, 1990).

Commercial bank failures in the USA between 1980 and 1988 were highly unevenly distributed geographically (figure 13.2). In terms of the total number of banks, Texas, with 216 bank failures affecting 2.37 million depositors, far exceeded any other state (more than twice that of second-ranking ones); other heavily affected states included Oklahoma and New York, as well as a broad swath of Midwestern states, Pennsylvania and California.

Fortunately for depositors with funds in failed banks, assets up to US $100,000 are insured by the FDIC. FDIC disbursements to failed

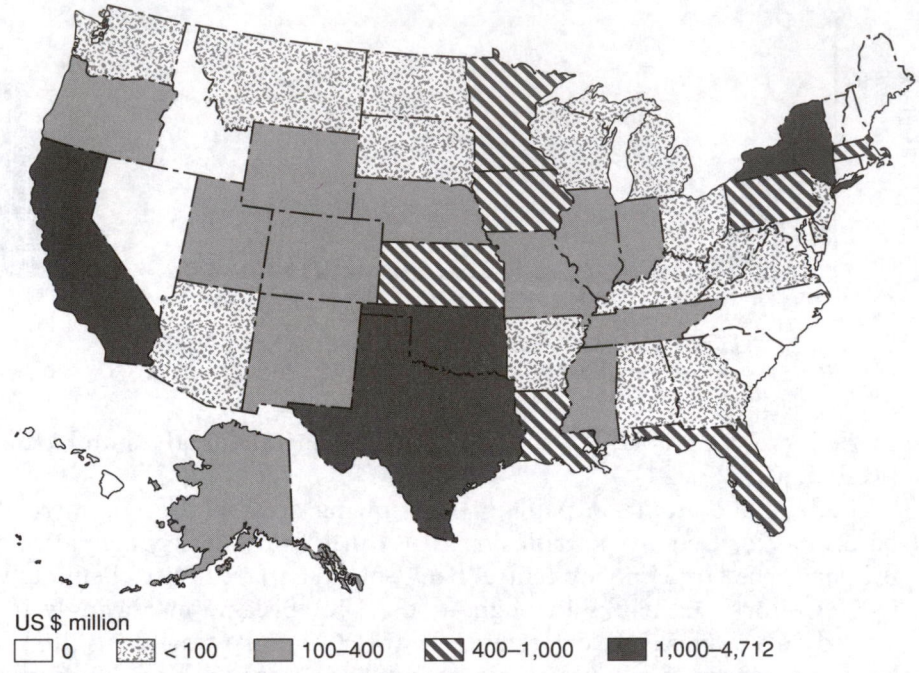

US $ million

| ☐ 0 | ▦ < 100 | ▨ 100–400 | ▧ 400–1,000 | ▩ 1,000–4,712 |

Figure 13.2 Total FDIC disbursements to failed commercial banks, 1980–1988.
Source: unpublished Resolution Trust Corporation data.

banks during the 1980–8 period – more than US $17 billion – were concentrated in the three largest states – New York, California and Texas – as well as Oklahoma (figure 13.2). Because some of these payments were drawn from tax revenues collected from the nation as a whole (while others came from membership fees levied on banks), it is evident that government intervention in the banking crisis involves important interregional transfers of public revenues, particularly from the Rustbelt to the Sunbelt (Rosenbaum, 1990).

Virtually a permanent fixture in the financial community, fraud and mismanagement rose greatly in importance under deregulation, prior to which large profit margins obscured errors and poor performance. Pantalone and Platt (1987) estimate that mismanagement and embezzlement are responsible for at least one-third of all US bank failures in the early 1980s. Insufficiently diversified banks became vulnerable to sudden changes in the fortunes of a particular industry (e.g. petroleum or agriculture), while banks with portfolios characterized by insufficient liquidity were susceptible to rapid changes in funding requirements (e.g. changes in the federally mandated reserve ratio).

An important consequence of deregulation was increased competition in banking, particularly as non-commercial banks invaded traditional commercial bank markets (e.g. commercial real estate). For many banks,

Table 13.1 Commercial real estate exposure of selected US commercial banks, 1990

	Total commercial loans (US $ billion)	Loans as % of net assets	Loans as % of net worth
Wells Fargo (CA)	8.3	14.9	252.9
Citicorp (NY)	7.0	3.2	67.7
Security Pacific (CA)	6.0	7.2	136.5
Bank America (CA)	5.2	4.6	77.7
Chemical Bank (NY)	3.6	6.0	92.0
Chase Manhattan (NY)	3.5	3.5	72.4
First Interstate (CA)	3.3	6.5	114.9
First Chicago (IL)	2.8	6.7	99.4
Bank of Boston (MA)	2.5	8.1	162.5
Sumitomo Bank (CA)	2.4	49.8	873.7

Source: Mahar, 1991, p. 20.

this result was most unwelcome given that the cost of funds to banks is greater today than in the 1970s, reducing interest rate margins. In response, many banks diverted funds in their investment and loan port-folios to higher risk/higher return opportunities, or by becoming more leveraged in commercial real estate. Table 13.1 reveals the extent to which some of the nation's selected largest banks are involved in com-mercial real estate, loans for which comprise between 67.7 per cent (Citicorp) and 252.9 per cent (Wells Fargo) of their net worth. Foreign owned banks such as Sumitomo, whose loans exceeded 837 per cent of its net worth, fared even worse. Small banks may be similarly involved in commercial real estate markets through syndicated loans shared by many lenders.

The degree to which commercial banks plunged into the orgy of commercial construction lending varied widely geographically (figure 13.3). Among the 100 largest US commercial banks, the heaviest lenders were located in New York and California, although New York banks faced the highest degree of foreclosures. Real estate loans as a percentage of total assets, on the other hand, were highest in south-eastern banks (Louisiana, Florida, South Carolina), while loans as a percentage of total net worth were highest in the northern Midwestern states (Minnesota, Wisconsin, Indiana, Missouri).

The Great Savings and Loan Robbery

One of the most important actors of the commercial building boom was the savings and loan (S&L) industry (Mayer, 1990; Pizzo et al., 1990; Sherrill, 1990). The story of the rise and fall of S&Ls in the 1980s throws

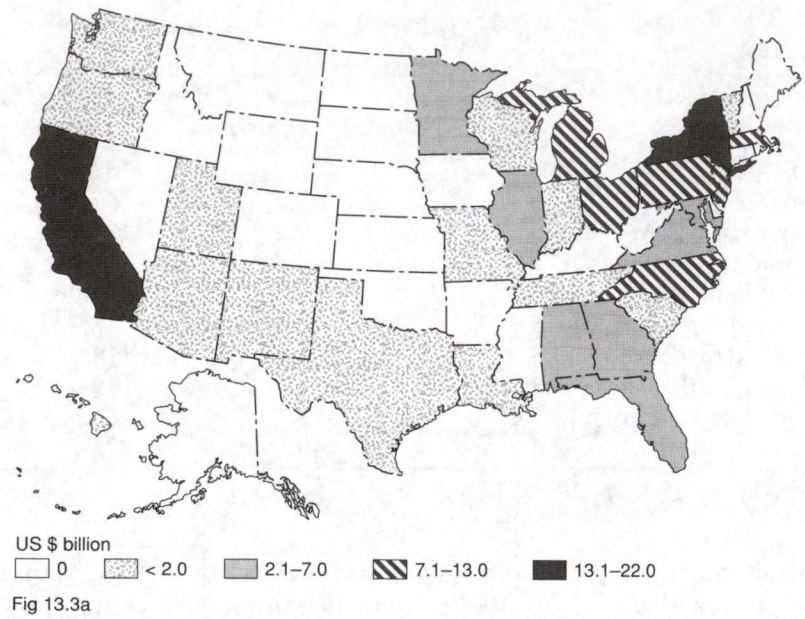

US $ billion

☐ 0 ░ < 2.0 ▨ 2.1–7.0 ▨ 7.1–13.0 ■ 13.1–22.0

Fig 13.3a

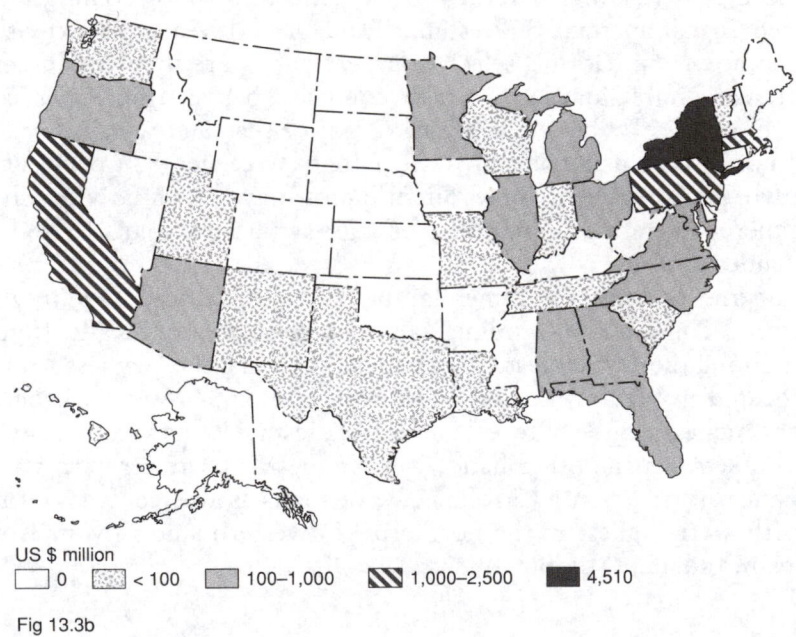

US $ million

☐ 0 ░ < 100 ▨ 100–1,000 ▨ 1,000–2,500 ■ 4,510

Fig 13.3b

Figure 13.3 Spatial patterns in US commercial real estate lending by 100 largest commercial banks, 1990 a, Total commercial real estate loans. b, Total foreclosed commercial property. c, Commercial real estate loans as a percentage of total assets. d, Commercial real estate loans as a percentage of total net worth.
Source: after Mahar, 1991.

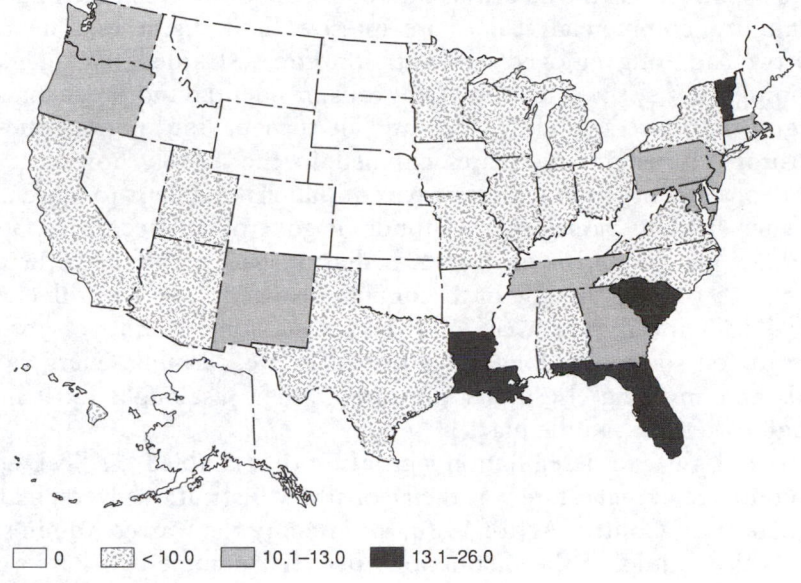

0 | < 10.0 | 10.1–13.0 | 13.1–26.0

Fig 13.3c

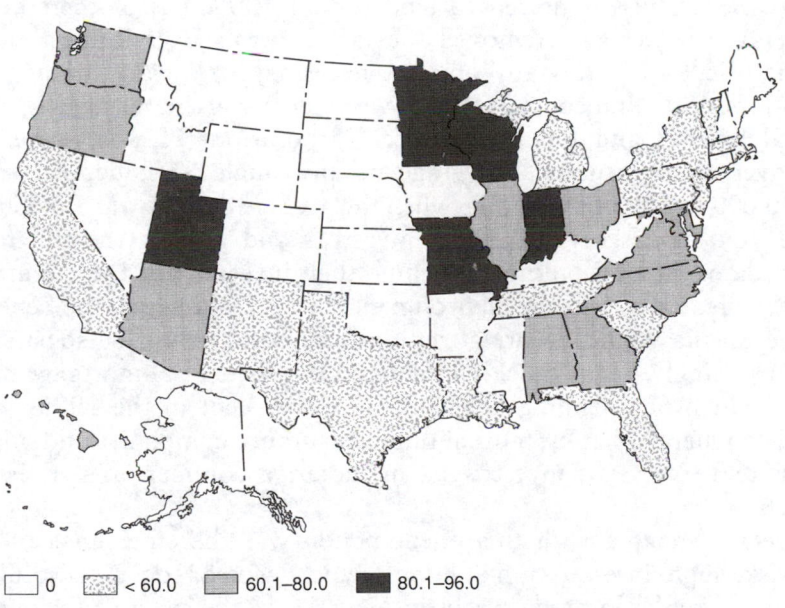

0 | < 60.0 | 60.1–80.0 | 80.1–96.0

Fig 13.3d

a harsh spotlight on the nefarious interconnections between the financial community, commercial real estate interests and the state. The S&L industry had long enjoyed a reputation for restrained management, confining itself to the safe, if unglamorous, residential mortgage market, charging borrowers modest rates and in turn paying modest ones to depositors. When interest rates climbed in the 1980s, however, and their depositors began to withdraw tens of billions of dollars to place them in higher yielding money market funds or government securities, S&Ls suffered a growing crisis of disintermediation, and many faced the critical choice of diversifying or becoming insolvent. As Sherrill (1990, p. 594) put it, 'if they were allowed to do some double-or-nothing gambling on some very long shots in real estate, farming, energy, junk bonds and anything else under the sun ... they just might hit it lucky enough to get back in the black.'

A critical piece of deregulation legislation that enabled the S&L entry into commercial real estate was the Depository Institutions Deregulation and Monetary Control Act of 1980, initiated by the Carter Administration, which muddled the distinctions between commercial banks and S&Ls and destroyed the traditional community orientation of the latter by eliminating all geographic limitations on their lending (previously, S&Ls were required to lend within 100 miles of their headquarters). The act also removed the last controls over interest rates, allowing S&Ls to offer any amount necessary to attract funds from depositors. Simultaneously, the government watchdog agency, the Federal Savings and Loan Insurance Corporation (FSLIC), increased the government insurance coverage of any single S&L deposit from US $40,000 to 100,000 at a time when the average deposit was US $6000, thus favouring large institutional investors and putting the full faith and credit of the US government behind their investments. Deregulation, in short, created a risk-free environment for S&Ls in which the benefits of investments would be privatized and the costs would be socialized. Not surprisingly, S&Ls quickly evacuated the residential mortgage market, in which new lending dropped by 50 per cent in the 1980s, and joined commercial banks, mutual funds, insurance companies and others in a massive wave of investments in lucrative commercial real estate projects.

Closely correlated with this phenomenon was the emergence of the high-risk, high interest 'junk' bond, which centred on a handful of investment banks located largely in New York, the most notorious of which was the now-defunct Drexel Burnham Lambert. Junk bonds provided large pools of brokered money that S&Ls needed to invest in commercial real estate – by 1989, S&Ls owned US $14 billion worth – and dramatically deepened their involvement in financing office towers, shopping plazas and hotels in numerous cities. When junk bonds lived up to their name and when a glut of office space began to appear in the late 1980s, depressing commercial rents, S&Ls found themselves increasingly destitute. By the late 1980s, hundreds of commercial banks and S&Ls, sliding down the same slippery deregulated slope, failed in the largest wave of collapse since the Great Depression of the 1930s. Thus did spatial relations reverberate back into the rarefied world of finance, creating a vicious circle in which the landscapes of overspeculation haunted the institutions that created them.

At this juncture, there enters a critical actor, the state: once more, the US financial community called upon the federal government to save it, all the while singing paeans of praise to the free market. The notoriously expensive S&L bail-out began to unfold as the FSLIC began to use taxpayer dollars to shore up threatened deposits extended primarily by commercial lenders. As more and more S&Ls became insolvent, the total cost of bailing them out rose exponentially. Even the federal government found itself short of funds for such a massive undertaking: in the mid-1980s, with almost *one trillion* dollars riding on the nation's thrifts, the FSLIC had a minuscule US $2 billion to cover depositor losses. Eager to protect one of its most powerful constituencies, the US Congress passed the Financial Institutions Reform, Recovery and Enforcement Act of 1989, which promised US $157 billion to save the thrift industry but

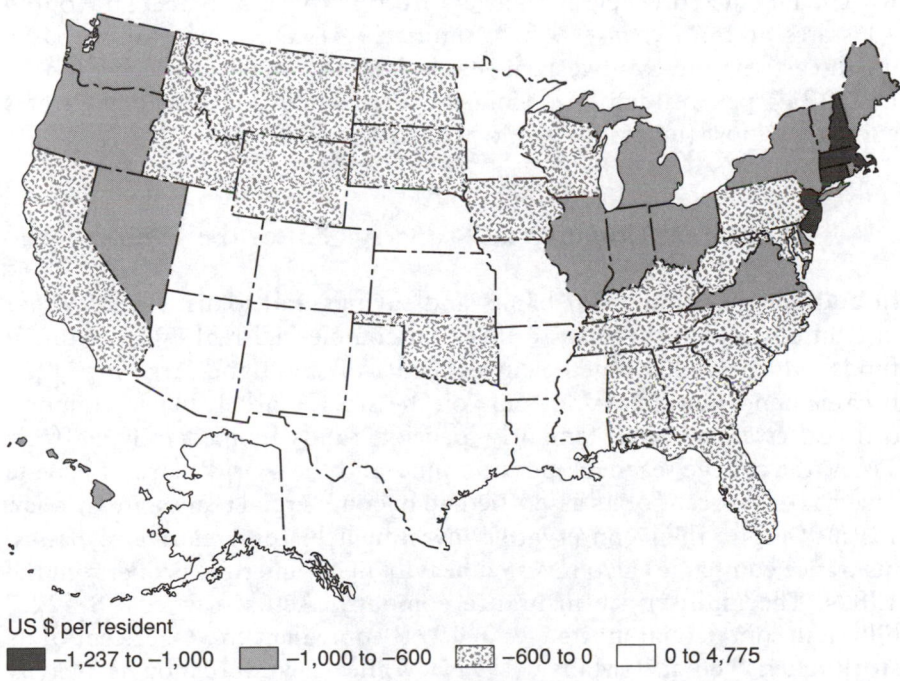

US $ per resident

■ −1,237 to −1,000   ■ −1,000 to −600   ▨ −600 to 0   □ 0 to 4,775

Figure 13.4 Per capita losses and gains of federal bail-out of savings and loan industry.
Source: after Rosenbaum, 1990.

offered initial funds of only US $50 billion. The bail-out would be managed through the newly created Resolution Trust Corporation (RTC), which would sell off insolvent S&Ls and their assets at breathtakingly subsidized prices to wealthy investors waiting in the wings, amounting to what Mayer (1990) aptly labels the nation's 'greatest-ever bank robbery'.

A disproportionate share of troubled S&Ls were located in the southwestern USA, particularly Texas. Long a region of rapid, unconstrained growth, the south-west enjoyed spectacular gains in real estate values in the late 1970s and early 1980s, particularly given rapid in-migration and rising global petroleum prices. Gorged by junk bonds and unfettered by deregulation, many S&Ls from around the USA invested heavily in commercial property in cities such as Houston, Dallas, Phoenix and dozens of other Sunbelt metropolises. When the price of oil dropped markedly in the 1980s and when the dimensions of real estate overinvestment and speculation became increasingly obvious, the same region suffered the most acutely. Because many of the insolvent S&Ls were located in this part of the nation, the federal government programme to sell them at subsidized prices became known informally as the 'Southwest Plan' (Sherrill, 1990). Thus, the bail-out of the S&Ls created a geography in its own right. Based on estimates by Edward Hill (see Rosenbaum, 1990), federal transfers from taxpayers to S&Ls favoured 13 states at the expense of 37 (figure 13.4). On a per capita basis, north-eastern and Midwestern states lost the most, suffering up to US $1237 per resident (in Connecticut), while south-western states gained the most (up to US $4775 per resident in Texas).

The Great Commercial Property Glut of the 1980s

In addition to commercial banks and savings and loans, several other institutions joined the rush to invest in commercial real estate. Mutual funds, which pooled together investments of small and large investors, became important actors not only on the stock market, but in commercial real estate as well. Similarly, pension funds jumped into the fray: TIAA, the college teachers' pension fund and the world's largest private one, has 43 per cent of its assets tied up in commercial real estate (Mahar, 1991). Despite their conservative investment history relative to banks, insurance companies also invested heavily in commercial property in the 1980s. The multiservice insurance company, Aetna, owned US $22.7 billion in commercial mortgages in 1991, equivalent to 36 per cent of its stockholders' equity (Mahar, 1991). While they were not as heavily involved in commercial real estate as banks, insurance companies' loans as a percentage of their net worth ranged as high as 44 per cent (table 13.2).

Table 13.2 Commercial real estate exposure of selected US insurers, 1990

	Total commercial loans (US $ billion)	As % of net assets
Prudential Life	28.8	26.9
Metropolitan Life	27.2	29.1
Teachers Ins. and Annuity	21.4	43.0
Equitable Life	13.0	35.9
J. Hancock Mutual Life	12.8	43.2
New York Life	6.9	17.9
Fidelity Mutual	0.5	44.5

Source: Mahar, 1991, p. 22.

The vast bulk of new commercial construction in the 1980s occurred in suburban areas (figure 13.5), part of the broader historical process that has created the highly commercialized, low density landscapes in which most Americans live and work. Despite much-heralded investments in central cities that initiated considerable gentrification, generally seen as indicative of Smith's (1982) 'rent gap' thesis, the predominant trend has been continued expansion at the urban periphery. In this context, the flood of construction of offices, hotels and shopping malls that washed over the United States in the 1980s contributed to the continued annihilation of agricultural land, the unbroken proliferation

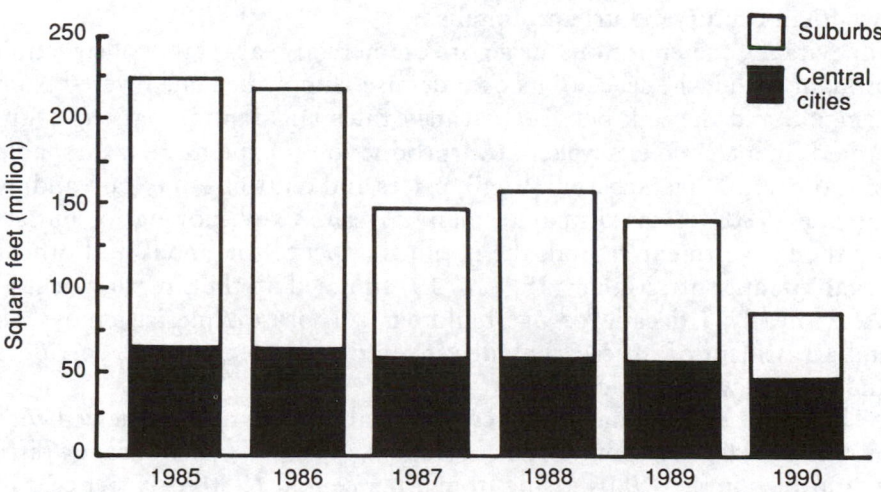

Figure 13.5 Suburban versus central city office construction, 1985–1990.
Source: after Mahar, 1991.

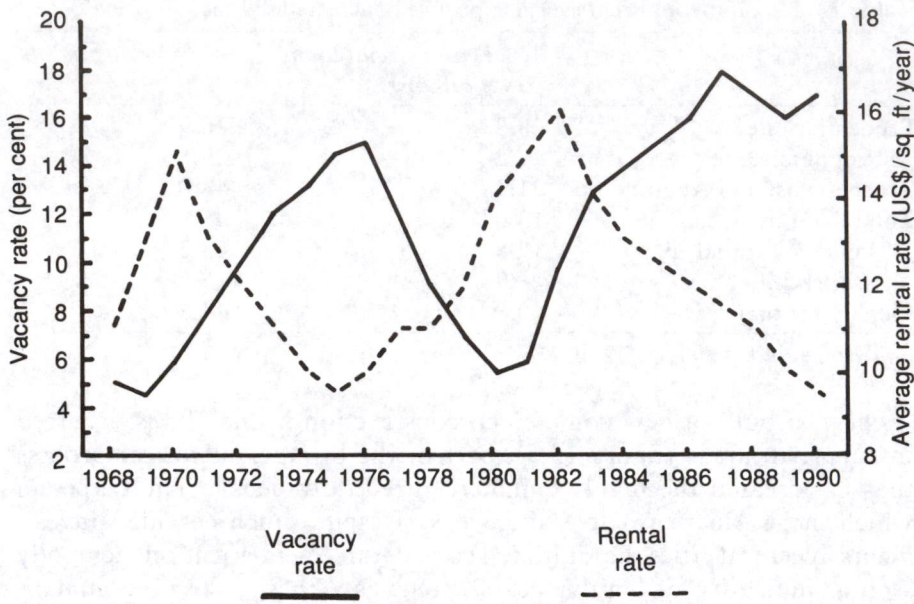

Figure 13.6   National office vacancy and rental rates, 1968–1990.
Source: after Port Authority of New York and New Jersey, 1991.

of small suburban municipalities and the uninterrupted migration of the middle class from the cores of metropolitan areas, all of which saw the proliferation of low density, multinucleated landscapes that define late twentieth-century US urban capitalism.

Inevitably, the enormous surge of commercial real estate construction brought with it the seeds of its own demise. Supply became severed from demand, and the link between vacancy rates and capital markets evaporated. In a classic example of overproduction (or the more fashionable Marxist term, 'overaccumulation'), prices and rents began to fall, and by the late 1980s, to the dismay of many investors still looking for outlets for their investment capital, the nation's appetite for hotels and offices began to taper off. Mahar (1991, p. 10) summed up the situation neatly: 'After nearly a decade of overbuilding, corporate America enjoys an embarrassment of offices, a hidden inventory of silent marble corridors and forlorn white cubicles.'

The signs of a national glut of commercial real estate were viewed with mounting alarm by commercial developers. National office vacancy rates quadrupled in the 1980s, rising from 5 per cent in 1980 to 17 per cent in 1990; meanwhile, real average rental rates plunged from US $16 per square foot in 1980 to less than US $10 in 1990 (figure 13.6). In some cities, the glut of office space climbed even higher. In Houston and Dallas, commercial vacancy rates in 1990 soared to 26.0 and 25.9 per

Table 13.3 Office market profiles of major US cities, 1990

City	Existing office space (million square feet)	Vacancy rate (%)	Median office rent (US $/square foot/year)
New York, NY	233.0	10.4	40.22
Chicago, IL	103.5	13.6	22.91
Washington, DC	63.4	10.0	31.70
San Francisco, CA	43.0	14.4	23.70
Boston, MA	35.8	8.9	36.46
Houston, TX	35.5	25.9	14.41
Dallas, TX	31.2	26.0	22.50
Pittsburgh, PA	28.8	15.5	20.63
Denver, CO	24.6	29.0	12.00
Los Angeles, CA	21.1	14.7	31.91
Seattle, WA	19.4	12.2	18.56
Phoenix, AZ	15.4	19.4	21.00
Detroit, MI	14.1	8.6	16.75
Portland, OR	13.0	20.2	17.50
Atlanta, GA	11.8	14.9	20.85
Miami, FL	11.6	28.0	26.80
Hartford, CT	7.4	7.2	25.14
Louisville, KY	6.3	12.9	17.09
Nashville, TN	5.1	17.0	19.27

Source: Port Authority of New York and New Jersey, 1991.

cent, respectively, Miami reached 28.0 per cent and in Denver they climbed to a near-catastrophic 29.0 per cent (table 13.3).

This overcapacity was highly unevenly distributed; office vacancy rates in 1990, for example, were considerably higher in Texas, Oklahoma and Louisiana – all of which had been severely hit by the collapse in the global price of petroleum – than they were elsewhere (figure 13.7). Geographically, the depression in real estate took the form of a 'rolling recession', starting with the 'oil patch' states of Texas, Louisiana and Oklahoma, moving north to New York and New England, and finally leaping across to the Los Angeles and San Francisco markets in California (Mahar, 1991), which were already depressed by reductions in military expenditures.

As commercial rents began to fall, investors saw dangerous drops in the revenues needed to cover their costs. Banks and savings and loans saw their non-performing loans rise alarmingly; in desperate attempts to compensate, many reduced their stock prices and dividends dramatically. In short, the causal chain that began with finance and ended with commercial property markets had been decisively reversed; by the late 1980s, the tail of excessive supply of commercial property began to wag the dog of investment capital. The overproduction of offices and

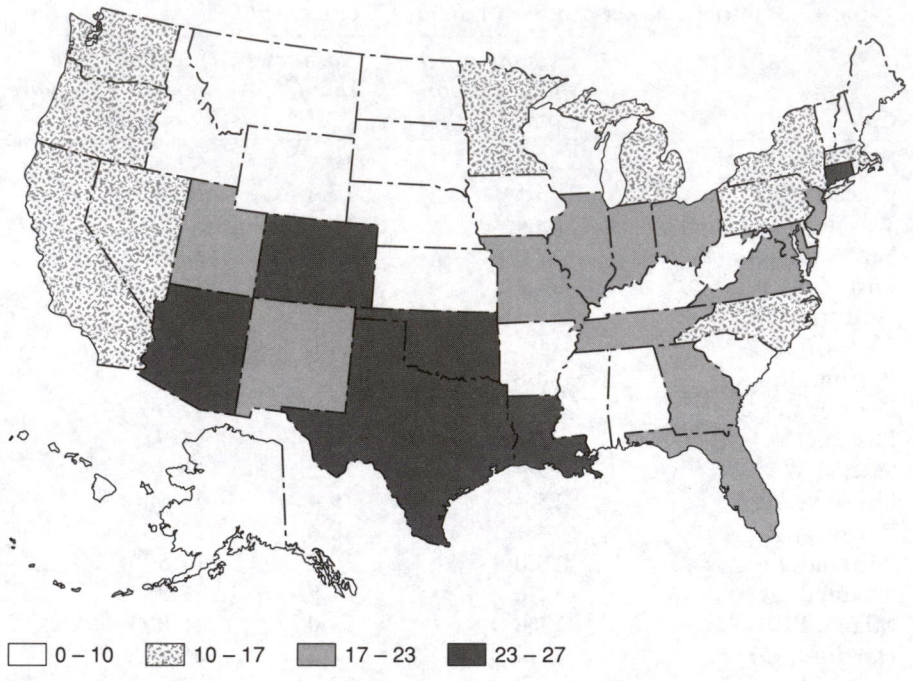

Figure 13.7   Distribution of office vacancy rates by state, 1990 (percentages).
Source: after Mahar, 1991.

shopping malls also had important effects on local governments: faced with a relentless erosion of their property tax base brought on by the drop in commercial property values, many were forced to increase local income and sales taxes just as federal taxes were declining.

Concluding Comments

Beginning in the 1970s, a widespread shift in production systems became increasingly evident in many industrialized nations, including the introduction of flexible production systems, the globalization of markets and sub-contracting networks, and changes in the structure and regulation of finance. At the same time, there occurred an equally powerful shift in public policy, manifested most dramatically at the national level in the post-Keynesian state and at the local level through accelerated local entrepreneurialism centred on the uncritical adoption of growth agendas (Harvey, 1989; Leitner, 1990; Gaffikin and Warf, 1993). It is within this broad context that the orgy of commercial lending and construction that occurred in the 1980s must be viewed. Deregulation, in particular, disrupted the stable division of markets (commercial banks and commercial loans, savings and loans and residential loans) that had existed since the emergence of the welfare state of the 1930s. Faced with low returns in their traditional markets (e.g. residential real estate), many investors, flush with excess capital (e.g. from junk bonds, pension and mutual funds), jumped headlong into the more lucrative market of commercial real estate. As a result, a surge of investor-driven construction projects sprouted up around the nation, actively abetted by local governments eager to attract growth-generating investments.

These comments point to three necessary reformulations in the theory of commercial property markets. In the first instance, it is readily evident that the enormously increased levels of liquidity and mobility that occurred in financial markets in the 1980s effectively dissolved the linkages between local capital and local property: rents were evidently no longer determined by locally created differentials, but on a national and international basis as financial institutions were freed from legal obligations to serve their local communities and began to invest within much broader markets. Second, within the context of reconfigured financial relations, commercial property has acquired exchange values far in excess of their previous levels, reducing the role of use values in land use deliberations and heightening the much underemphasized speculative aspects (Haila, 1988). Third, it is clear from the surge of investment-driven construction that swept the USA in the 1980s that finance capital is not some passive actor in the construction of landscapes, but an active participant with a logic of its own. Such observations reveal the bankruptcy of neoclassical economic theory and the myth that land markets unproblematically equilibrate supply and demand to form some Pareto-optimal equilibrium.

In this respect, commercial real estate markets reflect the endemic characteristics of capitalism in general: periodic overinvestment, oversupply and depressed earnings that define the inherently cyclical nature of capital accumulation. Indeed, from a historical perspective, the commercial boom of the 1980s is only the latest chapter in a long history of chapters. Having created one 'spatial fix' (Harvey, 1985) from the 1950s to the 1970s, American capitalists sought to create another in the 1980s. In the future, this process will surely play itself out again, undoubtedly in unexpected ways. In the process, geographies are made and destroyed, urban landscapes are created and recreated, and people's lives are uprooted. The task of critical social theory, then, is to illuminate the fundamentally political nature of this process, the winners and losers, the state strategies that unequally distribute the costs and benefits, and to articulate grounds for local action.

References

Budd, L. and Whimster, S. (eds) (1992) *Global Finance and Urban Living: a Study of Metropolitan Change*. London: Routledge.

Checkoway, B. (1980) Large builders, federal housing programmes, and post-war suburbanization. *International Journal of Urban and Regional Research*, 4, 21–44.

Downs, A. (1985) *The Revolution in Real Estate Finance*. Washington, DC: Brookings Institution.

Gaffikin, F. and Warf, B. (1993) Urban policy and the post-Keynesian state in the United Kingdom and the United States. *International Journal of Urban and Regional Research*, 17, 67–84.

Haila, A. (1988) Land as a financial asset: the theory of urban rent as a mirror of economic transformation. *Antipode*, 20, 79–101.

Harvey, D. (1974) Class-monopoly rent, finance capital and the urban revolution. *Regional Studies*, 8, 239–55.

Harvey, D. and Chatterjee, L. (1974) Absolute rent and the structuring of space by financial institutions. *Antipode*, 6, 22–36.

Harvey, D. (1985) *The Urbanization of Capital*. Baltimore: Johns Hopkins University Press.

Harvey, D. (1989) From managerialism to entrepreneurialism: the transformation in urban governance in late capitalism. *Geografiska Annaler*, 71, 3–17.

Holly, B. (1987) Regulation, competition, and technology: the restructuring of the US commercial banking system. *Environment and Planning A*, 19, 633–52.

Leitner, H. (1990) Cities in pursuit of economic growth: the local state as entrepreneur. *Political Geography Quarterly*, 9, 146–70.

Logan, J. and Molotch, H. (1987) *Urban Fortunes: the Political Economy of Place*. Berkeley: University of California Press.

Mahar, M. (1991) The great collapse: commercial real estate is on the skids across the nation. *Barron's*, 22 July, 10–26.

Mayer, M. (1990) *The Greatest-ever Bank Robbery: the Collapse of the Savings and Loan Industry*. New York: Scribner's.

Pantalone, C. and Platt, M. (1987) Predicting commercial bank failure since deregulation. *New England Economic Review*, July/August, 37–47.

Pizzo, S., Fricker, M. and Muolo, P. (1990) *Inside Job: the Looting of America's Savings and Loans*. New York: McGraw-Hill.

Port Authority of New York and New Jersey (1991) *Regional Perspectives: the 1991 Mid-year Report on the NY-NJ Economy*. New York: Port Authority of New York and New Jersey.

Quint, M. and Freed, J. (1991) Bank losses worst in 50 years, but no danger to system is seen. *New York Times*, 17 February, 1, 12.

Rosenbaum, D. (1990) Southwest to get economic benefits in savings bailout. *New York Times*, 25 June, 1, C5.

Sbragia, A. (1988) Finance capital and the city. In M. Gottdiener (ed.), *Cities in Stress: a New Look at the Urban Crisis*. Beverly Hills: Sage, 116–49.

Scott, A. (1980) *The Urban Land Nexus and the State*. London: Pion.

Sherrill, R. (1990) The looting decade: S&Ls, big banks and other triumphs of capitalism. *The Nation*, 251, 589–622.

Smith, N. (1982) Gentrification and uneven development. *Economic Geography*, 58, 139–55.

Thrift, N. (1987) The fixers: the urban geography of international commercial capital. In J. Henderson and M. Castells (eds), *Global Restructuring and Territorial Development*. Beverly Hills: Sage, 203–330.

14

On the Social and Cultural Determinants of International Financial Centres: the Case of the City of London

Nigel Thrift

Introduction

For the past eight years, I have been working on the history and geography of international financial centres, and especially of the City of London (e.g. Thrift, 1987, 1990; Thrift et al., 1987; Thrift and Leyshon, 1992; Amin and Thrift, 1992). In this chapter, I want both to summarize and to reflect upon this work. In particular, I want to ask – and give some tentative answers to – two linked questions that seem to me to be the most pressing in considering the future of international financial centres like the City, a future that is often depicted as tentative and insecure (London Planning and Advisory Council, 1990; City of London Research Project, 1992).

First of all, I want to ask whether there is any need for international financial centres like the City of London in a time when electronic communication is becoming so sophisticated. In other words, might a good part of their functions simply melt away into a generalized 'space of flows' (Castells, 1989), leaving money obligations to speed their way along the cables and through the aether, to and from many different terminals located in many different places? Certainly, this is the apocalyptic vision of the future conjured up by authors like O'Brien (1992). O'Brien writes of an 'end to geography', or rather a state of affairs in which 'geographical location no longer matters in finance, or matters much less than hitherto' (p. 1).

This chapter was written while I was a Fellow at the Netherlands Institute of Advanced Study. I would like to thank the Institute for its hospitality and its facilities.

Second, I want to ask whether the social and cultural structures of international financial centres like the City make any contribution to their success or failure. Do the social make-up and the various traditions of the City of London or Wall Street make any *economic* difference to their functioning or are they simply a decorative filigree?

These are not easy questions to forge answers to because the answers lie scattered across many literatures. Thus the first part of the chapter is an attempt to identify and summarize the literatures on which the chapter will draw for sustenance. In the second part of the chapter, I will then tap these literatures as part of an attempt to provide a general account of the locational determinants of contemporary international financial centres. Finally, in the third part of the chapter, I will turn to the specific example of the City of London pre and post the 1960s as both an illustration and an extension of the arguments made previously.

Six Literatures

In this chapter, I will be drawing on six main literatures in order to explain why international financial centres have not melted away into an electronic space of flows and why their social and cultural structures have become a more and more important determinant of their economic success. Each of these literatures has three characteristics in common. The first is that they try to problematize 'the economic' as a category and as a set of practices. The second is that they lie at the boundaries between accepted social science and humanities disciplines. Finally, they show signs of mutual convergence in that they are all beginning to stress many of the same themes.

The first literature is the so-called 'new international political economy', an attempt to link international politics, international economics, domestic (national) politics and domestic (national) economics together, in the belief that the distinctions between the economic and the political and the international and the national have become increasingly tenuous (e.g. Strange, 1986, 1988; Murphy and Tooze, 1991). In particular, this literature has been concerned to show that the construction of a capitalist class has increasingly become a worldwide task, which in turn has begun to make it possible to talk of 'transnational elites' that have attempted to construct systems of global economic guidance and money (Baker, 1987) that can only be maintained through more or less constant social interaction (e.g. Gill, 1990; Overbeek, 1990). Old ideas that a capitalist class could easily articulate its interests – because of the profit principle – have been replaced by notions of the active construction of interests by various elites that depend upon different forms of knowledge accumulation (and the 'epistemic communities' that generate them and 'critical readings' of this knowledge). The exact status of these transnational elites is, not surprisingly, a matter of considerable debate (e.g. Drainville, 1993), but that such elites exist, set agendas and need to be studied seems difficult to deny.

The second literature I want to draw on can be related to the first one largely through the work of Karl Polanyi: on high finance as the social linchpin of the hundred years' peace and on the 'social embeddedness' of economic processes in structural frameworks (Polanyi, 1944, 1957; Mendell and Salee, 1991). This is the so-called 'new economic sociology' or 'new sociology of economic life', with its emphasis on markets, power and culture (e.g. Granovetter, 1985; Swedberg, 1987; Zukin and Dimaggio, 1990; Granovetter and Swedberg, 1992). Economic sociology was revived in the early 1960s and has come to fruition since, based around three propositions (Granovetter and Swedberg, 1992): that economic action is a form of social action that is no different from other forms of human behaviour; that economic action is socially structured ('embedded') in networks and institutions; and that economic networks and institutions are social constructions of reality built without any necessary regard for efficiency but with regard to struggles over interests, a particular historical trajectory ('path dependence'), various traditions, gender, ethnicity and many other social variables. In other words, 'economic institutions are constructed by mobilisation of resources through social networks' (Granovetter and Swedberg, 1992, p. 18). Inspired by events like the clear difficulties of attempts to effect a great transformation in Eastern Europe over a short space of time, the EC 1992 Single Market project and the North America Free Trade Area, the new economic sociology radically questions the idea of markets as abstract, self-regulating entities and sees them instead as the result of long and long drawn-out processes of institution-building that must also incorporate prevailing relations of power and cultural formations.

I will also, therefore, draw upon the cultural studies literature. Cultural studies is, of course, experiencing an unprecedented international boom (e.g. Grossberg et al., 1992). To some extent, this boom can be explained by changes in the international political economy and, most especially, globalization. To some extent it is explained by the increasing importance of 'mass' media, accompanied by changes in the nature of audiences and technologies that in turn have privileged the production and consumption of signs and images. To some extent it is a function of the diffusion of the post-structuralist motifs of writers like Barthes, Foucault and Derrida. Whatever the reason, this boom has brought the ideas of textuality and discursivity to the fore. In this chapter, *textuality* is used to refer to the expanding world of texts and images and their associated techniques of reading and writing. More generally, *discursivity* refers to the process whereby the interpretation of texts and images by producers and consumers, through talk, and writing, and reading, is wrapped up in *narratives*, stories that construct 'what counts as a thing, what counts as true/false, and what it makes sense to do' (Dreyfus and Hall, 1992, p. 83). In other words, discursivity involves what we write and talk about, how we write and talk about it and how we come to a judgement about what it is good or bad to write and talk about.

A fourth literature that I will draw upon consists of recent work on reflexive modernization. Writers like Giddens (1991), Beck (1992) and Lash (1993) have sketched the outlines of a modern world that depends upon the presence of monitoring–learning systems and the knowledge generated by them, knowledge which is continually in the process of being revised. This new world has come about, among other reasons, because of the decline of traditional social structures (like class and the nuclear family), and a consequent move to more individualized societies that provide a greater degree of freedom to people to shape their biographies, because of the rise of media networks, which more easily allow people to monitor their place in the world, to see themselves as others see them, because of a burgeoning cosmopolitanism (Hannerz, 1992) and because of the increasing presumption that societies consist of thinking individuals working in and dependent upon 'expert systems' or 'knowledge structures' (thus, for example, the notion of 'reflexive accumulation': Lash and Urry, 1993). Most particularly, modern life depends upon an increasingly reflexive subjectivity, that is upon the deepening of the self through concerted work on the self, both as a project in itself and as a part of an increase in the learning capacity of networks and institutions.

A further literature that I will draw upon both influenced and is influenced by the previous one. This is the new ethnomethodological literature on social interaction in business (e.g. Boden, 1993; Boden and Molotch, 1993). This literature emphasizes the degree to which 'talk' (understood here in the broadest sense) plays a crucial role in economic systems. In particular, certain kinds of business talk, especially those involving a degree of uncertainty, still depend upon face-to-face interaction because of the way in which they allow particular kinds of communication and negotiation to take place (including non-verbal interaction), which are difficult or impossible to communicate or negotiate at a distance (for example, one study found that top management in business organizations spend 50 per cent of their time in face-to-face meetings). There is, in other words, a 'compulsion to proximity' in much business conduct, which it is difficult to surmount because

> features of co-present interaction make it fundamental to social order, both local and global. The immediacy and inherent indexicality of all human existence means that the fine, fleeting, yet essentially social moments of everyday life anchor and articulate the modern macro-order. Through the trust, commitment, and detailed understandings made possible in situations of co-presence, the essential time-space distanciation of modern society is achieved. (Boden and Molotch, 1993, p. 34)

There is one more literature that I want to draw upon. It is important to note that economics has itself begun to consider the ways in which the economy, and most especially markets, are socially constructed through at least three approaches. First, there are some of the more recent examples of the 'new institutional economics'. These have begun to move away from purely microeconomic foundations (e.g. Williamson, 1975). Second, there is a growing body of work on bubbles, fads and herd behaviour in markets (e.g. Camerer, 1989), which is part of the increasing amount of research on financial markets as inherently unstable entities (e.g. Goodhart, 1976). Finally, there is a small but growing body of work on the rhetoric of economics, which conceptualizes economics as the outcome of and as itself forms of rhetoric (e.g. McCloskey, 1985). Each of these approaches begins to problematize the idea of economic fundamentals and to point towards the idea of economics as a social and cultural construction that relies upon specific forms of textuality and discursivity.

These literatures are particularly important in hunting down the determinants of modern international financial centres because, as I want to argue, they stress social and cultural determinants of economic processes that have become increasingly important. In particular, the work in each of these literatures on money and markets is of vital importance to the understanding of international financial centres. Thus new international political economy stresses the importance of transnational financial elites and the weight of the task of maintaining these elites as relatively coherent social entities with relatively coherent ideologies (e.g. Marceau, 1990). The new economic sociology points to the importance of financial markets as socially constructed institutions and dealing in money as a social and cultural affair (e.g. Adler and Adler, 1984).

Cultural studies emphasizes how, as money has progressively dematerialized and become simply bits of information (Cencini, 1984), so the potential for discursive interpretation of money, and markets in money, has become greater and greater. Further, cultural studies makes it possible to emphasize the growing importance of textuality in this task of discursive interpretation. The literatures on reflexive modernization and talk amplify this emphasis on discursivity through their focus on subjectivity, the fashioning of the self, face-work and talk as vital components of modern expert systems of 'reflexive accumulation' (Lash and Urry, 1993). Finally, economics has also begun to be caught up in these kinds of themes, both through an emphasis on markets as permanently unstable, constantly rocked by fads and bubbles, and through an understanding of economics as itself a form of rhetoric bound up in the construction of money and markets.

No doubt other literatures could be called on to make the point that money and markets are not abstract and abstracted technical affairs, for example those from anthropology (e.g. Crump, 1990), social history or economic psychology (e.g. Cheal, 1988). However, I hope that the point is now made that money and markets are socially and culturally constructed and that the tasks of social and cultural construction may well be becoming more rather than less important.

In the next section I want to apply the insights gleaned from these six literatures to the case of the locational determinants of international financial centres. Quite clearly, this is a very general exercise, both in the fact that it stretches across many centres and in the fact that it takes in many different kinds of financial activity. There are clear variations in the importance of these determinants by centre and by type of activity. For example, banking is an industry that is much more clearly dependent upon social and cultural factors like expertise and contracts than foreign exchange, which is chiefly concerned with level of demand and the availability of associated markets like financial options on futures (Eccles and Crane, 1988; ter Hart and Piersma, 1990). However, such variations are to be expected and they are highlighted in the later section on the City of London.

The Locational Determinants of International Financial Centres

It can be argued that international financial centres consist of three main forms of 'actant' (Haraway, 1990), namely business organizations, markets and the discursive practices that institute them and define the borders within which they are regarded as effective. These actants are held together (if that is the right phrase) by social networks, which are often class, gender and ethnically specific, and by the 'flow' of money. Clearly a number of locational determinants of international financial centres are effectively exogenous, such as government regulation. However, recent studies (e.g. Davis, 1990; Cobham, 1992) suggest that these exogenous factors are rather less important as indices of a financial centre's success than endogenous factors. These endogenous determinants of the success or failure of international financial centres can be grouped under headings that relate to the chief characteristics of each of the three different kinds of actant described above.

Business Organizations in International Financial Centres

Business organizations in international financial centres are diverse and can often change their structure and function. However, as Eccles and Crane (1985) point out, because of their emphasis on marketing and on client bases, business organizations in international financial centres do tend to share a number of characteristics in common, of which they list five.

First, much of the production of financial products and services takes place at the boundaries of the firms. Firms tend to be client- rather than task-centred and to rely on repeat business. Second, firms tend to be flattened and non-hierarchical. Responsibility is often diffuse and vague with results coming from the efforts of small teams of relationship and product specialists. 'Each deal is unique' is a common cry (Eccles and Crane, 1988). Third, as a matter of course, firms need to cooperate with one another as well as compete, for example in syndicated lending or the placement of securities. Fourth, firms often find it difficult to judge their performance accurately. They can often only be sure of how they are doing through comparison with other firms' successes and failures. Thus market share is often important for firms simply as a way of getting to know what's going on. Fifth, it is difficult for financial services firms in international financial centres to build up the equivalent of inventories to buffer the firm. The result is that the employees of these firms have to be constantly 'on the go' to find new business. They must be able to respond swiftly to clients, and they must be able to work in a crisis mode, dropping everything to complete a task on time or to get work.

These shared characteristics already point to two important corollaries. First, in general, these firms must be sociable. Contacts are crucially important in generating and maintaining a flow of business and information about business. 'Who you know' is, in this sense, part of what you know. It is a part of the skill base of many employees and, in turn, part of the competitive edge of the firm: 'relationship management' is a vital task for both employees and firms. Second, this hunger for contacts is easier to satisfy if contacts are concentrated, are proximate. When contacts are bunched together they are easier to gain access to, and swift access at that. Furthermore, the possibility of informal, unplanned contacts, which may lead to unlooked for but very welcome new business, will also increase markedly (Cobham, 1992).

Quite clearly, this hunger for contacts has increased over the past twenty years, most particularly because of the move from one-to-one relationships between firms and clients to something nearer to business done on a competitive deal-by-deal basis as part of a search for cost savings by clients. The result is that clients are more 'transactional', and so are firms. This has led to greater uncertainty and a decline of trust, which in turn has meant that firms must try harder to get to know more people and to get to know them better. Relationship management is now crucial.

Markets in International Financial Centres

Like business organizations, markets in international financial centres are diverse. They can be primary or secondary. They can be organized as partnerships, or companies, or syndicates. They can trade electronically or through open outcry. However, whatever the exact cause, these financial markets do have three related characteristics in common.

First, they are usually very large. Indeed, one of the key determinants of success of an international financial centre is that its markets are sufficiently large to be continually liquid, making it easy for investors to enter and leave at will. The larger a market becomes the more socially differentiated it is likely to be. That is, it is more likely to consist of social 'micro-networks' of buyers and sellers, whose effect on price-setting can sometimes be marked. 'While under ideal-typical conditions large numbers and growth create a competitive and minimally differentiated market the opposite occurs in actual market situations' (Baker, 1984, p. 804).

Second, financial markets are based on rapid dissemination of information (Terleckji and Robinson's 'knowledge in a hurry'), which, as it is disseminated, may well lead to major market movements (Adler and Adler, 1984). But this information is often vague, ambiguous and difficult to interpret. 'One of the reasons people will often act differently in the market in response to a single piece of news is the often confusing over-abundance of conflicting interpretive schemes' (Adler and Adler, 1984, p. 13). Market participants are indeed forced to rely on a combination of texts, analytical schemes (e.g. chartists), social networks and influential opinion leaders (e.g. popular gurus) to generate interpretive schemes, leading not only to an uneven spread of information about markets but also to an uneven spread of interpretations.

Third, many financial markets are speculative and highly volatile. The speed of response needed to track and interpret these markets therefore almost demands being in a social network whether that network is some of the other traders on a trading floor or contact elsewhere. 'What's going on' is a question that, more often than not, has to be answered and responded to quickly.

Again, as with the case of organizations, there are the two obvious corollaries to these characteristics: the twin needs for sociability and proximity.

The Culture of International Financial Centres

The culture of international financial centres is often summarized in the phrase 'information, expertise, contacts'. That is, the need for information, for the expertise that allows that information to be interpreted and for the social contacts that generate trust, information, interpretive schemes – and business – is paramount. However, what is particularly important to note here is that it seems likely that these cultural aspects of international financial centres are actually increasing in importance. This increase in the importance of cultural aspects can be indexed in three related ways. First, international financial centres receive, send and interpret increasing amounts of information, especially, but not by any means exclusively, textual information. Second, international financial centres are the fount of increasing amounts of expertise, the result of a complex division of labour embodied in the skills of the workforce, in machines, in texts and so on. Third, international financial centres depend on contacts and the conduct of contact has become increasingly reflexive as trust based on common social background has been replaced by a more active construction of trust which involves working up and worrying about relationships. In other words, international financial centres are 'interactional proving grounds' (Boden, 1993) where there is often no set script with which to conduct business, and in which deals must therefore be worked out that will involve complex understandings, informal trade-offs and anticipated tensions. Such deals still require face-to-face contact.

These points may be put in another way (Amin and Thrift, 1992). Increasingly, the culture of international financial centres is based upon three correlates of information, expertise and contacts. The first of these is that international financial centres are centres of representation. They are the chief points of surveillance and scripting for the global financial services industry. They are where the stories are. Much of the world's financial press operates from these centres, so does much research and other analysis, information processing and so on. Concentration of these information-related industries in a few centres has the advantage that the international financial services industry can watch and script itself more easily. These centres are, in other words, centres of discursive *authority*, able to describe what constitutes 'news' and how that 'news' is interpreted.

The second correlate concerns expertise. Increasingly, international financial centres are, by virtue of their permanent place in the financial services 'knowledge structure' (Strange, 1988) or 'expert systems' (Giddens, 1990, 1991), able to act as proving grounds for product innovations. An important characteristic of financial services products is that product innovation and marketing are often closely tied together and that a product will not take off unless it is aggressively marketed in its early stages, usually to a few quite specific people in large client institutions (for example, in merchant banking 80 to 90 per cent of new products are the result of working with customers: Eccles and Crane, 1988). International financial centres allow these new, usually customized products to be evolved and tested quickly and efficiently since there are sufficient expertise and contacts that can be combined with sufficient liquidity and placement power. More than this, the availability in one place of representatives of many investment networks and companies means that products can be easily customized (e.g. many derivatives).

The third correlate concerns contacts. International financial centres have become centres of social interaction on an expanded scale. As a result of the expansion of transportation, and especially the massive expansion of business air travel, they have become the *meeting places* for the global corporate networks of the financial services industry, places that see a large and constant throughflow of visitors, as well as workers from other centres and people in each centre simply meeting and talking with each other. They function as these meeting places for a number of reasons: first, because of their accessibility to markets and firms in both research and electronic space; second, because of their knowledge base; third, because of the need to tap into the social networks that have evolved in them; fourth, because of a need for places from which to watch the competition; fifth, because the more complex deals are difficult to do at a distance, requiring, as they often do, the building of trust; sixth, and finally, because of their symbolic value as places associated with finance.

These correlates will of course vary in their intensity from product to product and centre to centre. For example, some financial activities like making primary issues or secondary trading in heterogeneous products require more trust and confidence on the part of customers and firms and therefore are likely to be more contact intensive (table 14.1) (Davis, 1990; Cobham, 1992). Again, some financial activities are more tightly controlled by law and more reliant on formal contracts than others.

Dynamic Economies

It is important to observe that international financial centres benefit substantially from so-called *external economies* of scale (or 'size externalities'), which occur simply because of the size of the concentration of industry; a firm's productivity (and profitability) 'directly benefits from the proximity of competitors or firms engaged in related activities' (Grilli, 1989, p. 391), from the presence of others.

Table 14.1 Sensitivity to physical proximity in international banking transactions

Low	Medium	High
Interbank payments	Trade-related finance	Mergers and acquisitions
Foreign exchange dealing	Participation in issuing	Management buy-outs
Small securities trades		Portfolio management for investors
International cash management for corporate customers		Swaps
Participation in syndicates for corporate customers		Large securities trades
		Lead management of syndicates

Source: Ter Hart and Piersma, 1990.

These economies tend to be *dynamic*, that is they increase as the number of firms, markets and discourses increases. A number of these dynamic economies can be thought of. First, the more firms there are, the more the fixed costs of running financial markets, like settlement systems, payment systems and document transportation systems, can be shared. Second, the concentration of markets attracts both greater information turnover and greater liquidity. Third, the greater the concentration of expertise the more likely it may be that product innovations will be sparked off. Fourth, the benefit of being able to make contacts rises with the number of possible contacts. Fifth, the concentration of financial firms and markets induces a similar concentration of firms supplying ancillary services, such as accounting, legal and computer programming services, thereby reducing the overall cost of these services. Sixth, a pool of skilled labour will be at hand. Seventh, and finally, the reputation of the centre as a place to do business attracts more business and more new firms. Further, the possibility of decline is at last warded off by the sunk costs associated with any centre: such costs as those associated with construction of buildings, installation of technology, build-up of a knowledge base, training systems for labour and construction of relationships with clients. These costs are quite clearly extensive.

Thus, to summarize, it is at least debatable that international financial centres will melt away into an electronic space of flows. Indeed, the volume and speed of such flows may make it even more imperative to construct places that act as centres of comprehension.

The next sections attempt to apply the insights gleaned above to the case of the City of London. I will argue that whereas the social and cultural structure of the City has always been quite particular, and as a result has clearly had some degree of influence on the City's economic well-being over and above external factors like government regulation, of late these social and cultural aspects have become, in a changed form, rather *more* important than before even as they have become less particular to the City.

In describing the City of London, it is important to note that the City is not a static object of study. In particular, the character of the City has varied over the course of its history in four significant ways. First, it has consisted of a differing mix of industries over time, which, to an extent, have had different social and cultural structures. For example, Michie (1992) distinguishes over time between a commercial or trading City, a credit or banking City, a capital market City, and a client or financial services City, each of which has shown some degree of dominance over time. Second, the size of firms in the City has varied over time. Until quite recently, the size distribution of firms in the City was overwhelmingly biased towards small firms but this has now changed. Third, it has varied over space. Until after the Second World War, the financial City of banking, capital markets and financial services occupied only a small part of the 'square mile', while it is only in recent times that the City has outgrown this boundary. Fourth, the numbers working in the City have fluctuated from 170,000 in 1866 to a peak of 500,000 in 1935, to about 300,000 in 1992 (even these numbers are difficult to rely on, since they depend upon what industries are counted as City industries).

All these comments made, it is still possible, and indeed conventional, to study the City as a relatively coherent whole and, in turn, to make a break between the 'old' City that existed before the late 1950s and the 'new' City that existed thereafter. The break takes in the point at which the City casts off the gloom of a moribund wartime and postwar trough and becomes a dynamic international financial centre again. The break also captures the point at which many social and cultural aspects of the City change decisively.

The City of London Pre-1960s

Before the 1960s, the City's power to reproduce itself rested on four foundation stones. The first of these was simply the City's relationship with the British state, which was essentially 'meso-corporatist' (Cawson, 1986). It consisted largely of a self-contained system of collective governance, with the Bank of England acting as a buffer against pluralist regulatory systems and politics. According to Moran (1991, p. 63), 'representation and regulation were fused'. As Michie (1992) makes clear, this statement is something of an exaggeration, since at various times the British state was in fact able to intervene in the economy in ways which were undoubtedly to the detriment of the City. However, it makes a valuable point. The second foundation stone of the City's power to reproduce itself consisted of a 'strong' social structure based upon highly visible class, gender and ethnic divisions, which in turn generated strong senses of identity, transgression of which was a potentially serious social and/or cultural offence.

In essence, until the 1960s, the City was composed of three relatively distinct class strata. At the top of the pile were the directors and partners of the numerous city firms (see, for example, Cassis, 1987). In the past, these directors and partners have often been seen as being drawn into the landed gentry over the course of the nineteenth century, their collective identity becoming increasingly bound up in aristocratic mores and practices. Such a depiction of a kind of mimetic aristocracy is now regarded with increasing suspicion, for at least four reasons. First, most studies have been based only on patterns of intermarriage with the aristocracy by partners and directors of merchant banks. Certainly, these partners and directors were both influential and visible in the City (for example, sitting on the Court of the Bank of England or, later, on the Accepting Houses Committee), but they were hardly the only partners and directors in the City. Second, these studies tend either to ignore or to play down the comparatively late arrival of a 'labouring aristocracy' (Cannadine, 1990) in the City. For example, the first lord only entered the Stock Exchange in 1865. These labouring aristocrats were often driven to the City by penurious circumstances and they were often regarded with some suspicion. Third, many studies have overstated the degree to which the City was impressed by the aristocracy. Recent research suggests that many were not, regarding the aristocracy as lazy and effete. Interestingly, the strongest patterns of intermarriage in the City were *between* banking families, suggesting that economic motives were much stronger than social ones. Fourth, previous studies have assumed that as city partners and directors took on the trappings of wealth (like country houses, hunting and so on) they interpreted them in the same way as aristocrats, but the evidence suggests that they often saw these trappings in more clearly economic terms: country houses were seen as investments, hunting as a means of obtaining new business contacts and so on. Current opinion on the class status of the partners and directors of the city is probably best summarized by Harris and Thane (1984, p. 83), who describe them as 'a distinct stratum, combining elements of bourgeois and aristocratic cultures but reducible to neither. It was a culture that (despite the trappings of landownership) was urban rather than rural, functionally progressive rather than reactionary, and combined grand dynastic aspiration with an unpretentious devotion to the ethic of work.' This description became, if anything, increasingly accurate after the professionalization of British society in the late nineteenth century (Perkin, 1989), with its systems of public schools, universities and so on, which offered the potential for City partners and directors to construct their own common background. Thus, through the nineteenth and into the twentieth century the proportion of partners and directors going through the mill of public schools, Oxbridge and so on gradually increased.

Of course, the directors and partners were not the only class stratum in the City. Increasingly, over time, they were joined by a professional and managerial middle class as a result of three main processes. The first of these was the expanding system of professional institutions described above, and the credentials that resulted from them. The second process was the increasing demand for managers as firms increased in size. There were managers in the City in the 1830s but the chief influx was after the middle of the nineteenth century, as the retail banks and insurance companies increased markedly in size. The third process was an increasing demand for professionals, especially from the late nineteenth century. Indeed, some parts of the City suffered skill shortages because of lack of appropriate professionals (e.g. actuaries).

There was one final class stratum that also needs to be noted. This was the clerical labour force. By 1866, commercial clerks in the City numbered 17,225 (20 per cent of all commercial clerks in Britain). At first, clerks tended to come from relatively elevated backgrounds, but after the 1860s working-class clerks became more common. Even so, clerical wages were relatively high compared with the rest of the country, but reduced over time, probably reaching their lowest point in the 1950s. Clerks worked in diverse conditions. In the private banks, conditions were often paternalist. By contrast, in the developing stock banks and insurance companies, they tended to be more regimented.

The social atmosphere of the City was not based only on class, of course. It was characterized by other divides as well. Of these, the most important was gender. The City was a classically 'homosocial' (Kanter, 1976) environment, based on the interaction of class and a severe form of masculinity that produced what, in retrospect, seem like stifling forms of masculine identity based on quaint uniforms, exact dress codes (thus items like brown suits, check suits and suede shoes were regarded with horror), various boyish market rituals and japes (particularly in the Stock Exchange, where the cry of '1400' would go up when a stranger was spotted on the floor and where throwing tickertape up into the balcony and setting fire to colleagues' newspapers were regarded as the height of wit), heavy drinking and the like. Of course, to a degree such forms of identity were only exaggerations of upper and upper middle class British Society at large, but it is difficult not to come to the conclusion that their weight was sufficient to have produced a distinctive City patina. Certainly in the early 1960s Sampson (1965, p. 394) found the atmosphere stuffy and uninspiring. 'Nearly everyone wears a dark suit and carries an umbrella, and discount brokers and gilt-edged stock-brokers still wear top hats. The restaurants are crowded with rows of pale faced, blackcoated men.'

The closed effect of this environment was considerably reinforced by a network of men-only social institutions that functioned inside and outside work and that were both mechanisms of social regulation and ways of extending contact networks and, by implication, trust. These social institutions were diverse. They included institutions with formal membership requirements like the City Corporation, the Livery Companies, the London clubs, Freemasons' lodges and so on. They also included more general social arenas of which the pubs and chophouses were perhaps the most important. All these institutions helped to dim the distinction between work and leisure: indeed, in a sense, for many a 'City man', work and leisure both involved mixing with the same round of people.

The effect of this homosocial environment was also to exclude women from the City's labour force. Women first made an appearance as City workers in this forbidding environment only in 1872, as clerks at the Prudential Insurance Company (only daughters of 'professional men' were allowed to apply). By 1890, there were 200 female clerks at the

Prudential. Then, in 1894, the Bank of England hired twenty-five female clerks, but, again, the conditions were strict: the women had to be nominated by directors of the Bank and they had to pass entrance examinations (in other words they had to be 'gentlewomen' of good family). Janet Courtney was one of these:

> When I first went to the Bank of England in 1894, women in the City were still few and far between. There were one or two copying offices; industrial typists were also working in most of the large City houses; and a few big businesses, such as the Prudential Insurance Company, employed a number of girl clerks. We also had within the City boundaries the General Post Office and the head-quarters of the Savings Bank, then still in Queen Victoria Street. But women in ordinary banks were unheard of, and their introduction into the Bank of England, of all places, caused a mild sensation, not to mention a series of tiresome jokes about 'old' and 'young' ladies of Threadneedle Street. How tired one got of trying to smile at them. (Courtney, 1926, p. 153)

The First and Second World Wars both saw large but temporary increases in female clerical labour in the City – for example, the Bank of England employed 400–500 women in the First World War, while in the Second World War women were allowed to become settling room clerks in that male bastion, the Stock Exchange (a 'privilege' promptly withdrawn in 1946) – but it was not until some time after the Second World War that women appeared in the City in large numbers. By 1961, the proportion of women office workers was actually greater than the average for England and Wales and even Central London (Pryke, 1989), chiefly as a result of three labour force factors: the advent of the typewriter and shorthand, which produced both a system of credentials and an occupational niche for women; the fact that women could be paid less than men; and the possibility of excluding women from any real career structure.

Another important social schism in the City was based on ethnicity. Various social groups were seen as 'foreign' to the City's collective body. But this sense of foreignness was deeply ambiguous, since the history of the City's success was in part based upon a constant infusion of foreign immigrants, often as a result of persecution elsewhere in Europe (e.g. the Hauguenots). There were three main 'foreign' presences in the City, often interconnected. The first of these was the Anglo-Jewish group that had built up in the City. This group was seen as insiders (for example, the Rothschilds and other Anglo-Jewish gentry) but also as outsiders. Indeed many of the group actively resisted assimilation into the City. Second, there was a constant stream of foreign immigrants, often German-Jewish, who set up in the City throughout the period and who were often very successful. Finally, note most be taken of the foreigners connected with the growth of foreign bank branches – which date from a surprisingly early point in the City's history. From the 1860s onwards, foreign banks had been established in the City. By 1910 there were twenty-eight such banks in the City, by 1913 there were thirty, including German, Japanese and Russian branches. These figures ignore the large number of colonial bank branches of the time. These branches fell off in number in the First World War but reappeared afterwards. By 1938 there were eighty-five foreign bank branches in the City, 'which was more than ever before despite the disappearance of German banks during the First World War and American banks in the wake of the 1929 crash' (Michie, 1992, p. 82).

The ambiguous relationship with foreigners only rarely seems to have given way to outright hostility, usually as a result of warfare. For example, 'both world wars led to discrimination against particular groups, especially the Germans, who were excluded from membership of such bodies as the Baltic Exchange. As Hodges reminisced concerning the impact of the First World War: "At last, it was brought home to the Mincing Lane fraternity that a foreigner really had no standing in this country" ' (Michie, 1992, p. 44).

A more generalized scepticism about foreigners does seem to have been present. In particular, foreign firms were often looked down upon by City partners and directors, who routinely only worked from 10.00 a.m. to 4.00 p.m., for starting work early and finishing work late (which, it is now generally acknowledged, gave these firms a major competitive edge).

The third foundation stone of the City's power to reproduce itself was its knowledge base, consisting of an expanding archive of knowledge, particular kinds of expertise, and extensive networks of interconnected contacts. This was vital to the City's reproduction, as is evidenced by the example of the two World Wars. Thus Michie (1992, p. 45) argues that 'the Second World War represented a disaster for the City's trading interests, not so much from the physical damage but from the loss of contacts and expertise. During the war, valuable contacts were lost, while key staff left with many not returning.'

The crucial element of this knowledge base was the narratives that structured it, which in turn produced particular judgements about the worth of people and practices. The most obvious of these was the narrative of the 'gentleman' [*sic*], a widespread narrative based on values of honour, integrity, courtesy and so on, and manifested in ideas of how to act, ways of talk, suitable clothing and so on. This gentlemanly narrative, in part imported from the aristocracy and in part from the new professionalization, was sustained by the City's high level of face-to-face contacts, and the consequent need to be able to value people or business. In those famous words, 'the first thing is character', by which was meant character of a gentlemanly type. Most especially, such a narrative en-abled people to scent when contacts did not 'fit', when something was 'wrong' and so on. In other words, the narrative enabled them to judge when to, and when not to, extend trust. However, this narrative was hardly the only one that circulated in the City. Many others did too, increasingly through the expanding medium of texts. In particular, through the nineteenth century the power of the financial press became much greater, as did the press's ability to distribute information, monitor actions and so on. In other words, increasingly texts constituted 'the City'. They 'kept the City informed about itself' (Michie, 1992, p. 184). Starting with *Lloyds List* in 1734, the financial press became increasingly important (Parsons, 1989). Thus in 1825 *The Times* started a regular City Feature. In 1843 *The Economist* began to publish. In 1888 the *Financial Times* started up (from a merger with the *Financial News*). In 1893 *The Investors Chronicle* began life. Finally, the knowledge of the City was also becoming increasingly specialized. This process was enshrined in a set of epistemic communities, each with its own particular vocabulary.

The fourth foundation stone of the City's power to reproduce itself came from spatial concentration. The City's activities were concentrated into a very small area and this concentration was strongly policed. From the micro-space of the partners' rooms in the merchant banks to the larger spaces of streets and squares the City was spatially regulated. In particular, a multitude of rules and rounds kept the City in the City. There were, first of all, the rules about spatial location. For example, all Stock Exchange members had to maintain an office within 700 yards of the Exchange to meet settlement deadlines. There was an (unwritten) Accepting Houses rule that all members had to locate within the City. The Bank of England insisted that all foreign bank offices were in close proximity to it. Second, there were rules that were the result of the need to intermesh time and space in various settlement systems. There were the daily discount house rounds. There were the walks of the banks, trodden each hour to pick up cheques and other paper to pay into the Bank of England. There were the various clearing systems. Most especially, there was the cheque clearing system, used by the banks routinely but then extended to cover the Stock Exchange, insurance companies and so on. 'General' clearing took place from 8.00 a.m. to 11.15 a.m. A later 'town' clearing took place at 3.50 p.m. Institutions had to be within a half mile radius of the Clearing House to be included in this system.

The City was not just reproduced by these intricate intermeshings of time and space, important though they were in producing a coherent City space. The spatial concentration of the workforce that resulted from these rules and rounds was mirrored by residential concentration. Until the early nineteenth century, this was the result of the isomorphism between City workplaces and residences. Then, over time, as commuting into the City grew and residence in the City declined, so specific City residential areas sprang up. By the end of the nineteenth century, a specific 'stockbroker belt' had formed in the Home Countries that persisted into the 1950s. But, in general, there were three main locations for the City workforce. Partners and directors tended to live in St Johns Wood, Hampstead and Mayfair (although 95 per cent of bank directors also had a country address and 20 per cent had only a country address). The middle class lived in the London suburbs, while the City's working class increasingly lived in East London (Cassis, 1984, 1987).

However, this emphasis on spatial concentration could be misleading. Even in the nineteenth century this was no walled City. The world economy impinged in numerous ways. The thriving port of London brought in a constant stream of visitors from overseas. There was a vast flow of bills and documents into and out of the City. Most importantly, the electronic space of flows so beloved of modern commentators had actually been a part of the City's operation over many years, the result of the invention and early application of the telegraph and telephone. The telegraph was first used in the City by Reuter in 1851 to transmit Stock Exchange prices between Paris and London. In 1866, the first telegraph connection was made between London and New York, with immediate effect on the rapidity of market adjustment between the two cities. The telegraph made it possible 'for the first time to trade systematically, and with a fair degree of confidence, in future delivery, rather than taking a gamble on a very risky speculation since it was possible to anticipate expected supply and demand with reasonable certainty. . . . The telegraph, and later the telephone, and their use by intermediaries meant a qualitative change in the degree of risk' (Michie, 1992, pp. 55–3).

Again, the City had the first telephone exchange in Britain, in 1879, and had large numbers of telephone users early on – by 1910 the number of telephone subscribers had reached more than 10,000. In 1937 a telephone link between London and New York was instated. By 1939 there were three City telephone exchanges, serving some 46,000 subscribers. By 1940 it was already possible for one commentator to describe a foreign exchange dealing room of the 1930s in terms not so very different from those used today.

> To describe exactly what goes on in the foreign exchange room of any of the big banks or foreign exchange brokers who compose the London Foreign Exchange market is beyond me. It is the nearest thing to Bedlam that I know – half a dozen men in a little room, shouting in incomprehensible jargon into Telephones, pushing switches up and down all the time in response to the flashing indicator lights. (Hobson, 1940, p. 85)

The innovations of the telegraph and telephone certainly reduced the need for physical proximity in certain cases, but this was not as strong a phenomenon as might have been expected. Rather, what seems to have happened is that to existing levels of contact was added the supplement of the electronic realm and the new markets it made possible. Thus, at times before the 1950s, the City, through this realm, became the centre of both a *global* foreign exchange market and an integrated *global* securities market. For example, even before the First World War,

> with international communications transformed with the coming of the telegraph, and later the telephone, and the need to mobilise funds on a world scale for the finance of infrastructure developments, there appeared the possibility of creating global trading in securities. Information and orders could be quickly transmitted between exchanges and there existed a substantial pool of commonly held securities, ownership of which could easily be changed between the nationals of different countries, especially in the absence of exchange controls. By 1913, securities with a paid-up value of $2bn were common to both the London and New York Stock Exchanges, and it took less than a minute to communicate between the two. (Michie, 1992, p. 79)

The City of London Post-1960s

Since the end of the 1950s or the beginning of the 1960s the City of London has changed its nature. To a degree, this shift has been prompted by a number of related changes in the nature and extent of international financial systems which have privileged the City, including: the rise of a privatized credit system on a global scale (and especially the Euro-markets); the dramatic increase in the number, size, speed of response, volatility and interaction of markets, with a consequent increase in the general indeterminacy of the markets; the increase in risk and the need for risk management; the increase in rates of product/market innovations; the rise of large oligopolistic financial service firms; the rise of large institutional investors, pension funds, insurance companies and block traders; large amounts of technological change, especially in the field of telecommunications, leading to greater computing power, the decline of fixed open outcry markets and the rise of paperless settlement systems; and the spread of North American-style regulatory systems.

Changes like these may have contributed to the success of the post-1960s City but they have also constituted actual or potential threats to the City's ability to reproduce itself, which the City has had to contend with in a number of ways. There are two chief threats. The first of these is technological change, which, in principle at least, allows financial markets to operate from anywhere. There are, in fact, formidable technological obstacles to such a vision. For example, paperless settlement and clearing systems have proved extremely difficult to implement (witness the recent TAURUS debacle in the City) and, even now, the financial system's appetite for paper and paper transactions is voracious. What seems less debatable is that financial markets have become more footloose and keeping them associated with a particular place like the City requires more work than previously to keep the competition from markets in other international financial centres at bay. The second threat to the City comes from its changed relationship with the British state. The old meso-corporatist structure has faced universal pressure from technological change, from scandals and crises, and from the changing character of the British state (and, in particular, a new fair trading ideology and a greater inclination by those in government to intervene in City affairs). In turn, these pressures have led to the death of the monopoly powers of many of its institutions, typified by the desertion of one of the bastions of old style regulation, the Stock Exchange, by the Bank of England in 1983 (Moran, 1991). The old meso-corporatist structure has been replaced by new North American-style regulatory structures, with the result that formal contracts have began to replace the old-style implicit contracts, based on social background. In turn, a constant quarrel has began to form over 'the meaning of an expanding, contradictory, and unclear body of jurisprudence' (Moran, 1991, p. 134).

If the City's power to reproduce itself has been under such threat, how has it managed to stay at least relatively successful? There are three possible answers: its social structure, its culture of narrativity and spatial policing. I will address each of these in turn.

The traditional social structures on which the City's collective self-definition in large part relied have quite clearly weakened and, in some cases, even faded away. Certainly, transgression of the identities forged by these social structures is a much less serious offence than before. Thus, as far as class is concerned, it is still possible to find a core of old-style white upper middle class homosocial merchant banks in which the directors and partners are recruited from only certain public schools and Oxbridge, as one 1986 survey found (Bowen, 1986). Such results are echoed by one of Pahl's (1989) respondents in the late 1980s, who noted that 'During most of those two years (in such a merchant bank), I was the only non-Etonian in the room and felt quite a social outcast.' But even these firms are nowhere near as closed as they were, especially if generational shifts are taken into account. Nor are they as influential: many of them are now relatively small firms in a larger, more international complex of large firms.

Increasingly, expertise and influence in the City resides in a reflexive group of managers and professionals. These managers and professionals have a more heterogeneous social background, partly because in the 1970s and 1980s the City was forced to recruit from a wider pool of people to satisfy its demand for more and more skilled labour and partly because, even though many managers and professionals are still recruited from independent schools and from Oxford, Cambridge and a 'milk run' of other universities like Bristol, Durham and Exeter, the social class constitution of these institutions has become more heterogeneous.

The influx of managers and professionals in such large numbers is relatively new. 'As late as 1965, few university careers advisors would mention finance as a possible choice for a first class honours student; it would be regarded as having rather low social status, and was seen to be unsuccessful and out of political fashion' (Fry, 1970, p. 23). In 1961, for example, the proportion of managers in the City was lower than in the rest of Central London, and England and Wales. By the 1980s it was much higher. The influx was the result of a number of processes (Thrift and Leyshon, 1992), including a more complex division of labour, an increasing foreign presence, which encouraged more meritocratic selection procedures, an increase in the requirements for credentials, greater financial rewards and early career responsibility.

The primacy of professionals and managers was underlined by a considerable decline in the number of clerical workers, especially as a result of the general decentralization of low-skill jobs out of London. In 1990 the percentages of clerical staff in various areas of the City were: banking, 46; other credit-granting institutions, 51; securities dealing, 30; insurance, 25; accountancy and management consultancy, 21; legal services, 40; software services, 13 (Rajan, 1990). Many of these clerical jobs were held by women, and this brings us conveniently to the question of gender.

The homosocial environment of the City has also weakened as the gender composition of the City has changed. After the Second World War, there was a rapid increase in the number of women working in the City, but nearly all these women were clerical workers who were socially and spatially segregated by prevailing codes of sexuality, by the gendered nature of the labour process and by these women's class position – many were working-class women from the East End. Even in the early 1970s Sampson (1972, p. 471) could still write of these female clerical workers as a separate race, which was 'automatically segregated in sandwich bars or canteens. The austere masculinity frightens away the more sophisticated secretaries who prefer the brightness and shops of the West End. The City remains the stronghold of male domination, whether social or financial, and women are kept out of nearly all the centres of its power.'

Since the 1970s, the social composition of women in the City has changed. Thus, even as clerical jobs have been declining, women have been able to keep, and in some cases increase, their proportional presence in the City because of the influx of professional and managerial women (table 14.2), especially into jobs that require skills and credentials, because they have increasingly been able to take up jobs that require high-level social interaction. The result is that women have to be admitted into what were segregated male-only spaces. In turn, this change has required a renegotiation of modes of identification by both men and women. Interestingly, most work has been on the problems of women (e.g. McDowell, 1993). Thus professional and managerial women have had to take care in how they are identified in matters like

Table 14.2 Women in the City (percentages)

	1984	1987	1990
Banking	44.1	44.7	46.3
Other credit-granting institutions	42.1	44.2	45.6
Securities dealing	33.3	35.7	37.5
Insurance	39.3	38.1	38.5
Accountancy and management consultancy	40.0	44.0	48.4
Legal services	62.0	74.2	65.9
Software services	28.6	27.7	30.4

Source: Rajan, 1988, 1990.

dress: 'if you dressed casually it would be quite difficult for people to distinguish between you and a secretary' (cited in Dix, 1990, p. 171).

Ethnic divisions within the City have also been declining as a result of its increasing cosmopolitanism (Hannerz, 1990). There are now a large number of foreign workers in the City. There are more British workers, working for the large number of foreign financial service firms. More British workers also have considerable overseas experience, especially as a result of secondments. Indeed, for many professionals and managers overseas experience is a vital part of their career (Beaverstock, 1991). In turn, the new cosmopolitanism has had other effects. For example, United States banks and securities houses are more likely to hire women, and more likely to promote them to positions of responsibility. (However, it is worth noting that lower down the hierarchy, the City's record in hiring British people who belong to ethnic minorities has not been outstanding: see Rajan, 1988, 1990.)

The weakening of the social structures on which the old City's integrity was based has had important consequences. In particular, it has heightened the City's reflexivity. In the past, the City's business was chiefly based on face-to-face contacts in order to stabilize relations of trust, but much of the content of these transactions was foreordained, since it involved reading 'badges of office', which were readily recognizable signs of class, gender and ethnicity. In current circumstances, the need for reflexivity has been much enhanced, because of a general tendency in society towards greater reflexivity, leading to a greater emphasis on presentation of self, face-work, negotiating skills and so on, because of the increasing requirement to be able to read people as the signs of their social positions are no longer so foreordained and because of the increasingly transactional nature of business relationships between firms and clients. Thus trust now has to be *constituted* through work on *relationships*, not read off from signs of trustworthiness. The formal gavottes of the Old City have therefore become much more complicated dances: 'the first thing is self'.

This increased emphasis on reflexivity in the City has another consequence. The City's thick network of social institutions not only still exists but is actually thriving. In the past, such institutions were the continuation of the social structures of work by other means: places where the extant social structures of the City were confirmed and reinforced. Now they have become places much more actively to do face-work: to make contacts, to check people out, to tap into and to transmit narratives. There is certainly an enormous web of such social institutions, including the City Corporation (with 18,000 on the electoral roll in 1990), the Livery Companies (there are eighty-three guilds in the City with new ones still coming into existence, such as the Company of Information Technologists), the London clubs (which have often been very successful in the 1980s), and the Freemasons' lodges (of which there are hundreds, including special lodges for the Bank of England, Lloyds and so on).

None of the aforegoing is to claim that social divisions no longer exist in the City. They clearly do. For example, women are still excluded from many City social networks because so many of the City's social institutions are still men-only (although it is also the case that women have set up their own networks, such as Women in Banking and the City Women's Network). However, it is to claim that these social divisions have weakened and that, as a consequence, the need for reflexivity has become greater. In this, the City has now become much closer to the rest of British society. For example, the managerial and professional women in the City that McDowell (1993) describes have the same problems of identification as in every other sector of British industry. If the City's social structure is still able to claim uniqueness, it is probably on the basis of its very high degree of reflexivity: the City is, even more than in the past, a 'communicative commotion' (Shotter, 1990).

To summarize, collective self-definition has widened and weakened in the City. People come from more diverse social backgrounds. As a result, the networks of contacts that run the City are increasingly constructed out of the demands of reflexivity and not just social structure. Personal relationships are still vital in the City but they have to be worked at rather than through, constructed for their own sakes rather than for the sake of maintaining social structures. Indeed, this tireless working on relationships is now, more than ever, the primary focus of the City. The City no longer looks for the signs of trust; it constructs them.

Such an emphasis on the City as a reflexivity machine also begins to account for why the third foundation stone of the City's power to reproduce itself has become more important. That is, quite simply, the City's role as a centre of knowledge, expertise and contacts, of narrativity. Clearly the City has seen an explosion of information on the financial services industry, and expertise in interpreting and disseminating that information, which has manifested itself in four related ways. First, and as already pointed out, the City is a nexus of *face-to-face* communication through which information is gathered and interpreted. Second, the City is a centre for *electronic* information gathering and transmission. For example, by 1989 Reuters 'maintained 184,300 screens worldwide, providing groups of customers not only with instant access to information, but also allowing groups of them to communicate with each other, and so provide an international electronic market-place' (Michie, 1992, p. 185). Third, the City is a centre of *textual* interpretation, from the voluminous research analysts' reports circulated to particular potential clients, even to humble tip sheets. In particular, the City is now a centre for the *global* financial press – including *Euromoney, The Banker, The Economist* and the *Financial Times*. The *Financial Times* started a continental European edition in 1979, with a New York edition following in 1985. By 1993, 40 per cent of the paper's circulation was abroad (Kynaston, 1989; *Financial Times*, 1993). Fourth, the City is increasingly home to many different global 'epistemic communities', occupational communities with their own specialized vocabularies, rhetorics, knowledges, practices and texts. From economists to foreign exchange dealers to Eurobond traders each of the communities tends to live in an increasingly specialized narrative world.

This emphasis on narrativity extends in other ways. Increasingly, the City markets itself as a centre of 'cultural authority' for global financial services. It is a place where people meet from around the world because of its associations with finance (and the knowledge, expertise and contracts concentrated there). In turn, the City has consciously begun to play to this role. The old gentlemanly discourse may have dissolved but the 'trappings of trust' still remain: quiet, wood-panelled dining rooms, crested china, discount round top hats, City police uniforms and so on are all used to 'brand' the City, to boost its image of solidity and trustworthiness. 'The rediscovery of tradition is the key to City trend-setting' (Pugh, 1989, p. 127). Indeed, so prominent has this heritage style become that it might be argued that it has spilled over even into City 'fashion' for men. In the 1960s, the City seemed to begin to reflect broader trends in British society. There were distinct signs of a loosening of the sartorial ties: one author of the time noted the presence of 'bright ties', 'soft collars', 'bright blue silky suits with a transatlantic feel', even 'ties with horizontal stripes in the continental fashion' (Ferris, 1968, p. 137). But by the 1980s a strict dress code had reasserted itself to an even greater extent than in Britain as a whole, one based on the dark suit: 'if you're not in a suit, you're invisible'; 'if you're not in a suit you must be a bike boy delivering sandwiches' (Pugh, 1989, p. 126). This dress code varied with age, with younger people tending to dress more sharply in bright shirts and ties and partners and directors clothed in tailored suits, but there were few signs of life outside the suit. Even the much vaunted working-class 'barrow boy' traders conformed. Only the bright trading floor jackets of LIFFE showed any measure of 'dissent'.

One might assume from all this that the last foundation stone of the City's power to reproduce itself, its tight spatial orbit, would melt away. Certainly there are at least three indicators of dissolution. First, the controls on the bounds of the City are much less strong than before. For example, in 1985 the Bank of England decided to take a less directive role in where foreign bank offices could locate (Pryke, 1991). Many of the walks and rounds are also dying out as electronic settlement systems come on line. Second, as this example shows, the City's space is itself increasingly electronic, linked into a global space of flows. Third, the City's denizens are now increasingly mobile. Many of them have lived abroad. Nearly all spend much of their time travelling.

Yet the City shows relatively few signs of deconstructing in the face of these tendencies. Since the 1960s it has become larger in extent, gradually extending its boundaries north and across the river. A few foreign banks' offices have moved to the West End. Back-office operations tend to be dotted around London. But few foreign bank offices have moved very far away. London Docklands never took off as an extension of the City. The spatial matrix of the City has enlarged only a little. Why? There are three main reasons.

First, the need for face-to-face contact has not diminished. Indeed, it is possible to argue that it has become greater as the need for reflexivity has increased as the whole process of international finance has speeded up. Second, there is little evidence to suggest that the growth of electronic space threatens the spatial integrity of the City. It may even help it to cohere. As already pointed out, the history of the City has been tied into this space of flows for over 100 years now and it continues to be. Thus, in 1956, the Foreign Exchange market requested an all-telephone market and has operated in such a mode ever since. Even in 1967, three million telephone calls were being made daily (excluding inter-office calls) (Dunning and Morgan, 1971). This figure has clearly increased since then as a result of expanding business, satellite communications, computing demands, faxes and so on. In other words, electronic communication seems to have acted as supplement to face-to-face communication, rather than an alternative, increasing the overall amount of communication in, into and out of the City (and this is to ignore the corresponding increase in paper communication, indexed by the rise in postal items delivered in, into and out of the City and by the rise of the motorbike messenger). Third, the increase in mobility actually seems to have helped the City to continue to cohere. The City is now an important transient space for international financiers, a place to do business. It has become a global node for circulating stories, sizing up people and doing deals. At any one time, much of the City's population will consist of visitors, but they are not incidental. They are part of why the City continues to exist. They are part of the communicative commotion that places the City.

Conclusions

Through the use of a coalescing set of literatures, and the example of the City of London, this chapter has sought the answers to two related questions: whether international financial centres like the City might melt away into an electronic space of flows and whether social and cultural structures are in any sense determinants of the success or failure of international financial centres. It seems clear that the first question can be relatively easily answered. International financial centres will continue because they satisfy essential communicative/interpretive needs that cannot be met through electronic communication. There will be no 'end to geography'. The answer to the second question is more difficult. It is clear that social and cultural structures do make economic difference and it seems possible that these structures are becoming rather more important, even as they have become less striking. However, the answer to this latter question clearly requires rather more empirical research before it can be answered definitively.

References

Adler, P. and Adler, P. (eds) (1984) *The Social Dynamics of Financial Markets*. Greenwich, CT: JAI Press.

Amin, A. and Thrift, N. J. (1992) Neo-marshallian nodes in global networks. *International Journal of Urban and Regional Research*, 16, 571–87.

Baker, W. E. (1984) Floor trading and crowd dynamics. In P. Adler and P. Adler (eds), *The Social Dynamics of Financial Markets*. Greenwich, CT: JAI Press, 107–28.

Baker, W. E. (1987) What is money? A social structural interpretation. In M. Mizruchi and M. Schwartz (eds), *Intercorporate Relations. The Structural Analysis of Business*. Cambridge: Cambridge University Press, 109–44.

Beaverstock, J. V. (1991) Skilled international migration: an analysis of the geography of international secondments within large accountancy firms. *Environment and Planning A*, 23, 1133–46.

Beck, U. (1992) *Risk Society. Towards a New Modernity*. London: Sage.

Boden, D. (1993) *The Business of Talk*. Cambridge: Polity Press.

Boden, D. and Molotch, H. (1993) The compulsion of proximity. In R. Friedland and D. Boden (eds), *Now/Here. Time, Space and Modernity*. Berkeley: University of California Press.

Bowen, O. (1986) Class of 86. *Business*, November, 34–41.

Camerer, C. (1989) Bubbles and fads in asset prices. *Journal of Economic Surveys*, 3, 3–41.

Cannadine, D. (1990) *The Decline and Fall of the British Aristocracy*. New Haven, CT: Yale University Press.

Cassis, Y. (1984) *Les Banquiers de la City à l'Epoque Edouardienne 1890–1914*. Geneva: Droz.

Cassis, Y. (1987) *La City de Londres, 1870–1914*. Paris: Belin.

Castells, M. (1989) *The Informational City. Economic Restructuring and Urban Development*. Oxford: Blackwell.

Cawson, A. (ed.) (1986) *Organised Interests and the State*. London: Sage.

Cencini, A. (1984) *Money, Income, and Time*. Oxford: Blackwell.

Cheal, P. (1988) *The Gift Economy*. London: Routledge.

City of London Research Project (1992) *The City Research Project Interim Report*. London: Corporation of London.

Cobham, D. (ed.) (1992) *Markets and Dealers. The Economics of the London Financial Markets*. London: Longman.

Courtney, J. E. (1926) *Recollected in Tranquility*. London: Heinemann.

Crump, T. (1990) *The Anthropology of Number*. Cambridge: Cambridge University Press.

Davis, E. P. (1990) International financial centers – an industrial analysis. Bank of England Discussion Paper No. 51.

Dix, C. (1990) *A Chance for the Top. The Lives of Women Business Graduates*. London: Bantam Press.

Drainville, A. C. (1993) International political economy in an age of open Marxism. University of Amsterdam Department of International Relations Working Paper 27.

Dreyfus, H. and Hall, H. L. (eds) (1992) *Heidegger. A Critical Reader*. Oxford: Blackwell.

Dunning, J. H. and Morgan, E. V. (1971) *An Economic Study of the City of London*. London: Allen and Unwin.

Eccles, R. G. and Crane, D. B. (1985) Managing through networks in investment banking. *California Management Review*, 30, 176–95.

Eccles, R. G. and Crane, D. B. (1988) *Doing Deals. Investment Banks at Work*. Boston, MA: Harvard Business School Press.

Ferris, P. (1968) *Men and Money*. London: Hutchinson.

Financial Times (1993) 100 years in the pink. *Financial Times*, 4 January, i–x.

Fry, R. (1970) *A Banker's World. The Revival of the City, 1957–1970*. London: Collins.

Giddens, A. (1990) *Consequences of Modernity*. Cambridge: Polity Press.

Giddens, A. (1991) *Modernity and Self-identity*. Cambridge: Polity Press.

Gill, S. (1990) *American Hegemony and the Trilateral Commission*. Cambridge: Cambridge University Press.

Goodhart, C. (1976) *Money, Information and Uncertainty*. London: Macmillan.

Granovetter, M. S. (1985) Economic action and social structure: the problem of embeddedness. *American Journal of Sociology*, 91, 481–510.

Granovetter, M. S. and Swedberg, R. (eds) (1992) *The Sociology of Economic Life*. Boulder, CO: Westview Press.

Grilli, R. (1989) Europe 1992: issues and prospects for the financial markets. *Economic Policy*, 4, 388–421.

Grossberg, L. M., Nelson, C. and Treichler, P. A. (eds) (1992) *Cultural Studies*. New York: Routledge.

Hannerz, U. (1992) *Cultural Complexity*. New York: Columbia University Press.

Haraway, D. (1990) *Simians, Cyborgs and Women. The Reinvention of Nature*. London: Free Association Books.

Harris, J. and Thane, P. (1984) British and European bankers, 1880–1914: an aristocratic bourgeosie. In P. Thane et al. (eds), *The Power of the Past*. London: Methuen.

ter Hart, H. W. and Piersma, J. (1990) Direct representation in international financial markets: the case of foreign banks in Amsterdam. *Tijdschrift voor Economische en Sociale Geografie*, 81, 82–92.

Hobson, O. R. (1940) *How the City Works*. London: Cassell.

Kanter, R. M. (1976) *Men and Women of the Organization*. New York: Basic Books.

Kynaston, D. (1989) *The Financial Times. A Centenary History*. London: Viking.

Lash, S. (1993) Reflexive modernisation: the aesthetic dimension. *Theory, Culture and Society*, 10, 1–23.

Lash, S. and Urry, J. (1993) *Economies of Signs and Space*. London: Sage.

London Planning and Advisory Council (1990) *London: World City*. London: HMSO.

Marceau, J. (1990) *A Family Business? The Making of an International Business Elite*. Cambridge: Cambridge University Press.

McCloskey, K. D. N. (1985) *The Rhetoric of Economics*. Madison: University of Wisconsin Press.

McDowell, L. (1993) The missing subject in economic geography (mimeo).

Mendell, M. and Salee, D. (eds) (1991) *The Legacy of Karl Polanyi: Market, State and Society*. London: Macmillan.

Michie, R. C. (1992) *The City of London. Continuity and Change, 1850–1990*. London: Macmillan.

Moran, M. (1991) *The Politics of the Financial Services Revolution*. London: Macmillan.

Murphy, C. N. and Tooze, R. (1991) *The New International Political Economy*. Boulder, CO: Lynne Rienner.

O'Brien, R. (1992) *Global Financial Integration. The End of Geography*. London: Pinter.

Overbeek, H. (1990) *Global Capitalism and National Decline. The Thatcher Decade in Perspective*. London: Unwin Hyman.

Pahl, R. E. (1989) St Matthews and the golden handcuffs (mimeo).

Parsons, W. (1989) *The Power of the Financial Press*. London: Edward Elgar.

Perkin, H. (1989) *The Professionalisation of English Society 1880–1980*. London: Routledge.

Polanyi, K. (1944) *The Great Transformation*. Boston: Beacon Press.

Polanyi, K. (1957) *Trade and Market in the Early Empires*. Glencoe, IL: Free Press.

Pryke, M. (1989) Urban land values and the changing role of financial institutions: a case study of the City of London. PhD thesis, Open University.

Pryke, M. (1991) An international city going global. *Environment and Planning D: Society and Space*, 9, 197–222.

Pugh, J. (1989) *The Penguin Guide to the City*. Harmondsworth: Penguin.

Rajan, A. (1988) *Create or Abdicate. The City's Human Resource Choices for the 1990s*. London: Wetherby.

Rajan, A. (1990) *Capital People*. London: Industrial Society.

Sampson, A. (1965) *The Anatomy of Britain*. London: Hodder and Stoughton.

Sampson, A. (1972) *The Anatomy of Britain*, 2nd edn. London: Hodder and Stoughton.

Sayer, S. (1992) The City, power and economic policy in the UK. *International Review of Applied Economics*, 6, 125–51.

Shotter, J. (1990) Social accountability and the social construction of you. In J. Shotter and T. Gergen (eds), *Texts of Identity*. London: Sage, 133–51.

Strange, S. (1986) *Casino Capitalism*. Oxford: Blackwell.

Strange, S. (1988) *States and Markets*. London: Pinter.

Swedberg, R. (1987) Economic sociology: past and present. *Current Sociology*, 35, 1–221.

Swedberg, R. (1991) Major traditions of economic sociology. *Annual Review of Sociology*, 17, 251–76.

Thrift, N. J. (1987) The fixers: the urban geography of international commercial capital. In M. Castells and J. Henderson (eds), *Global Restructuring and Territorial Development*. London: Sage, 219–54.

Thrift, N. J. (1990) Doing global regional geography: the City of London and the Southeast of England. In R. J. Johnston, J. Hauer and G. A. Hoekveld (eds), *Regional Geography. Current Developments and Future Prospects*. London: Routledge, 180–207.

Thrift, N. J. and Leyshon, A. (1992) In the wake of money. The City of London and the accumulation of value. In L. Budd and S. Whimster (eds), *Global Finance and Urban Living*. London: Routledge, 282–311.

Thrift, N. J., Leyshon, A. and Daniels, P. W. (1987) Sexy greedy. University of Bristol and University of Liverpool Working Papers on Producer Services No. 6.

Williamson, O. E. (1975) *Markets and Hierarchies. Analysis and Antitrust Implications*. New York: Free Press.

Zukin, S. and Dimaggio, P. (eds) (1990) *Structures of Capital*. Cambridge: Cambridge University Press.

15

The Battle of Bank Junction: the Contested Iconography of Capital

Jane M. Jacobs

Why is it that the present period of sustained growth in the wealth of Britain seems to be finding no monumental expression? (*William Waldegrave, Minister for Housing and Planning, Speech to the Royal Fine Arts Commission, London, 1988*)

Logic has its limits and . . . the City lies outside of them. (*Royal Commission on Local Government in Greater London, 1962*)

There was a time when the skyscraper was pointed to (sometimes with awe and at other times with disdain) as *the* architectural icon of capitalism in its modern formation (Tafuri, 1979; Gibbs, 1984; Domosh, 1987, 1988). Lefebvre (1991, p. 144) saw the skyscraper as a political space signifying 'arrogance, the will to power . . . the phallus . . . a spatial analogue of masculine brutality'. This association between verticality, capital, masculinity and power remains vital. For example, two recent books on the contemporary urban landscape (Relph, 1987; Short, 1989) connect concentrations of finance capital and the powers that direct capital (usually evoked as the faceless multinational corporation) with the phallic skyscraper. The persistence of the skyscraper as a symbol of capitalism is not surprising. It remains a very real element of the urban landscape, being, without question, the building form that most profitably utilizes highly valued central city land. Even if capital is expressing itself in more ambiguous or visually playful forms, in many cities the skyscraper remains the skeleton upon which postmodern skins are laid. Yet few would deny that in the city of the 1980s and 1990s the lean glass-walled skyscraper is no longer capable of symbolically carrying capitalism. Capital in the postwar years has been characterized by a new flexibility and there have been concomitant shifts in the shape and form of the city (see Jameson, 1984; Lash and Urry, 1987; Harvey, 1989b; Soja, 1989; Lash, 1990). The hegemony of capital may persist but its

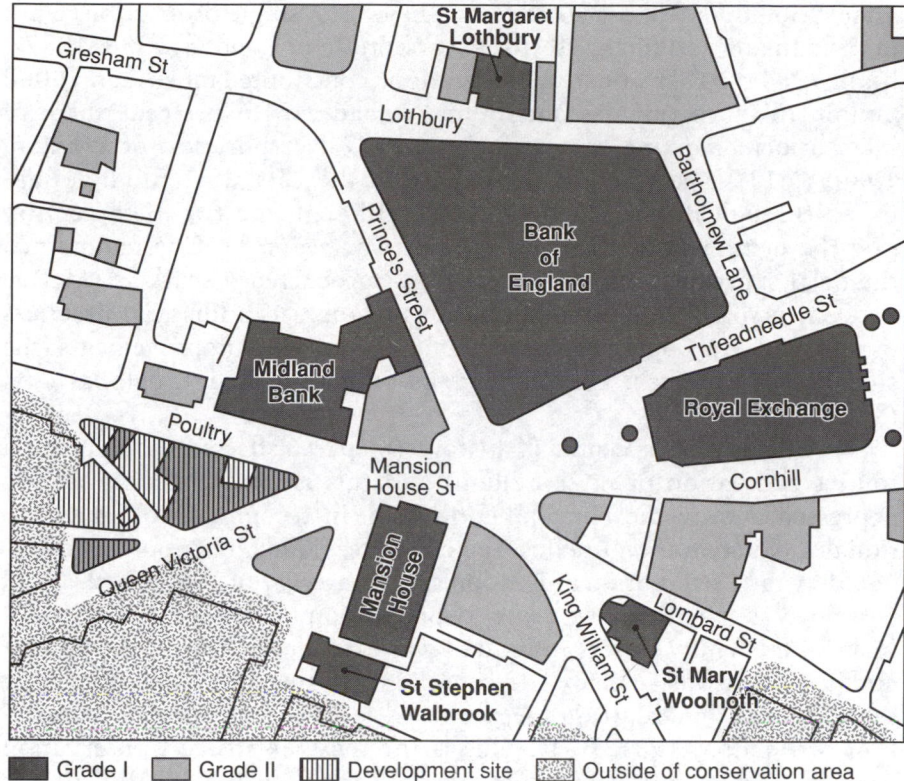

Grade I ■ Grade II ▥ Development site ▦ Outside of conservation area

Figure 15.1 The Bank Junction intersection, showing the development site, the key functions of finance and the local state, listed buildings and conservation area.

spatial patterning, its surface appearances, its intersection with cultural and social forms have fractured.

In this chapter I want to explore the cultural dimensions of money, power and space by focusing on one particular urban redevelopment effort: the thirty-year (1962–92) planning controversy surrounding proposals to redevelop part of Bank Junction at the centre of the City of London. Six major roads meet at Bank Junction. Around the Junction are sited three monumental buildings: the Bank of England, the Royal Exchange and the Mansion House. The radial street pattern, part medieval and part the product of Victorian road building, gives the sense of a focal point or hub. The buildings surrounding this hub are 'home' for three key City functions: banking, exchange markets and the Lord Mayor, head of the City's local government. In form and function, Bank Junction readily submits to the description 'Heart of Empire' (figure 15.1).

The City of London is a space given over to finance and business. During the 1980s, when the Bank Junction battle raged, the City had a resident population of only 5864 but a daily working population of almost 300,000. Almost 30 per cent, the largest single proportion, work in the banking and finance sector (Corporation of London, 1986, 1987a, b). In 1984 the City's financial institutions contributed more than £6000 million to the national economy and it had a 21.6 per cent share of international banking transactions in 1987 (Corporation of London, 1986, p. 13). The financial dominance of the City was initially established through Britain's imperial role. Although the twentieth century saw the demise of this role, in the postwar years the City maintained financial supremacy through growth in Eurocurrency markets (McRae and Cairncross 1985). Transformations of the City's financial practices in the 1980s, through deregulation and technological improvements (the so-called 'Big Bang'), consolidated its role as a leading 'global city' (Sassen, 1991).

The City is also a centre of history (in part reflected by an annual tourist population of three million) and this is nowhere more clearly expressed than in the Bank Junction area. In recognition of its exceptional architectural and townscape character, Bank Junction was designated by the Corporation of London as a Conservation Area in 1971 and described as 'a national set piece' (Corporation of London, 1970, p. 5). In 1974 the Bank Conservation Area was extended to the north and east and in 1981 it was again extended to the west, specifically incorporating those historic buildings on the proposed redevelopment site (Corporation of London, 1981, p. 1). This is the most extensive Conservation Area in the City and covers most of the central core. Bank Junction is surrounded by listed buildings. Of the eight major buildings which immediately face the junction, two are listed Grade A ecclesiastical buildings (Wren's St Stephen Walbrook and Hawksmoor's St Mary Woolnoth), four are listed Grade I (Dance's Mansion House, Soane's Bank of England, Lutyen's Midland Bank and the Royal Exchange) and the others are listed Grade II. Of the more modest mid-Victorian group of buildings on the development site itself, eight are listed.

For the past three decades, 'local' interests, conservationists, the Corporation of London and a City developer have been battling it out at Bank Junction over a proposed redevelopment of one part of the intersection. There have been numerous schemes proposed, two major planning inquiries, appeals to the Court of Appeal and the House of Lords, and a final decision (to allow redevelopment) made by the highest representatives of the law in Britain, the Law Lords. Conservationists and the local authority for the City (the Corporation) favoured restoration and refurbishment of the existing Victorian buildings on the site and argued for this in both inquiries. The developer proposed demolition and redevelopment. He initially suggested an 18-storey skyscraper designed by the famous, but by then dead, modernist Mies van der Rohe. Planning permission was provisionally granted, then refused, and the issue went to public inquiry where refusal of planning permission was ratified. The developer returned to the fray with an avowedly 'postmodernist' design by architect James Stirling.[1] In chronology this particular redevelopment controversy has followed closely the dramatic postwar period of economic restructuring, which has given rise to an expanded and more flexible finance sector with its associated service industry centred in the reinvigorated centres of the City of London, Tokyo and New York. The Bank Junction redevelopment saga reached its public peak during the 1980s; the very time that the economic, social and cultural implications of post-Fordism were becoming most apparent in global centres like London.

That this central site in one of the world's great cities should engender the interest of a developer says much of the economic potential of this piece of real estate and, in turn, the more familiar issues of the spatial patterning of value and cycles of reinvestment in the city. Yet this redevelopment bid is distinctive, for it resulted in the very centre of the City of London being frozen in controversy. At a time of massive economic restructuring, when the City was reinvigorated as a financial centre and was routinely listed as one of the three key financial centres in a new global system, one block of prime real estate did not get redeveloped, it did not have a new building erected with an architectural style that reflected the 'spirit of the age'. That the most valuable piece of City real estate could be 'locked out' of the most vigorous phase of economic growth the City of London has seen since the days of Empire says something of a more ambiguous City where (so it seems) the cycles of capital accumulation do not go uncontested.

Culture and Capital

The controversy over the redevelopment of Bank Junction provides a window on to the intersection between capital and a constellation of practices, artefacts, ideologies and values which can be loosely described as cultural. Dominant political economic perspectives in urban studies have begun to treat seriously the cultural dimension (Berman, 1982; Castells, 1983; Harvey, 1985, 1989a, b; King, 1988). Zukin (1988a, p. 432) notes that economic determinism has receded and been replaced by a 'more open materialist analysis that embraces culture and politics as well as economic structures'. Much spurred by Jameson's (1984) landmark article on the 'cultural logic' of late capitalism, urban studies has brought 'culture out of the superstructure' and set it as a 'basic determinant of material forms'.

The admittance of culture provides a more comprehensive understanding of the power dynamic of capital, for the hegemonic potential of

1 James Stirling died in 1992, not long after final permission for his scheme was granted.

capital is in part constituted through (and at times subverted by) the cultural. The power of capital is far from fixed or unidimensional, it must be 'continually renewed, recreated, defended', for it is also 'continually resisted, limited, altered [and] challenged' (Williams, 1977, p. 112). Cultural practices, objects and values play a key role in the way capital holds (or does not hold) and the forms that its takes in any one setting. A number of political economic accounts of recent urban and regional transformations have acknowledged the importance of culture in capital processes (Harvey, 1989b). The recent work on gentrification, for example, emphasizes taste and consumption practices in the revalorization of urban areas (e.g. Beauregard, 1986, 1989; Jager, 1986; Zukin, 1986, 1988b; Jacobs 1992). At a different scale, the British localities work has recognized the importance of local cultural practices and social formations in shaping the functioning and patterning of capital under restructuring. But as Jackson (1991) has noted, most locality studies have only touched on *how* culture and capital intersect in the local context. In the battle of Bank Junction the interests of capital 'hold' in the City of London through far more complex (and at times precarious) social and cultural forms than could ever be evoked by the skyscraper icon and its presumed author, the faceless multinational. Contemporary processes of capital accumulation intersect with residual and emergent social formations (the developer, the local state, the City worker, the urban conservationist) and their attendant structures of power, everyday practices and value systems.

The differential 'power' of these various interests is, in part, based on their relationship with capital in a material sense. It is also formed around their control of or access to 'symbolic capital'. Bourdieu's (1984, p. 1) 'economy of cultural goods' theorizes culture as part of a process of production and consumption in which certain cultural products circulate in a market. Like an economy of capital, Bourdieu's economy of culture has significant power differentials, for some forms of cultural capital are more privileged and have greater power or 'competence' than others. Those individuals and groups who have access to and can control privileged cultural capital are empowered. Lash (1990) suggests that Bourdieu's concept of 'cultural capital' is particularly relevant to the uniquely 'semiotic' society of late capitalism and argues that the urban environment is 'regulated' by a combination of the material and the representational.

The window on to the cultural opened out by this redevelopment controversy centred on 'heritage': artefactual (as in the interest in the historic built form), practical (as in the interest in traditional City practices) and ideological (as in the beliefs and values held about inherited artefacts and practices). 'Heritage' in contemporary society is politically weighted; certain pasts are privileged while others are marginalized, allowing 'heritage' to be construed as one dimension of cultural capital (Hobsbawm and Ranger, 1983; Lowenthal, 1985; Wright, 1985).

'Heritage' is also highly commodified; it is a resource in and a part of the surface form of the contemporary economy, particularly the service sector (Wright, 1985; Hewison, 1987; Thrift, 1989; Jacobs, 1992).

Surface and Space

The presence of a particular built form is itself a display of power. It is 'the material manifestation of dominant interests' (Gottdiener, 1986, p. 214–15). That I should take a site that has been locked in controversy and where virtually nothing has happened, in a material sense, as a template of the restructuring City of London may then seem contradictory. Surely the hallmarks of the post-Fordist city might be a range of more concrete forms generated by reinvestment in and revalorization of spaces and places previously under disinvestment? In the case of London, one might focus on the emergence of large-scale office developments on the City fringe, like the proposed Kings Cross, Broadgate or Spitalfields Market developments to name just a few of the many proposed in this area during the 1980s. Alternatively one might focus upon the London Docklands where the construction of the massive Canary Wharf development established this area as a serious competitor for the nearby City. At a different scale, there is the transformation of inner-city spaces to meet the residential and lifestyle needs of new social and class formations associated with restructuring (Williams, 1976; Wright, 1985; Smith and Williams, 1986; Zukin, 1986, 1988b; Raban, 1988). Sassen (1991), in describing London as a characteristic 'global city', links gentrification of inner London with the transformations occurring in the financial sector of the nearby City. The gentrification process is demographically more complex than simply inner-city homes and haunts for the new (or old) City finance worker. Yet there remains an important aesthetic collaboration between large-scale developments and the architecture revalorized in the finer-grained gentrification process (Jacobs, 1992). This collaboration is brought out in the Bank Junction controversy.

The visible spaces and surfaces of the restructuring city say something about dominant interests but they also act as 'false testimony' for they elide the constant struggle for the control of space (Gottdiener, 1986, p. 215). The Bank Junction saga elucidates spaces of desire, a place in its struggle to 'become' (Pred 1984, 1986; also Pryke, 1991, with reference to the City of London). It is through this struggle of becoming that the workings of power in the city are revealed: the discursive and representational constitution of symbolic space, the differentials of cultural capital, the struggle of visions to materialize or be resisted. The controversial, but unbuilt, redevelopment proposals for Bank Junction and the politics surrounding the absence of this development may reveal more about the emergent class formations, spatial configurations, visual forms and symbolic statements of the post-Fordist City of London than analyses of the existing or recently transformed built environment.

The examination of the struggle to remake this City space opens out a more ambiguous, contested and heterogeneous terrain of power. Among other things (and picking up the thread of my opening imagery), this redevelopment struggle lays bare the shift from skyscraper to more ambiguous and varied architectural forms; that is, the fracturing of the surface appearance of capital accumulation in the City of London. The two separate planning inquiries associated with the proposed redevelopment brought forth a number of distinctive architectural options which offer themselves as spatial and symbolic surfaces that can be 'read' semiotically (e.g. Broadbent et al., 1980; Jencks, 1987). The verbal, textual and visual representations that were generated to protect, to profane and to promote the distinct architectural visions for redevelopment provide alternative surfaces of understanding: iconographic and discursive representations of the architectural visions of Bank Junction as a setting and of the City as a place (Cosgrove, 1984; Burgess and Wood, 1988; Cosgrove and Daniels, 1988; Daniels, 1989).

Decoding the symbolism of surfaces is one strand in understanding the workings of cultural capital in the city. However, the passage from 'exterior surfaces' to inner meanings and experiences is fraught (Jackson, 1989, p. 177). Much of this work has suffered from a too literal transferral of linguistic analysis to the built environment. It can be highly codified and mechanistic and has been accused of privileging the material object as a source of meaning, giving little insight into the reflexive relationship between the object 'read' and its ideological, political and material constitution. Lefebvre (1991, p. 160), for example, argued that the reading of space in a strictly semiotic or iconographic manner passes over the 'nearside' and 'farside' of 'readability'; that is, the processes by which space is 'produced' (materially and socially) as well as the ways in which space is lived, both of which help to constitute the symbolic content of any space or surface. This accords with what has been called a socio-semiotic approach to space, in which symbolic meaning is sought not simply in material objects, but by attention to the differently empowered social groups producing, discursively constituting and living with and through these spaces (Gottdiener, 1985; Gottdiener and Lagopoulos, 1986). The case study of Bank Junction explores meanings associated with the urban environment as constituted and constructed, promoted and opposed, verbalized and visualized, acted upon or not acted upon by those who are directly involved in the politics surrounding the proposed changes to the urban environment of the City of London.

The Bank Junction redevelopment saga not only speaks of the symbolic meanings associated with surface forms (buildings and texts) but also of that more complexly constituted socio-spatial unit called place. This redevelopment struggle provides an insight into the intersections of symbolic meaning, social formation, political action and daily practices that constitute the specific place called the City of London. Exploring such intersections is of particular theoretical concern at present, with the renewed emphasis on locality and place specificity emerging out of a number of interlinked theoretical positions. Foucault's explicitly 'located' histories of social difference and control have demonstrated the value of attention to the sites and spaces of historical events and social relations. Soja (1989), for example, draws on Foucault's concept of 'heterotopia' in developing a self-consciously 'postmodern' geography of Los Angeles which seeks out the juxtaposition of the incompatible in one locale (Foucault, 1986, p. 25; quoted in Soja, 1989, p. 17). Philo (1992) culls a somewhat different geography from Foucault to press the case for the place specificity of historical processes (including, of course, the processes of capital). Foucault's work has demonstrated that to admit heterogeneity and diversity is not to refuse domination and subordination and that attention to place and space can elaborate the multiple processes and net-like organization of power. The detailed case study of Bank Junction, with its attention to vying interest groups with differing views, does evoke a fashionably postmodern sense of diversity but it does not divest the City of the notion of power. Rather, it suggests patterns of power that are complexly represented in and through space and place and that interweave with, embellish and at times challenge capital.

The Battle of Bank Junction

In the City of London the specificity of the local scene arises from its unique role as a finance centre, but also from its historical importance to the nation. The planning controversy associated with Bank Junction is an arena in which these two dimensions of the City rub together. Each participant in the battle of Bank Junction brought City 'heritage' and capital together in new configurations: not only in stark conflict but also in more subtle conflations pointing to the way capital is complexly embedded in the local cultural practices and values of City interests. In the following analysis I want to explore just three of the cases put in the Bank Junction battle: that of the local state (the Corporation of London), the developer (Peter Palumbo) and a group of 'locals' (the CARE group). I will touch upon the first proposed development (the Mansion House Square scheme), but will draw primarily on the controversy surrounding the second scheme for the site (the No. 1 Poultry scheme).

The Power of the State

The Corporation of London, like the various conservation interests, advocated the retention and refurbishment of the existing Victorian

Figure 15.2 Existing Victorian buildings at the Bank Junction site, eight of which
are listed under national heritage legislation.
Source: J. M. Jacobs private collection.

buildings on the redevelopment site (figure 15.2). The Corporation's
response to the Palumbo vision of redevelopment has been far from
consistent. In the late 1960s when Palumbo first mooted his vision for a
modernist office tower on this central site, he was granted provisional
planning permission. At this moment in City history the local state and
the developer were joined in their vision for Bank Junction. Only when
Palumbo applied for full planning permission in the early 1980s (after
acquiring adequate property rights over the site) did he face Corporation
resistance. By this stage there had been a sea-change in local and national
policy towards the historic built environment. The increasing commitment by the Corporation to conservation of the historic built environment in the City was evident in the listing of a wider range of buildings
(including more modest and younger buildings, like those on the development site) and in the implementation of conservation area policy
which ensured that whole sections of the City were protected for their

townscape quality; that is, the visual and architectural character of buildings in relation to one another (Lloyd, 1976).

The Corporation of London's commitment to the preservation and enhancement of the historic character of the City's built form was given clear expression in its local plan, strategically released in the midst of the redevelopment controversy (Corporation of London, 1986). Within the Plan, preservation and enhancement of the historic character of the City is set not in conflict with the City's role as a world finance centre but as a key ingredient in its aspirations to remain a centre of finance in a transforming global context:

> The City of London . . . is noted for its business expertise, its wealth of history and special architectural heritage . . . [giving it] . . . a world-wide reputation . . . and distinguish[ing] it from other international business centres. The . . . City's business activities, which are underpinned by the benefits of its precious heritage, further the wealth and opportunities of London and the surrounding region, and also provide a significant contribution to the well-being of the nation's economy. (Corporation of London, 1986, p. 3)

The historic built fabric is seen as an attraction to growth, not a deterrent. It is the basis of the City promoting itself as unique in a new global terrain, in which the City's status is more precarious, competing as it does with the financial centres of New York and Tokyo and, closer to home, Docklands and emergent centres of finance on the continent.

This broader policy commitment provides the context for the detail of the Corporation's case against the the Palumbo proposals. The Bank Junction saga became an arena in which the Corporation, through its opposition to the redevelopment schemes, attempted to reiterate and reinvent challenged structures of status and power associated with the decentred Empire and to find a place for them in this new global context. The historic built form became the repository and expression of structures of power and practice which were under challenge in the decentring City.

In its opposition to the Bank Junction schemes the Corporation focused specifically on issues of townscape and the anticipated impact of redevelopment on that existing character (Anderson, 1988). The Corporation advocated the preservation of the visual dominance of certain existing monumental buildings in the City: Mansion House, the Royal Exchange, the Bank of England and St Paul's. The intrinsic architectural and historical value of the existing Victorian buildings on the development site was acknowledged but primarily in terms of how they related to and enhanced surrounding monumental buildings. The townscape argument was put first in terms of the immediate vicinity of Bank Junction:

The visually subservient nature of the buildings on the Mappin and Webb site is crucially important. The existing buildings do not compete in scale with the dominance of the Royal Exchange forecourt and its Grade I listed buildings. The relationship of visual master and servant between the forecourt, with its major buildings, and the subject site must be retained if the Conservation Area designation is to be given any meaning. (No. 1 Poultry Public Inquiry 1988, Roy Worksett)

In drawing on the social metaphor of master and servant the Corporation reified in the built environment social structures familiar to the City scene. The Empire City was ethnographically specific: male, upper class and generally English. Sociological studies of the financial (merchant banking) sector of the City document its relatively 'informal' financial practices based on class- and gender-specific familial dynasties (Cassis, 1985a, b, 1988; Lisle-Williams, 1984a, b). The cohesive power of the merchant bankers has been enforced through attendance at the same schools and colleges (Eton and Oxbridge), intermarriage between banking families, common dress codes and membership of common clubs (Cohen, 1974). Upper-class values, expressed through the 'culture of the gentleman' and enacted through an 'old boy network', have provided a self-regulatory basis for financial practices in the City. The traditional geography of the financial City centred on Bank Junction and the Bank of England and the daily contact facilitated by this spatial proximity

Figure 15.3 The glimpsed view of the dome of St Paul's through the Bank Junction from Cornhill: existing view and after the 'irreverent' Poultry.
Source: Worksett, 1988.

reinforced social bonds and ensured that financial practices could be sustained informally (Cohen, 1974; Harris and Thane, 1984; Pryke, 1991). The Corporation's defence of a townscape relationship in which the Bank of England (along with the Mansion House and Royal Exchange) remains visually dominant is a symbolic reiteration of this traditional sociology and geography.

The townscape argument was also extended to another revered monument of the City. The dome of St Paul's can be glimpsed across the Junction from Cornhill to the east in what was cited as the only view of St Paul's from the financial centre of the City (figure 15.3). The Corporation defended the visual relationship between the 'master' dome and the 'servant' spire of the corner (Mappin and Webb) building on the redevelopment site. The visual relationship became a townscape metaphor for a desired hierarchy in which the church acted as moral guardian to the operations of money in Bank Junction. The reification of this relationship of morality and money draws on deeply rooted concepts of the immoral and godless city driven by capital (Williams, 1973). Thus constructed, the Palumbo scheme could be charged with 'irreverence' for interfering with this symbolic interplay between the financial and religious hubs of the City.

Through the townscape argument the Corporation was constructing a symbolic terrain which spoke of values of morality, civility, hierarchy and order once central to the triumphant City of old. The Corporation's case was brought to life by Lund's painting *Heart of the Empire*, which

Figure 15.4 Niels M. Lund's *Heart of Empire*, 1902, presented as 'evidence' in the Bank Junction public inquiries.

was presented to the Inquiry as evidence of 'the spirit of the place and the character that remains' and hung, an icon of City status, at the rear of the public inquiry room (figure 15.4). In referencing this icon the Corporation was reiterating within a new and challenging global context a set of ideas long associated with this distinctive part of the City. The townscape 'monument' being constructed through this planning struggle and the local plan spoke of increasingly imaginary City social orders and practices.

The recent global transformations in financial services had impacted significantly on the ethnography, practices and geography of the City of Empire. In the nineteenth-century City of Empire the financial sector was grounded in colonial structures of power and the trade of British manufactured goods for raw materials and food imports from the Empire (King, 1990, p. 9). In the postwar years the City shifted away from Empire-based internationalism to global internationalism (McRea and Cairncross, 1985, p. 18; Thrift 1986, 1987; King, 1990, pp. 83–7). The 'City revolution' is tied to the internationalization of banking and securities trading, the deregulation of the securities market and the introduction of new technology (Plender and Wallace, 1985, p. 2). These transformations have been apparent since the 1960s but have intensified from 1986, the time of the deregulation, the so-called Big Bang.

Deregulation has resulted in an opening up of the closed and closely regulated financial sector of the City. There has been an internationalization of banking and securities trading in the City. In 1914, there were only 30 foreign banks; by the 1930s this had expanded to over 80 and by the early 1960s there were over 100 (Goodhart and Grant, 1986, p. 9). From 1961 to 1971, the number of foreign banks in the City doubled and in the following decade doubled again. In 1987 there were 453 foreign banks either directly or indirectly represented in the City (King, 1990, p. 89). Similar shifts are apparent in the Eurocurrency market. In the 1950s there was only a small Eurocurrency market, but by 1973 total Eurocurrency deposits were US $315 million and by 1988 they exceeded US $4500 billion (Clarke, 1989, p. 113). The City now compares more favourably to its competitors of New York and Tokyo in terms of its share of global securities dealings (Thrift, 1987). Further internationalization of the City was anticipated with European monetary (and possibly political) union and the entry of Britain into the European Exchange Rate Mechanism. These changes hung over the redevelopment public inquiries as surely as Lund's *Heart of Empire* painting. Sampson (1982, p. 263) noted that 'the square mile of the City has become like an off-shore island in the heart of the nation'.

Along with deregulation has come a significant transformation in the technology of the City's financial sector. The new technology has meant that businesses can be more flexible. It is no longer crucial for financial services to locate close to each other or to cluster in and around the Bank of England and Bank Junction. Indeed, as will be shown, changes in technology have meant that existing office space in the City rarely meets the requirements of the restructured finance sector. The financial sector, which had traditionally clung to the area in and around Bank Junction, is not only able to relocate, but is finding that without redevelopment of existing building stock it simply must relocate (Pryke, 1991).

Thus the battle over Bank Junction was held during a deeply unstable moment for the City. As the City and its financial services were de-centring, the Corporation of London was trying to reiterate an increasingly imaginary City of Empire. Ironically, the very conservation-mindedness of the Corporation was party to the decentring of the City financial. Its impulse to preserve a built form that celebrated a fading City (and Britain) of Empire was preventing the very restructuring needed to ensure that the City retained a place in global finance. Conservation impulses in the City, which argued for the protection of the character of the area in townscape terms, were threatening the reinvention of the financial sector in its traditional locale.

The Power of Development

Clearly the developer and conservation interests (including the local state) disagreed over the value of the existing buildings in Bank Junction

Figure 15.5   The Mies van der Rohe Mansion House Scheme.
Source: Kutcher, 1976.

and had different visions for the site. Yet as the saga of Bank Junction continued there was an obvious conflation of the oppositional visions. Common threads of language and logic emerged, attesting to the pervasiveness of certain perceptions of the City and this emblematic site in the City. The developer's legitimation of change became rooted in references to traditions and historical precedents, and was as deeply imbued with historicism as the positions held by his opponents.

The first inquiry had seen the coming together of development and conservation around a building which in every way represented high modernism (figure 15.5). Mies van der Rohe, who designed the skyscraper Mansion House Square scheme in the 1960s, was acclaimed as a leading proponent of the International Style, once so persistently associated with the symbolic expression of capital in the City. The delay in Palumbo applying for planning permission meant that an emblematic 'battle' of the 1960s city (the old versus the new) was being enacted some twenty years late. It was hardly surprising that the modernist scheme was denied planning permission. In the inquiry over the second No. 1 Poultry scheme the 'battle' continued to rage but the lines were blurred.

Figure 15.6   James Stirling's No. 1 Poultry.
Source: James Stirling No. 1 Poultry Proof of Evidence 1988, illustration 40.

In his second attempt to redevelop Bank Junction, Palumbo commissioned a design by James Stirling (figure 15.6). Stirling too had an international reputation but his was a 'parochial' internationalism. James Stirling was a top *British* architect, a reputation stressed by Palumbo's expert witnesses. The equally famous architectural critic, Charles Jencks, was one such witness. He described Stirling as the founder of 'New Contextualism', referring to the second No. 1 Poultry scheme as 'site-specific architecture' based on the imaginative development of the classical proportioning and style of surrounding monumental buildings (No. 1 Poultry Public Inquiry, 1988, Charles Jencks, p. 13). In selecting Stirling as the architect for his second attempt to redevelop Bank Junction, Palumbo was consciously addressing the issues of context and relationship to the surrounding buildings which were so central to the rejection of his first proposal in the face of the strong conservation/townscape policy of the Corporation.

The defence of the Palumbo proposal could rely on the same concept of townscape used by those opposing redevelopment. Stirling's design, Palumbo's expert witness argued, was 'equal' to and 'did justice' to the surrounding monumental buildings of Bank Junction. The monumentality of the Poultry scheme was presented as a worthy addition to this site of special importance characterized by the presence of the other monumental buildings. It would be 'a building whose seriousness and monumental overtones much more appropriately accorded with [its] neighbours' and would sit in 'well mannered' harmony with the existing buildings (No. 1 Poultry Public Inquiry, 1988, St John Wilson, p. 13). The nomenclature, just like the building design, stressed a new sensitivity to surroundings. The intrusive and grand title of 'Mansion House Square' was replaced by a more modest title, a quaint address, 'No. 1 Poultry', which discursively slipped the planned addition unobtrusively into the existing street.

Perhaps the most difficult townscape issue for the developer's team was that the Stirling proposal would still impair the glimpsed serial view of the dome of St Paul's from Cornhill. Palumbo's expert witnesses counteracted this complaint by way of a strategy which appropriated the 'sacred space' of the dome of St Paul's and symbolically relocated it at No. 1 Poultry. Jencks argued that the central drum of the scheme was like an 'open dome' that would echo in absence the proportions and form of the dome of St Paul's. New views of St Paul's, it was argued, would be created from the No. 1 Poultry roof garden, creating a 'contemporary sacred site'. The developer's team replaced the Corporation's townscape metaphor of master and servant with their own metaphor of a 'dialogue between equals' (No. 1 Poultry Public Inquiry, 1988, Charles Jencks).

The presentation of a case for a grand building by a grand architect echoed the traditional cultural and social reputation of this central financial site. The developer's proposal may well have required the demolition of one part of the 'heritage' of the site but, in other respects, it conformed with the traditional lineage of the area, making a contemporary statement about the power of the City financial. Thus, while the cases for and against the proposed redevelopment referred to distinct social metaphors (one of hierarchy and one of grand equity), each celebrated a City of power.

Setting aside the competing 'heritage' rhetoric of the inquiry, perhaps the most overtly 'historical' act of the entire Bank Junction saga was Palumbo's desire to redevelop in the central core of the City. His vision of redevelopment began when the City financial still clung to its central core area around the Bank of England. By the time Palumbo had acquired all the property needed to apply for full planning permission on the initial Mansion House Square scheme, much had changed. City office requirements had begun to adjust to the new technology-based practices and needed to provide adequate floor to ceiling heights for electronic cabling and larger and more flexible open plan office space for computer-based trading (DEGW, 1985; King, 1985, 1990; Pryke, 1991). Clients were seeking quality buildings which would express corporate images. As one developer witness said, the 'power of the architectural statement' for tenants is 'greater than it has been at any time' (No. 1 Poultry Public Inquiry, 1988, Baker Harris Saunders, p. 15). For the most part these new requirements could not be met within the existing built fabric of the City, generating a development boom during the 1980s. When the second redevelopment scheme was in public inquiry it was estimated that 13 million square feet of office accommodation was under construction or to be started by the end of 1987, the majority of which was pre-let (Baker Harris Saunders, 1987, p. 3).

Most significantly, the property development and office rental booms had a new geography. Facilitated by the flexibility of the new technology, lured by the availability of larger single-owner sites and spurred by the conservation-mindedness of the Corporation, development in the City was pushing to the outer edges and non-City locations (Pryke, 1991). Between 1980 and 1983 there was an estimated 3.6 million square feet of office space scheduled for completion in the City but, of this, over half was outside the core part of the City (Jones Lang Wootton, 1986, p. 32). At a time when the rest of the City, including the traditional financial heartland, was looking for alternative locations away from that heartland, Palumbo's effort to redevelop the central core for financial use seemed in itself an act of the past, not the present.

Palumbo's dogged pursuit of the Bank Junction redevelopment vision against such persistent opposition, and at a time when most development consortia were looking to the edge of the City or non-City sites, transcends the logic of capital. This site became locked out of the contemporary moment in restructuring not simply because of fierce opposition, but also because of this unique developer's uncompromising commitment to being personally responsible for the production of an architectural icon for the twentieth-century City of London. In Palumbo the economic rationalism of development was fused with an extraordinary personality. Palumbo, a second generation City property man, was Chair of the Arts Council, and is a member of Friends of the Earth and Greenpeace, godparent to the first-born child of the Duke and Duchess of York, and a Peer of the Realm. Despite being cast in opposition to conservationist interests, Palumbo has himself promoted conservation, albeit with a modernist ilk. He has helped restore Wren's St Stephen Walbrook and he 'collects' modernist houses (owning examples by Van der Rohe, Frank Lloyd Wright and Le Corbusier) (Gardiner, 1990, p. 22). Unlike other developers he does not have a large number of concurrent, or even past, developments to his name. His career in development has largely focused on his dream of redeveloping the Bank Junction site: the 30-year effort to accrue 13 freehold properties and 348 leasehold interests, his insistence on designs by only top ranking architects and his engagement of large teams of the most expert of expert witnesses to take him through two public inquires. His extraordinary persona was not ignored by the media in its coverage of the saga. The media rarely referred to the developer by the company name of 'City Acre Property', preferring to stress the £65 million 'Peter Palumbo' persona. In his individualistic style, he is far from the modernist developer persona of a 'faceless' consortia.

This idiosyncratic developer was far from strictly oppositional to those who defended the existing built form of Bank Junction. His proposal actively engaged with ideas about the historical character of the Junction and the City more generally. The language of townscape used to defend the scheme was the language established in planning and urban design, largely through the efforts of conservationists. Conservationists may be keen to sustain an image of developers as enemies of the past but, increasingly, development in its contemporary manifestation is appropriating the logic of heritage. At a time of City boom and in a site long associated with expressions of British power and supremacy, it was the past that provided the rationale for and surface form of contemporary statements of success (Cooke, 1990, p. 88). The Corporation and the developer shared a commitment to creating a monument to this climate of success and to the City generally. The surface form and the scale of the 'monument' vary, but ostensibly oppositional interests spoke in the same historically imbued expert discourse and of the same City.

The Power of the 'Powerless'

Thus far the battle of Bank Junction has been confined to the dominant power intersects of capital and the state. While locked in battle for some 30 years, they are co-joined, first, by an acceptance of Bank Junction as a site of key economic and historic importance, and second, by a desire to protect or create a built environment which reflects a City of Power at a time when the City was being jettisoned into a more uncertain and threatening global order.

In the final part of this chapter I want to examine one other interest group which had a more ambiguous relationship with this variously expressed City of Power and instead participated in the battle of Bank Junction by way of a narrative of powerlessness. The CARE (the CAmpaign for REfurbishment) group was led by the priest of the local church, St Mary-le-Bow, and represented the interests of the 'non-experts', essentially independent shopkeepers on the development site. Their narrative of powerlessness was paradoxically linked to a range of residual nodes of power and influence in Britain. As such even this narrative of 'powerlessness' operated to reinforce and intensify the status of Bank Junction as a symbolic site of power.

In CARE's case against redevelopment, the plight of retailing activity on the site was presented as the plight of the 'ordinary person'. In the absence of a more usual residential population, those who used the site and the area in other ways became a substitute 'community'. The CARE group asserted an alternative symbolic value for the site based in part in the existing retail activity on the redevelopment site and its link with past City practices and social orders. The independent retailers involved in the CARE campaign lamented the demise in numbers and influence of their kind in the City. 'Local' traders were much affected by global trends in the retail sector. Cheapside/Poultry, which borders the northern edge of the development site, is one of only four retailing centres in the City of London. The 22 retailing units on the redevelopment site are occupied by small independent retailers and caterers who have taken advantage of reduced rents associated with redevelopment blight. The high proportion of independent retailers is incongruous with the character of the rest of Cheapside/Poultry and other retail centres in the City, where High Street multiples dominate. The redevelopment of this site was seen as the beginning of the demise of this last stronghold of the independent retailer in the City. It was a retail sector that prided itself on its long commitment to 'serving' the City. One retailer explained how his family's retail service to the City in sweets and confections was linked to a much more serious commitment to serve the nation:

> our family had a shop in Bow Lane . . . from 1911 to 1972. . . . My father served in the 1914–18 War, and I served for 6 years in the Army. My late brother lost an eye . . . Fire Watching in Cannon Street. . . . So you will appreciate our family and relatives, now retired, who served the City of London, still have a deep feeling for it. (Letter from retailer to CARE, 4 March 1987)

The desire of the independent retailers to resist the Palumbo schemes was compatible with that of conservationists, thereby opening the way for a coalitional opposition. The compatibility between conservation and the service sector has been evident throughout Britain during recent restructuring (Wright, 1985; Hewison, 1987; Thrift 1989). National conservation groups like Save Britain's Heritage, so closely involved with the CARE campaign and the Bank Junction redevelopment, have been instrumental in recasting conservation of the historic built environment not simply as an antiquarian exercise but as an economically viable alternative to new development. A Save Britain's Heritage report, 'Conservation and Jobs' (1976), outlined in detail the mutually beneficial relationship between conservation and small businesses (see also Binney and Hanna, 1978). Such businesses ensure that refurbished properties are economically viable. They also accord with the conservation aesthetic by contributing vitality and visual variety to the streetscape.

The independent retail activity on the site was seen as an example of 'a survival of the traditional . . . mix of uses' capturing a more humane, friendly and domestic way of life than that of the global City (No. 1 Poultry Public Inquiry, 1988, Save Britain's Heritage, pp. 6–7). This was a City redolent not of grand statements of power but a more diminutive, domestic and diverse City. As Save Britain's Heritage argued, 'the very essence of London's character' resides not in great set pieces or grand buildings but in the 'unexpected . . . relatively modest clusters of buildings that often have a village quality' (No. 1 Poultry Public Inquiry, 1988, Save Britain's Heritage, p. 5). The luxury goods Mappin and Webb store, whose spire was central to the conservation case, was diminutively described by the CARE group as the City's 'corner shop', while the entire collection of retail units on the redevelopment site were compared with a village high street (CARE, *The Threat Remains Exhibition*, St Mary-le-Bow, April/May 1988). CARE presented Bank Junction as a traditional retail centre in the City and this functional lineage was imparted with a redemptive capacity. The small shops and human scale of the retailing activity were seen to keep the ever-internationalizing and outward-facing City somehow rooted in a more domestic scene.

The symbolic transformation of the Heart of the Empire into the village scene could not be complete, not even in the City village, without a church spire. The CARE case reverberated with the townscape arguments of the Corporation and conservationists by advocating the protection of the view of St Paul's dome and its visual relationship with the more local spire of St Mary-le-Bow. The active participation of the church, by way of the CARE group, added enormous legitimacy to the townscape case for retaining the existing buildings. The church justified being outspoken about the Bank Junction case on the grounds that a 'very old, old deep thing' establishes the Anglican parish priest as 'a priest of a geographical area' over which he has responsibility for the 'well being of the place' (Interview with Victor Stock, CARE, 16 May 1988). Through CARE, the church directly reiterated the subtext of the

Corporation's case for the desirability of a visual presence of the Church within the financial heartland of Britain. Here again public opposition took recourse to past images of the City, in this case to Canaletto's London, in which the City skyline is dominated not by the NatWest tower or other statements of financial or commercial power, but by religion.

The transformation of the Heart of the Empire into a village established Bank Junction not as a site of power but as a symbolic site of 'powerlessness' where the 'ordinary person' battled it out against the powerful and the expert. Yet it was through this narrative of powerlessness that one of the more defiant residuals of power and influence in Britain intersected with the symbolic geography of Bank Junction. The CARE case for the right of the 'ordinary person' to defend the 'home patch' drew upon the recent comments by HRH the Prince of Wales on the state of British planning and architecture. The Prince of Wales' architectural polemic, *Visions of Britain* (a book, television programme and Victoria and Albert Exhibition) is framed as defiantly indigenous. His ten commandments of architecture, which he dubs 'pieces of folklore', bow to the natural and organic character of Britain, not to any global imperatives (HRH the Prince of Wales, 1989, p. 15). The Prince was presented as the heroic advocate of the powerless, leading them into battle against more powerful interests. His controversial description of the No. 1 Poultry scheme as 'an old 1930s wireless' was much cited proof of the unison of those who (once) 'mastered' the nation and those in its loyal 'service'.

Through the case of CARE the very same environment that was heralded as central to the traditional civic and financial City is reimagined as an alternative and possibly more pervasive *leitmotif* of English identity, the village. The City village is evoked by way of a particular community of social and cultural practices: independent retailers, the street life of a shopping precinct, the parish. The associated urban forms of the street-facing shopfronts and the church spire (or dome) reiterate this social world in the urban landscape. Through the village aesthetic 'local' interests could be expressed and preserved in the context of a City which is increasingly responding to global imperatives. Evoking the village produces a rural subtext in this centrally urban scene (Williams, 1973; Bagguley et al., 1990).

The village metaphor may rest as an oppositional image to the City as the Heart of Empire or Global Finance, but in the CARE evocation it does not seek to subvert the functional status of the financial City. The shops that are a part of the village scene will serve the class-specific financial City, as they always have. The village to be invented here in the heart of the City will assert an indigenous quality to help domesticate and give moral fibre to the international City. This is not a classic urban conflict of capital against community, new against old, but 'big capital' against 'small capital', a battle between different sectors of the service class (Bagguley et al., 1990). Thus the campaign of the church and the retailers, in collaboration with conservationists, worked both ideologically and materially to reinforce traditional social patterns of hierarchy and to reproduce grander processes of capital accumulation associated with this site.

Conclusion

This chapter is based on a 'reading' of the City that resisted privileging the existing built form as testament to the way capital is manifest and power operates. By examining a site locked out of the contemporary phase of economic restructuring it is possible to enter into some of the more elusive aspects of flexible accumulation. By focusing on a long-standing development controversy, in which real and desired 'Bank Junctions' come together in conflict, the chapter seeks to elucidate the more complex surfaces and spatial patterings of capital and its attendant terrain of power. The 'reading' makes explicit the way in which capital is in a mutually constitutive relationship with cultural practices, ideologies and artefacts that have local specificity.

To foreground a redevelopment that (as yet) remains unbuilt may also have an unexpected empirical accuracy. Current understandings of restructuring have rightly identified certain hallmark spatial adjustments and surface appearances. Yet if there was one distinctive feature of the restructuring City of London of the 1980s, it was that much of the decade was spent talking about massive urban changes which, by the close of the eighties, were still simply in the realm of media and public relations 'discourse and figure' (see Lash, 1990). The presence of a variously imagined and highly contested City of the 1980s gave way in the more economically sober days of the early 1990s to a City of blighted sites around which the remnants of the rhetoric and imagery of their promoters and their opponents floated, awaiting a lucrative landing.

The nexus of money, power and space evident in the battle of Bank Junction defies the simplistic iconography of the skyscraper and its associated faceless capital. Bank Junction provides an extreme but not unique example of the importance of the developer 'personality' in contemporary processes of capital accumulation. The self-conscious historicism of contemporary redevelopment in the City of London suggests that current cycles of capital accumulation are strategically alert to alternative sites of power, such as the conservation lobby and the local state. Current cycles of reinvestment may well be linked into global networks of capital, but they are more likely to have the surface appearance of things familiar (the old and the local). Bank Junction provides an excellent example of how residual practices, values, symbolic meanings, architectural aesthetics and patterns of power intersect with, reshape and indeed even halt the drive of globalizing capital. The Bank Junction saga is a testament to the way in which capital does indeed operate in very real and powerful local contexts that work to shape its particular expression.

Revised political economic accounts of the post-Fordist city tend to overemphasize the commodification of culture or the way capital 'uses' culture as legitimation. While these are both dimensions of the culture–capital nexus apparent in this case study it is only one part of the power dynamic of capital accumulation in the city. The battle of Bank Junction makes explicit the interlinking of 'small' and 'big' capital with complexly grounded sentiments about locality and nation, the past and the future. Furthermore, it demonstrates the way in which cycles of capital accumulation must negotiate locality-specific work practices that are deeply embedded in class, gender and ethnic structures and that themselves are the object of nostalgia and, at times, politicized defence.

The emergence in the Bank Junction saga of an exclusionary discursive field based on those having 'cultural capital' in the language and logic of 'townscape' elucidates the subtle formation of power. In the Bank Junction battle the 'local' retailers, keen to protect their traditional practices, could enter into the public debate because of an economic and aesthetic compatibility with the conservation agenda. More deeply oppositional interests, such as those refusing the conservation aesthetic or the confinement of the language and logic of townscape, may have been denied access to the public arena of debate (Jacobs, 1992). Thus understood, the discursive and representational are not simply 'reflections' of power, they are germane to the constitution of fields of power.

The battle of Bank Junction demonstrates that in this complex interlinking the surface appearance of conflict and struggle can be the spectacle through which the symbolic power of a place is reiterated, adjusted and at times reinvented. This gladiatorial planning struggle is a public ritual that verifies the importance of Bank Junction to the City and the City to the nation. The power of Bank Junction is constituted not simply from the presence of capital but from residual power nodes (the Empire, the Church, royalty, class) that operate inter-discursively and inter-textually. In the City of London, contemporary global imperatives negotiate their way through a net of nationalistic sentiments and residuals of power. In the case of Bank Junction the spatial product of this process is evident in its absence.

References

Anderson, R. (1988) Meaning in the urban environment. Unpublished PhD, Centre for Urban Design, Oxford Polytechnic.

Bagguley, P., Mark-Lawson, J., Shapiro, D., Walby, S. and Warde, A. (1990) *Restructuring: Place, Class and Gender*. London: Sage Publications.

Baker Harris Saunders (1987) *The City Office Market: an Examination of Supply, Demand and Debt*. London: Baker Harris Saunders.

Beauregard, R.A. (1986) The chaos and complexity of gentrification. In N. Smith and P. Williams (eds), *Gentrification of the City*. Boston: Unwin Hyman, 35–55.

Beauregard, R.A. (1989) Between modernity and postmodernity: the ambiguous position of US planning. *Environment and Planning D: Society and Space*, 7, 381–95.

Berman, M. (1982) *All That Is Solid Melts into Air: the Experience of Modernity*. London: Verso.

Binney, M. and Hanna, M. (1978) *Preservation Pays: Tourism and the Economic Benefits of Conserving Buildings*. London: Save Britain's Heritage.

Bourdieu, P. (1984) *Distinction: a Social Critique of the Judgement of Taste*. London: Routledge and Kegan Paul.

Broadbent, G., Bunt, R. and Jencks, C. (eds) (1980) *Signs, Symbols, and Architecture*. Chichester: John Wiley and Sons.

Burgess, J. and Wood, P. (1988) Decoding Docklands: place advertising and decision-making strategies of the small firm. In J. Eyles and D.M. Smith (eds), *Qualitative Methods in Human Geography*. Cambridge: Polity Press, 94–117.

Cassis, Y. (1985a) Bankers in English society in the late nineteenth century. *Economic History Review*, 38(2), 210–29.

Cassis, Y. (1985b) The banking community of London, 1890–1914: a survey. *Journal of Imperial and Commonwealth History*, 13(3), 109–26.

Cassis, Y. (1988) Merchant bankers and City aristocracy. *British Journal of Sociology*, 39(1), 114–20.

Castells, M. (1983) *The City and the Grassroots*. London: Edward Arnold.

Clarke, W. (ed.) (1989) *The City of London Official Guide*. London: Hobson Publishing.

Cohen, A. (1974) The lesson of ethnicity. In A. Choen (ed.), *Urban Ethnicity*. London: Tavistock Publications, ix–xxiv.

Cooke, P. (1990) *Back to the Future: Modernity, Postmodernity and Locality*. London: Unwin Hyman.

Corporation of London (1970) *Conservation Areas*. Report, Planning and Communications Committee, Corporation of London, Guildhall, London.

Corporation of London (1981) *Conservation Areas*. Report, Planning and Communications Committee, Corporation of London, Guildhall, London.

Corporation of London (1986) *City of London Local Plan*. Department of Architecture and Planning, Corporation of London, Guildhall, London.

Corporation of London (1987a) *1986 Survey of Office Ocupiers in the City of London*. Planning and Communications Committee, Corporation of London, Guildhall, London.

Corporation of London (1987b) *Population Census 1981: Information Report, City of London*. Department of Architecture and Planning, Corporation of London, Guildhall, London.

Cosgrove, D. (1985) *Social Formation and Symbolic Landscape*. London: Croom Helm.

Cosgrove, D. and Daniels, S. J. (eds) (1988) *The Iconography of Landscape*. Cambridge: Cambridge University Press.

Daniels, S. (1989) Marxism, culture and the duplicity of landscape. In R. Peet and N. Thrift (eds), *New Models in Geography, Vol. II.* London: Unwin Hyman, 196–220.

DEGW (1985) *Accommodating the Growing City.* Report by DEGW Research Consultants and Space Planners for Rosehaugh Stanhope plc. London: DEGW.

Domosh, M. (1987) Imagining New York's first skyscapers, 1875–1910. *Journal of Historical Geography*, 13(3), 233–48.

Domosh, M. (1988) The symbolism of the skyscaper: case studies of New York's first tall buildings. *Journal of Urban History*, 14(3), 320–45.

Foucault, M. (1986) Of other spaces. *Diacritics*, 16, 22–7.

Gardiner, S. (1990) Palumbo's Palaces. *The Observer Magazine*, 1 July, 22–7.

Gibbs, K. T. (1984) *Business Architectural Imagery in America, 1870–1930.* Ann Arbor, MI: UMI Research Press.

Goodhart, C. and Grant, A. (eds) (1986) *Business of Banking.* London: Gower Press.

Gottdiener, M. (1985) *The Social Production of Urban Space.* Austin: University of Texas Press.

Gottdiener, M. (1986) Culture, ideology and the sign of the city. In M. Gottdeiner and A. Ph. Lagopoulos (eds), *The City and the Sign: an Introduction to Urban Semiotics.* New York: Columbia University Press, 202–18.

Gottdiener, M. and Lagopoulos, A. Ph. (eds) (1986) *The City and the Sign: an Introduction to Urban Semiotics.* New York: Columbia University Press.

Harris, J. and Thane, P. (1984) British and European bankers 1880–1914: an 'aristocratic bourgeoisie'?. In P. Thane, G. Crossick and R. Floud (eds), *The Power of the Past: Essays for Eric Hobsbawm.* Cambridge: Cambridge University Press, 215–34.

Harvey, D. (1985) *Consciousness and the Urban Experience.* Oxford: Oxford University Press.

Harvey, D. (1989a) *The Urban Experience.* Oxford: Oxford University Press.

Harvey, D. (1989b) *The Condition of Postmodernity.* Oxford: Basil Blackwell.

Hewison, R. (1987) *The Heritage Industry: Britain in a Climate of Decline.* Methuen, London.

Hobsbawm, E. and Ranger, T. (eds) (1983) *The Invention of Tradition.* Cambridge: Cambridge University Press.

HRH the Prince of Wales (1989) *A Vision of Britain: a Personal View of Architecture.* London: Doubleday.

Jackson, P. (1991) Mapping meanings: a cultural critique of locality studies. *Environment and Planning A*, 23, 215–28.

Jacobs, J.M. (1992) Cultures of the past and urban transformation: the Spitalfields Market redevelopment in East London. In K. Anderson and F. Gale (eds), *Inventing Places: Studies in Cultural Geography.* Melbourne: Longman Cheshire.

Jager, M. (1986) Class definition and the aesthetics of gentrification: Victoriana in Melbourne. In N. Smith et al. (eds), *Gentrification of the City.* Hemel Hempstead: Allen and Unwin, 78–91.

Jameson, F. (1984) Postmodernism, or the cultural logic of late capitalism. *New Left Review*, 146, 53–92.

Jones Lang Wootton (1986) *City Offices* (June, July, December). London: JLW.

King, A. (ed.) (1980) *Buildings and Society: Essays on the Social Development of the Built Environment*. London: Routledge and Kegan Paul.

King, A. (1985) 'Capital City': physical and social aspects of London's role in the world economy. *Development and Change*, 16, 3–47.

King, A. (1990) *Global Cities: Post-imperialism and the Internationalization of London*. London: Routledge.

King, R. J. (1988) Urban design in capitalist society. *Environment and Planning D: Society and Space*, 6, 445–74.

Knox, P. L. (1984) Symbolism, styles and settings: the built environment and the imperatives of urbanized capital. *Architecture and Behaviour*, 2(2), 107–22.

Knox, P. L. (1987) The social production of the built environment: architects, architecture and the post-modern city. *Progress in Human Geography*, 11(3), 354–78.

Kutcher, A. (1976) The views of St Paul's Cathedral. In D. Lloyd et al. (eds), *Save the City*. London: SPAB.

Lash, S. (1990) *Sociology of Postmodernism*. London: Routledge.

Lash, S. and Urry, J. (1987) *The End of Organised Capitalism*. Cambridge: Polity Press.

Lefebvre, H. (1991) *The Production of Space* (trans. D. Nicholson-Smith). Oxford: Blackwell (originally published 1974).

Lisle-Williams, M. (1984a) Beyond the market: the survival of family capitalism in the English merchant banks. *British Journal of Sociology*, 35(2), 241–71.

Lisle-Williams, M. (1984b) Merchant banking dynasties in the English class structure: ownership, solidarity and kinship in the City of London, 1850–1960. *British Journal of Sociology*, 35(3), 333–62.

Lloyd, D. (ed.) (1976) *Save the City: a Conservation Study of the City of London*. London: SPAB.

Lowenthal, D. (1985) *The Past Is a Foreign Country*. Cambridge: Cambridge University Press.

McRae, H. and Cairncross, F. (1985) *Capital City: London and Financial Centre*. London: Methuen.

No. 1 Poultry Public Inquiry (1988) *Proofs of Evidence*. London.

Philo, C. (1992) Foucault's geography. *Environment and Planning D: Society and Space*, 10, 137–61.

Plender, J. and Wallace, P. (1985) *The Square Mile: a Guide to the New City of London*. London: Century Publishing.

Pred, A. (1984) Structuration, biography formation and knowledge: observations on port growth during the late mercantile period. *Environment and Planning D: Society and Space*, 2, 251–75.

Pred, A. (1986) *Place, Practice and Structure: Social and Spatial Transformation in Southern Sweden 1750–1850*. Cambridge: Cambridge University Press.

Pryke, M. (1991) An international city going 'global': spatial change and office provision in the City of London. *Environment and Planning D: Society and Space*, 9(2), 197–222.

Raban, J. (1988) *Soft City*. London: Collins Harvill.

Relph, E. (1987) *The Modern Urban Landscape*. London: Croom Helm.

Royal Commission on Local Government in Greater London (1962) *Written Evidence*. London: HMSO.

Sampson, A. (1982) *The Changing Anatomy of Britain*. London: Hodder and Stoughton.

Sassen, S. (1991) *The Global City: New York, London, Tokyo*. Princeton, NJ: Princeton University Press.

Save Britain's Heritage (1976) Conservation and jobs. *Built Environment Quarterly*, September, 211–26.

Short, J. R. (1989) *The Humane City: Cities as if People Matter*. Oxford: Basil Blackwell.

Smith, N. and Williams, P. (eds) (1986) *Gentrification of the City*. Winchester, MA: Allen and Unwin.

Soja, E. W. (1989) *Postmodern Geographies: the Reassertion of Space in Critical Social Theory*. London: Verso.

Tafuri, M. (1979) This disenchanted mountain: the skyscaper and the city. In G. Ciucci et al. (eds), *The American City: from the Civil War to the New Deal*. (trans. B. L. La Penta). Cambridge, MA: MIT Press, 389–528.

Thrift, N. (1986) The geography of international economic disorder. In R. J. Johnson and P. J. Taylor (eds), *A World In Crisis? Geographical Perspectives*. Oxford: Blackwell, 12–67.

Thrift, N. (1987) The fixers: the urban geography of international commercial capital. In J. Henderson and M. Castells (eds), *Global Restructuring and Territorial Development*. London: Sage, 203–33.

Thrift, N. (1989) Images of social change. In C. Hamnett, L. McDowell and P. Sarre (eds), *The Changing Social Structure*. London: Sage, 12–42.

Waldegrave, W. (1988) Speech to the Royal Fine Arts Commission by Minister for Housing and Planning, London.

Williams, P. (1976) The role of institutions in the inner London housing market: the case of Islington. *Transactions of the Institute of British Geographers, NS*, 3, 72–82.

Williams, R. (1973) *The Country and the City*. London: Chatto and Windus.

Williams, R. (1977) *Marxism and Literature*. Oxford: Oxford University Press.

Worskett, R. (1988) Mansion House: keeping the status quo. *Landscape*, 7, 56–7.

Wright, P. (1985) *On Living in an Old Country: the National Past in Contemporary Britain*. London: Verso.

Zukin, S. (1986) Gentrification: culture and capital in the urban core. *Annual Review of Sociology*, 13, 129–47.

Zukin, S. (1988a) The postmodern debate over urban form. *Theory, Culture and Society*, 5, 431–46.

Zukin, S. (1988b) *Loft Living: Culture and Capital in Urban Change*. London: Radius.

16

Money, Power and Social Movements: the Contested Geography of Finance in Southern Africa

Patrick Bond

Introduction: the Geographical Power of Finance

Money and the institutions that manage it have, in recent years, attained greater power over the commanding economic heights of many places, and as a result economic geography has been transformed at local, national and international scales. This chapter offers a Marxist interpretation of financial power, its spatial implications and, most importantly, popular resistance to that power.

As a first principle, Marxists hold that the power embodied in financial systems is never static – it ebbs and flows according to a broader trajectory of capital accumulation, closely correlated to the alternating strength and weakness of productive capital. The power of money is not static in spatial terms, either. During periodic upsurges of finance in relation to production, financiers are the best suited – of any and all capitalists – to identify geographical challenges, and then to conquer space and scale, and to reshape them in a different image. *The rise of finance accentuates existing tendencies towards uneven development* that are inherent in capitalist economies, and thereby sets the scene for political confrontations which have important spatial implications.

Across the world and at every geographic scale, the uneasy financial and geopolitical shifts engendered by periodic structural economic downturns provoke response by a diverse set of social movements. These movements have a strong chance of success because where financial power accumulates, so too a certain vulnerability emerges, which if properly conceptualized and strategically confronted by a sophisticated and militant social movement can actually produce dramatic upheavals. But to chart the contested geography of finance requires an appreciation of the enormous variance in the coherence of its power across different spatial scales. This is very much a geopolitical contest, featuring profoundly different ideological commitments to particular ways of organizing space and scale. It is not a contest easily reduced to the territorial–administrative disputes that are the bread and butter of orthodox geopolitical theory. Instead, it is about, quite simply, how the problems caused by financial power are *displaced* (but not solved) across space.

In resisting this displacement, the classic populist social movement can as easily turn to the right or simply become coopted, as it might – if conditions are potent – turn to the left to explore more democratic and grassroots-oriented approaches to money, power and space. Social movements in South Africa and Zimbabwe illustrate the relationship of strategy and tactics to the specificities of economic crisis management adopted by each set of local, national and international financiers.

Economic Crisis and the 'Financial Explosion'

Even at the zenith of victory over what was misnamed 'socialism' in the East, most of global capitalism (and in particular its financial circuits) still founders, and to understand why requires theoretical insights. Classical Marxist crisis theory offers an explanation for the long-term slow-down in growth, trade and productive investment that has plagued the world economy since the early 1970s, and for the phenomenal rise of finance – a veritable 'financial explosion' (Magdoff and Sweezy, 1987) – since the early 1980s. That rise is reflected in different ways in different national economies, but typically includes: extremely high real global interest rates; an explosion in stock markets and real estate; increasing debt burdens for consumers, corporations and governments; and a qualitative increase in the political clout of financiers.

To comprehend these in structural terms, consider first a permanent underlying tendency of capitalism, towards the *overaccumulation* of capital.[1] Overaccumulation refers, simply, to a situation in which excessive output is produced and cannot be brought to market profitably, leaving capital to pile up in sectoral bottlenecks or speculative outlets, without being put back into new productive investment. Other symptoms include: unused plant and equipment; huge gluts of unsold commodities; an unusually large number of unemployed workers; and the inordinate rise of financial markets (which serve increasingly as speculative vehicles for capital not reinvested in production). Debt also rises in the wake of inexorable declines in rates of corporate profits, workers' real wages and government tax revenues, as well as because of the increasing propensity to borrow in order to speculate.

1 For evidence of overaccumulation in the world economy since the early 1970s see Clarke (1988, pp. 279–360), Mandel (1989), Harvey (1989, pp. 180–97) and Armstrong et al. (1991, pp. 169–260).

When an economy reaches a decisive stage of overaccumulation, then it becomes difficult to bring together all these resources in a profitable way to meet social needs. The only 'solution' to overaccumulation – i.e. the only response to the crisis capable of re-establishing the conditions for a new round of accumulation – is widespread *devaluation*.

When overaccumulation becomes widespread, extreme forms of devaluation are invariably resisted (or deflected) by whatever local, regional, national or international alliances exist or are formed in specific areas under pressure. *Hence, overaccumulation has very important geographical and geopolitical implications*, as attempts are made to transfer the costs and burdens of devaluation to different regions and nations or to push overaccumulated capital into the built environment as a last-ditch speculative venture, in what David Harvey (1982, chapter 13) has termed the 'spatial fix'.

The rise and fall of financial power is most spectacular precisely because it is during these moments that spatial differentiation is most ambitiously generated. Space becomes much more crucial when the circulation of capital in productive sectors is overshadowed by increasingly futile attempts to accumulate capital not through production but through financial speculation. This is the basis for the spatial vision of a man like Thomas Johnson, President of New York's Chemical Bank, explaining the impact of the Third World debt crisis: 'There is a possibility of a nightmarish domino effect, as every creditor ransacks the globe attempting to locate his collateral' (cited in Smith, 1990, p. 161).

Across a variety of scales, uneven development is generally intensified during those periods when financial institutions increase their range of movement, the velocity and intensity of their operations, and simultaneously their power over debtors (whether companies, consumers or governments). Yet this situation cannot exist forever. The search for relief from overaccumulation crisis, through space, becomes ever more fruitless, as the restructuring of the space economy becomes, concomitantly, more frenetically finance-driven.

A sensitivity to scale and to space is therefore crucial to working out the modalities of financial power. One chilling example is the rise of Nazism, with the intellectual support of Haushofer's Geopolitical School. Hitler stitched together a coalition of the German middle classes and disenchanted national capitalists aimed at creating an expanding geographical barrier (*Lebensraum*) of economic autarchy against foreign finance. As van der Pijl (1984, p. 14) explains, 'The anti-Semitism of the Nazi movement portrayed the economic crisis as the result of "German, creative" capital throttled by a rapacious international finance capital personified by the Jews ("schaffendes" versus "raffendes Kapital") – an imagery that combined ancient prejudices with a distorted sense of Germany's actual subordination in the liberal world economy.' Thus by addressing space and scale explicitly we may determine which of several types of struggles – progressive grassroots-based, right-wing populist, nationalist and progressive internationalist – have the capacity to transcend what is sometimes an inordinate focus on financial power, and to root the struggle for a more democratic money in a longer-term approach to the *mode of production*.

Local and Regional Struggles against Financial Power

The local and regional scales, comprehensible to laypeople, provide a good taste of the conditions for successful popular interventions at the nexus of money, power and space. In advanced capitalist settings, these interventions typically occur against the 'redlining' (lending discrimination) of ghettos or the deindustrialization of regions. Alternatively, excessive financial investment (via gentrification or land speculation) can also reshape urban and rural space economies, and thus give rise to organized resistance. The same destructive principles governing inordinate flows of finance through space – alternately too little and too much – operate in the semi-periphery as well, where capitalist relations are often imposed on workforce and community in a vulgar way that heightens social tensions, as well as prospects for resistance.

The Township Bond Boycott

One of the world's strongest contemporary urban social movements has recently turned its attention to financial power, and the result is the most impressive tactic ever developed from the grassroots, one with important national implications as political transition in South Africa unfolds. Some two thousand urban community groups ('civic associations') in the late 1980s and early 1990s shared relatively uniform values, politics and methods. By most accounts, the existence of such 'organs of civil society', representing the material interests of poor and working-class black people, is crucial prior to and following formal democratization (Bond, 1991).

Regardless of the demise of apartheid, on its own the market system cannot provide a full set of the necessary subsistence goods to as much as 90 per cent of the black population, a fact readily conceded by many current state bureaucrats and capitalists. Huge subsidies will be needed to acquire land, build houses and provide minimal infrastructure and basic services. Civic associations are the basis of a social movement already demanding and struggling over these resources. Yet the issue is not only too little financial capital, but in some geographical situations too much.

This is illustrated well by the ebb and flow of housing credit during the last half of the 1980s, as banks invested more than US $2 billion in mortgages ('bonds') in black township space previously off-limit by apartheid decree. Politically, this addressed an oft-articulated need to identify a new outlet for surplus funds (black townships), which would both enhance the potential for piling on even more consumer credit once collateral (the house) had been established, and introduce an inherently conservatizing form of social control (repayment of a 20-year bond). But the US $2 billion was enough to saturate only the top 10 per cent of the market – those who could afford new houses costing in excess of US $15,000 (smaller loans are administratively too costly). The variable-rate bonds were largely granted at an initial 12.5 per cent interest rate (–7 per cent in real terms), reflecting an oversupply of money, due to several factors.

The main factor, dating from the late 1960s, was an overaccumulation crisis (especially affecting the white luxury consumer goods market), which led to a dramatic fall in new private fixed investment from the mid-1970s. The financial explosion kicked into gear, as the ratio of domestic bank credit to GDP soared from 28 per cent in 1978 to 46 per cent in 1990. With the official return to monetarist ideology (as well as the might of anti-apartheid financial sanctions and fear of capital flight), nominal interest rates on housing loans were pushed from 12.5 per cent in 1988 to 21 per cent (then + 6 per cent in real terms) in 1989. Moreover, the financial explosion infected both the stock market – the Johannesburg Stock Exchange was the world's fastest-growing major bourse from 1989 to mid-1992 (during the longest depression of the twentieth century) – and commercial real estate, which witnessed unprecedented, untenable levels of speculation.

Playing lightning rod for the deeper crisis, the financial markets were themselves becoming a nexus of combined power and vulnerability by the late 1980s. As stock market shares and real estate delinked from the productive economy, banks and insurance companies increasingly controlled the contours of development, but from an ever-shakier capital base. South African banks are among the world's most overextended, and several institutions have already collapsed, while others concede huge bad loans reserves yet still claim record profits on the basis of an unprecedented interest rate spread between loans and savings. The nature of these crisis tendencies affected social conditions and strategies of popular resistance in important ways.

If the current crisis is one that as a most fundamental characteristic will entail further divisions of privileged workers from the vast majority of poor people, then strengthening the unity of poor and working people – as against lender attempts to differentiate credit supply between the employed and the unemployed – is logically one vital aspect of resistance. There are countless examples of this unity, mainly drawn from community struggles, since apartheid has had the geographical effect of segregating and constraining, within the townships, the organic intellectuals who might otherwise have turned to a petty bourgeois existence away from the residential location of the majority.

Their response to financial power is telling. When interest rates mounted in the late 1980s, the monthly bond bill doubled, and repayment became impossible for many households (probably in excess of 25 per cent of all black borrowers). A rapid increase in retrenchments began in 1989, affecting hundreds of thousands of workers. Moreover, many houses were shoddily built by developers, and the only recourse of residents was to the financier. These conditions gave rise to the phenomenon of *bond boycotts* (collective refusal to repay loans) in several dozen townships. Because of the power of civic associations to prevent new residents from moving into occupied homes, banks often lack the ability to foreclose (especially when this involves hundreds of defaulters at a time). South Africa's best-known activist grounded in the politics of civil society, Moses Mayekiso, accurately labelled the bond boycott an 'atom bomb' against the vulnerable banks, in the course of a threat to jump scale with the tactic – from selected townships to the entire country.[2] This scale shift is worth some attention.

Once Mayekiso and other civic leaders formed the South African National Civic Organization (SANCO) in March 1992, the bond boycott became the basis for a radical national political strategy similar to that behind international 'financial sanctions' (see below). In June, immediately following the breakdown of 'Convention for a Democratic South Africa' multiparty negotiations (owing to South African government demands for a 25 per cent veto voting margin in drawing up the next constitution), there occurred a massacre of fifty shack-dwellers in Boipatong Township, apparently by Inkatha-aligned hostel-dwellers guided by the South African police. Outraged by government intransigence, the SANCO national leadership responded days later by declaring solidarity with African National Congress (ANC) and trade union 'mass action' plans against the government. In particular, SANCO reasoned that since South African banks had at least US $5 billion in outstanding loans to government (including apartheid agencies and homelands) – more than 10 per cent of total government liabilities – they had a responsibility to put pressure on Pretoria to democratize. Unless such financial power was used against the state, SANCO would campaign for a national bond boycott – in addition to the effective informal bond boycott underway owing to retrenchments and the rise in interest rates.

---

2 The first time Mayekiso and his coalition, the Civic Associations of the Southern Transvaal (CAST), made the threat was in September 1991, just prior to an inconclusive meeting with the South African Association of Mortgage Lenders. The day before the meeting, CAST's militant general secretary, Sam Ntuli, was assassinated, possibly by Inkatha or the South African Police, so follow-up on the threat did not occur. Mayekiso later became president of the national civic coalition.

Shortly thereafter ANC president Nelson Mandela condemned the national bond boycott as too extreme. Though contesting this point of view, SANCO did not subsequently engage actively in campaigns against the banks. (Simultaneously, efforts by the labour movement to persuade employers to support a one-day mass work stayaway came to naught – in part because a strike by South Africa's leading trade union had just been broken by the courts, and also because leading fractions of capital were coming to the conclusion, in mid-1992, that the ANC would adopt a neoliberal approach to post-apartheid economic management and would not punish big capital for its close alliance with the apartheid state.) Thus the banks refused SANCO's demands to put pressure on government, and also rebuffed SANCO attempts in late 1992 to address a variety of other complaints: bank redlining of desegregated inner-city areas (as well as townships); vast bank ownership of land which could be used for low-cost housing (following record levels of foreclosures on developers and farmers); repeated documented bank violations of the South African Usury Act; the lack of banking services (even cash machines) available within the townships; non-existent bank affirmative action policies; the need for a banking code of conduct; and capital flight facilitated by the banks. At this point, taking advantage of new-found spatial outlets for overaccumulated capital, the banks also rushed to buy foreign banks and open offices in Panama, the Cayman Islands, Guernsey, the Isle of Man, Zurich, etc.

What difference, then, did the bond boycott threat make to the evolving struggle between an unevenly developed social movement and financial capital? In the various local-level bond boycotts, the power of collective consumer action usually led bankers to the bargaining table on their knees, often with major concessions for militant civic leaders (there were also a few examples where the tactic instead set the civic movement back). But success for some well-organized civics did not automatically translate into an optimal vehicle for winning national demands, especially when the ANC opposed the tactic. SANCO could claim limited national success in raising issues and gaining concessions,[3] and indeed notwithstanding the ANC intervention the major banks agreed to negotiate their handling of township arrears and foreclosures with more sensitivity and community input. But other more serious conflicts continually emerged between banks and SANCO constituents and were left

---

3 For example, following the national bond boycott threat, the bank most exposed in the townships – 'the Perm' (US $800 million) – suffered the loss of US $180 million in holding company share value, as Johannesburg Stock Exchange investors feared the worst. The Perm immediately funded a Southern Transvaal community development trust, and established procedures to resolve local problems and even to give its 'properties in possession' to community-controlled 'housing associations'. SANCO accepted the perm concessions in large part because the bank had no loan exposure to government.

unresolved. These conflicts were, in a theoretical sense, over which party would bear the costs of devaluing the overaccumulated financial capital that was invested in township housing bonds, costs reflected in over-valued township land (owing in part to artificial group Areas Act restrictions when bonds were granted), the excessively high interest rates, poor quality housing construction and generalized 'negative equity' (where the outstanding bond amount is higher than the market value of the bonded house) as township housing prices dropped in the early 1990s. Such conflicts awaited further development at the local level before SANCO could effectively impose national solutions.

Nevertheless, the bond boycott had implications beyond the immediate problems with high interest rates and shoddy construction. Most civic associations have a development agenda that is profoundly anti-capitalist, drawing on the 1955 ANC Freedom Charter demand that housing be considered a 'right' (something capitalism is not about to concede). The bond boycott might therefore be considered an important aspect of the broader movement under way in the early 1990s for community-controlled development (replete with decommodified land, housing and services), which in time could lead to fulfilment of Mayekiso's and others' goal of a decentralized 'people's bank', consistent with subsidized funding from a desired 'strong but slim' ANC-led state.

Tactically, bond boycotts are an interesting example of grassroots resistance to high interest rates and other objectionable features that have accompanied the displacement of overaccumulation crisis into financial markets. The fact that resistance has emerged in townships to bankers' attempts to transfer the costs of devaluation and to the more general control of space by financial power gives many progressive strategists confidence about struggles for social justice in a post-apartheid society in which Freedom Charter promises simply won't be fulfilled by the first democratic government. If better developed at the national scale, the bond boycott in particular suggests a method for addressing the *unevenness* in both social and geographical development that corresponds to the restructuring of a space economy facing overaccumulation crisis and the ascendance of national financial power. Whether conditions will be appropriate for setting up an alternative framework of democratic, non-profit development finance remains to be seen. Ironically, the traditional front-line enemy of South African blacks, Afrikaner populism, offers an important historical precedent.

Regional Development, Financial Expansion and Afrikaner Resistance

Often, decisive regional aspects of uneven development and popular resistance can be traced through the confluence of money, space and power. Again, taking South Africa as an example, one discovers that the economic and geographical history of regional expansion and rural–urban relations in the crucial period of the late nineteenth and early twentieth centuries was strewn with extraordinary instances of Afrikaner ethnic-based resistance to excessive debt and financial speculation (Bond, 1991, 1992).

In some cases, the geopolitical machinations of international financial capital were overwhelming, but ultimately most important were indigenous crises of capital accumulation. In the end, following bouts of devaluation and spatial restructuring, local and regional struggles against financial capital were channelled into forming a new set of national institutions (especially Volkskas, Sanlam and Rembrandt), which in turn established Afrikaner finance as a power of its own, with its own (very politicized and ultimately contradictory) internal logic.

Financial speculation arising from overproduction crises haunted the agriculture-based Cape economy throughout the early nineteenth century. But when diamonds were found at Kimberley in 1867, the 'imperial banks' – especially the ancestor of Standard Chartered – became responsible for organizing the concentration of mining capital, leaving Cecil Rhodes at the head of an oligopoly that eventually became Anglo American–De Beers. The spatial and sectoral switch in accumulation was a function of the financiers' capacity to respond to – and to make – the market, and of its concurrence with that era's geopolitics, the deepening of colonialism.

Britain rediscovered South Africa during the 1870s, and carried out both the full-fledged subjugation of African kingdoms and the invasion of what was then the Afrikaner Transvaal Republic in 1877. The weak Transvaal government was the result of the 1830s Great Trek from the English-dominated Cape – but with its largely Boer peasant constituency, it was unable to withstand the expansive force of British colonialism. The Transvaal fighting can itself be traced, in part, to a financial foreclosure: the Cape Commercial Bank was having problems getting Transvaal government loans repaid in the mid-1870s. Once the British had (temporarily) annexed the province, Standard immediately moved in to set up branches. The ill-will thus created catalysed the Afrikaner nationalist movement, which subsequently fought the Anglo-Boer War (1899–1902) so vigorously.

The evolution of the anti-banking movement and its successors is worth considering, since it traces directly to the powerful, if increasingly flexible, Afrikaner ideology which remained in control of South Africa from 1948 through to the early 1990s. At grassroots level, the excessive indebtedness of both Afrikaner farmers and their black sharecroppers was a local problem that had important regional implications. Keegan (1986, pp. 44, 97) reports that 'a chain of debt leading to the wholesalers was the basis of agrarian exchange relationships' in the Orange Free State: 'As a result of the unrelenting pressures on landowners with heavy mortgage debts to meet, there was a strong resistance amongst many Boer farmers to bonding their property. The grip of mortgage capital was an irksome burden, and farmers were deeply conscious of the greatly unequal exchange relations that their own dependence on the credit of others imposed.' In response, from the early 1880s, the Afrikaner Broederbond gained political mileage from bank-bashing, claiming during one severe overaccumulation–speculation–devaluation crisis that bankers were 'draining the country'. Standard Bank, that 'gigantic devil fish', responded to the populist anger by officially dropping 'British' from its name in 1883. The Bond also started its own small banks in the Cape but without success. And in 1891, five years after gold was discovered in what became Johannesburg, the Transvaal Republic's president (Paul Kruger) founded the National Bank, in order that mining finance would not remain the preserve of the English-oriented banks. But the National Bank was poorly run, nearing bankruptcy when invading British forces took it over in 1901.

Following the Boer War, populist anger in the farming regions compelled the formation of a state land bank in 1912. However, its operations still reflected the power of bankers and large landowners, for it allowed them to liquidate land taken by foreclosure or speculation. There was, simultaneously, another major expansion of credit during the 1910s, as a new generation of potential farmers could now access state funding, even where speculation had pushed land values to new heights. Yet by 1915 this became a fertile breeding ground for what Giliomee (1989, p. 76) terms 'a more radical strain' of nationalism (led by D. F. Malan), which 'built on earlier exclusivist and assertive tendencies which had grown in the course of political and financial mobilisation'. Disaster struck farmers, in the process fuelling this new nationalism, when the next severe economic downturn arrived in 1920. By 1923, South Africa had eleven times as many insolvencies per capita as England. The banks were, perhaps now by habit, easy to blame. Even the conciliatory Prime Minister Jan Smuts castigated them for having 'granted credit too easily and then curtailed it too drastically'.

Thus the 'poor white problem' – Afrikaner farmers displaced from their land – which had been building since the debt crisis of the early 1920s, became severe as the Great Depression broke in 1929. As a result, pressure increased for an expansion in state welfare for whites. Once over the hump in 1933, however, the next two decades were good for the South African macroeconomy, thanks initially both to the speed at which devaluation was accomplished, and to the role of gold as the ultimate store of value during the course of massive global devaluation (for which a fitting title was given to South Africa: 'prosperous undertaker in a plague').

A sore point throughout the 1930s and 1940s continued to be the conflict between the English-speaking mining–financial elites and Afrikaner farmers. At this stage, even with overaccumulation temporarily muted and conditions for rapid growth in place, the power of the urban financial elites over rural daily life was so overwhelming and obnoxious that on the one hand, concomitant with the rise of German Nazism, Afrikaner anti-finance rhetoric turned anti-Semitic (against the Jewish head of Anglo American Corporation). On the other hand, a proactive Afrikaner Economic Movement was launched. According to O'Meara (1983, pp. 184, 205), Afrikaner strategists such as M. S. Louw surmised that 'With the centralisation and segmentation of latent money-capital generated in agriculture, a new class of Afrikaner financial industrial and commercial capitalists would be brought into existence.' Louw was indeed correct when he declared to the second Ekonomiese Volkskongres that the greatest achievement of 'the Afrikaner' as an entrepreneur in the 1940s was as the 'founder and controller of credit institutions'.

English-speaking capital was especially vulnerable when the National Party came to power in 1948 on a programme of nationalization of mining finance (from which the National Party leadership subsequently retreated). O'Meara argues that formal state support for Afrikaner capital – which helped to prompt a diversification of financial flows into commerce and industry via the Cape-based Sanlam insurance and Rembrandt conglomerates – ultimately engendered some serious internal contradictions:

> This weaning of Afrikaner financial capital from its dependence on accumulation in agriculture, and its increasing cooperation after Sharpeville [the 1960 massacre of unarmed blacks] with non-Afrikaner finance capital, led to important shifts and struggles in nationalist politics. . . . The *verligte* phenomenon ['enlightened' Afrikaners] was a response to the emergence of a class of aggressive, self-confident Afrikaner capitalists whose interests now went beyond those of the narrow class alliance out of which they had emerged. (O'Meara, 1983, p. 205)

There was, however, a natural backlash (replete with hints of political territoriality) against the enlightened Nationalists, by a group that eventually formed the Conservative Party (the official white opposition party in the late 1980s and early 1990s):

> The *verkramptes* [conservatives] attempted to use the traditional organisation of the Afrikaner petty bourgeoisie, the Bond, against what they labelled the 'finance power of the South' [Cape Province Afrikaner insurance capitalists]. A strong move was mounted to portray the factional struggle as a simple conflict between the Bond as the guardian and soul of Afrikaner values on one hand, and the *nouveau riche* 'money capitalists' of the south on the other hand. (O'Meara, 1983, p. 251)

This conflict played itself out in various ways, but finally led to severe splits in Afrikanerdom in the 1970s and 1980s. Nevertheless, until the 1960s, it is hard not to judge successful (on its own terms) this right-wing, regionally based populist social movement. After nearly six decades of false starts, Afrikaner nationalism finally, from the late 1930s, organized effectively on terrain set by English-speaking financiers, thanks in part to the particularly hospitable stage of the accumulation process, which combined financial power and vulnerability.

National and International Struggles against Financial Power

Across the world in the postwar era, financial power – even when muted – was most convincing as a phenomenon at the national scale (as signified by the rise of Afrikaner finance with protective state support), and subsequently became international as growth in the global productive economy slowed. Nationalist and national populist movements are especially susceptible to miscalculations of scale, as they tend to root their anti-systemic philosophy and sentiments in extremely localized experiences. Where this involves finance, the implications can be disastrous. Such is the lesson of Zimbabwean nationalism in the early 1960s. Conversely, if done strategically (and if objective conditions are more amenable), attacking the commanding heights of finance can boost a nationalist movement enormously, as the Afrikaner Economic Movement experience suggests. From a more progressive angle, the African National Congress in the 1980s was even more important in contesting (if only temporarily) financial power at an international scale.

Deferential Zimbabwean Nationalism[4]

Notwithstanding an official but insincere doctrine of Marxism-Leninism during the 1970s and 1980s, the most important roots of the modern Zimbabwean nationalist movement are in the black petty bourgeoisie: teachers, doctors, lawyers and the like. During the early 1960s, the black commercial petty bourgeoisie stumbled badly in Southern Rhodesia, as it was called then, in large part because they lacked the financing necessary to get major projects off the ground – and also because embryonic self-help efforts along these lines were beset by incompetence and corruption. More damning still, a crucial flaw in the strategy of black empowerment in the face of white financial power was the failure to 'think globally and act locally' (Bond, 1992, 1993).

The nationalist movement apparently did not consider the limits of 'fixes' to overaccumulation invoked by state and capital in the late

4   Zimbabwe was ruthlessly colonized by Cecil Rhodes and his British South Africa Company in 1890, and was generally known as Southern Rhodesia until 1965, when Ian Smith declared the Unilateral Declaration of Independence of Rhodesia. The guerrilla war waged by ZANU and ZAPU resulted in 40,000 civilian deaths, but led to the Lancaster House Agreement in 1979 and independence in April 1980.

1950s. These fixes included massive infrastructure provision and geo-graphical flows of funds within the Central African Federation (includ-ing what are now Malawi and Zambia), unprecedented real estate speculation in the capital city of Salisbury (now Harare) and a dramatic expansion of the national financial system.

In 1957, the Federation was crippled when the price of its mainstay, copper, collapsed. By 1958 'the credit system had got completely out of hand', according to an analysis presented by the Federation's Chambers of Commerce. 'Both commerce and industry had been over-encouraged by the "beckoning hand" of the banks, who had until recently extended over-generous credit facilities.' Under conditions of worsening overaccu-mulation, a decline in production, investment and consumption fol-lowed, and the last big Salisbury office building was completed in 1961. By 1962 the business association complained bitterly of 'considerable unutilized capacity', and a major government investigation found that 'The problems inhibiting the further expansion of manufacturing are deeply rooted in the small dimensions of the domestic market.'

In other words, each of the ameliorating features of 1950s spatial expansion and of the growth of the financial system had run out of steam by the early 1960s. The result, over the next couple of years, included geographical contraction (the Federation was dismantled), a dearth of new fixed capital investment, and a huge devaluation of financial assets (e.g. an 18 per cent default rate on housing bonds, a 25 per cent contraction of hire-purchase credit and the demise of five of the eight white building societies).

Yet just as the overaccumulation crisis began, the nationalists decided to move into banking, not to fight, but to join. A black 'friendly society' movement emerged to take deposits and offer small loans (for consumer goods and funeral expenses). White liberal capitalists were happy to champion community-based institutions, which (a) would distract the more radical of the nationalist leaders, (b) could easily be economically marginalized in terms of their potential competitive impact and (c) might draw more blacks into the credit system. This fit the broader 'partner-ship' strategy, which relied in part on debt to pacify black nationalists. In 1958 the state permitted home ownership and issuance of bonds to blacks, who until then were classic 'temporary sojourners' in the cities. 'There is a great deal of surplus cash in the country' (owing to the emerging overaccumulation crisis), one newspaper commented in 1959, 'The building societies are not unduly worried over the general fall in demand for bonds for European housing: as announced in the Southern Rhodesian Parliament, African home-ownership schemes will offer an outlet for their surplus funds.' However, black workers' wage levels were too low to permit bond repayments at increasing interest rates. The contrast between the black housing investment drought and overinvest-ment in luxurious commercial office space was stark, and ensured that flagrantly uneven metropolitan development would remain cemented into Salisbury's cityscape for decades to come.

Would the friendly societies fare better than the failing building societies, based as they were on the marketing appeal of nationalism? The Central African Mutual Association was even chaired briefly by the country's leading nationalist, Joshua Nkomo. But by 1962, after three years of operations, it had lost more than 60 per cent of the funds, and Nkomo denied any connection. The United Consumer's Co-operative Society lasted just four months in 1964, although it was chaired by the well-respected Leopold Takawira and included on its board a range of other nationalist notables. Earlier, in 1960, the managing director of a major white insurance firm had helped to establish the First African Friendly Society, whose trustees included Nathan Shamuyarira (then Editor-in-Chief of African Newspapers Ltd, later Zimbabwe's Foreign Minister) and several other prominent black politicians. But in 1961 the society failed and, according to a report, 'numbers of Africans wishing to transact business were somewhat disconcerted to find the doors locked'.

Unfazed, moderate nationalist leaders like Nkomo and Kenneth Kaunda (of Northern Rhodesia) looked to even greater financial challenges in 1961, and managed to frame them in a careful geopolitical light. A Conservative member of Britain's Parliament, John Foster, lauded

> a scheme initiated in the Central African Federation, known as the Bank of Africa Project, to which great importance is attached by African leaders, who regard its establishment as a useful counter to possible [radical] nationalist demands for the expropriation of European assets when the Africans attain political power. . . . African realisation of the importance of a sound banking system, would influence British investors who fear expropriation.

Raising Cold War fears, Foster warned fellow MPs that 'if British bankers refused to finance the project, black political leaders would look elsewhere' (in fact the bank project was ultimately aborted). Similarly, in 1960, when Chase Manhattan Bank agreed to grant a small loan to Southern Rhodesia as its international credit rating plummeted, this occasioned the involvement of Chase's David Rockefeller with leading nationalist politicians on the premise of providing 'up-to-date business training for Africans'.

In retrospect, black economic empowerment was pursued through coopted local alternatives to financial power, such as Friendly Societies, rather than full-fledged national resistance, and this social movement strategy failed. Other reforms of the racist system were applied half-heartedly by the liberals, meeting with resistance from most whites. With the rise of Ian Smith and the banning of the nationalist organizations –

the Zimbabwe African People's Union and the Zimbabwe African National Union – guerrilla war was the next (and perhaps only) logical strategy of resistance.

What should be clear from this review is that even if it ended in ultimate failure, an expansion of financial power into the nationalist movement was seen, from capital's perspective, as a way both to undergird the liberal social contract vision and to deal with overaccumulated financial capital. The strategy was sophisticated in terms of geography, for had the housing bond scheme worked it would have cemented blacks into their apartheid-style townships and simultaneously shifted the onus for reproduction of labour-power in the townships from employers and the state (which funded and built most housing at that time) to financial capital, and then to the individual. The spatial testimony of financial power during overaccumulation crisis is compelling because it also speaks to the geopolitical role of those, like Rockefeller, whose longer-term regional interests were increasingly threatened by nationalism. The cooptation of nationalists of every continent, country and stripe has since been perfected by financial capital.

It is telling, in this respect, that since the end of the guerrilla war in 1979 and independence in 1980, the most important Zimbabwean in international circles has been the Finance Minister, Dr Bernard Chidzero (runner-up candidate for UN Secretary General in 1991). Chidzero played a major role in what was meant to be the immediate post-independence 'national democratic stage' of Zimbabwe's 'transition to socialism'. On the domestic front, he helped to water down the liberation movement demand for bank nationalization – simply to starting new institutions that would ostensibly serve the majority. The most important of these was a 47 per cent government-owned local subsidiary of the Bank of Credit and Commerce International, a bank that ultimately served corrupt nationalists (and the CIA, among others) across the globe, without reference to needs of Third World majorities, as is well-known. Meanwhile, within Zimbabwe the five commercial banks (including BCCI) spent the first decade of independence making 97 per cent of their loans to whites, who comprise about 1 per cent of the total population.

Chidzero also failed to confront financial power on the international stage. Under his leadership, Zimbabwe borrowed from foreign lenders (including expensive commercial banks) far more money than could be comfortably repaid. The IMF deemed Zimbabwe 'underborrowed' at independence, and the World Bank provided hundreds of millions of dollars through project loans, for which strict conditionality was applied with increasing vigour. This culminated, a decade after independence, in the introduction of one of the continent's most widely criticized Structural Adjustment Programmes, which suggests that over the course of a quarter century, the black nationalist rulers of Zimbabwe didn't much improve their capacity to ward off self-destructive engagements with financial capital. As President Robert Mugabe put it in 1989, 'There exists among the membership of the new ZANU(PF) a minority, but very powerful bourgeois group which champions the cause of international finance and national private capital, whose interests thus stand opposed to the development and growth of a socialist and egalitarian society in Zimbabwe.'

Chidzero, for his part, was named a *Euromoney* 'Banker of the Year', was awarded membership on any number of important international commissions and chaired the IMF–World Bank 'Committee on the Transfer of Real Resources to the Developing Countries' from 1986 to 1989, a period in which the annual net transfer *from* the developing countries to northern bankers rose from nothing to US $50 billion. Similarly, Zimbabwe's leadership of the Non-aligned Movement from 1986 to 1989 was characterized by a studied avoidance of calls such as those of Julius Nyerere and Fidel Castro for a Third World debtor's cartel, or even of Peru's Alain Garcia for limits on debt servicing to 10 per cent of export earnings. The Zimbabweans were acting globally but thinking locally (i.e. solely in terms of maintaining their own solid international credit rating).

In 1987, Zimbabwe's nationalist leadership cut its citizens' food and transport subsidies, education spending and health programmes in order to make foreign debt repayments worth 35 per cent of export earnings, with hardly a murmur about the structural conditions of global overaccumulation and the rise of financial power that the dire situation reflected. Domestically, financial power exploded as well, as real estate speculation soared, and as the value of industrial shares on the smallish local stock market rose by a factor of *100* from 1984 to the early 1990s, while productive capital stock withered.

At that stage, the Structural Adjustment Programme portended even more severe trials for the 1991–5 period: 150 per cent more hard currency debt; price, wage and agricultural marketing decontrol; the phasing out of parastatal subsidies with consequent price increases; cuts of 25 per cent in the civil service; an end to import controls with the predicted loss of 10 per cent of manufacturing jobs; and trade and financial liberalization (in other words, extreme forms of spatial and temporal fix). Beginning in September 1991, short-term interest rates were doubled at the World Bank's insistence, the stock market promptly crashed by 65 per cent, real estate prices fell 35 per cent and a credit crunch sent many overexposed companies and individuals into bankruptcy. According to a panicky ZANU MP later that year, 'This is why the party is dead. People are no longer keen on following the leadership because it has betrayed the people economically.'

The early 1990s suggested some mild prospects for grassroots-based resistance to financial power, including university demonstrations and a threat from the leading trade unionist that 'mass action' would follow the intensification of structural adjustment. As the main business newspaper put it in September 1991,

The socio-economic hardships may force many Zimbabweans to go into the streets and show their disenchantment with the system. Many will remember the so-called IMF riots in places like Sudan and Zambia . . . While we do not advocate the oppression and suppression of the masses, it would be very unfortunate if the government were to be swayed by the popular view to abandon the programme because of the difficulties that it would have necessitated. (*Financial Gazette*, 5 September 1991)

It is no exaggeration to suggest that as the 1990s unfold, key decisions about Zimbabwe are made by the organs of international financial power, and no longer by ZANU. Notwithstanding the intervening period of armed struggle and revolutionary theorizing, little in the way of the deferential nationalists' capacity for global deliberation and militant local action against financial power – or even the capacity to identify the appropriate mix of financial power and vulnerability they confront in their domestic project of national development – seems to have changed in the past three decades.

Financial Sanctions against Apartheid

In the South Africa of the early 1990s, a disturbingly similar set of conditions to 1960s Southern Rhodesia is in place, including overaccumulation crisis, limited scope for further spatial fixes and the turn by enlightened state bureaucrats and liberal capital to finance as a cornerstone of social contract formation. The latter is emblematized by the Rockefeller Foundation's highly touted (but unlikely) US $5 billion 'Trust for Equity and Development', which is only one of several major financing initiatives that reek of geopolitical intentions – namely, putting the ANC so deeply into foreign debt that post-apartheid South Africa is ruled from Washington, DC (along the lines of the Zimbabwe model), while paving the way for the full penetration of financial power into the irrational terrain of apartheid geography.

However, the crucial difference between Southern Rhodesia in the early 1960s and South Africa in the early 1990s, as explained above and below, is the power of a social movement to address finance from a class-conscious perspective with powerful tactics like bond boycotts. An international component of the attack against financial power – the financial sanctions movement of the 1980s – completes the case studies. As with the bond boycott, it may be the most powerful tactic ever developed by a social movement to influence the spatial orientation of financial capital (Ovenden and Cole, 1989; Bond, 1991).

The campaign to cut Pretoria off from foreign loans began in the early 1960s, as ANC leader Chief Albert Luthuli and Dr Martin Luther King began calling for anti-apartheid sanctions. In the USA in 1965, Students for a Democratic Society (SDS) lodged the first direct anti-apartheid protests against a US bank – David Rockefeller's Chase Manhattan. *Ad hoc* anti-apartheid groups with names such as Committee to Oppose Bank Loans to South Africa and End Loans to South Africa sprang up in the USA and Europe during the 1970s, working closely with the mainstream anti-apartheid movement. Some of their initial government-lobbying campaigns – against guarantees of loans by the US Export–Import Bank or against new International Monetary Fund credits – were, by the early 1980s, surprisingly successful.

Minor banks were also harassed periodically by the anti-apartheid campaigners. In many cities in the USA, bank connections to South Africa provided activists with excellent linkages to their own local concerns. Banks were redlining inner-city ghettos, but at the same time making funds available to Pretoria. This provided the conditions for many a campaign based on the 'think globally, act locally' theme, involving students, labour, community groups and the anti-apartheid movement. Because such banks have very little other than public relations to distinguish themselves from their competitors, being smeared with the apartheid brush hurt a great deal. Likewise, the British anti-apartheid movement featured thousands of student activists transferring funds from Barclays to other banks, which helped persuade the bank to sell its South African operations in 1987.

Meanwhile in South Africa, declining corporate profits, the high cost of imported oil, extremely uneven gold revenues, the 1975–8 recession, the 1976 Soweto uprising and the state's desire to expand major infrastructural investment projects in a last-ditch spatial fix, all created pressures on foreign exchange and resulted in a dire need for foreign loans. South Africa's debt quickly grew to more than US $20 billion in the early 1980s.

Following the early SDS protests, Chase Manhattan Bank weathered a great number of creative attacks over the years, including sophisticated church and pension fund investment campaigns, which placed before Chase shareholders formal resolutions calling on the bank to leave South Africa. But in July 1985, with the State of Emergency and the belligerence of State President P. W. Botha sending clear signals to foreign investors, Chase withdrew a US $500 million line of credit.

The resulting uproar was the strongest proof possible that sanctions 'worked'. Botha was forced to close the Johannesburg Stock Exchange for fear of a meltdown, to introduce a new devalued currency – the financial rand – in order to stem the torrent of capital flight and to declare a debt repayment 'standstill'. Corporate leaders immediately jetted to Lusaka for unprecedented meetings with ANC leaders. Unfortunately for Botha, the standstill came at a moment when the country's townships were in flames and its factories besieged by militant workers. The international solidarity movement grew in strength.

Relations between Pretoria and international finance were, as a result, even more hotly contested by the ANC and the internal Mass Democratic

Movement, in a manner that also threatened banks in the USA, Britain, Canada, Germany and Switzerland. US bankers were fleeing South Africa as if in the proverbial herd, and although some European banks held on temporarily and two subsequent reschedulings were organized, the end of apartheid South Africa's access to new foreign long-term loans was certain.

It is often acknowledged by South African business leaders that this was the single most important event in bringing National Party politicians to the realization that they would have to share some degree of power with the black majority. But the pressure was not over. The ANC monitored the subsequent rollover of South Africa's foreign debt in early 1986 and mid-1987, and by late 1988 devised an international programme to prevent banks from bailing out Pretoria when the repayment pressure would be strongest, in June 1990.

Throughout 1989, anti-apartheid bank campaigns were launched in international financial centres, at the ANC's behest. By the time of the IMF–World Bank meetings in October 1989, a US banker remarked to *Business Day*, 'To be seen dealing with South Africa is equivalent to being tested positive for AIDS.' Yet at those meetings South African officials managed to gain a behind-the-scenes rescheduling deal on the US $13 billion outstanding, thus relieving the immediate pressure (which included extensive official Commonwealth action in support of financial sanctions). Nevertheless, South Africa would have to continue to run huge balance of payments surpluses in order to make periodic repayments. Pretoria remained vulnerable to the power of international banks. The ANC continued to call for tightened financial sanctions, even after their February 1990 unbanning. Indeed, in order to discourage foreign bankers before the culmination of the democratic transition, ANC leaders were quoted in late 1991 as suggesting that the ANC would review Pretoria's loan commitments once in power. In the words of a 1991 ANC handbook on banking and finance, 'Morally, it could be argued that this debt, used to bolster apartheid, should be used to assist economic reconstruction in South Africa.'

Nevertheless, the danger clearly on the horizon – and indeed concretized by the bond boycott controversy in mid-1992 – is that unless strategic insights from the financial campaign expand, rather than fade, Zimbabwe's post-independence experience could be repeated: the commanding heights of the post-apartheid South African economy would be left intact; foreign lenders (like the World Bank, IMF and US aid) would smother the country with loans, and dependency relations; and Chidzeroesque figures would multiply within the nationalist camp. Such danger, in turn, inspires renewed commitment to the grassroots movement for an independent, class-conscious civil society, and to the notion of a socialist seedbed of decommodified, community-controlled development.

Strategic Conclusions and Questions

Social movements can form one line of defence against the devaluation of overaccumulated capital, as we have seen, and financial power will always offer an enticing target for strategic resistance, even if there are any number of dangers involved. Aside from those in southern Africa, there are plenty of other contemporary movements against financial power at the national and international scales (there are also plenty of unorganized, localized movements, or 'IMF riots') (Walton, 1987).

In Brazil, the Workers Party built a strong following – and nearly came to power in 1989 – in part based on a platform of foreign debt repudiation. The Philippine Freedom from Debt Coalition engaged in a variety of pressure tactics and won a debt cap (10 per cent of export earnings) in the national legislature's General Appropriations Act of 1991. Northern Europeans also attacked international financial power at the 1988 Berlin IMF and World Bank meetings, which attracted 80,000 protesters.

There was plenty for activists to concentrate on in the advanced capitalist countries, for in the early 1990s, as in the early 1930s, domestic crises of overaccumulation followed by financial explosion were becoming nearly universal. Even Norway and Sweden, paragons of social-democratic respectability, in 1991 witnessed enormous banking crises. In Japan, where the rise of financial power appeared unstoppable during the 1980s, vigorous right-wing populist protests subsequently arose because domestic financial scandals moved from political influence-peddling to playing favourite with corporations (against pensioners) over who would bear the brunt of Tokyo stock market devaluation.

In the USA, the demise of several hundred thousand family farms in the 1980s fostered similar tendencies. But the USA also has a long tradition of progressive resistance to financial power, dating from the populist movement of the late nineteenth century (Goodwyn, 1978). A present-day Financial Democracy Campaign (FDC), a coalition of hundreds of organizations led by the national ghetto-based ACORN network, is operating with this tradition firmly in mind (Bond, 1990).

The optimal direction, according to FDC strategists, is a new set of 'public banks' that can operate outside the existing logic of financial power. (This may also be the optimal route for addressing chronic gender bias in finance (Berger, 1989), as most successful informal savings schemes are dominated by women.) Recall the dangers, however, of putting excessive weight on alternative institutions – whether based in credit and savings, or in community-controlled development – in the context of financial devaluation, as reflected in the problems of the Zimbabwean nationalists.

Nevertheless, at a very basic level, the devaluation process is one in which people are continually discharged from formal employment and the circuits of capital. Alternative institutions are therefore not a luxury but a necessity. Especially where the value of the currency is itself thrown into question by a collapse of domestic *vis-à-vis* international financial power (as has happened with devastating effect throughout the Third World in recent years), an alternative savings and payments system may well be required. Such is the argument of Fantu Cheru (1989), whose *Silent Revolution in Africa* suggests that peasant delinking from formal state-run crop marketing and exchange systems – to be replaced by barter networks – is one ongoing response to the austerity regimes imposed by financial power. But economic semi-autarchy probably must jump in scale to make a dent in financial power. 'Popular demonstrations against such officially constructed austerity plans are reported almost daily', report Arrighi et al. (1989, pp. 73–4):

> The more these popular struggles focus in each national setting on what-ever regime is in office, and so become focused on who speaks in the name of that national people as a whole, the more will such struggles weaken the workings of the world-scale class-forming process and strengthen the interstate system. The more, on the other hand, the popular movements join forces across borders (and continents) to have their respective state officials abrogate those relations of the interstate system through which the pressure is conveyed, the less likely they are to weaken, and the more likely they are to strengthen, the pivotal class-forming process of the world-economy.

There may be important national and local particularities, but the fact that the austerity plans are becoming ever similar throughout the inter-state system, under the broad determination of financial power, should be clear. This heightens the urgency of internationalist campaigns, of which anti-apartheid financial sanctions are the best example to date – and of which resistance to the IMF and World Bank (of the type that Zimbabwe's nationalists spurned) must be the next step. In this respect, it may also be true that, as in the 1930s, the only prospect for an entirely new direction of accumulation that would give hope for the majority of people in the world in the 1990s, through hastening the fall of financial power, lies in widespread default on the Third World debt, increased South–South cooperation and semi-autarchic, inward-oriented accumu-lation (Amin, 1990).

The case studies from Southern Africa suggest that it is essential to think globally and act locally, but act nationally and internationally as well. With the decline of industrial power relative to financial power, it is revealing that working-class movements have broadly given way to new social movement challenges to the uneven development of inter-national capitalism, and that anti-systemic struggles remain strong even in the downturn phase of the global accumulation cycle (Frank and Fuentes, 1990).

A tentative conclusion, therefore, is that the *revolutionary* social movement cannot primarily be grounded in proletarian point-of-production
politics, yet needs to maintain *class-conscious politics of civil society*
(like those of South African civic associations) in the context of financial
power over nation states and of the compradorization of nationalist
movements (such as ZANU and, probably, the future ANC). But if a
social movement with such characteristics is right-wing populist and
successful, it is as liable to tend towards Afrikaner-style corporatism (some
say fascism) in order ultimately to make peace with capital, and this has
its own self-destructive tendencies (in addition to its dangers to 'others').

Can social movements walk this tightrope, and react to financial power
in an internationalist manner that one day addresses the causes – in
industrial overaccumulation – rather than merely the symptoms? If there
is not a worldwide socialist movement to emerge in the short term to
confront and transform financial power, shall we then embrace, perhaps,
progressive populism in its diverse forms and at different scales, in order
to contest the geography of financial power and sow some tentative seeds
of a new mode of production?

References

Amin, S. (1990) *Delinking*. London: Zed Books.
Armstrong, K., Glyn, A. and Harrison, J. (1991) *Capitalism Since 1945*.
Oxford: Basil Blackwell.
Arrighi, G., Hopkins, T. and Wallerstein, I. (1989) *Anti-systemic Movements*.
London: Verso.
Berger, M. (1989) Giving women credit: the strengths and limitations of credit
as a tool for alleviating poverty. *World Development*, 17(7), 1017–32.
Bond, P. (1990) The new US class struggle: financial industry power vs. grass-
roots populism. *Capital and Class*, 40, 150–81.
Bond, P. (1991) *Commanding Heights and Community Control*. Johannesburg:
Ravan Press.
Bond, P. (1992) Finance and uneven development in Zimbabwe. PhD disserta-
tion, Department of Geography and Environmental Engineering, Johns Hop-
kins University, Baltimore.
Bond, P. (1993) Economic origins of black townships in Zimbabwe: contradic-
tions of industrial and financial capital in the 1950s and 1960s. *Economic
Geography*, 72–89.
Cheru, F. (1989) *The Silent Revolution in Africa*. London: Zed Books.
Clarke, S. (1988) *Keynesianism, Monetarism and the Crisis of the State*. Alder-
shot: Edward Elgar.
Frank, A. G. and Fuentes, M. (1990) Civil democracy: social movements in recent
world history. In S. Amin, G. Arrighi, A. G. Frank and I. Wallerstein (eds),
Transforming the Revolution. New York: Monthly Review Press, 139–80.
Giliomee, H. (1989) Aspects of the rise of Afrikaner capital and Afrikaner
nationalism in the Western Cape, 1870–1915. In W. G. James and M. Simons
(eds), *The Angry Divide*. Cape Town: David Philip, 63–79.

Goodwyn, L. (1978) *The Populist Moment*. New York: Oxford University Press.

Harvey, D. (1982) *The Limits to Capital*. Oxford: Basil Blackwell.

Harvey, D. (1989) *The Condition of Postmodernity*. Oxford: Basil Blackwell.

Keegan, T. (1986) *Rural Transformations in Industrializing South Africa*. Johannesburg: Ravan Press.

Magdoff, H. and Sweezy, P. (1987) *Stagnation and the Financial Explosion*. New York: Monthly Review Press.

Mandel, E. (1989) Theories of crisis. In M. Gottdiener and N. Komninos (eds), *Capitalist Development and Crisis Theory*. London: Macmillan.

O'Meara, D. (1983) *Volks-kapitalisme*. Cambridge: Cambridge University Press.

Ovenden, K. and Cole, T. (1989) *Apartheid and International Finance*. Harmondsworth: Penguin.

Smith, N. (1990) *Uneven Development*. Oxford: Basil Blackwell.

van der Pijl, K. (1984) *The Making of an Atlantic Ruling Class*. London: Verso.

Walton, J. (1987) Urban protest and the global political economy: the IMF riots. In M. P. Smith and J. Feigin (eds), *The Capitalist City*. Oxford: Basil Blackwell, 364–86.

17

Oil as Money: the Devil's Excrement and the Spectacle of Black Gold

Michael J. Watts

Introduction

Gold which the devil gives his paramours turns into excrement after his departure. (*Freud, 1955, p. 174*)

I call petroleum 'the devil's excrement'. It brings trouble. . . . The [oil money] hasn't brought us any benefits. . . . We are drowning in the devil's excrement. (*Juan Pablo Perez Alfonso, founder of OPEC, 1976, cited in Karl, 1982, p. 316*)

After what has been said money is seen to be nothing other than deodorized, dehydrated shit that has been made to shine. (*Ferenczi, 1950, p. 327*)

This black gold [petroleum], the magical *élan vital* for . . . economic takeoff. (*Amuzegar, 1982, p. 814*)

Gold by itself is fraught with problems, first of all because of its mysterious origins. It comes from the bowels of the earth. . . . Gold is instant wealth [yet] it produces corruption . . . [it] can signify the loss of the soul . . . it scorches fingers and hearts; it is odorless but it is the 'devil's dung'. (*Gille, 1986, pp. 258–9*).

In 1975, the founder of OPEC and former Venezuelan oil minister Perez Alfonso wrote a book entitled *Hundiendonos en el excremento de diablo*

I have benefited from the comments and criticisms of members of the Berkeley Labor Process Group, specifically Gill Hart, Michael Burawoy, Dick Walker, Peter Evans, Harley Shaiken, Anno Saxenian and Michael Johns. Mary Beth Pudup was, as usual, the most demanding of critics.

(*We Are Sinking in the Devil's Excrement*). Oil, says Perez, is the Third World's black gold. Like gold it brings untold wealth and yet it is a supremely powerful and ultimately uncontrollable force. Like gold in the world of the alchemist, petroleum is a pure fruit of 'the subterranean workings of the telluric forces' (Gille, 1986, p. 258), yet it is a brilliant threat. In Perez's powerful and compelling vision, the natural bounty of oil had, in the magical and mysterious process of being transformed into money, become a a putrid and toxic waste. It was as if the Venezuelan 'body' suffered from bulimia; an excessive, orgiastic appetite was matched by periodic sickness, which contaminated the national metabolism. Indeed, for Perez the digestion of petroleum – what was referred to in Venezuela as 'sowing the oil' – gave birth to a weak and corrupt society, decadent and degenerate under the accumulated weight of waste and excrement (Coronil, 1987; Karl, in press). 'Manna or malediction?' was how one Venezuelan commentator opened his discussion of the legacy of petroleum in Venezuela (Izard, 1986, p. 205). Oil had vastly increased the national appetite and the capacity to consume, yet ingesting petroleum only served to contaminate everything.[1] Black gold, like the devil's counterpart, had turned into excrement. As Coronil puts it in describing Venezuela during the oil boom,

> Venezuela had lost control over itself; intoxicated by oil as waste it had become transformed into waste. . . . The identification of both the nation and individuals with excrement became an ever more common short hand expression for everyday problems . . . 'somos una mierda', 'es que este es un pais de mierda' ('we are pieces of shit', 'it's that this country is made of shit'). (Coronil, 1987, p. 233)

At about the same time that Venezuela's oil wealth was being debated explicitly in terms of waste, corruption and degeneracy, the Iranian, or more properly the Shah Pahlavi's, petrolic vision of 'the Great Civilization' was being derailed by an Islamic revolution made in the name of disciplined Muslim renewal and an autocratic moral order. Several thousand miles away from Caracas, black gold ushered in the collapse of the world's most powerful monarchy and, in its wake, a massive bloodletting.

Oil wealth, the magical *élan vital* of economic and social transformation, had proven to be a very mixed blessing. Perez Alfonso put it bluntly: *nothing* was better in 1980 than 1974, not even the economic growth rate (cited in Amuzegar, 1982, p. 821).

---

1 See Le Goff (1988) for a similar discussion of usury and money in the Middle Ages, Shell (1982, especially chapter 1) and Brown (1959).

El Dorado: Oil Wealth as Spectacle, Display and Illusion

The spectacle is not a collection of images, but a social relation among people, mediated by images. (*Debord, 1978, para. 4*)

Oil creates the illusion of a completely changed life, life without work, life for free. . . . The concept of oil expresses perfectly the eternal human dream of wealth achieved through lucky accident. . . . In this sense oil is a fairy tale and like every fairy tale a bit of a lie. (*Kapuściński, 1982, p. 35*)

For many commentators and critics, the oil bonanza of the 1970s was seen to presage the dawn of prosperity for the privileged few. As the West looked on in horror, oil prices ran out of control, soaring effortlessly, quadrupling in 1973–4 alone, then reaching their zenith during the second boom of 1980. Government revenues of OPEC states mushroomed by over 1000 per cent between 1970 and 1980 (table 17.1, see also figure 17.1). Five years after the first boom, nine of the thirteen OPEC members devoted close to 50 per cent of their now bloated gross domestic product (GDP) to domestic investment. State treasuries were literally awash with money.

So began the era of blind ambition, 'the Great Civilization' in Iran and 'La Gran Venezuela'. Jahangir Amuzegar describes this sensibility as a 'lyrical illusion', an exhilarating state of euphoria in which state planners, blinded by the refulgence of the great God petroleum, came to

Table 17.1 Estimated growth of government oil revenues of major OPEC countries, 1970–1980 (US $ billion)

	1970	1980	*Ratio*
Saudi Arabia	1.2	102.4	85.3
Kuwait	0.895	18.3	20.4
Iran	1.136	12.7	11.2
Iraq	0.521	26.1	50.1
United Arab Emirates	0.233	19.4	83.3
Qatar	0.122	5.4	44.3
Libya	1.295	22.6	17.5
Algeria	0.325	11.4	35.1
Nigeria	0.411	24.5	59.6
Venezuela	1.406	17.8	12.7
Indonesia	1.185	11.3	9.5
Total	7.729	271.9	39

Source: *The Petroleum Economist*, March 1975 and June 1982

Figure 17.1 Rolando Pena's gold oil-drum sculpture, 'Diagonales', at the National Gallery, Washington, DC.

believe that oil wealth could solve all problems (Amuzegar, 1982, p. 827). El Dorado was finally located, and it was an oil well.

From its inception, the oil boom was a spectacle, with new social relations mediated by images (Debord, 1978). Reza Shah predicted, that, in a decade, Iran would have the same living standard as Germany and France (Kapuściński, 1982, p. 53); in twenty years, he bragged, 'we shall be ahead of the United States' (Shah Pahlavi, in Zonis, 1991, p. 65). In the era of the Great Civilization that lay ahead, the Shah saw a world of unbridled material prosperity, thousands of electric buses to shuttle well-endowed workers to and from their workplace and a three-day work week. The monetary deluge that floated this modern utopia was truly biblical in scale. Hector Hurtado, the Minister of Finance in Venezuela, saw money cascading into the state treasury, money 'beyond our wildest dreams' (cited in Karl, in press, p. 2). Boundless money produced boundless ambition, what was dubbed 'Pharaohism' by the popular press. During the 1970s, for example, over three-quarters of the top twenty states classified by scale of public investment (the number of projects exceeding US $100 million) were oil producers. Saudi Arabia and Iran each accounted for over 100 projects costing in excess US $1 billion dollars a shot! (Gelb, 1984, p. 33). To add an extra frisson, the cost overruns on each of these Herculean projects averaged 109 per cent!

Anything was possible, even the defeat of nature. Saudi Arabia, for example, aggressively promoted domestically produced wheat, grown in the most inhospitable of desert environments. After massive production subsidies, Saudi wheat could be purchased for US $1050 per ton. US wheat, of vastly superior quality, could be acquired on the world market for less than US $150 per ton (Chaudhry, 1989, p. 128). Oil money conferred the power to change everything, even time: on 19 March 1976, the Shah changed, by imperial decree, the Iranian calendar.[2]

Commodity booms are not unusual in themselves, of course. The value of several commodities grew in excess of 20 per cent per annum during the 1970s.[3] On a larger historical canvas, the gold and bullion boom in the Americas during the sixteenth century resembles in certain respects the oil windfall four centuries later. Some 450 million pesos of precious metals poured into Spain between 1503 and 1660, stimulating feverish activity in the economy. Seville became a world city for a short while, driven by a manufacturing boom and a cycle of inflationary spending and borrowing (see Braudet, 1973; Wallerstein, 1974; Anderson, 1984; Vilar, 1984). The bullion bonanza lasted a century and a half, producing

2   The Iranian calendar based on the flight of the Prophet Mohammed from Mecca to Medina was changed to 'the Imperial Year' based on the founding of the first Iranian kingdom.

3   The annual growth in value of exports over the period 1970–80 was as follows: coffee 22 per cent (Brazil), rubber 23 per cent (Malaysia), tin 23 per cent (Thailand). See Roemer (1983, p. 4).

in its wake inflation, debt and a crippled Castillian state. Some aspects of the oil boom appear strikingly similar. Both commodities were, after all, central to the mercantilist and capitalist world economies of the time and each, in different ways, contributed to state centralization and state building.

Naturally, there are also radical dissimilarities. These contrasting forms of money were inserted into vastly different political economies and put to quite different uses. The sheer magnitude, duration and density of the booms also diverge markedly. None the less, these money booms, and the crises they precipitated, if rooted in their historical and cultural specificities, do both provide an opportunity to illuminate the working of societies into which vast fluxes of money are injected, and by extension enable one to outline the social, cultural and political contours of money. Oil as El Dorado speaks powerfully to what Simmel (1978, p. 175) saw as money's specific role in 'reified social functions', as the reified representation of impersonal capitalism. The spectacular manifestations of oil wealth reveal, first, something of the social relations of peripheral capitalisms and, second, how the growth of money in societies often presumed to be partly 'traditional' reveals something of how money itself is a 'frightful leveller' whose colourlessness and indifference 'hollows out the core of things' (Simmel, 1978, p. 414).

Meanings of Oil Money

Oil *is* almost like money. (*Robert O. Anderson, Chairman of ARCO, cited in Yergin, 1991, p. 13*)

Three categories – the imaginary, the symbolic and the real – correspond to the three functions of money: in its capacity as a measure of value money is 'imaginary'; as a medium of exchange, money is 'symbolic'; and as an instrument of reserve or of hoarding, money is 'real'. (*Goux, 1989, p. 52*)

A very great difficulty in talking about money arises from its multiple functions and representations. 'Everybody who earns it and spends it every day in order to live knows that money is money', said Gertrude Stein, but 'anybody who votes it to be gathered in as taxes knows that money is not money. That is what makes everybody go crazy' (Stein, 1989, p. 3). To simplify such complexity greatly, in this chapter I am going to pursue two broad lines of argument. The first starts from Marx's discussion of the functions of money: as a universal equivalent, as a measure of value, as a medium of exchange and as social power. But, following Goux (1989), I want to identify these multiple functions as the inseparable symbolic, imaginary and real aspects of money. Money is both an objectified relation of production (see Marx) and a system of culturally encoded symbols, a sort of transactional order which signifies itself (Smelt, 1980). The specific cultural, social and historical forms in which these attributes are expressed will vary enormously, giving rise to the multiple meanings of money in capitalist and non-capitalist societies (Zelizer, 1989). Underlying this heterogeneity, however, is a general presumption that money is always in part an abstraction and one that portrays the character, what Simmel (1978, p. 251) called the 'modern spirit', of capitalist society.[4]

The second line is taken directly from Simmel's *Philosophy of Money* (1978). The central argument here is tripartite in form: first, that the rise of complex and more abstract monetary systems corresponds to a *Gemeinschaft–Gesellschaft* shift; second, that the growing dominance of money represents a progression towards abstraction and convention, which is itself a reflection of impersonal and abstract social relations (as Turner, 1986, p. 97, says, 'abstract money is the symbol of abstract relations'); third, money promotes increased personal freedom and social exchange at the same time that it subjects human life to growing calculability, bureaucratization and quantitative regulation (Turner, 1986). For Simmel, money spoke to estrangement under modernity: reification, alienation and objectification.

I wish to trace these two broad problematics – the symbolic, imaginary and real unity of money on the one hand, and the simultaneous integrative and disintegrative effects of money *à la* Simmel on the other – as they are played out in oil-based economies awash with money during the 1970s. In this case – and I shall focus primarily on Nigeria – money takes the form of *oil rents*.[5] There are two particular significances to money as rent. First, oil money – as a form of money – must be theorized in terms of specific forms of state landed property (Haussman, 1981). In other words, as owner of the means of production of petroleum, the state mediates the particular social relations by which oil is exploited (royalties, commissions, state-owned enterprises) and converted into money. Changes in the ownership of the state take place through political transformations in the ruling class alliances that govern the state apparatuses. Once the oil rents are realized as money at the international level, they provide what Haussman (1981) calls a 'right of access to the world market' for the state, which in turn allocates this right to various domestic agents (importers, contractors), including itself. There are two

4   In this most general and abstract sense money is typically part of a more general logic of exchange (Goux, 1989) or transactional order (Parry and Bloch, 1989). This idea is explored in Shell (1982).

5   The rise of OPEC as a major force capable of shaping oil prices reflects in this sense a shift from a rent determined by the market price to a market price determined by the level of rent and hence indicates a radical shift in the power relations between transnational capital and (organized) state landed property.

moments in the genesis of oil monies, therefore: the *realization* (in dollars) at the international level and the *localization* of oil rents (in local currency). This 'double nature' of the oil rent appears as a function of the right of access to the world market, which is perceived by the state as access to the domestic market. The realization of oil rents (the magical genesis and ingestion of oil monies) requires, in political-economic terms, an adaptation between state spending and imports (Imam-Jomeh, 1985). As Haussman (1981) points out, however, there can be discrepancies between these two processes which may create a crisis for the state (abundance or shortage of capital) and the domestic economy (shortage or abundance of imported goods). Oil money, as a specific form of money, is thus situated at the intersection of internationalized rents on the one hand and localized consumption on the other.

The second significance of money as rent derives from the dominance of extractive and rentier capitals, which underlie money booms and particular patterns of commodity circulation. In other words, I want to argue that money (or commodity) booms based on extractive and rentier activity rather than on productive capital produce a particular sort of money fetishism. Unlike wealth created through industrial accumulation – in which there is some direct relation between productive labour, investment, work and money – oil money is effaced and disguised, appearing as it were out of thin air. To put it crudely, the form of capital which corresponds to the proliferation of wealth fundamentally shapes the cultural economy, the particular social and cultural constructions and fetishisms, of money itself.[6]

The Midas Touch: Ingesting Petrodollars and Manufacturing Modernity in Iran and Venezuela[7]

[Your] old socialism is finished. Old, obsolete, finished.... I achieve more than the Swedes.... Huh! Swedish socialism! It didn't even nationalize forests and water. But I have ... my White Revolution ... believe me, in Iran we're far more advanced than you and really have nothing to learn from you. (*Shah Pahlavi, interview with Oriana Fallaci, New Republic, 1 December 1974, pp. 17–18*)

6 I am especially grateful to Michael Johns, who has written of a similar phenomenon in late nineteenth-century Argentina and whose ideas and criticism have been extremely helpful.
7 This draws upon a comparative study that I directed on the comparative political economy of oil producing states (Nigeria, Venezuela, Iran) funded by the National Science Foundation; the researchers on the project were myself, Iraj Imam-Jomeh and George Leddy.

The decision to build a modern industrialized economy was mine. There were others who wanted to move more slowly. But we had to take advantage of this moment given to us, pull Venezuela out of her underdevelopment, and propel her into the twentieth century. (*Interview with President Carlos Andres Perez, cited in Karl, in press, p. 351*)

There are about thirty developing countries that are net exporters of oil but they differ markedly in terms of area, size, oil endowment, dependence on petroleum revenues and economic structure (Watts, 1984). There is a fundamental distinction between the oil-producing city or desert states (Kuwait, Saudi Arabia), which are land and labour poor and in capital surplus, and states such as Iran, Venezuela and Nigeria, which are large and well-populated, with diversified economies and a substantial domestic economy and home market. In this chapter I shall address oil money in the context of the latter, the so-called 'high absorbers' (Gelb, 1984). These petroleum-based economies embarked upon ambitious, and not infrequently disastrous, state-led development programmes during the 1970s, ingesting huge quantities of oil revenues. A decade later these same economies were plagued by hyperinflation, economic stagnation, structural balance of payments problems, periodic devaluations and a massive foreign debt.[8]

What the high absorbers have in common for the purposes of my discussion are the following contradictory traits:

- A dependence on oil as a fully internationalized commodity. All transactions are in dollars (oil *is* money) and the petro-state, as the landlord and entrepreneur, is 'internationalized' (i.e. expands its reliance on the world market through a growing monocultural dependence on oil revenues).
- The enclave character of the oil industry within oil producing states, which implies an absence of linkage effects to non-oil sectors. The petroleum industry does not constitute itself as a major determinant of the organization of social life. Hence its impact on the national economy will be determined by the landed property relation (the social relations by which oil is exploited) and the realization of oil rents. What distinguishes an oil country, then, is 'not so much the presence of petroleum as the *expenditure of petrodollars*' (Haussman, 1981, p. 75, emphasis added).
- The nationalization of the oil sector such that oil monies flow directly (via taxes, rents, concessions and sales) to the state treasury, which accordingly acts as a strong centralizing force. Oil accrues to the state as an independent source of revenue, which affords it an unusual degree of political and economic autonomy (i.e. the state is 'suspended' from civil society; Katouzian, 1981).

8   There is a substantial literature on oil-exporters: for a representative sampling see Hallwood and Sinclair (1981), Amuzegar (1983) Watts (1984), Gelb (1984) and Chaudhry (1989).

● The centralizing impact of oil revenues confers a central role for the public sector (fiscal linkages) via state investment ('the entire system . . . depends on the size and strategy of state expenditure'; Katouzian 1981, p. 246), and to this extent the state is 'domesticated' (i.e. projected into civil society). The state, in other words, takes on the primary role of 'localizing' money capital (oil rents).

The broad outlines of petroleum-based accumulation, the so-called 'oil economy syndrome', are by now well documented, particularly for Iran and Venezuela.[9] Both the Accion Democratic government of Carlos Perez (1974–8) in Venezuela and the Pahlavi regime in Iran saw oil as the ticket to modernity on a grand scale. In Venezuela the centrepiece of 'La Gran Venezuela' was the US $52 billion industrial complex in Ciudad Guayana. For the Shah it was the spectacle of modernism; in 1974 he initiated a monumental downtown project in Tehran bearing his name (Shahestan Pahlavi), not simply the largest concentration of service activities in the world but 'the equivalent of the Persepolis' (Costello, 1981, p. 170). Grandiosity rested in both instances on extreme political centralization. It took the form of a monarchical clique under an auto-cratic Shah in Iran, a small power bloc consisting of family, high ranking state bureaucrats and a group of industrial and financial bourgeoisies who surrendered political power as a condition of access to oil monies. Under Perez, a bureaucratic oligarchy supported state ownership but actively promoted a domestic capitalist class, 'the big manufacturers, large commercial farmers, construction contractors and real estate inter-ests and the large import-exporters who have received the bulk of the investment funds' (Petras and Morley, 1983, p. 26). In both cases the critical institutions mediating between oil monies and the national eco-nomy were state development banks: the Fondo de Inversiones de Vene-zuela (FIV), which was granted US $23 billion between 1974 and 1977 (20 per cent of state revenues), and the Industrial and Mining Develop-ment Bank of Iran (IMDBI), whose share capital and reserves increased by 43 times between 1961 and 1977 (its loan activity in 1977 was 81.3 billion riales).

The Perez government operationalized a two-prong strategy: sectoral nationalization (iron ore, petrochemicals) and massive investments in upstream sectors (steel); and the redirection of foreign investment into downstream non-oil economic activities (see Coronil and Skurski, 1991). The Shah recycled oil money through state development banks which favoured large Iranian private capital – in essence a small court clique – particularly in the heavy and capital goods sectors. The small-scale bazaar economy was marginalized and income inequality increased pre-cipitously (Imam-Jomeh, 1985).

9 This section draws upon Haussman (1981), Petras and Morley (1983), Imam-Jomeh (1985), Coronil (1987), Karshenas (1990) and Karl (in the press).

Table 17.2 Oil booms and petrolic accumulation: Iran and Venezuela, 1970–1980

	Oil exports (US $ billion)	Ratio of oil to total exports	Ratio of oil resources to gov't revenues	Annual rate of growth of gov't revenues (%)	Annual rate of growth of gov't expenditures (%)	Rate of growth of credit to private sector (%)	Rate of annual growth of money supply (%)	Annual growth of export debt (%)	Annual rate of growth of output of non-oil (%) sector	Annual rate of growth of consumer price index (%)
	1980	1980	1980	1970–80	1970–80	1970–80	1970–80	1976–82	1971–9	1971–80
Iran	13.45	94.4	64.3	5.5	5.0	6.9	34.8	25.0	9.9	13.7
Venezuela	18.24	91.4	65.5	9.0	8.6	10.8	22.5	46.1	6.7	10.1

Source: Amuzegar, 1983, pp. 11–20; IMF, *International Financial Statistics*, 1985.

In spite of the differences of emphasis there are striking macroeconomic empirical regularities, as table 17.2 suggests. First, oil money fuels a rapid growth and expansion of state expenditures and parastatal organizations. A huge share of money capital is, in other words, localized by the state to reproduce itself via expenditures on administration and defence/repressive apparatuses.[10] Second, an urban construction boom is stimulated by public investment projects and a vast import boom of both consumer durables and capital goods. Third, there is an increased demand for non-tradables, which promotes an appreciation of the real exchange rate (and hence further stimulates imports). Fourth, a deliberate effort is made to encourage local industrialization through import substitution behind high tariff walls. Fifth, non-oil sectors lag (the so-called Dutch Disease), especially in agriculture. Finally there is a tendency towards 'overshooting', that is to say a difficulty in scaling back lumpy state investments, a process compounded by inflation and additional borrowing to cover project completion.

In both Venezuela and Iran, the 1970s witnessed a period of rapid urbanization, industrial growth and social change. In both cases what emerged was a sort of rentier capitalism in which the state redistributed oil revenues through rents, subsidies and outright corruption. In Iran a small clique of Pahlavi cronies benefited from the Shah's largesse. In Venezuela state contracts were awarded to a small group of merchant-contractors. Corruption, cronyism and outright theft flourished. Huge quantities of public oil monies were privately appropriated and exported; according to Morley and Petras (1983, p. 15) some US $2.3 billion left Venezuela in 1977 for the purchase of property in southern Florida! Sowing oil monies invariably meant seeding foreign bank accounts. Criminality emerged as the normal, and to a degree acceptable, form of sociality and display.[11] For the popular classes, inflation, real estate speculation, administrative chaos and escalating costs of living (especially food) defined the lived reality of the oil years. The Shah's Great Civilization was, as Kapuściński (1982) noted, 'the Great Injustice'. Within several years of the first oil boom, both countries were running substantial balance of payments deficits and were borrowing heavily.

Against this backdrop there are three relevant aspects of the oil boom that provide the vantage point for grasping the form, function and meaning of petrodollars. The fetishization of money, and the intense

10 Imam-Jomeh (1985, p. 158) shows that in the case of Iran in the 1970s the 'reproduction of the state' functions accounted for close to half of all central expenditures of money capital, substantially in excess of the 'reproduction of labour' (services, education, subsidies etc.) and the 'reproduction of capital' (economic investment, infrastructure) functions. For Venezuela see Haussman (1981, p. 335).

11 In Venezuela the ideals of criminality were 'brought out into the open. Its heroes left the clandestine world and proudly paraded in public places' (Coronil, 1987, p. 238).

activity, much of which was patently and publicly illegal, focused on the acquisition of wealth without apparent effort. Petroleum came to be synonymous with money and the defining force in society. Second, petro-states emerged as rentier and redistributive in form though their social character is locally specific (autocratic and highly centralized personal monarchical rule in Iran, complex political pacts and alliances orchestrated through a powerful oligarchical bureaucracy in Venezuela). Oil, insofar as it *is* money and state property, amplifies central power but this is typically combined with weak authority and limited administrative and institutional capacity in the context of intense competition for state resources. The state appears suspended above society – it is represented as *the* source of power since oil *is* power – yet is projected into society as it spends simultaneously to develop and purchase political consent.[12] Finally, the state mediates the contradiction between public petro-wealth and individual appropriation of it. The state distribution of oil monies as rents dominates the investment of money as productive capital. A culture of corruption flourishes in such a way that the state paradoxically becomes *the* major blockage to development (understood as systematic capitalist accumulation) at the same moment that the state is *the* vehicle to promote it.

How, then, can money be traced through the various social, cultural and political circuits of petrolic capitalism as it is constituted through this trilogy of processes? In the remainder of the chapter I shall focus on another high-absorber oil state, namely Nigeria, seeking to trace how money is a general ether which colours, and is coloured by, the cultural and political economy of petroleum booms and busts in Africa's most populous state.

Paradoxes of Prosperity: Oil Money in Nigeria

Oil is crude or dirty and so are the actions it often inspires. Oil is volatile and so are the expectations that are based on it; oil is a diminishing or vanishing asset, so is the false sense of political power which it could confer. (*Festus Marinho, managing director, Nigerian National Petroleum Company, The African Guardian, 5 March 1990, p. 19*)

Dutch born Englishmen in ten gallon hats and snakeskin boots brought us
the putrid curse of crude oil
which suffocates our soul . . . Oil commands, dictates, warps and distorts

12 This is clearly the case in Kuwait, Qatar and Saudi Arabia, where oil monies allow the state to buy off merchant opposition. See Chaudhry (1989).

we seek aromas without the smell
lightning without the flash . . . so we get instead
growth without development.
(*Emeka Ezera, 'Ode to Crude Oil', unpublished poem, Berkeley, 1988*)

She has been called the Texas of Africa: big, brash and, for a while, oil rich. For a decade oil flowed out and money flowed in. At the peak of production, the mangrove swamps of southeastern Nigeria pumped two million barrels a day and sold them for US $41 a piece. As in Iran and Venezuela, the oil boom created huge windfall profits, a transfer large enough to lay the basis of an economic revolution in Africa's largest nation. The Nigerians chose a capitalist road, an ambitious import-substitution industrialization strategy that required roads, banks, electrification, capital goods and a developmental state. What they got was a sort of organized chaos: 'a massive foreign debt whose size nobody knows, a mountain of expensive equipment that mostly does not work, and a military dictatorship' (*Economist*, 3 May 1986, p. 3). The oil boom unleashed a spasm of consumption and construction; money and commodities circulated apace and disreputable salesmen from every corner of the globe competed to sell to all manner of Nigerians artefacts they could not possibly make use of. The proliferation of everything from stallions to stereos suggested a sort of African cargo cult.

In the 1970s, Nigeria felt, to me at least, like a vast and wild frontier settlement. Sometimes it was very surreal.

Two memories.

The first is of a child strolling through a massive, hot and sweaty Lagos traffic jam, which had not moved for close to half a day, selling glass paperweights, each containing a small plastic Santa Claus and his reindeers trudging through a small snow storm. The other occured in the Muslim north, in Sokoto township, a dusty and then provincial traditional city on the edge of the desert. A small store had been mysteriously burned down during the night; nothing remained but a pile of smouldering ashes. As I walk through the charred remains, there is the sound of a siren and out of the morning haze emerges a bright, fierce-red fire engine, newly minted and imported from England. Barreling toward the scene at a terrifying speed about twelve hours too late, the fire engine roared over a small hump-backed bridge and literally took flight. Magisterially airborne, it rolled to one side, landed in an adjacent peanut field and exploded. It all appeared perfectly normal, if not exactly natural.

An independent Nigeria inherited in 1960 an archetypical agrarian export economy dominated by groundnuts, cotton, palm oil, cocoa and rubber. This economy was starkly regional. Three semi-autonomous regions, each associated with a primary export commodity and a marketing board, tightly circumscribed the power of the federal centre. Regional

Table 17.3 Nigeria: national accounts, 1965–1990

	Account						Rate				
	1965	1973	1980	1988	1989	1990	1965–73	1973–80	1980–9	1989	1990
	Share of gross domestic product from current price data						*Growth rate (% per year) from constant price data*				
Gross domestic product	100.0	100.0	100.0	100.0	100.0	100.0	6.6	3.5	− 0.5	5.8	4.9
Agriculture	49.4	33.1	25.3	33.7	30.0	29.9	2.8	− 1.4	1.3	4.0	4.5
Industry	12.2	25.7	40.5	35.8	43.1	43.2	19.6	5.7	− 2.1	8.8	5.2
Manufacturing industry	5.9	4.6	8.9	10.1	8.6	8.4	15.0	7.2	0.8	0.0	3.0
Services	30.5	39.0	31.0	28.1	24.7	24.7	6.6	5.4	− 0.4	2.8	5.0
	Billions of 1987 naira						*Growth rate (% per year)*				
Gross domestic product	60	87	113	103	109	114	6.6	3.5	0.1	5.8	–
Capacity to import	13	41	140	29	38	– etc.	16.9	13.5	− 14.1	33.7	–
Terms of trade adjustment	− 16	− 17	57	− 7	− 3	–	–	–	–	–	–
Gross domestic income	44	69	170	96	106	–	7.5	8.4	− 6.1	10.3	–
Gross national product	56	78	103	96	101	–	6.0	3.7	− 0.3	5.4	–
Gross national income	40	60	160	89	98	–	6.8	9.0	− 6.4	10.3	–
	Consumer prices (1987 = 100)						*Inflation rate (% per year)*				
	1975	1980	1986	1988	1989	1990					
	22.0	44.7	90.7	138.3	208.1	224.0	7.1	19.0	19.1	50.5	7.5

Mid-1989 population 113.8 million; 1989 per capita GNP US $250.
Source: World Bank, *Trends in Developing Countries*, 1991, p. 405; Central Bank of Nigeria, *Annual Report*, 1982, pp. 30–1.

economies were also distinguished by powerful ethnic and religion identifications which produced a fragile and fractured national polity presided over by the Muslim Hausa-speaking north. Behind the facade of political independence during the 1960s lay vicious interregional competition over political office, public contracts and state resources. Indeed, this delicate federalism exploded into civil war in 1966 and it was into this fragmented political economy, presided over by a military government, that the oil monies of the 1970s were inserted.

The oil revenues flowed directly to the state via the Nigerian National Petroleum Company (NNPC),[13] which both centralized and expanded central (federal) power. Federal revenues grew at 26 per cent per annum during the 1970s (table 17.3) and expanded state activity unleashed a torrent of imports (capital goods increased from N422 million in 1971 to N3.6 billion in 1979[14]) and urban construction (the construction industry grew at over 20 per cent annum in the mid-1970s). The state invested heavily in industrial development and infrastructure[15] – manufacturing output increased by 13 per cent per annum between 1970 and 1982 (figure 17.2) – but the intense competition for public resources along regional and class lines produced unthinkable corruption and administrative chaos. While serious under the military governments of the 1970s, corruption and state indiscipline radically increased under the civilian government of President Shagari between 1979 and 1983. Cities such as Warri, Port Harcourt and Lagos doubled (and in some cases tripled) in size during the boom. Consumer prices leapt upward, agriculture collapsed and the real exchange rate rose steadily, feeding the import boom. Nigeria became ever more a monocultural economy; it simply shifted from one oil (vegetable) to another (petroleum).

The collapse of the boom in 1981 exposed Nigeria to the structural weaknesses of oil-based rentier capitalism. A foreign exchange crisis – the visible trade balance in 1981 was N12 billion – was compounded by mounting external debt obligations. By 1982 the President and his advisors talked of the need for sacrifice and denial: the 1970s, they said,

13 The Nigerian oil scene is complex. Since 1974 the government (NNPC) has been a majority shareholder in all of the producing consortia. Oil revenues flow to the government via profit taxes, royalties, premiums for oil concessions and miscellaneous fees. The NNPC had an annual turnover in 1987 of US $11 billion, making it the largest firm in Africa.

14 Non-oil imports as a percentage of GDP grew from 10 per cent in 1970 to 29 per cent in 1980 (Struthers, 1990, p. 322). Consumer durables and non-durable imports grew from N338.4 million in 1971 to N2.1 billion in 1979 (Watts, 1984).

15 State expenditure as a proportion of GDP doubled during the 1970s. The growth sectors were social and community services (from 2 per cent of government expenditures in 1970 to 16 per cent in the late 1970s) and economic services, which includes investment in industry, transport, agriculture and utilities (which rose from 6 per cent in 1970 to almost 30 per cent in the late 1970s). See Struthers (1990, p. 336).

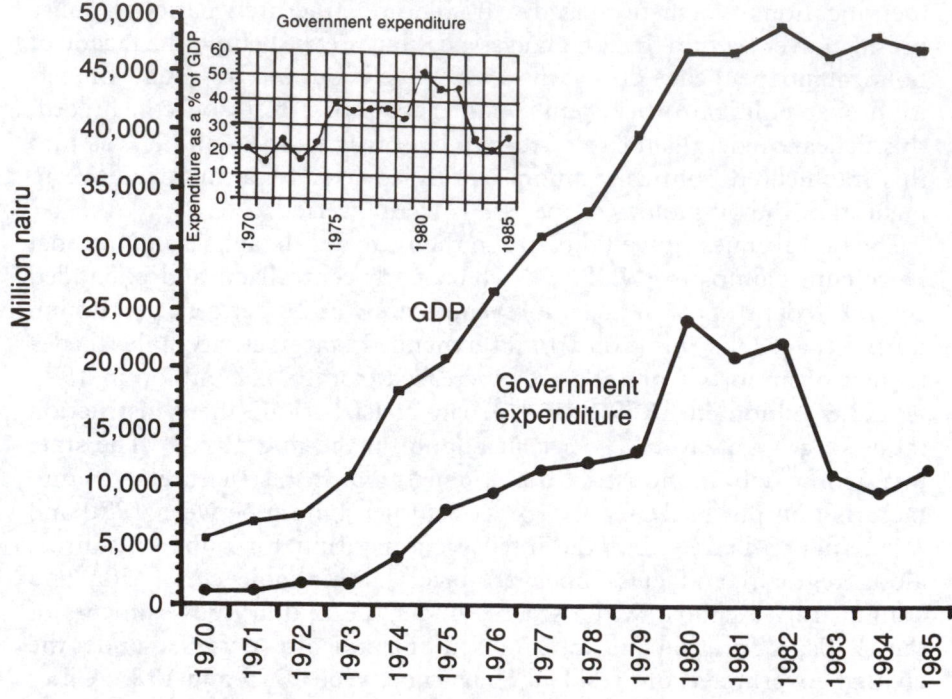

Figure 17.2   The growth of the Nigerian public sector (at current factor cost), 1970–1985.
Source: Central Bank of Nigeria, *Economic and Financial Review*, various issues.

had been a time of illusion.[16] They were promptly ousted in a military coup in 1983. By 1984 the 'boom was over' and the watchword was austerity (figure 17.3). By 1986 Nigeria had signed a structural adjustment programme (SAP) with the IMF and the World Bank, and the medicine was bitter. The economy contracted, the naira collapsed from US $1.12 to ten cents, and the real wage of industrial workers was savaged. Money was scarce and popular discontent widespread, as the anti-SAP riots in 1988 and 1989 revealed with some clarity.

What began with petro-euphoria and bountiful money in 1973 ended, some fifteen years later, with scarcity, a huge debt, urban looting and bodies in the streets. Over this period oil money coursed through the Nigerian economy and polity, a sort of a barium meal which charted the decomposing metabolism of Nigerian political economy.

16 In the late 1980s President Perez of Venezuela made the same claim: 'Venezuelans had been living in a world of illusion and false expectations. They had to face the Great Turn [*El gran viraje*], the shift from artificial to real capitalism via the free market' (Coronil and Skurski, 1991, p. 313).

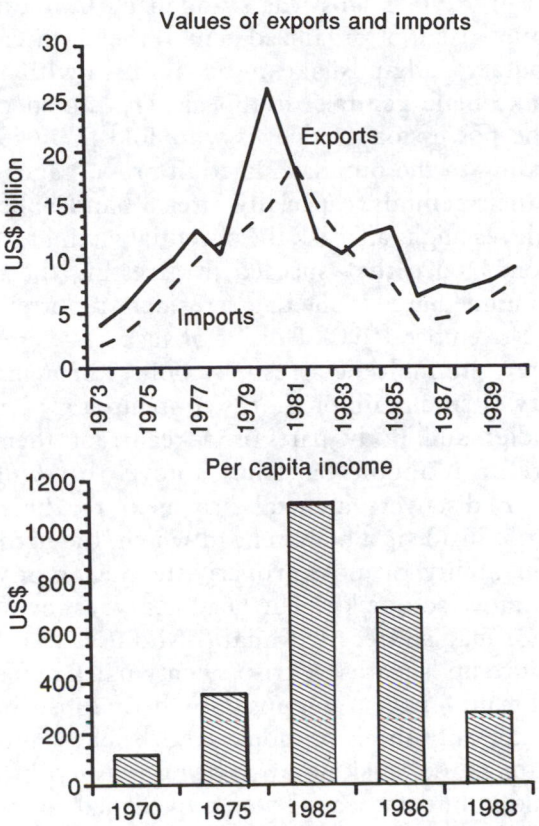

Figure 17.3 The boom and bust cycle: Nigeria, 1970–1990.
Source: *African Recovery*, 1990, vol. 4, no. 1.

The Nigerian naira. Sometimes plentiful, sometimes scare, sometimes valuable, often worthless. As with all money under capitalism, an analysis of the petro-naira requires a phenomenological vision which sees it as a medium by which social reality is experienced but also a thing to be uncovered and unmasked insofar as it mediates and obscures social and economic relations. The naira provides 'an insight into the total workings of [Nigerian] society' (Turner, 1986, p. 95), while the structure of Nigerian society provides the context within which money as a social and cultural phenomenon can be fully comprehended.

Money Magic: Petro-naira as Reification

[Oil] is a filthy, foul smelling liquid that squirts obligingly up into the air and falls back to earth as a rustling shower of money. (*Kapuściński, 1982, p. 34*)

In the autumn of 1990, Lagos was scandalized by the rumour, widely believed and publicized, of organized genital theft. Unscrupulous people used bodily contact – a handshake, a casual brush with a stranger in the street – to make male genitals disappear. The stolen organs later re-appeared in the possession of thieves who sold them for thousands of dollars. According to the popular Nigerian press, Lagos residents regularly checked their genitals, especially after a handshake. Beside bodily contact, the thieves might also ask the potential victim for the time of day or for directions: 'once they succeed in arresting their attention, the genitals vanish immediately', one Lagos resident reported (*San Francisco Chronicle*, 15 November 1990). Dozens of suspects were beaten by irate mobs and there were multiple arrests by police throughout the sprawling, chaotic city of seven million that is contemporary Lagos.

Theft of bodies and body parts is a recurrent theme in Nigerian popular culture. In Akinbolu Babarinsa's novel *Anything for Money*, a Fulani herdsman discovers a metal box next to the railway line in northern Nigeria. Inside is a human head which, the herdsman assumes, accounts for the ability, or more properly the power, of white people to make the train move so quickly. The head is in fact the possession of an influential Lagos magistrate, Mr Kadara, who uses it as juju or 'money magic', to conjure up 'sheaths of crisp twenty naira banknotes'. Kadara is a selfish and brutal magistrate, unsympathetic to the poor and down-trodden, who can only think of money and bribery, and who embarks upon a career of money-making after being rejected by several lovers. His money-making human head is stolen by armed robbers and Kadara turns to bribing just about everyone in a desperate effort to regain the box, an obsession that ultimately leads to a hideous death.

This is of course a fictional account, but Bastiat's (1991) description of body parts apparently discovered in a suitcase in an Onitsha market (in Ibo-speaking south-eastern Nigeria) during late 1987, purportedly en route to influential landlords or notables for money-making purposes, speaks of how widespread local beliefs in juju and money magic are (see also Barber, 1982). In all these narratives, there is of course a strong Faustian echo.

According to local Nigerian opinion, head-hunting comes in cycles and in the recent past it has been associated with making medicines that will 'make the owner a millionaire in just a matter of weeks' (*Topmagazine*, cited in Bastiat, 1991, p. 2). A head may bring anything between three and nine thousand naira. The trade in body parts is part of a larger cultural terrain, however, in which juju or money magic refers to personal gain (money wealth) without apparent effort. In this sense the body part business is a way of capturing the productivity of the murdered person which can be transposed into money without personal or physical effort. These are what Elechi Amadi, writing as a Nigerian on Nigerian ethics, calls 'ritual murders', in a sense the violent appropriation of labour power, 'committed by people who use parts of the human body aimed at making them richer, [and] stronger' (Amadi, 1982, p. 19). Money magic speaks not to a cultural antipathy in Nigeria to wealth or money in general, but rather to the specific cultural question of how money as wealth is acquired and legitimated in relation to work and effort, and secondarily to what sorts of practices can be monetized or commodified, that is to say the morality of monetary practice.

Shipton (1989, p. 28) has described this moral dimension among the Luo in Western Kenya: what is seen locally as 'bitter money' is typically associated with some type of theft, whether actual theft or *de facto* via the sale of certain commodities such as land or tobacco. In all these instances the bitter or 'dirty' money derives from the abrogation of critical social relations, and from the activities of people rather than of things. In a similar vein, the Hausa of northern Nigeria, who have a long and complex association with mercantile activities and various sorts of monies, articulate a basic cultural distinction between fertile capital (*uwa mai anfi*, literally a mother that gives birth) and ominous capital (*jarin tsaya*) which has been accrued through illegitimate means. This distinction between good and bad money[17] is rooted within the local hermeneutics of Muslim practice and, in the mercantile sphere, in normative patterns of Hausa patronage.

In the Nigerian popular imagination, oil wealth is not understood as the product of work (Barber, 1982). Indeed, there is an extensive popular fiction dealing with ill-gotten petro-wealth and money magic during the 1970s and 1980s. Buchi Emecheta's *Naira Power* (1982) and Lekan Oyegoke's *Cowrie Tears* (1981) are perhaps the most widely known English-language novels dealing with this issue but there is also a large indigenous 'popular literature'; for example, in the Yoruba-speaking south-west Olatubosun Oladapo's *Aroye Akewi* and a substantial number of plays reproduced in the Yoruba-language photoplay magazine *Atoka* that explicitly deal with money magic, greed and robbery.[18] Barber's (1982) work with the Oyin Adejobi and the Lerer Paimo Theatre Companies near Ife[19] is especially apposite in this regard because she documents how two dominant themes – armed robbery and the gigantic baseless oil fortune – coalesce around a compelling image in Yoruba drama: the child stealer who makes medicine from their blood and then, by uttering the right incantations, causes unlimited quantities of money

---

17 A Mossi farmer is quoted by Robert Lacville as saying: 'Warm money is what you earn yourself, when you have earned it through the heat of your own work. . . . Cold money comes from outside and does not belong to us' (*Guardian*, 23 June 1991, p. 19).

18 Larwaju Adepoju's play *Sagba di were* deals explicitly with money magic (personal communication, Karin Barber, 30 April 1989, Birmingham University).

19 These theatres, staffed and run by farmers, workers, minor civil servants and so on, tour throughout Yorubaland (and have done so since the 1940s when they began as operatic renderings of Bible readings) and are enormously popular.

to shower down into a calabash placed on the child's head. The play *Gbanga dEkun*, for example, is set in a robber-gang's headquarters and is a sort of morality play in which good and evil wealth, baseless and well-founded money, real work and fake work, traditional and dubious medicine are counterposed. In the play the good rich man is rescued from a bad rich man by the forces of traditional morality (*orisa*). Oil wealth generates a social contradiction because, as one character in the play *Ona Ola* says of the *nouveau riche* Laosebikan, 'you eat like an elephant, you work like a mouse'. The possibility of legitimate money is displaced by the oil boom, in other words, to robbery and money magic.

The idea, taken from a well-known Yoruba proverb, that 'the roots of riches are a shameful secret' is a powerful image translated, via popular theatre, into culturally meaningful discourses that contain the material realities of the oil boom. For many in the popular sector – workers, peasants, informal sector craftsmen – oil wealth *was* baseless; those well placed with respect to the state prospered from kick backs and contracts and became multi-millionaires overnight. Black Mercedes, big houses, lace gowns, commodities of all sorts seemingly appeared out of thin air. The popular press, moreover, regularly invoked extraordinary oil fortunes that were typically revealed in extravagant acts of consumption and display.[20] The normal running of the economy required clandestine deals, fraud, embezzlement and corruption. Equally, the unplanned and chaotic growth of the cities triggered by the construction boom, and the stark polarization between rich and poor in the major cities, contributed to a violent and anarchic urban environment. Lagos was, as the *Washington Post* (26 December 1980, p. 2) put it, 'a modern day Dodge City'. During the 1979–83 civilian interregnum the development of private political armies was *de rigeur*, indicative of a larger culture of terror and violence. Armed robbers such as Lawrence Anini (a.k.a. Anini the Law) declared outright war on the police and as a consequence became nationally recognized figures (*West Africa*, 15 December 1986, p. 2596). Anini himself was thought to possess magical powers and successfully avoided capture through juju. Organized teams of armed bandits regularly raided entire neighbourhoods, becoming so bold that they posted bills in the quarter giving details of their future attack! (*West Africa*, 17 January 1983, p. 128).[21] The fact that power was so frequently off – it gives the

20 A dozen supporters of a political party donate N5 million in a half-hour ceremony, high-ranking officials are involved in drug smuggling, contractors and politicians are found at airports carrying enormous quantities (millions of dollars!) of cash in their briefcases. The Nigerian press was chock full of such stories in the late 1970s and 1980s.

21 'A new dimension was introduced into burglary this week when a group of robbers set a house ablaze [in Lagos] because it did not contain anything worth stealing' (*West Africa*, 17 January 1983, p. 126). See also Lindsay Barrett on violence and fear in the major cities in the 1980s (*West Africa*, 2 June 1986, pp. 1156–7).

city a pulsating glow, said one commentator (*Wall Street Journal*, 22 September 1982, p. 32) – meant in effect that urban crime was uncontrollable, not least by a police force popularly seen as a total shambles.

Money magic, whatever the empirical status of its liturgy of body parts and juju narratives, captured perfectly in this respect the magical and fetishistic (and violent) qualities of the petro-naira. Oil money bred more money. Inherent in money was a sort of occult power akin to what Virginia Woolf (1929, p. 37) called 'the power of my purse to breed ten-shilling notes automatically'. Juju did not so much appear with the oil boom as much as it came to embody the contradictions of oil monies and the perilous qualities of life on the petroleum roller coaster. Money magic is, I think, what Benjamin (1973) had in mind when he referred to the 'fantastic' combination of the old and new thrown up by the vortex of capitalist modernization.

Visions of Excess: Nigerian Steel and Petrolic Ambition

Oil fills us with such arrogance that we begin believing we can easily overcome such unyielding obstacles as time. With oil . . . I [Shah Pahlavi] will create a second America in a generation! (*Kapuściński, 1982, p. 35*)

According to a World Bank official, it is the eighth wonder of the world.[22] When completed the state-owned Ajaokuta Steel Complex (ASC) in Kwara state will be the largest plant of its kind in sub-Saharan Africa and one of the largest in the world. It covers a total land area of over 24,000 hectares with a steel township of a further 7000 hectares. Sprawling, massive, unthinkably huge, it resembles, in scale and tenor, some sort of hideous offspring of Stalinist industrial gigantism and Charles Dickens's worst nightmare from *Hard Times*. It is a technical disaster – Soviet and Czech technologies, platoons of French, German, East European and British workers – and a contractor's wet dream. Still unfinished with over US \$5 billion already spent, the first steel is unlikely to roll out of the mill until 1995. When, and if, it is completed, Nigerian steel will cost somewhere between six and seven times the prevailing world price.[23] Despite 'gross mismanagement' and massive 'theft of equipment and machinery' (EIU, 1990, p. 20), the hopelessly antiquated Soviet(!) blast furnace technology provided by MSVO Tiajpromexport is designed to produce, initially, 1.3 million tons per year, substantially in excess of current domestic requirements. Export prospects are not exactly rosy. Hatch Associates of Canada, who undertook an assessment of

22 Interview conducted by the author, World Bank, Washington, DC, 12 May 1990.
23 Interview with Professor Akin Mabogunje (Washington, DC, May 1990), who headed a government sponsored assessment of the steel sector in the late 1980s.

ASC in 1987, estimate that the importation of high quality coal to run the relatively remote plant would, alone, be a huge drain on foreign exchange. The same report questioned the viability of using Nigeria's low grade iron ore around which the Ajaokuta plant was planned in the first place.

In 1989 there were 2500 Soviet workers at the site; the French and German contractors had another 2000. Delays in payment and huge cost overruns have dogged the project to the extent that the prospects for completion remain extremely tentative.[24] The government is, of course, unlikely to write off the monies already invested. The World Bank, a heavy but increasingly reluctant funder, prefers a 'minimal outlay' plan deferring some of the projects, cutting back expenditure to 'only' N300 million per year and essentially mothballing Ajaokuta for another three years, thereby temporarily shutting down one of the rolling mills and postponding the flat products plant. In a world-class myopic gesture, the federal government decided to 'privatize' part of ASC, putting it on the block with three steel rolling mills bizarrely located in other remote parts of the country. As the *Economist* put it in a masterpiece of British understatement, these 'are not the most attractive assets on the disposals list and sales [may] be slow' (Synge, 1989, p. 72).

The origins of the state steel sector can be traced to what President Shagari in his 1983 budget speech called the 'oil boom hysteria' in which 'money was . . . said to be no longer a problem in the execution of projects' (*New Nigerian*, 30 December 1983, p. 1). Steel would stimulate the economy and herald technological progress. Plans drawn up in the 1970s focused on two steelmaking plants and a network of rolling mills across the country, a vision hatched ironically at a moment of falling prices and substantial overcapacity in the global steel industry. Like other gargantuan state projects (the US $5 billion federal capital project at Abuja is the obvious comparison), the rolling mills proved to be the casualty of regional politics, their location – to say nothing of the extraordinary corruption and inefficiency associated with their construction and operation – reflecting no known form of economic rationality. Located in the extreme north of the country, and for the most part marginal to the required industrial infrastructure, the Katsina rolling mill stands amidst peanut fields almost a thousand miles from coal deposits and from the steel billets. The three rolling mills have operated, at best, at about 28 per cent of capacity, producing the most expensive steel in the world (EIU, 1986, pp. 200–21).

Nigeria's first steelmaking unit, the Delta Steel Company (DSC) at Aladja in Bendel state, opened in 1982 but its performance has been mixed (it has rarely operated at more than 25 per cent of capacity). It

24   By 1989 the French and Soviet contractors were being paid in oil in lieu of foreign exchange (*Third World Reports*, 15 February 1989, p. 4).

Figure 17.4 NEPA lampooned.

requires stiff import quotas to avoid South Korean competition, and has been fundamentally handicapped by equipment shortages and inadequate infrastructure. In particular the state has been incapable of providing stable electricity and the nationalized electricity company (NEPA) is legendary for its chronic inefficiency and decrepitude (figure 17.4); in the mid-1980s the head of NEPA resigned, declaring that not even Allah could make NEPA work! A study by the World Bank (1989) showed that 92 per cent of firms cannot depend on NEPA and require their own electricity generators. A frustrated management of the Jos steel rolling mill incurred N75 million in equipment loss owing to irregular power supply.[25]

State incapacity has, in other words, fundamentally compromised the ambitious project that the public sector itself initiated when flush with oil monies. Professor Tam-West put it succinctly: the steel industry founders on 'the lack of working capital, inadequate power supply, and the absence of forward planning' (EIU, 1986, p. 20). Steel production has steadily increased throughout the 1980s (from 176,000 tons in 1982 to 1,079,000 tons in 1985), but structural adjustment since 1986 has reduced output by close to half. Indeed at the heart of the problem is the contradiction between grandiose planning on the one hand (ASC alone was planned to produce a staggering 5.2 million tons!) and the real size of the local market in the era of adjustment on the other.

Ajaokuta stands as a pathetic monument to oil, to oil politics and to oil money. Like Perez's 'Gran Venezeula' or the Shah's 'Great Civilization', it represents Nigeria's commitment to serious money, to greatness and to petrolic visions of excess. Money in one of its manifestations is 'the Holy Grail' of modern society (Marx, 1974, Vol. 1, p. 133), the 'glittering incarnation of its own life'; as such money 'has the power to lay down forms and directions for contents to which [it is] indifferent' (Simmel, 1978, p. 441). Yet this vision and ambition conferred by money was cross cut, and ultimately crippled, by a state incapable, largely for political reasons, of providing a rational foundation for its magisterial industrial ambitions. In this sense Ajaokuta must also be explained by kick backs and rents collected by state officials from foreign contractors (Lubeck, 1991).

Naira Power: State Degeneracy and the Dikko Affair

> Oil is a resource that anesthetizes thought, blurs vision, corrupts. . . .
> Look at the ministers from oil countries, how high they hold their
> heads, what a sense of power. (*Kapuściński, 1982, p. 35*)

> If you haven't got Naira power here, Auntie, you are lost. Money
> can buy you everything, even justice; and as Auntie replies, 'Ah yes,
> you must be ready to bribe your way openly here, or perish'.
> (*Emecheta, 1982, p. 10*)

Stansted Airport, 5 July 1984. British customs officers and Scotland Yard's anti-terrorist squad, responding to a reported abduction in central

25 Fifty per cent of NEPA's capacity is idle, and only 15 per cent of its repair vehicles and crews are operable.

London, intercept two wooden crates addressed to the Ministry of External Affairs, Lagos, that are about to be loaded on board a privately chartered Boeing 707 purportedly containing four tons of catering equipment. In one crate is an Israeli would-be leather manufacturer and a Nigerian employee of the political division of the Nigerian Ministry of External Affairs. In the other, a rather embarrassed Israeli anaesthetist by the name of Dr 'Lou' Shapiro, and Alhaji Umaru Dikko, former Minister of Transportation and Aviation during the Shagari regime (1979–83), heavily drugged and shackled. Drawn by a 'medical smell' that emanated from one of the crates, customs officers forcibly opened the first wooden container to discover Dikko with a tube forced down his throat. As he saw the light of day, Dr Shapiro, a reserve major in the Israeli army, was heard to say: 'Well gentleman, what do we do now?' (*Africa Now*, August 1984, pp. 11–15).

Dikko, Nigeria's 'most wanted fugitive' (*West Africa*, 16 July 1984, p. 1433), had fled Nigeria early in 1984 in the wake of a military coup, hiding out in Lagos for several days and then driving to the Benin border where he ditched his black Mercedes and casually walked across the border at a rural bush location to avoid capture. Subsequently, having taken up residence in Britain and 'living comfortably' in West London according to the *Guardian*, he became an outspoken critic of the new military regime, calling for a *jihad* to overthrow the Buhari military government. Rumour had it that Dikko had put aside US $300 million to fund an army to overthrow the military government (*Africa Now*, August 1984, p. 14). With other high-ranking politicians and 'multi-millionaire exiles' – most conspicuously Joseph Wayas (former President of the Nigerian Senate) and arms dealer Isyaku Ibrahim (*The Observer*, 24 June 1984, p. 12) – Dikko arrived in Britain under a dark cloud of accusation, and quite specifically amidst rumour of massive corruption and illicit gain. Dikko himself was estimated to be worth a staggering US $1.4 billion (*Daily Sketch*, 23 January 1984, p. 1).

The Nigerian government denied all knowledge of the kidnapping in spite of the fact that the Israeli abductors claimed to be in the pay of the Nigerian secret police. Extradition orders served by the Nigerian government had placed a good deal of pressure on the Tory Government in Britain to assist in the return of Nigerian exiles to face *in camera* trials before the Tribunal on the Recovery of Public Property (so-called Decree No. 3). Coupled with the rather dim view of the abduction in the British popular press, the Nigerian generals' aggressive prosecution of ex-President Shagari's National Party of Nigeria (NPN) ruling elite[26] produced

26 Immediately prior to the abduction the former governors of Kano (Bakin Zuwo), Anambra (Jim Nwobodo), Plateau (Solomon Lar) and Kwara (Adamu Attah) states had been sentenced by the Special Military Tribunal to respectively 44, 44, 88 and 126 years for corruption and fraud during the Shagari government (*West Africa*, 2 July 1984, pp. 1374–5).

an extremely tense diplomatic environment in which the 'special relationship' between Britain and Nigeria was severely jeopardized.

What appears on the surface to be the stuff of B-grade movies and pulp
spy novels is, I believe, yet one more manifestation of the, in this case
political, visage of petrodollars. Umaru Dikko personified Nigerian politics during the euphoric phase of the oil boom and perhaps more than
any other personality captured the ethos of a monumentally venal Second Republic (1979–83): the brash and aggressive civil servant–contractor,
the corrupt party machine politician, the avaricious rent-seeker for
whom public office simply conferred the means to ransack state oil
revenues for private gain. The explosion of oil revenues during the 1970s
vastly expanded the number and distribution of public offices (there
were 850 federal and state parastatals by the late 1970s!)[27] but oil rents
were channelled through state apparatuses already cross cut by deeply
sedimented regional, ethnic and religious affiliations and identities. As a
consequence, the explosive growth of federal petrodollars had the effect
of deepening and intensifying competing claims over highly lucrative
state offices and resources. Nigerian political scientist Claude Ake put it
well: politics was a ferocious contest to gain access to state monies. The
Nigerian public sector became, in this sense, a tool to manufacture a sort
of political consent through an unstable and delicate web of pacts and
alliances purchased by the distribution of rents (import licences, contracts) and the seemingly endless extension of federal and state-level
employment opportunities. To this extent, the more vast (and myopic)
the project – the massive new federal capital project at Abuja, a multi-
billion iron and steel programme – the greater its political attractiveness
as a means to lubricate critical constituencies with petroleum monies.
Only in this way can one understand why the costs of irrigation projects
or state-funded educational construction throughout the oil boom were
obscenely inflated, at least 300–400 per cent higher than anywhere else
in sub-Saharan Africa.[28]

The intersection of centralized (state) oil monies and a highly segmented, and regionalized, class structure in which northern Muslims
maintained, or endeavoured to maintain, a precarious hegemony produced a seemingly unsatiable source of rents for the privileged, and
corruption and fraud of Hobbesian proportions. Chinua Achebe in *The
Trouble with Nigeria* put the matter starkly: 'Nigeria is without shadow
of a doubt one of the most corrupt nations in the world' (Achebe, 1983,
p. 42). Not only did Nigerian public servants become 'more reckless and
blatant' (ibid., p. 43) as oil revenues continued to roll in, but in addition

27 By 1980 the public sector accounted for 50 per cent of GDP and provided 66 per
cent of all modern sector employment (Synge, 1989, p. 12).
28 The costs of completed irrigation schemes in Nigeria in 1978 were ten times
higher than in Liberia, five times higher than in Ivory Coast and three times higher
than in Ghana. See Usman (1986, p. 170).

there was a conspicuous failure to apprehend, prosecute and punish perpetrators.[29] The *Economist* (3 May 1986, p. 18) described the culture of corruption this way:

> Contracts might be perfectly innocent . . . but from the first, money told. Contracts, by convention, were inflated . . . by an item called 'public relations'. This extra amount was divided in an orderly way among the officials or ministers. . . . In the early years it was all quite gentlemanly. But [with oil] the pay offs grew . . . to involve literally millions on big construction contracts. The quality of work was very often skimped to allow for the payments. The beauty of it was that everybody could bribe or steal without feeling particularly dishonest. . . . Theft from the state brought mysterious largesse to extended families, to towns, to local political factions.

During the Second Republic, the second oil boom in 1979 unleashed a spasm of fraud and rent-seeking in which the state was mercilessly pillaged.[30] Nigeria 'lost' US $16.7 billion in oil income ('Oilgate', so-called) owing to fraudulent activities and smuggling of petroleum between 1979 and 1983 (*New African*, April 1984, p. 11); US $2 billion (over 10 per cent of GDP) was 'discovered' in a private Swiss bank account; and government ministries regularly went up in flames, the product of arson immediately prior to federal audits. Special military tribunals set up after the December 1983 coup prosecuted governors and high-ranking politicians for spectacular feats of corruption.[31] Governor Lar accumulated N32.6 million in four years; Governor Attah made N2 million through illegal activities associated with a single state security vote in the Kwara state legislature (*West Africa*, 2 July 1984, p. 1373, 23 July, p. 1511). Military officers who raided the home of the governor of Kano state, Bakin Zuwo, discovered millions of naira in cardboard boxes piled up in his bedroom. With money, says Marx, 'each individual holds social power in his pocket in the form of a thing' (Marx, 1953, pp. 986ff).

Umaru Dikko was the consummate oil politician. Not only did he preside over the presidential re-election campaign, which suffered from ballot-rigging on a gargantuan scale, he was also the central figure in the Ricegate scandal in the early 1980s. Dikko headed a presidential task

29 '[The] manner by which identified fraud cases are handled often appears more as if designed to encourage fraud than deter it . . . culprits are hardly ever prosecuted' (*National Concord*, 20 May 1983, p. 4).

30 Nigerian journalist Dele Giwa says that while the military stole with forks during the 1970s, the Shagari government stole with shovels.

31 Within the first eight months (December–September 1984) ten former governors from nine states were convicted of corruption charges; sentences were severe (variously between 15 and 126 years). However, the Tribunals failed to convict a number of offenders whose ethnicity and/or political affiliation conferred a political immunity.

force charged with alleviating food shortages by the distribution of N500 million of rice. Domestic production stagnated during the 1970s, largely as a result of overvalued exchange rates and undervalued producer prices. By 1980 staple food imports amounted to over US $1 billion. While the Shagari government pretended to limit rice imports to conserve foreign exchange and stimulate local production, the presidential task force actually gave out import licences and foreign exchange authorizations to well-connected businessmen and politicians to import low-quality Thai rice. It was not only that rice reached the Nigerian docks at US $480 per ton and miraculously appeared on the local market at five times that amount (*Washington Post*, 27 December 1980, p. 17); it was also that the distribution of licences was linked to the ruling NPN, which was popularly referred to as the 'Naira Party of Nigeria'. In 1984, one million bags of hoarded rice were discovered in a Lagos warehouse owned by a party functionary. Businessmen with connections to the party imported rice and recycled some of the profits to party election funds (*The Economist*, 3 May 1986, p. 23). Dikko himself was directly implicated; the military discovered rice stashed away in his home in early 1984: primitive accumulation of another sort.

Skyrocketing food prices, corruption in high places, hoarding and speculation. Ricegate was yet another manifestation of the pillaging of state oil monies, much of which was of course exported. Capital flight not only produced a lack of investment funds, however, but signalled a state fundamentally incapacitated by corruption and rent seeking. A hugely overvalued exchange rate,[32] in other words, certainly distorted the economy but highlighted how state apparatuses were functionally crippled by a culture of public theft. The bureaucratic inefficiency and administrative anarchy of Nigerian state organizations is, of course, legendary. Electricity and water became the scarcest national resources; the central bank and federal financial institutions were often incapable of providing basic national accounts data; Chase Manhattan was contracted to try and compute the outstanding Nigerian public debt.[33] This is, in other words, the antithesis of the 'developmental state'; the public sector is entirely incapable of laying the foundations for systematic capitalist accumulation (as opposed to a flabby and corrupt 'pirate' capitalism).

In this regard, the discovery of Umaru Dikko drugged in a wooden crate as part of a pathetic abduction scheme perfectly embodied two features of a Nigerian political economy bloated with oil monies: first, the state as the vehicle for, and obstacle to, capitalist accumulation;

32 By the early 1980s, a live chicken cost N20 and a packet of local cigarettes N4. At an official exchange rate of N1 = $1 these prices were ridiculous.
33 Contracts not only contained pay-offs and kick backs but were often unfinished, the state lacking any form of enforcement or accountability.

second, money as Naira power (to employ the title of Nigerian novelist Buchi Emecheta's popular novel), a general condition that Marx described as the process by which 'social power becomes the private power of private persons' (Marx, 1974, p. 133).

Money, Modernism, Millenarianism: the Maitatsine Insurrection[34]

> And oil's relation to the Mosque? What vigor, glory and significance this new wealth has given its religion, Islam, which is enjoying a period of accelerated expansion and attracting new crowds of faithful. (*Kapuściński, 1982, p. 35*)

The body of a self-proclaimed Muslim prophet, Maitatsine, is exhumed from a shallow grave near Rigiyar Zaki village on the outskirts of Kano, a massive, sprawling metropolitan area in the commercial and religious heart of Hausa-speaking northern Nigeria. Concerned to prevent any sort of martyrdom after ten days of insurrectionary struggle between the prophet's followers ('yantatsine) and the Nigerian military, the authorities embarked upon a campaign to discredit the movement as the brainchild of a psychopath, a 'fanatic' and 'heretic'. According to one Muslim intellectual, Maitatsine was 'witchcraft married to cannibalism' (Yusuf, 1988). He was, in fact, a brilliant Qu'ranic student schooled in the science of Qu'ranic exegesis, and had lived and taught in Kano city for almost twenty years in the 'Yan Awaki quarter. However, throughout the 1970s his public teaching became increasingly idiosyncratic and unorthodox; anti-modernist and syncretic in style, damning all those who read any text other than the Qu'ran, who carried money, who rode on bicycles or in cars, who smoked cigarettes, wore buttons or watched TV. Highly critical of established Sunni practice, Maitatsine vilified the local Muslim clergy and gradually built a community of followers within the traditional walled city of Kano. Radical and literalist in thrust, Maitatsine articulated an alternative Muslim project. By 1980 he had mobilized some 10,000 footsoldiers to advance his millenarian vision.

Maitatsine's community lived in a sort of liminal space between the old and the new Kano, a transition zone of motor parks, markets, cinemas and low income houses, a sort of urban jungle. Followers and students scavenged for work and alms in this informal sector, living in makeshift dwellings, preaching and begging at major intersections. By 1977 the followers were increasingly visible, vigorously attacking corrupt and unjust leaders and clergy (*ulema*) and more generally denouncing materialism. Several clashes between 1974 and 1979 had escalated tensions between Maitatsine and the police. On 18 December 1980, four police

---

34 For a more detailed discussion of Maitatsine, see Watts (1992).

units were sent to arrest some of the preachers after rumours of conflagrations and attacks on the central mosque. Disorganized police forces were attacked by Maitatsine's followers, armed with bows and arrows and daggers. Police arms were seized, vehicles burned and by late afternoon a plume of smoke hung over the city. Amidst growing chaos and confusion, the police were unable to control the situation, and by 22 December large numbers of Maitatsine supporters were reportedly entering Kano while trucks full of corpses were leaving the city. After five days of escalating violence, the Nigerian army intervened on 29 December with ten hours of mortar barrage. According to the official tribunal 4177 were killed but the figure is a huge underestimate; 15,000 were injured and 100,000 rendered homeless. Maitatsine was killed in the fighting and buried by his followers as they retreated from the city. Close to 1000 of the 'yantatsine were subsequently arrested and imprisoned.

What is striking about the Maitatsine insurrection is that at about the same time in another oil-producing state, namely Iran, a society was in the midst of a popular Muslim *revolution* which swept the Pahlavi regime from power. Indeed, there is a sense in which both phenomena need to be rooted in the material and cultural experience of the oil boom, and in the growing commodification of social life, lubricated, so to speak, by money. Quite specifically, oil money stands at the confluence of two world systemic processes which frame these Muslim 'fundamentalist' politics: on the one hand, the political economy of oil-based, and state-led, capitalist transformation, and on the other a Muslim world system in which debates over Muslim identity and modernity had become, in a historically unprecedented fashion, thoroughly interrogational. This confluence is especially vivid in the case of Maitatsine and his followers (Watts, 1989). The 'yantatsine constituted a sort of archetypical Fanonite class, for the most part relatively recent migrants to Kano (*'yan cin rani* and *gardi* in Hausa), drawn into the city through long standing Qu'ranic networks by the urban construction boom unleashed by state invested petro-dollars. They brought with them a sort of jacobin or populist reading of Islam acquired through a vital rural Muslim educational system, and an experience of social relations rooted in the moral economy of the peasantry. Their consciousness was very much that of the 'commoner' class, *talaka* in Hausa, a complex and dense term which originated in relation to the genesis and growth of the tributary Hausa states, and subsequently the Sokoto Caliphate, in the eighteenth century (Watts, 1984; Lubeck, 1985). But the 'yantatsine's experience of urban life and of proletarianization was directly mediated by the particular form of petroleum-capitalism that I sketched previously: corruption, illicit gain of magic money, rapid inflation, escalating land prices and rentals, and a sort of city life that combines commodity fetishism (the consumer boom of the 1970s) with Hobbesian anarchy. The state became *the* expression of corruption and moral degeneracy; its local representatives, the police, were despised and described as *daggal*, literally the devil.

The historic role of Maitatsine was, in a sense, to interpret this experience in cultural terms in ways that resonated with everyday life. Maitatsine articulated a particular experience through what one might call the local hermeneutics of Islam. Rather than being prescriptive in simple ways, Islam is a text-based religion that is made socially relevant through enunciation, performance, citation, reading and interpretation. It is this interpretive and dialogic tradition within Islam that points to how texts are used, by whom and with what authority (Fischer and Abedi, 1990). Maitatsine drew upon a legitimate Muslim tradition at a moment when Islam as a whole was embroiled in debates over modernity and change. Indeed, within Nigeria the oil monies had exacerbated tensions within the Muslim *umma* precisely by funding state education, which came into conflict with traditional Muslim educational institutions, and by drawing the powerful Muslim brotherhoods (and the clergy) into the circuits of money circulation. Maitatsine focused solely on the Qu'ran and gave a literalist reading in a way that cobbled together a sense of community in the context of a wide-ranging series of debates within the Muslim community and a total collapse of moral authority and state legitimacy associated with oil wealth. As the Hausa adage put it, 'money corrupts truth'.

To put the matter succinctly, what seems like a fundamentalist eruption led by a fanatical heretic is more about a particular class, and cultural, reading of oil monies; that is to say, a reading of the speeding up of modern life and an acceleration of commodities in circulation against a backdrop of wide-ranging debates within Islam over modernity itself. Maitatsine's concern with money was to reject it in the context of the petro-naira having eroded the moral basis of the Muslim community itself. It sought to limit the impact of the Midas touch of money, a cultural and political expression of what Simmel (1978) and Marx (1973) saw as the reification effect of money under capitalism and its dissolving influence on the community.

The Oil Bust: Scarce Money and the 'Great IMF Debate'

Oil kindles extraordinary emotions and hopes, since oil is above all a great temptation. It is the temptation of ease, wealth, fortune, power. [But] oil, though powerful, has its defects. (*Kapuściński, 1982, pp. 34–5*)

The great disappearing act. On 23 April 1984, the Nigerian Chief of Staff, Tunde Idiagbon, announced via a nationwide broadcast that Nigeria's borders were to be sealed. Simultaneously, all money was to be withdrawn from circulation. The Nigerian naira was to vanish overnight. A new currency was to be issued on 25 April, though individuals would be permitted to change only N5000 old naira for new notes. Amounts in excess of that amount would be deposited in special bank accounts until the depositor provided a sworn affidavit attesting to the source and ownership of the money (*West Africa*, 30 April 1984, p. 912). Currency exchange was to render worthless the hundreds of millions of naira smuggled out of the country, to force into the open those unscrupulous individuals who accrued untold millions during the civilian binge and who held much of this money outside of the banking system, and not least to squelch large-scale currency counterfeiting. A huge naira 'factory' was uncovered in Taiwan in 1984. The new money was printed in London to maintain the veil of secrecy and flown into Nigeria amidst tight security.

While the Central Bank withdrew N5.3 billion from circulation, it issued only N2.45 billion in new notes, which accordingly generated a huge money scarcity. By the middle of the exercise old bank notes were exchanged for receipts, and almost everybody, business organizations included, was broke (*West Africa*, 28 May 1984, p. 1108). In the large cities, money was so scarce that the working poor walked to work and pooled food. What was most striking about this disappearance of Nigerian money was that it occurred at a time when the government was rumoured to be negotiating a loan from the IMF which involved a substantial currency devaluation. Five years after the second oil boom, Nigeria had a huge external debt and a money that bore no semblance to its value; it was very close to bankruptcy. The oil boom was unequivocally over; 40 per cent of the reserves and some US $101 billion in oil revenues had been, to be charitable, 'used up'.

'One of the effects of the oil boom', said E. C. Edozien, President Shagari's economic advisor, in 1982, 'is to make it difficult to engender the necessary spirit of self-sacrifice and self-denial' (*Wall Street Journal*, 2 August 1982, p. 12). The population had simply come to 'expect too much from the government'. But why should there be a need for self-sacrifice to begin with, and why should there be denial among those, the countless millions of peasants, workers and informal sector operatives, who had little to show from oil in any case? And how could money, the much touted petro-naira, come and go, how could its value evaporate? How could the expectation and ambition of the boom turn to the disillusionment and austerity of the bust? During the height of the boom, the World Bank classified Nigeria as a middle income country; by the end of the 1980s it was reclassified as 'poor'. By 1985, talk in Nigeria was of 'oil doom' (*West Africa*, 26 August 1985, p. 1735).

The first austerity package had in fact been introduced in September 1981 following a 30 per cent fall in oil prices. Further cuts were announced in 1982 but external borrowing increased substantially as the national elections approached. In April 1983 Nigeria initiated negotiations with the IMF to borrow US $2 billion, facing strict conditionalities in the form of devaluation, a tightening of money supply, reductions in current expenditures and a relaxation in exchange and import controls. Despite progress throughout 1983, three major issues blocked any advance: devaluation, trade liberalization and petroleum subsidies. By September the parties were stalemated. Three months later the Shagari government was overthrown by a military coup.

The Buhari military government came to power emphasizing discipline, austerity, self-reliance and populist conservatism. Like Shagari before him, Buhari continued negotiations with the IMF but these stalled over devaluation and subsidies. Nigerian officials feared the destabilizing political consequences of inflation induced by devaluation and the elimination of import licences (i.e. potential rents for key political constituencies). Trade liberalization would crush the manufacturing sector. As a consequence, Buhari decided to go it alone with a domestically hatched austerity plan wherein 44 per cent of the foreign exchange earnings went to debt service. Rather than borrowing from private banks, Nigeria turned to counter-trading oil for current imports. Faced with crashing oil prices (from a high of US $41 per barrel in 1980 to the low teens by 1985) and a severe deflationary budget package, Buhari turned to authoritarian rule in the name of discipline and patriotic self-reliance. In August 1985 he was overthrown in another military coup.

The new Babangida regime immediately confronted the great oil crash; prices slumped below US $10.00 per barrel (in 1986 Nigerian oil earnings were US $6.5 billion compared to US $25.00 billion in 1981) and he declared his intention to break the deadlock with the IMF (Bierstecker, 1988). In an extraordinary populist twist, Babangida took the IMF loan to the people: so began, in October 1985, 'the Great Debate' (figure 17.5) (see *West Africa*, 14, 21 and 28 October, 25 November and 2 December 1985). It consisted of a flurry of speeches, street demonstrations and extensive debates in the press and news media (see, for example, Ekpo, 1985; ORC, 1985; Usman, 1986; Phillips, 1987). The articulate middle classes represented the IMF in explicitly nationalist terms; Nigeria would be sold for a mess of pottage. Indeed, in spite of the fact that the Babangida regime mounted a campaign for IMF-type reform, within a short time a broad-based opposition to taking the loan began to form and mobilize. The IMF demands – devaluation, liberalization, anti-inflationary measures – were published and subject to a lively critique by students, organized labour and academics. To live in debt and bondage or not was the issue.

What began as a thinly disguised effort to build a corporatist alliance around austerity produced a vociferous resistance to cutting petroleum subsidies and devaluation. But what also emerged was a strong popular sentiment against *any* form of borrowing; borrowed money would disappear just had quickly as it had in the past (Lubeck, 1993)! In the wake

Figure 17.5   Trapped: Nigeria and the IMF.

of popular protest and strikes, the Nigerian government broke off negotiations with the Fund in December 1985. Yet within two weeks the
annual budget speech combined nationalist assertion for economic autonomy with savage austerity taken directly from the IMF blueprint: a
'realistic exchange rate', an 80 per cent reduction in petroleum subsidies,
large scale privatization. Six months later came Babangida's new two-
year structural adjustment programme (SAP): hardship but 'Made in

Nigeria' as the popular press put it. The SAP's cornerstone was a second-tier foreign exchange market (essentially designed and presided over by the World Bank), in effect an auction for foreign exchange large enough to handle foreign transactions. Access to oil monies accordingly shifted to the financial sector and to rent-seeking within and between the private and public banking communities. Within a year, however, the value of the naira had fallen from US $1.12 to 20 cents. By January 1987 an IMF standby loan of SDR650 million had been signed by the Babangida government along with the full battery of SAP cutbacks. The real minimum monthly wage crashed from US $201 to US $16 (Watts and Lubeck, 1989).

The Great Debate proved to be about the conditions of getting new money and not about accounting for the loss of the old. Foreign money was rejected and as a consequence local money lost its value. In this sense the state had broken its promise, its obligation, to back the value of the naira, and hence further contributed to its own illegitimacy. Devaluation eroded what Simmel (1978) saw as the precondition for paper money: inter-social trust and social stability. The Great IMF Debate highlights, I would suggest, a long-standing conflict in Western discourse over the possibility of monetary order and in particular the incompatibility of money as a tool of state action and money as a symbol of social trust (Frankel, 1977, p. 86). As Gunnar Olsson (1991, p. 67) puts it: 'the institution of money is nothing outside a complicated network of promises'.

Serious Money

Money simultaneously exerts both a disintegrating and unifying effect. (*Simmel, 1978, p. 345*)

If money is the bond which ties me to human life and society to me, which links me to nature and to man, is money not the bond of all bonds? Can it not bind and loose all bonds? Is it therefore not the universal means of separation? It is the true agent of separation and the true cementing agent, it is the chemical power of society. (*Marx, 1975, p. 377*)

The dense symbolism and imagery of oil money as the devil's excrement suggests a sort of money fetishism in which extraordinary powers, of a magical and occult variety, are seen to reside in dirty lucre. In this sense it speaks directly to Marx's concern with money fetishism, money's obfuscatory qualities, money endowed with fecundity; in capitalism, money breeds money, he said, 'much as it is an attribute of pear trees to bear pears' (Marx, cited in Parry and Bloch, 1989, p. 6). But there is also a much larger motif here with a very long history in Western thinking (dating at least to Aristotle), in which money has a dark and sinister face, as a source of evil and moral confusion; in short, money as threat.

Marx pursues this line of thinking when he talks of money as the God of commodities, and it is seen in Simmel's vision of money as subversive of 'moral polarities', 'turning what was formerly black and white into grayness' (Simmel, 1978, p. 72); 'honor and conviction, talent and virtue, beauty and salvation of the soul are exchanged against money' (ibid., p. 256). For Chaucer money was filth, for Dickens an awful offal, for Edgar Allen Poe gold was death itself. For Hegel money was a 'monstrous system' that required 'continual dominance and taming like a beast' (cited in Shell, 1982, p. 154). The particular cultural constructions by which this view of money is articulated across time and space are, as is clear from this chapter, extremely varied. But underlying all these articulations is a strong sense of money as eroding the bases of sociability, as an acid that dissolves social ties and as a dark almost satanic force that tears asunder the integument of the community, giving rise to greed, avarice and alienation.

There is, however, a counterweight, another vision of money which stands in a dialectical relation to money as threat (it is also associated with Simmel, and to an extent with Marx), in which money enhances personal freedom, trust, rationality, calculability and expanded forms of social exchange (Frankel, 1977; Simmel, 1978; Martin, 1986). The community of money tends to be 'strongly marked by individualism and certain conceptions of liberty, freedom and equality' (Harvey, 1985, p. 4). Rather than a bland greyness, money produces what Emily Martin (1986, p. 4) calls 'the most intense, clear and passionately directed feelings'. Both Marx and Simmel recognized that money can fulfil both these functions – integrative and disintegrative – simultaneously, which produces complex and contradictory tendencies in social, cultural and political relations. Martin (1986) has brilliantly argued in a comparison of Taiwan and the USA that in the former money works primarily as a form of social integration and in the latter it creates social disintegration.

I have sought to show how the infusion of oil monies in an industrializing capitalist state in Africa provides a vantage point from which one can show that money contributes to, and reflects, how social integration and disintegration are at work simultaneously. In this light, some of the symbolic, cultural and socio-political expressions of money in Nigeria seem to endeavour to hold money operations within certain social limits. In other respects, oil money – as social power, as state corruption and degeneracy, as blind ambition and illusion – has eroded sociability, turning everything it touches into shit: oil money as deodorized faeces that has been made to shine. Oil money provides a means to pry open the black box of society, while the structure of society provides the entry point into understanding the complex ways in which money simultaneously mediates social relations and provides a fundamental means of experiencing them.

References

Achebe, C. (1983) *The Trouble with Nigeria*. Ibadan: Heinemann.

Amadi, E. (1982) *Ethics in Nigerian Culture*. Ibadan: Heinemann.

Amuzegar, J. (1982) Oil wealth: a very mixed blessing. *Foreign Affairs*, 60, 814–35.

Amuzegar, J. (1983) *Oil Exporters' Economic Development in an Interdependent World*. OP-18. Washington, DC: The International Monetary Fund.

Anderson, P. (1984) *Lineages of the Absolutist State*. London: Verso.

Barber, K. (1982) Popular reactions to the petro-naira. *Journal of Modern African Studies*, 20(3), 431–50.

Bastiat, M. (1991) 'My head was too strong': body parts and money magic in Nigerian popular discourse. Paper delivered to the Institute for Advanced Study and Research in the African Humanities, Northwestern University, Evanston, Illinois, 9 October.

Benjamin, W. (1973) *Charles Baudelaire*. London: Verso.

Bierstecker, T. (1988) Reaching agreement with the IMF: the Nigerian negotiations 1983–1986. Unpublished manuscript, School of International Relations, University of Southern California, Los Angeles.

Braudel, F. (1973) *The Mediterranean and the Mediterranean World in the Age of Philip II*. New York: Harper and Row.

Brown, N. O. (1959) *Life against Death*. New York: Vintage.

Chaudhry, K. (1989) The price of wealth: business and state in labor remittance and oil economies. *International Organization*, 43(1), 101–45.

Coronil, F. (1987) The black El Dorado: money fetishism, democracy and capitalism in Venezuela. PhD Dissertation, University of Chicago.

Coronil, F. and Skurski, J. (1991) Dismembering and remembering the nation: the semantics of political violence in Venezuela. *Comparative Studies in Society and History*, 26, 288–337.

Costello, V. (1981) Tehran. In M. Pacione (ed.), *Problems and Planning in Third World Cities*. New York: St Martins, 137–56.

Debord, G. (1978) *Society of the Spectacle*. Detroit: Black and Red Books.

EIU (1986) *Quarterly Economic Review of Nigeria*. London: Economist Intelligence Unit.

EIU (1990) *Quarterly Economic Review of Nigeria*. London: Economist Intelligence Unit.

Ekpo, E. (1985) *IMF Loan Comes to Nigeria*. Apapa: Nigerian Problems and Issues.

Emecheta, B. (1982) *Naira Power*. London: Macmillan.

Ferenczi, S. (1950) *Sex in Psychoanalysis*. New York: Holmes.

Fischer, M. and Abedi, M. (1990) *Debating Muslims*. Madison: University of Wisconsin Press.

Frankel, H. (1977) *Money: Two Philosophies*. Oxford: Blackwell.

Freud, S. (1955) *Standard Edition of the Complete Psychological Works*. London: Hogarth Press.

Gelb, A. (1984) Adjustment to windfall gains: a comparative analysis of oil exporting countries. Working Paper, The World Bank, Washington, DC.

Gille, D. (1986) Maceration and purification. In *ZONE 1/2*, New York: Urzone, 226–83.

Goux, J.-J. (1989) *Symbolic Economies after Marx and Freud*. Ithaca, NY: Cornell University Press.

Hallwood, P. and Sinclair, S. (1981) *Oil, Debt and Development*. Hemel Hempstead: George Allen and Unwin.

Harvey, D. (1985) Time, space, money and the city. In *Consciousness and the Urban Experience*. Baltimore: Johns Hopkins University Press, 1–35.

Haussman, R. (1981) State landed property, oil rent and accumulation in Venezuela. PhD Dissertation, Cornell University, Ithaca, New York.

Imam-Jomeh, I. (1985) Petroleum-based accumulation and the state in Iran: aspects of social and geographical differentiation, 1953–1979. PhD Dissertation, University of California, Los Angeles.

Izard, M. (1986) *Tierra Firme: Historia de Venezuela Contemporanea*. Madrid: Alianza America.

Kapuściński, R. (1982) *Shah of Shahs*. New York: Harcourt Brace Jovanovich.

Karl, T. (1982) The political economy of petro-dollars: oil and democracy in Venezuela. PhD dissertation, Stanford University, California.

Karl, T. (in the press) *The Paradox of Plenty: Oil Booms and Petro-states*. Princeton, NJ: Princeton University Press.

Karshenas, M. (1990) *Oil, State and Industrialization in Iran*. Cambridge: Cambridge University Press.

Katouzian, H. (1981) *The Political Economy of Modern Iran 1926–1979*. New York: New York University Press.

Le Goff, J. (1988) *Your Money or Your Life*. Boston: Zone.

Lubeck, P. (1985) Islamic protest under semi-industrial capitalism. *Africa*, 55, 369–89.

Lubeck, P. (1993) Restructuring Nigeria's urban-industrial sector within the West African region. *International Journal of Urban and Regional Research*, forthcoming.

Martin, E. (1986) The meaning of money in China and the United States. Lewis Henry Morgan Lectures, University of Rochester, New York, unpublished (cited with author's permission).

Marx, K. (1967) *Capital, Volume 1*. New York: International Publishers.

Marx, K. (1973) *Grundrisse*. New York: Vintage.

Marx, K. (1975) *Early Writings*. New York: Vintage.

Olsson, G. (1991) *Lines of Power/Limits of Language*. Minneapolis: University of Minnesota Press.

ORC (Opinion Research and Communications) (1985) *The Great Debate: What Is IMF?* Owerri: Gunson Headway Press.

Oyegake, L. (1981) *Cowrie Tears*. London: Heinemann.

Parry, J. and Bloch, M. (eds) (1989) *Money and the Morality of Exchange*. Cambridge: Cambridge University Press.

Petras, J. and Morley, M. (1983) Petrodollars and the state: the failure of state capitalist development in Venezeula. *Third World Quarterly*, 5, 8–27.

Philips, D. (1987) *Structural Adjustment of What, by Whom, for Whom?* Lagos: Centre for Management Development.

Roemer, M. (1983) Dutch disease in developing countries; swallowing the bitter medicine. Development Discussion Paper no. 156. Cambridge, MA: Harvard Institute of International Development.

Shell, M. (1982) *Money, Language and Thought: Literary and Philosophic Economies from the Medieval to the Modern Era*. Los Angeles: University of California Press.

Shipton, P. (1989) *Bitter Money: Cultural Economy and Some African Meanings of Forbidden Commodities*. Washington, DC: American Ethnological Association Monograph.

Simmel, G. (1978) *The Philosophy of Money*. London: Routledge.

Smelt, S. (1980) Money's place in society. *British Journal of Society*, 31(2), 204–23.

Stein, G. (1989) *Money*. New York: Workman Publishing.

Struthers, J. (1990) Nigerian oil and exchange rates: indicators of Dutch disease. *Development and Change*, 21, 309–41.

Synge, R. (1989) *Nigeria to 1993: Will Liberalisation Work?* London: Economist Intelligence Unit.

Turner, B. (1986) Simmel, rationalisation and the sociology of money. *Sociological Review*, 34(1), 93–114.

Usman, B. (1986) *Nigeria against the IMF*. Kaduna: Vanguard Printers.

Vilar, P. (1984) *A History of Gold and Money*. London: Verso.

Wallerstein, I. (1974) *The Modern World System*. New York: Academic Press.

Watts, M. (1984) State, oil and accumulation: from boom to crisis. *Society and Space*, 2, 403–28.

Watts, M. (1989) The shock of modernity: money, protest and fast capitalism in an industrializing state. Wallace Atwood Lecture Series no. 6, Clark University, Graduate School of Geography, Worcester, MA.

Watts, M. (1992) The shock of modernity. In A. Pred and M. Watts (eds), *Reworking Modernity*. New York: Rutgers University Press, 21–64.

Watts, M. and Lubeck, P. (1989) Structural adjustment, academic freedom and human rights in Nigeria. Special Issue of *Bulletin of Concerned Africanist Scholars*, no. 28, Fall.

Woolf, V. (1957) *A Room of One's Own*. London: Harcourt Brace Jovanovich.

World Bank (1989) Manufacturers' response to infrastructural deficiencies in Nigeria. Discussion paper, Infrastructure and Urban Development Department, World Bank, Washington, DC.

Yergin, D. (1991) *The Prize: the Epic Quest for Oil, Money and Power*. New York: Simon and Schuster.

Yusuf, A. (1988) *Maitatsine: Pedlar of Epidemics*. Kano: Syneco Press.

Zelizer, V. (1989) The social meaning of money: special monies. *American Journal of Sociology*, 95(2), 342–77.

Zonis, M. (1991) *Majestic Failure: the Fall of the Shah*. Chicago: University of Chicago Press.

Index